COMMONLY USED SYMBOLS

SYMBOL	TERM	PAGE WHERE SYMBOL IS FIRST INTRODUCED
Y	GDP	33
C	Consumption	33
I	Investment	33
G	Government spending	33
X	Net exports	33
F	Government transfers	51
V	Net factor payments from abroad	51
T	Taxes	51
S_p	Private saving	51
S_g	Government saving	51
S_r	Rest of world saving	51
M	Money	54
B	Bonds	54
W	Wage	94
U	Unemployment	84
L	Labor force	84
t	Tax rate	157
R	Interest rate	179
P	Price level	94
N^*	Full employment	97
K	Capital stock	91
N	Employment	93
n	Labor force growth rate	99
s	Net saving rate	100
Y^*	Potential GDP	98
π	Rate of inflation	215
π^e	Expected inflation	215
Z	Exogenous price shock	260
R^K	Rental price of capital	314
E	Exchange rate	349
RE	Reserves of the Fed	414
M_B	Monetary base	415
m	Monetary base multiplier	416
D	Deposits at banks	430
U^*	Natural unemployment rate	496

MACROECONOMICS

FOURTH EDITION

To Accompany This Text

STUDY GUIDE, Fourth Edition, by David H. Papell

MACRO

ECONOMICS

FOURTH EDITION

ROBERT E. HALL
JOHN B. TAYLOR

W · W · NORTON & COMPANY · NEW YORK · LONDON

Macintosh System Software © 1983–1990
IBM® is a registered trademark of the International Business Machines Corporation.
Apple® is a registered trademark of Apple Computer, Inc. Macintosh™ is a trademark of Apple Computer, Inc.

Printed in the United States of America.

The text of this book is composed in Garamond with the display set in Leawood.
Composition by TSI Graphics.
Manufacturing by Von Hoffman Press, Inc.
Book design by Natasha Sylvester.

Library of Congress Cataloging-in-Publication Data
Hall, Robert Ernest, 1943–
    Macroeconomics: theory, performance, and policy
    Robert E. Hall, John B. Taylor—4th ed.
    p. cm.
    Includes bibliographical references and index.
    1. Macroeconomics.   I. Taylor, John B. II. Title.
    HB172.5.H35   1992
    339—dc20   92-9921

ISBN 0–393–96307-1 (text)
ISBN 0–393–96360-8 (IBM 5 1/4" disk and text)
ISBN 0–393–96361-6 (IBM 3 1/2" disk and text)
ISBN 0–393–96362-4 (Macintosh disk and text)

W.W. Norton & Company, Inc. 500 Fifth Avenue, New York, N.Y. 10110
W.W. Norton & Company, Ltd., 10 Coptic Street, London WCIA IPU

1 2 3 4 5 6 7 8 9 0

To our families

Contents

Preface   xix

PART

1

FUNDAMENTALS OF MACROECONOMICS

CHAPTER
1

The Macroeconomy: Growth and Fluctuations   3

1.1	Recent Performance of the Macroeconomy	6
	EMPLOYMENT 9 INFLATION 10 INTEREST RATES 11	
1.2	Explaining Long-Run Economic Growth: A Preview	14
	EXPENDITURE AND OUTPUT SHIFTING 18 THE GROWTH OF POTENTIAL GDP 18	
1.3	Explaining Fluctuations: A Preview of the Complete Model	19
1.4	Currents of Thought in Macroeconomics	21
	How Did Today's Macroeconomists Come to Study Economics? 25	
1.5	The Macroeconomic Model Used in This Book	26
Review and Practice		27
	MAJOR POINTS 27 KEY TERMS AND CONCEPTS 27 QUESTIONS FOR DISCUSSION AND REVIEW 28 PROBLEMS 28 MACROSOLVE EXERCISES 30	

CHAPTER
2

Measuring Economic Performance: Output and Income   31

2.1	Gross Domestic Product	31
2.2	Measuring GDP through Spending	32
	CONSUMPTION 33 INVESTMENT 33	
	Portfolio Investment and Macro Investment 35	
	GOVERNMENT PURCHASES 36 IMPORTS AND EXPORTS 36	
	THE RECENT COMPOSITION OF SPENDING 36	
	Bringing Astronomical Numbers Down to Earth 38	
	WHICH SPENDING ITEMS SHOULD BE INCLUDED? 38	
	REAL GDP 38 A TALE OF TWO RECESSIONS 38	
	Quarterly GDP Statistics and the 1990–91 Recession 42	
	ECONOMIC GROWTH AND CONVERGENCE IN THREE COUNTRIES 42	
2.3	Measuring GDP through Production: Value Added	44
2.4	Measuring GDP through Income	45
	What Happened to GNP? 46	

2.5   Savings and Investment   50
       SAVING AND INVESTMENT IN AN OPEN ECONOMY 50
       SAVING AND CHANGES IN ASSETS 54
2.6   Transactions with the Rest of the World: The Current
       Account and the Exchange Rate   55
       FROM THE MERCHANDISE DEFICIT TO THE CURRENT
       ACCOUNT DEFICIT 56   THE EXCHANGE RATE 58
Review and Practice   59
       MAJOR POINTS 59   KEY TERMS AND CONCEPTS 60
       QUESTIONS FOR DISCUSSION AND REVIEW 60
       PROBLEMS 61   MACROSOLVE EXERCISES 65

CHAPTER
3

Monitoring the Economy: Inflation and Employment   66

3.1   Measuring Inflation   67
       PRICE INDEXES 67   DEFLATORS 69
3.2   Measuring Employment, Unemployment, and Wages   70
       HOURS PER WEEK AND TOTAL HOURS 71   DATA ON
       UNEMPLOYMENT AND ITS USES 72   UNEMPLOYMENT IN TWO
       RECESSIONS 73   UNEMPLOYMENT AND THE NATURAL
       RATE 75
       The Labor Market in the 1960s and the 1980s   76
       OKUN'S LAW 77   WAGES 77
3.3   The Productivity Slowdown   79
       Review and Practice   81
       MAJOR POINTS 81   KEY TERMS AND CONCEPTS 82
       QUESTIONS FOR DISCUSSION AND REVIEW 82
       PROBLEMS 83   MACROSOLVE EXERCISES 85

CHAPTER
4

The Long-Run Growth Model   87

4.1   The Determinants of Economic Growth   88
       LABOR 88   CAPITAL 91   TECHNOLOGY 91
       THE PRODUCTION FUNCTION 91
4.2   Full-Employment and Potential GDP   93
       THE DEMAND FOR LABOR 94   THE SUPPLY OF LABOR 95
       EMPLOYMENT WHERE SUPPLY EQUALS DEMAND 97
       POTENTIAL GDP 98
4.3   Saving and Balanced Growth   98
       CONDITIONS FOR BALANCED GROWTH 100   WHY THE
       GROWTH PATH IS STABLE 101   THE EFFECT OF SAVING ON
       GROWTH 102   TECHNOLOGICAL CHANGE 103
4.4   The Economic Growth Formula   104
4.5   Policies to Stimulate Growth   105

POLICIES TO IMPROVE TECHNOLOGICAL GROWTH AND
PRODUCTIVITY 106   POLICIES TO STIMULATE CAPITAL
FORMATION 107   POLICIES TO INCREASE LABOR SUPPLY 109
NEW RESEARCH IN PRACTICE Endogenous Growth Theory
and International Trade Liberalization 110

4.6   Real Business Cycle Explanations of Fluctuation   112
WHAT CAUSES SHIFTS IN LABOR DEMAND? 114   CRITIQUE OF
THE REAL BUSINESS CYCLE MODEL 114
Review and Practice   116
MAJOR POINTS 116   KEY TERMS AND CONCEPTS 117
QUESTIONS FOR DISCUSSION AND REVIEW 117
PROBLEMS 118   MACROSOLVE EXERCISES 119
Appendix: Deriving the Growth Formula   119

CHAPTER
5

The Effects of Fiscal and Monetary Policies in the Long Run

121

5.1   The Effects of Macroeconomic Policy on Real GDP in the
Long Run   122
5.2   The Effects of Fiscal Policy on the Shares Output   124
INTEREST-RATE SENSITIVITY OF CONSUMPTION, INVESTMENT,
AND NET EXPORTS 125   GOVERNMENT PURCHASES 126
THE BUDGET DEFICIT AND THE TRADE DEFICIT 126
OTHER FISCAL POLICY CHANGES 129   IMPORTANCE OF THE
LONG-RUN ASSUMPTION 129
NEW RESEARCH IN PRACTICE Governing the $5 Trillion
Economy   130
5.3   The Money Market and the Price Level   132
THE DEMAND FOR MONEY 132   THE SUPPLY OF MONEY 134
EQUILIBRIUM IN THE MONEY MARKET 135
5.4   Inflation   137
NEW RESEARCH IN PRACTICE International Policy
Coordination   138
5.5   Summary: The Classical Dichotomy   139
Review and Practice   140
MAJOR POINTS 140   KEY TERMS AND CONCEPTS 140
QUESTIONS FOR DISCUSSION AND REVIEW 141
PROBLEMS 141   MACROSOLVE EXERCISES 143

CHAPTER
6

Short-Run Fluctuations and Spending Balance

144

6.1   The Labor Market Out of Equilibrium   144
6.2   Forces that Push the Economy Off Its Growth Path   146

6.3   Aggregate Demand and Spending Balance   149
      THE BASIC CONCEPT OF AGGREGATE DEMAND 151
      THE UNRESPONSIVENESS OF THE PRICE LEVEL 152
      AN EXAMPLE: GENERAL MOTORS 153
6.4   The Point of Balance of Income and Spending   154
      THE INCOME IDENTITY 154   THE CONSUMPTION
      FUNCTION 154   GRAPHICAL ANALYSIS OF SPENDING
      BALANCE 158   ALGEBRAIC SOLUTION 160
      Graphs, Slopes, and Intercepts versus Algebra and Coefficients   161
      HOW SPENDING BALANCE IS MAINTAINED 162
      THE MULTIPLIER 163   SPENDING BALANCE WHEN NET
      EXPORTS DEPEND ON INCOME 168
      The Decline of the Multiplier   170
Review and Practice   171
      MAJOR POINTS 171   KEY TERMS AND CONCEPTS 172
      QUESTIONS FOR DISCUSSION AND REVIEW 172
      PROBLEMS 173   MACROSOLVE EXERCISES 175

CHAPTER
7   **Financial Markets and Aggregate Demand**   **176**

7.1   Investment and the Interest Rate   176
      THE INVESTMENT DEMAND FUNCTION 177   THE MEANING
      AND INTERPRETATION OF R 179
7.2   Net Exports and the Interest Rate   180
7.3   The IS Curve and the LM Curve   181
      Key Macro Relationships   182
      THE IS CURVE 182   THE LM CURVE 185   ALGEBRAIC
      DERIVATION OF THE IS AND LM CURVES 188   FINDING
      INCOME Y AND THE INTEREST RATE R 190
7.4   Policy Analysis with IS-LM   191
      MONETARY POLICY 191   FISCAL POLICY 192
      IS-LM in the Business Pages   193
      IS-LM AT WORK IN THREE COUNTRIES, 1990–91 194
      THE RELATIVE EFFECTIVENESS OF MONETARY AND
      FISCAL POLICIES 195   THE IS-LM INTERPRETATION 196
      NEW RESEARCH IN PRACTICE Monetary and Fiscal
      Policy Coordination in 1990   199
7.5   Deriving the Aggregate Demand Curve   200
      MONETARY AND FISCAL POLICIES 202
Review and Practice   203
      MAJOR POINTS 203   KEY TERMS AND CONCEPTS 204
      QUESTIONS FOR DISCUSSION AND REVIEW 204
      PROBLEMS 204   MACROSOLVE EXERCISES 206

CHAPTER
8   **The Complete Model**   **209**

    8.1   Price Stickiness and the Determination of Output and
           Unemployment in the Short Run   209
           DETERMINATION OF OUTPUT 210   DETERMINATION OF
           UNEMPLOYMENT 212

    8.2   Price Adjustment   214
           WHAT DETERMINES EXPECTED INFLATION? 218

    8.3   Combining Aggregate Demand and Price Adjustment   219
           ALGEBRAIC DERIVATION 224

    Review and Practice   225
           MAJOR POINTS 225   KEY TERMS AND CONCEPTS 225
           QUESTIONS FOR DISCUSSION AND REVIEW 225
           PROBLEMS 225   MACROSOLVE EXERCISES 228

CHAPTER
9   **Macroeconomic Policy: A First Look**   **229**

    9.1   Shocks and Disturbances to the Economy   230
           SHOCKS TO AGGREGATE DEMAND 231   ANALYZING THE
           EFFECTS OF AGGREGATE DEMAND SHOCKS 232   SHOCKS
           TO THE PRICE LEVEL 233
           Model Validation: Four Oil Price Shocks   234

    9.2   Responding to Aggregate Demand Shocks: Stabilization Policy   236
           WHEN DO MACROECONOMISTS DISAGREE ABOUT STABILIZATION
           POLICY? 237

    9.3   Responding to Price Shocks   240

    9.4   Monetary Policy as a Rule: How the Fed Picks the Aggregate
           Demand Curve   242
           OKUN GAPS AND HARBERGER TRIANGLES 243
           NEW RESEARCH IN PRACTICE The Budget Enforcement
           Act of 1990   246
           WHY FOCUS ON POLICY RULES? 248

    9.5   Disinflation   249
           SETTING POLICY TO HIT A TARGET LEVEL OF GDP 250
           ALTERNATIVE DISINFLATION PATHS 251
           Other Schools of Thought on Disinflation   256

    9.6   Monetary Versus Fiscal Policy 257

    Review and Practice   258
           MAJOR POINTS 258   KEY TERMS AND CONCEPTS 259
           QUESTIONS FOR DISCUSSION AND REVIEW 259
           PROBLEMS 259   MACROSOLVE EXERCISES 263

PART

2

THE MICRO FOUNDATIONS OF AGGREGATE DEMAND

CHAPTER

10   **Consumption Demand**   **267**

10.1   Fluctuations in GDP, Consumption, and Income   268
 GDP AND PERSONAL DISPOSABLE INCOME 270
 THE RELATION BETWEEN REAL DISPOSABLE INCOME AND
 CONSUMPTION 272

10.2   Defects in the Simple Keynesian Consumption Function   273
 THE EFFECT OF CONSUMPTION ERRORS ON FORECASTING AND
 POLICY 275 SHORT-RUN VERSUS LONG-RUN MARGINAL
 PROPENSITY TO CONSUME 275

10.3   The Forward-Looking Theory of Consumption   278
 THE INTERTEMPORAL BUDGET CONSTRAINT 279
 PREFERENCES: STEADY RATHER THAN ERRATIC
 CONSUMPTION 281 PREFERENCES: HOW LARGE AN
 INHERITANCE FOR THE NEXT GENERATION? 282 THE
 MARGINAL PROPENSITY TO CONSUME OUT OF TEMPORARY
 VERSUS PERMANENT CHANGES IN INCOME 282 ANTICIPATED
 VERSUS UNANTICIPATED CHANGES IN INCOME 285

10.4   How Well Does the Forward-Looking Theory Work?   286
 THE SHORT-RUN AND LONG-RUN MPC: A ROUGH CHECK OF THE
 THEORY 287 ANDO AND MODIGLIANI: DO ASSETS MATTER
 FOR CONSUMPTION? 287
 Why is the Saving Rate Higher in Japan than in the United
 States? 288
 FRIEDMAN: DOES PAST INCOME MATTER FOR
 CONSUMPTION? 289 WHERE DO WE STAND NOW? 290
 NEW RESEARCH IN PRACTICE How Consumers Deal
 with Uncertainty and Changes in their Incomes 292
 DEFECTS IN THE FORWARD-LOOKING MODEL 295

10.5   Real Interest Rates, Consumption, and Saving   296
 EFFECT OF REAL INTEREST RATES ON WORK 297

10.6   Consumption and the IS Curve   298
 THE SLOPE OF THE IS CURVE 299 SHIFTS IN THE IS CURVE
 DUE TO TAX CHANGES 299

Review and Practice   300
 MAJOR POINTS 300 KEY TERMS AND CONCEPTS 300
 QUESTIONS FOR DISCUSSION AND REVIEW 301
 PROBLEMS 301 MACROSOLVE EXERCISES 305

APPENDIX: A GRAPHICAL APPROACH TO CONSUMPTION
PLANNING 305

CHAPTER
11   Investment Demand   308

11.1   Fluctuations in Investment Spending   309
11.2   How a Business Looks at the Investment Decision   312
       DETERMINATION OF THE RENTAL PRICE OF CAPITAL 316   THE
       RENTAL PRICE AND THE DECISION TO BUY NEW CAPITAL
       GOODS 317   EXPECTED CHANGES IN THE FUTURE PRICE OF
       CAPITAL 318
11.3   The Investment Function   319
       DEPRECIATION AND GROSS INVESTMENT 321   LAGS IN THE
       INVESTMENT PROCESS 322   THE AGGREGATE INVESTMENT
       DEMAND FUNCTION 323
11.4   Taxes and Investment   323
       PERMANENT TAX CHANGES 324   ANTICIPATED TAX
       CHANGES 325
       NEW RESEARCH IN PRACTICE Getting Investments
       Moving Again in Recessions   326
11.5   Residential Investment   328
       HOUSING INVESTMENT AND MONETARY POLICY 329
11.6   Inventory Investment   330
11.7   The Investment Function and the IS Curve   333
Review and Practice   334
       MAJOR POINTS 334   KEY TERMS AND CONCEPTS 335
       QUESTIONS FOR DISCUSSION AND REVIEW 335
       PROBLEMS 336   MACROSOLVE EXERCISES 340
Appendix A: Capital Budgeting and the Rental Price of Capital   341
Appendix B: Tobin's q and the Rental Price of Capital   343

CHAPTER
12   Foreign Trade and the Exchange Rate   345

12.1   Foreign Trade and the Aggregate Demand   346
12.2   The Exchange Rate   348
       THE EXCHANGE RATE AND RELATIVE PRICES 350
12.3   The Determinants of Net Exports   352
       THE EFFECT OF THE EXCHANGE RATE 352   THE EFFECT OF
       INCOME 353   THE NET EXPORT FUNCTION 353
12.4   The Exchange Rate and the Interest Rate   355
12.5   The IS Curve and Economic Policy in an Open Economy   358
       ALGEBRAIC DERIVATION OF THE OPEN-ECONOMY IS CURVE 358

EFFECTS OF MONETARY AND FISCAL POLICY ON TRADE IN THE
SHORT RUN 359   PRICE ADJUSTMENT 359
The Budget Deficit and the Trade Deficit   360

12.6   The Exchange Rate and the Price Level   362
12.7   Protectionism versus Free Trade   363
Dumping and Predatory Pricing   364
MACROECONOMIC EFFECTS OF PROTECTIONISM 365

12.8   Stabilizing the Exchange Rate   366
Review and Practice   369
MAJOR POINTS 369   KEY TERMS AND CONCEPTS 369
QUESTIONS FOR DISCUSSION AND REVIEW 370
PROBLEMS 370   MACROSOLVE EXERCISES 373

Appendix: The Interest Rate and the Exchange Rate under Rational
Expectations   374
INTEREST-RATE PARITY 374   TESTING INTEREST-RATE PARITY
USING FUTURES MARKETS 376   THE EXCHANGE RATE AND ITS
EXPECTED DEPRECIATION 377   THE INTEREST-RATE
DIFFERENTIAL AND THE U.S. INTEREST RATE 379

CHAPTER
13

The Government's Budget Deficit and Aggregate Demand — 383

13.1   Government Budgets   384
THE FEDERAL GOVERNMENT BUDGET AND DEFICIT 384
STATE AND LOCAL GOVERNMENT BUDGETS 386

13.2   Fluctuations in the Deficit: Purchases, Transfers, and Taxes 387
13.3   The Effect of the Government Deficit   392
CYCLICAL VERSUS STRUCTURAL DEFICITS 393   HAVE DEFICITS
BEEN RELATED TO INTEREST RATES IN RECENT U.S.
HISTORY? 394   THE DEFICIT AND THE EXPLOSION OF
GOVERNMENT DEBT 395   PROBLEMS IN MEASURING THE
FEDERAL BUDGET DEFICIT 397   ECONOMIC SIGNIFICANCE OF
THE NATIONAL DEBT 398

13.4   The Government and the IS Curve   401
Review and Practice   402
MAJOR POINTS 402   KEY TERMS AND CONCEPTS 402
QUESTIONS FOR DISCUSSION AND REVIEW 402
PROBLEMS 403   MACROSOLVE EXERCISES 407

CHAPTER
14

The Monetary System — 409

14.1   The Elements of a Monetary System   410
14.2   Money Supply: How the Fed Controls It   413
REQUIRED RESERVES AND EXCESS RESERVES 417

BORROWED RESERVES AND THE DISCOUNT RATE 418   THE
FEDERAL OPEN MARKET COMMITTEE 419   DISTINGUISHING
BETWEEN MONETARY AND FISCAL POLICIES 419
Financing Government through the Printing Press   420

14.3   The Demand for Money: Currency and Checking Deposits   421
WHAT ARE THE OPPORTUNITY COSTS OF HOLDING FUNDS AS
MONEY? 422   THE TRANSACTIONS DEMAND FOR MONEY: AN
INVENTORY THEORY 424   MONEY AS A STORE OF
WEALTH 426   THE DEMAND FOR CHECKING DEPOSITS TO
PAY FOR BANKING SERVICES 427   DEMAND FUNCTIONS
FOR MONEY 428

14.4   The LM Curve and the Fed's Policy Rule for the Monetary Base   432
MONEY SUPPLY (M_1) TARGET 433   INTEREST-RATE
TARGET 434   GDP TARGET 434

14.5   How the Fed's Rule Determines the Effect of Fiscal Policy   435
14.6   Unavoidable Shocks to the IS Curve and LM Curve   437
14.7   Lags in the Effect of Monetary Policy   440
Review and Practice   441
MAJOR POINTS 441   KEY TERMS AND CONCEPTS 442
QUESTIONS FOR DISCUSSION AND REVIEW 442
PROBLEMS 443   MACROSOLVE EXERCISES 446

PART

3

THE MICRO FOUNDATIONS OF OUTPUT DETERMINATION AND PRICE ADJUSTMENT

CHAPTER
15

The Labor Market and Flexible-Price Theories of Fluctuations   451

15.1   Labor Supply   452
LONG-RUN VERSUS SHORT-RUN LABOR SUPPLY 452
ALTERNATIVE ACTIVITIES DURING RECESSIONS 454
FIXED COSTS OF GOING TO WORK 455

15.2   Labor Demand   456
15.3   Models with an Effect of Real Interest Rates on Labor Supply   458
15.4   Imperfect Information: The Misperceptions Model   462
POLICY IMPLICATIONS OF THE MISPERCEPTIONS MODEL 465
CRITIQUE OF THE MISPERCEPTIONS MODEL 466

Review and Practice   467
MAJOR POINTS 467   KEY TERMS AND CONCEPTS 468
QUESTIONS FOR DISCUSSION AND REVIEW 468
PROBLEMS 469   MACROSOLVE EXERCISES 472

CHAPTER
16   **The Firm and the Labor Market with Price**
          and Wage Rigidities   **473**

          16.1   Real Wage and Price Rigidity   474
                  NEW RESEARCH IN PRACTICE Why Does the Employer
                  Choose the Level of Employment? Why Does the
                  Customer Choose the Quantity Sold?   476
                  PRICE DETERMINATION 477
          16.2   Nominal Wage and Price Rigidity   482
                  STICKY NOMINAL WAGES 484   THE RELATION OF WAGE
                  STICKINESS TO PRICE STICKINESS 485
          16.3   How Wages Are Set in the U.S. Economy   486
                  WAGE DETERMINATION IN THE LARGE UNION SECTOR 486
                  WAGE DETERMINATION IN THE NONUNION SECTOR 489   WHY
                  ARE WAGES SET FOR LONG PERIODS WITH FEW
                  CONTINGENCIES? 490   WHY IS WAGE SETTING
                  STAGGERED? 493
          16.4   A Simple Model of Staggered Wage Setting   494
          16.5   Policy Implications   498
                  DISINFLATION AND THE REAL EFFECTS OF MONETARY
                  POLICY 498
          16.6   Summary and Appraisal   501
          Review and Practice   502
                  MAJOR POINTS 502   KEY TERMS AND CONCEPTS 503
                  QUESTIONS FOR DISCUSSION AND REVIEW 503
                  PROBLEMS 504   MACROSOLVE EXERCISES 506

CHAPTER
17   **Aggregate Dynamics and Price Adjustment**   **507**

          17.1   The Wage-Price Process as a Whole   507
          17.2   Changes in the Coefficients of the Price-Adjustment Model   509
                  THE EFFECT OF WAGE INDEXING 509   LENGTH AND SEVERITY
                  OF BUSINESS CYCLES 510
          17.3   Models of the Expected Inflation Term   511
                  CHANGES IN THE MODEL OF EXPECTED INFLATION 512
                  EXAMPLE 1: EFFECT OF A 1-YEAR STIMULUS 513   EXAMPLE 2:
                  EFFECT OF A MATERIALS PRICE SHOCK 515   EXAMPLE 3:
                  EFFECT OF EXTENDED HIGH OUTPUT 515
          17.4   The Combined Operation of Price Adjustment and Aggregate
                  Demand   518
                  The Four Relationships of the Numerical Example   519
                  EXAMPLE 1: RECOVERY FROM A DEMAND-DEFICIENT
                  RECESSION 520   EXAMPLE 2: RECOVERY FROM
                  STAGFLATION 522   EXAMPLE 3: A BOOM 522   EXAMPLE 4:
                  AN OIL PRICE SHOCK 524

17.5   Inflation-Output Loops in the United States, Germany, and the
         United Kingdom   525
         Why Are Output Fluctuations in Japan So Small   526
Review and Practice   529
         MAJOR POINTS 529   KEY TERMS AND CONCEPTS 530
         QUESTIONS FOR DISCUSSION AND REVIEW 530
         PROBLEMS 531   MACROSOLVE EXERCISES 532

P A R T

4

MACROECONOMIC POLICY

CHAPTER
18

Designing and Maintaining a Good Macro Policy   537

18.1   General Principles of Macro Policy Analysis   537
18.2   Instruments and Targets   543
18.3   Uncertainty and Timing Considerations   545
18.4   The Benefits of Full Employment and Price Stability   546
         WHY IS INFLATION UNDESIRABLE? 548   COSTS OF OUTPUT
         LOSS AND UNEMPLOYMENT 550
18.5   The Policy Frontier between Inflation Loss and
         Unemployment Loss   552
18.6   The Optimal Policy for Dealing with Price Shocks   556
         What Would Have Been an Optimal Policy in 1979 to
         1991?   558
         THE MESSAGE FOR POLICYMAKERS 560   NOMINAL GDP
         TARGETING: A REASONABLE WAY TO EXPRESS POLICY? 560
         NEW RESEARCH IN PRACTICE Using Indicators to Guide
         Policy   561
18.7   Changing the Policy Frontier   564
         STREAMLINE THE LABOR MARKET 565   IMPROVE
         INDEXATION 566   AVOID GOVERNMENT PRICE SHOCKS 566
         CONTROLS AND INCENTIVES 567   TRADE POLICY 568
Review and Practice   569
         MAJOR POINTS 569   KEY TERMS AND CONCEPTS 569
         QUESTIONS FOR DISCUSSION AND REVIEW 570
         PROBLEMS 571   MACROSOLVE EXERCISES 574

CHAPTER
19

The World Economy   575

19.1   The International Financial and Monetary System   576
         HOW A CENTRAL BANK CARRIES OUT ITS EXCHANGE-RATE
         POLICY 579   STERILIZED INTERVENTION 580
         CAPITAL OR EXCHANGE CONTROLS 581

19.2   History of the World Financial and Monetary System   581
        THE DEVALUATION OF THE DOLLAR AND THE COLLAPSE OF
        BRETTON WOODS 584   CURRENT EXCHANGE-RATE POLICIES
        AROUND THE WORLD 584
19.3   Macroeconomic Policy, Exchange Rates, and Inflation   588
        POLICY WITH FLOATING RATES 588   POLICY WITH A FIXED
        EXCHANGE RATE 590   EQUILIBRIUM ANALYSIS OF FIXED- AND
        FLOATING-RATE POLICIES 591   WORLD INFLATION WITH
        FLOATING EXCHANGE RATES 592
19.4   International Macro Policy Coordination   594
19.5   Monetary Union   596
        NEW RESEARCH IN PRACTICE Does Western Europe
        Need a Central Bank? Does Russia?   598
Review and Practice   600
        MAJOR POINTS 600   KEY TERMS AND CONCEPTS 601
        QUESTIONS FOR DISCUSSION AND REVIEW 601
        PROBLEMS 601   MACROSOLVE EXERCISES 603

APPENDIX **Introduction to MacroSolve**   **605**

        Instructions for the IBM PC Version of MacroSolve   606
        EQUIPMENT REQUIRED 606   INSTALLING MACROSOLVE 606
        STARTING MACROSOLVE 607   MENUS AND OPTIONS FOR
        THE IBM PC 608
        Instructions for the Macintosh Version of MacroSolve   610
        EQUIPMENT REQUIRED 610   RUNNING MACROSOLVE FROM
        THE DISKETTE 610   MENUS AND OPTIONS FOR THE
        MACINTOSH 611   TRANSPORTING MACROSOLVE DATA AND
        GRAPHS TO OTHER PROGRAMS 613   INSTALLING
        MACROSOLVE 615

        Index   617

Preface

In writing the first edition of this book, we set ourselves the goal of presenting the new macroeconomics in a manageable form. The content and emphasis of our book have changed some over three editions, but the enthusiastic response to each one has encouraged us to stick to our original goal: build in the new developments, but keep the presentation manageable. This fourth edition includes important research and policy developments through the early 1990s. New research has been particularly substantial on endogenous economic growth and on banking and credit markets. New policy issues have arisen from concerns about the U.S. recession in the early 1990s and about the low projections for long-term economic growth.

Weaving up-to-date, real-world policy examples into the text has proven to be a useful pedagogical feature which we have tried to preserve in each writing. Earlier editions drew many examples from the disinflation and the recessions of the early 1980s. In preparing this fourth edition, we reviewed all of these examples, and where we felt we could enhance readers' interest, we replaced the examples with events from the recession of the early 1990s. The recent recession has provided new developments on the international front, which we also explore.

The major revision of the National Income and Product Accounts (NIPA) provides a new lens through which to examine macroeconomic fluctuations in the United States. And the new emphasis on Gross Domestic Product (GDP) in the NIPA receives a corresponding emphasis in the text. The fourth edition makes extensive use of the new data. It also defines, explores fully, and focuses on GDP as the primary measure of output.

Our professional experience since the first edition has allowed us to do something entirely new with real-world examples in this fourth edition: to examine how *new* macroeconomic research is being used in practical policymaking. This new research is not only everywhere apparent in the discipline, it is also, in our view, everywhere apparent in practical policymaking. In order to share this experience, we have developed a series of essays—placed at appropriate locations throughout the book—that highlight how new research has been used in practice. We portray how successful, or unsuccessful, each application has been. Of course, many noneconomic factors—security, diplomatic, or political—influence practical policy decisions, and we try to sort out the effects of one influence from another on policy decisions. This is difficult. Policymakers themselves may be unfamiliar with the research and therefore may deny its influence, but still may be influenced indirectly. In highlighting applications of new research, we do not mean to denigrate old research. Indeed, much early macroeconomic research is more important than ever. It is fully embedded in the basic model used in the book, with practical examples routinely woven into the text.

New technological developments outside economics are also seen in this fourth edition. All diagrams and charts have been reconstructed using a full multicolor design. In preparing for this reconstruction, we reviewed all the charts and diagrams and selected a color coding that we felt would help the reader understand, sort out, and remember the material. Moreover, several new charts have been added that exploit the advantages of a multicolor design. Overall we feel that this is an enormous pedagogical improvement.

Economic fluctuations—recessions and booms—continue to be a key theme of the book. Recessions cause serious hardship and economic loss. We continue to view them, however, as temporary departures of the economy from its full-employment long-run growth path. We emphasize in this fourth edition—in keeping with much recent research—that this long-run growth path is not exogenous. As with the third edition, we describe the determinants of growth—labor, capital, and technological change—early in the book (Chapters 4 and 5), but we now also discuss the determinants of these determinants.

We take the view that many types of shocks are responsible for departures of the economy from its long-run path. These include changes in monetary and fiscal policies, as well as sudden increases in world oil prices, a factor that was of great importance in the 1990 recession and its two direct predecessors. They also include technological shocks, which have been featured in real business cycle research as a major source of economic fluctuations.

In our view full employment is not restored immediately after a shock because the economy adjusts slowly, a sluggishness primarily due to price and wage rigidity. We study rigidities within an overall framework in which expectations and other features of people's behavior are basically rational, and we provide a microeconomic account of the way in which price and wage rigidities delay the return to full employment.

Changes in the instruments of monetary and fiscal policies have powerful effects in this kind of model. We see ourselves as part of a newly evolving consensus that recognizes the value of clearly stated, credible, and systematic monetary and fiscal policies. We examine how such policies should be designed and implemented.

As in the earlier editions, Part I is a short course in macroeconomics by itself. The *complete* model is developed in this part. It focuses on three major ideas: the fundamental determinants of output in the long run, the determination of output and employment in the short run through the aggregate demand curve and the predetermined price, and the process of price adjustment that takes the economy back to the long-run growth path after a shock causes a recession or boom. Part I also introduces our analysis of monetary and fiscal policies.

Part II gives a systematic treatment of the microfoundations of aggregate demand. Consumption, investment, imports, exports, government spending, taxes, and the monetary system are studied in detail. Part III considers the microfoundations of price and wage setting and the dynamic adjustment of the economy. Models with flexible prices as well as models with wage and price rigidities are studied. Part IV looks in detail at the design and implementation of monetary and fiscal policies using the fully embellished model with wage and price rigidities and rational expectations, both in a national and an international setting.

Distinctive Features at a Glance

A number of important features have made this book work well in the classroom:

- Consistent development of a *complete working macro model* with short-run fluctuations, price adjustment, and long-run growth.
- Thorough examination of how macroeconomics is used in *practical policy applications*.
- Consistent *numerical values* of the coefficients of the complete model give a sense of the magnitudes involved and provide a bridge between the text and the end-of-chapter problems.
- *Computer software* that displays the same complete model and permits many kinds of experiments with the model.
- Discussion of the *determinants of long-run growth* before describing fluctuations around the growth path.

- Treating the *price level as a predetermined variable* consistently throughout the book.
- Considering the United States as an *open economy* throughout the book, rather than adding trade and exchange rates late in the book.
- Attention to the *microeconomic foundations* of all subjects discussed.
- Careful exposition of the *empirical regularities* of the U.S. economy at the start of each chapter on microfoundations.

Summary of Pedagogical Features

Teachers and students who have used the text have found many pedagogical features that enhance the student's understanding of the material. Here is how those features work:

- *Summary boxes.* Key ideas are drawn together at appropriate places within each chapter. The boxes serve a reinforcing function by allowing readers to check their understanding of one aspect of the analysis before tackling new material. And they also serve a review function; they help readers locate the building blocks of the analysis without rereading entire chapters.
- *Topic boxes.* Special concepts that are related to the discussion in the text are introduced. These include computing growth rates, quarterly Gross Domestic Product statistics, budget projections, indexing taxes, and the relationship between graphs and algebra. The boxes also present discussions of historical examples, current policy issues, and other illustrations of points in the text.
- *Problems and policy simulations.* At the end of each chapter there are questions for review and three types of problems: numerical, analytical, and computer simulation exercises to be used with the *MacroSolve* program. The numerical problems require the use of a hand calculator and usually take more time. We have found these useful for special projects. The analytical questions can be done with graphs or simple algebra. We have found much enthusiasm for putting *MacroSolve* Exercises in the text in the third edition. In this fourth edition we have made the computer problems more interesting by simulating decisions facing policymakers in a practical setting.
- *References.* We have tried to keep footnotes to a minimum. Footnotes are used mainly to document a specific statement or reference in the text.
- *Parallel graphical and algebraic presentation.* In most cases arguments are presented in both graphical and algebraic form. We have found that some students learn better with graphs and some learn better with algebra, especially if the algebra is presented in a way that does not intimidate. Graphical arguments are not necessarily easier for all students, and the algebra is provided to help those with a preference for algebra. Of course, graphical presentation usually helps with the intuition, and we

expect even the less graphically inclined students to learn basic diagrams. A special effort has been made to demonstrate that graphs and
algebra are just two ways to describe the same economic concepts.

- *Multicolor figures.* All diagrams and charts of data are now shown with
several colors to highlight different ideas. Shifting curves are easier to visualize with these colors. Micro relationships are generally given special
colors to distinguish them from macro relationships.

- *Policy essays: New Research in Practice.* In order to highlight how new
research is used in practice, a series of policy essays have been placed at
appropriate spots throughout the text.

- *Real-world examples.* Seeing how economic theory works in practice is
the best way to learn. Too often, however, these lessons of experience
are placed at some distance from the analysis, with the result that students often sense that a barrier exists between macroeconomic models
and the real world from which they are drawn. We have chosen to make
the performance of the economy an integral aspect of the exposition,
with new concepts constantly illuminated by examples.

- *Teaching supplements.* An excellent *Study Guide* prepared by David H.
Papell of the University of Houston is available for student purchase. An
Instructor's Manual that we have prepared jointly with Michael Knetter
of Dartmouth College and Gary W. Yohe of Wesleyan University is available to teachers from the publisher. This *Instructor's Manual* contains
many teaching "tricks" to prompt students to become actively involved
in the subject. These include macro-forecasting contests, policy projects
on Federal Reserve monetary targeting and federal budget projections,
debate formats for lectures, classroom skits to illustrate the forward-
looking theory of consumption and other models, and formats for class
participation in financial decision-making. There are also references to
more complicated material related to the text and a large number of test
questions. A *Test-Item File* of roughly 700 questions has been prepared
by Michael Knetter and Gary W. Yohe and is available either in printed
form as part of the *Instructor's Manual* or on diskette for most personal
computers. *Transparencies* suitable for use with an overhead projector
are available in full color for all the key figures.

- *Highly regarded computer software.* The MacroSolve package, written by
Stephen R. King and Rick M. McConnell, embodies the IS-LM and price-
adjustment equations developed in the text. This innovative software has
received rave reviews from students and teachers and can now be or-
dered as part of the text. The user can shift curves on the graphical display and see immediately how the economy reacts.

- *Data sources.* Whenever possible the data in charts and tables are taken
from the most recently available *Economic Report of the President.* This
makes it easy for students and instructors to explore the data in more
detail.

A Guided Tour

The book starts with a short course in macroeconomic analysis in Part I. All the major topics are covered. We review the basic facts of macroeconomic fluctuations and develop a simple but complete model of the macroeconomy. We present the determinants of long-run growth and relate factor inputs to output. We consider short-run fluctuations around the long-run growth path. We use the aggregate demand curve to explain the determination of output in the short run when the price level is predetermined. Our approach to aggregate demand is standard, through the IS-LM apparatus. The aggregate demand curve also has an important role in long-run calculations, where the price level is determined.

The path to full employment is governed by the price-adjustment process. Our analysis shuttles back and forth from price adjustment to output determination. Once the price level has adjusted, output is found at the point of the new price level on the aggregate demand curve. We do not drop the predetermined-price assumption when we trace the economy's move to its long-run path. IS-LM remains our theory of output determination in each period of the dynamic analysis.

The expositional simplification we achieve in this way is enormous. We do not feel that the empirical evidence justifies the complexity of simultaneous determination of prices and output in each period. There is certainly no contradiction to the predetermined-price assumption if the period is a quarter of a year, and the assumption is valid as a close approximation if the period is a full year.

The adaptation of price adjustment to inflation ranks high among the ideas that have evolved in macroeconomics over the past two decades. We avoid characterizing this adaptation solely as a matter of changing expectations. Even with rational expectations, price adjustment depends partly on recent inflation experience since contracts and other rigidities prevent quick adjustments. We discuss how the adaptation of expectations to inflation depends on how prices and wages are set.

After the short course in macroeconomic analysis, we go on to develop the micro foundations of aggregate demand in Part II. At the start of each chapter we present the key facts or puzzles that need to be explained. At the end of each chapter we look at the implications for IS-LM. The consumption chapter (10) develops a forward-looking theory of consumption based on the life-cycle and permanent-income formulations, emphasizing the role of rational expectations. By establishing an intertemporal budget constraint, we avoid present discounted values and forbidding summations. Chapter 11, on investment, focuses on Dale Jorgensen's model. The foreign trade chapter (12) focuses on flexible exchange rates, with a rational expectations model of the exchange rate as its centerpiece. Chapter 13, on government, presents material on the deficit and government debt alongside a standard treatment of automatic stabilizers and related subjects. When the intertemporal budget constraint for the government is presented, the idea is already familiar to the student from consumption and investment. Chapter 14, on the monetary system, takes up money demand and describes the role of the Federal Reserve using financial balance sheets developed in Part I. We emphasize the credit, or intermediation, role of banks in addition to their role in determining the money supply. This role has received increased attention in recent research and policy discussion.

Part III contains much that we think is novel for an intermediate text. This part takes up the microeconomic foundations of wage and price setting. Chapter 15 considers market-clearing or equilibrium views, including Robert Lucas's imperfect information model of aggregate supply. Chapter 16 considers alternative views emphasizing the microfoundation of wage and price rigidities. Chapter 17 discusses the implications of gradual price adjustment for the dynamic behavior of the macroeconomy and compares these implications with actual experience.

Part IV pulls the analysis together into a comprehensive treatment of macroeconomic policy evaluation. Chapter 18 takes up general policy issues such as time inconsistency, multiplier uncertainty, targets and instruments, and the rational expectations critique of policy evaluation. The emphasis is on policy rules, rather than on one-time policy changes. The inflation/unemployment trade-off appears as a policy frontier between output stability and price stability. Chapter 19 then considers macroeconomic policy in the world economy, including a review of how the international monetary system evolved from Bretton Woods and how policy works in countries with fixed exchange rates.

Acknowledgments

Michael Knetter of Dartmouth University provided valuable assistance in preparing this edition, as he did for the previous edition.

We thank the students, teaching assistants, and instructors in numerous sections of intermediate macro at Stanford for their many helpful comments and corrections throughout the development of this book. We are also deeply grateful to the many teachers and students at other universities who wrote to us with comments on earlier editions. This edition is immeasurably better than it would have been without their feedback. In particular, we would like to single out the following: Francis Ahking, University of Connecticut; Ugur Aker, Hiram College; Robert Barry, College of William and Mary; Dan Ben-David, University of Houston; Ernst Berndt, Massachusetts Institute of Technology; Olivier Blanchard, Massachusetts Institute of Technology; Dwight M. Blood, Brigham Young University; Ronald Bodkin, University of Ottawa; Norman G. Clifford, University of Kansas; Gregory Crawford, Stanford University; Betty Daniel, SUNY-Albany; Wilfred J. Ethier,

University of Pennsylvania; George Evans, London School of Economics; Craig Furfine, Stanford University; Rajendra Gangadean, Stanford University; Frederick Goddard, University of Florida; Pete Gomori, St. Francis College (New York); Rae-Joan B. Goodman, U.S. Naval Academy; Harvey Gram, City University of New York; Howard Gruenspecht, Carnegie-Mellon University; Joseph Guerin, St. Joseph's University; John Haltiwanger, University of Maryland; James Hamilton, University of Virginia; Daniel Himarios, University of Texas at Arlington; Brad Humphreys, University of Maryland; Takatoshi Ito, University of Minnesota; Demetrius Kantarelis, Assumption College; Stephen R. King, Chemical Bank; Michael Knetter, Dartmouth College; John Laitner, University of Michigan; Julia Lane, American University; Bennett McCallum, Carnegie-Mellon University; Basil Moore, Wesleyan University; Richard F. Muth, Emory University; Neil B. Niman, University of New Hampshire; Ian Novos, University of Southern California; Ernest H. Oksanen, McMaster University; David H. Papell, University of Houston; Edmund S. Phelps, Columbia University; Mikko Puhakka, Cornell University; Garey Ramey, University of California, San Diego; Duane J. Rosa, West Texas State University; Michael Sattinger, SUNY-Albany; Edward Trubac, University of Notre Dame; J. Kirker Stephens, University of Oklahoma; Michael Truscott, University of Tampa; Larkin Warner, Oklahoma State University; Shinichi Watanabe, University of Kansas; John Williams, Stanford University; and Hou-Mu Wu, Tulane University.

Finally, we would like to thank Drake McFeely, Donald Lamm, Debra Makay, Kelly Nusser, and Nancy Palmquist of W. W. Norton for outstanding editorial help and advice.

Stanford   R.E.H.
December 1992   J.B.T.

PART

1

FUNDAMENTALS OF MACRO- ECONOMICS

CHAPTER

1

The Macroeconomy: Growth and Fluctuations

What is the outlook for the United States economy next year? Will it be a good year? A bad year? More precisely, by what percent will the economy grow from this year to next year?

Two and a half percent might seem like a good guess. That was about the average annual growth rate for the last 25 years in the United States. If you said 2.5 percent, however, you are very likely to be wrong. First of all, 2.5 percent is a long-term—25-year—growth rate, and economic growth from year to year rarely equals the long-term average. History shows that the United States economy, and all other economies, fluctuate widely around the long-term average from year to year. In 1991, for example, growth was *negative* .7 percent, far from the 2.5 percent average. The year 1991 was not a good one for the economy: production declined, workers were laid off, unemployment and poverty rose, new college and university graduates had trouble finding jobs, and many other people throughout the country felt economic hardship. Growth also slumped in 1970, 1974, 1975, 1980, and 1982—five other negative growth years from recent history, which generated similar hardships.

But in many other years economic growth was well above average. For example, the economy boomed by more than 5 percent in 1973 and by more than 6 percent in 1984. In fact, growth was above average for the six consecutive years from 1983 to 1988, one of the longest periods of above average growth in United States history. Economic history teaches that booms and slumps—economic fluctuations—are temporary. Even the persistent, above average growth of the 1983–88 period proved temporary.

There is a second reason why a 2.5 percent forecast is likely to be off the mark for next year. Long-term economic growth appears to be slowing down in the United States. Many economists feel that the growth rate will average less than 2.5 percent in the 1990s. This low projection for future economic growth is a cause for concern. If long-term economic growth decreases in the future then living standards will not rise significantly, and we will not have the resources either to increase consumption in the future or deal with pressing problems such as the environment. And increased economic growth is the only way to achieve significant and lasting reductions in poverty.

Macroeconomics is the branch of economics that tries to explain how and why the economy grows and fluctuates over time. The general upward path of the economy is the result of slow-moving forces—increasing population, more factories and machines, and better technology. Recessions—periods of declining total output—and other fluctuations divert the economy from a smooth growth path. Macroeconomics tries to explain growth and fluctuations using the standard principles of economic analysis.

The other branch of economics is **microeconomics**—the study of the behavior of individual consumers, firms, and markets. There are two ways that microeconomics differs from macroeconomics. First, microeconomics is more concerned with how one market differs from another than with how the economy as a whole grows and fluctuates over time. Second, macroeconomics explains the determination of variables that microeconomics considers given. These variables include national income, the price level, and interest rates. Although it has different objectives, macroeconomics employs the basic ideas of microeconomics. When macroeconomists try to explain growth and fluctuations, they must look at the behavior of consumers and firms, the organization of labor markets and industry, the workings of financial markets, and even the machinations of government. They rely on microeconomics when they do so. Good microeconomics is a necessary but not sufficient condition for good macroeconomics.

Long-run economic growth and short-term fluctuations—the subject matters of macroeconomics—have dominated discussions of economic performance in recent years. For example, all the major candidates in the 1992 presidential campaign presented programs both to end the economic slowdown which continued into 1992 and stimulate economic growth during the rest of the 1990s.

Other important variables change as the macroeconomy grows and fluctuates. For example, inflation and interest rates in the United States rose toward the end of the 1983–88 high growth period and declined as production and employment fell in 1990 and 1991. Although the high inflation of the 1970s is becoming a fading memory, it is important to remember that it caused great harm to the economy, and ending it brought on the pain of two recessions in the early 1980s. Exchange rates and the foreign trade deficit also fluctuate with changes in the macroeconomy. Inflation, interest rates, exchange rates, and the foreign trade deficit are part of the natural focus of macroeconomics.

What is macroeconomics good for? One answer is that macroeconomics is essential for good economic policy. Used appropriately by policymakers, it has the potential greatly to improve economic welfare in the United States and other countries, including the less-developed economies of Africa, Asia, and Latin America and the newly emerging market economies of Eastern Europe and the former Soviet Union. That is why we have devoted most of our careers to the subject. Consider the following applications of macroeconomics.

Macroeconomics can help policymakers decide what to do to help avert recessions and to ensure that recessions are as short and mild as possible when they occur. Fluctuations are not unique to the last 25 years. They have been recorded for hundreds of years in the United States and other countries, and they will undoubtedly continue into the future. Hence, the possibility of another recession in the economy will remain a continual concern to policymakers. When the next recession strikes, it will have substantial effects on our welfare, just as the last recession did. Unemployment and poverty rise in all recessions. Even those who don't lose their jobs may be forced into part-time jobs. Lower national income during a recession reduces the funds available to make new investments that fuel long-term growth.

Macroeconomics can also help policymakers sort through various government spending and tax proposals to increase long-term economic growth. Production *per hour* by U.S. workers grew by only .9 percent per year since 1973, way down from the 2.8 percent per year from 1959 to 1973. The slowdown in the growth of *total* production was not as bad because of the rapid growth of the number of workers as the postwar baby boom generation entered the work force and more women chose to work outside the home.

Macroeconomics can help policymakers keep inflation low and stable without making the economy unstable in the short run. Many analysts feel that low and stable inflation is essential for strong long-term economic growth. Suggestions about how government institutions can be designed to best ensure low and stable inflation are some of the more important recent contributions of macroeconomics.

Finally, macroeconomics tells us how broad policy changes affect the types of goods produced in the economy. Even when overall economic growth is relatively smooth, there are major fluctuations in the kinds of goods being produced. For example, during the late 1980s, production of defense and nondefense goods for the federal government slowed to a standstill, while the production of goods for export abroad soared. During this same period of steady overall growth the production of new houses actually fell. These developments in the government, export, and housing sectors of the economy represented sharp reversals of developments in the mid-1980s. As we will see, they led to large changes in the trade deficit. The trade deficit rose in the mid-1980s and fell in the late 1980s. The trade deficit is largely a macroeconomic phenomenon.

RECENT PERFORMANCE OF THE MACROECONOMY

Figure 1–1 documents the fluctuations of the U.S. economy over the last quarter century. The red line in the figure traces **real gross domestic product (GDP),** a concept we will examine in more detail in the next chapter. Real GDP measures the actual physical production of cars, trucks, TV sets, rock concerts, Hollywood films, medical care, and every other good or service that people in the United States produce for trade with one another or with the rest of the world. We get real GDP by summing up the dollar value of production, and then adjusting for any price changes that have occurred from year to year. Frequently, real GDP is simply called real *output,* as it represents the total output of goods in the economy.

The vertical axis in Figure 1–1 shows the values of real GDP in 1987 dollars. The horizontal axis indicates the year. GDP rose fairly consistently during this period at an average growth rate of 2.5 percent. Growth in the labor force and in the capital stock, the two key inputs to production, accounted for part of the total growth. The rest came from technological improvements. The black line in the chart indicates the steady upward trend that underlies the behavior of real GDP. This trend line measures the amount of output that would have been produced had the economy been in neither boom nor recession.

During the period shown in Figure 1–1, the U.S. economy experienced five **recessions**—periods when real GDP declined. The recessions are highlighted with boxes in the figure. Recessions start just after the **peak** of the previous expansion. The end of each recession is called a **trough.**

Figure 1–2 gives a more detailed look at the deviations of real GDP from trend. The ups and downs are exactly the same as in Figure 1–1, but the **percentage** deviations of real GDP from trend are shown.

Fluctuations do not occur at regular intervals. They certainly cannot be anticipated with great accuracy, and this is what makes macroeconomic

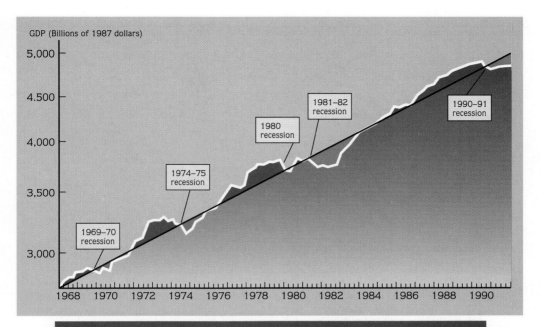

FIGURE 1–1   Real GDP in the United States, 1968–91

The white line shows what has happened to real GDP. The black line shows what real GDP would have looked like if it had grown smoothly at about 2.5 percent per year during the period instead of fluctuating as it did.
Source: *Economic Report of the President*, 1992.

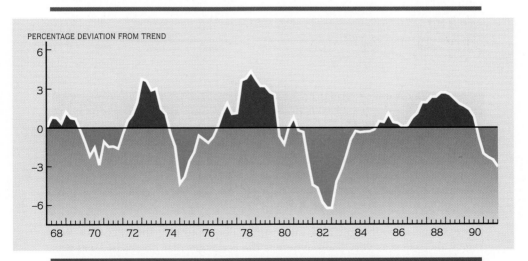

FIGURE 1–2   Fluctuations of real GDP around the smooth trend.

The chart shows the *percentage* deviations of real GDP from trend. Real GDP was more than 6 percent below trend in 1982 and about 3 percent below trend at the end of 1991.

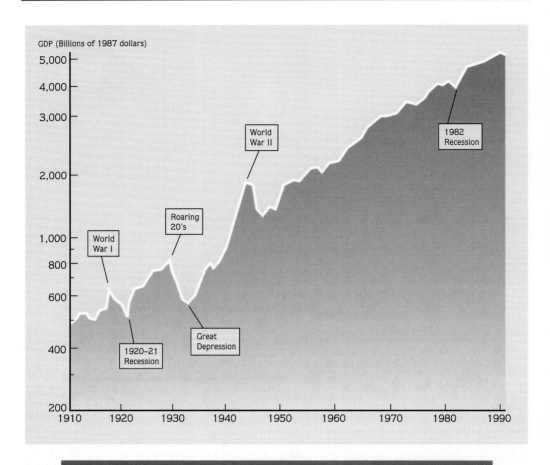

GDP (Billions of 1987 dollars)

FIGURE 1–3 Real GDP, 1910–91

The largest decline in real GDP occurred from 1929 to 1933, the years of the Great Depression. Another important contraction occurred in the early 1920s. Both were more serious than any recession since 1950.
Source: *National Income and Product Accounts of the U.S.* (U.S. Department of Commerce) and *Economic Report of the President*, 1992, Table B–2.

forecasting both difficult and interesting. For example, the recovery that began in 1982 was very long, whereas the recovery that began in 1980 was short.

Figure 1–3 gives a longer perspective on the growth and fluctuations in economic activity, showing the ups and downs in the economy over the last 80 years. The most noticeable single fluctuation during this period was the downturn during the Great Depression of the early 1930s. Note, however, that the recession in the early 1920s and the subsequent boom in the late 1920s were also comparatively large in magnitude. Although economic fluctuations in the United States have not ceased, they appear to have diminished in magnitude compared with this earlier period.

Employment

Fluctuations in employment follow closely the fluctuations in real GDP. Figure 1–4 shows the ratio of employed workers to the working-age population for the same period covered by Figure 1–1. Employment fell rapidly as the economy went through each of the five recessions during this period. Firms laid off workers as the economy's production fell and hired fewer new workers as well. As the economy began to recover after each downturn, employment again grew as firms called workers back to work and hired many new workers. This close association between production and employment as the economy fluctuates is one of the key facts of macroeconomics. Recurrent recessions are serious social problems, because they involve large-scale job losses.

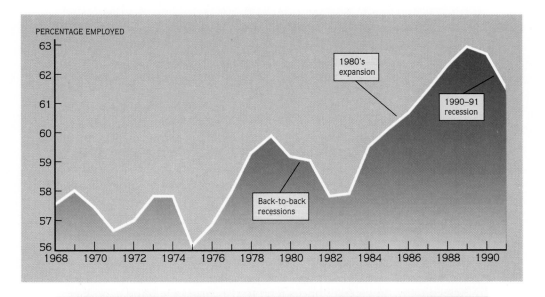

FIGURE 1–4   Employment as a percentage of working-age population

Recessions are periods of declining employment, measured as a fraction of the working-age population. Because of the fluctuations in employment, recessions influence a large fraction of the public. The percentage of the working-age population who are working reached an all-time high in 1989.
Source: *Economic Report of the President*, 1992, Table B–30.

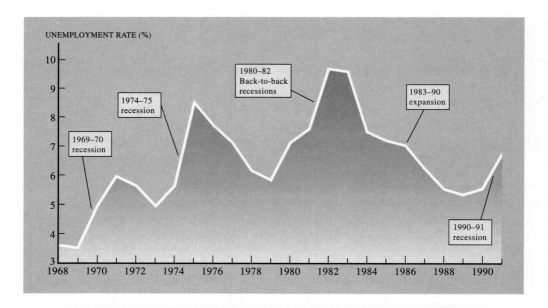

UNEMPLOYMENT RATE (%)

1969–70 recession

1974–75 recession

1980–82 Back-to-back recessions

1983–90 expansion

1990–91 recession

FIGURE 1–5   Annual unemployment rate, 1968–1991

The unemployment rate rises during recessions and falls during recoveries.

Mirroring the fluctuations in employment are the fluctuations in the **unemployment rate,** which is the percentage of the labor force who are not working but who are looking for work. When employment falls, the unemployment rate rises as workers are laid off. Figure 1–5 shows the unemployment rate. In 1982 the unemployment rate rose to about 10 percent. In 1989 it had fallen to about 5 percent. Unemployment then began rising again and reached nearly 8 percent for 1992.

Inflation

Another important fact of economic fluctuations is their correlation with the rate of **inflation**—the percentage change in the average price of all goods in the economy. In general, prices tend to rise faster when the economy is operating near its peak. Conversely, prices tend to rise less rapidly when the economy is near a trough. These rises and falls lag behind the fluctuations in real GDP.

Figure 1–6 shows the rate of inflation. One of the most striking aspects of inflation is that it was much higher and much more volatile in the 1970s than in the 1980s. This is clearly demonstrated in the chart. Almost all

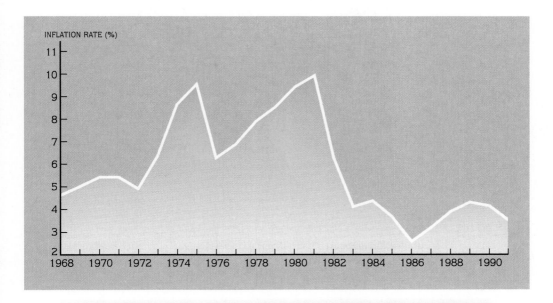

FIGURE 1–6   The rate of inflation

Inflation was high and volatile in the 1970s. In the 1980s it declined and remained relatively steady. Bursts of inflation have preceded or accompanied recessions. Typically, inflation subsides during and just after recessions.
Source: *Economic Report of the President*, 1992, GDP deflator in Table B–3.

the significant increases in the rate of inflation preceded recession periods. Declines in inflation usually follow recessions. Do increases in inflation cause recessions? Are recessions a necessary part of the disinflation process? These are two of the central concerns of this book.

Interest Rates

Interest rates also tend to fluctuate over the business cycle. The interest rate is the amount charged for a loan by a bank or other lender per dollar per year, expressed as a percent. For instance, if your roommate lends you $100, for which she asks you to pay her $110 a year from now, the interest rate is 10 percent. Figure 1–7 shows one representative interest rate, the federal funds rate, during the same period that we previously considered. The federal funds rate measures how much banks pay to borrow funds from each other overnight. As we will see, the federal funds rate is a key measure of the effect of the Federal Reserve Board, the central bank of the United States. There was a general rise in interest rates starting in the 1960s

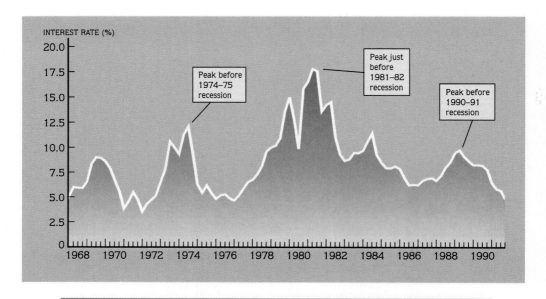

INTEREST RATE (%)

Peak before 1974–75 recession

Peak just before 1981–82 recession

Peak before 1990–91 recession

FIGURE 1–7   The federal funds interest rate

Like other interest rates, the federal funds rate reaches a peak just before a recession and then usually falls sharply.
Source: *Economic Report of the President*, 1992, Table B–69.

as inflation rose. Interest rates usually rise with inflation to compensate lenders for the falling purchasing power of the dollar. The interest rate minus the expected rate of inflation is called the **real interest rate.**

However, the fluctuations of interest rates during recessions are most dramatic. Interest rates are **procyclical;** they rise during booms and fall during recessions. They are also one of the most volatile of macroeconomic variables, and the most difficult to predict. Nevertheless, as Figure 1–7 makes clear, these interest-rate fluctuations are intimately related to the fluctuations in production and employment. A thorough understanding of interest-rate behavior is crucial to any explanation of economic fluctuations.

A variable closely related to the interest rate is the **money supply.** The money supply consists of currency and the deposits that people have at banks and certain other financial institutions. The money supply is controlled by the Federal Reserve Board.

The behavior of the money supply is shown in Figure 1–8. The chart shows the money supply divided by the price level, or **real money.** There seems to be a relationship between money and the timing of recessions

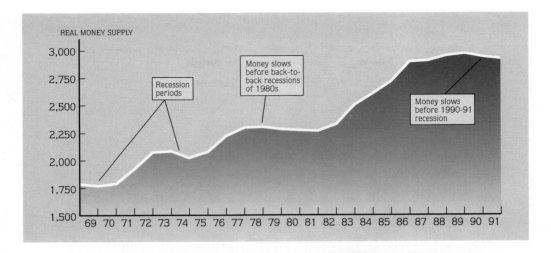

FIGURE 1–8   The money supply

The money supply divided by the price level—real money—seems to decline before recessions. The general trend in real money is positive because the growth in the economy creates a need for more money to assist in buying and selling goods.
Source: *Economic Report of the President*, 1992, Tables B–3 (GDP deflator) and B–65 (M_2).

and booms. The relationship suggests that changes in the money supply may be causing the fluctuations in the economy. In the theory that we develop in this book, the money supply is a primary force in economic fluctuations.

The ideas, theories, and models we study in this book endeavor to explain why GDP and employment fluctuate so much. They will also try to provide reasons for the cyclical movements of inflation, interest rates, and the money supply as well as a number of other macroeconomic variables.

GROWTH AND FLUCTUATIONS

1. In most years, the economy grows. The long-run growth path of the economy depends on population growth, capital accumulation, and technological progress.
2. The economy undergoes recessions, recoveries, and other fluctuations at irregular intervals. Recessions are periods of contracting economic activity; recoveries are periods of above-average economic growth following a recession.

3. The physical volume of output—measured by real GDP—contracts in a recession and expands in a recovery.

4. Employment moves closely with output. Recessions are periods of job loss, that is, rising unemployment.

5. The period between World War I and World War II saw two very large contractions. Recessions have continued since World War II. In the early 1980s the overall contraction was the worst since the Great Depression. The recession that began in 1990 was less severe.

6. Inflation generally increases before a recession and subsides in the wake of a recession.

7. Interest rates usually reach a peak just before a recession starts and then fall considerably during the recession.

EXPLAINING LONG-RUN ECONOMIC GROWTH: A PREVIEW

The aim of this book is to develop a theory that explains growth and fluctuations. In this section and the next we give a brief preview of this theory. While a preview of coming attractions is necessarily incomplete, it helps visualize what the story is about. Of course, it is by no means a substitute for the complete story, which is laid out in Part II of the text.

At the core of any macroeconomic theory is an explanation of how the economy responds to economic forces. How does GDP adjust when a new technology is introduced, when foreigners decide to purchase a smaller amount of U.S. exports, or when Americans decide to import rather than buy similar domestically produced goods? What if there is a decrease in demand for new factories and machines because of a massive reduction in defense spending? What if the price of oil is quadrupled because a cartel of foreign producers cuts back on oil production?

In constructing an explanation of how the economy responds to these forces, the macroeconomist constructs a **model.** A model is simply a description of the economy expressed in graphs or equations. It shows how the decisions of consumers and firms interact with each other in markets to determine output and other variables.

Macroeconomists use a long-run growth model to study the general upward path of the economy over time. Studying the growth model is the

Computing Growth Rates

The growth rate of a variable between two periods, in percent, is defined as *the change in the variable divided by the value of the variable in the first period multiplied by 100.* Thus, the growth rate of real GDP from 1989 to 1990 is

   100 × (real GDP in 1990 — real GDP in 1989) / (real GDP in 1989)

= 100 × (4,884.9 – 4,836.9) / (4,836.9)

= 100 × (48)/(4,836.9)

= 1.0 percent.

Growth rates are usually converted to "annual rates" because everyone is used to annual rates. For a change from one year to the next, the growth rate is already at an annual rate. For the growth rate from one quarter to the next, the annual rate is approximated by multiplying the quarterly growth rate by 4.

first step in understanding the complete model we develop in this book. The growth model focuses on the amount of labor and capital that go into the production of goods and services. Labor and capital work together to produce output. The long-run growth model also shows how the resulting output goes partly to consumers and partly to businesses in the form of investment in additional factories and equipment.

The long-run growth model looks at the economy after it has adjusted completely to a shock, such as an increase in foreign demand or a decline in defense spending. This is an important simplification, because such shocks are frequent and the economy is always in the process of adjusting to one shock or another. The complete model will consider the adjustment process through which the economy responds to shocks. As we will see, the adjustment can sometimes last a long time and can involve recessions and other departures from the economy's longer-term growth path. We start from the simplified long-run growth model because it has an important role in the full model and because it has some important lessons of its own.

Elementary economics emphasizes how changes in prices play a key role in the adjustment of a market economy to shocks. If there is an increase in the demand for cars, for example, the price of cars will increase. Higher car prices give car companies greater incentive to produce more cars and also tend to offset the higher demand for cars. The increase in car prices is what brings about the realignment of car production and car demand. If car prices adjusted rapidly—in economic terminology, if prices were perfectly *flexible*—then we could skip over the adjustment process and focus immediately on the new alignment of supply and demand with higher car prices. On the other hand, if car prices adjusted more slowly—in economic terms, if prices were *sticky*—then the adjustment process itself would take time and would be a central part of the economic analysis. These two alternative assumptions about prices—flexible versus sticky— lead to two different types of models. The assumption of flexible prices leads to a long-run model, which describes the long-run position of the economy but skips over the adjustment process. The assumption of sticky prices leads to a more complete model, which describes not only the new long-run position but also how the economy gets there.

The distinction between flexible prices and sticky prices is the key difference between the long-run growth model and the more complete model developed in this book. In the long-run growth model, car prices and all other prices in the economy, including wages, are assumed to be perfectly flexible. In the complete model prices are sticky; the adjustment process takes time. In fact, this adjustment process is an essential part of the model. It is at the heart of the explanation of recessions and other departures of the economy from its long-run growth path. But the long-run growth model is essential too: *Describing where the economy eventually goes after a shock is the first step in describing how it gets there.*

The determination of GDP in the long-run growth model can be described as follows: At a given moment, there is a certain amount of productive capacity in the economy. The level of the capacity depends on the number of factories and machines and the number of workers. Full employment will prevail in the economy, because if unemployment developed it would quickly disappear as wages fell enough to stimulate the demand for labor. The basic theory of supply and demand assumes that prices or wages would adjust quickly so that supply would equal demand. Wages and prices for the whole economy would adjust quickly to *keep labor and machines fully employed*. Prices are assumed to be *flexible* enough to bring about a complete and quick adjustment.

According to the long-run growth model, a change in overall demand in the economy results in a change in the price level, but not in the level of production. The workings of such a model with flexible prices are shown in the simple diagram in Figure 1–9.

The productive capacity of the economy is shown as a vertical line. The productive capacity is determined by the volume of productive factors—capital and labor—and is unrelated to the price level. Productive capacity determines **potential output,** or **potential GDP,** labeled Y^* in Figure 1–9. Potential output is the amount of output that can be produced from the existing capital stock and labor force.

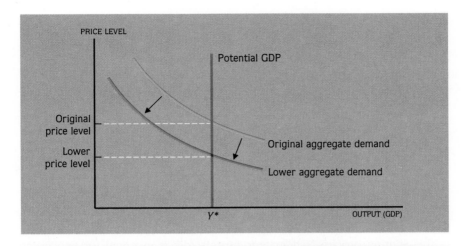

FIGURE 1–9   The aggregate demand curve determines the price level in the longer run

In the longer run, the price level is flexible and output is at the level of potential GDP. The vertical line shows potential GDP. The point where it intersects the aggregate demand curve is the longer-run price level.

Figure 1–9 also shows an **aggregate demand curve,** which slopes downward. Aggregate demand is the total amount of demand throughout the economy. Demand depends on the price level—demand is higher if the price is lower. The negative relationship is due to financial factors: A higher price level increases the demand for money and credit and raises interest rates. Higher interest rates then lower demand. We will have much more to say in later chapters about aggregate demand, which has a central role in all macroeconomic theories.

With perfectly flexible prices the economy always operates at the intersection of aggregate demand and potential output. If the price level happened to be too high, so that demand fell short of the economy's potential, and unemployment threatened, then the price level would fall immediately by just enough to stimulate demand and restore equilibrium.

What is interesting and important about this model is that demand influences only the price level, not the level of output. If a change in economic policy shifts demand downward, prices fall immediately. Output remains unchanged. With perfectly flexible prices, *shifts in demand cannot explain recessions and booms*. Shifts in demand explain only variations in inflation.

Expenditure and Output Shifting

The long-run growth model's prediction that total output remains unchanged when there is a shift in demand has an important corollary. A decline in the output of one kind of good—brought about perhaps by a decline in the demand for that good—must be accompanied by an increase in the output of some other goods. Suppose, for example, that there is a decline in defense spending on planes, tanks, and missiles. According to the long-run growth model, total output remains unchanged. Hence, spending on some other goods—consumption goods, investment goods, or goods for sales abroad—must increase. There is a *shift in production from one type of good to another.*

An important task in developing the long-run growth model is to explain the mechanism through which this shift takes place. As we will see in later chapters, changes in interest rates and exchange rates play a key role in this shifting process. Understanding this role is essential for explaining economic developments during the middle and late 1980s when such expenditure shifts were large but output remained at its potential level. It is also essential for analyzing appropriate macroeconomic policy responses to expected declines in defense spending in the 1990s.

The Growth of Potential GDP

Potential GDP grows over time. One reason is that employment grows. The population rises over time, and, at least in the past two decades, a growing fraction of the population chooses to work. Growth in labor input causes a growth in potential GDP.

Other factors enable the economy to make more output from a given level of employment. An increase in the capital stock is one factor: Workers can produce more if they have more capital to work with. A more important reason is technological improvement. During recent years, the output of the economy has grown by at least 1 percent per year more than can be explained by the growth of labor and capital inputs. Economists ascribe this extra growth to improved means of production. The 1 percent of recent years has been a severe disappointment in comparison with earlier periods. For instance, during the 1950s and 1960s, technological improvement ran at a pace of 2 to 3 percent per year.

A smooth growth path of potential output results from the smooth upward trend in labor supply, gradual capital accumulation, and technological progress. There are none of the hills and valleys we saw earlier in Figures 1–1 and 1–2. To understand short-run movements, we need to expand the model to include an explanation of short-run fluctuations. This is where the role of sticky prices comes into the model.

THE LONG-RUN GROWTH MODEL

1. Economists use the long-run growth model to study the general upward path of the economy over time.
2. In the long-run growth model, the price level is flexible. Output is always at its potential level. The price level is determined by the intersection of aggregate demand and potential output.
3. The level of production is determined by capital and labor; demand determines only the price level, not the level of output.
4. The economy grows as labor, capital, and technological know-how increase.

1.3 EXPLAINING FLUCTUATIONS: A PREVIEW OF THE COMPLETE MODEL

At any particular moment, the level of output is not necessarily equal to potential GDP, as in Figure 1–9. Instead, output can be lower or higher than potential. In the short run, output can depart from potential for a year or more, and our model must describe these movements as well. Prices and wages are not so responsive in the short run as to keep output equal to potential in each year. In contrast, the long-run growth model posits that output is pinned down to a particular value determined by capital and labor. The price level adjusts to make this possible. In the short run, we reverse things, taking the price level as sticky and the level of output as flexible. In short-run analysis, we put Figure 1–9 aside and consider the price level as fixed or sticky instead. The idea that it is useful to consider the price level as fixed in the short run was one of the important contributions of the great macroeconomist John Maynard Keynes.

If we know the economy's aggregate demand curve and the price level, then we can figure out the level of output, as shown in Figure 1–10. The horizontal line shows the given price level, and the position where it intersects the aggregate demand curve is the level of output. Figure 1–10 shows the basic idea about economic fluctuations that we will develop in later chapters. If the aggregate demand curve moves inward, the level of output must fall. The inward movement means that spending has declined. Because the price level is fixed, less spending means less output.

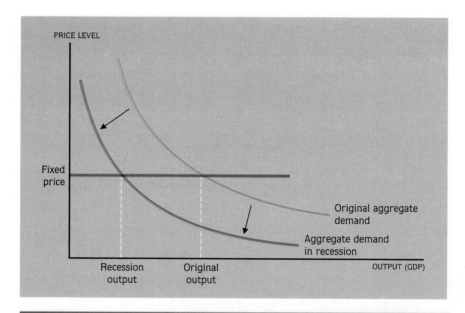

FIGURE 1–10   A recession occurs when the aggregate demand curve shifts inward

The horizontal line expresses the idea that the price level remains fixed, or sticky, in the short run. When the aggregate demand curve shifts inward, output falls. The economy moves to the left along the horizontal line. When the aggregate demand curve shifts inward, it means that total dollar spending has fallen. With the price level unchanged, this means that output must fall, so a recession occurs.

What kinds of forces might make spending fall? Some originate in the private sector of the U.S. economy. For example, in some years there is a spontaneous decline in the amount that families spend on cars, appliances, and houses, or that businesses spend on new plants and equipment. Another source of shocks to spending is public policy. The Federal Reserve has a powerful influence on spending because it controls the money supply. Congress sets income taxes on families and these affect consumption spending; business taxes and the investment tax credit are important determinants of investment spending. Policy can also influence the levels of exports of U.S. goods to other countries and of imports to the United States from other countries.

Eventually, the economy moves back toward its potential. The process seems to take years, not days, weeks, or months. Hence, the intervening period deserves a lot of attention.

How does the economy move back to potential? The answer is by *gradual price adjustment*. When the economy is away from its potential, there are incentives to move back toward potential. Over time, firms and workers respond to these incentives. The response takes the form of adjustment of prices and wages. As prices and wages change, so do output and employment.

The complete model tells the following story about the economy. Shocks hit the economy from time to time. Sometimes they come from changes in the behavior of firms or consumers. Sometimes new developments in foreign economies disturb the economy. Sometimes there is a surprise in monetary or fiscal policy. Initially, the aggregate demand curve moves but the price level does not, so output and employment change. This is the short-run response. Then the price level begins to adjust. As prices change, the economy moves along the aggregate demand curve to the point of potential GDP. In the long run, the price level absorbs all or part of the shock.

THE COMPLETE MODEL

1. Because the determinants of potential output grow from one year to the next, recessions—years of output decline—involve departures from potential.
2. The departures of output from its potential level are temporary.
3. In the short run, the price level hardly changes at all. Output is determined by the intersection of the aggregate demand curve and the price level.
4. As the price level adjusts, the economy moves toward potential.

1.4 CURRENTS OF THOUGHT IN MACROECONOMICS

The story we previewed briefly in the last two sections draws from two major strands of thinking in macroeconomics. The analysis of long-run growth with the emphasis on flexible prices comes from **classical macroeconomics.** The classical school dominated macroeconomic thinking before the Great Depression in the 1930s. Classical macroeconomics is basi-cally the application of standard supply-and-demand analysis to the whole economy. The growth model builds on this analysis, showing how the growth of capital and labor determines the growth of potential GDP. On the other hand, our analysis of short-run departures from the growth path comes from the tradition started by Keynes as a result of the experience of the Great Depression of the 1930s. That experience seemed to Keynes and his followers to be very different from the predictions of the classical model.

The acceptance of Keynesian ideas brought recognition of the impor-tance of maintaining a steady growth of aggregate demand. After many years of research, the importance of controlling aggregate demand has now been well documented both theoretically and empirically, though there is still debate among macroeconomists about the best method of control.

One important school, the **monetarists,** usually identified with Nobel Prize winner Milton Friedman, formerly of the University of Chicago, now of the Hoover Institution at Stanford University, holds that steady money growth will best stabilize the growth of aggregate demand.

The **new classical school,** including economists such as Robert Lucas of the University of Chicago and Thomas Sargent of the University of Chicago and Stanford University, also places great importance on the stabil-ity of aggregate demand. The new classicals maintain that prices adjust very quickly, as the classical economists assumed, and that expectations are ra-tional. In their models, departures from potential are due to firms' and workers' misinterpretations of surprise price and wage changes. These models place importance on keeping the growth of demand stable in order to minimize the size and frequency of such price surprises. Steady money growth is also their recommendation.

Macroeconomists in the **Keynesian school** have argued that changes in taxes and government spending are also desirable. James Tobin of Yale University, Robert Solow of M.I.T., and Franco Modigliani of M.I.T. (all Nobel Prize winners) are macroeconomists usually identified with this school. They also favor the active use of monetary policy to offset other sources of instability, in place of the passive, steady growth policy of the monetarists and new classicals.

There is also a more recent **new Keynesian** school of economists who continue to base their theory on the Keynesian assumption that prices and wages are sticky, but who examine the microeconomic foundations of this stickiness and use many of the same assumptions about expectations as the new classical economists. Edmunds Phelps of Columbia University and Olivier Blanchard of M.I.T. have been contributors to this school. A representative collection of papers by economists in this group has been put together by N. Gregory Mankiw of Harvard University and David

Romer of the University of California at Berkeley in a two-volume book entitled *New Keynesian Economics.*

Perhaps the only modern school of macroeconomics that does not emphasize the importance of stabilizing aggregate demand is the **real business cycle school,** led by Finn Kydland of Carnegie-Mellon University and Edward Prescott of the University of Minnesota. This school contends that the analysis of Figure 1–9 applies year by year, not just in the longer run. They explain recessions and other movements in employment as the result of shifts in the economy's potential, due to factors like technical change, rather than as departures from potential. Sticky prices do not play a role in generating economic fluctuations in the real business cycle model, and neither does aggregate demand. However, even this school recognizes that increases in the money supply cause inflation. Many economists in this school would therefore recommend stable money growth as a policy prescription.

In the 1960s, some economists began to think that controlling aggregate demand could virtually eliminate economic fluctuations; for example, in 1969 Martin Bronfenbrenner wrote a book entitled *Is the Business Cycle Obsolete?* arguing that it was. More recent research and the actual experience in the 1970s, the 1980s, and 1990s have shown this to be a false hope, and few economists ask questions about the obsolesence of the business cycle. We know that aggregate demand management will not eliminate economic fluctuations, or be able to bring unemployment permanently to very low levels.

In recent years, new research in macroeconomics has been substantial in four areas: price adjustment, rational expectations, economic growth, and banking and credit markets.

Price adjustment is the process through which firms adjust their prices in response to changing demand and supply conditions in their markets. The new theories of price adjustment attempt to fill in gaps in the simple model with sticky prices. First, in an inflationary environment many prices are continually increasing. Price-adjustment theories have to describe how price setting would incorporate the steadily rising trend in prices. Second, early theories of price adjustment were vague about the microeconomic reason for the slow adjustment. New theories of price adjustment have provided better explanations based on labor contracts, monopolistic power on the part of firms, or lack of information by firms about the nature of the changes in demand. All the newer theories about price adjustment show explicitly that potential GDP matters in the long run. In fact, in the long run, the economy returns to potential.

The concept of **rational expectations** has influenced macroeconomic thinking deeply, and many parts of this book show the influence. Consumption, investment, and price adjustment are areas where we have to deal forthrightly with the issues of how people form their expectations. In *The General Theory of Employment, Interest, and Money,* Keynes emphasized the erratic nature of expectations, that they could shift around randomly with no rational explanation.

The hypothesis of rational expectations holds that firms and consumers make the most of the information that is available to them. If they know from past experience that the Federal Reserve lowers interest rates whenever there is an increase in unemployment, then they will expect the Federal Reserve to act the same in the future. The rational expectations assumption is used so much in this book that you may find the idea somewhat routine. Frequently, "rational expectations" is taken as a shorthand phrase to stand for propositions that economic policy is ineffective. We will explain later in the book why we think the propositions are wrong.

Economic growth theory has experienced a resurgence of research interest in the last few years. Disappointments about growth in the United States and persistent disparities of income per capita in countries around the world—made more vivid by the careful statistical studies of Robert Summers and Robert Heston of the University of Pennsylvania—have been two key reasons for this renewed interest. New research goes beyond the path-breaking neoclassical model of Nobel Prize–winning economist Robert Solow to try to explain the determinants of technological change. Hence, the new research is sometimes called *endogenous* growth theory. It points to the importance of education and training, research and development, and increased international integration of economies, as well as physical capital, in generating technical progress. Robert Lucas of the University of Chicago and Paul Romer of the University of California at Berkeley have contributed to the latest theoretical developments in endogenous growth theory.

Banking and credit markets have also been an active area of macroeconomic research in recent years. The problems in the savings and loan industry in the United States, concerns that similar problems could occur in banks in the 1990s, perceived increases in financial market volatility associated with the stock market break in 1987, greater riskiness due to heavy borrowing by firms and households in the late 1980s, and wide public attention on the "credit crunch" in the early 1990s have helped to motivate this research. Much of this research is related to financial institutions' role in intermediation—channeling funds from lenders to borrowers, a role which is emphasized in this book. New research has explored the microeconomic foundations of financial intermediation and the empirical importance of bank credit in economic fluctuations. Many of the researchers in this area argue that changes in the supply of bank credit underlie the empirical relationship between money growth and economic fluctuations which we pointed out in Figure 1–8. R. Glenn Hubbard of Columbia University has pulled together some of this recent research in a new volume entitled *Financial Markets and Financial Crises.*

How Did Today's Macroeconomists Come to Study Economics?

Macroeconomists—whether traditional Keynesian, monetarist, or new classical—began studying economics for many different reasons. Some got interested because the hardships of the Great Depression of the 1930s touched them personally. For others it was pure chance. But whatever the reason, they all liked it and stuck with it. Here are some answers to the question "How did you come to study economics?" from some macroeconomists whose work we will study in this book.*

Franco Modigliani

[Laughter] That's a good question. I'd say, by chance. I started my university years with the expectation that I would become a doctor, because my father was one. . . . At the last moment I realized that I wasn't cut out for that profession; I cannot stand the sight of blood. So I went into law, which is in Italy very general.

Then there was a national competition among university students to write an essay about the effect of price controls. I decided to participate. . . . I wrote my essay and won first prize. The judges said that I should pursue the study of economics and so I began.

James Tobin

I went into economics for two reasons. One was that as a child of the Depression I was terribly concerned about the world. It seemed then that many of the problems were economic in origin. If you thought that the world should be saved, and I did, then economics looked like the decisive thing to study. The second thing was that you could have your cake and eat it too, because it was an intellectually fascinating subject.

Robert E. Lucas, Jr.

I have always liked to think about social problems. It may have something to do with my family. We always argued about politics and social issues. I studied history. . . . But I came around to the view that economic forces are central forces in history, and started trying some economics. It was a big shock to me to find books in English that were incomprehensible to me. . . [Like] Keynes's *General Theory.* I still can't read Keynes. [Laughter] I realized I couldn't pick it up as an amateur. So I got into economics in a professional way and got my Ph.D. at Chicago.

Thomas J. Sargent

[Long pause and hesitation] I liked it when we studied it in college. But also I was truly curious, ever since I was a kid, about what causes depressions. The Great Depression had a big effect on me: a lot of people in my family got wiped out. My grandfather ran a quarry in the construction business, and he got wiped out. My other grandfather was in the radio business, and he got wiped out. It was the common story.

*The answers come from separate interviews published in Arjo Klamer, *Conversations with Economists* (Rowman and Allanheld, 1984).

1.5 THE MACROECONOMIC MODEL USED IN THIS BOOK

Although many alternative theories are discussed, a main model appears throughout this book. This model combines new theories of sticky prices and new theories of rational expectations. It explains recessions as temporary departures from the long-run potential growth path of output. It shows how shifts in production from one sector to another can occur without large departures from the potential growth path. And it places great emphasis on how labor, capital, and technological change affect that growth path.

There is an interesting question of what to call this type of model. Because of the use of sticky prices, many economists use the term *Keynesian* for this model. A problem with this name is that "Keynesian" is also a term used to refer to traditional models that do not incorporate the ideas of rational expectations. A related problem with this name is that "Keynesian economics" is also a term used to describe a certain set of positions on policy issues. Some writers use the name "Keynesians" to mean economists who believe in aggressive government intervention, high government spending, and use of taxes and spending to offset recessions. A simple way to see the difference is to consider the opinions of the world's leading conservative macroeconomist, Milton Friedman. Friedman strongly opposes all of the policies that go by the name Keynesian. Yet Friedman has adopted a sticky-price model as the centerpiece of his macroeconomic theory.[1]

An alternative would be to use the term "rational-expectations model," but this term is frequently used to refer to models used by the new classical school with perfectly flexible prices. "Rational expectations" is commonly used to refer to theories in which monetary policy has no effect in stabilizing the economy. On the contrary, the model used in this book says that monetary policy can play an important role in improving economic performance.

Because of the alternative misleading interpretations of these more popular names, we usually refer to the model in this book simply as the **complete model**—a model with all its essential parts. The complete model is developed in a rudimentary or "no-frills" form in Chapters 4 through 9, with the important microeconomic foundations and more advanced policy analysis provided later in the book. In developing the rudi-

[1]Milton Friedman, "A Theoretical Framework for Monetary Analysis," *Journal of Political Economy,* Vol. 78 (March/April 1970), pp. 193–238.

mentary form of the complete model, we begin with the determinants of long-term potential growth (Chapters 4 and 5) and then discuss departures from the potential growth path (Chapters 6 through 9).

REVIEW AND PRACTICE

Major Points

1. Output and employment expand and contract at irregular intervals.

2. Other measures of the state of the economy, like interest rates and inflation, also track fluctuations.

3. The goal of macroeconomics is to develop models that give us an understanding of the determinants of both short-term economic fluctuations and long-term economic growth. Such an understanding will permit us to design fiscal, monetary, and other government policies that promote growth and mitigate fluctuations.

4. According to the long-run growth model, output is set by supply conditions alone; output is always at its potential level. The model with flexible prices has problems explaining short-term declines in output, but describes long-term growth quite well.

5. The complete model with sticky prices says that output need not be equal to potential output. In the very short run, output is determined by aggregate demand given a fixed price level.

6. In the model with sticky prices, fluctuations in output can be caused by shifts in aggregate demand. In the long-run model, the only source of change in output is a change in potential.

7. The price-adjustment process describes the transition from the short run to the long run. Prices fall when output is below potential GDP and rise when it is above. The price adjustment moves the economy in the direction of potential GDP.

8. Economists agree about the importance of stabilizing aggregate demand, but disagree about how government should try to influence it through fiscal and monetary policy.

Key Terms and Concepts

fluctuations	rate of inflation	sticky prices
recession	rate of interest	flexible prices
recovery	unemployment rate	John Maynard Keynes
trough	price adjustment	Keynesians
peak	procyclical	monetarists
gross domestic product	long-run growth model	new classicals
real GDP	complete model	real business cycle model
potential GDP	aggregate demand	

Questions for Discussion and Review

1. Which of the following are procyclical?
   - a. Interest rates
   - c. Inflation
   - b. Employment
   - d. Money supply
2. Explain the difference between potential GDP and real GDP.
3. Describe a typical macroeconomic fluctuation, starting from a peak.
4. What are the determinants of potential GDP?
5. How have economic fluctuations changed during the last 80 years?
6. How does GDP respond to aggregate demand when prices are perfectly flexible?
7. How does GDP respond to aggregate demand when prices do not adjust?
8. What could cause a recession in the long-run growth model with flexible prices?

Problems

Numerical

1. Real output in the United Kingdom from 1960 through 1991 is given below. All data are in billions of 1985 pounds.

1960	200.4	1971	271.9	1982	322.9
1961	206.4	1972	278.0	1983	335.4
1962	208.1	1973	300.1	1984	341.3
1963	217.4	1974	297.3	1985	354.0
1964	229.0	1975	295.4	1986	366.2
1965	234.0	1976	306.3	1987	382.0
1966	238.8	1977	309.5	1988	392.0
1967	245.3	1978	321.7	1989	401.0
1968	255.7	1979	328.9	1990	404.2
1969	259.1	1980	322.5	1991	396.5
1970	265.1	1981	318.9		

   - a. Plot U.K. real output over the 32-year period. Put real output on the vertical axis of the graph and the year on the horizontal axis.
   - b. Estimate potential output by drawing a smooth trend line through the points on the graph. Identify any shifts in the trend of potential. By what percent did real output grow during this period?
   - c. Identify the fluctuations of real output around potential output. How many complete (peak-to-peak) economic fluctuations occurred during this period? How does the frequency of economic fluctuations during this period compare with that of the United States during the same period?
2. Suppose that the aggregate demand curve in a particular year is given by the algebraic expression $Y = 5,000 + 1,000/P$, where Y is output and P is the price level. Potential output is $Y^* = 6,000$.
   - a. Draw the downward-sloping aggregate demand curve and a vertical line showing potential GDP to scale on a diagram with the price level P on

the vertical axis and output Y on the horizontal axis.

b. Suppose that prices are flexible. Find the price level and show it on the diagram.

c. Now suppose that the following year the aggregate demand curve is given by $Y = 5,000 + 1,100/P$. In what direction has the curve shifted? If output remains at potential, what is the new price level? What was the rate of inflation between the two years?

d. If prices are instead assumed to be sticky, what will the new level of output be? Will there be pressure on the price level to move upward or downward? Explain.

3. We have the following data on interest rates and the price level (in the United States) for the years 1977–91:

Year	Price Level (1982–84=100)	Interest Rates
1977	60.6	5.5%
1978	65.2	7.6
1979	72.6	10.0
1980	82.4	11.4
1981	90.9	13.8
1982	96.5	11.1
1983	99.6	8.8
1984	103.9	9.8
1985	107.6	7.7
1986	109.6	6.0
1987	113.6	6.1
1988	118.3	6.9
1989	124.0	8.0
1990	130.7	7.5
1991	136.2	5.5

a. Calculate the rate of inflation for the years 1978–91.

b. Calculate the expected rate of inflation for the years 1979–91 assuming (i) people expect the rate of inflation to be the average rate of inflation in the two previous years and (ii) people have perfect foresight and expected inflation just equals actual inflation.

c. For each of the assumptions in Part b, calculate the real interest rate for the years 1977–91.

d. In light of this example, explain why economists have such a difficult time measuring the real interest rate.

e. How do you think people forecast inflation? What information do they use? Do you think they systematically underestimate changes in the price level?

Analytical

1. What explains the fluctuations in output in models where prices are flexible? In models where prices are sticky?

2. Comment on the following two explanations of the large drop in output in the early 1980s in the United States:

   a. "There was a decline in potential output because the number of people available for work declined."

   b. "There was a decline in aggregate demand. With very high interest rates, consumers and firms purchased fewer goods so that production and employment declined."

   Which statement seems more plausible? Which statement is consistent with the macro model with flexible prices and which with the model with sticky prices?

3. Would Keynes have argued that prices in the 1930s were too low or too high? Explain.

4. Is it reasonable to ignore departures from potential GDP in the study of change in real GDP over periods of 10 years or more? Why or why not?

5. The notion that departures from potential GDP are important is a necessary, but not sufficient, condition to warrant active use of government policy to offset recessions. Why is some belief in departures from potential GDP essential to rationalize activist policy to fight recessions? Why is it not sufficient to make activism superior to nonintervention?

MacroSolve Exercises

1. Plot, using the **PLOT** option, the GDP gap (the percentage deviation of real GDP from potential GDP) using annual data. Identify the years when troughs and peaks occur. (It will be useful to tabulate the data to identify the exact years when these occur. Peaks occur in periods when the GDP gap is greater than the surrounding observations, and troughs occur when the GDP gap is more negative than the surrounding observations.)

   a. On average, how frequent are recessions? Has this frequency increased or decreased since the Second World War? Why might the frequency have changed?

   b. Are business fluctuations symmetric? In other words, is the period of decline between peaks and troughs longer or shorter than the upswing from troughs to peaks? Can you think of any reasons for this?

2. Using annual data, graph the GDP gap on the horizontal axis against the unemployment rate on the vertical axis. Is unemployment procyclical or countercyclical? In other words, when output is high relative to potential output, is the unemployment rate high (so that unemployment is procyclical) or low (countercyclical)? Explain why.

3. Plot both the real interest rate and the inflation rate on the same screen using quarterly data from 1967 to 1991. When the inflation rate changes, do the real and nominal interest rates generally move in the same direction or in opposite directions? Why?

4. Do the real interest rate and the GDP gap generally move in the same direction or opposite directions? Can you think of any explanations for this?

CHAPTER

2

Measuring Economic Performance: Output and Income

In Chapter 1 we examined the behavior of several key macroeconomic variables—production, employment, and inflation. In this chapter and the next we show how these and other important variables are defined and measured.

2.1   GROSS DOMESTIC PRODUCT

We begin with gross domestic product (GDP). GDP refers to production during a particular time period, which we will usually take to be a year or a quarter of a year. GDP is the *flow* of new products during the year or the quarter. GDP is measured in dollars. When we adjust GDP for the effects of inflation, we get real GDP, the measure of physical output discussed in Chapter 1.

There are three different ways to think about and measure GDP. First, we can measure **spending** on goods and services by different groups— households, businesses, government, and foreigners. Second, we can measure **production** in different industries—agriculture, mining, manufacturing, and so on. Last, we can measure the total wage and profit **income** earned by different groups producing GDP. Each of these measures has its own special purpose, but they all add up to the same thing. We consider each in turn in the next three sections.

How do we know that the total amount of spending is equal to the total value of production, which in turn is equal to the total amount of income? Think about an individual firm. Suppose the value of its production is $1 million. It is unlikely that its sales are exactly $1 million in that year—suppose its sales are $900,000. For accounting purposes, we treat the remaining $100,000 as spending. It is the firm's investment in inventories of its own goods and is included as part of total investment. Both at the level of the firm and at the level of the whole economy, the equality of production and spending is the result of considering inventory investment as part of spending.

The equality of the value of production and income also derives from accounting principles. Our firm takes in $900,000 in one year. In addition, we add in the $100,000 value of its inventory accumulation as sales, for a total value of production of $1 million. The firm pays out $450,000 in wages. That amount is counted in the incomes of the workers. The firm pays $50,000 in interest, which is counted in the incomes of whoever holds the firm's bonds. It pays $400,000 for its raw materials, which is counted in the incomes of the sellers of materials or of their employees, bondholders, etc. The residual, $1,000,000 − $450,000 − $50,000 − $400,000 = $100,000, is the profit that is earned by the owner of the firm and that counts as part of the owner's income. All the receipts of the firm from its sales are paid out to somebody as income. The value of production and the total amount of income generated are the same.

As a result of the two accounting rules—including inventories in spending and computing profit as the residual between sales and expenses—it is always true that production, spending, and income are exactly the same. This kind of relation is called an **identity;** it is the inevitable outcome of the accounting system, not a statement about how the economy works.

The alternative measures of GDP are gathered together in the national income and product accounts (NIPA). Economists and statisticians at the Bureau of Economic Analysis (BEA), an agency of the United States government in Washington, D.C., are responsible for collecting the GDP data and publishing the NIPA. Many of the ideas behind the GDP were developed by the late Simon Kuznets of Harvard University. He won the Nobel Prize in economics in 1971 for this work.

2.2   MEASURING GDP THROUGH SPENDING

Total spending on goods and services produced by Americans during any period can be broken down as follows:

Gross domestic product = Consumption
+ Investment
+ Government purchases
+ Net exports (or exports minus imports).

Using symbols, this key identity can be written on one line:

$$Y = C + I + G + X$$
where Y = Gross domestic product
C = Consumption
I = Investment
G = Government spending
X = Net exports (exports minus imports).

Consumption

Consumption is defined as spending by *households*. It includes purchases of (1) **durable goods,** such as washing machines, stereos, and cars, (2) **nondurable goods,** such as food, clothing, and gasoline, and (3) **services,** such as haircuts, medical care, and education. Spending on new houses is the only type of household spending that is not included in consumption. Instead it is included in fixed investment.

Investment

Investment is the sum of spending by firms on plant, equipment, and inventories and spending by households on housing. We separate total investment into **fixed investment** and **inventory investment.** Fixed investment is the purchase of new factories, machines, and houses. Inventory investment is the change in inventories at business firms. We first discuss fixed investment.

FIXED INVESTMENT.   Fixed investment is broken down into **nonresidential** fixed investment and **residential** fixed investment. Nonresidential fixed investment is spending on structures and equipment for use in business. Steel mills, office buildings, and power plants are examples of structures. Trucks, lathes, and typewriters are examples of equipment. Residential fixed investment is spending on construction of new houses and apartment buildings. The term "fixed" connotes that these types of investment goods will be around for a long time and thus distinguishes them from inventory investment, which is much more temporary, as we will see below. The term "fixed" is conventionally dropped when the meaning is implicit from the context, and we will follow this convention.

Investment is a *flow* of new capital during the year that is added to the *stock* of capital. The **capital stock** is the total physical amount of productive capital in the economy; it includes all the buildings, equipment, and houses. The capital stock increases from one year to the next as a result of investment. However, because the capital stock is constantly wearing out, part of the investment reported in each year's GDP is actually devoted to replacing worn-out capital, not increasing the capital stock. What is reported in GDP is *gross* investment. This accounts for the term "gross" in GDP. Statisticians have a number of ways of estimating the loss of the existing capital stock from one year to the next. This loss is called **depreciation. Net investment** is defined as follows:

$$\text{Net investment} = \text{Gross investment} - \text{Depreciation.}$$

We have the following relation:

Capital stock at the end of this year = Capital stock at the end of last year
  − Depreciation during this year
  + Gross investment during this year.

By rearranging this equation and putting in the definition of net investment, we have:

Net investment = Capital stock at the end of this year
  − Capital stock at the end of last year.

These equations hold whether we are looking at total investment or separately at nonresidential and residential investment.

INVENTORY INVESTMENT. Now consider inventory investment, which is simply the change in the stock of inventories held at businesses.

Inventory investment this year = Stock of inventories at the end of this year
  − Stock of inventories at the end of last year.

For example, when a publisher produces and stores 10,000 copies of a newly printed book in its warehouse, the books are counted in GDP as inventory investment. Even though no one has yet purchased the books, they must be counted in GDP because they have been produced. If subsequently you purchase a book directly from the publisher, consumption is up by one book and inventory investment is down by one book; GDP does not change, nor should it since there is no new production. When the publisher sells a book to a bookstore, the publisher's inventory investment is down by one book and the bookstore's inventory investment is up by one book. Total inventory investment does not change, and neither does GDP.

Inventory investment is positive when inventories are increasing, and negative when inventories are decreasing. In 1989 inventory investment was $36 billion. In 1991, a recession year, it was −$20 billion. If inventory investment were not added to spending when computing GDP, we would underestimate production when inventory investment was positive, as in 1989, because spending would be less than production; similarly we would overestimate production when inventory investment was negative, as in 1991, because spending would be more than production.

As the data for 1989 show, inventory investment adds to the fluctuations of GDP. **Final sales** is a measure that excludes inventory investment. Final sales is defined as GDP minus inventory investment. Final sales fluctuates less than GDP.

Portfolio Investment and Macro Investment

The difference between the macroeconomist's use of the term "investment" and its use in casual conversation may be a stumbling block. Macroeconomic investment, *I*, is limited to purchases of newly built houses, plant, equipment, and inventories. When a business or a family buys stocks, bonds, existing real estate, or other portfolio items, they also think of them as investments because these assets (should) provide a financial return. Such investments are not counted as macroeconomic investment, however, because they are just movements of existing assets from one person to another. They do not create any new productive facilities. When one person buys stock, somebody else sells that stock; one person's investment is another's disinvestment.

But portfolio opportunities still matter, because they always loom as an alternative to macroeconomic investment. A business can invest in plant, equipment, and inventories, and presumably it will enjoy a high return, or else why would it stay in that industry? But if its corporate treasurer recommended investing in a new plant predicted to provide a 5 percent return at a time when government securities were paying 6 percent, the trea-

surer would soon enjoy the status of ex-corporate treasurer.

What kind of competition is macroeconomic investment up against? In 1991, portfolio investments scored the following returns:

1991 Stock market dividend rate	3.2%
3-month Treasury bills	5.4
Aaa corporate bonds	8.8
Baa corporate bonds	9.8
Tax-free municipal bonds	6.9

The returns to bonds generally grow higher as they get riskier, but in the case of tax-free municipals they can pay less and make their owners just as happy as corporate bond owners because no taxes are paid on the proceeds. Interestingly, the best investment historically has been the stock market, where capital gains have more than made up for the lower dividend rates.

If a business concludes that the likely return to a new plant is better than any of these other returns, taking into consideration taxes, capital gains, future inflation, and so on, then it will decide to build the plant. Hence the returns on alternatives, such as bonds, are an important determinant of the level of investment.

Government Purchases

Government purchases are the sum of federal government and state and local government purchases of goods and services. In 1991, state and local government purchases were 59 percent of total government purchases. Schools, road construction, and military hardware are examples of government purchases. Government purchases are only part of the total government *outlays* that are included in the government budget. Government purchases exclude such items as welfare payments and interest payments on the public debt that are included in government outlays.

The distinction between consumption, investment, and government is based primarily on the type of purchaser rather than on the type of product that is purchased. If a Chevrolet is purchased by a household it goes into consumption—as a consumer durable. If it is purchased for use by a business, it goes into investment—as business fixed investment in equipment. If it is purchased by government, it goes into government purchases. The only exception to this rule is residential investment, which includes all housing purchases whether by households, businesses, or government.

Imports and Exports

The United States has an open economy. An open economy is one with substantial interaction with other countries. The United States has experienced a growing volume of transactions with the rest of the world, and GDP has to take these into account. **Exports** are deliveries of goods and services from the United States to foreigners. Sales of transportation services, such as when foreigners travel on U.S. airlines, is an example of service exports. **Imports** are deliveries of goods and services from foreigners to the United States.

Part, but not all, of United States exports represent goods and services *produced* by Americans. The other part has been imported to the United States and then sold abroad, perhaps as part of manufactured products. For example, General Motors might put a radio imported from Japan into a Chevrolet that is exported to Mexico. We want to subtract the radio from the exported car if we are measuring goods produced by Americans. More generally, if goods are imported from abroad and purchased by United States consumers, businesses, or governments, the goods should not be counted in a measure of U.S. production. For these reasons imports are subtracted from spending and exports are added to spending when computing GDP. In other words, only **net exports,** that is, *exports less imports,* are added to the total volume of spending when computing GDP. Note that this decomposition of GDP does not tell you what part of consumption was imported and what part was produced in the United States. Nor does it break down investment, government purchases, or exports between domestic and imported components. The total of net exports is sometimes referred to as the **trade balance.** When net exports are positive there is a **trade surplus.** When net exports are negative there is a **trade deficit.**

The Recent Composition of Spending

Table 2–1 shows how U.S. GDP broke down in 1991. Consumption is the biggest component—about two-thirds—of GDP. Services is the biggest component of consumption—about 56 percent. Services (restaurants, utilities, housing, transportation, medical care, and the like) have been growing as a share of consumption. In the early 1950s services accounted for less than a third of consumption. Medical services have grown most rapidly.

Fixed investment is about 13 percent of GDP. Nonresidential fixed investment is much larger than residential fixed investment. Government purchases are larger than investment, at about 19 percent of GDP. Imports are about 11 percent of GDP. Exports are 10 percent of GDP. Foreign trade is now a much bigger factor in the United States than it was 20 or 30 years ago. In the early 1950s exports and imports each were about 5 percent of GDP.

These shares fluctuate from year to year but the two-thirds consumption share is fairly typical of recent years in the United States. Inventory investment and net exports fluctuate dramatically and can be negative as well

TABLE 2–1 Gross Domestic Product in 1991—The Spending Side (billions of dollars)

Gross domestic product	5671.8
Consumption	3886.8
Durables	445.2
Nondurables	1251.0
Services	2190.5
Investment	725.3
Fixed investment	745.6
Nonresidential	550.4
Residential	195.1
Inventory investment	−20.2
Government purchases	1086.9
Net exports	−27.1
Exports	593.3
Imports	620.4
Final sales	5692.0

Note: Final sales is GDP less inventory investment. Details in the table may not add to totals because of rounding.

Source: *Economic Report of the President,* 1992, Table B–1.

Bringing Astronomical Numbers Down to Earth

Table 2–1 shows that GDP was $5,671.8 billion, or about $5.7 trillion, in 1991. With all the zeros this looks like $5,671,800,000,000. An astrophysicist would write it 5.6718×10^{12} dollars. How can we make intuitive sense of such large numbers?

The best way to bring numbers like these down to size is simply to divide by the population—that is, to calculate GDP per person, or GDP per capita. The population in the United States in 1991 was 252.6 million. GDP per capita in the United States is thus $22,454 (5,671,800,000,000/252,600,000 = 22,453.68).

U.S. consumption in 1991 was $3,886.8 billion. This amounts to about $15,387 per capita for food, clothing, transportation, and other consumer items. On average, every man, woman, and child in the United States consumed $15,387 of goods and services in 1991.

Government purchases of goods and services were $1,086.9 billion in 1991. This amounted to $4,303 per capita for national defense, schools, highways, police, and so on. Net exports were –$27.1 billion in 1991, or about –$107 per capita. In other words, on average every person in the United States bought $107 more goods that were made abroad than they made goods that were sold abroad.

as positive; no year is typical. Since exports were slightly smaller than imports in 1991, net exports were negative. Final sales were slightly more than GDP in 1991 since inventory investment was negative.

Which Spending Items Should Be Included?

In deciding which spending items to include in computing GDP, we must be careful to avoid double counting. For example, the purchase of a 10-year-old house should not be counted; that house was counted 10 years ago when it was constructed. Similarly, the purchase of the assets of Gulf Oil by Chevron should not be counted; the Gulf building in Pittsburgh and Gulf's offshore oil rigs were included in business fixed investment when they were built.

To avoid double counting, we also do not include the purchase of **intermediate goods.** These are goods that are converted into other goods in the production process (for example, steel is an intermediate good used in the production of cars). We only include purchases of the **final goods,** such as the cars themselves. The value of the steel is included in GDP as part of a car when someone buys the car. The purchases of steel by automobile manufacturers are not counted.

In computing GDP, we value different types of goods, such as apples and oranges, using the price of each good that is paid by the purchaser. The price includes sales and excise taxes. If apples cost twice as much as oranges, then each apple will contribute twice as much to GDP as will each orange.

Real GDP

GDP is a dollar measure of production. In comparing one year with another, we run into the problem that the dollar is not a stable measure of purchasing power. In the 1970s especially, GDP rose a great deal, not because the economy was actually growing rapidly but because the dollar was inflating. For comparisons across years, we need a measure of output that adjusts for inflation. We want *GDP in constant dollars,* or, as we will generally call it, **real GDP.** In contrast, the GDP that we have looked at so far is sometimes called **nominal GDP.** From 1972 to 1990 nominal GDP grew by 357 percent from $1,207.0 billion to $5,513.8 billion. During the same period real GDP grew by about 57 percent. The conversion from nominal to real makes a big difference.

The concept of real GDP is straighforward. We want to measure consumption, investment, government purchases, and exports in physical rather than dollar units. Further, we want to subtract imports in the same physical units, so that real GDP is a measure of production.

To compute consumption in real terms, the national income statisticians gather data on the prices of consumption goods in great detail. They take the data on the corresponding detailed flows of goods to consumers and restate them in 1987 dollars. For example, suppose the retail price of a typical shirt rose from $10.00 in 1987 to $12.00 in 1991. The flow of shirts to consumers was $3 billion in 1987 and $5 billion in 1991. Consumption of shirts in real terms was $3 billion in 1987 dollars in 1987 and $4.17 billion in 1987 dollars in 1991. The $4.17 billion is computed as

(5 billion 1991 dollars) x [(10/12) 1987 dollars per 1991 dollar]
= 4.17 billion 1987 dollars.

The same type of adjustment for price change is applied to each detailed category of consumption, investment, government purchases, exports, and imports. Then real GDP is real consumption plus real investment plus real government purchases plus real exports less real imports.

A Tale of Two Recessions

Table 2–2 shows the breakdown of real GDP for the three-year period that spans the deep 1981-82 recession in the United States. This recession was

TABLE 2–2   Components of Real GDP, 1981–83 (billions of 1987 dollars)

	1981	1982	1983
Gross domestic product	3843.1	3760.3	3906.6
Consumption	2476.9	2503.7	2619.4
Durables	264.6	262.5	297.7
Nondurables	867.9	872.2	900.3
Services	1344.4	1368.9	1421.4
Investment	631.1	540.5	599.5
Fixed investment	606.5	558.0	595.1
Nonresidential	455.0	433.9	420.8
Residential	151.6	124.1	174.2
Inventory investment	24.6	−17.5	4.4
Government purchases	713.2	723.6	743.8
Net exports	22.0	−7.4	−56.1
Exports	326.1	296.7	285.9
Imports	304.1	304.1	342.1
Final sales	3818.6	3777.8	3902.2

Source: *Economic Report of the President,* 1992, Table B–2.

preceded by record high interest rates in the summer of 1981. As we will see later, the high interest rates were the result of policy actions at the Federal Reserve Board. Table 2–3 shows a similar breakdown for 1990, 1991, and 1992—a period that contains a similar downturn.

There are many figures in Tables 2–2 and 2–3. The job of a professional macroeconomist is to interpret such numbers and develop an account of what happened to the U.S. economy. With a close look, at least five interesting facts can be gleaned.

1. Real GDP fell from 1981 to 1982. It also fell from 1990 to 1991. After both declines, real GDP rose. This decline and subsequent rise is the essential feature of an economic cycle. Each cycle begins with a contraction of real GDP, reaches a trough, begins an expansion, and then reaches a peak. The next cycle starts with the next contraction. The decline in real GDP in 1982 was by 2.2 percent while the decline in 1991 was by much less, 0.7 percent.

2. Real GDP fell by more than final sales in both 1982 and 1991, since inventory investment declined in both recessions. In fact, inventory investment became negative in both years; firms drew down their inventories

TABLE 2-3 Components of Real GDP, 1990-92
(billions of 1987 dollars)

	1990	1991	1992
Gross domestic product	4884.9	4848.4	4921.1
Consumption	3262.9	3256.7	3312.0
Durables	438.9	412.5	414.6
Nondurables	1050.8	1042.3	1046.5
Services	1773.0	1801.9	1848.7
Investment	744.5	672.6	699.5
Fixed investment	744.2	687.7	699.4
Nonresidential	548.8	512.7	500.4
Residential	195.5	175.1	199.1
Inventory investment	.2	-15.1	2.7
Net exports	-51.3	-17.6	-16.5
Exports	505.7	539.6	582.2
Imports	557.0	557.2	596.2
Government purchases	929.1	936.7	925.5
Final sales	4884.7	4863.6	4917.0

Source: *Economic Report of the President*, 1992, Table B-2 and *The U.S. Economic Outlook*, Lawrence H. Meyer and Associate, March 9, 1992 (the figures for 1992 are based on the latter report).

because they anticipated lower sales during the recession. The decline in inventories made both recessions worse than they otherwise would have been.

3. Consumption increased only slightly in 1982 and actually fell a bit in 1991 as automobile, furniture, and appliance purchases dropped. People postponed purchases of big-ticket items until better times.

4. Residential investment and nonresidential investment fell sharply both in 1982 and in 1991. The high interest rates made it difficult to borrow to finance both housing and factory construction.

5. Net exports fell in 1982 but rose in 1991. This was the *biggest difference* between the two recessions as evidenced from these tables. The decrease in net exports worsened the decline in GDP in 1982, while the increase in net exports in 1991 lessened the decline in GDP in that year. Amazingly, if net exports had behaved the same in 1982 and 1991, then the declines in GDP would have been the same. In this sense, the foreign trade sector is what made 1991 a mild downturn compared with 1982.

Quarterly GDP Statistics and the 1990–91 Recession

The spending data reported in Tables 2–1 through 2–3 are *annual*. They give the flow of spending for a year. *Quarterly* GDP data are also available in the United States. These give the spending flows for a quarter of a year. Quarterly data are useful for understanding shorter-run movements of business cycles. Private forecasting firms and government agencies all use quarterly models of the economy. Quarterly data on real GDP are reported in the newspapers as soon as they are available, usually a few weeks after the quarter is over. The traditional rule of thumb for a downturn to qualify as a recession is two consecutive quarters of declining GDP. Note how real GDP declined in the fourth quarter of 1990 and the first quarter of 1991. Real GDP in 1991 was lower for the year as a whole than in 1990. Some important conventions of the reporting of quarterly data are illustrated in the following comparison.

Year:Quarter	Real GDP	Year	Real GDP
1989:1	4,809.8	1989	4,836.9
1989:2	4,832.4		
1989:3	4,845.6		
1989:4	4,859.7		
1990:1	4,880.8	1990	4,884.9
1990:2	4,900.3		
1990:3	4,903.3		
1990:4	4,855.1		
1991:1	4,824.0	1991	4,848.4
1991:2	4,840.7		
1991:3	4,862.7		
1991:4	4,866.3		

Source: *Economic Report of the President*, 1992, Table B-2.

The flow of GDP in each quarter is stated at an annual rate, which means that the actual flow each quarter is multiplied by 4. If you add up the four quarterly flows for each year and divide by 4, you get the annual figure reported at the right.

Economic Growth and Convergence in Three Countries

Data on real GDP can also be used to compare economic performance in different countries. Figure 2–1 shows real GDP in three countries: the United States, Germany, and Japan. GDP is divided by the number of workers in each country to give a comparable measure of economic perfor-

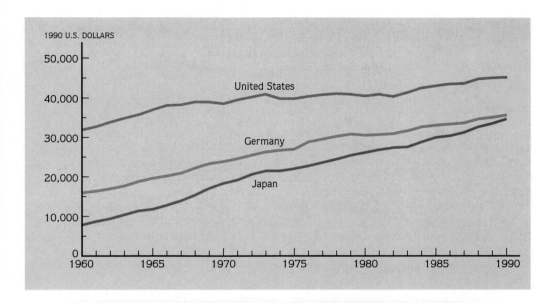

FIGURE 2-1   GDP per worker in three countries

Of the three countries, growth is highest in Japan and lowest in the United States.

mance. Moreover, GDP in Germany and Japan, measured in marks and yen respectively, has been translated into dollars by the use of an exchange rate that takes account of different costs of living in each country. (Exchange rate measures are discussed in the last section of this chapter.)

GDP per worker is a measure of the productivity of workers in each country. Despite many claims to the contrary, American workers were still the most productive according to these measures. In Japan and Germany, real output per worker was about 80 percent of that in the United States in 1990. However, the three economies have been converging. The growth rate has been higher in Germany, and especially in Japan, than in the United States. In fact, these three countries show an interesting inverse relationship between the level of GDP per worker and the growth rate of GDP per worker: the country with the lowest GDP per worker (Japan) is growing fastest, and the country with the highest GDP per worker (United States) is growing slowest. Ongoing research suggests a similar pattern for other countries around the world.

An important objective of this book is to explain these different growth trends and the evident convergence. As we emphasized in Chapter 1, macroeconomics is concerned with both economic growth and economic fluctuations.

2.3   MEASURING GDP THROUGH PRODUCTION: VALUE ADDED

GDP can also be computed by adding up production of goods and services in different industries. As we observed on the spending side, we must avoid counting the same items more than once. Many industries specialize in the production of intermediate goods that are used in the production of other goods. If we want each industry's production to include the contribution of those industries to total GDP, then we want to take the production of intermediate goods into account.

The concept of **value added** was developed to prevent double counting and to attribute to each industry a part of the GDP. The value added by a firm is the difference between the revenue the firm earns by selling its products and the amount it pays for the products of other firms it uses as intermediate goods. It is a measure of the value that is added to each product by firms at each stage of production.

For General Motors, for example, value added is the revenue from selling cars less the amount it pays for steel, glass, and the other inputs it buys.

For a car dealer, value added is the revenue from selling cars less the wholesale cost of the cars. The value added to a car by a car dealer takes the form of a convenient showroom, ample selection, advice (for what it's worth), and final preparation and testing. The car dealer produces these services by hiring salespeople and car mechanics, renting showroom and garage space, borrowing money to hold a big inventory of cars, and keeping the profits. Wages, rents, interest, and profits are thus what make up value added at each firm.

GDP is the sum of the value added by all the firms located in the United States. If a firm sells a final product, the sale appears in that firm's value added but does not appear anywhere else. On the other hand, if a firm sells its output as an input for another firm, that sale appears negatively in the other firm's value added. Products sold by one firm to another are called **intermediate products.** When the two firms are added together in the process of computing GDP, sales of intermediate products wash out. When a firm imports a product, the transaction appears negatively in that firm's value added, but does not appear positively in the value added of any U.S. firm.

A breakdown of real GDP in terms of the value added by various industries is given in Table 2–4 for 1970 and 1988. These figures tell some interesting stories about the modern U.S. economy. Perhaps most striking, given all that we have heard about the deindustrialization of America, is that manufacturing as a share of GDP was higher in 1988 than in 1970 (23 percent versus 21 percent). (Employment in manufacturing has declined,

TABLE 2–4 Value Added by Industry in 1970 and 1988
(billions of 1982 dollars)

	1970	1988
Gross domestic product	2402.9	4023.9
Agriculture	68.8	94.5
Mining	134.5	127.3
Construction	168.0	176.9
Manufacturing	506.8	927.5
Transportation and utilities	203.9	392.0
Wholesale and retail trade	367.6	693.9
Finance, insurance, and real estate	320.7	583.7
Services	295.7	613.9
Government	339.6	422.2
Statistical discrepancy	−2.7	−8.0

Source: *Economic Report of the President,* 1991, Table B–11 (more recent data not available).

however, because labor productivity in manufacturing has grown rapidly.)
Manufacturing is the largest sector, but the wholesale and retail trade sector,
whose only function is to take produced goods and make them available to
the public, is almost as large as the manufacturing sector. The finance, insurance, and real estate sector is also large.

Near the bottom of the list is a small item called **statistical discrepancy.** Although the value-added computation of GDP should give the same
answer as total spending, in practice there are measurement errors that
cause a slight discrepancy between the two.

2.4   MEASURING GDP THROUGH INCOME

The Americans who produce GDP receive income for their work. This income provides a third way to compute GDP. To see the relation between
GDP and income, think again about the value added of a car dealer. Value
added is the difference between the revenue from selling cars and the
wholesale cost of cars. That difference must be somebody's income. Part of
the difference is the wages the car dealer pays to salespeople and mechanics. Another part is the rent that the car dealer pays to a landlord for the use
of the showroom and garage. Another part is the interest that the car dealer
pays to a bank for loans to finance inventory. The rest of the difference is
profit, which goes into the income of the owner of the car dealership.

What Happened to GNP?

Ever since the Department of Commerce started measuring income in the United States, statisticians and accountants have emphasized Gross National Product (GNP) rather than Gross Domestic Product (GDP). GNP is GDP plus *net* payments of factor incomes from abroad. GNP measures the value of goods and services produced by residents of the United States, while GDP measures the value of goods and services produced within the borders of the United States. GDP is a better measure of what is going on in the United States and is more closely associated with employment and other measures of production. However, the difference between the two has been very small.

Starting in 1991, the Bureau of Economic Analysis began to emphasize GDP in all publications and press releases.

There are two reasons for the switch. First, foreign transactions are becoming larger for the United States economy; factor payments are rising both into and out of the United States. Hence, GNP is gradually becoming less reliable than GDP as an indicator of economic activity within the United States. Second, the GDP concept is used in most other countries of the world. The latter reason represents a new effort to make the United States National Income and Product Accounts conform more closely with those of other countries. For example, during the 1990s, the U.S. national accountants will start to use the standard United Nations accounting framework called the system of national accounts (SNA). This will make it easier to compare the United States with other countries.

rent, interest, or profit. Since we know that the sum of all firms' value added is GDP, the sum of all incomes must also equal GDP.

Because of taxes and certain other complications, there are several concepts of income. The most comprehensive is **national income.** It is a broad measure of the incomes of Americans, including income taxes and several other items that are deducted before people receive actual payments. There are three important reasons why national income is different from GDP. First, some Americans earn at least part of their income abroad, and some have invested capital abroad and earn income on that capital. This income from work or capital is called factor income *from* the rest of the world. It must be added to GDP to get a measure of income. On the other hand, some of U.S. GDP is earned by foreigners who work in the United States or who have invested capital in the United States. This is called factor income *to* the rest of the world and must be subtracted from GDP to get a measure of income. GDP plus factor income from the rest of the world minus factor income to the rest of the world is called Gross National Product (GNP). It is a measure of goods and services purchased by Americans rather than in America. Until 1992 it was the most common measure of U.S. output. Starting in 1991, GDP was emphasized by government national income accountants.

A second reason that GDP is different from national income is that depreciation must be subtracted to get national income. Third, national income is measured in terms of the prices firms receive for the products they sell, whereas GDP is measured in terms of the prices paid by purchasers. Prices received differ from prices paid by the amount of sales and excise taxes.

There are two other minor conceptual differences. Business transfer payments—such as business gifts—are deducted from national income. Subsidies paid by the government to the businesses it runs are added to national income.

Finally, there is the statistical discrepancy. Conceptually, the income calculation should be numerically the same as the spending calculation of GDP. But because of measurement errors, there is a small discrepancy. (This discrepancy is identical to the discrepancy in the calculation of value added, which attributes incomes to the various industries.)

The relation between GDP and national income is shown below in Table 2–5.

A large amount of national income is diverted by the government and by businesses before it reaches wage earners or shareholders. But government and businesses also augment the income of some people by paying social security and other benefits. The NIPA contain two concepts of income that take account of these diversions and augmentations. **Personal income** is total income received by the public before income taxes, and **disposable personal income** is total income after income taxes.

For wage income, the social security tax is one of the important differences between wages paid by businesses and wages received by work-

---

TABLE 2–5   The Relation between GDP and National Income in 1990 (billions of dollars)

Gross domestic product	5513.8
plus: Net factor payments	10.7
equals: Gross national product	5524.5
less: Depreciation	594.8
equals: Net national product	4929.8
less: Sales and excise taxes	439.2
less: Business transfers	27.7
less: Statistical discrepancy	8.1
plus: Net subsidies to government business	4.8
equals: National income	4459.6

Source: *Economic Report of the President*, 1992. Table B–20.

ers. The aggregate amount of social security tax, called **contributions for social insurance,** is one of the items that is subtracted from national income to get personal income.

All the profits of corporations are included in national income, but only the cash payments of dividends by corporations are included in personal income. The difference between profits and dividends consists of **retained earnings** and the income taxes paid by corporations. These two items are excluded from personal income.

People have two important sources of income other than the production of goods and services. First, the government pays social security and other benefits. Second, people receive interest from the government debt and from other nonbusiness sources. Both of these are included in personal income. Note that social security contributions by employers are taken out of personal income, but the benefits financed by the contributions are added back into personal income.

The relationship between the three concepts of income is shown in Table 2–6. Disposable personal income was $4,058.8 billion, or $16,138 per capita. Consumption per capita was $14,881, so all but $1,257 of income per capita was consumed.

How much of national income is earned by workers and how much is profit? Table 2–7 shows the breakdown for 1990. About 74 percent of national income was earned by labor; this includes payments to workers in wages and salaries as well as fringe benefits. The profit share includes not only corporate profits, but also rental income, proprietors' income, and net interest income. Since labor plus profits exhausts income, the profit share was 26 percent in 1990. These relative shares are fairly stable from year to year. In 1970 the labor share of national income was also 74 percent.

TABLE 2–6   National Income, Personal Income, and Personal Disposable Income in 1990
(billions of dollars)

National income	4459.6
less: Contributions for social insurance	501.7
less: Corporate retained earnings	194.2
plus: Nonbusiness interest	231.2
plus: Transfer payments from government and business	684.9
equals: Personal income	4679.8
less: Income taxes	621.0
equals: Personal disposable income	4058.8

Note: Wage accruals less disbursements, a trivial accounting item, is omitted from the list of adjustments to national income.

Source: *Economic Report of the President,* 1992, Tables B–21 and B–24.

TABLE 2–7 Labor and Profit Shares of National Income in 1990
(billions of dollars)

Compensation of employees	3290.3	} Labor share 74 percent
Proprietors' income	373.3	
Rental income of persons	−12.9	} Profit share 26 percent
Corporate profits	319.0	
Net interest	490.1	
National income	4459.6	

Source: *Economic Report of the President*, 1992, Tables B–22 and B–23.

THE NATIONAL INCOME AND PRODUCT ACCOUNTS

1. Gross domestic product (GDP) is the production of goods and services in the United States. The spending, value added, and factor income measures of GDP are all equal.
2. Consumption, investment, government purchases, and net exports are the four basic components of spending. Consumption is the largest component and investment is the most volatile component.
3. The investment component of GDP includes the replacement of depreciating capital. It is thus gross investment. Net investment is gross investment less depreciation.
4. Real GDP is a measure of production that is adjusted for the effects of inflation. It measures the physical volume of production. Nominal GDP measures the dollar volume of production.
5. Final sales is GDP less inventory investment. It fluctuates less than GDP.
6. To avoid double counting, we measure the contribution of each industry by its value added and do not include any goods that were produced in an earlier year.
7. Disposable personal income is the amount of national income that is available for households to spend. It excludes retained earnings of corporations. It includes what is left of wage and salary income, fringe benefits, rents, dividends, interest, and small business income after all taxes are paid to governments.

2.5   SAVING AND INVESTMENT

Saving is defined as income minus consumption. An important, but some-times confusing, fact is that *saving must equal investment*. To see this, con-sider first a closed economy with no government and therefore no taxes. Then,

$$\text{Spending on GDP} = \text{Consumption} + \text{Investment.}$$

Also, from the definition of saving,

$$\text{Income} = \text{Saving} + \text{Consumption.}$$

Since spending on GDP equals income, we know that

$$\text{Consumption} + \text{Investment} = \text{Saving} + \text{Consumption}$$

or

$$\text{Investment} = \text{Saving.}$$

The equality of saving and investment follows from nothing but the defini-tions of GDP and income. As long as the statisticians adhere to these defin-itions, there is no possibility that investment can ever differ from saving. We don't have to say, "If our theories hold, saving and investment will be equal." No matter how investors and consumers behave, saving and invest-ment will be equal.

The simple identity that saving equals investment becomes more complicated for an open economy interacting with other economies in the world. By borrowing, a country can invest more than it saves. By lending, a country can save more than it invests. The ability to borrow or lend permits investment to be undertaken at the most efficient place and time. Borrow-ing means accumulating financial liabilities. Lending means accumulating financial assets. These financial assets and liabilities have implications for macroeconomic behavior. An important example is the borrowing of the United States government to finance its budget deficit. As the stock of gov-ernment bonds (liabilities of the government) grows, the interest payments on the debt may require increasing future taxes or printing more money, ei-ther of which has macroeconomic implications.

Saving and Investment in an Open Economy

We now look at saving and investment flows at the sector level. The econ-omy is divided into three sectors: private (households and private businesses), government, and the rest of the world. Some more symbols will save space. Let

F = Government transfers to the private sector
N = Interest on the government debt
T = Taxes
V = Factor income and transfer payments from abroad (net)
S_p = Private saving (saving of the private sector)
S_g = Government saving
S_r = Rest of world saving

and recall that we previously defined

Y = GDP
C = Consumption
I = Investment
G = Government spending
X = Net exports.

PRIVATE SAVING. From the definition of saving we know that private saving is disposable income $(Y + V + F + N - T)$ minus consumption (C):

$$S_p = (Y + V + F + N - T) - C. \qquad (2\text{--}1)$$

GOVERNMENT SAVING. The NIPA use the convention of treating all government expenditures as government consumption. That is, investment is always assumed to equal zero for the government sector. Hence, government saving equals income (tax receipts, net of transfer payments and interest payments)[1] minus purchases of goods and services:

$$S_g = (T - F - N) - G. \qquad (2\text{--}2)$$

Government saving is also called the government **budget surplus** or **budget deficit.** The budget is in surplus when G is less than $(T - F - N)$ and in deficit when G is greater than $(T - F - N)$.

REST OF THE WORLD SAVING. The rest of the world saving vis-à-vis the United States is defined as payments received from the United States less payments made to the United States. We need to keep track of three

[1]The United States government also sometimes makes payments to and receives payments from foreigners. For example, in 1991 there was a huge transfer from foreign governments to the U.S. government to help pay for the war in the Middle East. These payments are included in our definition of V. They are not usually as large as they were in 1991.

types of payments. Payments received from the United States include (1) payments for our imports, (2) factor payments to foreigners, and (3) transfer payments to foreigners. Payments made to the United States include (1) payments for our exports, (2) factor payments to Americans, and (3) transfer payments to Americans.

Rest of the world saving is the sum of the net payments for each type: (1) imports less exports, or *net* exports with the sign reversed, (2) factor payments to foreigners less factor payments from foreigners, or *net* factor income from abroad with the sign reversed, and (3) transfer payments to foreigners less transfer payments to Americans, or *net* transfer payments from abroad with the sign reversed. In terms of our notation, (1) is equal to -X, and (2) plus (3) is equal to -V. Thus

$$S_r = -X - V. \qquad (2-3)$$

The sum $V + X$ is sometimes called *net foreign investment of the United States*. Recall that X is sometimes called the trade deficit. As we will describe in the next section, $V + X$ is sometimes called the surplus (or deficit) on the *current account*. Hence, foreign saving is positive in the United States when the United States is running a current account deficit. The rest of the world saving is used either to buy financial assets in the United States or to reduce foreign financial liabilities. Either is called a *capital inflow*. Put another way, the United States finances any excess of imports over exports by borrowing from abroad. Then rest of the world lending is equal to U.S. borrowing.

It is important to note that these equations do not imply that saving equals investment for any of the sectors individually. However, for the three sectors as a whole, saving must equal investment. The sum of the three sectors' saving is

$$S_p + S_g + S_r = (Y + V + F + N - T) - C + (T - F - N - G) - V - X. \qquad (2-4)$$

Everything cancels out on the right-hand side except $Y - C - G - X$, which from the income identity is equal to investment, I. Thus, private saving plus government saving plus saving from the rest of the world equals investment. This identity is of great importance in interpreting movements in investment and saving. Because of large shifts in the saving of these three sectors in recent years, the identity deserves particular emphasis, as is illustrated in Table 2–8.

Table 2–8 shows gross investment in the United States in 1990 and where the saving came from. The large saving from abroad was a positive factor. The government deficit was a large negative factor. *National saving* is the sum of private plus government saving and in 1990 equaled $851.3 billion + (−139.5) billion = $711.8 billion. Investment in new factories and

TABLE 2–8 Gross Saving and Investment, 1990
(billions of dollars)

Gross private domestic saving	851.3
plus: Government saving	−139.5
plus: Foreign saving	82.8
plus: Statistical discrepancy	8.0
equals: Gross private domestic investment	802.6

Source: *Economic Report of the President,* 1992, Table B–26.

equipment in the United States was larger than national saving because of the willingness of foreigners to save in the United States.

Figure 2–2 shows the trends in investment and savings in the 1980s. Throughout this period investment has been greater than national saving, so that foreign saving has been positive. That foreign saving is, of course,

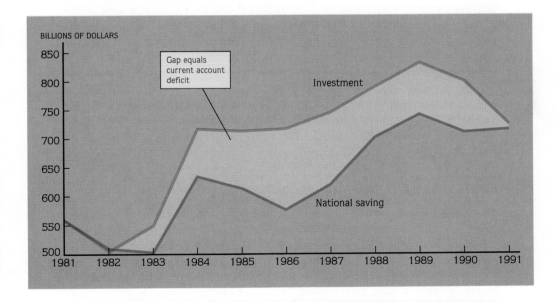

FIGURE 2–2 Investment and national saving in the United States.

The gap between investment and national saving (private plus government saving) rose and then fell during the 1980s. The gap equals the current account deficit.

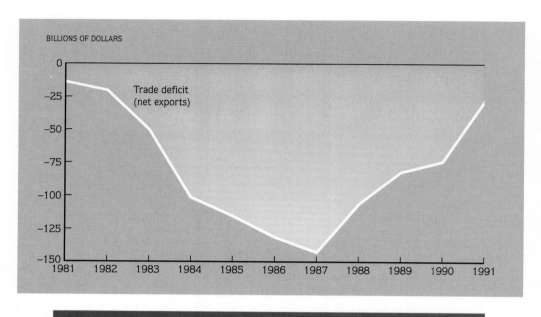

BILLIONS OF DOLLARS

Trade deficit
(net exports)

FIGURE 2–3 The U.S. trade deficit

The trade deficit is closely related to the gap between investment and national saving shown in Figure 2–2. As the gap widened, so did the trade deficit. (The gap equals $X + V$ where X is the trade deficit and V is other net payments to foreigners.)

related to the trade deficit. As the gap between investment and national saving rose and then fell in the 1980s, the trade deficit also rose and fell. Figure 2–2 shows how dramatic that pattern was. Figure 2–3 shows how the trade deficit (X) has the same pattern.

Saving and Changes in Assets

To illustrate how these saving and investment decisions relate to the accumulation of assets and liabilities, consider two types of financial assets: government bonds and government money (currency). Money and bonds are financial liabilities of the government and are financial assets of the private sector. We call bonds B and money M. Let the symbol Δ represent a change from one year to the next. Then ΔM means change in money and ΔB means change in bonds.

The excess of saving over physical investment can be used to increase assets or reduce liabilities. In the NIPA the government is treated as if it does not undertake any physical investment. The entire government saving can be used either to reduce the national debt or to reduce money.

The relation between government saving and asset accumulation is thus summarized as

$$S_g = - (\Delta M + \Delta B). \qquad (2\text{--}5)$$

Since the government deficit is $-S_g$, Equation 2–5 equivalently says that the deficit must be financed by issuing money or by issuing bonds. Sometimes Equation 2–5 is called the **government budget identity.** If the private sector restricts itself to money and bonds, then the excess of private saving goes into either money or bonds. That is,

$$S_p = I + \Delta M + \Delta B_p. \qquad (2\text{--}6)$$

The subscript "p" on B means that this is the private holding of bonds. Finally, if the rest of the world invests only in government bonds, then we have

$$S_r = \Delta B_r. \qquad (2\text{--}7)$$

The subscript "r" on B means that this is foreign holdings of U.S. government bonds. By adding the assets for these three equations together, we find again that $I = S_p + S_g + S_r$, the saving equals investment identity for the economy as a whole. As is clear from these equations, a government deficit generates an increase in either money or government bonds or both. A capital inflow from abroad results in an accumulation of U.S. debt abroad. In this sense the U.S. trade deficit is used to help finance the government budget deficit.

2.6 TRANSACTIONS WITH THE REST OF THE WORLD: THE CURRENT ACCOUNT AND THE EXCHANGE RATE

We have already discussed transactions with other countries: imports and exports of goods, factor payments from and to foreigners, and capital inflows and outflows with the rest of the world. There are many different ways that these can be added up and summarized. For example, you frequently hear about various types of deficits. It is important to understand what these mean. In addition, transactions with other countries require that U.S. dollars be exchanged for foreign currency—Japanese yen, German marks, Italian lire, Canadian dollars, and so on. The *exchange rate* is the price at which these exchanges of dollars for foreign currencies take place.

From the Merchandise Deficit to the Current Account Deficit

International transactions are divided into *current account transactions* and *capital account transactions*. The current account keeps track of net exports as well as government grants and interest payments from the U.S. government abroad.

The capital account keeps track of borrowing and lending. When an American lends to a foreigner, by making a loan, buying a bond, or some similar transaction, the lending appears with a negative sign in the capital account. When an American borrows by taking out a loan in another country or by selling stocks and bonds, the borrowing appears with a positive sign. The term "balance of payments" refers to the current account or the capital account.

The current account is broken into a number of subsidiary accounts. These accounts are illustrated in Table 2–9 with data for 1990. The *merchandise account* keeps track of trade in manufactured goods, agricultural products, raw materials, and all other items except services. In recent years the United States has imported more of these products than it has exported; since 1976 there has been a merchandise trade deficit every year, and in 1990 the merchandise deficit was $109 billion. The trade deficit was as high as $160 billion in 1987.

TABLE 2–9   The United States Current Account, 1990 (billions of dollars)

1. Merchandise trade balance		−109.2
Exports	398.2	
Imports	507.4	
2. Services trade deficit		34.8
Exports	152.2	
Imports	117.4	
3. Net factor payments		10.8
Receipts	147.7	
Payments	137.0	
4. Net transfer payments		−19.2
5. Balance on current account		−82.8

Source: *Economic Report of the President,* 1992, Table B–18. Note that the current account is defined here as net foreign investment.[2]

[2]These data are tabulated as part of the national income and product accounts and are thus consistent with other data reported in this chapter. A slightly different measure of the current account is published as part of the balance of payments statistics, but the two measures are conceptually the same and usually very close.

On the other hand, the United States exports more services—including financial services, transportation services, and education services—than it imports. The *services trade account* was in surplus at $35 billion in 1990. The current account also includes factor incomes, much of which is earnings on capital. Since World War II the United States consistently has had a surplus; we have earned more overseas from our capital than foreigners have earned from their capital in the United States. The factor incomes surplus was $11 billion in 1990.

The last item in the current account is *unilateral transfers*. The U.S. government and the U.S. public make gifts, pension payments, and other transfers to the rest of the world. These enter the current account with a negative sign.

An important principle of the balance of payments accounts is that the current account and the capital account should sum to zero. When the United States imports more than it exports, it must be borrowing from the rest of the world to finance its current account deficit. There should be a positive balance in the capital account equal in magnitude to the current account deficit. This principle is what underlies Equation 2–3. When Americans buy more than they sell, they must borrow from abroad. Figure 2–4 shows the net effect of U.S. borrowing and lending abroad in the 1980s and

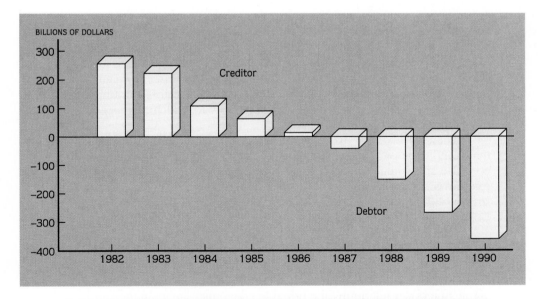

FIGURE 2–4   Net creditor/debtor position of the United States

A new data series that endeavors to measure U.S. assets at market values shows that the United States has moved from being a creditor nation to being a debtor nation in the last 10 years.
Source: *Economic Report of the President*, 1992, Table B–99.

early 1990s. The U.S. current account deficit meant that we were increasing our net indebtedness to foreigners. Our net asset position—assets less liabilities—went from positive to negative.

The current account and the capital account are measured independently in the balance of payments accounts. Thus, in practice, the sum of the two is not zero; there is a statistical discrepancy. In recent years the discrepancy has been quite large and volatile. For example, in 1990 the discrepancy was $64 billion—more than 1 percent of GDP! And even though the data in Figure 2–4 indicate that the United States is a net debtor nation, we are receiving more in interest and profits abroad than we are paying out.

The Exchange Rate

The dollar exchange rate measures the *price of dollars* in terms of foreign currencies. For example, the exchange rate between the U.S. dollar and the Japanese yen in the last quarter of 1991 was 130 yen per dollar. That is, one could go to a bank and get 130 yen with 1 dollar. The *price* of 1 dollar was 130 yen. When Americans purchase foreign goods—such as a cup of coffee in Tokyo—they must pay for these goods with foreign currency—such as yen. Hence, the exchange rate is important for international transactions. A cup of coffee that costs 260 yen in Tokyo would cost an American 2 dollars if the exchange rate is 130 yen per dollar. If the exchange rate rises to 260 yen per dollar, that same cup of coffee would cost "only" 1 dollar.

The exchange rate determines how expensive foreign goods are compared with American goods. When the exchange rate rises, foreign goods become cheaper compared with home goods. As we will see in Chapter 7, this causes Americans to buy more goods abroad and foreigners to buy fewer goods in the United States.

There is a dollar exchange rate for every foreign currency. Rather than keep track of all of these exchange rates, it is a useful simplification to consider an average of the different exchange rates. The **trade-weighted exchange rate** is an average of the exchange rates between the dollar and several different currencies, with those countries that trade more with the United States getting more weight.

The trade-weighted dollar exchange rate against 10 major currencies is shown in Figure 2–5, along with the dollar-yen exchange rate. Note that both exchange rates fluctuate by large amounts. Some of these fluctuations are associated with the fluctuations in real GDP in the United States. For example, the dollar fell during the boom in economic activity in the late 1970s and rose during the slump in economic activity in the early 1980s. But there are many other movements in the exchange rate. During the period from 1968 to 1991 the dollar was generally falling relative to the yen. As we will see, this was a result of the higher rate of inflation in the United States compared with Japan during these 20 years.

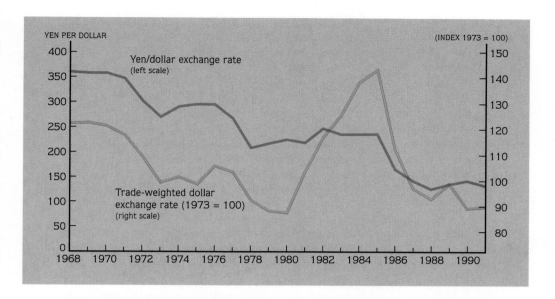

FIGURE 2–5 Yen-dollar and trade-weighted dollar exchange rates

The exchange rate has had large fluctuations during the last 13 years. Some of these fluctuations are associated with the movements in U.S. output. The dollar fell during the boom of the late 1970s and rose during the slump of the early 1980s. Other fluctuations seem unrelated to the state of the U.S. economy.
Source: *Economic Report of the President*, 1992. Table B–107.

REVIEW AND PRACTICE

Major Points

1. There are three ways to measure and think about GDP: the spending side, the production side, and the income side. The components of spending are consumption, investment, government spending, and net exports. The components of production are the values added by each industry. The components of income are wages, profits, and interest.

2. Real GDP is the physical volume of production, after the effects of rising prices have been removed. Real GDP growth has averaged about 3 percent per year since the end of the Second World War, but there have been many fluctuations. Potential GDP is real GDP after the economic fluctuations have been removed. Nominal GDP is just GDP without adjustment for inflation or for economic fluctuations.

3. Value added by a firm is the difference between the revenue of the firm and its purchases of goods and services from other firms. It is the firm's contribution to GDP. GDP for the whole economy is the sum of value added across all producers.

4. Depreciation is the loss of capital from wear and tear. Net investment is gross investment less depreciation.

5. Conceptually, income and production are equal. All value added is somebody's income. In the national accounts, there are various measures of income. National income is GDP less depreciation and less sales and excise taxes and adjusted for net factor payments. Personal income is national income less social security taxes and corporate retained earnings plus transfer payments and interest paid by the government to consumers. Disposable personal income is personal income less income taxes.

6. The international accounts consist of a current account and a capital account. The two sum to zero except for the statistical discrepancy. The current account is in surplus when the United States is exporting more than it is importing. At the same time, the capital account is in deficit—capital is flowing out because the United States must be lending to the rest of the world if the United States is importing less than it exports.

7. The exchange rate is crucial for international transactions. It is the price of dollars in terms of foreign currency. When the exchange rate rises, more foreign currency can be bought with each dollar. This makes foreign goods cheaper in terms of dollars.

8. An important implication of the equality of income and product is the equality of saving and investment. It will always be the case that investment equals private saving plus the government surplus plus the capital inflow from abroad.

Key Terms and Concepts

gross domestic
   product
value added
consumption
gross national
   product
fixed investment
national income
inventory investment

government purchases
imports
exports
depreciation
net investment
final sales
factor incomes
private saving
personal disposable
   income

intermediate goods
government saving
real GDP
nominal GDP
balance of payments
current account
capital account
exchange rate
trade-weighted
   exchange rate

Questions for Discussion and Review

1. Explain why spending on GDP is equal to income earned from producing GDP.

2. Identify which of the following are flows and which are stocks: consumption; government bonds outstanding at the end of last year; government purchases; inventories; inventory investment; depreciation; factories and equipment in the United States on December 31, 1991; the budget deficit.

3. Explain how real GDP is calculated.

4. Which components of spending fluctuate the most over the cycle?

Problems

Numerical

1. The following are data for the U.S. economy for 1990 in billions of dollars.

Net rental income of persons*	−12.9
Depreciation	594.8
Compensation of employees	3290.3
Personal consumption expenditures	3742.6
Sales and excise taxes	439.2
Business transfer payments	27.7
Statistical discrepancy	8.1
Gross private domestic investment	802.6
Exports of goods and services	550.4
Net subsidies of government business	4.8
Government purchases of goods and services	1042.9
Imports of goods and services	624.8
Net interest	490.1
Proprietors' income	373.2
Corporate profits	319.0
Net factor income from rest of world	10.7

   a. Compute GDP using the spending approach.
   b. Compute net domestic product.
   c. Compute national income two ways.

2. Fill in the blanks.
   a. If investment is $700 billion, private saving is $650 billion, and capital inflow from abroad is $100 billion, then the government budget deficit is _____ billion.
   b. If the stock of inventories in the economy is $500 billion at the end of 1988 and $520 billion at the end of 1989, then inventory investment for 1989 is _____ billion.
   c. If production by Americans and American capital abroad is $50 billion and GNP is $4,000 billion, then GDP is _____.

*Adjusted for capital consumption.

3. (Warning: This problem is difficult.) Data on the U.S. economy are given in the following tables (billions of dollars).

   Assume that consumer and government purchases from abroad are zero and that there is no inventory investment.

   a. Compute consumption, investment, government purchases, exports, and imports. Compute GDP from these.

   b. Compute value added for each industry. Calculate GDP by summing all value added. Is it equal to GDP from Part a? (Hints: Government value added is its wage payment. In calculating value added, do not subtract capital inputs.)

   c. Compute profit for each industry as sales less purchases of current inputs (do not subtract investment). Compute national income as total profit plus total wages. Is it equal to GDP?

   d. Compute net exports.

Purchases of Intermediate Inputs from

Industry	Agriculture	Mining	Manufacturing	Transportation and Utilities (T&U)	Trade	Finance, Insurance, and Real Estate (FIRE)	Services
Agriculture	—	1	19	14	7	7	18
Mining	8	—	21	4	18	18	8
Construction	21	21	22	23	18	15	5
Manufacturing	54	153	—	139	20	106	11
T&U	1	60	20	—	25	55	12
Trade	9	7	464	79	—	76	8
FIRE	0	13	24	36	14	—	7
Services	4	9	104	29	56	73	—

Purchases of Capital from

Industry	Construction	Manufacturing	Abroad
Agriculture	2	3	1
Mining	11	12	2
Construction	0	8	1
Manufacturing	21	132	14
T&U	8	17	3
Trade	27	25	0
FIRE	143	6	0
Services	19	15	1

Industry	Imports of Inputs	Sales to Government	Sales to Consumer	Exports	Wages
Agriculture	12	8	12	37	60
Mining	90	9	1	21	88
Construction	2	23	0	0	98
Manufacturing	181	188	21	206	315
T&U	5	5	101	13	132
Trade	2	6	935	15	287
FIRE	3	11	178	5	256
Services	6	4	583	21	195

Government wages: 337
Earnings of U.S. factors abroad: 49

4. Consider a closed economy with expenditure totals for a year given by

Consumption	1,300
Investment	500
Government purchases	500
Government tax receipts	400
Depreciation	200

Suppose that the financial assets in the economy consist of money and bonds. Assume that money equals 500 at the start of the year and that government bonds equal 700 at the start of the year.
   a. Assuming that 90 percent of government deficits are financed by bonds, calculate the new levels of bond and money holdings for the private sector and for the government.
   b. Show how the total change in government liabilities—money (M) + bonds (B)—can be computed in two ways.

Analytical

1. Identify which of the following purchases is counted as part of GDP: You purchase a used lawn mower at a garage sale. General Motors purchases tires from Goodyear to equip new Chevrolets. General Motors purchases tires from Goodyear to replace worn tires on executives' company cars. A neighbor hires you to baby-sit for an evening. You purchase a share of AT&T. A neighbor breaks your window with a golf ball, and you purchase a new window. You pay your tuition for the semester.

2. As part of its drive to replace welfare with workfare, the government decides to redesignate $100 billion in welfare benefits as government wages. The recipients become government employees.
   a. For each of the methods used in calculating GDP, describe the effect of this policy change.

b. Suppose now that the workfare recipients are removed from the government payroll and are moved into the payroll of the newly incorporated Workfare, Inc. As part of its support for the workfare program, the government stands ready to subsidize Workfare, Inc., if its sales do not cover its costs. Since Workfare, Inc., has no products to sell, the subsidy ends up being the full $100 billion. How does this arrangement affect your answers to Part a?

3. Suppose that automobile purchases were to be treated like housing purchases in the national income accounts. How would that affect saving? Investment?

4. Determine whether the following statements are true or false, and explain why.
   a. The trade deficit is equal to the government budget deficit plus investment less private domestic saving.
   b. If GDP were measured at the prices firms receive for the products they sell, then sales and excise taxes would not be subtracted from GDP in computing national income.
   c. The importance of different goods in GDP is determined by their relative price: for example, the production of one ounce of gold counts much more in GDP than the production of one ounce of steel.

5. In 1987, spending by Americans on personal consumption, private investment, and government operations totaled 103 percent of GDP. How is that possible?

6. Explain how the trade deficit in the 1980s helped finance the large government budget deficit as well as the large increase in private gross investment in the United States. Should Americans care whether foreigners or other Americans hold the U.S. public debt?

7. Suppose initially that exports are zero and imports are $100 billion. Then assume that the government places a ban on imports. Assume that the spending habits of consumers, firms, and government remain the same (i.e., they spend the same amount but substitute domestic goods for imports).
   a. What happens to GDP?
   b. What happens to each category of savings (assume taxes remain unchanged)?
   c. Does total savings still equal investment?

8. Suppose that in a given year U.S. foreign trade consists of some consumer importing a single Toyota Tercel for $12,000 (1.8 million yen). Here are some possible financial transactions to accompany the purchase: (i) The consumer pays with $12,000, which Toyota puts in its American bank account. (ii) The consumer pays with 1.8 million yen that happens to be in a Japanese bank account. (iii) The consumer pays with $12,000; Toyota invests the proceeds in U.S. Treasury bills. (iv) The consumer purchases 1.8 million yen on the foreign exchange market from some anonymous American foreign exchange trader and then pays for the car.
   a. Is the United States running a current account surplus or deficit?
   b. For each of the financial transactions described above, explain the effect the transaction has on the U.S. capital account. What is the sum of the current account and capital account balances?

9. Net domestic product is considered to be a better measure of welfare than GDP, since it adjusts for the fact that part of GDP must be devoted to replacing

physical capital that has worn out during the course of the year. If we took this principle of adjusting for depreciation more seriously, what other expenditures would you want to deduct from GDP to get a clearer measure of net national product?

10. With the exception of housing expenditure, consumption and investment spending are delineated by the decision-making unit responsible for each type of expenditure. An alternative accounting scheme might be based on the durability of goods. Suppose investment was equal to total expenditures on goods that last one year or more. All other expenditures count as consumption. How would this revised scheme affect consumption, investment, depreciation, and the capital stock relative to the current accounting system? Which system do you think is more informative and why? Which system would be more costly to manage?

MacroSolve Exercises

1. Tabulate annual data on the ratios of investment in GDP. Describe how the ratio of investment to GDP has changed since the 1930s. Why does the share of investment in GDP fall during recessions? Why do you think that the ratio investment to GDP may have fallen in the 1940s when the GDP gap was high?

2. Tabulate annual data on the ratios to GDP of saving, investment, the government deficit, and net exports.
   a. Confirm that saving equals investment plus the government deficit and net exports. Explain intuitively rather than algebraically why this must always be the case.
   b. According to the above identity, $S_p = I + \text{Deficit} + X$. Equivalently, $S_p - \text{Deficit} - X = I$. Private saving and investment should be positively related (everything else constant), the government budget deficit and investment should be negatively related (everything else constant), and net exports and investment should be negatively related (everything else constant). Graph each relationship using annual data. Historically, have these relationships existed? Do the data support the argument that government deficits crowd out investment? Are high government deficits correlated with low net exports?

3. Plot the ratio of the government deficit to GDP. Why do you think that the government deficit was such a large share of GDP in mid-1975?

4. Plot the trade-weighted exchange rate using quarterly data from 1967 to the present. Between 1981 and 1985, the exchange rate rose sharply.
   a. Does this mean that the U.S. dollar became worth more or less in terms of foreign currencies during that period?
   b. In this period, would foreign goods become relatively more expensive or cheaper for U.S. consumers to buy?

Monitoring the Economy: Inflation and Employment

We cannot overemphasize the importance of carefully monitoring the economy. The successful conduct of monetary and fiscal policy requires that policymakers have an up-to-the-minute assessment of the state of the economy. Businesses deciding whether to invest or to hire more workers want to know if there is going to be a recession. Investors in the stock and bond markets know that the release of new information about the economy can move markets by large amounts.

The national income and product accounts discussed in Chapter 2 are important measures of economic performance. But two other measures—inflation and employment—are released to the public at more frequent intervals and have formed the basis of most policy initiatives of the past 25 years. Data on inflation and employment are released every month. When the data are released at 8:30 in the morning (Eastern time), financial investors are watching the news monitors carefully. By that time, however, key policy officials including the President of the United States are already aware of the numbers. In this chapter we take up these two measures and show how important they are not only for determining whether a recession is coming but also for assessing long-term trends. We examine a disturbing slowdown in labor productivity growth beginning in the early 1970s.

3.1 MEASURING INFLATION

Almost everybody watches the rate of inflation. It is a major indicator of how the economy is doing, and changes in inflation are closely related to fluctuations in real GDP. The *rate of inflation* is defined as the percentage rate of change in the general price level from one period to the next. The general price level is a measure of the purchasing power of the dollar, or the amount of goods and services the dollar can buy. For example, one measure of the price level was 117 in 1991, which means that the same basket of goods that cost $100 in 1987 cost $117 in 1991. In this example, 1987 is the base year. Much of the original economic research on measuring the general price level was done by Irving Fisher of Yale University in the 1920s. There are now two approaches to measuring the general price level: constructing **price indexes** directly from data on the prices of thousands of goods and services, and calculating **deflators** by dividing a component of nominal GDP by the same component of real GDP.

Price Indexes

A price index is a ratio showing the price of a basket of goods and services in various years in relation to the price of the basket in a base year. The index is 100 in the base year and correspondingly higher in later years if the prices of the things in the basket have risen. The most conspicuous price index is the **consumer price index (CPI).** This index measures the cost of living for a typical urban family. The Bureau of Labor Statistics (BLS) of the Department of Labor computes it in the following way: Once every 10 years or so, the BLS makes a survey of the buying habits of American families. The survey covers not only the products they buy in stores, but other expenditures like the purchases of houses. Then the BLS makes a long list of goods and services whose prices they can determine once a month. From the survey of buying habits, they estimate the quantities of each item bought by the average family. The list includes tomato soup, for example. However, the amount of tomato soup in the CPI basket is greater than the fraction of income that the typical family spends on tomato soup. The price of tomato soup is considered representative of the prices of similar products that are not included in the index.

Every month, the BLS sends surveyors into stores to write down the actual prices of goods and services. When discounts are available, they take them into account. The BLS is particularly careful about new car prices because cars have a large role in the price index and few people actually pay the sticker price for a new car.

Each month, the BLS computes the new level of the price index by using the detailed prices to compute the cost of the CPI basket. The basket is chosen so that its price was 100 in 1983, which means that the index had the value 100 in 1983. In 1991, the index was 136.2, so prices rose by 36 percent over 8 years. Some prices rose more than others. The 1991 level of the medical care price index was 177, while the level for energy was only 102.5. Both started at 100 in 1983.

Figure 3–1 shows the rate of inflation, the percent change in the U.S. price level as measured by the CPI, since 1968. Inflation was moderate in the early 1960s, but, as shown in Figure 3–1, gained momentum in the late 1960s and early 1970s, and reached two peaks in 1974 and 1980. Inflation moderated in the 1980s and early 1990s.

The CPI is the most widely used measure of the purchasing power of the dollar. When people make an agreement that is set in dollars and want to protect themselves against inflation, they can write in a provision that payments rise in proportion to the increase in the CPI. This practice is called **cost-of-living adjustment (COLA)** and is used for social security

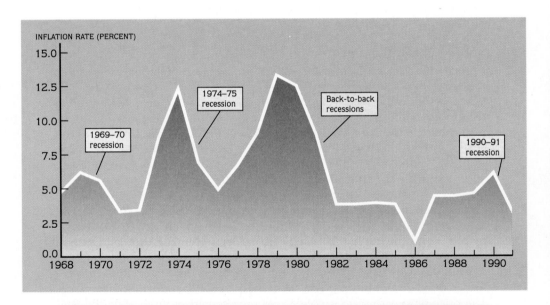

FIGURE 3–1   Consumer price inflation

The consumer price index measures the price of a bundle of goods and services representative of the purchases of a typical family. The chart shows the percent change in this index (December to December) for each year.
Source: *Economic Report of the President,* 1992, Table B–56.

payments and in many collective-bargaining agreements that spell out the terms of employment for unionized workers.

The government puts out another major price index in addition to the CPI. Formerly the wholesale price index, it is now called the **producer price index (PPI).** Instead of measuring the prices actually paid by consumers, it measures the prices charged by producers at various stages in the production process. There is no clear basis for the choice of weights for the PPI, comparable to the market basket that gives the weights for the CPI. As a result, there is much less interest in the monthly value of the PPI. However, the BLS reports all the detailed prices going into the PPI and these prices and the price indexes computed from them are the best source of information about prices of crude materials and intermediate goods. Some economists think that the PPI for crude materials is one of the most sensitive early warning indicators of future inflation.

Deflators

The construction of data on nominal and real GDP results in another type of price index. The purpose of measuring real GDP is to get rid of the price effects in nominal GDP. Thus, the ratio of nominal GDP to real GDP is a measure of prices. It is called the **GDP implicit price deflator.** For example, in 1990 nominal GDP was $5,514 billion. Real GDP was $4,885 billion 1987 dollars. The GDP deflator for 1990 was $100 \times 5,514/4,885 = 113$. That is, with a base of 100 in 1987, the price level according to the GDP deflator was 113.

Each component for GDP has a deflator. For example, the ratio of nominal consumption to real consumption is the **consumption deflator.** It is widely used as an alternative to the CPI as a measure of the cost of living.

Remember that GDP does not include imports. Correspondingly, the GDP deflator does not count the prices of imported goods. When the world oil price jumped in 1974, the GDP deflator did not rise by as much as the deflators for consumption, investment, and government purchases, which do include the prices of imports. The GDP deflator rose by 8.7 percent from 1973 to 1974. At the same time, the consumption deflator rose by 10.2 percent, the investment deflator by 11.1 percent, and the government deflator by 10.0 percent. The deflator for exports rose by 21.6 percent and the deflator for imports by 43.4 percent. Had it not been for the increase in export prices, the 43 percent increase in import prices caused by the oil price increase would have driven up product prices in the United States by even more compared with the GDP deflator. But import price shocks have been sufficiently small that the GDP deflator and the consumption deflator tell pretty much the same story about the U.S. price level.

INFLATION, PRICE INDEXES, AND DEFLATORS

1. Inflation is the rate of increase in the price level. The price level is an average of all prices in the economy.

2. There are two types of measures of the price level: price indexes and deflators. The consumer price index (CPI) and the producer price index (PPI) are the two major price indexes. The weights on the individual prices in the CPI are based on a survey of consumer buying habits. The GDP deflator is the ratio of nominal GDP to real GDP. It is a measure of the prices of all goods and services produced in America.

3. The CPI is used for cost-of-living adjustments in many union contracts and in many government programs.

MEASURING EMPLOYMENT, UNEMPLOYMENT, AND WAGES

Employment falls along with production during recessions and rises again during recoveries. Over the long haul, employment grows along with potential GDP as firms hire more workers to produce the growing output. Information on employment in the United States comes from two surveys, one of *households* and the other of *establishments*—the offices, factories, stores, mines, and other places where people work.

The household survey—called the Current Population Survey—is conducted each month by the Bureau of the Census, and the data are tabulated and reported by the BLS. About 100,000 adults are interviewed each month to find out whether they are employed during the calendar week that includes the 12th of the month. Everyone who worked an hour or more during that week is counted as employed for that month. The results are blown up by multiplying by about 1,000 so that they are good estimates of the total number of workers employed that month in the whole economy (each person in the survey stands for a little over 1,000 people in the population). Some other people who did not work—notably those on vacation—are also counted as employed.

Total civilian employment by this measure was 116.9 million in 1991, down by about 1 million from its level of 117.9 million in 1990 and up by 17.3 million from its level of 99.5 million in the recession year of 1982. The long recovery and expansion of the mid-1980s involved substantial growth in employment, as expansions generally do. On the other hand, employment falls during recessions; this is evidenced by the behavior of employment during the 1990s.

The establishment survey interviews employers to find out the number of people on the payroll at each workplace. The survey excludes farm employees. Because it is based on payrolls, it also omits people who are self-employed. Total nonagricultural payroll employment was 109.9 million people in December 1990.

Hours per Week and Total Hours

The number of hours worked each week varies among workers and over time. Some people normally work part time for only a few hours a week and others work 60 to 70 hours. The average factory worker now puts in about 41 hours per week, while the average store worker puts in about 29 hours. Also, the number of hours per week falls during recessions and rises during expansions. When demand is booming, many workers are asked, or choose, to work overtime. For example, in the 1981–82 recession, average weekly hours for the whole economy fell from 35.3 hours in July 1981 to 34.7 hours in November 1982 and rose again to 35.2 hours in December 1983. The decline in hours in the 1990–91 recession was similar in magnitude; average weekly hours fell from 34.5 hours per week in July 1990 to 34.0 in April 1991. The data also verify the fact that the average workweek has declined. However, average weekly hours for store workers fell from about 40 hours per week in 1947 to about 29 hours per week now, and average weekly hours in manufacturing have remained steady at about 40 hours per week since 1947.

For all these reasons, employment by itself is not a complete measure of labor input to the economy. Total hours of work—the number of people working multiplied by the hours of work of the average worker—is a better measure. The BLS index of total hours for the business sector is shown in Figure 3–2 for the period from 1968 to 1991. The upward trend in hours is clear in the figure, but so are the fluctuations. Total hours declined by 1.7 percent from 1990 to 1991. That was larger than the 0.8 percent decline for real GDP (see Chapter 2), because the business sector excludes government and agriculture, which did not decline as much as the rest of the economy.

When the level of real output of the economy declines, total hours of work decline. The work force feels the effects of a recession in the form of fewer hours of work per week; they feel it as well in the possibility of being laid off. In either case, their pay declines even if the wage rate does not change.

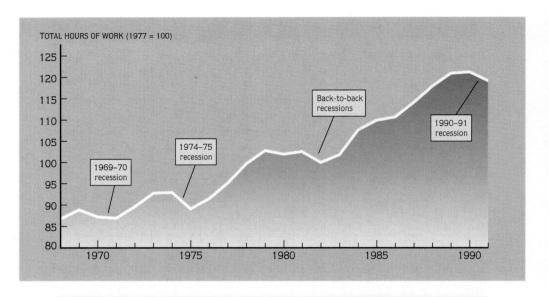

TOTAL HOURS OF WORK (1977 = 100)

FIGURE 3–2   Growth and fluctuations of hours worked

The total amount of work performed in the United States, measured by the hours of all workers, fluctuates along with the business cycle. In each of the five recessions shown here —1969–70, 1974–75, 1980, 1981–82, and 1990–91—total hours declined. In general, total hours have been growing. Growth was particularly strong from 1975 to 1979 and from 1982 to 1988.
Source: *Economic Report of the President*, 1992, Table B–44.

Data on Unemployment and Its Uses

One of the most important questions in macroeconomics is why the economy does not provide work for the entire labor force. Even in the best of times, some people are unemployed. They are interested in working and are available for work, but have not found jobs. One of the principal purposes of the Current Population Survey is to determine how many people are unemployed each month. High unemployment is the single most important signal of distress in the economy.

The Current Population Survey counts you as unemployed if you did not work at all during the survey week and you are looking for work. In each survey, several million people are found to be unemployed. The **labor force** is defined as the number of persons 16 years of age or over who are either working or unemployed. The **unemployment rate** is the percentage of the labor force that is unemployed.

There are millions of people who are not working but who are not counted as unemployed. They are considered out of the labor force because they are retired, in school, at home looking after their own children, sick, or not looking for work for some other reason. The **labor force participation rate** is the percentage of the working-age population that is in the labor force. Whether one is in the labor force or not is sometimes a matter of opinion; this has lead some economists to look at other less subjective measures of labor market conditions. One example is the **employment/population ratio.** This is the percentage of the working-age population that is employed.

The BLS collects many different unemployment statistics. One of the series is available with very little lag on a weekly basis. This is the series on the number of workers who file **initial claims for unemployment benefits** under unemployment insurance programs. During times of economic turbulence, policymakers watch this series carefully, because it can give the earliest warnings of an impending recession or an emerging recovery. As we will study in later chapters, the Federal Reserve Board adjusts its monetary policy depending on what is happening to the economy. By the time monthly data, and especially quarterly data, are released, the economy could already be in recession or a recovery could have started long ago.

The BLS data can also be used to tell us the reasons for unemployment—a job loss, a quit, or simply someone who just entered the labor force. Of the 8.9 million people unemployed in January 1992, 54 percent had lost their jobs, 11 percent had quit, and 35 percent had newly entered or reentered the labor force. In a year with less unemployment like 1989, 46 percent of the unemployed had lost their jobs.

The BLS data also tells us how long people are unemployed. The duration of unemployment rises during recessions. For example, in January 1992, 16 percent of unemployed workers had been unemployed for more than 27 weeks. In 1989 it was 10 percent. These data were one of the reasons that a bill was passed in 1991 to extend the period of time that unemployed workers could receive unemployment benefits. Similar extensions occurred as a result of the 1981–82 recession. See Figure 3–3 for a comparison of 1983 and 1989.

Unemployment in Two Recessions

Table 3–1 shows the number of people in the population aged 16 or over along with the labor force, employment, and unemployment in two recession periods, 1981–82 and 1990–91. The unemployment rate got up to 10.7 percent in 1982, a level it had not reached since the depression of the 1930s. The unemployment rate at the 1981 peak was higher than normal because the economy had not fully recovered from the 1980 recession when the 1981–82 recession began. The unemployment rate also rose in

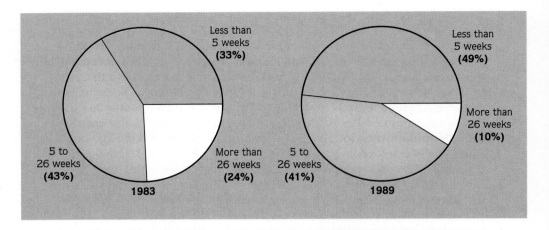

FIGURE 3–3   Unemployment duration in a slump and in a boom

The figures show the percentage of workers unemployed for different lengths of time in a bad year just at the end of a recession (1983) and in a good year just before the start of a recession (1989). Long-term unemployment is relatively high in a bad year.

the 1990–91 recession but to a level well below that of 1982. According to these figures, the 1990–91 recession was not as severe.

The labor force participation rate sometimes falls during recessions, because some workers get discouraged looking for work and leave the labor force to retire early, go back to school, or do something else. This did not happen in the 1981–82 recession, because it was offset by other factors that increased the labor force. The labor force participation rate for women

TABLE 3–1   Unemployment, Labor Force, and the Population

	1981	1982	1990	1991
Millions of people:				
(1) Aged 16 or over	170.1	172.3	188.0	189.8
(2) In labor force	108.7	110.2	124.8	125.3
(3) Employed	100.4	99.5	117.9	116.9
(4) Unemployed	8.3	10.7	6.9	8.4
Percentage:				
Labor force participation rate, (2)/(1)	63.9	64.0	66.3	66.0
Unemployment rate, (4)/(2)	7.6	9.7	5.5	6.7
Employment/population ratio, (3)/(1)	59.0	57.8	62.7	61.6

Source: *Economic Report of the President*, 1992, Table B–30.

has been increasing in the last few decades, and this continued during the 1981–82 recession. The labor force participation rates for teenagers and for males over 20 did decline during the recession, but were offset by the increased participation rate for women. On the other hand, the labor force participation rate did decline in 1991. These other factors affecting the labor force were not as significant as in 1981–82.

Note that the employment/population ratio tells about the same story as the unemployment rate during both periods. However, in the nearly 9 years in between, the employment to population ratios had risen as we discussed in Chapter 1.

Unemployment and the Natural Rate

Figure 3–4 shows how the average annual unemployment rate behaved during the period since the Second World War. Unemployment moves with the business cycle. When real GDP is high relative to the trend path of po-

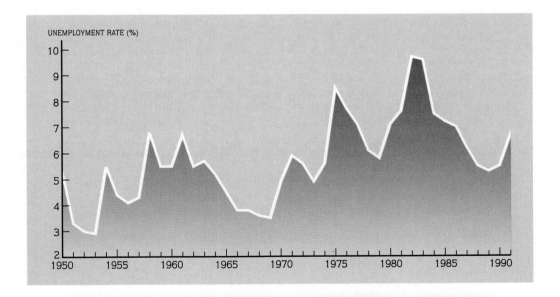

FIGURE 3–4   The unemployment rate

The unemployment rate has fluctuated between 3 and 10 percent since 1950. Unemployment rises during recessions and falls during expansions. There has also been an upward drift in the unemployment rate.
Source: *Economic Report of the President,* 1991, Table B–37.

The Labor Market in the 1960s and the 1980s

The 1960s and the 1980s both had economic expansions of unusual length. The middle years of these expansions show the labor market under more or less standard conditions—neither suffering from a recent recession nor enjoying superheated conditions. In 1964 the unemployment rate was 5.0 percent. In 1985, the same unemployment rate was 7.1 percent. By that measure, unemployment was considerably worse in the 1980s than in the 1960s. Jobs seemed to be harder to find.

By another measure, the insured unemployment rate, the situation was the reverse. In 1964, 3.8 percent of workers eligible for state unemployment insurance benefits were unemployed. In 1985, the rate was only 2.9 percent. The job situation seemed much better in 1985 than it did in 1964; fewer insured workers were out of work in any given week.

A third measure, the volume of help-wanted advertising, tells a story partway between the two unemployment rates. Katherine Abraham of the Brookings Institution has created an index of help-wanted advertising that adjusts for the growth of the labor market and for other factors. Her index was 95 in 1964 and also 95 in 1985. Employers were placing about the same volume of help-wanted ads in 1985 as in 1964. The index is a sensitive indicator of labor market conditions; it reached an all-time low of 75 in the severe recession of 1982 and a high of 136 in the extreme boom of 1969.

Experts are still uncertain about why unemployment has risen in comparison with other indicators of how easy it is to find a job for a worker or how much effort it takes an employer to find a suitable worker. One important factor is that more of the unemployed are people who have not worked recently. These people are not eligible for unemployment insurance. That is why insured unemployment is so low compared with total unemployment.

---

tential GDP, unemployment is low. When output is at low levels in the depths of recessions, unemployment is high.

Note that in normal times—when real GDP is equal to potential GDP—unemployment is not zero. Even in boom times there is some **frictional unemployment.** When workers enter the labor force for the first time or after a spell out of the labor force, they need some time to find a job. During this period they are counted as unemployed. Similarly, when workers quit their jobs, there will frequently be a span of time before they find new jobs. Movements from one job to another are particularly common for young workers as they find out what type of job they are best suited for. This is one reason why young workers have higher unemployment rates than older workers. In addition, there are some low-skilled workers who are frequently unemployed. Additional training for such workers would reduce the unemployment rate. The term economists use for the unemployment rate that prevails in normal times is the **natural rate of unemployment.** The natural rate of unemployment now seems to be about 6 percent. It was apparently closer to 5 percent in the 1960s. The reasons for the increase in the natural employment rate in the past three decades are not well understood. Although the labor force was younger, on the average, in the 1980s and 1990s in comparison with the 1960s, the labor force was also quite a bit better educated. The first factor may have increased the natural rate but the second should have lowered it.

Okun's Law

There is a useful shorthand formula that closely approximates the cyclical relationship between unemployment and real GDP. It is commonly called **Okun's law,** after its discoverer, Arthur Okun, who used it to illustrate the effects of macroeconomic policy when he was on the staff of the Council of Economic Advisers during the early days of the Kennedy administration in the 1960s. Okun's law says that for each percentage point by which the unemployment rate is *above* the natural rate, real GDP is 3 percent *below* potential GDP. The percentage departure of GDP from potential is called the **GDP gap.** For example, if unemployment is 8 percent, 2 percentage points above the natural rate of 6 percent, the real GDP is 6 percent below potential. The GDP gap is minus 6 percent. The historical accuracy of the formula is illustrated in Figure 3–5.

Wages

Remember that the income side of the national income and product accounts reports the total earnings of workers. Total annual earnings divided by total annual hours of work gives a measure of the average hourly wage paid to workers in the United States. The BLS calls this compensation per hour. Compensation per hour includes the value of fringe benefits as well as cash wages. Wages are the most important component of the cost of production.

Wages and prices generally moved together throughout the swings in inflation in the 1970s. The **real wage** is the hourly average wage divided by

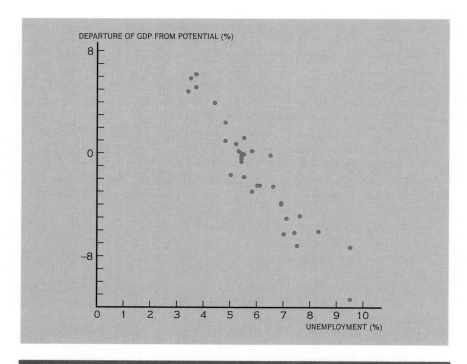

FIGURE 3–5   Okun's law

The movements in unemployment are closely related to the movements in the percentage departures of real GDP from potential GDP. We examined those departures in Chapter 1. The slope of the relationship is roughly 3 percentage points of real GDP for each percent of unemployment.

the cost of living. From the point of view of workers, it measures the purchasing power of the wage—the amount of goods and services that can be bought with 1 hour of work. From the point of view of employers, it measures the real costs of labor input. The real wage does not fluctuate in any systematic way during recessions or booms. The most noticeable thing about the real wage is how it grows over time. The real wage since 1960 is shown in Figure 3–6.

After steady growth in the 1960s, the upward path of the real wage was interrupted in the early 1970s. Since then real wage growth has been much lower. One of the most pressing problems facing the U.S. economy is the slowdown in real wage growth. The most promising explanation is a slowdown in productivity growth. We look at productivity in the next section.

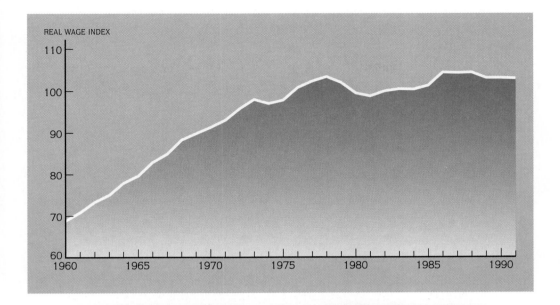

FIGURE 3–6   The slowdown in real wage growth

The real wage is the ratio of the dollar wage (compensation per hour) to the cost of living (the consumer price index). Real wage growth slowed down significantly in the early 1970s and has not yet picked up.
Source: *Economic Report of the President*, 1992, Table B–44.

3.3   THE PRODUCTIVITY SLOWDOWN

Productivity is the amount of output produced per unit of input. Because labor is the most important input, the most popular measure of productivity is **labor productivity**, or output per hour of labor. When economists talk about productivity, they usually mean labor productivity. A broader measure of productivity, called **total factor productivity,** is output per generalized unit of input ("factor" is a general term for an input like labor or capital). The generalized unit counts capital, energy, and materials as inputs in addition to labor. However, output per unit of labor and total factor productivity for the United States as a whole tell about the same story in recent years.

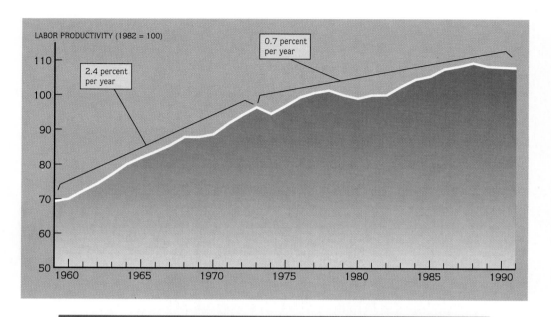

FIGURE 3-7   The slowdown in labor productivity growth

Productivity is the amount of output produced per hour of work. The general trend in productivity has been upward, but growth slowed down in the early 1970s. Productivity also fluctuates during recessions and booms.
Source: *Economic Report of the President*, 1992, Table B-44.

The BLS computes labor productivity for the economy as the ratio of real GDP originating in the business sector to the total hours of work in that sector. The recent history of labor productivity is shown in Figure 3–7. Productivity has generally been increasing as workers have become more efficient and have had more and better machines to work with. This increase in productivity underlies the growth in real wages that we saw in the previous section. But productivity is also procyclical. It rises in booms, and falls in recessions. Firms tend to keep skilled workers on the payroll and let them produce fewer items in slack times, rather than lay them off and run the risk that they will find jobs elsewhere. They make up for their low productivity in bad times with higher productivity in good times.

Productivity growth slowed down in the early 1970s, and this is the main reason that real wage growth has slowed down. Economists disagree about the reasons for the productivity slowdown. Some stress the role of the increases in oil prices, but the real price of crude oil is not much different from what it was in the 1950s and 1960s. Others point to a reduction in expenditures on research and development and say that technical innovation has slowed down as a result. Still others say that we are not investing enough in new machines and factories. Of all the puzzles about the recent performance of the U.S. economy, the slowdown in productivity growth is perhaps the most difficult for economists to solve. We look at the productivity growth slowdown carefully in Chapter 4 and consider some of the suggestions that have been made to halt the decline.

EMPLOYMENT AND PRODUCTIVITY

1. Employment data are collected in a household survey and in an establishment survey. Employment fluctuations are closely related to output fluctuations.

2. The unemployment rate is the percentage of the labor force that is unemployed. The participation rate is the percentage of the working-age population that is in the labor force.

3. The unemployment rate is closely related to the deviations of real GDP from potential GDP. This relation is called Okun's law.

4. The wage rate is the amount paid to workers per hour of work. The real wage measures the purchasing power of the wage payment. The real wage grew steadily in the United States until the early 1970s, when its growth slowed down.

5. Labor productivity is defined as output per unit of labor input. Labor productivity has been growing for a long time, though with fluctuations during business cycles.

6. In the United States productivity growth slowed down in the early 1970s. Growth of productivity permits the real wage to grow, and the slowdown in productivity is the main reason for the slowdown in real wage growth in the United States.

REVIEW AND PRACTICE

Major Points

1. The consumer price index is the number of dollars required to purchase a market basket of goods and services typical of the consumption patterns of Americans.

2. Price indexes called deflators can be calculated by dividing a component of nominal GDP by the same component of real GDP. The consumption deflator is widely used by economists as an alternative to the CPI. The overall GDP deflator is a measure of the price of domestic production; it does not include the price of imports.

3. The best measure of total labor input to the economy is the total number of hours worked by all workers each year. That measure tends to fluctuate in the same direction as real GDP.

4. A good measure of hourly wages is total labor earnings divided by total hours worked. The real wage is the ratio of the hourly wage to the price level. The real wage in the United States grew smoothly until the oil price jumps of the 1970s, after which almost no growth occurred.

5. The unemployment rate is the percentage of the labor force that is actively looking for work but has not found work. Many people who are not working are not counted as unemployed because they are not looking for work. The unemployment rate has varied between 3 and 10 percent since 1950. Okun's law describes the relation between unemployment and real GDP: For every 3 percent by which real GDP departs from its trend path, the unemployment rate departs in the opposite direction from its normal level by 1 percentage point.

6. A simple measure of productivity is the ratio of real GDP to labor input. In the United States, productivity grew smoothly from 1950 until the oil shock recessions in the 1970s. Growth has continued since then, but more irregularly and at diminished rates.

Key Terms and Concepts

price indexes	unemployment rate	Okun's law
consumer price index	participation rate	GDP gap
producer price index	rate of inflation	real wage
price deflators	frictional unemployment	labor productivity
labor force	natural rate of unemployment	

Questions for Discussion and Review

1. What is the difference between high prices and inflation?
2. What is the difference between being unemployed and not working? Give some examples of people not at work who are not unemployed.
3. Explain why unemployment falls when output rises. In the process, mention what happens to employment.
4. Describe how the real wage, employment, and hours of work influence the purchasing power of earnings.

Problems

Numerical

1. Suppose that Okun's law between unemployment and GDP is given by

$$(Y - Y^*)/Y^* = -3(U - U^*),$$

where U is the unemployment rate, U^* is the natural rate of unemployment, Y is GDP, and Y^* is potential GDP. Unemployment is measured as a fraction. Suppose that the natural rate is 6 percent; that is, $U^* = .06$.
   a. Calculate the GDP gap for each of the years in 1987–91 using the following unemployment data: $U = 6.1$, 5.4, 5.2, 5.4, and 6.6 percent, respectively.
   b. GDP for these same years is as follows: $4,540, $4,719, $4,837, $4,885, and $4,848 billion. Using these data and your answers to Part a, calculate potential GDP for each of these years. What is the average growth rate of potential GDP?

2. The consumer price index for the 1978-82 period and the GDP deflator are listed below. This was a period of unusually high, but declining, inflation. (The CPI is equal to 100 in the base years, 1982–84; the GDP deflator is equal to 100 in the base year 1987.)

	CPI	GDP Deflator
1978	65.2	60.3
1979	72.6	65.5
1980	82.4	71.7
1981	90.9	78.9
1982	96.5	83.8

   a. Calculate the rate of inflation according to both measures from 1979 through 1982. What might explain the differences between the two?
   b. Suppose that the hourly wage rate for a group of workers that sign an employment contract for the 3-year period starting in 1979 is indexed to the CPI according to the formula

$$\Delta W/W = .03 + .5 \, \Delta \, \text{CPI}/\text{CPI}$$

   Calculate the actual increase in the wage during each year of the contract period. If the wage is $12.00 in 1979, what was it in 1980, 1981, and 1982? What happens to the real wage measured in terms of the CPI?
   c. Repeat your calculations with .03 reduced to 0 and .5 increased to 1. What indexing formula would the workers' employer have preferred? Is there any reason for the employer to have been happy with the other formula before the actual inflation experience was known?

3. The CPI is calculated for a fixed market basket. It measures the change in the cost of the market basket from the base year until the current year. An index

with the market basket fixed in the first year—like the CPI—is called a Laspeyres index. An alternative index—called the Paasche index—is based on a market basket in the end year. It measures the change in the cost of a market basket fixed in the end year. Suppose that the base year is 1993. Suppose that the market basket contains only two items, peanut butter and gasoline, and that the quantities consumed in 1993 and 1994 are:

	Peanut Butter	*Gasoline*
1993	100 jars	50 gallons
1994	150 jars	45 gallons

Suppose that the price of peanut butter increases from $1.00 per jar in 1993 to $1.20 per jar in 1994 and the price of gasoline increases from $.50 per gallon to $2.00 per gallon.

a. Calculate the rate of inflation for the Laspeyres (CPI) index and the Paasche index.

b. Will inflation calculated using the Laspeyres index always exceed inflation calculated with the Paasche index? (Hint: Use standard indifference curve analysis).

c. Workers often receive an adjustment in their wages equal to only a fraction of inflation as calculated using the CPI. In view of the preceding analysis explain why workers would likely be better off than they were before if they were fully compensated for inflation. Would this also be the case if inflation was calculated using the Paasche index?

Analytical

1. Okun's law suggests that over the course of the business cycle a change in the unemployment rate of 1 percentage point will be accompanied by a 3 percent change in output. Using the formula

$$Y = (Y/H)(H/N)(1 - U)L,$$

where Y/H is output per hour worked, H/N is hours per worker, N is the number of employed workers, U is the unemployment rate, and L is the labor force, explain in what direction and why some of the factors other than Y and U might change. (Note that if $W=XYZ$, then for small changes, the percentage change in W is given by the sum of the percentage changes in X, Y, and Z. Note also the $1 - U = N/L$ and that a change in the unemployment rate of 1 percentage point corresponds to approximately a 1 percent change in N/L.)

2. An empirical regularity in the U.S. economy is that roughly 25 percent of output goes to capitalists in the form of earnings of capital, while 75 percent goes to workers in the form of wages.

a. Using the formula given in Question 1, show that the increase in the average hourly wage will be given by the growth in productivity per worker-hour, *Y/NH*.

b. From Figures 3–6 and 3–7 it appears that real wage growth slowed even more than productivity growth through 1989. Does this imply that there has been a rise in the share of output going to the owners of capital?

3. Suppose that on January 1, 1995, the government creates a million new jobs. Only those currently without jobs may apply. The new jobs attract 3 million applicants, half of whom would not otherwise be looking for work in January.

a. Is the labor force for January changed from what it would have been in the absence of these new jobs? By how much?

b. Assuming that without the new jobs the labor force would have been 100 million and the unemployment rate 6 percent, what will the unemployment rate for January now be?

4. It has been facetiously proposed that if reducing unemployment were our main objective, banning the use of farm equipment might be a solution. What effect would this have on:

a. The real wage.

b. Employment.

c. Unemployment.

d. Labor productivity.

5. Describe the implications of each of the following for the behavior of productivity during the 1970s and 1980s:

a. Secondary workers enter the labor force in greater proportion than they had in the past.

b. Technological change has been underaccounted for in measuring output.

c. Oil shocks made part of the existing capital shock obsolete.

6. With the collapse of the Soviet Union and the Eastern Bloc there has been a large increase in the migration of foreign workers into Germany. What impact will large scale migration have on each of the following labor market indicators?

a. The number of persons employed in Germany.

b. The unemployment rate.

c. The real wage.

d. The employment rate.

MacroSolve Exercises

1. Plot the quarterly growth rates of the CPI and the GDP deflator ["Inflation (CPI)" and "Inflation (GDP)", respectively]. Why are the two not always the same? (Hint: What *exactly* do the two indexes measure?)

a. What major event helps explain why the growth of the CPI was larger than the growth in the GDP deflator in 1979-80?

b. Why was the CPI inflation rate less than the GDP inflation rate in 1986?

2. Okun's law states that "for each percentage point by which the unemployment rate is *above* the natural rate, real GDP is 3 percent *below* potential GDP. The percentage departure of GDP from potential is called the **GDP gap**." Using quar-

terly data, graph the unemployment rate (on the horizontal axis) against the GDP gap (on the vertical axis).

a. You will see that the curve seems to shift outward over time. Does this imply that the natural rate of unemployment has risen over time? (Hint: If the GDP gap is zero for any length of time, then unemployment should be close to the natural rate.)

b. Compute the slope of the Okun relationship between 1933 and 1944 by tabulating the data for the GDP gap and the unemployment rate. The slope is given by the change in the GDP gap divided by the change in the unemployment rate. Make the same calculation between 1978 and 1983. Has the slope changed? What factors might account for such a change?

3. Plot inflation (GDP) and real GDP growth using annual data. Does inflation seem to lag behind real GDP growth? Explain why this relationship may exist.

CHAPTER
4

The Long-Run Growth Model

In this chapter we assemble a model of **long-run economic growth**—the first part of a complete theory of economic growth and fluctuations. The long-run economic growth model is designed to explain the general upward path of output over time. Sometimes it is called the *neoclassical growth* model because it builds on the classical models used before Keynes and his followers.

By describing the upward trend in the economy, the long-run growth model enables us to address many crucial economic policy issues. Most importantly, it can help to explain why the trend in economic growth has declined in the United States in the 1970s and 1980s or why economic growth differs greatly in different regions and countries of the world. Small differences in the economic growth rate make enormous differences in economic well-being. A growth rate difference of only .5 percent per year enabled income per capita in the U.S. South to rise from only 40 percent of the North's after the Civil War to almost the same today. If the growth rate in the United States had been the same in the 1970s and the 1980s as it was in the 1950s and 1960s, then production in the United States would be about one trillion dollars more in 1993. That would be $4,000 per year for every man, woman, and child in the United States, or about 3 times the national defense budget. That "lost" production could have been put to use in many ways: to reduce poverty, increase funds for the environmental cleanup, help assist the emerging market economies in Eastern Europe and the nations of the former Soviet Union, or simply increase private consumption. But because the growth rate slowed down, those funds have not been available to spend.

The long-run growth model does not try to explain the departures of the economy from its growth trend. Hence, it does not explain important events like the 1990–91 recession or the increase in unemployment that occurred at that time. Unlike the complete model, which is examined in Chapter 6, the long-run growth model abstracts from these short-run fluctuations. You can think of the long-run growth model as a description of the economic climate. The complete model describes the weather as well. On any given day, it is either hotter or colder than normal, but it is necessary to know what to expect under normal conditions. For example, in deciding where to live, you would want to know about the average temperatures at different times of the year. Thus, even though the long-run growth model does not explain short-term movements from year to year, it must be part of any complete model of the economy. We use it to project economic conditions in the more distant future and to understand variations in growth rates.

4.1 THE DETERMINANTS OF ECONOMIC GROWTH

The long-run growth model describes the economy in a state where supply and demand for both goods and workers are in balance. Wages and prices have moved as needed to equate supply and demand. Incentives are having their full effect in inducing an efficient level of production.

The important determinants of the long-run growth path of output are:
1. *Labor*—the people available for work.
2. *Capital*—equipment, structures, and other productive facilities.
3. *Technology*—the knowledge about how to use labor and capital to produce goods and services.

Labor

Growth in the number of people available for work is an important source of the growth of GDP. During the 1970s and 1980s growth in the number of workers was strong as the postwar baby boom generation came of working age. Growth in the future is expected to be weaker.

Not everybody in the population is in the labor force. It is against the law for children to work; many adults are in school, working at home, or in retirement and quite a few others are unable to work because they are disabled or sick. Some people are committed to working full time no matter what the incentives; others will choose the level of their work effort depending on the incentives provided by the labor market. As we learned in Table 3–1, about 66 percent of the working-age population was in the labor force in 1991. This percentage—the **labor force participation rate**—has been steadily increasing during the last 20 years, primarily because of increasing participation rates for women.

Another important fact about the labor market is that not everybody who is in the labor force and available for work is actually employed at any given time. Unemployment is a feature of the economy even when supply and demand appear to be in balance. In 1989, a good year for the economy, 5.2 percent of the labor force was unemployed during the typical week. Unemployment rises in recessions and falls in booms, but there is a certain level of unemployment (as we noted in Chapter 3) called the **natural rate of unemployment.** The natural rate is the amount of unemployment when the labor market is in equilibrium. One simple measure of the natural rate is the average rate of unemployment over several decades. The natural rate appears to lie between 5 and 6 percent in the United States.

Part of the natural rate of unemployment is *frictional.* Every month, millions of people move from one activity to another. In the spring, for example, high school and college students finish the school year and move into the labor market, hoping for either summer work or permanent work. Even more important, people are constantly changing jobs, either because they feel they can find better jobs or because their earlier jobs have ended. Frictional unemployment occurs because it takes time for people to find jobs. During the period when they are looking, they count as unemployed.

Another important reason for significant unemployment in equilibrium is the adverse experience suffered by certain groups in the labor market. Young people, members of racial minorities, and the unskilled contribute disproportionately to the unemployment that is found when the economy as a whole is at full employment. These people spend long periods between jobs because of their difficulty in finding work; to the extent that they meet the survey's requirement for having some type of job-seeking effort in the 4 weeks before the survey, they are counted as unemployed. They tend to find jobs that last only a few months, so they are thrown back into the market fairly quickly. Of all the weeks of unemployment suffered in the economy, a large number is contributed by a fairly small fraction of the labor force who tend to spend many weeks each year looking for work and relatively few weeks working.[1]

---

[1]See Kim Clark and Lawrence Summers, "Labor Market Dynamics and Unemployment: A Reconsideration," *Brookings Papers on Economic Activity,* Vol. 1, 1979, pp. 13–61.

The natural rate is not a fixed number. It can change gradually over time as labor market conditions change. When some industries are shrinking at unusual rates and others are expanding to take their places, more than the usual number of workers will be looking for new jobs. Some economists have concluded that abnormal sectoral shifts were responsible for a high natural rate of unemployment in the 1970s.[2] Similarly, when the baby boom generation was entering the labor force, also in the 1970s and early 1980s, the natural rate may have been temporarily higher. Teenagers and young adults typically have higher unemployment rates because they have not settled into long-term jobs.

The actual unemployment rate is equal to the natural unemployment rate when the economy is close to potential—in neither a recession nor a boom. In Chapter 6 we will begin to study departures of the actual unemployment rate from the natural rate. In a recession, when labor demand contracts, unemployment rises above the natural rate. For example, in the recession year of 1991 the unemployment rate was 6.6 percent, well above the natural rate. Workers lose jobs more frequently than they do in normal times and they spend longer periods finding new jobs. As a result, unemployment is higher than the natural rate until the recovery takes the economy back to potential GDP. Similarly, in a boom, the demand for labor increases, and the unemployment rate can fall below the natural rate. Higher rates of inflation typically accompany such episodes.

If we subtract the number of unemployed workers from the number of workers in the labor force, we get the number of workers employed. Production depends not only on the number of workers employed but also on the amount of hours they work each year. Hence, when looking at the effects of employment on production and growth, we only count the hours that workers actually work. The total number of hours worked in the economy in a given year is what we mean by labor input. We frequently refer to labor input simply as employment and label it N.

LABOR AND THE NATURAL RATE OF UNEMPLOYMENT

1. Growth of the labor force is one of the three key factors explaining growth.
2. Even when there is equilibrium in the labor market, not all those available for work are working. The natural rate is the amount of unemployment present when the overall economy is in equilibrium.

---

[2]See David M. Lilien, "Sectoral Shifts and Cyclical Unemployment," *Journal of Political Economy,* Vol. 90 (August 1982), pp. 777–793.

3. The natural rate is positive because people are continually entering the labor market to find work or moving from one job to another. A third reason is that some disadvantaged groups spend a large fraction of each year out of work.

4. The average amount of unemployment since 1950 has been about 5.5 percent, and there is an argument that the natural rate is not too far from this average. However, there are reasons to believe that the natural rate rose in the 1970s and began to fall in the 1980s.

Capital

In any given year, the volume of physical capital—aircraft factories, computers, trucks, tractors, barns, clothing stores, etc.—is determined by investment in previous years. An increase in the amount of capital in the economy will enable the economy to produce more output. For example, a farmer with a tractor can produce tons more wheat than a farmer without a tractor. Boeing couldn't produce any 747s without manufacturing plants. The capital stock increases from one year to the next as long as gross investment is greater than the depreciation of the capital stock. As long as net investment is positive, the capital stock is growing. However, any investment project undertaken this year to increase the capital stock will not add to the stock until the project is complete, a process that takes time. Moreover, the capital stock is so large that the flow of new investment can have little effect on it in a short span of time. Chapter 11 will provide more detail on this point. For now all that matters is that the amount of capital in the economy in any one year does not depend much on other macro variables in any one year. We use the symbol K for the existing capital stock.

Technology

The third determinant of production—technology—tells us how much output can be produced from the amount of labor and capital used in production. Technology includes anything that influences the productivity of workers or capital. It includes technology in the usual sense of the word, such as a communications technology that enables a firm to fax a supplier an order form, rather than send it by regular mail. It also includes how efficiently businesses are organized and managed.

We use the symbol "A" to represent technology. Technology is perhaps the most abstract of the three determinants of growth, and it is more difficult to measure than labor and capital. Fortunately, there are many vivid examples that can reduce the level of abstraction, such as the following automobile example.

One of the great—and most visible—technological advances of the twentieth century was Henry Ford's idea of mass production through the assembly line. Mass production greatly increased the productivity of workers and capital employed in the automobile industry, and eventually other industries as well. It represents an example of an increase in technology—an increase in A.

Ford's innovation occurred in 1913 at his Highland Park factory in Detroit, where he arranged an assembly line in which cars moved past workers who remained in place, rather than having the workers move around the factory. Observers at the time calculated that this one technological advance reduced the time it took a group of workers to assemble the major components into a complete car from $12\frac{1}{2}$ to $1\frac{1}{2}$ hours! With this increase in productivity it is not surprising that Ford could double wages to $5 a day and still cut prices.

In the 1990s we are seeing the effects of another change in the technology of car production. It has been called lean production by a team of researchers at M.I.T. who wrote a book about it called *The Machine That Changed the World*. With lean production, car-producing machines—for example, those that shape steel sheets into fenders and doors—are designed so that they can quickly be modified to handle different cars. This reduces down time, allows for low inventory levels, and permits the manufacturing plants to be smaller. Estimates suggest that productivity can be doubled as a result. Apparently originating in Japan, lean production promises to affect automobile production as much as the idea of mass production. It is already being used in car production in countries around the world, including Mexico and the United States.

Technical change increases the productivity of both labor and capital. Labor and capital are factors of production. Technical change may increase the productivity of both factors in a neutral way such that the marginal productivities of both factors increase in the same proportion. It is then useful to define technical change as something that increases *total factor productivity*. Total factor productivity should be distinguished from productivity, which we discussed in Chapter 3.

The Production Function

A simple way to represent how the three determinants of production combine to produce output is through the **production function,** which shows how much output can be produced from given amounts of labor, capital, and technology. The production function can be represented using symbols as follows:

$$Y = F(N, K, A). \quad \text{The Production Function} \quad (4\text{--}1)$$

This is simply shorthand notation for saying that output Y depends on em-

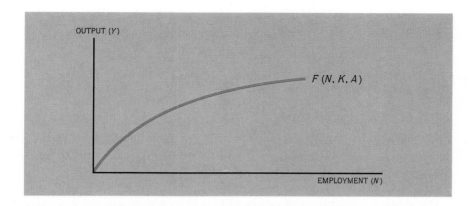

FIGURE 4–1   The production function in terms of labor input

With a given capital stock and technology, the volume of output Y produced from various levels of employment N shows the diminishing marginal product of labor.

ployment N, capital K, and technology A. (Reading out loud we say "Y is a function F of N, K, and A.") The notation F with parentheses after it means a general function of the variables listed in parentheses. With such a notation we are not specific about what the function actually looks like, whether it is linear or the square root of N or whatever.

The production function relates output to employment, capital, and technology whatever their levels. It would tell us how much real GDP would be produced, for example, if there were a very severe depression and only half the normal number of people were at work.

Figure 4–1 shows how production depends on labor for a given capital stock and a given level of technology. The production function curves toward the horizontal axis. The **marginal product of labor** is the additional output that is produced by 1 additional unit of work. The marginal product of labor is the slope of the production function in Figure 4–1. Note how the production function gets less steep as more labor is employed. This means that the marginal product of labor declines as the amount of employment increases.

4.2   FULL EMPLOYMENT AND POTENTIAL GDP

We define potential GDP as the amount of production that occurs when labor is fully employed and the unemployment rate is equal to the natural rate of unemployment. In order to determine potential GDP, we must therefore calculate the level of N corresponding to full employment. We consider the level of technology A and the level of capital K as determined from previous decisions. The focus is on the determination of full employment in the labor market. For this we must consider the demand for, and supply of, labor.

The Demand for Labor

A first principle of microeconomics is that a profit-maximizing firm in a competitive market will choose the level of employment so that *the marginal product of labor equals the real wage.* The real wage is the dollar wage W divided by the price level P, that is, W/P. If firms had employment below this level, the marginal product of labor would exceed the real wage and an opportunity for improved profit would exist. A firm could hire a worker for the wage W, produce more output in the amount given by the marginal product of labor, sell that output at price P, and make a profit on the deal. Firms will pursue this opportunity for profit until their additional hiring pushes the marginal product of labor down to the real wage. The point of maximum profit is shown in Figure 4–2.

The demand function for labor is a negative function of the real wage because the marginal product of labor declines with increased labor input, as shown in Figure 4–3.

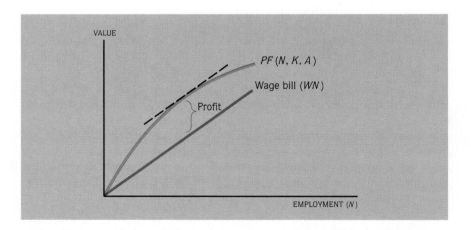

FIGURE 4–2 Profit maximization

Profit is the difference between the value of output, P times $F(N, K, A)$, and the wage bill, W times N. It reaches a maximum when the slope of P times $F(N, K, A)$ equals the slope of W times N; that is, the value of the marginal product of labor equals the wage.

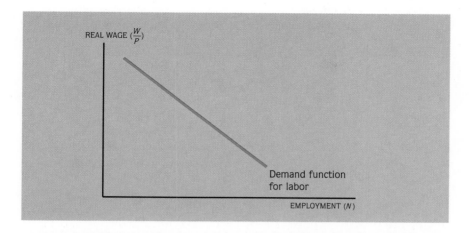

REAL WAGE $(\frac{W}{P})$

Demand function
for labor

EMPLOYMENT (N)

FIGURE 4–3   The demand function for labor

The demand function for labor is a downward-sloping relation between the real wage, W/P, and the level of employment, N. For each real wage, it gives the level of employment that firms will choose by equating the marginal product of labor to the real wage.

The Supply of Labor

The supply of labor is determined by the decisions of individual workers about how much of their time to spend working. The real wage measures the incentive to work. At higher real wages, those already at work will want to work more. In addition, a higher real wage may draw people into the work force who would not work at all with a lower real wage. A higher real wage has an incentive effect toward more work. For most people, therefore, wages are the dominant source of income. When wages rise permanently, they are better off. People who are better off choose to spend more time at home and away from the job. On this account, permanently higher real wages bring lower labor supply. Microeconomic theory labels these two contrasting influences the substitution effect and the income effect.

SUBSTITUTION EFFECT.   As something becomes more expensive, people substitute away from it. In the case of labor supply, as time at home becomes more expensive (as its opportunity cost, the real wage, rises), people substitute away from time at home and toward time in the labor market. To put it another way, the real wage provides an incentive for work, and people substitute toward work when the real wage rises.

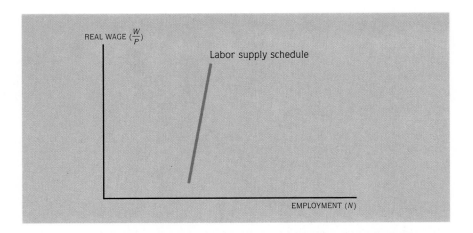

FIGURE 4–4 Long-run labor supply schedule

The labor supply schedule gives the amount of labor offered in the labor market for various levels of the real wage. When real wages rise permanently, the incentive to work is greater, but people have more income, and this tends to offset the incentive. The evidence suggests that the long-run labor supply schedule is almost vertical.

INCOME EFFECT. As income rises, people tend to consume more of most things. In this case, they consume more of their own time at home and offer less of their time in the labor market. Permanently higher real wages make people better off, and they work less on that account.

The long-run labor supply schedule, illustrated in Figure 4–4, shows the net effect of these two offsetting influences. Research by a number of economists has agreed rather closely that the net effect of the two influences of real wage on labor supply is roughly zero.[3] However, it is important to keep in mind that the agreement is that the net effect is approximately zero, not that each of its components is zero. The substitution effect, prompting people to work more when the real wage rises, has been shown to be strong in some studies. In these studies the income effect happens to be equally strong in the opposite direction. If the substitution effect is large, then an increase in work incentives without an increase in income could increase labor supply dramatically.

[3]The most recent econometric studies have used experimental data or panel data of the type we describe in Chapter 10 in our analysis of consumption. A useful survey of available results is found in John Pencavel, "Labor Supply of Men: A Survey," in Orley Ashenfelter, ed., *Handbook of Labor Economics* (Amsterdam: North-Holland, 1987).

Employment Where Supply Equals Demand

Another principle of microeconomics is that employment will be at the intersection of the labor supply and labor demand schedules. The equilibrium is shown in Figure 4–5. On the vertical axis is the real wage, which is the ratio W/P of the dollar wage to the price level. In equilibrium at the real wage W/P, the quantity of labor N chosen by firms equals the quantity supplied by the public. For simplicity, we omit the relatively small amount of frictional unemployment that exists in every labor market. In Figure 4–5, the labor market is in a standard microeconomic equilibrium. Every worker is able to find a job. If the real wage were too high to provide jobs for everyone interested, the real wage would fall. The fall would stimulate labor demand by firms and discourage work effort by workers. The real wage would fall immediately to the point where supply and demand were equal and everybody had work.

We define **full employment,** N^*, as the volume of employment at the intersection of supply and demand in Figure 4–5. It is the total amount of work that would be done if each worker could find a job after a brief search and earn as much as similar people are already earning. Notice that full employment is not the absolute maximum amount of work that the population is capable of doing. It is the amount people want to work given the real wage that employers are willing to pay. If productivity rises, so the

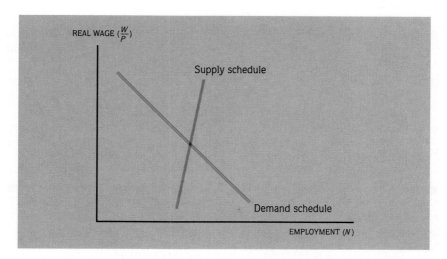

FIGURE 4–5 Labor market equilibrium

In the model with perfectly flexible wages and prices, the real wage fluctuates to equate the supply of and demand for labor.

labor demand schedule shifts upward, the equilibrium level of employment rises. Moreover, as the population grows, the labor supply schedule will shift to the right and equilibrium employment will rise.

Potential GDP

Potential GDP, denoted Y^*, is the amount of output produced when the labor market is at full employment:

$$Y^* = F(N^*, K, A). \qquad (4-2)$$

The level of output, Y^*, is the amount of output that would be produced if everybody who wanted to work could find a job. For this reason, Y^* is also frequently called the **full-employment level of output.** Recall that in Figures 1–1 and 1–2 we compared actual GDP with estimates of potential GDP. We found that potential GDP grows steadily, whereas actual GDP fluctuates around a growth trend.

POTENTIAL GDP AND THE LABOR MARKET

1. Potential GDP is the level of real GDP when labor is fully employed. Prices and wages have moved so that markets are in balance.
2. The determinants of potential GDP are the labor force and its willingness to work as expressed by the labor supply schedule, the capital stock, and the technology of the economy.
3. In the labor market, the real wage adjusts as needed to keep the market in balance. Full employment is the common value of labor supply and labor demand after the real wage has made the two equal.
4. When the labor market is in balance, there is still some unemployment. The natural rate of unemployment is between 5 and 6 percent in the United States.

4.3   SAVING AND BALANCED GROWTH

Having defined the production function and potential output in the previous two sections, we are now prepared to explore the behavior of the economy as it steadily grows through time. In particular, we want to look at the relationship between labor growth, capital growth, and saving growth and to examine whether the growth process has any inherent tendencies to slow down. We focus on a most practical real-world example: the growth path of the United States economy from now into the first part of the twenty-first century.

The growth of the labor force is predicted by the Bureau of Labor Statistics (BLS) to average around 1 percent per year from now through the year 2010. The forecast is very reliable, because most of the people who will be in the labor force—which is limited to those who are 16 years of age and over—during this time have already been born. Projecting the labor force much beyond 2010 is more difficult because it requires forecasting future birth rates.

Now consider the growth of the capital stock over the same future period. Capital growth will depend on how much investment there is each year, which in turn depends on how much Americans save and how much foreigners invest in the United States. Forecasting future saving and foreign investment is much more difficult than forecasting the growth of the labor force. Saving will depend not only on what private individuals do, but also on whether the federal government succeeds in reducing the budget deficit. Instead of trying to forecast future capital growth, we consider the implications of a future in which the growth rate of capital exactly equals the growth rate of labor, so that the amount of capital available for each worker neither rises nor falls. Such a steady growth path—called a **balanced growth path** because the growth rates of capital and labor are balanced—would be a useful baseline from which to make judgments about how alternative economic policies would affect the future. But first we need to check whether the economy tends to follow a balanced growth path.

In 1956, Robert Solow of M.I.T., who won the Nobel Prize in 1987, wrote a paper using the neoclassical growth model to study balanced growth paths such as the hypothesized one.[4] In fact, the long-run growth model was introduced for the first time in that paper. The Solow analysis makes extensive use of the production function, the identities we discussed in Chapter 2, and a simple assumption about saving.

Like Solow, we will assume, at the start, that the economy is closed (no foreign investment) and that there is no technological change (the term A is ignored). Both assumptions can be modified, but they make it easier to see what is going on. Labor force growth is assumed to be a steady 1 percent per year. Solow used the symbol n for the growth rate of labor. For our case, $n = .01$. Each year the labor force increases by .01 times N, the level at the start of the year.

---

[4]R. M. Solow "A Contribution to the Theory of Economic Growth," *Quarterly Journal of Economics*, Vol. 70 (February 1956), pp. 65–94.

Conditions for Balanced Growth

We saw in Chapter 2 that the change in the capital stock equals net investment. If capital is to grow at the same 1 percent rate as the labor force, then each year capital must increase by 1 percent; that is, by .01 times K or, as Solow put it, by nK. By definition net investment equals the change in the capital stock, so that if capital is to grow at the same rate as labor, then net investment must equal nK. In other words, nK represents the amount of investment needed to maintain balanced growth. We can think of nK as *balanced growth* investment. For example, if the capital stock is $10 trillion, then net investment must equal $100 billion (.01 times $10,000 billion) if the capital stock is to grow at the same 1 percent rate as labor. To summarize, we have derived the first key condition for balanced growth:

$$\text{Net investment} = nK. \tag{4–3}$$

To complete the Solow analysis, we consider the link between saving and investment, also discussed in Chapter 2. In particular, net investment equals net saving (saving less depreciation). Saving depends on (1) the fraction of national income that is saved and (2) the level of national income. Let s be the fraction of income that is saved; s is called the **saving rate.** Thus, saving in the economy is equal to s times income. We know from Chapter 2 that income equals output Y. Hence,

$$\text{Net saving} = sY. \tag{4–4}$$

For example, if income Y is $5 trillion and the saving rate is .02, then net saving (saving less depreciation) would be $100 billion. Since net saving equals net investment, we see that sY equals that *actual* amount of net investment in the economy.

Now by equating *actual* investment in Equation 4–4 with *balanced growth* investment in Equation 4–3, we get Solow's basic condition for balanced growth,

$$\underset{\substack{\nearrow \\ \text{Net saving}}}{sY} = \underset{\substack{\nwarrow \\ \text{Net investment}}}{nK,} \tag{4–5}$$

which we rewrite simply as

$$\frac{K}{Y} = \frac{s}{n}. \tag{4–6}$$

The ratio of capital K to output Y on the left-hand side of Equation 4–6 is called the **capital-output ratio**—the value of all factories and equipment in the United States divided by output. When Equation 4–5 holds, the growth rate of capital equals the growth rate of labor; growth is in balance. Note that if sY is greater than nK, then actual investment is greater than balanced growth investment; hence, capital grows faster than labor. Analogously if sY is less than nK, then the growth rate of capital is less than the growth rate of labor.

Equation 4–6 has several profound implications. It says that when an economy is growing *along a balanced growth path, the capital-output ratio is given by the ratio of the saving rate to the labor force growth rate.* For example, the net saving rate in the United States has recently been about 2 percent ($s = .02$). With the 1 percent labor growth rate ($n = .01$), we immediately have that the capital-output ratio must equal 2 (from .02 divided by .01) along our hypothesized balanced growth path.

The stock of capital in the United States in 1991 was about $10 trillion. National income was about $5 trillion. Hence, the capital-output ratio at the start of the 1990s was close to the 2 figure required for the hypothesized balanced growth path through the year 2010. The United States economy appears to be on a balanced growth path, at least according to these calculations.

Why the Growth Path Is Stable

Even if the economy were not on a balanced growth path, Solow pointed out that there are natural forces at work in the economy that would automatically bring the capital-output ratio into line with the s/n value and with the growth rate converging to the balanced growth path. Growth economists before Solow worried that discrepancies between K/Y and s/n would cause serious instabilities in the economy, leading either to ever deepening recessions or uncontrollable booms. Solow showed that they were wrong, that, on the contrary, the economy is stable.

SOLOW'S STABILITY PROOF. Solow reasoned as follows. Suppose sY is greater than nK (or K/Y is less than s/n), so that capital is growing faster than labor. With each worker using more and more capital, the capital-output ratio (K/Y) would rise[5] until it equaled s/n and the economy would be back on the steady growth path. Similar reasoning shows that if sY is less than nK (or K/Y is greater than s/n), so that capital grows more slowly than labor, then the capital-output ratio falls. Therefore, even if the economy starts out in a position where Equation 4–6 does not hold, the capital-output ratio will either rise or fall until the equation does hold and the economy is on a balanced growth path. Rather than being unstable as earlier economists had feared, Solow showed that the balanced path was

---

[5]The capital-output ratio rises—that is, more capital is required for each unit of output—because of the diminishing marginal product of capital. For example, suppose that $Y = K^{.3}L^{.7}$. Then $K/Y = (K/L)^{.7}$. Hence, a rise in K/L implies a rise in K/Y.

stable. If the economy was off the path, the capital-output ratio would rise or fall until the balanced growth rate was reached.

The Effect of Saving on Growth

Another profound implication of Equation 4–6 is that *the growth rate of output along the balanced growth path does not depend on the saving rate*. Because the capital-output ratio is fixed along the balanced growth path, the growth rate of output must equal the growth rate of capital. Hence, labor N, capital K, and output Y all grow at the same rate on the balanced growth path. What then is the impact of increasing the saving rate in the Solow analysis? The answer comes directly from Solow's stability argument.

Suppose that the saving rate suddenly rises from .02 to .04 and stays there. Then the balanced growth condition in Equation 4–6 is violated with $K/Y = 2 < s/n = 4$. According to Solow's stability argument, capital will increase more rapidly than labor, and because of diminishing returns to capital, the capital-output ratio increases. The ratio will continue to increase until it reaches 4 and the economy returns to the balanced growth rate of 1 percent. There is a **transition period,** however, during which the growth rate of the economy is greater than the balanced growth rate. This is illustrated in Figure 4–6, which shows how the level of output rises as a result of the increase in saving, but the growth rate of the economy returns to the

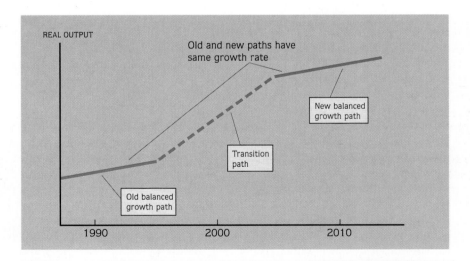

FIGURE 4–6 Transition between balanced growth paths

A higher saving rate starting in the mid-1990s leads to a higher level of real output. During a transition period growth is higher. The growth rates in the old and new balanced growth paths are the same.

balanced growth rate after the transition period. Hence, greater saving benefits the economy by raising future GDP, but not by increasing the long-term growth rate, according to the Solow model.

Technological Change

The above discussion may paint too rosy a picture of saving and balanced growth. It seems to suggest that the United States economy is on a balanced growth path with a (net) saving rate of only 2 percent. But recall that output only grows by 1 percent per year on that balanced growth path. The introduction to this chapter indicated that most economists thought the growth rate of output would average closer to 2 percent in the 1990s. The difference is technological change, which we now must consider.

Suppose that technological change is expected to increase the effectiveness of workers by 1 percent per year. For example, this year only 100 workers produce the same output that it took 101 workers to produce last year. However, if those 100 workers can produce the same output as 101 workers, they need as much capital as those 101 workers would have. In others words, technological progress requires more capital even if the number of workers does not increase. This type of technological progress increases the capital requirements just as the growth of the labor force does. With technology growth of g and labor force growth of n, we now have the need for capital growth of $n + g$ percent per year. Net investment equals .01 + .01 = .02 times K, rather than .01 times K. For balanced growth we therefore must have $K/Y = s/(n + g)$. For the same capital-output ratio of 2 to be on the balanced growth path, the saving rate must now be .04 rather than .02. Hence, a doubling of the net saving rate would be required to generate a balanced growth path of 2 percent per year in the future. This is a much less sanguine assessment and demonstrates the importance of increasing saving in the United States.

BALANCED GROWTH AND THE SOLOW ANALYSIS

1. Balanced growth occurs when the labor force, capital stock, and real output all grow at the same rate.
2. Along a balanced growth path, the ratio of capital to output equals the ratio of the saving rate to the labor force growth rate.
3. Solow showed that the balanced growth path is stable: if the economy is off a balanced growth path, it will naturally tend to return to that path.
4. A higher saving rate will raise GDP in Solow's analysis of the long-run growth model, but it will not permanently raise the growth rate.

4.4   THE ECONOMIC GROWTH FORMULA

The economy is not always on a balanced growth path. Transitions from one balanced growth path to another are the rule rather than the exception. For example, in Chapter 2, Figure 2–1, we observed that the growth rate in Japan with a lower level of GDP per worker is higher than that in the United States with a higher level of GDP per worker. The higher growth rate in Japan may represent a transition to a higher level of GDP per worker. If there is a negative relationship between the level of GDP per worker and the growth rate, then there is a tendency for countries to *converge* in GDP per worker. This is the *convergence hypothesis* implied by the neoclassical model. There is another possible explanation for the growth differences, however: technological growth might be greater in Japan than in the United States. Distinguishing one explanation from the other requires a framework to measure the contributions of the three different determinants of economic growth.

Solow also developed a framework that can be used even if the economy is not in balanced growth to determine the contributions of labor, capital, and technical change to economic growth.[6] His formula is used by growth specialists, such as Edward Denison of the Brookings Institution, to assign credit for growth. In its simplest form Solow's formula says the rate of growth of output equals technology growth plus the weighed rates of growth of labor and capital:

$$\frac{\Delta Y}{Y} = \frac{\Delta A}{A} + \frac{.7\Delta N}{N} + \frac{.3\Delta K}{K}. \tag{4–7}$$

The derivation of this formula is shown in the appendix to this chapter. The growth formula shows how total growth relates to growth in the three determinants. In words the formula says that the rate of growth of output is equal to the rate of growth of technology plus .7 times the rate of growth in labor input plus .3 times the rate of growth of capital input. What is interesting about the formula is its lack of dependence on the details of the production function. All that matters is that technology increases the productivity of both factors in a neutral way. The weight .3 and its complement .7 can then be derived from data on the relative shares of capital and labor in national income. In Chapter 2 we saw that these income shares are roughly .3 and .7.

---

[6]Robert M. Solow, "Technical Change and the Aggregate Production Function," *Review of Economics and Statistics.* Vol. 39 (August 1957) pp. 312-20.

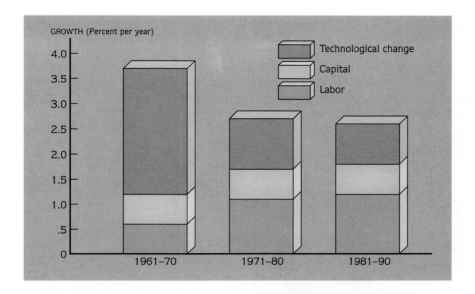

FIGURE 4–7   Sources of growth

The height of each bar shows the actual annual growth rate of real GDP over 10-year intervals. Each bar is broken into blocks showing the contributions from labor growth, from capital growth, and from technological change. The contributions are calculated using Equation 4–7 in the text.
Source: Data on real output growth are from the *Economic Report of the President*, 1992, Table B–2; the labor growth data are from Table B–44; and the capital stock data are calculated from investment data in Table B–15.

The formula can be used to study the contributions of each factor to long-term growth in the United States over the last 30 years. In order to smooth out the business cycle fluctuations, it helps to look at average contributions over longer periods. The data are shown over 10-year intervals in Figure 4–7. Growth reached its peak around 1970. According to the data, the major reason for the decline in growth was a decline in technological change. Because of the baby boom, labor growth rose, but is declining again in the 1990s.

 4.5   POLICIES TO STIMULATE GROWTH

The government can influence all three of the determinants of growth—technological change, capital formation, and labor input. Disappointing rates of growth since the beginning of the 1970s have led to a number of federal policies to stimulate growth. Under what circumstances might a

free-market economy deliver an inadequate rate of growth in potential output that could be improved by government intervention? In general, government intervention is justified if a market failure exists. A market failure
exists when there is a divergence between social and private costs or benefits of a particular activity. Many activities that generate growth have social
benefits that exceed private benefits. Government can encourage such activities.

Policies to Improve Technological Growth and Productivity

Figure 4–7 shows that, of the three factors, technological change—or the
productivity growth of labor and capital—has fallen most significantly.
Hence the idea of stimulating productivity has been attractive to policymakers. But there have been few proposals for concrete action. Unfortunately, the process of improving technology and productivity growth is not
well understood by economists.

Perhaps the most important role that the government can play in improving productivity growth is in the area of education. In the United
States, state and local governments provide most of the support for primary
and secondary schools and universities. A highly skilled labor force is obviously a key ingredient to successful productivity growth.

The federal government also has played a role in sponsoring research
in science and engineering. Figure 4–8 shows the expenditures on research
and development (R&D) in the United States and four other countries. The
United States spends more on R&D than other countries, but as a share of
GDP the amounts are nearly the same. Note that much more of U.S. R&D
has been devoted to defense. The end of the Cold War will likely reduce
defense R&D. An important policy-question is whether efforts should be
made to increase research in other areas to offset this decline. Many experts
feel that the U.S. government could do more. The federal government now
provides about 47 percent of the funds for R&D in the United States. Like
education, basic research may provide social benefits in excess of the private benefits that accrue to those engaged in these activities. Left to their
own, individuals and firms will choose levels of spending on education and
research that fall short of the social optimum. Government may want to encourage these activities through grants and subsidies.

The Research and Experimentation Tax Credit in the United States has
provided tax incentives for research and development expenditures. This
special tax credit allows firms to reduce their taxes by 20 percent of their
research and development expenses. Some have argued that the credit
should be made permanent. If R&D programs are an important source of
productivity growth, then tax incentives like these should yield some further growth. The use of public funds for this purpose, through the tax sys-

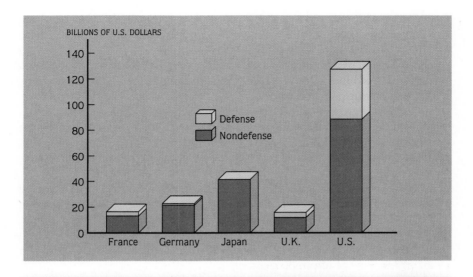

BILLIONS OF U.S. DOLLARS

Defense
Nondefense

France   Germany   Japan   U.K.   U.S.

FIGURE 4–8   R & D spending in 1987

The United States spends the most on R & D, but much has been related to defense. Nondefense spending as a share of GDP is less in the United States than in Germany and Japan.

tem, is justified if the sponsors of R&D are unable to capture the full benefits themselves.

Policies to Stimulate Capital Formation

Until recently, government policy to stimulate growth concentrated almost entirely on capital formation. A rising capital stock will add to economic growth; the growth formula in the previous section made this clear. Numerically, an extra percentage point of capital growth will add about .3 percentage point to growth in output. To get an added 1 percent of growth in output, the capital stock would have to grow 3.3 percent per year.

Consider a numerical illustration. At the end of 1991, the capital stock was about $10,000 billion, counting plants, equipment, housing, and inventories. The 3.3 percent growth in capital needed to add a point to growth of output would be

3.3 percent times $10,000 billion = $330 billion in added investment.

Total fixed investment in 1992 was about $800 billion. Investment would have to rise by 330/800 = 41 percent to add just 1 percentage point to growth in output. Of course, 1 percent more growth would take us a long way to restoring the growth path that the United States experienced in the mid-1960s and would compound itself to an impressive increase in living standards in 20 years. Moreover, it is possible that the increase in new plants and machines would bring forth additional technical innovations which could spur productivity growth.

Increased growth in the capital stock requires consistently high levels of investment spending. This can occur only if there are fewer competing demands on output from households and government purchases. To expand investment, we need to reduce consumption, government purchases, or net exports.

Under the right combination of economic conditions, a large increase in investment is possible. For example, investment was at depressed levels in 1962 when President Kennedy sponsored the first investment tax credit. The new investment incentive plus generally expansive conditions caused investment to rise from 306 billion 1987 dollars in 1962 to $401 billion in 1966, an increase of about 30 percent.

Although an increase in investment of 30 percent is feasible, it does not appear to be sustainable. Output growth can be raised by a percentage point for a few years, but then investment tends to decline to more normal levels. For example, annual growth of the capital stock reached its peak from the Kennedy stimulus at 7 percent per year in 1966, but then subsided to about 5 percent through 1974. During most of this period, the investment tax credit was in effect. Between 1975 and 1982, the growth of the capital stock fluctuated between 1 and 4 percent per year. The investment credit was in effect at a higher rate throughout these disappointing years.

GROWTH THROUGH CAPITAL FORMATION

1. Because the coefficient of capital growth in the growth formula is about .3, it takes about 3.3 percent of growth in capital to add 1 percent to output growth.
2. In 1990, it would have taken a 31 percent increase in the amount of investment to raise the growth of the capital stock by 3.3 percent.
3. Increases of this magnitude in investment have occurred in the past, but only when special incentives were combined with other favorable conditions. Even then, the high levels of investment were sustained for only a few years.

Policies to Increase Labor Supply

In the growth equation, employment growth has over twice the leverage of capital growth. Each percentage point of extra growth of employment adds .7 percent to output growth. To put it the other way around, it takes 1.4 percent of added employment growth to increase output growth by 1 percent per year. Reductions in income tax rates are one way to stimulate work effort by improving incentives. Major tax rate cuts occurred in the United States in 1981 and 1986.

The income tax depresses the incentive to work by reducing the wage that workers receive for their work. On this account, one might expect that a cut in income taxes would stimulate work by improving incentives. A prime selling point of the policies put into place in 1981 and 1986 was precisely this incentive argument. But a cut in income taxes also makes people better off, which depresses labor supply. The net effect of a simple tax cut could therefore be quite small. This is illustrated in Figure 4–9. If the labor supply curve is steep, as statistical evidence seems to suggest, the intersection of supply and demand occurs at almost the same level of em-

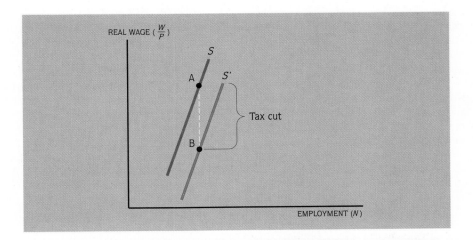

FIGURE 4–9 Shift in labor supply from a tax cut

A tax cut shifts the labor supply function downward in proportion to the cut. *S* is the labor supply schedule before the tax rate cut; *A* is an arbitrary point on it. *S'* is the supply schedule after the cut. *B* is a point on *S'* where the real wage after tax is the same as the real wage after tax on *S* at *A*. *B* is below *A* by the amount of the tax cut. The amount of labor supplied at *B* is the same as at *A* because the real wage received by workers is the same at *B* as at *A*. A downward shift in a schedule that is nearly vertical has almost no substantive effect on employment.

NEW RESEARCH IN PRACTICE
Endogenous Growth Theory and International Trade Liberalization

An important area of new research in macroeconomics during the 1980s and 1990s has been called "endogenous" growth theory. Paul Romer of the University of California, Berkeley and Robert Lucas of the University of Chicago have been two of the key contributors, though the research can be traced to work in the 1960s by Kenneth Arrow of Stanford University and Hirofumi Uzawa of the University of Tokyo.

Compared with Solow's neoclassical growth theory described in Section 4.3 of this chapter, endogenous growth theory focuses more on explaining the three factors that underlie economic growth—technology, labor, and capital. Technological growth, in particular, had typically been treated as exogenous, either explained outside the model or not at all. In contrast, much of the new research has been devoted to technology growth and how it depends on, or is endogenous to, investment in research, education, and government influence on incentives. In Section 4.5, for example, we discussed how improvements in education as well as research and development can increase technological growth and productivity. This discussion reflects the influence of endogenous growth research. Economists have long known that economic incentives play a major role in how resources are directed toward improving technology and human capital (education and job training). Recent research provides valuable insights into the short- and long-run effects of these policies. Another strand of endogenous growth theory looks at how changes in taxes or other government policies might have a permanent effect on the rate of growth of output, not only on the level of output as in Solow's original research.

There has been much interest in applying endogenous growth theory to economic policy. An important example is international trade policy—the policy of reducing barriers to international trade. Indeed, this is an area where the new research has been used in practice and has influenced public debate.

Trade policy is much in the news in the 1990s. Two major initiatives to reduce trade barriers in the 1990s are the Uruguay Round of multilateral trade negotiations (under the General Agreement on Trade and Tariffs), which aims to reduce or eliminate tariffs in many sectors worldwide, and the North American Free Trade Area, which aims to eliminate tariffs among the United States, Mexico, and Canada.

Estimating the benefits of these trade liberalization efforts is important. While the classical theory of comparative advantage tells us that there are gains from trade, public debate can be influenced by the perceived magnitude of the gain, because in the short run, certain interests can be harmed by trade liberalization.

How much effect does trade liberalization have on the economy? Estimates that ignore growth seem surprisingly small. In the traditional analysis, there is an increase in the level of real GDP, due to the more efficient allocation of resources among different economies. However, increased trade may raise the return to investment (in physical capital, human capital, and research and development). For example, access to a world market may increase the return to a new product or invention. If so, then investment will increase, and this will raise the economy's growth rate for a while. The total increase due to the trade liberalization equals the static gain in income plus the dynamic gain achieved over time as investment responds to the change in policy.

In a 1992 paper in the *Journal of Political Economy*, Richard Baldwin of Columbia University provides some quantitative estimates of these effects. He found that if trade liberalization leads to a 1 percent increase in productivity (the *A* coefficient in the production function increases), then the long-run increase in output is 1.6 percent with the additional .6 percent due to capital accumulation. Hence, approximately 6/16 = 3/8 of the long-run increase in output is due to capital accumulations. Of course, output is not the sole variable of interest to policymakers. Increased capital accumulation requires an increase in saving. Thus, although capital accumulation fostered by trade liberalization leads to a large increase in output, the effect on consumption is less.

These calculations share the characteristic with the Solow model that the long-run growth rate is unaffected by policy. Other models of endogenous growth explicitly consider the implications of economic policy on the long-run rate of growth. In such models, trade liberalization may lead to greater R&D and human capital investment as firms and workers take advantage of the larger markets and the greater flow of ideas and knowledge across borders. The market return to productivity-increasing investments is increased, and this leads to an increase in the rate of growth. In this case, the long-run effect of trade liberalization is not only a higher

level of output in the future, but a higher rate of growth of output. Trade liberalization thus may lead to a permanent increase in the rate of growth of output and consumption. If this type of model is more appropriate for describing the economy, the estimates of the benefits of a free trade agreement discussed above may underestimate the true values.

The estimates of the effect of trade liberalization under the Uruguay Round used by the Office of the United States Trade Representative in 1992 incorporated the increase in growth due to the increase in investment as described above. However, endogenous growth theory has yet to provide a quantitative way to assess the importance of the effects that induce a permanent increase in growth. Hence, they are not incorporated in the quantitative estimates.

---

ployment. A prediction of large stimulus to employment and output from tax cuts would be contrary to the evidence.

Growth policies need not take the exclusive form of tax cuts. In fact, the federal government's need for revenue makes it impossible to improve work incentives dramatically by cutting taxes. Another type of policy is *tax reform*. A tax reform keeps revenue the same although tax rates are cut. This could be done by eliminating deductions and lowering tax rates on earned income. Because revenue is the same, the typical taxpayer pays the same amount of tax and there is no income effect. The cut in taxes due to the lower tax rate is offset by the increase in taxes due to the elimination of deductions. This type of reform necessarily involves a reduction in the progressivity of the income tax. What matters for work incentives is the *marginal* tax rate, the rate applied to the last dollar of earnings. A flat tax system that puts roughly the same tax rate on all dollars of earnings above the first few thousand dollars of income could raise the same amount of revenue with lower marginal rates. The Tax Reform Act of 1986 significantly reduced rates while leaving revenue unchanged. This type of tax reform has no income effect to depress work. The labor supply schedule shifts by the full amount of the substitution effect. The 1987 *Economic Report of the President* estimated that labor supply would increase by 3.1 percent as a result of the tax reform. This would increase real GDP by about 2.2 percent. These are one-time permanent effects on the level of labor supply and output.

GROWTH THROUGH INCREASED WORK EFFORT

1. The classical model provides a good way to analyze programs to stimulate growth through improved work incentives. However, the analysis applies only in the long run.
2. Because the labor supply schedule is nearly vertical, even a large tax cut has only a small effect on employment. The substitution effect of lower tax rates raises incentives to work, but the higher level of income depresses work.
3. If the tax change is a tax *reform,* which keeps tax receipts constant, rather than a tax *cut,* it improves incentives without changing average income. Then the substitution effects are not offset by income effects.

4.6 REAL BUSINESS CYCLE EXPLANATIONS OF FLUCTUATIONS

In Chapter 1, we noted that most macroeconomists see potential GDP as evolving smoothly over time. They view a recession or a boom as a temporary departure from potential. Fluctuations in employment occur as shocks hit the economy and push employment away from the potential. An important group of macroeconomists disputes this idea. They believe that potential GDP, as defined above, fluctuates significantly. This group is the **real business cycle school,** which has been prominent in recent years.[7]

The real business cycle school argues that employment is always at the intersection of demand and supply. If so, employment can change only if the demand curve shifts or the supply curve shifts. The real business cycle model considers shifts in the labor demand schedule—caused by shifts in the production function—to be the basic moving force of booms and recessions. We will study that view in this section.

Figure 4–10 shows the basic idea of shifts in labor demand. When some adverse force makes the demand for labor fall, the equilibrium level

---

[7]A more detailed introduction to this school of thought is Charles Plosser, "Understanding Real Business Cycles," *Journal of Economic Perspectives,* Vol. 3 (Summer 1989), pp. 51-77.

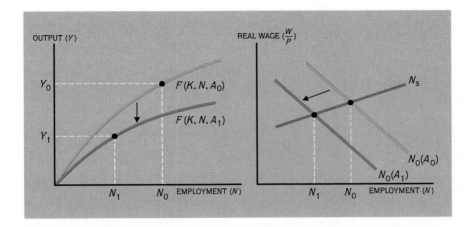

FIGURE 4-10   A recession according to the real business cycle view

The left-hand panel shows how an adverse shock to technology causes a downward shift in the production function for a given level of the capital stock. The labor demand schedule is the marginal product of labor, which shifts inward as a result of the adverse technology shock. As a result, the real wage is lower at any level of employment. The right-hand panel shows that employment falls in the recession and the real wage falls as well.

of employment declines. The real wage declines as well. An increase in the world oil price is one example of a negative shock. The economists Finn Kydland of Carnegie-Mellon University and Edward Prescott of the University of Minnesota are leaders of the real business cycle school.[8] They stress the distinction between changes in real wages in the short run and in the long run. Recall that the income effect from a permanent increase in the real wage may offset the substitution effect, so that wage increases produce no corresponding increases in labor supplied. But if the increase in the real wage is temporary, the income effect is much weaker. The substitution effect is just as strong or even stronger, so individuals will supply more labor. A brief period of unusually high wages is a good time to work very hard; time off can be scheduled when wages are briefly below normal at some time in the future. For an auto worker, a period of strong demand for cars will raise the real wage temporarily and stimulate extra work. For workers throughout the economy, it takes an economywide surge of productivity to raise real wages everywhere.

[8]Edward Prescott, "Theory Ahead of Business Cycle Measurement," *Quarterly Review of the Federal Reserve Bank of Minneapolis* (Fall 1986), pp. 9-22.

What Causes Shifts in Labor Demand?

Recall that the labor demand schedule has a very particular microeconomic interpretation—it is the marginal product of labor. In a competitive economy, the labor demand schedule shifts only if the production function shifts. Consequently, the real business cycle model holds that booms are times of unusually favorable productivity and recessions are times when productivity drops below normal. Advances and declines in technology are a major driving force in the economy, according to the real business cycle view. In an agricultural economy, changes in rainfall and temperature could cause shifts in productivity sufficiently large to produce important fluctuations in employment. Workers concentrate their effort during periods of favorable weather and spend their time in nonwork activities when conditions for growing crops are poor. Certainly this idea is supported by the seasonal pattern of work activity of farmers—they work much harder during the summer and early fall than they do in the winter.

Industrial economies do not have productivity shocks as obvious and pervasive as the effects of weather on agriculture. Technology improves because of innovations, and some of these improvements might take effect sufficiently quickly to create a boom. Sudden changes in financial conditions or in world relative prices might generate shifts in labor demand. Proponents of the real business cycle view have only just begun to try to measure and identify the driving forces that make the labor demand curve shift back and forth.

The real business cycle school has one important fact on its side. When shifts in technology are measured from year to year with the standard method we discussed in Section 4.4, the shifts are large. Productivity rises at the same time that output and employment rise in a boom, and productivity drops sharply in a recession. The real business cycle view is that these shifts in productivity are exogenous events that cause the ups and downs of the economy. The timing and magnitude of the movements in productivity fit the real business cycle story. By contrast, critics of the real business cycle model believe the productivity shifts are the result of other shocks to the economy, not the underlying cause of fluctuations.

Critique of the Real Business Cycle Model

Although the real business cycle model has attracted some support among macroeconomists, it has influential critics. Most of the criticism focuses on the idea the productivity shifts are an important driving force in the short-run fluctuations of the economy.

Many economists find it hard to think of exogenous contractions in productivity big enough to explain recessions.[9] What adverse technological shock explains the decline in output and employment in 1991? Sticky-price models assign responsibility for that contraction to monetary policy. But the real business cycle model has no role for monetary policy in the determination of employment. Figure 4–10 shows the level of employment, and neither supply nor demand is influenced by monetary policy.

Critics of the real business cycle view have an alternative explanation for the fact that measured productivity moves along with output and employment, just as the real business cycle model predicts. The critics answer that the changes in measured productivity are caused by the changes in output and employment, rather than being the cause of those changes. Three factors make measured productivity rise along with output and employment, even when there is no shift in the production function.[10] One is sometimes called "labor hoarding." Firms find it costly to lay off skilled workers when production declines. Hence employment does not drop as much as production, and productivity falls. Similarly, during the upturn these workers become more productive when output rises. A second factor is market power. If firms have market power, then they will be able to pay a real wage lower than the marginal product of labor. Productivity measurement methods that assume that the real wage equals the marginal product of labor have an important bias because they give labor too little credit. The third factor is increasing returns—a 1 percent increase in output requires much less than 1 percent increases in capital and labor. Standard productivity measures record the difference as productivity gains. Then every expansion shows rapid productivity growth and every recession a decline in productivity. But these movements in productivity are the result of the expansions and recessions, and are not the exogenous cause of them.

It would make a big difference for economic policy if the real business cycle model were right about the sources of macro fluctuations and the complete model described in this book were wrong. The macroeconomist who believes that the economy can move away from potential GDP right after a shock counsels the Fed to try to stabilize GDP against short-run fluctuations while keeping the price level stable in the longer run. The real business cycle macroeconomist says the fluctuations are the natural and desirable consequence of productivity fluctuations and policy should not try to offset them.

[9]Lawrence Summers, "Some Skeptical Observations on Real Business Cycle Theory," *Quarterly Review of the Federal Reserve Bank of Minneapolis* (Fall 1986), pp. 23–27.

[10]Robert Hall, "Invariance Properties of Solow's Productivity Residual," in Peter Diamond, ed., *Essays in Honor of Robert Solow's 65th Birthday* (Cambridge, Mass.: M.I.T. Press, 1991), pp. 71–112.

REAL BUSINESS CYCLE THEORY

1. Real business cycle theory views movements in GDP as movements in potential GDP rather than departures from potential GDP.
2. The real business cycle interpretation of a recession requires an inward shift in labor demand or supply. Real business cycle theory emphasizes inward shifts in labor demand resulting from adverse technology shifts.
3. Critics of real business cycle theory are skeptical that productivity fluctuations are an exogenous driving force in the economy. They tend to attach more importance to financial factors and price rigidities in explaining recessions.

REVIEW AND PRACTICE

Major Points

1. The long-run growth model is one in which the economy is always operating at full employment. Output is determined by the labor force, the capital stock, and technology.

2. Even when the economy is operating at potential, there is some unemployment. The rate of unemployment when the labor market is in equilibrium is called the natural rate.

3. At any one time, the capital stock and technology are predetermined. Thus, output is determined in the labor market. Employment is given by the equality of labor demand and labor supply.

4. Potential GDP is the amount of output predicted by the long-run growth model. It is the amount of output the economy would produce if it were at full employment.

5. Balanced growth occurs when labor and capital grow at the same rate.

6. GDP growth can be divided into three sources: growth in labor input, growth in capital stock, and technological (or productivity) change.

7. The 1970s and 1980s had reduced rates of growth in output. The slowdown is attributed primarily to slower growth in productivity and the capital stock.

8. Government policies can improve economic growth through increased expenditures on education and basic research or through tax incentives to encourage labor supply or capital accumulation.

9. Tax reform can improve incentives without reducing the tax revenue collected

by government. Such a reform usually requires flattening marginal tax rates on income.

10. While the long-term growth model is used by almost all macroeconomists to study growth, it is more controversial when used to explain short-term fluctuations in GDP. Real business cycle theorists interpret all the economy's movements in terms of equilibrium in the labor market.

11. Real business cycle theories of recession involve adverse shifts that cause labor demand to shift inward. If short-run labor supply is relatively flat, employment and output may fall substantially as a result.

12. Critics of the real business cycle model are skeptical of the role assigned to labor demand in explaining recessions in output. They are also skeptical of the short-run neutrality of money that holds in the long-run growth model. The critics find monetary contraction to be a more plausible explanation of the recession of the early 1980s.

Key Terms and Concepts

long-run growth model	production function	potential GDP
balanced growth capital- output ratio	labor demand	economic growth formula
natural rate of unemployment	labor supply	real business cycle model
	labor market equilibrium	
	full employment	

Questions for Discussion and Review

1. What are the three basic determinants of long-run growth?

2. Why is there unemployment when the economy is in equilibrium?

3. Why is the demand for labor a negative function of the real wage?

4. Explain why microeconomic theory predicts that for labor supply the income effect is negative and the substitution effect is positive. What do empirical studies indicate about the sum of these two effects?

5. Explain why the long-run growth model predicts that the level of real GDP in any one year is determined solely in the labor market. What would happen to the real wage, the price level, and the nominal wage if the money supply were increased?

6. What is potential GDP?

7. Does an increase in the rate of growth of labor add more or less to the growth rate of output than the same size increase in the rate of growth of capital? Explain why.

8. Describe three different policies that could be used to increase the growth rate of potential GDP. Identify whether the policy is aimed at productivity, capital formation, or labor supply.

9. Explain what happens in the labor market in a recession according to the real business cycle model.

Problems

Numerical

1. a. The labor supply function is given by $N = 1{,}000 + 12\,(W/P)$ and labor demand is $N = 2{,}000 - 8\,(W/P)$. Draw a diagram showing these schedules. Find the equilibrium level of employment and the real wage.
    b. Given existing technology and the capital stock, output is given by the function $Y = 100\,\sqrt{N}$. Graph the production function. Does the production function exhibit diminishing marginal product of labor?
    c. Using the labor market from Part a and the production function from Part b, determine the equilibrium level of output for this economy.

2. Assume that over a 10-year period the growth rate of capital is 4 percent, the growth rate of employment is 2 percent, and the growth rate of real output is 5 percent. Calculate the growth rate of total factor productivity. Suppose that a permanent cut in the budget deficit increases investment, and the growth rate of capital rises by 1 percent. How much does the growth rate of output increase? Suppose that a tax reduction increases the supply of labor by 1 percent in one year. What happens to the growth rate of real output?

3. Suppose that the production function takes the special form $Y = AN^{.7}K^{.3}$. By taking logarithms and first differences of this production function, show that the growth formula is satisfied. (If you have had calculus, calculate the marginal products of labor and capital. Derive the labor demand function. Calculate the labor share and the capital share.)

Analytical

1. Explain the relationship between the following terms: equilibrium employment, the natural rate of unemployment, and potential GDP.

2. Suppose you thought technological change or productivity always improved from year to year. Using the long-run growth model, describe two other ways in which it may be possible for equilibrium employment to decline in spite of positive growth in productivity.

3. Suppose the target rate of long-run equilibrium per capita GDP growth is 1 percent per year. Labor input and population are expected to grow at 1 percent.
    a. What rate of GDP growth is required to achieve the target for per capita GDP growth?
    b. Using equation 4–7 (also called Solow's formula), what is the required growth in the capital stock necessary to achieve the target assuming productivity growth of .5 percent? What is the required growth in the capital stock if there is no growth in productivity?

4. Can tax reform that increases labor supply permanently raise the rate of growth of GDP? Explain.

5. Suppose that the labor supply schedule is vertical. Can the real business cycle model still account for fluctuations in GDP? Explain. What feature of business cycles cannot be explained with vertical labor supply?

6. About half the growth in output in the 1980s can be attributed to the growth in labor input, as shown in Figure 4–7. Given the behavior of productivity and real wages (see Figures 3–6 and 3–7) during the same period, do you think the growth in labor input was due to the growth in labor demand or labor supply? Explain. What factors might account for the growth in labor demand or supply?

7. The unification of Germany created a nation with a much lower capital to labor ratio relative to what previously existed in West Germany. What impact do you think unification had on the level of productivity compared with what existed in West Germany alone? What impact will unification have on the growth rate of labor productivity after the initial shock? Explain.

MacroSolve Exercises

1. Plot the unemployment rate using quarterly data. What level should the rate of unemployment ideally approach if the labor market is in equilibrium? What does the time series indicate? How does the long-run growth model account for this discrepancy?

2. How does the real business cycle model explain fluctuations in labor supply? (Hint: Plot real interest rates and unemployment using quarterly data.) How well do the data support the theory? What problems does the theory face?

3. How does the long-run growth model explain fluctuations in output? Plot real GDP growth and the unemployment rate on the same screen using annual data from 1930 to 1991. How credible is the long-run growth model's explanation in light of the data? What might contribute to the high correlation in these two series that the long-run growth model overlooks?

APPENDIX: Deriving the Growth Formula

Suppose that A, N, and K grow by rates $\Delta A/A$, $\Delta N/N$, and $\Delta K/K$. We will derive a formula for the growth rate of output, $\Delta Y/Y$. First, with neutral technological change we can write the production function as $F(N, K, A) = Af(N, K)$. Then the growth rate of output is approximately

$$\Delta Y/Y = \Delta A/A + \Delta f(N, K)/f(N, K). \qquad (4–8)$$

In other words, the growth rate of the *product* of A and $f(N, K)$ is the *sum* of the growth rates of A and $f(N, K)$.

Second, the part of the change in output that comes from changes in employment and capital can be further broken down using the marginal products of the two. Let M_N be the marginal product of labor and M_K be the marginal product of capital. Then

$$\Delta f(N, K)/f(N, K) = M_N \Delta N/Y + M_K \Delta K/Y. \qquad (4–9)$$

In words, this expression states that the proportional change in f can be divided into two components that measure the contributions of the proportional changes in N and K. (If you have had calculus, this formula can be derived by taking the total derivative of f and dividing by Y.) Putting this into the formula for $\Delta Y/Y$, we get

$$\Delta Y/Y = \Delta A/A + M_N \Delta N/Y + M_K \Delta K/Y. \tag{4-10}$$

If firms are using labor and capital up to the points where their marginal products are equal to the real wage and real rental prices, then

$$M_N = W/P \quad \text{and} \quad M_K = R^K/P. \tag{4-11}$$

Now the formula is

$$\Delta Y/Y = \Delta A/A + (W/P)\Delta N/Y + (R^K/P)\Delta K/Y. \tag{4-12}$$

We can rewrite this as

$$\Delta Y/Y = \Delta A/A + (WN/PY)\Delta N/N + (R^K K/PY)\Delta K/K. \tag{4-13}$$

WN/PY is the fraction of revenue, PY, paid out to labor in the form of compensation, WN. Similarly, $R^K K/PY$ is the fraction of revenue earned by capital. From the national income and product accounts, we find that these fractions are about .7 and .3. Thus,

$$\Delta Y/Y = \Delta A/A + .7\Delta N/N + .3\Delta K/K,$$

which is the growth formula (Equation 4–7).

The Effects of Fiscal and Monetary Policies in the Long Run

The long-run growth model introduced in the previous chapter provides a simple framework for establishing some of the most fundamental long-term properties of monetary and fiscal policies. The framework is simple because the long-run growth model does not deal with the complexities of the departures of the economy from the full-employment level of output. Although a complete treatment of the short-run effects of monetary and fiscal policies must await the development of the complete model in Chapters 6 through 9, it is useful to establish the long-run properties now. They are an integral part of the complete analysis and important principles in their own right.

The long-run growth model is useful for evaluating the effects of monetary and fiscal policies over long spans of time; 10 years or more would be ideal and in most applications a minimum of about 3 years is necessary. For example, fiscal policy in the United States during the 1980s was more expansionary than during the 1960s. The federal deficit averaged 4 percent of GDP in the 1980s and 1 percent of GDP in the 1960s. What was the effect of this difference on interest rates? On exchange rates? On the trade balance? The full-employment model can provide good answers to these important questions. Another long-term fiscal policy issue is the effect on the economy of an expected reduction in defense spending in the

1990s, reflecting dramatic changes in Eastern Europe and the demise of the Soviet Union.

We also address important properties of monetary policy in this chapter. Again the focus is on the long term and we do not deal with the departures of the economy from potential. For example, money growth was much higher in the 1970s than in the 1980s in the United States. The long-term growth model indicates that the main effect of this change on the economy would be a higher rate of inflation in the 1970s than in the 1980s. In fact, inflation was higher in the 1970s than in the 1980s.

5.1 THE EFFECTS OF MACROECONOMIC POLICY ON REAL GDP IN THE LONG RUN

Fiscal policy, by definition, involves changes in government purchases *(G)*, taxes *(T)*, transfer payments to the private sector *(F)*, and interest payments on the government debt *(N)*. (The symbols in parentheses were introduced in Chapter 2.) Changes in any of these four items cause changes in the federal budget deficit, which is simply defined as total expenditures less taxes:

$$\text{Budget deficit} = G + F + N - T. \qquad (5\text{--}1)$$

Fiscal policy is determined by the President and the Congress. The primary focus of fiscal policy in recent years has been to find a way to reduce the federal budget deficit. One of the purposes here is to understand why this would be a good policy for the long term.

Monetary policy involves changes in the money supply. In the United States the money supply is controlled by the Federal Reserve System (the Fed)—the country's central bank established by Congress in 1913. There are important interactions between monetary and fiscal policies; this means that Congress, the President, and the Fed have a joint role to play in determining the overall stance of monetary and fiscal policies, or simply macroeconomic policy.

What are the effects of monetary and fiscal policies on output in the long run? Although we did not emphasize these effects in the previous chapter, they can be derived fairly easily from the results we obtained in that chapter. We know that in the long-term growth model with perfectly flexible prices, GDP is always equal to potential GDP and therefore depends only on the supply of the three productive factors: labor, capital, and technology. If monetary and fiscal policies are to affect GDP in this model, they must affect one or more of these three factors.

Consider first the effects on potential GDP of government spending, a key component of fiscal policy. A change in government spending, such as a decline in defense spending on nuclear missiles, does not immediately have any substantial effect on the *supply* of the three productive factors. If the government decides to build fewer missiles, there is no tendency for the supply of labor to decline. Nor, in the absence of a reduction in R&D spending, is there a change in technological know-how. If there is some increase in private investment in the economy to fill the gap left by the decline in the production of missiles, then eventually this will increase the supply of private capital; however, this increase in the supply of capital will be small relative to the existing size of the capital stock and will not have a noticeable effect on GDP for several years.

What about the effect of the other major components of fiscal policy? In the previous chapter we showed how changes in tax rates affect worker incentives. A reduction in tax rates, for example, will increase the incentive to work and thereby increase the supply of labor; GDP is thus increased. However, a change in taxes that does not affect incentives but merely changes tax revenues will not affect the supply of labor. It is tax revenues T that appears in the budget calculation as described in Equation 5–1. An increase in tax revenues paid by consumers to the government will reduce income available for consumption and thereby decrease consumption. If investment increases as a result, then the capital stock will grow and real GDP will rise. But the effect on GDP will be relatively small for several years. Changes in interest payments or transfers from the government that do not affect incentives or investment will have no impact on real GDP.

Similar reasoning suggests that a change in the money supply will not affect the supply of the productive factors. There is no reason to expect an increase in the money supply—currency and deposits at banks—to change the incentive to work or to be more inventive. In the long-term growth model with perfectly flexible prices, an increase in the money supply will

MACROECONOMIC POLICY AND GDP IN THE LONG RUN

1. In the long run, GDP depends only on the supply of the three productive factors: labor, capital, and technological know-how.
2. Unless fiscal policy changes the supply of these factors, it will not affect GDP in the long run.
3. A change in monetary policy will affect the price level. Higher inflation reduces real GDP in the long run.

leave GDP unchanged. But with more money persistently chasing the same amount of goods, prices will rise. Hence, monetary policy can increase the inflation rate. Some economists feel that higher inflation reduces productivity and thereby reduces GDP—a possibility that we will pursue later in the book. If so, then monetary policy affects real GDP by affecting the rate of inflation.

5.2   THE EFFECTS OF FISCAL POLICY ON THE SHARES OF OUTPUT

In Chapter 2 we presented the components of output using the simple accounting identity

$$Y = \underbrace{C + I + X}_{\substack{\text{Nongovernment}\\\text{purchases}}} + \underbrace{G,}_{\substack{\text{Government}\\\text{purchases}}} \qquad \text{The Income Identity} \qquad (5\text{--}2)$$

where Y is GDP, C is consumption, I is investment, X is net exports, and G is government purchases. All four components are measured in real terms as discussed in Chapter 2.

We also saw in Chapter 2 that after subtracting depreciation, indirect taxes, and certain other items from GDP, we get income. This relationship between GDP and income is important. To keep the analysis simple for now, we will assume that income and GDP are the same; this implies that there is no depreciation or indirect taxation. If so, the variable Y on the left-hand side of Equation 5–2 is income as well as GDP. The identity says that income equals the sum of consumption, investment, net exports, and government purchases. For this reason it is called the **income identity.** Because GDP is equal to income, we will frequently use the words interchangeably in our discussions. To avoid confusion, keep in mind that GDP (or simply *output*) and *income* take on the same value and are represented by the same symbol Y.

Many of the long-run questions about fiscal policy involve the effects of changes in government spending as a *share* of output. For example, we might want to know what will happen if government purchases in the 1990s are 20 percent rather than 15 percent of GDP. Or what difference it makes for interest rates if the deficit as a share of GDP is 1 percent in the 1990s instead of 4 percent as it was in the 1980s. Equation 5–2 can be rewritten and interpreted in terms of shares of GDP if we simply divide both sides of the equation by Y. This gives

$$1 = \frac{C}{Y} + \frac{I}{Y} + \frac{X}{Y} + \frac{G}{Y}. \tag{5-3}$$

In other words, the shares of the different components of spending must sum to 1.

We now want to use Equation 5–3 to determine what happens to the components of output when fiscal policy changes. A quick glance at the equation shows that *a change in government purchases as a share of GDP must bring about a change in nongovernment purchases as a share of GDP by the same amount, but in the opposite direction.* For example, a decrease in government purchases of 3 percent of GDP must bring about an *increase* in nongovernment purchases of 3 percent of GDP. An increase in government purchases of 3 percent of GDP implies that nongovernment purchases must fall by 3 percent of GDP. This is straightforward arithmetic. It is also straightforward logic.

How much do consumption, investment, and net exports individually rise? Would consumption C, income I, and net exports X each rise by 1 percent of GDP in the case of a cut in government purchases of 3 percent of GDP? Or would some other combination of percentages occur? The answer depends on how sensitive each of these items is to interest rates.

Interest-Rate Sensitivity of Consumption, Investment, and Net Exports

What brings about a change in consumption, investment, and net exports in the long-term growth model? We have simply used arithmetic and logic to show that such a change must take place. The economic mechanism involves interest rates. An increase in interest rates will tend to reduce investment, net exports, and consumption. A decrease in interest rates will have the opposite effect. Later in the book we will show in detail why consumption and especially investment and net exports depend negatively on the interest rate. These changes in interest rates, which accompany changes in fiscal policy, are what bring about the changes in the nongovernment components of output.

Why do consumption, investment, and net exports depend negatively on the interest rate? Consider consumption first. Consumption is expenditure by households. Higher interest rates mean that consumers will have to pay more to finance consumption of automobiles and other durables. These higher finance costs discourage consumption. For example, higher required payments on a car loan discourage purchases of cars. Higher interest rates discourage investment for similar reasons. Recall that investment is expenditures by firms on machines and equipment. Higher interest rates mean that firms will have to pay more to finance their investments, and thus higher interest rates discourage investment.

The relationship between interest rates and net exports is more complicated, involving two steps. First, recall from Chapter 2 that the exchange rate determines how expensive foreign goods are in comparison with American goods. When the exchange rate rises, foreign goods become cheaper compared with home goods (see page 58). Hence, with a higher exchange rate, Americans want to import more and foreigners want less American exports. With American exports falling and imports rising, net exports—exports less imports—decline. In other words, a higher exchange rate reduces net exports. Now the second step: Higher interest rates in the United States make U.S. assets a more attractive financial investment and drive up the value of the dollar. Hence, a higher interest rate tends to be associated with a higher exchange rate. Now combining these two steps, we see that higher interest rates tend to reduce net exports by raising the exchange rate.

Figure 5–1 shows the three negative relationships between the interest rate and (1) consumption, (2) investment, and (3) net exports. Note that in the diagram the slope of the consumption relationship is less steep than that of investment and net exports. This reflects historical observations that the sensitivity of consumption to interest rates is smaller than that of investment and net exports. Note also that the bottom panel in Figure 5–1 is the sum of consumption, investment, and net exports shares and illustrates how the total nongovernment share depends negatively on the interest rate. Having derived the interest-rate sensitivities of the major components of output, we now can proceed to derive the impact of a change in government purchases and other fiscal actions on the composition of output.

Government Purchases

When government purchases fall, we know that nongovernment purchases rise. Figure 5–2 on page 128 on nongovernment purchases shows how a decrease in interest rates brings about this increase in consumption, investment, and net exports. The bottom panel shows that lower interest rates must be associated with higher spending on nongovernment purchases. This panel also tells us how much interest rates must fall. The top three panels can then be used to determine by how much consumption, investment, and net exports individually rise. According to Figure 5–2, consumption rises by a smaller amount than does investment because consumption is less sensitive to interest rates than investment is. Net exports rise because the lower interest rates cause a decline in the exchange rate.

The Budget Deficit and the Trade Deficit

Note that this analysis illustrates the close connection between the budget deficit and the trade deficit. The cut in government purchases as a share of

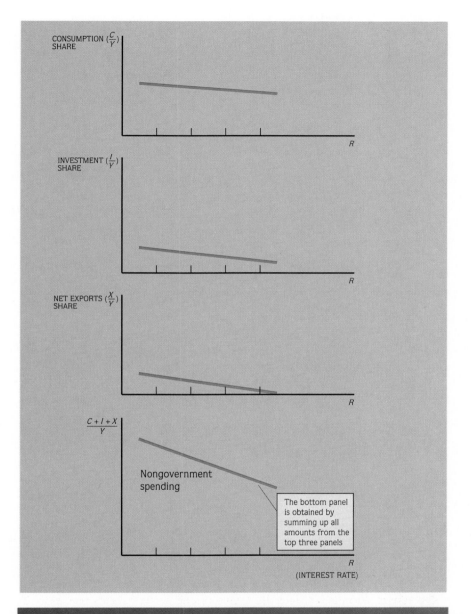

FIGURE 5–1 Interest-rate sensitivity of consumption, investment, and net exports

Consumption, investment, and net exports shares all depend negatively on the interest rate R. Therefore, the sum of the shares depends negatively on the interest rate. The bottom panel is simply the sum of the top three panels. Note that consumption is not as sensitive to the interest rate as are investment and net exports. The consumption graph is very flat.

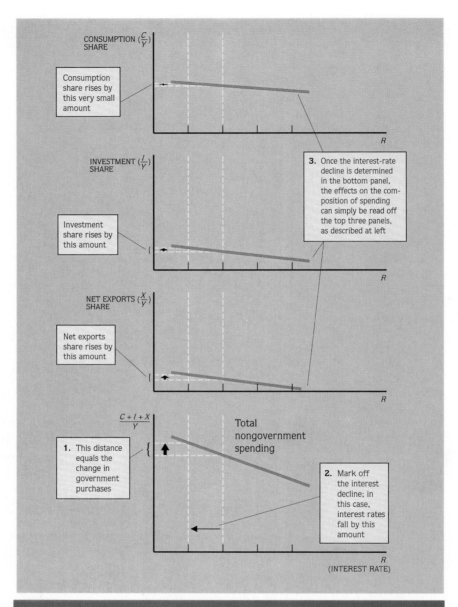

FIGURE 5–2 Effects of a decrease in government purchases

The nongovernment share of GDP must rise by the same amount as the fall in the government share of GDP . This rise is brought about by a decline in interest rates. The decline in interest rates also causes the exchange rate to fall.

GDP will reduce the budget deficit as a share of GDP, as is clear from Equation 5–1. But as we have seen, the cut in government purchases also reduces the trade deficit (net exports rise). That is, the government's attempt to reduce the budget deficit has reduced the trade deficit.

Experience in the 1980s lends validity to this analysis. As the U.S. budget deficit rose in the early 1980s, so did the U.S. trade deficit. And starting in 1987, when the budget deficit began to fall as a fraction of GDP, the trade deficit also began to fall. Also in keeping with the model was the behavior of the dollar exchange rate. In the early 1980s as the deficit rose, the dollar exchange rate rose to very high levels. Then when the budget deficit began to fall, the dollar fell rapidly. All these patterns are consistent with the long-run growth model and the graphical analysis in Figure 5–2.

Other Fiscal Policy Changes

The analysis of other types of fiscal policy changes in the long run is very similar to the above analysis of a decline in government purchases. The analysis of an increase in government purchases is just the reverse of a decline in government purchases. In this case, the interest rate rises to depress the demand for consumption, investment, and net exports in order to make room for a greater government use of resources. The term **crowding out** is used to describe this process—higher government spending crowds out investment and net exports. If consumption does not depend on the interest rate in the long-run growth model, a dollar of government purchases crowds out a dollar of investment and net exports. This is an important contrast to the complete model used for short-run analysis, where higher government purchases raise GDP and thus crowd out investment and net exports less than dollar for dollar.

Changes in taxes will affect consumption. For example, higher taxes will reduce consumption because people have less to spend. But the reduction in consumption does not affect potential GDP because the supply of the three productive factors does not change. Hence, the decline in consumption must result in an increase in net exports and investment. The effects can be illustrated in a diagram similar to Figure 5–2 and are left as an exercise at the end of the chapter.

Importance of the Long-Run Assumption

You might ask where the assumption about the long run fits into these calculations. Clearly, the shares of output add up to 1 in both the long run and the short run. The answer is that the long-run assumption makes sure that other things besides interest rates do not affect the shares of spending in GDP.

NEW RESEARCH IN PRACTICE
Governing the $5 Trillion Economy

Figures 5–1 and 5–2 may seem remarkably simple given the complexity of the policies being considered. That is the beauty of the long-run framework. It does not require an elaborate system of equations to derive results about the allocation of GDP among different uses—consumption, investment, government, and net exports. It demonstrates how, if the government uses a larger share of GDP, the private sector has to use less. Interest rates play the role of determining whether it is investment, consumption, or net exports that gets crowded out.

Herbert Stein of the American Enterprise Institute and formerly chairman of the Council of Economic Advisers has suggested a framework for the analysis of the federal budget, which is based on this notion of allocating different components of GDP to different uses. He argues that federal budget policy should be viewed more broadly as "budgeting GDP" rather than simply budgeting federal expenditures. His book on the subject, which is called *Governing the $5 Trillion Economy*, describes his proposals in detail. The theoretical framework that underlies his practical suggestions is essentially the long-run framework in Section 5.2.

Stein's basic point is that decisions about the federal budget should be based on two considerations: (1) an ordering of national priorities and (2) a view of the relation between the budget and the achievement of those priorities. Clearly, people will have widely different views about priorities. One can see this in political campaigns, and the 1992 Presidential campaign was no exception. To some, national health insurance is a high priority. Others feel that we need more roads and bridges or fiber optic cable lines. People have different views about defense spending in the aftermath of the end of the Cold War. Others are concerned that we are not spending enough on the poor.

But people also have different views on the efficacy of budget policy for achieving those objectives. Here the long-run economic analysis can be very useful in analyzing both incentives to work, save, invest, and innovate and the mechanism through which GDP is allocated to different uses.

To see how Stein's proposals would work, consider the following figures adapted from Stein's book:

Shares of GDP in 1980 and 1986

	1980	1986
Defense	5	7
Education	6	6
Consumption	64	67
Health	9	11
By poor	2	2
By nonpoor	53	55
Investment	19	14
Other government	6	6
Total	100	100

Stein subtracts foreign saving in the United States (S_r using the notation of Chapter 2) from private investment in computing the investment share. That is why there is no entry for net exports in the table; it is contained in the line for investment. He also includes investment by the government—roads, schools, etc.—in the line for investment, although the government accountants include this in G. "Other government" is therefore mainly nondefense government consumption. He also breaks down nonhealth consumption into the share consumed by poor people and the share consumed by nonpoor people.

The figures show three essential facts about the mid-1980s compared with the early 1980s: (1) defense spending was higher, (2) consumption was higher, and (3) investment was lower, much lower. Recall that Stein subtracts out foreign saving in the United States from the usual definition of investment; foreign saving grew dramatically in the early 1980s as the trade deficit widened. Nonhealth consumption by the poor did not increase at all as a share of GDP.

Now consider two options for budgeting GDP in the 1990s using Stein's approach. For convenience focus on a single year:

Options for Shares of GDP in 1997

	Option 1	Option 2
Defense	5	3
Education	7	8
Consumption	65	64
Health	10	10
By poor	2	3
By nonpoor	53	52
Investment	17	19
Other government	6	6
Total	100	100

Compared with the mid-1980s, both options involve much lower expenditures on defense, reflecting the end of the Cold War. The defense share for Option 1 is the same as for 1980. The defense share for Option 2 is even lower. Both options also have more expenditures on investment. That reflects a general consensus that national saving in the United States in the late 1980s was too low. Option 2 is more investment oriented. The other differences relate to consumption spending and its distribution.

Choosing between these two options—or indeed many other possibilities—is one of the functions of our political system and government. Especially in comparison with the shares of the mid-1980s, these options represent significant differences in economic policy and would have profound effects on the evolution of the United States economy. A shift in the composition of spending from the levels in the late 1980s to either of the two options will involve movements in interest and exchange rates. The model in Figure 5–1 can tell us how this will happen and by how much interest and exchange rates will change. It is hard to imagine a more practical application of the simple long-run model.

For example, as we will show in later chapters, if we cut government spending by 3 percent of GDP in one fell swoop, real GDP itself will fall in the short run, probably by more than 3 percent. A fall in real GDP will result in an even sharper decline in investment as businesses see their sales falling. The share of investment in GDP will fall rather than rise. The results in this section would be all wrong and terribly misleading to policymakers if applied in the very short run. The long-run assumption allows us to view the economy on its long-run potential growth path. Hence, there will be no sharp movements in GDP.

Of course, as was argued in Section 5.1, changes in the shares of different components of spending in GDP will have effects on potential GDP through changes in the supply of the productive factors. But all these effects will be spread out over time and will thereby make our share analysis more accurate and reliable.

The relationship between the short run and the long run will be clearer after we have studied the departures of real GDP from potential. Then we will see that the results obtained through these simple share calculations are exactly the same as long-run calculations that will be obtained with the more complex complete model.

FISCAL POLICY AND THE COMPOSITION OF OUTPUT

1. In the long-run growth model, an increase in government purchases will raise interest rates and reduce (crowd out) investment and net exports. The exchange rate will also rise. If consumption is sensitive to the interest rate, the production of consumption goods will fall as well.
2. The budget deficit and the trade deficit are closely related. A decrease in government spending which lowers the budget deficit will also lower the trade deficit.
3. The crowding out of investment which accompanies an increase in government spending will eventually cause the capital stock in the economy to grow less rapidly. This will reduce the economy's potential GDP.
4. The interest rate is a key factor in the analysis of fiscal policy. Consumption and especially investment and net exports are negatively affected by higher interest rates.

5.3 THE MONEY MARKET AND THE PRICE LEVEL

In the previous section, we determined the equilibrium real interest rate, consumption, investment, and net exports. We showed how fiscal policy affects these variables. The long-run behavior of another important macroeconomic variable, the price level, remains to be determined. In order to explain the price level, we need to consider the demand for and supply of money. In the long-run growth model, the price level is determined by equating money demand to money supply.

The Demand for Money

When we speak of **money,** we have a rather special meaning in mind. Money is the currency issued by the Federal Reserve—for example, coins and dollar bills—together with the checking account balances held by the public in banks. Money is used to facilitate the purchase and sale of goods. When we buy goods, we usually pay with currency or with a check. Money does not include the much larger amounts of wealth held in mutual funds, bonds, corporate stock, and other forms, even though these forms of wealth are measured in dollars, because they are not usually used to pay for goods.

Three basic propositions about the demand for money are important for macroeconomics.

1. *People will want to hold less money when the interest rate is high and, conversely, will want to hold more money when the interest rate is low.*

This means that there is a negative relation between the demand for money and the interest rate R. People hold money for transactions purposes, to pay daily expenses and monthly bills. But they could obtain higher earnings by keeping their wealth in other forms, such as savings accounts or bonds. Currency pays no interest. And even though many checking deposits now pay interest, the rate is less than on other forms of wealth. Because of this, people tend to economize on the use of money for transaction purposes. A common way to do this is to go to the bank more often to withdraw money from a high-interest savings account to obtain currency, or simply to transfer funds to a lower-interest checking account. With more frequent trips to the bank, a smaller amount can be withdrawn each time from savings accounts. This means that, on average, a smaller amount of currency or checking balances will be held by the individual. For example, you could go to the bank every week, rather than every month, to obtain currency and thereby hold a smaller amount of currency on average.

How much economizing will occur will depend on the interest rate. The interest rate R represents how much a consumer or firm could earn by holding more of their wealth in forms that pay full interest instead of in currency, which pays no interest, or checking deposits, which pay less than full interest. Clearly the more that can be earned by holding those other forms—the higher is R—the less money an individual will want to hold.

2. *People want to hold more money when income is higher and, conversely, less money when income is lower.*

The more a family receives as income, the more the family will normally be spending, and the more money the family will need for transaction purposes. When income increases, the transaction demand for money increases. More money will be needed to buy and sell goods.

This means that there is a positive relationship between income Y and the demand for money. As income in the economy increases, on average each family's income increases and the demand for money in the entire economy increases.

3. *People want to hold more money when the price level is higher and, conversely, less money when the price level is lower.*

If the price level rises, people will need more dollars to carry out their transactions, even if their real income does not increase. At a higher price level, goods and services will be more expensive; more currency will be needed to pay for them and checks will be written for larger amounts. This means that the demand for money is an increasing function of the price level.

To summarize these three basic ideas, the demand for money depends negatively on the interest rate R, positively on income Y, and positively on the price level P. An algebraic relationship that summarizes the effect of these three variables on the demand for money is presented in the following equation:

$$M = (kY - hR)P. \hspace{2cm} (5-4)$$

Here M represents the amount of money demanded by firms and consumers. The other variables in Equations 5-4 have been defined already: P is the price level, R is the interest rate, and Y is income or GDP.[1] The lowercase symbols k and h are positive coefficients. The coefficient k measures how much money demand increases when income increases. The coefficient h measures how much money demand declines when the interest rate increases. Equation 5-4 is called the **money demand function.** It is a more complicated algebraic expression than the equation we used previously for consumption and investment demand. The money demand function shows that money demand depends on three variables (the interest rate R, income Y, and the price level P), whereas consumption demand and investment demand each depend on only one variable.

EXAMPLE. If k equals .1583 and h equals 1,000, then Equation 5-4 looks like

$$M = (.1583Y - 1,000R)P.$$

If income Y is $6,000 billion, the interest rate is 5 percent ($R = .05$), and the price level P is 1, then the demand for money is equal to $900 billion. An increase in income of $10 billion will increase the demand for money by $1.583 billion. An increase in the interest rate of 1 percentage point will decrease the demand for money by $10 billion.

The Supply of Money

The Federal Reserve System determines the level of the **money supply.** In Chapter 14 we will study the interesting question of how the Fed goes

---

[1]Note that the appropriate interest rate for the money demand function is the nominal rate. Most alternatives to holding currency such as bonds pay a nominal interest rate. In order to keep our analysis simple, we place the real interest rate R in the money demand function. If inflation is low, this is a very good approximation.

about setting the money supply. For now, we will assume that the Fed has picked a certain level for the money supply.

We will also assume that the demand for money and the supply of money are equal. For this reason we do not introduce a new symbol to represent the money supply. The variable M means both money supply and money demand. Since these are always equal, this should cause little confusion. (Recall that the symbol Y also refers to two variables: income and GDP.)

How does the demand for money become equal to the supply of money? Suppose that the demand is greater than the supply. Since the supply of money is fixed by the Fed, the demand for money must fall if the two are to be equal. The demand for money can adjust down by an increase in the interest rate, a decline in the level of income, or a decline in the price level. For example, an increase in the interest rate will cause people to demand less money. In principle, all three variables could move, but in the long-run model income and the interest rate are determined outside the money market. Thus, only the price level can move to equilibrate the money market.

MONEY AND THE INTEREST RATE

1. Money is currency plus the balances in checking accounts.
2. The demand for money falls if the interest rate rises, if income falls, or if the price level falls.
3. The Federal Reserve determines the money supply.

Equilibrium in the Money Market

We will continue to assume that the economy is on the long-run growth path; GDP is at potential Y^*, and the interest rate is at the value R^* determined in Figure 5–2. Money demand is

$$M = (kY^* - hR^*)P. \qquad (5-5)$$

Money demand is proportional to the price level; if P rises by 10 percent, people will want to hold 10 percent more money. Money supply is fixed by the Fed. The price level equates money demand to money supply, as

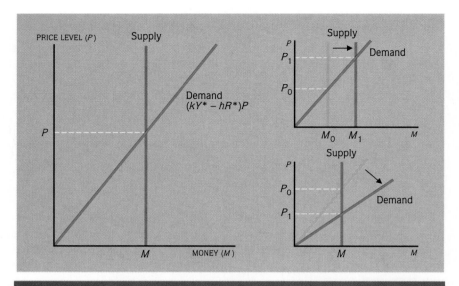

FIGURE 5–3 Determination of the price level in the money market

On the left, the demand for money depends positively on the price level. The supply of money is fixed by the Fed. Equilibrium occurs at the intersection of supply and demand. On the top right, if the money supply rises, the price level rises in the same proportion. On the bottom right, if potential GDP is higher, the price level is lower.

shown in Figure 5–3. The algebraic expression for the price level that clears the money market is

$$P = \frac{M}{kY^* - hR^*} . \tag{5–6}$$

When the Fed raises the money supply M by 10 percent, the price level rises by the same 10 percent. With money more plentiful, its purchasing power falls and the price level rises. If potential GDP rises and the money stock remains the same, the price level falls; money becomes more valuable when the economy is producing a higher volume of goods and services. If government spending or some other determinant of demand falls, the equilibrium interest rate R^* falls, and the price level also falls, to offset the rise in money demand.

In the long-run growth model, monetary policy is a very simple matter. The price level is proportional to the money stock. The money supply has no influence on output or the interest rate. This property is known as the **neutrality of money.** Another term for the independence of real variables like output from the money stock is the **classical dichotomy.** We can think first about the determination of employment and output and then, separately, about the price level.

5.4   INFLATION

Inflation is the rate of increase of the price level. In an economy where GDP doesn't change, the price level is proportional to the money supply (see Equation 5−6). More money simply raises prices. The Fed can choose whatever rate of inflation it wants just by raising the money supply by that percentage each year. For price stability, the Fed should keep the money supply constant from one year to the next. For 5 percent inflation, it should raise M by 5 percent each year.

In a growing economy, the rate of inflation will be less than the rate of money growth. If Y^* is growing over time, some money growth is needed just to keep the price level from falling from one year to the next.

Figure 5−4 shows the relationship between money growth and inflation in a group of seven countries. Money growth is measured over an

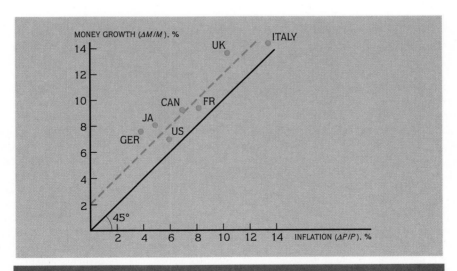

FIGURE 5−4 Money growth and inflation in seven countries, 1973–90

The vertical axis shows the average annual growth rate of money supply over an 18-year period. The horizontal axis shows the average annual rate of inflation. Generally, the observations appear to lie about 2 percent above the 45-degree line, clustered around the dashed line. Growth in real output absorbs about 2 percent of annual money growth, and the remaining money growth leads to inflation.

NEW RESEARCH IN PRACTICE
International Policy Coordination

Because net exports (X) appear in the income identity, the long-run analysis of the composition of GDP has applications for international macroeconomic policy. For example, a reduction in government spending raises net exports (reduces the trade deficit). This analysis underlies many international discussions of fiscal policy that occur at multilateral forums such as the Organization for Economic Cooperation and Development (OECD) in Paris, the International Monetary Fund in Washington, and, more frequently, the group of finance ministers of the seven largest industrial countries (commonly called the G-7). The analysis also forms the underpinning of bilateral negotiations.

One particular application illustrates very well how this type of analysis is used in practice. The application occurred as part of a bilateral coordination effort between the United States and Japan known as the Structural Impediments Initiative (SII). One of the objectives of the SII was to reduce both the United States trade deficit and the Japanese trade surplus. Such a reduction, it was hoped, would help reduce trade friction between the two countries and ease protectionist pressures. The SII talks were always meant to be a two-way street: both the United States and the Japanese would make policy changes.

The United States government's economic analysis stressed that the U.S. trade deficit as a share of GDP would go down if the U.S. budget deficit as a share of GDP went down, assuming that no other factors that would offset this changed. The same analysis suggested that the Japanese surplus would go down if the Japanese increased the share of GDP devoted to public infrastructure investment in Japan. These are both long-run propositions that can be handled with the long-run model. Both propositions can be proved with the simple diagrams in Figure 5–2. You should try to do it. What would happen to interest rates and exchange rates?

As part of the SII, the government of Japan agreed to increase government infrastructure investment in Japan over a 10-year period. The government agreed to increase such investment by 430 trillion yen during the 1990s. That would raise the share of investment in GDP about 1 percent by the end of the 10 years compared with what it otherwise would have been. For its part, the United States offered the 5-year $500 billion reduction in the U.S. budget deficit in the 1990 budget agreement.

International policy coordination seems mysterious to outsiders. How much influence does one sovereign government have on another? Some argue, for example, that coordination efforts like SII or the work of the G-7 have little effect. Governments only agree to do what they would have done anyway. For example, even before SII started many Japanese had argued that more public infrastructure investment was needed. And in the United States there was already a consensus that something should have been done to reduce the budget deficit. So maybe these and other actions would have occurred without coordination efforts. It is difficult to know for sure. Certainly, in the discussions there is a notion of making concessions, for example, increasing infrastructure investment in Japan in exchange for something else from the United States. There is also the element of diplomacy and international goodwill, the importance of which is hard to measure.

Note that there would have been other ways for the Japanese to reduce their trade surplus. Increasing consumption as a share of GDP was discussed in the preliminaries to the SII talks, but the United States government felt that it would not be good economic policy to promote antisaving in any country, especially in a decade in which there appeared to be a shortage of saving around the world. Hence, the United States position was that the gap between saving and investment in Japan would be better reduced by increasing investment rather than by reducing saving.

18-year period, so the long-run analysis should apply even if recessions or booms are important over a 3- or 5-year period. If the relationship were as simple as 1 percent of inflation for each percent of money growth, all the observations would lie along the 45-degree line that equates inflation and money growth in the figure. Because growth of output also affects the relation between money growth and inflation, all the points lie above the 45-degree line. But it remains clear that money growth and inflation have a close relationship over a period of this length.

In the United States and all other economies, monetary policy and inflation are contentious issues. The United States has had episodes of inflation at rates of 10 percent and more, and some countries suffer hyperinflations with rates of price increase of thousands of percent. Why does this happen if the central bank has direct control over inflation? There are two reasons that central banks don't deliver an inflation-free economy. In the United States, the reason is mainly that the long-run growth model does not describe the year-to-year movements of the economy. Instead, the economy can move away from potential. A monetary contraction is one of the forces that may cause a recession—a period when GDP is below potential. The fear of setting off a recession may prevent the Fed from cutting money growth, even though the reduced growth is just what the long-run growth model says is needed to end inflation.

In some smaller countries with less efficient tax systems, the second reason for inflation is important. The central bank—an arm of the government—issues large amounts of new money each year because the government is spending more than it takes in as taxes or from issuing bonds. The deliberate creation of high rates of inflation is one of the ways of financing government, though not a very good way. Severe deliberate inflation has not been part of U.S. economic policy since the Civil War.

5.5 SUMMARY: THE CLASSICAL DICHOTOMY

The analysis of fiscal and monetary policies in this chapter illustrates an important property of the long-run growth model. Real variables like the interest rate and the composition of spending in the long-run growth model can be analyzed solely by looking at other real variables like government purchases. Nominal variables such as the money supply do not influence the level of GDP, the composition of GDP, or the level of interest rates. The diagrams in Figure 5–2 enabled us to determine the interest rate and the composition of output without considering monetary policy. In other words, to study the real economy, we could conveniently restrict ourselves to real variables in the economy. Once we know the stance of fiscal policy, we know all we need to know to determine the interest rate. Information about the money supply would not tell us anything else about the interest rate. Monetary variables such as the money supply affect only other nominal variables like the price level.

In the next chapter we begin to develop the complete model in which this classical dichotomy does not always hold. But even in the complete model the results of this chapter are useful and important. They tell us the effects of monetary and fiscal policies that must hold in the long run in the complete model. Hence, the results derived in this chapter, with a minimum of algebra and technical detail, provide us with a benchmark from which to judge our results in the more complete model.

REVIEW AND PRACTICE

Major Points

1. The long-run growth model is a good guide to the effects of fiscal and monetary policy over periods of 3 years or more.
2. Fiscal policy involves changes in government purchases, transfers, and taxes.
3. Monetary policy involves changes in the money supply.
4. In the long-run growth model, changes in government purchases crowd out investment and thereby affect the long-run path of GDP.
5. An increase in the money supply has no effect on real GDP in the long run.
6. A decrease in government purchases as a share of GDP causes an equal increase in nongovernment purchases as a share of GDP.
7. Consumption, investment, and net exports depend negatively on the interest rate.
8. A decrease in government purchases causes a decline in the interest rate.
9. In the long run, the price level moves as necessary to equate the money demand to the money supply set by the Fed.
10. The price level is proportional to the money supply in the long run.
11. The Fed chooses the long-run rate of inflation by choosing the rate of money growth.

Key Terms and Concepts

fiscal policy	money market	neutrality of money
monetary policy	demand for money	inflation
crowding out	supply of money	money growth
interest rate	money-market equilibrium	classical dichotomy
interest-rate sensitivity		

Questions for Discussion and Review

1. What is the difference between fiscal and monetary policies?

2. Explain why an increase in government purchases decreases nongovernment purchases by the same amount.

3. How does monetary policy affect real GDP?

4. What determines the interest rate in the long-run growth model? In what sense does the interest rate guide resource allocation?

5. What effect does an increase in government purchases have on output and the interest rate in the long-run growth model?

6. Describe how the price level is determined in the long-run growth model. Is the price level a good indicator of economic welfare?

7. What is meant by the neutrality of money?

Problems

Numerical

1. Consider a closed economy in which net exports $X = 0$. Suppose that consumption is insensitive to the interest rate, but that the share of investment in GDP rises by 2 percent for every 1 percent decline in the interest rate.
   a. By how much does investment rise as a share of GDP if government purchases decrease by 4 percent of GDP?
   b. By how much does the interest rate change?
   c. Using the growth accounting formula from Chapter 4, calculate how much more real GDP there would be if the capital-output ratio starts at 2.

2. Suppose that output is equal to potential at 4,000 and the equilibrium interest rate is .05. Money demand is given by

$$M = (.3Y-4,000R)P.$$

   Money supply is set at 1,000 by the Fed.
   a. What price level is required for equilibrium in the money market?
   b. Suppose the Fed increases the money supply by 100. What is the new price level? What is the percentage change in the money supply? In the price level?
   c. Starting with a money supply of 1,000 and price level of 1.0, how does an increase in the interest rate from .05 to .10 affect the equilibrium price level? What could cause such an increase in the real interest rate?
   d. Starting again with $M = 1,000$ and $P = 1.0$, what effect does an increase in output from 4,000 to 4,500 have on the equilibrium price level?

Analytical

1. Investment spending and net exports are negatively related to the interest rate. In the hopes of increasing output in the economy, a regulation is imposed that precludes the interest rate from exceeding 5 percent. Suppose that in the absence of this regulation, the interest rate would be 6 percent. What effect will

the regulation have on the level and allocation of output according to the long-run growth model? Explain why in the absence of such regulation the interest rate reflects the scarcity of output while preventing shortages.

2. Describe the qualitative effect of each of the following on output in the long-run growth model.
   a. An outward shift in the labor supply schedule.
   b. An improvement in technology.
   c. An increase in the money supply.
   d. A reduction in the tax rate t on income.

3. In the long-run growth model, money is neutral. Changes in the supply of money influence the price level, but not the level of output. Reconcile this fact with the observation that labor supply and labor demand—which do determine output—are a function of the real wage W/P which depends on the price level. How would you determine the nominal wage W in the long-run model?

4. Suppose government purchases go toward refurbishing bridges and freeways in major metropolitan areas that suffer from congestion. What are the short-run (before the project is completed) and long-run (after the project is completed) effects on interest rates and investment assuming other factors are unchanged? (Hint: Think about how potential GDP is affected in the long run.)

5. Higher real interest rates today make current income worth more in terms of future consumption. For this reason, some people argue that labor supply is positively related to interest rates.
   a. If this is true, how is the diagram that plots output against the interest rate affected?
   b. Explain why fiscal policy has more influence over output in a model where labor supply is positively related to interest rates.

6. Suppose that there is a reduction in investment incentives in the long-run growth model. Investment as a share of GDP is lower for any given interest rate.
   a. Show what happens in a diagram like Figure 5–1.
   b. Assume that neither consumption nor net exports vary with the interest rate. Does investment fall? Why or why not?
   c. Now assume that net exports vary negatively with the interest rate. What happens to investment?

7. Suppose the Fed attempted to keep the price level constant over time—a zero-inflation policy. Describe how the money supply would have to change in response to each of the following situations:
   a. An increase in potential GDP.
   b. An increase in income taxes with no change in potential GDP.
   c. A change in investment incentives that increases investment at any interest rate.
   d. An exogenous increase in foreign demand for U.S. goods.

8. In the early 1980s government purchases grew as a share of GDP. Simultaneously, the current account moved from near balance in 1980 to a large deficit in the mid- to late 1980s. Use the long-run model to explain the behavior of net exports in relation to the growth of government purchases.

9. Describe the qualitative effect of each of the following on the price level in the long-run growth model.
   a. An increase in the labor supply.
   b. A decrease in the sensitivity of investment to the interest rate.
   c. A widespread, increased taste for consumption rather than saving.
   d. A decrease in government purchases.
   e. An increase in the average tariff rate on imports.

10. The end of the Cold War will presumably enable the United States to reduce government expenditure on national defense. Suppose the administration believes it can cut defense by 2 percent of GDP. Using the long-run model, analyze the impact of this defense cut in combination with each of the following policies for allocating the "peace dividend." In each case, indicate what would happen to the real interest rate, consumption, and investment relative to the situation prior to the defense cut.
    a. The full amount of the cut in defense is applied toward a tax cut for households.
    b. The full amount of the cut is put toward government expenditure on infrastructure and education.
    c. No tax changes or other changes in government spending are combined with the defense cut.
    d. Rank the policies according to how much they will increase real GDP growth in the long run.

MacroSolve Exercises

1. Plot the real interest rate with investment using quarterly data. What relationship do you find. What might explain this relationship?
2. Plot the rate of inflation and the rate of money growth using annual data. Comment on the strength of this relationship. Does the evidence support the implications of the long-run model? Why or why not?
3. Plot the growth rate of real GDP and the investment/GDP ratio. Are the two closely related? Does growth in the investment/GDP ratio seem to have a temporary or permanent effect on GDP?

CHAPTER

6

Short-Run Fluctuations and Spending Balance

The long-run model of Chapters 4 and 5 is an important part of modern macroeconomics. But it does not explain recessions such as those that occurred in 1981–82 and in 1990–91 when the economy deviated from the long-run path. The long-run model is incomplete.

Why does it take several years for the economy to return to potential GDP after a shock? What forces push output away from its potential? The complete model, to which we now turn, will try to answer these two key questions. In the complete model, demand can affect output in a way not considered in the long-run growth model. When GDP drops below potential, there are unutilized resources, especially unemployed labor, in the economy. Unemployment can persist above the natural rate if the incentives for firms to restore full employment are not very great. We will begin the discussion with a consideration of these incentives.

6.1 THE LABOR MARKET OUT OF EQUILIBRIUM

Consider a recession with output below potential GDP and unemployment in excess of the natural rate. Why don't market forces correct the excess supply quickly and restore full employment? Figure 6–1 shows the labor market in recession. When employment is at a recession level, there are incentives facing both employers and workers to raise the amount of work. The difference between the marginal product of labor (the labor demand schedule) and the real wage is the incentive facing the employer. One added worker will increase the firm's revenue by the marginal product, but the worker only has to be paid the real wage. The difference is a profit opportunity for the firm; it provides an economic incentive to expand output.

The difference between the real wage and the worker's value of time (the labor supply schedule) is the incentive facing the worker. Another hour of work will earn the worker the real wage, but the cost (forgone time in other activities) is a smaller amount. The difference is an economic opportunity for the worker; it provides an economic incentive to increase hours worked.

Both firms and workers have incentives to raise employment when employment is at a recession level, below equilibrium. How long does it take for these incentives to bring about an expansion of employment back to equilibrium? Macroeconomists debate this question frequently and intensely. We will consider many ideas about it in Chapter 15. For now, we will simply make the practical observation that recessions do occur every

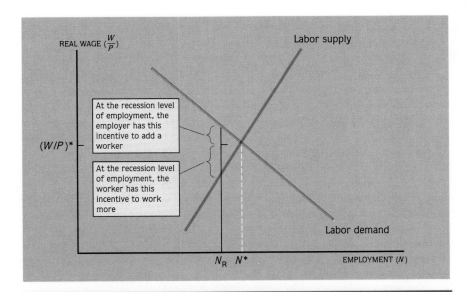

FIGURE 6–1   Incentives when employment is below equilibrium

If employment is at the recession level N_R, and the real wage is at its equilibrium level $(W/P)^*$, both employers and workers have incentives to increase the amount of work. The incentives are measured in dollars per hour on the vertical (real-wage) axis.

few years and each one lasts a year or two. We conclude that incentives operate over years, not days, weeks, or months. Until incentives do their job, the level of employment can remain below equilibrium. In this chapter, we begin the development of a short-run model to describe the transitory departures of the economy from its long-run growth path.

THE LABOR MARKET OUT OF EQUILIBRIUM

1. Sometimes the level of employment is lower than the full-employment level.
2. When employment is below this level, firms and workers face incentives to expand employment.
3. These incentives take time to operate. High unemployment can persist for several years.

6.2 FORCES THAT PUSH THE ECONOMY OFF ITS GROWTH PATH

We have seen that the economy can deviate from full employment and the forces pushing it back to full employment take time. What kinds of forces are responsible for departures from equilibrium? In order to answer this question, macroeconomists have to take a stand on which relationships in the economy hold in both the short and long run and which hold only in the long run. The view that we take in this book is that equality of supply and demand in the labor market (the condition of equilibrium) holds only in the long run. A second idea is that the price level is unresponsive to current developments; it moves only gradually over time. On the other hand, certain key relationships involving spending hold even in the short run. Accordingly, the complete model we develop considers spending relationships. It takes the price level as given for now from the past history of the economy. In the short run unemployment can be above the natural rate.

In the short run, we assume that firms stand ready to supply whatever output their customers want, given existing prices. Firms do not consider production incentives. When firms let their customers determine their level of output and employment, demand becomes the ruling force. If demand is

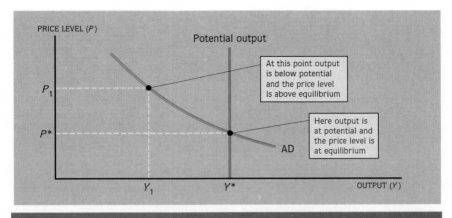

FIGURE 6–2 The aggregate demand curve

The aggregate demand curve shows the different levels of output that the spending process generates at different price levels. At price level P_1 output is Y_1 below the potential level Y^*. At price level P^*, the economy is at potential.

strong, employment exceeds its equilibrium. In recession, when demand is weak, employment drops below its equilibrium. The period out of equilibrium is temporary in either case. Fairly soon, firms adjust their prices to get back toward equilibrium. Price adjustment eventually takes the economy back to its long-run growth path. Chapter 8 will consider this transition process of price adjustment.

The spending relationships that affect demand add up to the *aggregate demand (AD) curve*. Figure 6–2 illustrates the basic use of the aggregate demand curve. Given a price level on the vertical axis, we can find the amount of output generated by the spending process by moving across, on a horizontal line, to the aggregate demand curve.

Any event that shifts the aggregate demand curve will move the economy away from potential. Figure 6–3 illustrates the effect of a leftward (inward) shift of aggregate demand. The shift leaves output below potential. In accord with our assumption that the price level does not respond immediately to this type of shift, the price level remains unchanged. In the next two chapters, we will consider the types of changes that would shift the aggregate demand curve. They include changes in the government's tax and spending policies, spontaneous changes in consumption and investment, and changes in purchases of U.S. goods by foreigners. Changes in monetary policy and in financial markets also shift the AD curve.

A second event that could move the economy away from potential is a shift in the price level. Changes in world prices, especially oil prices, are the most common source of price shocks. Figure 6–4 shows the effect of a

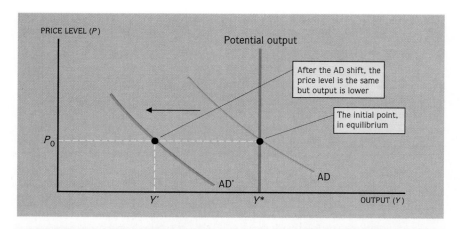

FIGURE 6–3   Output declines when AD shifts inward

A shock moves the AD curve and pushes the economy away from potential. The economy starts in equilibrium at output Y^* and price level P_0. Because of a negative shock, the AD curve shifts to the left, to AD'. The price level stays at P_0. The new level of output is Y', which is below Y^*.

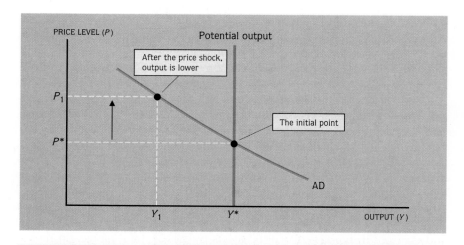

FIGURE 6–4   A price shock

A price increase moves the economy to a point on the AD curve with lower output.

price increase. From an initial position, the economy moves to a lower level of output. Again, the AD schedule tells how a price increase leads to a decline in output.

THE AGGREGATE DEMAND MODEL

1. In the short-run model, demand sets output; firms provide the level of output their customers demand at existing prices.
2. The aggregate demand curve shows the resulting level of output.
3. Any event that shifts the AD curve pushes the economy away from potential. Fiscal and monetary policy, consumption, investment, and foreign purchases can all shift the AD curve.

6.3

AGGREGATE DEMAND AND SPENDING BALANCE

To derive the aggregate demand curve, we consider a particular price level. Then we ask what level of output goes with this price level, considering the spending decisions of households, firms, and foreigners and the decisions made by the fiscal and monetary authorities. In the long-run growth model GDP is independent of demand factors; it depends only on production factor supply—labor, capital, and technology. Now, in the aggregate demand analysis, we have to determine GDP along with the interest rate (R). We still need the equality of GDP and spending, but we need to bring in the money market in order to get two equations with two unknowns so as to solve for both Y and R. Figure 6–5 illustrates the difference between the long- and short-run analyses.

Even though the long-run growth model explains one more variable—the price level—it is easier to solve the long-run growth model than the aggregate demand model. That is why we could rely on such simple diagrams. In the long-run growth model, we consider just the labor market to get the levels of employment and output. Then we can figure out the interest rate from the demand for output schedules. Finally, we can find the price level given output, the interest rate, and the money supply. We never have to solve simultaneous equations. With the aggregate demand model, on the other hand, we start with the demand for output and the money

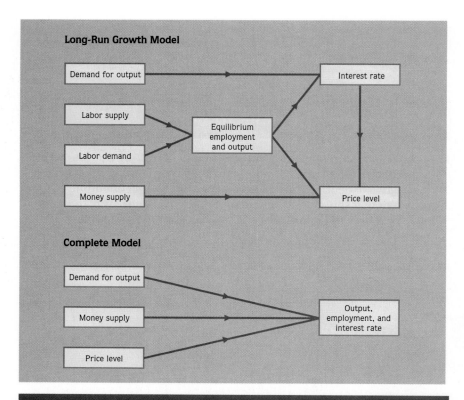

FIGURE 6–5   Comparing the long-run growth model with the complete model

The long-run growth model determines the levels of employment and output, the interest rate, and the price level given labor supply, labor demand, and output demand schedules and the money supply. It can be solved step by step: Labor supply and demand give employment and output, output demand gives the interest rate, and money supply, output, and the interest rate give the price level. The complete model does not assume equilibrium in the labor market; instead, it assumes that the price level is given. We have to solve simultaneous equations to find employment, output, and the interest rate.

supply, which are the same as in the long-run model, and we also start with the price level as a prescribed input. Then we have to solve simultaneous equations to find the levels of output and the interest rate that satisfy spending balance. We use the production function in reverse to find the level of employment that accompanies the level of output. Note that we do not make use of the supply and demand schedules for the labor market; they drop out because we do not assume that supply and demand are equal.

As Figure 6–5 shows, derivation of the aggregate demand schedule is a challenge; it involves solving multiple equations simultaneously. In fact, it is the most complicated piece of analysis in this book. In the rest of this chapter, we will say a little more about the assumption of price rigidity that underlies the aggregate demand curve. Then we will get started on the output demand part of the aggregate demand analysis. To focus on certain key issues relating to spending, we drop the interest rate out of the discussion temporarily. This means that we do not have to worry about the money market for this part of the discussion. Then in Chapter 7, we solve the entire problem laid out in Figure 6–5. The ultimate result is a full derivation of the aggregate demand curve.

The Basic Concept of Aggregate Demand

In Chapter 2 we noted that GDP could be defined and measured in three alternative ways: as **spending** on goods and services, as **production** of goods and services, and as **income** received by workers and firms. It is a simple matter of accounting identities that these three alternatives will give the same answer for total GDP, aside from measurement error and statistical discrepancies. When we move beyond accounting identities to a theory of what determines the fluctuations of GDP, however, it makes quite a difference which one of these concepts is used. In practice, it has turned out to be useful to focus first on the spending side.

Firms produce goods because people have decided to buy them. Aggregate demand theory starts by examining spending decisions. For example, consider how a macroeconomist goes about projecting the growth of GDP for the upcoming year. The macroeconomist begins with a projection of the spending demands of consumers, firms, and governments. If a personal tax cut is coming up, then the macroeconomist will naturally anticipate a larger amount of demand for consumption goods by households. If interest rates are projected to rise because of a change in monetary policy, then investment demand from firms is likely to be lower. If there is a public clamor for decreased defense spending, then government demand is likely to fall. By adding up the spending demands of the various sectors of the economy the macroeconomist obtains an estimate of aggregate spending. This total then serves as the projection for GDP for the upcoming year. While it will be necessary to check whether these spending projections are consistent with incomes—in a way to be made clear below—the basic forecast is obtained from an analysis of the spending decisions in the economy. Because the total spending forecast is an aggregation of demand in all sectors of the economy, we refer to the total as aggregate demand. Implicitly the macroeconomist is making an assumption that aggregate demand determines the amount of goods produced in the economy. This assumption is central to our analysis of economic fluctuations.

The Unresponsiveness of the Price Level

To see why the macroeconomist's assumption that prices are unresponsive and therefore that aggregate demand determines output is usually a reasonable assumption, we need to consider the typical behavior of business firms at the microeconomic level. Under normal conditions most business firms operate with some excess capacity and respond to increases in demand by producing more goods. In the United States the average level of capacity utilization in manufacturing industries is about 84 percent. Some machines are left idle on standby; others are run for only two of three shifts. Hence firms have considerable leeway to produce more by increasing capacity utilization when demand increases. If additional labor is necessary to operate the equipment more intensively, it is usually possible to have some workers increase their hours per week, to recall some workers from layoff status, or even to hire additional workers. The natural rate of unemployment is between 5 and 6 percent; this indicates that additional workers can be hired in the short run, even at full employment. Hence, for both capital and labor inputs to production, there is considerable short-run flexibility for firms to meet an increase in the demand for their products. And though we have been speaking entirely in terms of increases in demand, the same response occurs for declines in demand. A firm will produce less when the demand for its product declines. In sum, both increases and decreases in demand for a firm's product get translated into increases and decreases in production. In the economy as a whole, short-run fluctuations in aggregate demand result in similar fluctuations in GDP. In this sense, the assumption that "demand determines output" is a reasonable one for analyzing most short-run fluctuations of GDP from its long-run growth path.

Firms not only adjust their production in response to changes in demand, they also adjust their prices. When an increase in demand results in a firm producing at above-average operating levels, it usually increases its prices as well. Similarly, a decline in demand that brings the firm to below-normal operating levels will result in a price adjustment below what would have been appropriate otherwise. By adjusting its price in this way, the firm can usually both increase its profits in the short run and encourage a change in quantity demanded to a more desirable level from the firm's point of view.

There is a crucial difference, however, between the adjustment of production and the adjustment of prices in response to a change in demand: *Prices appear to be very "sticky" compared with production; the adjustment of prices occurs gradually, whereas the adjustment of production and employment occurs almost instantaneously.* Economists have only recently begun researching the reasons for this slow price adjustment on the part of firms, and we will summarize this exciting and important research in

Part III. The implication of this slow price adjustment is that changes in aggregate demand first result in changes in production, much as described above, and only later in changes in prices. In fact, in the very short run it is usually a good approximation to ignore price adjustment and focus on the changes in production.

We have left out one important aspect of firm behavior in our discussion so far. Many firms maintain a stock or inventory of their finished products on their shelves, so that when there is an increase in demand, the immediate response is usually to meet the demand out of the inventory. Conversely, a drop in demand can be matched by an accumulation of inventory. Clearly, changes in demand that are exactly matched by changes in inventory will not affect production or GDP. However, for the economy as a whole, increases in sales are met with increases in production. Thus, as an approximation it is possible to ignore inventory adjustments and assume that changes in demand are directly translated into changes in production. A full treatment of the process of inventory adjustment is given in Chapter 11.

An Example: General Motors

Production in the automobile industry rises and falls by large magnitudes in response to changes in demand, and automobile purchases are a very large part of total spending, so this is an important example. During the large downturn from 1929 to 1933, for instance, annual production of automobiles in the United States fell from about 5 million to about 1 million cars. In the downturn from 1979 to 1982 production of cars at GM plants in the United States fell from 4.8 million to 3.1 million cars per year.

Consider what happens at GM when there is a change in the demand for automobiles. Suppose, for example, that there is an increase in demand for automobiles, as there typically is in a recovery period following a recession like the one that ended in 1982. In the short run this increase in demand results in more automobiles being produced; some workers are asked to work more hours, others are recalled from layoff, some new workers are hired, plants are worked an extra shift, and plants that were closed earlier are reopened. Employment and capacity utilization in the automobile industry are increased in response to the increase in demand.

In 1984, for example, the demand for cars was increasing rapidly in the United States, as the economy was recovering rapidly from the previous recession. People bought 4.6 million cars from GM dealers in 1984, up 13 percent from the 4.1 million purchased in 1983. As a result, production of cars increased and the number of workers at GM plants in the United States increased to 375,000 in 1984, up 12 percent from 336,000 in 1983. With more workers on the job for longer hours, wage payments to GM workers increased by 19 percent to $13.6 billion during the same period. GM profits also rose dramatically, and dividends paid to holders of common stock increased from $900 million to $1.5 billion. Bonuses to managers were increased. Some of the increased profits—about $282 million—were shared with workers under a profit-sharing plan instituted during the previous recession. GM workers, managers, and owners thus had more income to spend, and this added further to the demand for goods in the economy. By the end of 1984 GM was building about the same number of cars that it was in 1979, before the downturn.

6.4 THE POINT OF BALANCE OF INCOME AND SPENDING

We rely on the principle of **spending balance** to determine GDP. In order to understand spending balance, recall first that income and output are both measured by GDP. In other words, when we add up total spending in the economy to get GDP, we also are calculating total income. Spending balance expresses this idea in the complete model. Spending balance occurs when the level of income used by consumers and other spenders in making their spending decisions is the same as the sum of the spending of all the spenders.

To show how this principle works, we will start with the simple case where investment, government purchases, and net exports are all fixed and do not depend on income or the interest rate. We will consider these variables to be determined outside the model (exogenous).

The Income Identity

We have already looked at the income identity in Chapters 2 and 5. This income identity says that

$$Y = C + I + G + X, \qquad \text{The Income Identity} \qquad (6-1)$$

where Y is GDP, C is consumption, I is investment, G is government purchases, and X is net exports. GDP, consumption, investment, government purchases, and net exports in this identity are all measured in real terms as discussed in Chapter 2.

We now consider the components of spending. We start with consumption.

The Consumption Function

How do consumers make their spending decisions? The **consumption function** is a description of the total consumption demand of all families in the economy. It states that consumption depends on **disposable income.** Disposable income, as we saw in Chapter 2, is income less taxes. The consumption function is based on the simple idea that the larger a family's disposable income, the larger that family's consumption will be. Thus, total consumption for all families in the economy will be larger if disposable income in the economy is larger.

The consumption function should be viewed as a simple approximation of actual consumption demand. Clearly consumption depends on other things besides current income: wealth, expected future income, and the price of goods today compared with tomorrow. We will discuss these and other factors that affect consumption in Chapter 10. The more elementary consumption function used in this chapter was first introduced to the study of macroeconomics by Keynes. Despite its simplicity, it has proved remarkably versatile as a macroeoconomic tool.

The consumption function can be written algebraically as

$$C = a + bY_d. \qquad \text{The Consumption Function} \qquad (6\text{--}2)$$

Specifically, this algebraic formula says that consumption C is equal to some constant a plus another constant b times disposable income Y_d. Both constants (a and b) are positive and b is less than 1. The constant a describes an element of consumption that is independent of disposable income. Less formally, Equation 6–2 simply says that consumption depends positively on disposable income.[1]

When studying algebraic relationships like the consumption function in macroeconomics, it is very important to distinguish between the constants and the variables. Sometimes the constants are called **coefficients.** In this consumption function the variables are C and Y_d. The constants, or coefficients, are a and b. Variables move around; constants stay fixed. To highlight this important distinction, we use lowercase letters for constants and uppercase letters for variables. This convention is used throughout this book.

EXAMPLE. If the coefficient a = 220 and the coefficient b = .9, then the consumption function looks like this:

$$C = 220 + .9Y_d.$$

---

[1]Note that in Chapter 5 we allowed for the possibility that consumption depends on the interest rate. Here we do not consider the effects of the interest rate on consumption, but we come back to that possibility in our detailed analysis of consumption in Chapter 10.

If disposable income is $4,000 billion, then consumption will be 220 + .9 × 4,000, or $3,820 billion. If disposable income rises to $5,000 billion, then consumption will rise to 220 + .9 × 5,000, or $4,720 billion. If disposable income increases by $1,000 billion, consumption increases by $900 billion. Note how the variables, consumption and disposable income, change in this calculation but the coefficients stay fixed.

The coefficient b is called the **marginal propensity to consume.** It measures how much of an *additional* dollar of disposable income is spent on consumption. For the numerical values stated in the last paragraph, 90 percent of each additional dollar of income is spent on consumption.

We can also represent the consumption function graphically, as in Figure 6–6. The vertical axis measures consumption. The horizontal axis measures disposable income. The consumption function is shown as a straight, upward-sloping line. It indicates that as disposable income increases, so does consumption.

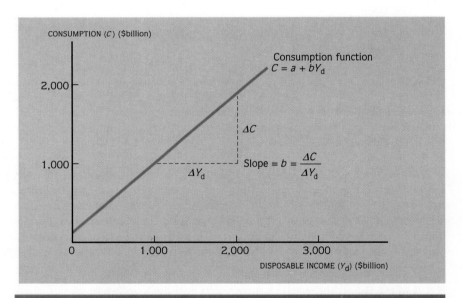

FIGURE 6–6   The consumption function

Consumption depends on income. The upward-sloping line shows that higher levels of disposable income correspond to higher levels of consumption. The slope of the line tells us how much consumption changes when disposable income changes. The slope of the line equals the marginal propensity to consume.

THE CONSUMPTION FUNCTION

1. Disposable income is the amount of income that people have available to spend after taxes.
2. The consumption function says that there is a predictable relationship between disposable income and consumption. The higher disposable income, the higher consumption.
3. The marginal propensity to consume is the fraction of an increase in disposable income that is consumed.

We can also write the consumption function in terms of income rather than disposable income. Disposable income is obtained by subtracting income taxes from income. If the tax *rate* is given by the constant t, then total tax payments are tY. Disposable income Y_d equals income Y minus taxes tY. Thus, we can write disposable income as $Y_d = (1 - t)Y$. For example, if the tax rate t is .3 and income Y is \$6,000 billion, then taxes are \$1,800 billion and disposable income is \$4,200 billion. By replacing disposable income Y_d with $(1 - t)Y$, the consumption function can be written

$$C = a + b(1 - t)Y. \qquad (6\text{--}3)$$

This says that consumption depends positively on income. For example, if the marginal propensity to consume b is .9 and the tax rate t is .3, then $b(1 - t) = .63$. An increase in income of \$100 billion will increase consumption by \$63 billion. This alternative way to write the consumption function is useful because it has the same income variable Y that appears in the income identity.

So far we have discussed the determinants of only one of the components of spending—consumption—but we already have the ingredients of an elementary theory of income or GDP determination. Before considering the determinants of the other components of spending—investment I, government G, and net exports X—we illustrate how this theory works. To do this, values for investment, government spending, and net exports must be taken from *outside* the model. Variables determined outside a model are called **exogenous variables.** Of the five variables that we discussed so far (income Y, consumption C, investment I, government spending G, and net exports X), this leaves two, consumption C and income Y, to be determined *inside* the model. Variables that are determined inside a model are called **endogenous variables.**

This basic idea that the endogenous variables must simultaneously satisfy a number of relationships is central to macroeconomic analysis. In the chapters that follow we will elaborate on this simple theory by adding more endogenous variables and more relationships that they must satisfy.

The elementary model consists of two basic relationships: the income identity, summarized algebraically in Equation 6–1, and the consumption function, summarized algebraically in Equation 6–3. These two relationships can be used to determine values for the two endogenous variables of the model: consumption C and income Y. *The values for C and Y are determined by requiring that both the consumption function and the income identity are satisfied simultaneously.*

Once we determine income and consumption in this way, we will have also determined GDP, of course, because income equals GDP. We illustrate the determination of income and consumption first using graphs and then using algebra.

Graphical Analysis of Spending Balance

In Figure 6–7 spending is measured on the vertical axis and income on the horizontal axis. Two intersecting straight lines are shown, a **spending line** and a **45-degree line.**

The spending line (the flatter of the two) shows how total spending depends on income. Total spending is the sum of consumption, investment, government spending, and net exports. In this model only consumption depends on income, through the consumption function. Investment, government spending, and net exports are exogenous. The spending line is obtained by adding the consumption function in Equation 6–3 to investment, government spending, and net exports. The equation corresponding to the spending line is

$$\text{Spending} = \underbrace{a + b(1-t)Y}_{\substack{\text{Consumption} \\ \text{from} \\ \text{Equation 6–3}}} + \underbrace{I}_{\substack{\text{Exogenous} \\ \text{investment}}} + \underbrace{G}_{\substack{\text{Exogenous} \\ \text{government} \\ \text{spending}}} + \underbrace{X.}_{\substack{\text{Exogenous} \\ \text{net exports}}}$$

The spending line thus incorporates the consumption function. The spending line is flatter than the 45-degree line because consumers spend only part of each added dollar of income. They save the rest.

The 45-degree line is drawn halfway between the vertical spending axis and the horizontal income axis. For any point on the 45-degree line, income equals spending. This line thus represents the income identity. The line makes a 45-degree angle with the horizontal axis; hence its name. Sometimes Figure 6–7 is called a **Keynesian 45-degree diagram,** or a

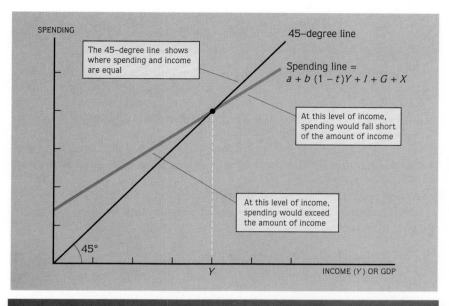

FIGURE 6–7 Spending balance

The intersection of the two lines shows where consumption and income satisfy both the consumption function and the income identity. The point of intersection is the solution to the model consisting of Equations 6–1 and 6–3.

Keynesian cross diagram, because of its early use to illustrate this simple model with a Keynesian consumption function.

The point of intersection of the spending line and the 45-degree line is the point where consumption and income satisfy both relationships of the model. On the 45-degree line, the income identity is satisfied. On the spending line, the consumption function is satisfied. The intersection of the two lines thus gives the value of income that we are looking for. At this point total spending in the economy equals total income, and consumption spending satisfies the consumption function. Income and spending are in balance.

The 45-degree line is steeper than the spending line. The 45-degree line has a slope of 1. The consumption function has a slope $b(1 - t)$, which is less than 1. For example, if $b = .9$ and $t = .3$, then $b(1 - t) = .63$. Because the lines have different slopes, they will always intersect.[2]

---

[2]See the box on p. 161 for a review of the concept of slope.

SPENDING BALANCE

1. The simple model of income determination consists of two relationships, the consumption function and the income identity. The model determines two endogenous variables: consumption and income. Three exogenous variables — investment, government spending, and net exports — are determined outside the model.
2. Spending balance occurs when consumers are choosing their consumption levels, C, on the basis of a level of income that is the same as the level $Y = C + I + G + X$.
3. In terms of the equations, spending balance occurs at levels of consumption C and income Y that obey both the consumption function and the income identity.

Algebraic Solution

The levels of consumption and income can also be found algebraically. Substitute the consumption function, Equation 6–3, into Equation 6–1. The result is

$$Y = \underbrace{a + b(1 - t)Y}_{C} + I + G + X. \tag{6–4}$$

The brace below Equation 6–4 shows where C in the income identity has been replaced by the consumption function. Equation 6–4 has one endogenous variable: Y. Recall that I, G, and X are exogenous variables. The variable Y appears on both sides of Equation 6–4. To solve the equation for Y, we gather together both terms involving Y on the left-hand side of the equation. Doing so, we see that the value of Y that solves Equation 6–4 is given by

$$Y = \frac{a + I + G + X}{1 - b(1 - t)}. \tag{6–5}$$

This is the solution of the model and corresponds exactly to the value of Y, which is at the point of intersection in Figure 6–7. The solution value for consumption can then be obtained by plugging this value into the consumption function (6–3). That is,

Graphs, Slopes, and Intercepts versus Algebra and Coefficients

Figure 6–6 and Equation 6–2 express exactly the same idea—that consumption depends positively on disposable income—in two different ways: graphically and algebraically. A third way is *verbal* presentation and analysis, which, although sometimes less precise, is necessary if you want to explain your economic ideas to those without economic training.

In general a graph is a diagram with a line or lines showing the relationship between two variables. The lines can be straight, as with the consumption line, or they can be bending, as with the aggregate demand curve (Figure 6–2). Relationships that are shown by straight lines are called *linear* relationships to distinguish them from those represented by bending lines. Sometimes lines are called **schedules,** a term that derives from the presentation of the relationship numerically as two columns of numbers that look like a train schedule. Graphs provide a more intuitive understanding, and, because visual images are sometimes easier to recall, graphs are good memory aids.

Algebra frequently provides more accurate and direct answers, and is needed in more complex problems. Sometimes only a rough sketch is needed for a graphical analysis, but it is important to know that there is a precise connection between a graphical and an algebraic representation of an economic relationship. The variable on the vertical axis of a graph is usually the one on the left-hand side of the equal sign in the algebraic expression. For the consumption function, the variable on the left-hand side is consumption. The variable on the horizontal axis is usually the one on the right-hand

side of the equal sign in the algebraic expression. For the consumption function, the variable on the right-hand side is disposable income. The place where the vertical axis and horizontal axis cross sometimes represents the zero value for both variables, but this is not necessary. It is important to look carefully at the scale on a diagram. For diagrams that are simply rough illustrations, no numerical scale will appear.

The place where the consumption line crosses the vertical axis in Figure 6–6 is called the **intercept.** It equals the coefficient a in the algebraic expression Equation 6–2. It gives the value of consumption when disposable income is zero. More generally, the intercept of any line is the place where the line crosses the vertical axis.

The steepness of the consumption line is measured by its **slope.** The slope tells us how much consumption increases when income increases by 1 unit. The slope of the line is the coefficient b in the algebraic expression. Thus, if disposable income increases by an amount ΔY_d, then consumption increases by an amount ΔC given by b times ΔY_d. On the graph we move to the right by ΔY_d and up by b times ΔY_d. In general, a perfectly flat horizontal line has a slope of zero, and a perfectly vertical line has a slope of infinity. If the slope is positive, then we say that the line slopes *upward* as we move from left to right; if the slope is negative, then the line slopes *downward* as we move from left to right. The slope of the consumption function is positive (b is greater than zero), and clearly the consumption line slopes upward.

$$C = a + b(1 - t)Y,$$

where Y comes from Equation 6–5.

EXAMPLE. Suppose that investment equals $900 billion, government spending equals $1,200 billion, and net exports equal –$100 billion. Suppose, as in previous examples, that the marginal propensity to consume b equals .9, the constant a equals 220, and the tax rate t equals .3. Then, according to the formula in Equation 6–5, income equals

$$\frac{220 + 900 + 1,200 - 100}{1 - .9(1 - .3)} = \frac{2,220}{.37},$$

or $6,000 billion. GDP is also equal to $6,000 billion. Using the consumption function (Equation 6–3), we get that consumption equals

$$220 + .9(1 - .3)(6,000),$$

or $4,000 billion.

How Spending Balance Is Maintained

It is important to understand the logic of finding the values of consumption and income that satisfy both the consumption function and the income identity. When people consume more in stores, firms will produce more. As we discussed in the microeconomic example, the firms will then employ more workers or have their existing workers spend more time on the job. Their added production increases the wage incomes of their existing and new workers and adds to the profits of the owners of the firms. This added income in turn stimulates more consumption. When spending is in balance, the income that consumers are receiving is the same as the income generated by their spending.

What happens if spending is not in balance? Suppose that consumers are spending too much relative to their incomes. The economy would then be in an untenable situation. Consumers would notice that they were spending too much and would contract their consumption. But then firms would produce less and workers' incomes would fall. The process of contraction would continue until consumption fell to a point of balance with income.

How do we know that the contraction of income and consumption will ultimately reach a point of balance rather than continuing to a complete collapse of the economy? When families contract their consumption because their incomes fall, the contraction in consumption is less than the fall in income. Some of the fall in income results in reduced taxes, so that disposable income does not fall as much as national income. Moreover, the marginal propensity to consume is less than 1, so that the fall in disposable income results in a smaller reduction in consumption. The smaller reduction in consumption thus generates a smaller drop in income on the second round. So the process of consumption and income contraction converges to a new lower point of balance. A numerical example of this type of convergence is presented in Table 6–1, page 166.

We do not present a formal model of the detailed process by which the economy reaches spending balance. The reason is that the process seems to operate quickly—more quickly than the business cycle or price adjustment. Our model assumes that the economy has already reached spending balance over each period of observation. Balance is not achieved by magic. But it is a useful simplification to talk about the economy after it has gone through the process.[3]

The Multiplier

In order to show how the elementary model can be used to analyze the short-run fluctuations in the economy, we consider what happens to income when there is a change in one of the exogenous variables. Suppose, for example, that there is a *decrease* in investment *I*. The exact reasons for the decrease are not important at this time, but for concreteness you may think of a sudden decline in expected profitability that reduces firms' desire to invest. What are the implications of this decline in investment demand?

We first consider the situation graphically using the spending line and 45-degree line in Figure 6–7, reproduced in Figure 6–8. The new diagram shows the impact of a decline in exogenous investment. It *shifts* the spending line downward by the amount of the decline in investment. If investment falls by $1 billion, then the spending line shifts down by $1 billion. To see this, note that the intercept of the spending line is $a + I + G + X$. Hence, the change in the intercept is the same as the change in investment; government spending and net exports are not changing and a is constant. Figure 6–8 shows that income is lower as a result of the downward shift in the spending line.

Note that the decline in income is larger than the shift in the spending line, because the slope of the spending line is greater than zero. The econ-

---

[3]Some elementary texts describe the adjustment process by focusing on inventories: If output is greater than spending, inventories begin to rise and this leads firms to cut back on output. Output and spending are thus brought into equality. We prefer not to introduce inventories at this stage of the analysis. We feel that the description in the text is a close approximation to reality. Many types of businesses—medical services, education—do not hold inventories of finished products, yet their production responds to changes in demand.

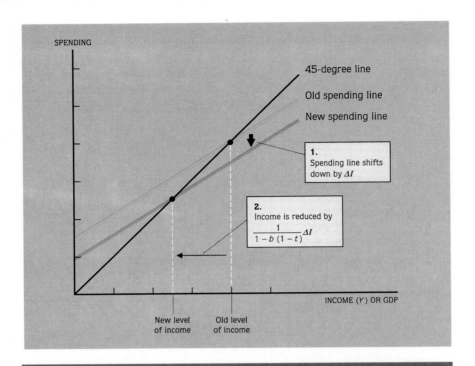

FIGURE 6–8   The multiplier

A decrease in investment demand shifts the spending line down. The new point of intersection is at a lower level of GDP. The decline in GDP is larger than the decline in investment; this illustrates the multiplier mechanism. (Note that the drop in investment shown in the diagram is much larger than would be possible in the U.S. economy. The drop is exaggerated here so that it can be easily seen in the diagram.)

omy thus "multiplies" the decline in investment into an even larger decline in income and GDP. This mechanism is called the **multiplier.** The steeper the spending line, the larger the decline in income.

The effect of the decline in investment on income can be calculated algebraically. Looking back to Equation 6–5, if we change investment by an amount ΔI, then the change in income will be given by

$$\Delta Y = \underbrace{\frac{1}{1 - b(1 - t)}}_{\text{The Multiplier}} \Delta I. \qquad (6-6)$$

This is obtained by writing Equation 6–5 in terms of the changes in the variables, and noting that neither government spending, net exports, nor the coefficient changes. All that is left is the change in investment.

The term $1/[1 - b(1 - t)]$, which multiplies the change in investment in Equation 6–6, is the multiplier. It is a general expression for the change in income associated with a change in investment. Since $b(1 - t)$ is less than 1, the value of the multiplier in expression 6–6 is greater than 1. Hence, the change in GDP is greater than the change in investment, just as we found using the graphical anlaysis. Note that the larger the marginal propensity to consume b, the larger the multiplier.

EXAMPLE. If the marginal propensity to consume b is equal to .9 and the tax rate t is .3, then the multiplier is equal to 1/.37 or about 2.7. A $10 billion *decrease* in investment results in a $27 billion decrease in income or GDP. Similarly, a $10 billion increase in investment results in a $27 billion increase in income or GDP.

This example can be used to illustrate the explicit actions of consumers and firms that result in the multiplier process. Suppose that a $10 billion decrease in investment occurs because Hertz, Avis, and several other large car rental companies in the United States suddenly get pessimistic about future profitability and stop buying new cars from General Motors, Ford, and Chrysler. Initially, the decreased purchases of new cars decrease income and GDP by $10 billion. But the reduced automobile production means that the incomes of workers in those companies will be reduced as they work fewer hours or are laid off. The income of shareholders of GM, Ford, and Chrysler will also be reduced, because of the decline in profits. In this example, the income of workers and shareholders falls by the full $10 billion. If the workers and shareholders have a marginal propensity to consume of .9 and pay taxes equal to 30 percent of their income, then they will reduce their consumption by $6.3 billion. Hence, GDP is cut by another $6.3 billion. The total reduction in GDP is now $16.3 billion.

But this is not the end. There is a third round. The workers and owners of the firms where the owners and employees of GM, Ford, and Chrysler cut their purchases by $6.3 billion will have a reduction in their income of this same amount. With the same taxes and marginal propensity to consume, they will thus cut their consumption by .63 times $6.3 billion, or by $3.969 billion. The total reduction in GDP is now $20.269 billion. The process will continue for a fourth and fifth round and so on, but by this time the reduction in income will be diversified across many different firms in the economy. Some of the reduced consumption demand will certainly get back to GM, Ford, and Chrysler.

If we keep summing the reduction in GDP at all these rounds, we will eventually get a $27 billion reduction in GDP—the same as the direct com-

TABLE 6–1   Example of the Multiplier Process (billions of dollars)

| | Reduction in GDP | | |
	This Round	Sum to Date	Calculation
Round 1	10.000	10.000	Exogenous drop in investment
Round 2	6.300	16.300	$b(1-t)(10) = (.6300)(10)$
Round 3	3.969	20.269	$[b(1-t)]^2(10) = (.3969)(10)$
Round 4	2.500	22.769	$[b(1-t)]^3(10) = (.2500)(10)$
Round 5	1.575	24.344	$[b(1-t)]^4(10) = (.1575)(10)$
Round 6	.992	25.336	$[b(1-t)]^5(10) = (.0992)(10)$

putation using the multiplier. As we mentioned above, the total effect of these spending reductions on GDP would usually occur in a fairly short period, certainly less than a year. The different rounds of production are summarized in Table 6–1. Note how the eventual $27 billion reduction of GDP that we calculated directly through the multiplier is almost reached after just a few rounds. Note also how convenient it is to use the multiplier rather than go through all these tedious calculations.[4]

Fluctuations in investment have always been associated with cyclical fluctuations in GDP. Such fluctuations in investment were emphasized by Keynes as an essential source of business cycle fluctuations. One of Keynes's main contributions was to show that relatively small fluctuations in investment could lead to large fluctuations in GDP. The mechanism underlying Keynes's theory was the multiplier; our example of a decline in investment leading to a large decline in GDP provides a simple illustration of Keynes's theory.

Changes in the other exogenous variables—government spending and net exports—also result in changes in income. The analysis is exactly

---

[4]The formulas for the calculations in the far right column of Table 6–1 add up to the formula for the multiplier: that is,

$$\frac{1}{1 - b(1 - t)} = 1 + b(1 - t) + [b(1 - t)]^2 + [b(1 - t)]^3 + \cdots.$$

This result can be shown using the formula for a geometric series. A formal algebraic model of the adjustment process could come from putting *past* income rather than current income in the consumption function. This leads to a dynamic model—called the dynamic multiplier—that describes how consumption adjusts over time after a sudden change in investment.

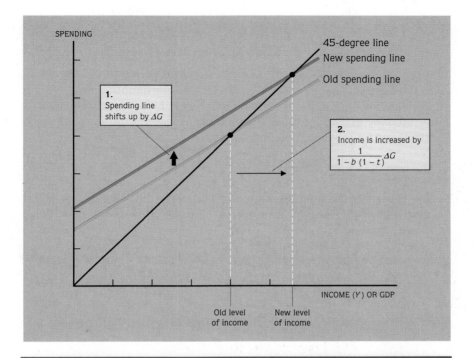

FIGURE 6–9 The government spending multiplier

An increase in government spending shifts the spending line up. Income or GDP expands by the multiplier times the increase in government spending.

the same as investment. For example, an increase in government spending will raise income and GDP by a greater amount. The same multiplier process is at work. In fact, the formula for the government spending multiplier—the amount that income increases when government spending increases—is exactly the same as the investment multiplier.

The government spending multiplier can be derived in the same way that the investment multiplier was derived. To show this, we have again reproduced the 45-degree line and spending line from Figure 6–7 in Figure 6–9. An increase in government spending will *raise* the spending line in Figure 6–9. This has an even larger effect on income, because of the multiplier process. Knowing the size of the government spending multiplier is important for accessing the impact of a change in government policy on the economy.

THE MULTIPLIER

1. When investment rises, GDP rises; investment is part of total GDP.

2. As GDP rises, disposable income also rises, so consumption rises.

3. The increase in GDP is larger than the increase in investment, because of the increase in consumption. The multiplier measures the amount of GDP stimulated by an increase in investment.

4. The formula for the multiplier is $\dfrac{1}{1 - b(1 - t)}$.

5. The government spending multiplier is exactly the same as the investment multiplier. When government spending increases, GDP increases by a larger amount.

Spending Balance When Net Exports Depend on Income

The next step is to drop the assumption that net exports are exogenous. We need to consider the influence of foreign trade and the value of the dollar on the macroeconomy. It is time to bring these crucial variables into the model—to consider the subject of **open-economy macroeconomics.**

As we saw in Chapter 2, foreign trade is divided into exports, sales of goods and services to the rest of the world, and imports, purchases of goods and services from the rest of the world. **Net exports** are simply exports less imports. When exports are greater than imports, there is a **trade surplus;** conversely, when exports are less than imports, there is a **trade deficit.**

Recall the income identity, Equation 6–1:

$$Y = \underbrace{C + I + G}_{\substack{\text{Domestic} \\ \text{purchases}}} + \underbrace{X.}_{\substack{\text{Net exports} = \\ \text{Exports} - \text{Imports}}}$$

This income identity tells us two things: (1) Income and GDP are the same thing, and (2) aggregate demand—as measured by total spending—determines GDP. In thinking about how imports and exports affect the aggregate demand for goods produced in the United States, keep in mind that consumption C, invesment I, and government spending G by Americans all include some purchases of goods and services abroad. In order to get a measure of how much of American demand is for U.S.-produced goods, we need to subtract imports. For example, if Americans buy 1 million more cars, then consumption rises by 1 million cars. But if all these cars are imported from abroad, then imports increase by 1 million cars and aggregate demand for U.S. goods (Y) does not change. The reason we add exports to the identity is straightforward: When foreigners increase their purchases of U.S.-produced goods, aggregate demand increases.

We will develop a relation between net exports and the level of U.S. income. The relation is negative. There is no reason to think that U.S. exports are much affected by U.S. income; they are affected instead by incomes in the countries purchasing the imports. But imports are affected by U.S. income. When U.S. income rises, consumers increase their spending on imported as well as domestic goods.

We can summarize the relation between income and net exports in a **net export function:**

$$X = g - mY. \tag{6-7}$$

Here g is a constant and m is a coefficient. For each dollar that GDP rises, imports rise by m dollars. Exports remain unchanged, so net exports fall by the same m dollars.

Compare the net export function with the consumption function, which we discussed earlier in this chapter. Net exports, like consumption, depend on income. But net exports *decline* by m dollars for each dollar increase in income, whereas consumption *rises* by b dollars for each dollar increase in income (b is the marginal propensity to consume). The reason that net exports decline with income is that imports rise by m dollars for each dollar increase in income. For this reason the coefficient m is sometimes called the **marginal propensity to import.** The dependence of net exports on income means that we need to take account of the response of net exports to income when we calculate the effects of monetary and fiscal policy, much as we took account of the response of consumption earlier in this chapter.

Now we can proceed exactly as we did before to develop an equation for spending balance by putting the net export function and the consumption function into the income identity. We did that before to get Equation 6-4. The corresponding equation is

$$Y = a + b(1 - t)Y + I + G + g - mY. \tag{6-8}$$

Again, we can solve for the value of Y at the point of spending balance. Previously, we got Equation 6-5. Now we get

$$Y = \frac{a + I + G + g}{1 - b(1 - t) + m}. \tag{6-9}$$

Note how the impact of a change in government spending on output is

$$\frac{1}{1 - b(1 - t) + m}.$$

This is the **open-economy multiplier.** Note that the multiplier is smaller when the marginal propensity to import is larger. By setting m equal to zero, the multiplier is the same as the multiplier for a closed economy. For example, if the marginal propensity to consume b is .9, the tax rate t is .3, and the marginal propensity to import m is .1, then the multiplier is $1/.47 = 2.1$, compared with a multiplier of $1/.37 = 2.7$ for the closed economy.

At this point, we can begin to analyze how policy or other economic forces affect the trade deficit. Recall from Chapter 2 that the trade deficit, as measured in the national income accounts, is just the negative of net exports. Anything that lowers net exports will raise the deficit. Looking at the net export function, Equation 6–7, we can see that net exports, in turn, respond negatively to the level of GDP. Combining the two, we can say that forces that raise GDP will also raise the trade deficit. In particular, an increase in government spending G will raise GDP according to the multiplier derived in Equation 6–9. Thus, increases in G raise the trade deficit.

The Decline of the Multiplier

At your first exposure to the multiplier, you may be very impressed. If the marginal propensity to spend b is .9 and there are no taxes, then the multiplier is 10! But then when you consider the role of taxes in reducing disposable income, you get the multiplier in Equation 6–6, which we said might be about 2.7. Then when we considered the fact that some of the purchasing power stimulated by growth in demand would go into imports rather than domestic spending, the multiplier dropped some more, to perhaps 2.1.

Other factors, which we will study in later chapters, will further reduce the multiplier. In the next chapter, we will consider the fact that higher demand raises interest rates, and these in turn discourage investment and net exports. Then the multiplier in our standard example will be only 1.1.

Some monetarists think that the multiplier is virtually zero. The real business cycle school asserts that the multiplier is low; moreover, to the extent that they believe that government spending stimulates output, it is through a different mechanism than the one we developed in this chapter. Briefly, in the real business cycle model, higher government spending raises the interest rate, and a higher interest rate stimulates more work effort. We will discuss this mechanism in Chapter 15.

Since increases in G also raise the fiscal deficit, we can see that the two deficits are related; when the government takes an action that raises its own deficit, it causes the trade deficit to rise as well.

In Chapter 2, we noted that the trade deficit is also the total amount that Americans are borrowing from overseas. An increase in the trade deficit means an increase in borrowing. Thus, we can express the relation between fiscal and trade deficits in the following way: When some force such as higher government spending raises government borrowing, part of the borrowing is done overseas. Instead of obtaining all the resources to be devoted to government spending from the domestic economy, some of them come from foreign economies.

In the rest of the book, the models we develop will all consider net exports endogenous.

SPENDING BALANCE IN AN OPEN ECONOMY

1. The net export function describes the negative relation between income and net exports. It arises because higher U.S. income causes higher U.S. imports from other countries.
2. The multiplier in an open economy is smaller than in a closed economy.
3. Events that raise GDP, such as higher government spending, cause net exports to fall and the trade deficit to rise. Part of an increase in the fiscal deficit is financed overseas through a higher trade deficit.

REVIEW AND PRACTICE

Major Points

1. Many economists feel that in the short run employment may deviate from full employment.
2. Incentives to restore full employment take a number of years to operate.
3. In the short run output is determined by the aggregate demand for goods and services in the economy.
4. In the short run firms respond to an increase in demand by producing more output rather than by raising prices.
5. The consumption function expresses the positive relation between income and consumption.

6. Spending balance occurs when consumption plus investment plus government purchases plus net exports add up to the level of GDP on which the consumers made their consumption plan.

7. The investment multiplier expresses the relation between investment and GDP. When investment rises by $1 billion, GDP rises by more than $1 billion because consumption rises as GDP rises.

8. Spending balance for an open economy occurs when the sum of all spending, including net exports, equals GDP.

9. The multiplier for an open economy is less than the multiplier for a closed economy.

10. An increase in government spending increases both the fiscal deficit and the trade deficit.

Key Terms and Concepts

spending balance	exogenous variable	marginal propensity
aggregate demand	endogenous variable	to import
income identity	multiplier	net exports
consumption function	investment multiplier	net export function
marginal propensity to	government spending	trade deficit
consume	multiplier	price shocks

Questions for Discussion and Review

1. Explain the role of labor supply and labor demand in determining the incentives to return to equilibrium.

2. What factors can push the economy out of equilibrium in the short run?

3. How is the level of employment determined in short-run disequilibrium situations?

4. What does the aggregate demand schedule measure?

5. How do firms typically respond to an increase in demand in the short run?

6. What happens to consumption if income rises? If taxes are cut?

7. What is true at the point of spending balance? What happens if the economy is not at a point of spending balance?

8. What happens to GDP if consumers change their behavior in such a way that the constant *a* in the consumption function increases?

9. Why does an increase in investment or government purchases bring about a large increase in GDP?

10. Explain why the open-economy multiplier is smaller than the closed-economy multiplier.

11. How does an increase in government spending affect the trade deficit?

Problems

Numerical

1. Suppose that the model of the economy is given by

$$Y = C + I + G + X$$
$$C = a + bY_d$$
$$Y_d = (1 - t)Y$$
$$X = g - mY$$

where I = \$900 billion, G = \$1,200 billion, and the constants take the following values: a = 220, b = .9, t = .3, g = 500, and m = .1.

a. Show that the value of GDP at the point of spending balance is \$6,000 billion. Compared with the example on page 165 with exogenous net exports, is the multiplier larger or smaller?

b. What proportion of investment is private saving? Government saving? Saving by the rest of the world?

c. Now suppose that I increases by \$100 billion. By what proportion of the increase in investment do each of the three categories of saving increase?

2. Consider a closed-economy model given by the following equations:

$$Y = C + I + G$$
$$C = 160 + .8Y_d$$
$$Y_d = (1 - t)Y - Z$$

Investment and government spending are exogenous and each is equal to 200. The tax system has two components: a lump-sum tax denoted by Z and an income tax of rate t.

a. Assume Z is equal to 200 and t is .25. Find the level of income that satisfies spending balance. How much does the government collect in taxes at that level of income? What is the level of government saving?

b. Suppose the lump-sum tax is reduced to 100. Find the new level of income that is consistent with spending balance. What is the lump-sum tax multiplier? What are the new levels of tax collections and government saving?

c. Comparing your answers in Parts a and b, does the tax cut increase or decrease tax receipts? By how much? Explain why tax receipts do not simply fall by 100 with the cut in lump-sum taxes.

d. One of the arguments of "supply-side" economists in the early 1980s was that a tax cut could actually reduce the budge deficit. Can that happen with a lump-sum tax cut in the model used in this problem? Does the spending balance model ignore factors that the "supply-siders" think are important for this problem? If so, name them.

Analytical

1. Imagine that you operate an economic forecasting firm. Your stock in trade is that you know the true model of the U.S. economy. It is given by

$$Y = C + I + G + X$$
$$C = a + bY_d$$
$$Y_d = (1 - t)Y$$
$$X = g - mY$$

where I and G are exogenous, and it is assumed that you have numerical values for all of the constants in the model.

a. Of the four spending components, which must you forecast before arriving at a forecast for the U.S. GDP? Explain.

b. Now suppose that you are trying to forecast GDP for a centrally planned economy in which the production schedules for all goods are determined a year in advance. Would forecasting C, I, G, and X be a very good way of forecasting GDP?

2. For the model given in Problem 1, explain why private saving, government saving, and saving by the rest of the world are all endogenous variables.

3. Suppose the economy is described by the following simple model:

$$Y = C + G$$
$$C = a + bY_d$$
$$Y_d = (1 - t)Y$$

a. Give an expression that relates private saving S_p to disposable income. This is called the saving function.

b. What must the relationship be between private saving and the government budget deficit? (Hint: Refer back to the discussion in Chapter 2 concerning the relationship between saving and investment.)

c. Solve for the values of S_p and the budget deficit; that is, derive an expression for each that is a function only of the exogenous variable G and the constants in the model. Are your expressions consistent with your answer to Part b?

4. Balanced budget multiplier: Consider the following simple model with investment and government spending exogenous.

$$Y = C + I + G$$
$$C = a + bY_d$$

Disposable income Y_d is given by $Y - T$ where T is total taxes. Suppose that taxes are not directly related to income so that T can be increased or decreased independently of income.

a. Derive the change in Y associated with an increase in taxes T. Show the results graphically and algebraically. What is the tax multiplier? That is, what is $\Delta Y/\Delta T$?

b. Compare the tax multiplier with the government spending multiplier derived in the text. Aside from the difference in signs, which is larger? Why?

c. Now increase government spending G and taxes T by the same amount. For this change the government budget deficit $G - T$ does not change. If the budget was balanced before, it will still be balanced. What happens to income Y in this case? Perhaps surprisingly it increases. Calculate by how much. That is, using algebra, calculate $\Delta Y/\Delta G$; $\Delta G = \Delta T$. The result is called the balanced budget multiplier.

5. For the model given in Problem 1, which of the following statements are true?
   a. An exogenous increase in net exports (i.e., an increase in g) lowers the trade deficit and the government budget deficit.
   b. An increase in investment lowers the government budget deficit but raises the trade deficit.
   c. An increase in government spending and taxes of the same amount leaves both the government budget deficit and the trade deficit unchanged.

6. Imagine an economy in which the government spent all its tax revenues, but was prevented (by a balanced budget amendment) from spending any more; thus $G = tY$, where t is the tax rate.
   a. Explain why government spending is endogenous in the model.
   b. Is the multiplier larger or smaller than the case in which government spending is exogenous?
   c. When t increases, does Y increase, decrease, or stay the same?

7. This question focuses on the differences in the structure of the long-run growth model of Chapter 4 and the short-run spending balance model introduced in this chapter.
   a. In the long-run model, what exogenous factors determine the level of output?
   b. In the spending balance model, what exogenous factors determine the level of output?
   c. In the spending balance model, is employment an exogenous or endogenous variable? How is the level of employment determined in this model?
   d. Which of the two models is best described by the statement "Demand creates its own supply"? Which model is best described by "Supply creates its own demand"?

MacroSolve Exercises

1. Plot the quarterly growth rates of real GDP and the GDP deflator ["Inflation (GDP)"]. Which would you describe as being more variable? Is this finding compatible with the view that prices are more sticky than output? Is the same true for the entire sample of annual data from 1930 to 1991?

2. Using quarterly data, graph consumption expenditure on the vertical axis against disposable income.
   a. What is the approximate slope of the consumption function (the marginal propensity to consume)?
   b. If the tax rate were zero, what would this marginal propensity to consume imply would be the value of the multiplier for a closed economy?
   c. If the tax rate were 30 percent, what would be the value of the multiplier?
   d. If, in addition, the marginal propensity to import were .1, what would be the value of the multiplier?

3. Tabulate the ratio of consumption to disposable income using quarterly data. How can the average propensity to consume be different from the marginal propensity to consume? What does this imply for the value of consumption when income is zero?

Financial Markets and Aggregate Demand

Spending balance, as we discussed in the last chapter, involves finding the level of GDP that makes the spending plans of consumers and others consistent with their actual levels of income. In this chapter, we will complete the discussion of spending balance by bringing back in another key variable, the interest rate. Spending depends on the interest rate because of the sensitivity of investment and net exports to the interest rate. In order to tell the full story of the interest rate, we have to consider the money market. We introduce the IS-LM framework to help develop the story. The IS-LM framework combines the money market and the spending process. We will use the IS-LM approach in the rest of the book to describe the determination of output and interest rates in the short run.

7.1 INVESTMENT AND THE INTEREST RATE

In the aggregate demand system we developed in Chapter 6, there were two exogenous forces that potentially could affect aggregate demand—investment and government spending. In this section we present an extension of that aggregate demand model. The extension has two important features: First, **financial variables**—interest rates and the supply of money—are shown to play an important role in the determination of aggregate demand, and, second, investment depends on these financial variables. Investment is no longer determined outside the model. Investment now becomes an endogenous variable. The addition of financial variables to the model means that we will be concerned with the effects of changes in the money supply and interest rates, as well as with government spending.

In the basic system of Chapter 6, you may have noticed that aggregate demand was independent of the price level. We talked about the possibility of firms adjusting their individual prices, but the general or average level of prices had no direct effect on demand. As soon as we add financial variables, we will find that aggregate demand depends on the price level: As the price level increases, aggregate demand decreases. Aggregate demand, and hence real GDP, will also change if there is a shock to the price level, such as when the price of oil jumped upward in 1973, 1979, and 1990, and collapsed in 1986. Such shocks can affect the overall price level significantly. Unless monetary or fiscal policy offsets the shock, there will be a recession or a boom. The issue of how policy should respond to price shocks is one of the most important macroeconomic problems facing policymakers today.

The Investment Demand Function

When we change investment from an exogenous variable to an endogenous variable, we need to specify a behavioral relationship to explain how investment is determined within the model. The relationship we use to describe investment is a simple but fundamental one. It states that investment depends negatively on the interest rate. This means that the demand for investment goods—the new factories, offices, and equipment used by business firms, as well as the new houses built for residential use—is low when interest rates are high, and vice versa.

The major reason for this negative relationship is that business firms and consumers finance many of their investment purchases by borrowing. When borrowing costs are high because of high interest rates, firms and consumers will tend to make fewer investment purchases. High borrowing costs effectively make investment goods more costly. Note that even if borrowing is not the source of funds for investment—such as when the funds come from selling financial securities—the interest rate still matters. If interest rates are high, then not holding those securities will represent a larger loss of income on those securities than if interest rates were low. Hence, if interest rates are high, people will be reluctant to sell those securities in order to purchase physical investment goods.

In algebraic terms the relationship for investment demand, called the **investment function,** can be represented as

$$I = e - dR. \tag{7–1}$$

As before, I is investment, R is the interest rate, and e and d are constants. Investment is measured in billions of dollars, and the interest rate is measured in percentage points. Equation 7–1 says that investment demand is equal to a constant e minus another constant d times the interest rate. The coefficient d measures how much investment falls when the interest rate increases by 1 percentage point. Note that we have kept the convention that lowercase letters represent constant coefficients, while uppercase letters represent variables. The investment function is shown graphically in Figure 7–1. It is a downward-sloping line.

EXAMPLE. Suppose e equals 1,000 and d equals 2,000; then Equation 7–1 looks like

$$I = 1,000 - 2,000R.$$

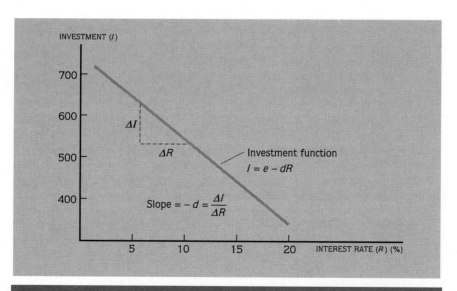

FIGURE 7–1 The investment function

When the interest rate rises, the demand for investment falls. A higher interest rate means that the cost of funds required for investment is higher; only those investment projects that are particularly profitable will be undertaken.

When the interest rate is 5 percent, investment I is 1,000–2,000(.05), or $900 billion. An increase in the interest rate of 1 percent reduces investment by $20 billion. Note that we speak about the interest rate R as a percent, but use decimals in algebraic formulas: "The interest rate is 5 percent" means $R = .05$. This convention is used throughout the book.

The Meaning and Interpretation of R

Note that, in changing investment from an exogenous variable to an endogenous variable, we have introduced a new endogenous variable into the model: the interest rate R. There are, of course, many different interest rates in a modern economy: rates on *long*-term securities, rates on *short*-term securities, rates on *risky* securities, and rates on *safe* securities. When we use the term "*the* interest rate," we are therefore simplifying the financial structure of the economy. In thinking about this simplification—that is, in trying to relate R to something you can read about or look up in a newspaper—it is useful to imagine an average or representative interest rate that represents the behavior of all the different types of rates. For many purposes this abstraction is not too bad; interest rates on different types of securities—while not equal—tend to move in the same direction. That is, when interest rates on risk-free Treasury bills are abnormally high, so are interest rates on more risky corporate bonds. Of course, there are sometimes differences between short- and long-term interest-rate behavior. Long-term interest rates depend on expectations of future short-term rates. However, we will focus on the average representative interest rate R.

It is also important to distinguish between the **real interest rate** and the **nominal interest rate.** The nominal interest rate is simply the rate that you read about in the newspaper or that banks place in their windows to indicate what they will pay for different types of deposits. The real interest rate corrects the nominal rate for expected changes in the price level. Specifically, the real interest rate is the nominal interest rate minus the expected rate of inflation. For example, if your bank is paying 10 percent on deposits for a year and you expect inflation to be 6 percent for the year,

THE INVESTMENT FUNCTION

1. Investment demand is negatively related to the interest rate. When funds are more expensive, less investment takes place. The investment function describes this negative relationship.
2. The interest rate R that is in the investment function is an average of the many interest rates that we observe at banks and in the financial markets.

then the real rate of interest for you is 4 percent. The real rate of interest measures how much you will earn on your deposit after taking account of the fact that inflation will have increased the price of goods that you might purchase in a year. We usually mean the real interest rate when we use the symbol R in this book, but we do not generally add the adjective "real," unless the meaning is ambiguous or we want to point out a particular reason to distinguish between the real and the nominal rates. For low rates of inflation the real rate and the nominal rate are very close.

7.2   NET EXPORTS AND THE INTEREST RATE

Another factor that we want to consider in building a complete model of aggregate demand is that net exports depend negatively on the interest rate. In Chapter 12, we will consider the reasons for this important relation in more detail. For now, we will look at the relation in the following way: When the U.S. interest rate is higher than interest rates in other countries, it becomes attractive for people in those countries to put their funds in *dollars,* that is, to lend funds to businesses in the United States and to the U.S. government. By the same token, it is less attractive for people in the United States to put their funds in other currencies, that is, to lend overseas, where returns are lower. This means that dollars become more attractive, and this drives up the price of dollars, that is, the exchange rate rises. But a higher exchange rate makes U.S. goods more expensive to foreigners and it also makes foreign goods less expensive to U.S. residents. Less expensive foreign goods will make U.S. imports rise. Similarly, more expensive U.S. goods will make U.S. exports fall. On both accounts *net exports—exports minus imports—fall when the U.S. interest rate rises* because the exchange rate rises.

How do we incorporate this negative relationship between net exports and the interest rate into our complete model of aggregate demand? We must add another term to the net export function of Equation 6–7 to incorporate the negative effect of the interest rate R on net exports:

$$X = g - mY - nR. \qquad (7\text{–}2)$$

The new coefficient n measures the decrease in net exports that occurs when the interest rate rises by 1 percentage point.

EXAMPLE. Suppose g is 525, m is .1, and n is 500. Then the net export function is

$$X = 525 - .1Y - 500R.$$

7.3   THE IS CURVE AND THE LM CURVE

We have now developed all the economic relationships needed to understand the full short-run spending model. We can thus tackle the problem of short-run output and interest-rate determination. Recall that this is a challenging problem because output and the interest rate are simultaneously determined. The IS and LM curves are convenient ways to describe the solution to the problem.

In the short-run model, we take the price level as given or **predetermined.** There are five economic relationships to consider: the income identity, the consumption function, the investment demand function, the net export function, and the money demand function. The theory implies that all five relationships must hold at the same time.

The method of analysis proceeds as follows. We take as given the values for the variables determined outside our model in any year, for example, 1992. These are the exogenous variables: the money supply M and government spending G. They are determined by the Fed, the President, and Congress. We want to find values for income, consumption, investment, net exports, the interest rate, and the price level that are implied by the model and by the values of the money supply and government spending for that year. We also want to find out what happens if the money supply or government spending changes. Will interest rates and output rise or fall, and by how much? The economic relationships and the key macroeconomic variables are summarized in the box on page 182.

Suppose that $P = 1$. Then the five macro relationships will determine values for the five remaining endogenous variables. The situation is analogous to that in Chapter 6 where we had to find values for two variables to satisfy two relationships. We first use graphs and then algebra.

Because graphs only allow for two variables, we need to reduce the five relationships to two relationships. A way to do this was originally proposed in 1937 by the late J. R. Hicks, the British economist who won the Nobel Prize in 1972. Hicks's graphical approach, called the IS-LM approach, is still used widely today because of its great intuitive appeal.[1]

---

[1] See J. R. Hicks, "Mr. Keynes and the Classics: A Suggested Interpretation," *Econometrica,* Vol. 6, pp. 147–159, 1937. The IS curve gets its name because, when all relationships are satisfied, investment demand, "I," must equal income less consumption demand, or saving, "S." The "M" in the LM curve stands for the money supply and the "L" stands for liquidity preference, which is a synonym for money demand. (Money is more liquid—easier to exchange for goods and other items—than bonds or corporate stock.)

KEY MACRO RELATIONSHIPS

Macro Variables

The *Endogenous* Variables:

Name	Symbol
Income	Y
Consumption	C
Investment	I
Net exports	X
Interest rate	R

The *Exogenous* Variables:

Name	Symbol
Government purchases	G
Money supply	M

The *Predetermined* Variable:

Name	Symbol
Price level	P

Five Relationships (How the Variables Interact with Each Other)

Algebra		Name	Numerical Example
$Y = C + I + G + X$	(6-1)	Income identity	
$C = a + b(1 - t)Y$	(6-3)	Consumption function	$C = 220 + .63Y$
$I = e - dR$	(7-1)	Investment function	$I = 1,000 - 2,000R$
$X = g - mY - nR$	(7-2)	Net export function	$X = 525 - .1Y - 500R$
$M = (kY - hR)P$	(5-3)	Money demand	$M = (.1583Y - 1,000R)P$

The IS Curve

The **IS curve** is shown in Figure 7–2. *The IS curve shows all the combinations of the interest rate* R *and income* Y *that satisfy the income identity, the consumption function, the investment function, and the net export function.* In other words, it is the set of points for which spending balance occurs. The left-hand panel of Figure 7–2 shows how higher levels of the interest rate are associated with lower levels of GDP along the IS curve.

SLOPE. The first thing to remember about the IS curve is that it is downward sloping. Understanding the intuitive economic reason for this downward slope is very important. *The IS curve is downward sloping because a higher interest rate reduces investment and net exports and thereby reduces GDP through the multiplier process.* To find a specific point on the

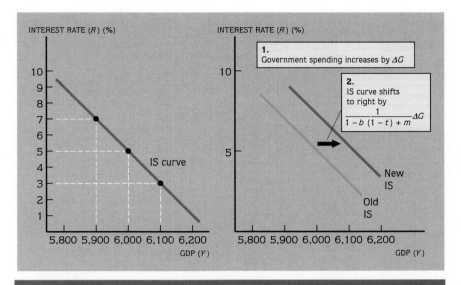

FIGURE 7–2 The IS curve

The IS curve shows all the combinations of the interest rate R and income Y that satisfy the consumption, investment, and net export functions and the income identity. As shown in the left-hand panel, it is downward sloping; an increase in the interest rate reduces investment and net exports. Through the multiplier, GDP falls. The right-hand panel illustrates how the IS curve shifts to the right when government spending increases.

IS curve, choose an interest rate and calculate how much investment and net exports will result using the investment function and the export function. The higher the rate of interest, the lower the level of investment and net exports. Pass this level of spending through the multiplier process to find out how much GDP will result. The less of both, the less GDP. The interest rate and this level of GDP are a point on the IS curve. A self-contained explicit graphical derivation of the IS curve is shown in Figure 7–3.

SHIFTS. The second thing to remember about the IS curve is that *an increase in government spending shifts the IS curve to the right.* An increase in government spending increases GDP through the multiplier; as GDP increases, we move the IS curve to the right. Note that, conversely, a decrease in government spending pushes the IS curve to the left.

To find how much the IS curve shifts, pick an interest rate R and calculate a corresponding level of investment and net exports. Now increase government spending. Through the multiplier process, output will increase by the multiplier times the increase in government spending. Holding the

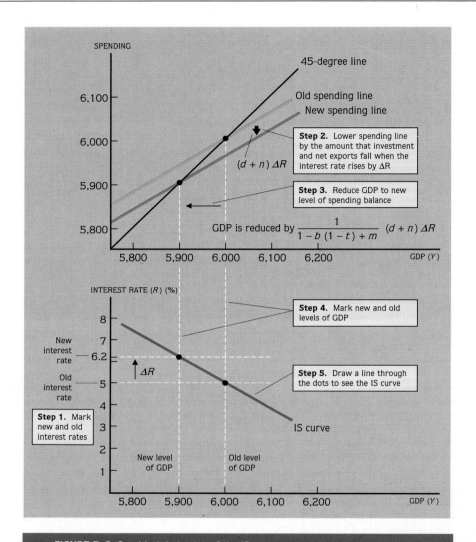

FIGURE 7–3 Graphical derivation of the IS curve

The upper part of the diagram shows the 45-degree line and the spending line. The lower part of the diagram is the graph where the IS curve is to be drawn. The lower diagram has the interest rate on the vertical axis, and GDP on the horizontal axis. Points on the graph are obtained as described in the instructions placed in boxes on the diagram. Start with an interest rate and find the position of the spending line for that interest rate. (Higher interest rates will lower the spending line because they reduce investment and net exports.) Then find the resulting level of GDP that satisfies the requirements of spending balance. Note how the slope of the IS curve will depend on the marginal propensity to consume b, the tax rate t, and the marginal propensity to import m, because these affect the multiplier. Note also that the slope depends on the sensitivity of investment and net exports to changes in the interest rate, controlled by the coefficents d and n.

interest rate constant, the IS curve shifts to the right along the horizontal GDP axis by the amount of the multiplier times the increase in government spending. This is shown in the right-hand panel of Figure 7–2.

The LM Curve

The **LM curve** is shown in Figure 7–4. *The LM curve shows all combinations of the interest rate* R *and income* Y *that satisfy the money demand relationship for a fixed level of the money supply and for a predetermined value of the price level.* The left-hand panel of Figure 7–4 shows that higher levels of the interest rate are associated with higher levels of GDP along the LM curve.

SLOPE. The first thing to remember about the LM curve is that it slopes upward. The reason for this is somewhat involved, but important to keep in mind. Imagine that the interest rate increases. What must happen to income if money demand is to remain equal to money supply? An increase in the interest rate *R* reduces the demand for money. But the money supply is fixed. Hence, income must adjust to bring money demand back up. A rise in income is what is required. A rise in income will increase the demand for money and offset the decline in money demand brought about

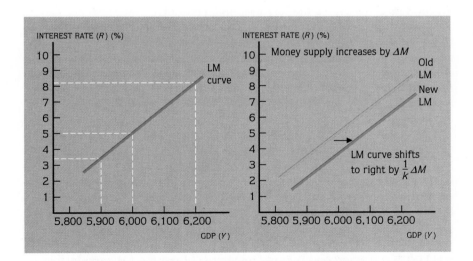

FIGURE 7–4 The LM curve

The LM curve shows the values for the interest rate and income such that the supply of money is equal to the demand for money. As shown in the left-hand panel the LM curve is upward sloping. The right-hand panel shows how an increase in the money supply shifts the LM curve to the right.

by the rise in the interest rate. In sum, the increase in the interest rate is associated with an increase in income. Thus the LM curve is upward sloping.

To understand better the derivation of the LM curve, it is helpful to introduce the concept of **real money.** Real money is defined as money M divided by the price level P. Because the term "real money" is used so much in macroeconomics we sometimes use the term **nominal money** when we mean just plain money M. Real money M/P is a convenient measure of money that corrects for changes in the price level. For example, if money increases by 10 percent and the price level increases by 10 percent, then real money does not change. The money demand function back in Equation 5–4 can be written in terms of real money if we simply divide both sides by the price level. That is,

$$M/P = kY - hR. \tag{7–3}$$

This says that the demand for *real* money depends positively on real GDP and negatively on the interest rate. The real money demand equation is an attractive way to think about money demand because it depends on two rather than three variables. Looking at Equation 7–3, we see that real money demand consists of two parts: One part, kY, increases with income, while the other part, $-hR$, decreases with the interest rate. Of course the same economic principles apply whether we write the money demand function in terms of real money or nominal money.

Looking at Equation 7–3, we see clearly why the LM curve slopes up. If the Fed is holding nominal money constant and the price level isn't moving, then the real money supply is also constant. If the real money supply is constant, then an increase in the interest rate R, which reduces money demand by hR, must be offset by an increase in Y, which increases money demand by kY. Hence, when the interest rate R increases, income Y increases.

A self-contained graphical derivation of the LM curve, based on this line of reasoning, is shown in Figure 7–5. The left-hand panel of Figure 7–5 is a graph of the demand for real money as a function of the interest rate. Real money demand decreases with the interest rate. But note that an increase in GDP increases money demand and this shifts the money demand line to the right. If money demand is to stay equal to money supply, then the interest rate must increase, as shown in the diagram.

SHIFTS. The second thing to remember about the LM curve is that *an increase in the money supply shifts the LM curve to the right.* Conversely, a decrease in the money supply shifts the LM curve to the left. Looking again at Equation 7–3, we can get an economic understanding for this. An increase in the money supply increases the variable on the left-hand side, M/P. If money demand is to remain equal to money supply, then either output Y must rise or the interest rate R must fall. If we hold the interest on

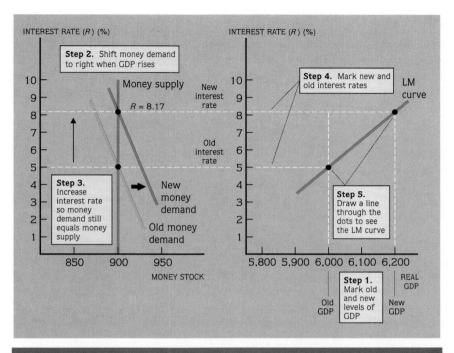

FIGURE 7–5 Graphical derivation of the LM curve

The left-hand panel shows the demand for real money as a function of the interest rate. The demand schedule slopes downward because higher interest rates make the public conserve on money holdings. Money demand shifts to the right if real GDP rises. Higher GDP causes the public to hold more real money at a given interest rate. The LM curve is constructed in the right-hand panel. The instructions show how to get points on the curve. Start with a level of GDP and find the money demand suitable for that level. Then find the interest rate that equates money demand and money supply. The LM curve traces out the market-clearing interest rate for different levels of GDP.

the LM diagram at a particular value, then output Y must increase as the LM curve shifts to the right. This is shown in the right-hand panel of Figure 7–4.

Changes in the price level also shift the LM curve. Again, look at the symbols in Equation 7–3 to keep track of what is going on. An increase in the price level reduces real balances. Hence, an increase in the price level does exactly the same thing to the LM curve as a decrease in the money supply. *An increase in the price level shifts the LM curve to the left*. The rationale: An increase in the price level means that less real money is available for transactions purposes. This means that either the interest rate must rise or real income must fall to reduce money demand. Either way the LM curve shifts to the left. Conversely, a decrease in the price level shifts the LM curve to the right, just like an increase in the money supply.

Algebraic Derivation of the IS and LM Curves

The algebraic statement that defines the IS curve is the expression of spending balance; that is, the GDP, Y, generated as total spending, is equal to the level of income Y, assumed by consumers and importers in making their spending decisions:

$$Y = a + e + g + [b(1 - t) - m] Y - (d + n) R + G. \qquad (7\text{–}4)$$

Note that the right-hand side is just the consumption function plus the investment function plus the net export function plus government spending. We want to express the IS curve as an equation giving the value of R that gives spending balance at a specified level of Y. We solve Equation 7–4 for R by moving the R term to the left-hand side and dividing by $d + n$:

$$R = \frac{a + e + g}{d + n} - \frac{1 - b(1 - t) + m}{d + n} Y + \frac{1}{d + n} G. \qquad \text{IS Curve} \qquad (7\text{–}5)$$

Government spending G increases the interest rate for a given level of income. Graphically, this looks like a shift of the IS curve to the right, a result that we saw in Figure 7–2. A higher value of G raises the IS curve or, equivalently, shifts the IS curve to the right.

The coefficient

$$\frac{1 - b(1 - t) + m}{d + n}$$

that multiplies Y in Equation 7–5 is the slope of the IS curve. Note that the slope of the IS curve depends on the sensitivity of investment to the interest rate, represented by the coefficient d. The algebraic formula shows that the slope of the IS curve is small—this means that the IS curve is fairly flat—if investment is very responsive to the interest rate. Then, small changes in the interest rate result in large changes in investment and hence large fluctuations in GDP. Similarly, the IS curve will be flat if net exports are highly sensitive to the interest rate, that is, if the coefficient n is large. What matters is the sum of the two interest-rate coefficients, $d + n$. Note also that the IS curve will be flat if the marginal propensity to consume b is large, if the tax rate t is small, or if the marginal propensity to import m is small. In these cases, the multiplier is large and changes in the interest rate have large effects on GDP.

AN EXAMPLE OF AN IS CURVE. With the numerical values summarized in the box on page 182, the IS curve is

$$R = \frac{1,745}{2,500} - \frac{1 - .53}{2,500}\, Y + \frac{1}{2,500}\, G$$

or

$$R = .698 - .000188\,Y + .0004\,G. \qquad \text{Numerical Example} \qquad (7\text{--}6)$$
$$\text{of IS Curve}$$

The slope of the IS curve is - .000188: Along the IS curve, when GDP rises by $100 billion, the interest rate falls by 1.88 percentage points. The IS curve that appears in Figure 7–2 is drawn accurately to scale for this numerical example. The IS curve on the left is drawn for government spending G equal to $1,200 billion. The shift in the IS curve to the right in Figure 7-2 is due to an increase in government spending of $40 billion.

The algebraic expression for the LM curve is obtained simply by moving R to the left-hand side of the money demand equation (7-3) and dividing by the coefficient h. That is,

$$R = \frac{k}{h}\, Y - \frac{1}{h}\, \frac{M}{P}. \qquad \text{LM Curve} \qquad (7\text{--}7)$$

Equation 7–7 says that an increase in real money balances M/P lowers the interest rate for a given level of income. This means that the LM curve shifts to the right, a result that corresponds to the graph in Figure 7–4. The slope of the LM curve is k/h. Note that the slope of the LM curve k/h is small—meaning that the LM curve is fairly flat—if the sensitivity of money demand to the interest rate is large, that is, if the coefficient h is large. Then, a small decline in the interest rate raises the demand for money by a large amount and requires a large offsetting increase in income. The small change in the interest rate combined with the large change in income trace out a flat LM curve. Note also that the LM curve is flat if the sensitivity of money demand to income k is small.

$1 - .8(1 - .2)$

AN EXAMPLE OF AN LM CURVE. With the numerical values summarized in the box on page 182, the LM curve is

$1 - .8(.8)$

$$R = \frac{.1583}{1,000}\, Y - \frac{1}{1,000}\, \frac{M}{P}$$

$1 - .64 = .36$

or

$$R = .0001583\,Y - .001\frac{M}{P}. \qquad \text{Numerical Example} \qquad (7\text{--}8)$$
$$\text{of LM Curve}$$

$1 - .8(1 - .4)$

$1 - .48 =$

This LM curve is drawn to scale in Figure 7–4. The shift of the LM curve for an initial money stock of 900 in the right-hand side of Figure 7–4 corresponds to an increase in the money supply of $40 billion.

Finding Income *Y* and the Interest Rate *R*

Finally we are ready to find the values of the interest rate and income that are predicted by the theory. We first proceed graphically. To satisfy all five relationships of the model, the values of *R* and *Y* must be on both the LM curve and the IS curve, that is, at the intersection of the LM curve and the IS curve. The IS curve takes care that the theory of consumption, investment, and net exports and the income identity are satisfied, while the LM curve takes care that the theory of money demand and money supply is satisfied. The values of the interest rate and income that we are looking for are thus at the intersection of the LM curve and the IS curve. The intersection is shown graphically in Figure 7–6.

Once we have determined the levels of income *Y* and the interest rate *R*, we can determine consumption *C,* investment *I,* and net exports *X.* Con-

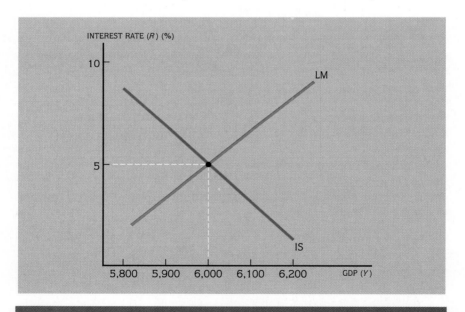

FIGURE 7–6 The intersection of the IS curve and the LM curve

The values of the interest rate and income predicted by the macro model occur at the intersection of the IS curve and the LM curve. For these values, all five relationships of the model are satisfied. Along the IS curve consumption demand, investment demand, net export demand, and the income identity are satisfied. Along the LM curve money demand equals money supply.

sumption is obtained by putting the value of income into the consumption function, investment is obtained by putting the value of the interest rate into the investment function, and net exports are obtained by putting income and the interest rate into the net export function.

Recall that all these predictions of the model are made with the price level fixed, on the "back burner." This is fine for the short run—for about a year or so—but for no longer. We look at what happens to the price level in the next chapter.

THE IS-LM FRAMEWORK

1. The IS curve shows all combinations of the interest rate and income that satisfy spending balance.
2. The LM curve shows all combinations of the interest rate and income that satisfy money market equilibrium.
3. Given the price level, the IS-LM diagram tells the levels of GDP and the interest rate, at the intersection of the IS and LM curves. This is the only combination of Y and R that satisfies both spending balance and money market equilibrium.

7.4   POLICY ANALYSIS WITH IS-LM

Monetary Policy

We are now ready to make the IS-LM approach go to work. Consider monetary policy. What happens if the Fed increases the money supply? We now know that an increase in the money supply shifts the LM curve to the right. The effect of such a change on the interest rate and income is shown in Figure 7–7. As the left-hand panel indicates, the theory predicts that *when the money supply increases the interest rate falls and GDP rises*. This increase in GDP will probably put upward pressure on prices, but we are saving the details for the next chapter.

What is actually happening in the economy when the Fed increases the money supply? Immediately after the increase there is more money in the economy than people demand. This tends to make the interest rate fall, so the demand for money increases. The lower interest rate then stimulates investment and net exports; this raises GDP through the multiplier process. In sum, GDP rises and the interest rate falls.

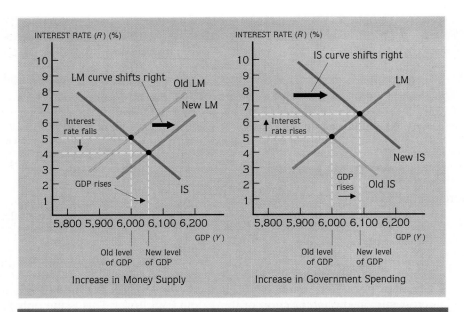

FIGURE 7–7 Effects of monetary and fiscal policies

In the left-hand panel, an increase in the money supply shifts the LM curve to the right; this raises GDP and lowers the interest rate. In the right-hand panel, an increase in government spending shifts the IS curve to the right; this raises GDP and the interest rate. A comparison of the two panels illustrates a fundamental difference between monetary policy and fiscal policy: An expansionary monetary policy lowers interest rates, and an expansionary fiscal policy raises interest rates.

Fiscal Policy

Suppose that Congress passes a bill that increases defense spending. We now know that an increase in government spending pushes the IS curve to the right. Figure 7–7 shows what happens to interest rates and GDP. In the right-hand panel *an increase in government spending increases the interest rate and increases income.*

What is going on in the economy when the government purchases more goods? First, the increase in government demand increases GDP through the multiplier. But the increase in GDP will increase the demand for money: More money is needed for transactions purposes. Since the Fed does not change the money supply, we know that interest rates must rise to offset the increase in money demand that came from the increase in GDP. This increase in the interest rate will reduce investment demand and net exports and thus offset some of the stimulus to GDP caused by government spending. The offsetting negative effect is called **crowding out.**

IS-LM in the Business Pages

Not many reporters are versed in the IS-LM model. It's not surprising to find statements like this one in the financial pages:

> A new recession is feared because higher government spending for business bailouts is raising interest rates. Those higher rates are discouraging housing purchases and plant and equipment investment.

More bailout spending shifts the IS curve outward. The economy moves up and to the right along the LM curve. It is true that interest rates are higher, but this is a symptom of higher GDP, not something that will cause a decline in GDP. How about:

> There is concern about declining sales and employment because of the collapse of the dollar. That collapse will be accompanied

by higher interest rates, which will lead to lower investment and total spending.

Same error. The lower dollar will lead to a diversion of demand to domestic products, which will shift the IS curve outward. GDP and the interest rate rise as the economy moves up the LM curve. And:

> The only way to head off the impending recession is to bring the government's deficit under control. Otherwise, high interest rates will choke off economic activity.

It is true that an antideficit move (lower spending or higher taxes) will lower interest rates by moving the IS curve inward, but the result will be to worsen, not head off, an incipient recession.

NUMERICAL EXAMPLE. Explicit numerical values for the effect of changes in the money supply and government spending can be obtained from the numerical IS-LM curves in Equations 7–6 and 7–8. By setting the right-hand side of Equation 7–6 equal to the right-hand side of Equation 7–8 and solving for Y, the level of income that satisfies the IS-LM model can be written as a function of constants, the real money supply, and government purchases:

$$Y = 2{,}015 + 2.887\,\frac{M}{P} + 1.155\,G. \qquad (7\text{–}9)$$

Suppose that the money supply M is \$900 billion, that government spending G is \$1,200 billion, and that the price level is 1. Then Equation 7–9 says that GDP is equal to \$6,000 billion. Plugging this value for Y into either the equation for the IS curve or the equation for the LM curve, we find that the interest rate is 5 percent. Figure 7–6 is drawn accurately to scale for these values. Equation 7–9 says that an increase in government spending of \$1 billion increases real GDP by \$1.155 billion, for a ratio of 1.155. Compare this effect with the government spending multiplier of 2.1 that we found in Chapter 6 in the model where investment is exogenous and net exports depend only on income. The effect is smaller when we take account of the financial system, because interest rates rise and crowd out investment spending. As for monetary policy, if the price level is 1, then an increase in the money supply of $1 billion increases GDP by $2.887 billion.

IS-LM at Work in Three Countries, 1990–92

The U.S. economy entered a recession in 1990, but the slowdown in economic growth actually began more than a year before, in early 1989. Surprisingly, the other major economies did not slow down at the same time as the United States—a development unlike the economic fluctuations for the 1970s and the early 1980s. The German and Japanese economies continued to boom through 1990 and much of 1991. Only in 1992 did these economies slow down. The IS-LM framework provides an explanation.

UNITED STATES. The United States economy was booming in 1987, continuing the long expansion that began in 1982. But there were also signs that inflation was beginning to heat up. To counteract inflationary pressures, the Fed began in early 1987 to tighten monetary policy (that is, it moved the LM curve to the left). The Fed began to tighten more earnestly in 1988 (after it became clear that the 1987 market crash would have no major effects on the economy), and by the end of 1989 the short-term interest rate had risen from under 6 percent to about 10 percent. This tightening of policy led to high interest rates on business and consumer loans. Business investment and purchases of automobiles and other durable goods declined. As a result of the drop in demand, the economy began to slow down in 1989.

As inflationary pressures eased, the Fed lowered interest rates. But monetary policy works with a lag, and slow economic growth continued into 1990 culminating in the recession that began in July 1990. The United States might have avoided a recession if there had not been a drop in consumer confidence and a rise in oil prices associated with Iraq's invasion of Kuwait. But the growth slowdown would have occurred anyway because of these monetary policy developments.

JAPAN. The timing in Japan was almost the opposite of that in the United States. In 1987, when inflationary pressures were rising in the United States, prices were falling in the Japanese economy and there were concerns that economic growth was declining. In any case, by 1987 the Bank of Japan—the central bank of Japan—felt the need to ease monetary policy (that is, it moved the LM curve to the right). Interest rates declined. The Japanese short-term rates eventually got as low as 2.5 percent. As a result, the Japanese economy boomed in 1989 and 1990.

Because of the boom, the Bank of Japan began to raise interest rates again. This occurred as U.S. interest rates began to fall. By late 1991, we were in the unusual situation where interest rates in Japan were higher than in the United States. Interest rates were over 6 percent in Japan and under 4 percent in the United States.

GERMANY. Like the Japanese, the German economy continued to grow through much of 1991. But it was not an easier monetary policy that led to the boom in Germany. Rather it was a shift to an expansionary fiscal policy. Government expenditures related to the reunification of Germany rose substantially in 1990 (that is, the IS curve shifted out). Taxes did not rise as much, and the German deficit rose. This caused the German economy to continue to grow rapidly despite the tightening policies that the Bundesbank—the central bank of Germany—began at almost the same time as the Federal Reserve Bank. However, because the boom continued, inflationary pressures in Germany persisted and monetary policy tightening continued. In 1991 and 1992, interest rates were much higher in Germany than in the United States.

The Relative Effectiveness of Monetary and Fiscal Policies

Monetary and fiscal policies differ in how effective they are in shifting aggregate demand. Two important issues must be faced in determining the relative effectiveness of monetary and fiscal policies:

1. The sensitivity of **investment demand** and **net exports** to interest rates.
2. The sensitivity of **money demand** to interest rates.

The issues can be given graphical interpretations in terms of the *slopes* of the IS curve and the LM curve. First, think about it intuitively.

WHEN IS FISCAL POLICY RELATIVELY WEAK? An expansionary fiscal policy will have a relatively *weak* effect on aggregate demand if interest rates rise a lot and have a large negative effect on investment and net exports. The fall in investment and net exports will offset the positive effect that government spending has on aggregate demand. The fall in investment and net exports will be large under two circumstances, corresponding to the two issues listed above.

1. If the sensitivity of investment demand and net exports to the interest rate is *very large*, then a rise in interest rates will reduce investment and net exports by a considerable amount.

2. If the sensitivity of money demand to the interest rate is *very small*, then the increase in money demand that arises as a result of the increased government expenditures will cause a big rise in the interest rate. (The small interest-rate sensitivity means that the interest rate has to move a lot.)

Another property of the economy that affects the strength of fiscal policy is the spending multiplier (see page 163). A high spending multiplier means more effective fiscal policy. However, if the economy has high interest sensitivity of investment and net exports and low interest sensitivity of money demand, even a very large multiplier will not result in strong effects of fiscal policy.

WHEN IS FISCAL POLICY RELATIVELY STRONG?
An expansionary fiscal policy will have a relatively *strong* effect on aggregate demand if interest rates don't rise by much or have a small effect on investment and net exports. This occurs under circumstances opposite to those listed under weak fiscal policy.

WHEN IS MONETARY POLICY RELATIVELY WEAK?
An expansionary monetary policy will have a relatively *weak* effect on aggregate demand if the drop in interest rates that occurs when the money supply is increased is small or has little influence on investment and net exports. This occurs under two circumstances.

1. If the sensitivity of investment demand and net exports to interest rates is *very small*, then investment is not stimulated much by the decline in interest rates.

2. If the sensitivity of money demand to interest rates is *very large*, then the increase in the money supply doesn't cause much of a drop in interest rates. (A small drop in interest rates is sufficient to bring money demand up to the higher money supply.)

WHEN IS MONETARY POLICY RELATIVELY STRONG?
An expansionary monetary policy will have a big effect if interest rates fall by a large amount and stimulate investment and net exports in a big way. This occurs under circumstances opposite to those listed under weak monetary policy.

The IS-LM Interpretation

The IS curve is relatively flat if investment demand and net exports are very sensitive to interest rates, because small changes in interest rates are associated with big changes in demand. Conversely, the IS curve is relatively steep if investment and net exports are very insensitive to interest rates.

The LM curve is relatively flat if money demand is very sensitive to interest rates, because small changes in interest rates are sufficient to reduce money demand when it increases with a change in income. Conversely, the LM curve is relatively steep if money demand is very insensitive to interest rates.

With these IS slope and LM slope interpretations of the interest-rate sensitivities, we now can review the previous discussion using the IS-LM diagrams. Eight cases exhaust the possibilities, and are shown in Figures 7–8 and 7–9.

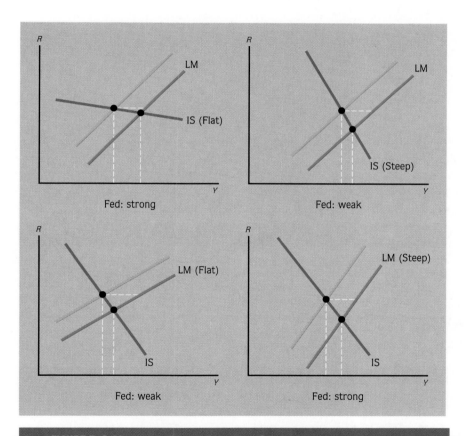

FIGURE 7–8 Monetary policy: weak or strong?

The four IS-LM diagrams illustrate all the possibilities that have bearing on the strength of monetary policy. In some cases the IS curve is flat; in other cases the LM curve is flat. In every case the LM curve is shifted outward by the same amount. At the bottom of each diagram the answer to "Weak or strong?" is given.

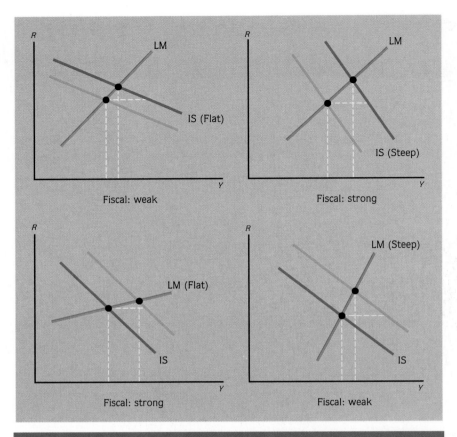

FIGURE 7–9 Fiscal policy: weak or strong?

The four IS-LM diagrams illustrate all the possibilities that have bearing on the strength of fiscal policy. In some cases the IS curve is flat; in other cases the LM curve is flat. At the bottom of each diagram the answer to "Weak or strong?" is given. In all four cases, we assume that the multiplier is the same. A higher multiplier makes fiscal policy stronger in all cases.

WEAK AND STRONG POLICY

1. Monetary policy is strong if the IS curve is flat or the LM curve is steep. Monetary policy is weak if the IS curve is steep or the LM curve is flat.
2. Fiscal policy is strong if the IS curve is steep or the LM curve is flat. Fiscal policy is weak if the IS curve is flat or the LM curve is steep.
3. For given slopes of the IS and LM curves, fiscal policy is more effective if the spending multiplier is large.

The IS-LM diagrams of Figure 7–7 show how monetary *and* fiscal policies affect real output. The Fed controls monetary policy. The President and the Congress control fiscal policy. Ideally, however, these two types of macroeconomic policy should be coordinated. Suppose, for example, that a decline in government spending is planned in order to reduce the budget deficit. The IS-LM diagram tells us that real output will fall in the short run (a leftward shift in the IS curve). A coordinated monetary policy could be used to offset the fall in real output: Just the right amount of a reduction in the interest rate, brought about by an increase in the money supply (a rightward shift in the LM curve), would increase output in the short run by just enough to offset the decline in output brought about by the cutback in government spending. The IS-LM diagram can even be used to calculate the right amount of the decline in interest rates. The intersection of the new (rightward shifted) LM curve and the new (leftward shifted) IS curve gives the value of the interest rate.

Recent research on rational expectations says that these calculations would need to be modified if the decline in the budget deficit were to occur in the future and if it were *anticipated* in advance. With a credible pledge to reduce the budget deficit in the future, people would figure that interest rates in the future would decline. But if future interest rates were expected to decline, then long-term interest rates would decline right away. The rationale is mentioned in Section 7.1: long-term interest rates are affected by expectations of future short-term interest rates. In any case, the decline in long-term rates would increase the demand for investment and thereby begin to offset the contractionary effects of monetary policy right away. This modification implies that the IS curve with the short-term interest rate on the vertical axis should not shift to the left as much. Hence, the decline in short-term interest rates brought on by the Fed would be smaller than if the contractionary fiscal policy were unanticipated.

Fiscal and monetary policymakers were confronted with exactly this coordination problem in 1990 when President Bush and the Congress adopted a multiyear deficit reduction plan. The agreement called for a decline in the deficit—compared with what it would otherwise have been—of about $500 billion over the *future* 5-year period from 1991 through 1995. About $50 billion was to occur in 1991. The Fed—under the chairmanship of Alan Greenspan—indicated that an adjustment of monetary policy would be appropriate if such an agreement on fiscal policy could be worked out and was credible. On October 4, 1990, just after the budget agreement was made, a *Washington Post* headline proclaimed "Fed Chairman Endorses Budget Agreement." Greenspan stated that the administration and Congress had "crafted what appears to be a credible, enforceable, reduction in the budget deficit over a number of years." (*New York Times*, October 5, 1991.)

But what was the right amount of adjustment of monetary policy? Simulations with empirical models based on the IS-LM analysis, but with rational expectations much like that discussed in the previous paragraph suggest a deficit reduction of this magnitude would require a cut in short-term interest rates of about 1½ percentage points to keep real output from being affected in the short run.

The Fed did allow short-term interest rates to decline around the time of the budget agreement, but the actual decline was only about 1/4 percentage point. To be sure, short-term interest rates declined by a larger amount later in 1990 and in 1991, but this was after it was clear that the economy had actually entered a recession.

One interpretation of this episode might be that empirical macro models did not affect the policy decision by much. Another interpretation is that there were doubts at the Fed about the budget deficit reduction package itself. The first version actually did not pass in Congress, and only after a month of further deliberations was a package put together. And despite Chairman Greenspan's initial endorsement, perhaps other monetary policymakers at the Fed had questions about the credibility of the budget deficit reduction. Others did. For example, economists at the Wall Street firm of Salomon Brothers denigrated the budget agreement saying it was "riddled with loopholes." Leonard Silk, economic columnist of the *New York Times*, had faint praise; he wrote, "These numbers look optimistic but are still fairly credible." If budget deficit reduction in the future was not to take place as promised, then monetary ease might be viewed as inappropriate. But whatever interpretation one prefers, the episode illustrates the complexities of macroeconomic research in action.

7.5 DERIVING THE AGGREGATE DEMAND CURVE

With the IS-LM diagrams, we are in a position to derive formally the aggregate demand curve previewed in Chapter 6. The aggregate demand curve is shown in Figure 7–10. The aggregate demand curve tells how much people will demand at a given level of prices. The higher the price level, the less aggregate demand. Hence, as with most demand curves in microeconomics, the aggregate demand curve is downward sloping.

Except as a mnemonic device to remember which way the aggregate demand curve is sloped, the analogy between the standard microeconomic demand curve and the aggregate demand curve of macroeconomics is a weak one, and should not be emphasized. The ideas behind the aggregate

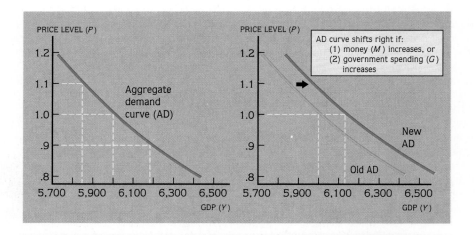

FIGURE 7–10 The aggregate demand curve

On the left is the aggregate demand curve (AD). It shows that aggregate demand is a declining function of the price level. On the right, the aggregate demand curve shifts to the right if either monetary or fiscal policy is expansionary.

demand curve are much different from those that underlie the typical demand curve of microeconomics. In particular, it is important to keep in
mind that the financial system—the demand and supply for money—lies
behind the aggregate demand curve.

   Figure 7–11 is a graphical derivation of the aggregate demand curve.
In the top part of Figure 7–11 is an IS-LM diagram. Recall that changes in

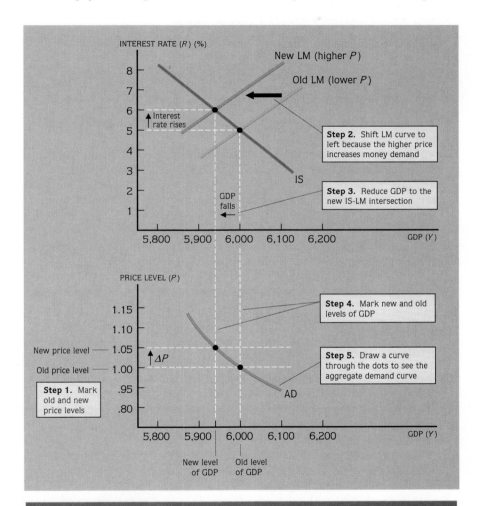

FIGURE 7-11 Derivation of the aggregate demand curve

An increase in the price level shifts the LM curve to the left. This raises interest rates and reduces output. The resulting negative relationship between the price level and GDP is summarized in the aggregate demand curve.

the price level shift the LM curve. Higher prices shift the LM curve to the left, and lower prices shift the LM curve to the right.

Now suppose that the price level rises. The LM curve shifts to the left; this raises the interest rate, lowers investment and net exports, and ultimately lowers GDP. Thus, a higher price level reduces GDP because it increases the demand for money. The increase in demand causes interest rates to rise and causes GDP to fall. The different values for the price level and GDP constitute the aggregate demand curve.

THE AGGREGATE DEMAND CURVE

1. The aggregate demand curve shows what level of GDP will be demanded given a particular price level.
2. The two economic principles governing the aggregate demand curve are spending balance and the equality of the demand and supply of money.
3. The aggregate demand curve slopes downward. A higher price level means that real money balances are lower and therefore that the interest rate is higher. This means that investment, net exports, and GDP are lower.
4. An increase in government spending or an increase in the money supply shifts the aggregate demand curve to the right.

Monetary and Fiscal Policies

Changes in the money supply and in government spending both shift the aggregate demand curve. This is shown in the right-hand panel of Figure 7–10. Suppose that the money supply increases. At a given price level, aggregate demand rises. More money means that a lower interest rate equates money demand with money supply. A lower interest rate stimulates more investment and net exports, which in turn require a higher level of GDP for spending balance. In sum, the aggregate demand curve shifts to the right when the money supply increases.

Fiscal policy also shifts the aggregate demand curve. An increase in government spending shifts the aggregate demand curve to the right. At a given price level, more government spending means more aggregate demand. Conversely, a decrease in government spending shifts the aggregate demand curve to the left.

The effects of fiscal and monetary policies are easily seen by using Equation 7–9. Recall that this equation gives the level of income that satisfies spending balance and money market equilibrium. But that is precisely the aggregate demand curve. All combinations of Y and P that satisfy Equation 7–9 for given values of G and M represent points on the aggregate demand curve. Inspection of this equation shows clearly that increases in M or G will increase Y for a given P; they shift the curve outward.

REVIEW AND PRACTICE

Major Points

1. Investment depends on the interest rate. A higher interest rate discourages some investment projects and lowers total investment.

2. Net exports also depend negatively on the interest rate. A higher interest rate attracts capital from other countries; this drives up the exchange rate and lowers net exports.

3. The IS-LM model determines output, the interest rate, and each of the spending components in the short run. It does not require that the economy operate at its long-run equilibrium.

4. The IS curve shows the level of GDP that brings spending balance for each interest rate. It slopes downward.

5. The LM curve shows the interest rate that brings equality of supply and demand in the money market for each level of GDP. It slopes upward.

6. The IS-LM model answers questions about the effect of policy over the period when it is reasonable to consider prices fixed. Monetary expansion raises output and lowers the interest rate. Fiscal expansion raises output and raises the interest rate.

7. Fiscal policy is most effective when money demand is sensitive to the interest rate and investment and net exports are insensitive to the interest rate.

8. Monetary policy is most effective when money demand is insensitive to the interest rate and investment and net exports are responsive to changes in the interest rate.

9. The intersection of the IS and LM curves tells the levels of GDP and the interest rate for a given price level and fiscal-monetary policies. It corresponds to a point on the aggregate demand schedule.

10. The aggregate demand schedule shows all combinations of GDP and the price level that satisfy spending balance and money market equilibrium for given fiscal and monetary policies. Fiscal and monetary expansions shift aggregate demand out.

Key Terms and Concepts

interest rate   net export function   LM curve
real interest rate   monetary policy   aggregate demand
nominal interest rate   fiscal policy   curve
investment function   IS curve

Questions for Discussion and Review

1. What are the important determinants of aggregate demand? For each one, trace out what happens if it changes.

2. Why does a higher price level raise the interest rate? What could the Fed do to prevent the increase in the interest rate?

3. Explain why the IS curve slopes downward.

4. Explain why the LM curve slopes upward.

5. Explain why the aggregate demand curve slopes downward.

6. Why does a decrease in government spending reduce interest rates?

7. Why does an increase in the money supply reduce interest rates?

Problems

Numerical

1. This problem pertains to the numerical example listed in the box on page 182. Set the price level equal to 1.
   a. Use the algebraic form of the aggregate demand curve to find the level of GDP that occurs when the money supply is $900 billion and government spending is $1,200 billion.
   b. Use the IS curve and the LM curve to find the interest rate that occurs in this same situation. Explain why you get the same answer in each case.
   c. Use the consumption function to find the level of consumption, the investment function to find the level of investment, and the net export function to find the level of net exports for this same situation.
   d. Show that the sum of your answers for consumption, investment, government spending, and net exports equals GDP.
   e. Repeat all the previous calculations if government spending increased to $1,300 billion. How much investment is "crowded out" as a result of the increase in government spending? How much are net exports crowded out?

2. Savings and budget deficits: This problem pertains to the numerical example in the text and makes use of the answers to Problem 1.
   a. Set government spending at $1,200 billion and the money supply at $900 billion. Calculate government saving (the budget surplus). Calculate the level of private saving, and show that private saving plus government saving plus rest of world saving equals investment.

b. Now repeat your calculations for a level of government spending equal to $1,300 billion. Does private saving plus government saving plus rest of the world saving still equal investment? How does each element in the identity change?

c. Explain why private saving increases as a result of government spending. In light of your calculations evaluate the statement: "Government budget deficits absorb private saving that would otherwise be used for investment purposes."

3. Compare the IS curve in the numerical example on pages 188–189 with the IS curve that you get by increasing the coefficient d to 4,000.

   a. What is the slope of each IS curve? Explain in words why the second IS curve is flatter.

   b. For which value of d does an increase in the money supply have a larger effect on output? Why?

   c. Derive the aggregate demand curve in each case. Which has a larger coefficient for M/P? Is this consistent with your answer to Part b?

4. Compare the LM curve in the numerical example on page 189 with the LM curve you get by increasing the coefficient b to 2,000.

   a. What is the slope of each LM curve? Explain why the slopes are different.

   b. For which value of b is monetary policy more powerful? Explain.

   c. Derive the aggregate demand curve in each case. Which has a larger coefficient for M/P? Is this consistent with your answer to Part b?

5. Using the numerical example of the chapter, calculate values for the money supply and government spending that will increase GDP from $6,000 billion to $6,100 billion *without changing the interest rate at all*.

6. The following relationships describe the imaginary economy of Nineland:

$$
\begin{aligned}
Y &= C + I & \text{(Income identity)} \\
C &= 90 + .9Y & \text{(Consumption)} \\
I &= 900 - 900R & \text{(Investment)} \\
M &= (.9Y - 900R)P & \text{(Money demand)}
\end{aligned}
$$

Y is output, C is consumption, I is investment, R is the interest rate, M is the money supply, and P is the price level. There are no taxes, government spending, or foreign trade in Nineland.

The year is 1999 in Nineland. The price level is 1. The money supply is 900 in 1999.

   a. Sketch the IS curve and the LM curve for the year 1999 on a diagram and show the point where interest rate and output are determined. Show what happens in the diagram if the money supply is *increased* above 900 in 1999.

   b. Sketch the aggregate demand curve. Show what happens in the diagram if the money supply is *decreased* below 900 in 1999.

   c. Derive an algebraic expression for the aggregate demand curve in which P is on the left-hand side and Y is on the right-hand side.

   d. What are the values of output and the interest rate in 1999 when the money supply is 900?

Analytical

1. Higher interest rates reduce investment and increase foreign saving. What then must happen to the combination of private and government saving after a rise in interest rates? If neither private nor government saving depends directly on the interest rate, how can this change come about?

2. Graphically derive the LM curve, as in Figure 7–5, using instead a graph that relates money demand to income. (Hint: Put the stock of money on the vertical axis and income on the horizontal axis, and set this diagram above the LM diagram.)

3. Consider the following statements: (i) The IS curve is steep when investment is insensitive to the interest rate. (ii) The LM curve is flat when money demand is insensitive to income. (iii) The LM curve is flat when money demand is sensitive to the interest rate. (iv) The IS curve is flat when the marginal propensity to consume is high.
   a. Explain in words why each of these statements is true.
   b. Confirm algebraically that each statement is true. (Hint: Begin by deciding which coefficient in the model changes. Then show how a change in that coefficient affects the expression for the slope of the IS or LM curve.)

4. Suppose that money demand depended only on income and not on interest rates.
   a. What does the LM curve look like in this case?
   b. Show graphically that G has no effect on the level of output Y. What does G affect?
   c. Show the same thing algebraically. Explain why the LM equation becomes the aggregate demand equation.

5. Show how the IS curve and the LM curve can be shifted to get an increase in output without a change in interest rates. What kind of mix of monetary and fiscal policy is needed to do this? Will a reduction in interest rates while holding output constant do this?

6. Suppose that two administrations, one Democratic and the other Republican, both use fiscal and monetary policy to keep output at its potential level, but that the Democratic administration raises more in taxes and maintains a larger money supply than the Republican administration.
   a. On a single graph, show how the IS and LM curves of these two administrations differ.
   b. Indicate whether the following variables will be higher under the Democratic or Republican administration, or whether they'll be unchanged: consumption, investment, net exports, government saving, and private saving.
   c. Under which administration will foreign holdings of U.S. financial assets grow more slowly?

Macrosolve Exercises

The model "ISLM, Closed Econ" in the Select Model option is described by the following equations:

$$Y = C + I + G$$
$$C = 220 + .63\,Y$$
$$I = 1,000 - 2,000R$$
$$M/P = (.1583 - 1000R)$$

We assume that the tax rate is .1875, so that the marginal propensity to consume out of disposable income is .77538.

The equations for the IS and LM curves for this model are derived in the text as

IS curve: $R = .698 - .000188\,Y + .0004G$
LM curve: $R = .0001583\,Y - .001\ M/P$

1. *Policy Decisions 1997.* You have been hired to work for the Federal Reserve Board and your friend has been hired to work at the Council of Economic Advisers. Although you recognize the Fed's independence, you and your friend decide that is no reason for you not to agree on the correct model of the U.S. economy. You both settle on MacroSolve's "ISLM, Closed Econ." First, get warmed up. Tabulate the results with no change in government spending or the money supply. Confirm that the equilibrium interest rate and the level of GDP are 5 percent and $6,000 billion, respectively.

   a. Your friend is asked by the Council to investigate fiscal policy. Of course you work together. Increase government spending by $50 billion. Display the shifts of the curves (using the Display Model option) to ensure that you understand what is being done. Tabulate the model to find the value of the government spending multiplier. Do you get the same multiplier if you increase government spending by $100 billion? Why?

   b. Convince your friend that this spending increase would be a mistake. How much is investment "crowded out" by a $50 billion increase in government spending? Explain why investment is crowded out by the increase in government spending. If the money supply is constant, under what conditions on the slopes of the IS and LM curves would there be no crowding out in response to an increase in government spending?

   c. Your friend argues that it would not be so bad if the Fed would just accommodate a bit. What is your opinion? By how much would the Fed have to increase the money supply to keep investment from being crowded out at all (i.e., keeping investment constant at $900 billion)? If the Fed increases the money supply to avoid any crowding out of investment, what is the value of the government spending multiplier? The size of this multiplier depends on only two parameters in the model. Which are they?

   d. Just after you finish your simulations the Fed chair calls you in and says a major spending bill ($100 billion) has just been signed by the President. The chair asks you what the Fed should do. What do you say?

2. a. Using the "ISLM, Closed Econ" model, increase the responsiveness of investment to interest rates. Increase government spending by $50 billion (with no change in the money supply). Is the multiplier larger or smaller in this case then in Question 1? What happens to the IS curve? How is fiscal policy affected? Explain in words why the multiplier changes the way it does.

   b. Reset the interest elasticity of investment to its default value, but decrease the marginal propensity to consume. What happens to the IS curve? How is the fiscal policy affected? Explain in words why the multiplier is larger or smaller than it was in your answer to Question 1.

c. Reset the marginal propensity to consume to its default value. Increase the interest elasticity of money demand. What happens to the IS curve? How is fiscal policy affected? Explain in words how and why the multiplier changes.

3. Select the model "ISLM, Closed Econ" and reset all parameters to their default values using the Change Params option. By how much does GDP increase when the money supply is increased by $50 billion?

a. If the interest responsiveness of money demand is increased, explain why a given change in money supply has a smaller effect on GDP than in the default case. What happens to the LM curve? How is monetary policy affected?

b. Reset the interest responsiveness of money demand to its default value, and decrease the interest elasticity of investment. How is monetary policy affected? Explain why this reduces the effect on GDP of a $50 billion increase in the money supply.

c. Is output more responsive to changes in the money supply when the income elasticity of money demand is increased? How is monetary policy affected? Explain why.

CHAPTER
8

The Complete Model

The long-run growth model developed in Chapter 4 is one of the basic components of our complete model. The aggregate demand schedule is the second. In this chapter, we will develop the third major component—the adjustment process that takes the economy from a position out of equilibrium (described by the aggregate demand analysis) back to potential. For the reasons we discussed in Chapter 6, the move to potential is slow. The economic incentives that push the economy toward its equilibrium are relatively weak.

8.1 PRICE STICKINESS AND THE DETERMINATION OF OUTPUT AND UNEMPLOYMENT IN THE SHORT RUN

Recall that prices are sticky in the sense that they are not adjusted quickly by firms in response to demand conditions. Firms wait a while before adjusting their prices. For some period of time, therefore, the price level is stuck at a predetermined level. It is during this time that sellers are waiting to see how demand conditions change before they adjust their prices again. Prices eventually adjust, of course, but not until the next time period—a year or quarter later, for example. For the time being the price level is predetermined.

Determination of Output

Figure 8–1 shows how aggregate demand determines output at a predetermined price. The aggregate demand curve is the same one derived in the previous chapter. The predetermined price is shown by the horizontal line drawn at P_0. GDP is determined by the point of intersection of the aggregate demand curve and the flat predetermined-price line.

Shifts in the aggregate demand curve—caused perhaps by changes in the money supply or government spending—will result in increases or decreases in output. A rightward shift in the aggregate demand curve results in an expansion of output; a leftward shift in the aggregate demand curve results in a contraction of output.

The price level inherited from last year, when combined with the aggregate demand curve, determines the level of output. Output can be below potential output. Then we will observe unemployment and other unused resources. Or output can exceed potential output. These two possi-

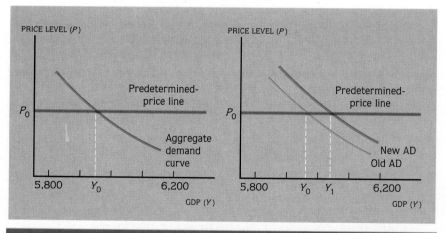

FIGURE 8–1   Determination of output with a predetermined price

The horizontal line shows the price level predetermined for this year at level P_0. This year's output is at the intersection of the aggregate demand schedule and the horizontal line. In the left-hand panel the intersection occurs at the level of output marked Y_0. In the right-hand panel the aggregate demand curve shifts right, and output expands from Y_0 to Y_1.

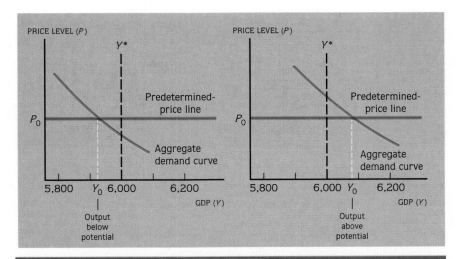

FIGURE 8–2　GDP can be above or below potential GDP

On the left, the level of output is below potential. On the right, the level of output is above potential. Both of these positions will exert pressure on firms to change prices. On the left there is pressure to lower prices. On the right there is pressure to raise prices.

bilities are shown in Figure 8–2, where we have superimposed the vertical potential GDP line to indicate potential. In the left-hand panel of Figure 8–2, output is below potential. In the right-hand panel, output is above potential.

Although the price level doesn't change immediately when firms find themselves producing above or below equilibrium, there is an incentive to move back to equilibrium, as we discussed in Chapter 6. The incentive is to lower prices when output is below potential and raise prices when it is above. A price cut will raise output and a price increase will lower output, so these moves will take the firm and the economy back toward equilibrium.

These adjustments lead to a changed price level for the *next year* or period—not this year. For example, if output is above potential in the year 2001, then the price level will be higher in 2002. When the aggregate demand curve is drawn to determine output for the year 2002, the predetermined price will be drawn at a higher level. If the intersection of the aggregate demand curve for the year 2002 and this new price line is still not at an output level equal to potential, then there will be a further adjustment in prices, but this will not occur until the year 2003. The process continues this way until aggregate demand equals potential output, at which point the desire for firms to adjust their prices will no longer be present. Whether

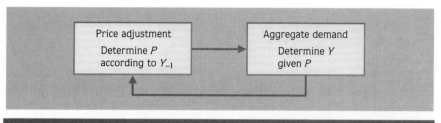

FIGURE 8–3   Dynamic analysis and predetermined variables

The price-adjustment process is shown on the left. It determines the current price level based on the recent past level of output. Then the aggregate demand schedule, shown on the right, determines the level of output given the price level.

or not the process converges depends on the explicit price-adjustment process, which we consider in the next section.

The process by which the price level changes from one year to the next is *dynamic* in the sense that the variables are changing from one period to the next. The impact of a change in the money supply, for example, has effects on the price level that take place over a number of years. The model that we use to describe this dynamic process is an example of a **dynamic model.** The dynamic model is illustrated in Figure 8–3.

DETERMINATION OF OUTPUT IN THE SHORT RUN

1. In the short run, the price level is predetermined. It can change over time but, in a given year, the events of that year have almost no impact on the price level.
2. The level of output is predetermined by the point on the aggregate demand schedule corresponding to the price level.
3. In the short run, output can be below or above its potential level.

Determination of Unemployment

We noted in Chapter 3 that Okun's law establishes a close relation between real GDP and unemployment. When an adverse shock shifts the aggregate demand curve inward, real GDP falls. Figure 8–4 starts with that shift and shows how it generates an increase in unemployment as well. From the decline in real GDP, the lower left-hand diagram converts it into a change in the percentage deviation of GDP from potential, $(Y - Y^*)/Y^*$. Then the right-hand part of the diagram computes the resulting increase in unemployment by applying Okun's law.

A number of important mechanisms are at work in the process described in Figure 8–4. If GDP declines, employers need a smaller amount of labor input. They cut the length of the workweek, they reduce the intensity of work, and they cut the size of the work force. Most of the workers who are laid off become unemployed. In addition, people who are looking for work find it harder to locate jobs. Because of the importance of hours

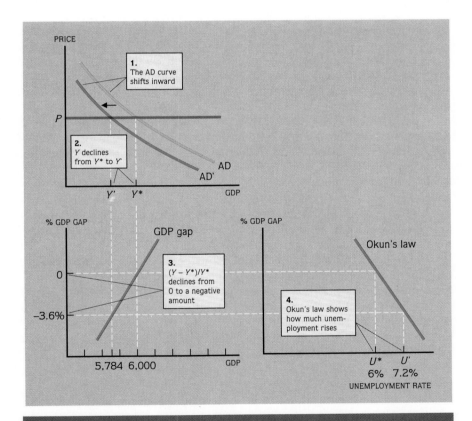

FIGURE 8–4 Determination of unemployment

The upper left-hand diagram shows the aggregate demand curve in its original position and after it shifts inward. Output declines from Y^* to Y'. The lower left-hand diagram translates the GDP decline into percentage terms. The right-hand diagram uses Okun's law to show the amount of increase in unemployment that occurs as a result of the decline in GDP.

reductions and the common pattern of retaining workers during temporary declines in demand (called labor hoarding), a 3 percent decline in GDP is associated with only a 1 percentage point increase in unemployment. This close negative relation is one of the most reliable generalizations that macroeconomists have found. Whenever some force causes GDP to decline, you can be confident that unemployment will rise.

8.2   PRICE ADJUSTMENT

Decisions about prices are made by individual firms. But, moving from the level of the firm to the macro level is tricky. Finding a good way to model aggregate price adjustment has occupied much of the research time of macroeconomics during the last 25 years. Mistakes in understanding price adjustment have generated some of the most glaring errors in the field of macroeconomics.

Firms adjust their prices in response to conditions in their markets. If demand has been strong and they are producing more than they think is appropriate given their current prices, they will raise their prices. If demand has been weak and they are producing less than is appropriate, they will lower their prices. When we look at the process in terms of aggregate variables—GDP and the price level—prices will tend to rise when GDP has been above potential and will tend to fall when it has been below potential. We have already mentioned this aspect of price adjustment in illustrating the dynamic analysis in the previous section.

Specifically, if demand in the previous period Y_{-1} is greater than Y^*, then the price level P in this period will be raised (the subscript "-1" indicates the previous period). Conversely, if demand in the previous period Y_{-1} is below Y^*, then the price level P will be bid down. The percentage difference $(Y_{-1} - Y^*)/Y^*$ measures the pressure on prices to change. Note that, because P depends on Y_{-1}, it is *predetermined*, or set, according to demand conditions prevailing in the recent past.

Firms make their price decisions with the prices of their inputs in mind. The most important input is labor. Hence, the behavior of the wage rate is a major determinant of price adjustment. Wages tend to rise when conditions in the labor market are strong. Remember that, when real GDP is high relative to potential, unemployment is low and employment is high. These are conditions that are likely to lead to rising wages. Wage pressure comes at the same time as the direct pressure on prices, and these two pressures combine to give a relation between the deviation of GDP from potential and inflation.

Economic intuition and historical experience both support the notion that market pressure, as measured by $(Y_{-1} - Y^*)/Y^*$, and inflation should be related. There is a different way to think about the relationship. Suppose a firm and its workers realize that it is in their mutual interest to raise the level of employment. In terms of Figure 6–1, they find themselves at a level of employment below equilibrium, where the value of the workers' time (measured by the labor supply schedule) is below the value of what they produce (measured by the labor demand schedule). The firm decides to produce more output. How can the firm gets its customers to buy the additional output? By setting or accepting a lower price. Thus, even firms that do not have much control over their own prices will obey the positive relation between the output gap, $(Y_{-1} - Y^*)/Y^*$, and price change.

A second factor in the rate of change of prices is inflationary momentum. In times when prices have risen consistently in past years, they will rise this year even if there is no pressure from the market. For example, in 1989, prices rose by almost 5 percent even though the economy was not much above full employment. Inflation in 1987 and 1988 was also close to 5 percent, so it appears that the continuation of inflation at about the same level was the result of momentum. Macroeconomists usually explain the momentum in terms of expectations: When firms and workers expect a particular level of inflation, that level occurs even without any pressure from the output or labor market.

The relation between the change in the price level and its determinants is called the **Phillips curve,** after A. W. Phillips, the British economist who first studied it.[1] We let the Greek letter π stand for the rate of inflation, $(P - P_{-1})/P_{-1}$, and let π^e stand for the expected rate of inflation. The Phillips curve is

$$\pi = \pi^e + f \frac{Y_{-1} - Y^*}{Y^*} \qquad \text{The Phillips Curve} \qquad (8\text{-}1)$$

The coefficient f controls the slope of the Phillips curve. If f is large, inflation responds quickly and the economy moves back to equilibrium rapidly. If f is small, a difference between output and potential persists for many years. Figure 8–5 shows the Phillips curve as a graph. When inflation becomes expected at the rate π^e, it shifts the Phillips curve upward.

The Phillips curve with the expectation term has an important property: If real GDP is above potential GDP on a permanent basis, then the

---

[1]A.W. Phillips fit this type of relationship to data for the United Kingdom from 1861 to 1957. The fit was very good. Phillips actually related percentage changes in wages to the unemployment rate. See "The Relationship between the Unemployment Rate and the Rate of Change in Money Wage Rates in the United Kingdom, 1861–1957," *Economica,* November 1957, pp. 283–299.

rate of inflation will never stop increasing. As actual inflation rises, expected inflation π^e will also begin to rise; as firms see actual inflation increasing, they will begin to expect higher inflation. But then actual inflation will have to be even higher, because GDP can exceed potential only if actual inflation exceeds expected inflation. This property of the price-adjustment equation has been called the **accelerationist** or, equivalently, the **natural rate property.** The terminology comes from the property that if real GDP is brought above its potential level Y^*, then the inflation rate will rise and the price level will accelerate. There is no way for real GDP to be held constantly above its natural level without inflation constantly rising with no limit. In an economy with reasonably stable prices, the level of real GDP will tend to be near potential on the average.

This relationship between expectations and price adjustment was developed in the late 1960s by Edmund Phelps of Columbia University and independently by Milton Friedman. At the time that they developed the relationship, most economists had not considered the role of expectations in the Phillips curve. Friedman presented his controversial theory at a large convention of economists in his presidential address to the American Eco-

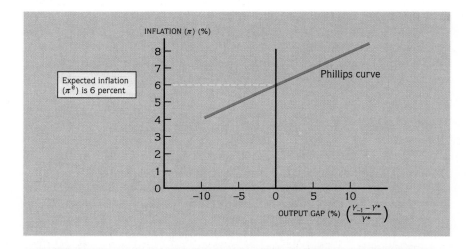

FIGURE 8–5   The Phillips curve

The higher GDP is relative to potential, the higher will be the rate of inflation. When GDP is below potential, the Phillips curve predicts that inflation will be below the expected rate of inflation. In booms, when GDP is above potential, actual inflation will exceed expected inflation. The higher the expected rate of inflation, the higher is actual inflation. The expectational shift is important in explaining persistent inflationary periods, like the 1970s, in the United States.

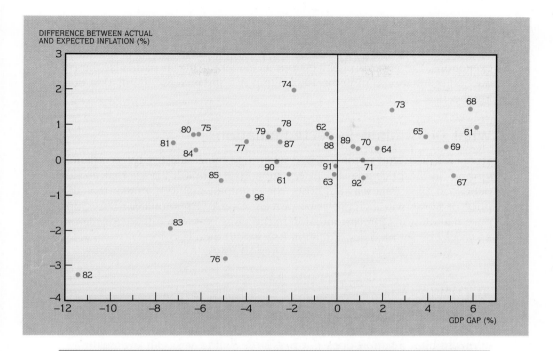

FIGURE 8–6   Price adjustment in the United States since 1960

The horizontal axis shows the percentage departure of GDP from potential. The vertical axis shows the amount of inflation relative to the expected amount. Years in the upper right are ones when output was above potential and inflation exceeded expectations. Years in the lower left are recession years when output was low and inflation subsided. Most, but not all, years fit into the general pattern predicted by the price-adjustment relationship. In this diagram, the expected inflation rate is measured as the inflation rate in the year before.

nomic Association in 1967.[2] At that time inflation in the United States was pretty low and many economists were skeptical of the Friedman-Phelps theory. As it turned out, data that became available in the 1970s showed that Friedman and Phelps were right.

Figure 8–6 shows that there has been a stable Phillips curve price-adjustment relationship of the type proposed by Phelps and Friedman for the period since 1960. The vertical axis measures the amount by which infla-

[2] Friedman's presidential address is found in Milton Friedman, "The Role of Monetary Policy," *American Economic Review,* March 1968, pp. 1-17. Phelps first published his results in Edmund S. Phelps, "Money Wage Dynamics and Labor Market Equilibrium," *Journal of Political Economy,* July–August 1967, pp. 678-711.

tion exceeds expectations and the horizontal axis measures the gap between actual and potential GDP. According to the theory, this relationship should be stable over time and upward sloping. Although there are many exceptions, the general positive slope is evident. Note in particular the reduction in inflation during the 1982 slump and the increase in inflation during the 1968 boom.

What Determines Expected Inflation?

So far we have said nothing about what determines the expected inflation term π^e in the price-adjustment equation. The simplest idea is that π^e depends on past inflation. Suppose, for example, that GM thinks that the price of Fords will increase at 60 percent of last year's inflation rate. Suppose that all firms forecast inflation in the same way. Then the expectation π^e would be set to $.6\,\pi_{-1}$. Equation 8–1 would then become

$$\pi = .6\pi_{-1} + f\frac{Y_{-1} - Y^*}{Y^*}. \tag{8–2}$$

This Phillips curve is based on a particularly simple model of expected inflation. It is a rational way for firms to forecast in an economy where abnormally high inflation does not persist year after year but eventually returns to lower inflation, so that the best guess of inflation would be simply a fraction (like .6) of past inflation. On the other hand, if high inflation tended to last a long time, then people would expect inflation to come down only a little if at all. They might simply extrapolate from the past and set $\pi^e = \pi_{-1}$. In more complex inflationary environments, expected inflation would probably also be more complex, perhaps depending on inflation in the previous two years. Or firms might attempt to guess where inflation was heading based on what they expect the Fed to do with the money supply: If they expect the Fed to start fighting inflation, they might forecast less inflation.

But even if firms attempted to bring future policy changes into their calculations, the past rate of inflation would probably have some influence on expected inflation. Firms know that some prices will continue to rise for a while, even if they suspect that the Fed would start fighting inflation right away. Some price increases would already have been announced by other firms, and these will take place in any case. Wage setting is also a factor in price decisions, and wage increases negotiated in earlier years would continue. For unionized workers, such as the United Automobile Workers, the contractual nature of wage setting is conspicuous. Contracts frequently set wages for as much as 3 years in advance. The contracts of different unions are set at different times. When wage contracts are renegotiated, they are influenced by the wages currently being paid to workers under contracts settled in previous years and by what other workers are likely to get in upcoming years. The expected rate of increase in prevailing wages is thus influenced by past wage decisions, as well as by upcoming wage decisions. Overlapping contracts mean that expected inflation will be related to past inflation even if forecasters are perfectly rational and forward-looking.

We will come back to alternative ideas about expected inflation in Chapter 17. For now we will use Equation 8–2 as our Phillips curve.

Note that the larger the difference between real GDP and potential GDP, the faster will be the change in inflation. Suppose, for example, that the coefficient f in the price-adjustment equation is equal to .2. This value implies that a 5 percent gap between real GDP and potential GDP, which lasts for 1 year, will reduce the rate of inflation by 1 percent. When output is 10 percent below normal for one period, the rate of inflation will be reduced by 2 percent. Of course, the price-adjustment equation works the other way around as well. If real GDP is above potential GDP, then there will be an increase in inflation.

PRICE ADJUSTMENT

1. The process of price adjustment moves the economy toward potential GDP. When the price level is too high, GDP is less than potential, prices fall, demand rises, and eventually full employment is restored.
2. If no inflation is expected, the price-adjustment equation relates the rate of inflation to the deviation of GDP from potential.
3. Under conditions of expected inflation, the price-adjustment relation is shifted upward by the amount of the expected inflation. When output exceeds potential, inflation will exceed expected inflation.
4. A simple model of expected inflation is that expected inflation is given by a fraction of last year's inflation.

8.3

COMBINING AGGREGATE DEMAND AND PRICE ADJUSTMENT

The aggregate demand curve, in combination with price adjustment, governs the dynamic response of the economy to a change in economic conditions. As an example, we will look at what happens to the economy when the money supply is increased. We assume the economy starts out with zero inflation and GDP equals potential GDP. The increase in money initially pushes the aggregate demand curve to the right and increases output. Gradually prices rise to bring the economy back into equilibrium at potential GDP. We now trace out the path of GDP as it returns to potential.

On the left in Figure 8–7 we show the aggregate demand curve intersecting the predetermined-price line. The intersection occurs where output is equal to potential GDP. Suppose that this is the situation in the year 2000 but that starting in 2001 the Fed increases the money supply. The aggregate demand curve shifts to the right, and GDP expands. The economy goes into a boom during 2001, and GDP is above potential GDP. Since the stimulus to aggregate demand comes from monetary policy, we know from the IS-LM model of the last chapter that the interest rate falls, and this stimulates investment spending. Then GDP expands via the multiplier. All this occurs during the year that the money supply increased.

With firms now operating above potential, they will adjust their prices upward. The price line will shift up. We can easily calculate the exact size

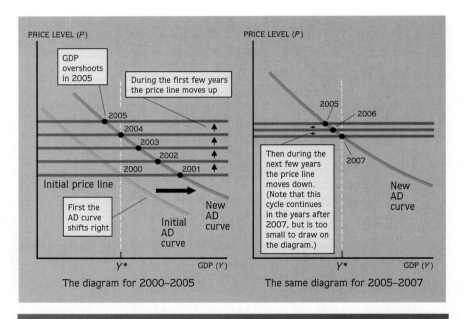

FIGURE 8–7   Aggregate demand and price adjustment

The diagram on the left shows the aggregate demand curve intersecting the predetermined-price line at potential GDP (Y^*). After an increase in the money supply the aggregate demand curve shifts to the right. Then the price line begins to shift up and output declines. GDP falls below potential GDP, but then there is downward pressure on prices and the price line begins to fall. This is shown in the diagram on the right, where we see the same aggregate demand curve during the years after 2005.

of the price adjustment in 2002 using the price-adjustment equation (8–2): Calculate the inflation rate $(P - P_{-1})/P_{-1}$ associated with the level of GDP for 2001. Multiply this inflation rate by the previous price level P_{-1} to get the absolute change in the price level, $P - P_{-1}$, and hence the price level P for 2002. We shift the price line in Figure 8–7 upward by the amount of this price increase. Assuming that the Fed does not increase the money supply again, the same aggregate demand curve continues to apply in 2002. Thus, the new point of intersection of aggregate demand and the price line occurs at a lower level of output compared with 2001. The economy moves up and to the left along the aggregate demand curve.

What is happening in the economy? At a higher price level more money is demanded by people for transactions purposes. But since the Fed doesn't increase the money supply again, this puts upward pressure on the interest rate. The higher interest rate reduces investment below what it was in 2001, and this reduction has multiplier effects throughout the economy. Hence, GDP falls.

According to Figure 8–7, GDP is still above potential in 2002. Thus there will be another upward adjustment in the price level. This time the price adjustment will be the sum of two effects. The two effects correspond to the two terms on the right-hand side of the price-adjustment equation (8–2). Because there was inflation the year before, there will be expectations of continuing inflation in 2002. This factor will add to inflation. On the other hand, output is no longer so far above potential. The contribution from that term in the Phillips curve will be smaller. In the scenario in Figure 8–7, the price rises by about the same amount in 2003 as it did on 2002. Again the aggregate demand curve doesn't move, so output falls again in 2003. As before, the interest rate rises because of the increased demand for money, and this reduces investment.

If output is still above potential or if inflation is still above where it started in 2000, there will be another price adjustment. Hence, GDP will continue to fall. Note that GDP will fall below—overshoot—potential because expected inflation keeps the price line moving up.

This overshooting is shown in Figure 8–7, where GDP falls below potential GDP in the year 2005. But this overshooting creates forces that reverse the decline in GDP and bring it back to potential GDP. When actual GDP is below potential GDP, the depressed economic conditions place downward pressure on prices. As firms bid down their prices, the price line begins to shift down as shown in the right-hand panel of Figure 8–7. As the price line reverses its previous movement and begins to shift down, GDP will start to rise. The process continues period after period until GDP eventually returns to potential. In Figure 8–7 we show GDP getting very close to potential in the year 2006 though there are tiny movements (too small to see on the diagram) after that. By 2007 inflation has returned to zero, where it began in 2000, though the price level has permanently increased.

The price level has increased by the same proportion that the money supply increased.

Note how the graphical analysis in Figure 8–7 is divided into different phases. In the first phase (on the left), the price line is moving up. In the second phase (on the right), the price line is moving down. The graphs are divided into phases because it is confusing to draw in the new price lines for 2006 and 2007 on top of the previous ones for 2000 to 2005. Rather, the new diagram on the right has simply omitted the previous price lines. The important thing to imagine visually is that the price line moves up and then reverses direction and moves down. Getting out a pencil and paper and shifting the price lines yourself will convince you of the dynamic nature of this adjustment process. Alternatively this movement can be shown very nicely with computer graphics in which you can see the price line moving gradually over time. The MacroSolve Exercises at the end of this chapter are designed to illustrate this process.

The fact that the economy returns to potential GDP, as shown in Figure 8–7, is a key result of macroeconomic theory. In the long run, an increase in money does not increase GDP. The increase in money eventually leads to an increase in the price level of the same proportion. This raises interest rates back to where they were before the monetary expansion and eventually reduces investment back to its original level. Note that all other variables—except the price level—are also back to where they were before the increase in the money supply. In the long run the increase in money had no effect on real variables. Thus, our complete model has the property of monetary neutrality in the long run. But money is not neutral in the short run. It has a powerful effect on output in the short run before prices have had a chance to adjust. The same analysis holds in reverse for a decline in the money supply. This short-run effect of money on real output distinguishes our complete model from the real business cycle model of fluctuations. Recall that monetary neutrality holds in that model, even in the short run.

Figure 8–8 is a summary of how GDP and the price level move over time according to the calculations given above. The upper panel shows GDP and the lower panel shows the price level. Notice how GDP returns to potential after overshooting and how the price level permanently rises to a new level.

Fiscal policy works a little differently from monetary policy. Suppose that in the same circumstances government spending, rather than the money supply, is increased in 2001. Again the aggregate demand curve shifts to the right just as in Figure 8–7, and GDP rises. But now, from IS-LM results of the previous chapter, we know that interest rates rise during the first year and thus crowd out investment and net exports and partly offset the stimulus to demand from government spending. As the price level begins to rise, interest rates rise further, and more investment and exports are crowded out.

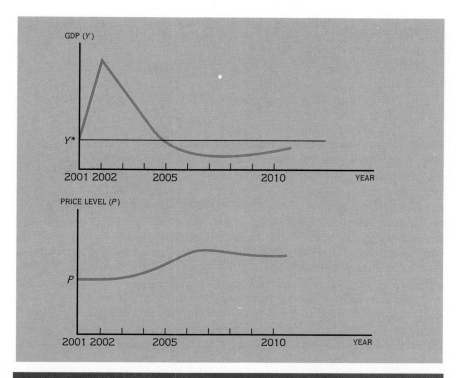

FIGURE 8–8 GDP and the price level after an increase in money

The top panel shows GDP and the bottom panel shows the price level. Time (years) is measured on the horizontal axis of both diagrams. The money supply is increased in the year 2001, which is marked on both graphs. At first, GDP increases and the price level does not move. In 2002 the level of GDP begins to fall, and the price level begins to rise. The movements continue in 2003 and so on until GDP returns to potential GDP, and the price level rises by the full proportion that the money supply increases.

In the long run GDP returns to potential GDP even though government spending has been increased. As a result we know that in the long run investment spending and net exports must have been reduced by exactly the same amount that government spending was raised. Otherwise, the income identity would be violated. In the long run fiscal policy completely crowds out investment spending and net exports. The rise in the price level increases the demand for money; this leads to higher interest rates and less investment spending and net exports. Again, notice that in the long run our complete model preserves the policy implications of the long-run growth model. But since shifts in demand are capable of causing employment to diverge from its equilibrium level in the short run, both fiscal and monetary policy can influence real output in the short run.

Algebraic Derivation

The response of the economy to a change in the money supply can also be analyzed with algebra. Suppose the aggregate demand curve is

$$Y = 3{,}401 + 2.887 \, \frac{M}{P}, \tag{8-3}$$

where we have set government spending to $1,200 billion. We combine this aggregate demand curve with the price-adjustment equation (8–2) to describe the evolution of the economy. We then use Equation 8–2 along with Equation 8–3. The algebraic calculations proceed in flip-flop fashion, just like the graphical analysis: Take the price level as given, use Equation 8–3 to find output Y, and plug the value of output into Equation 8–2. Calculate the inflation rate π and the price level P for the next year. Then go back to Equation 8–3 with the new price level, determine a new output level, and so on. The answers you get at each stage are the same as the ones that can be read off the numerical scales in Figure 8–7.

We have now completed our first description of the complete macroeconomic model. In the short run, the price level inherited from the previous year together with the current aggregate demand schedule determine the level of output. In the medium run, the process of price adjustment moves the economy closer to potential GDP. Eventually, the economy will reach potential GDP. Our next step is to use this complete model to examine the important issues of monetary and fiscal policy.

THE MOVEMENT TO POTENTIAL GDP

1. The aggregate demand curve and the price-adjustment line govern the movement to potential GDP. After being pushed away from potential GDP by monetary policy or fiscal policy—whether toward slack or overfull employment—the economy will eventually reach potential GDP.
2. Because expected inflation responds to past inflation, the economy overshoots potential GDP. However, it will still eventually reach potential GDP.
3. An increase in the money supply increases GDP in the short run, but eventually this effect wears off as the price level rises. In the long run an increase in the money supply has no effect on GDP.
4. An increase in government spending also increases GDP in the short run, though there is some reduction in investment and net exports. In the long run, the stimulus to GDP is completely offset by a decline in investment and net exports as interest rates rise. In the long run fiscal policy completely crowds out investment spending and net exports.

REVIEW AND PRACTICE

Major Points

1. In the long run, the economy moves to potential GDP.

2. In the short run, the price level is predetermined. GDP is determined by aggregate demand at the predetermined price level.

3. The process of price adjustment takes the economy to potential GDP over time. When output is above potential, prices rise; when output is below potential, prices fall.

4. If inflation becomes expected by the public, the price-adjustment schedule is shifted upward by the amount of the expected inflation.

5. The economy reaches potential GDP through the repetition of price adjustment year after year. Each year, conditions in the previous year determine the price level coming into the year. Then the aggregate demand curve determines GDP.

6. Because expected inflation fluctuates according to recent actual inflation, the economy overshoots its potential on the way to its final resting point at potential.

Key Terms and Concepts

predetermined-price level	price adjustment	expected inflation
dynamic model	Phillips curve	accelerationist property

Questions for Discussion and Review

1. Explain how the Phillips curve is derived from a model of relative price setting. What happens to the Phillips curve if firms expect inflation?

2. Explain why money is neutral in the long run but not in the short run.

3. Does government spending completely crowd out private investment and net exports in the long run? What about the short run? Why?

4. Why does the economy overshoot potential GDP when expectations of inflation depend on last year's inflation?

5. What is the accelerationist hypothesis? What would happen to inflation if policymakers attempted to hold unemployment below the natural rate year after year?

6. If firms expect the Fed to start fighting inflation with an aim to bringing it to zero, will their expectations of inflation suddenly drop to zero? Why?

Problems

Numerical

1. Suppose the economy has the aggregate demand curve

$$Y = 3{,}401 + 2.887 \frac{M}{P},$$

and the price-adjustment schedule

$$\pi = 1.2 \left(\frac{Y_{-1} - 6{,}000}{6{,}000} \right).$$

The money supply is $900 billion.
  a. Plot the aggregate demand curve and the potential GDP line. Explain why the *aggregate demand curve is not a straight line.*
  b. If $P_0 = .5$, what will Y_0 be? Will this place upward or downward pressure on prices?
  c. Compute the path of the economy—that is, calculate GDP, the price level, and inflation—for each year until GDP is within 1 percent of potential.
  d. Diagram the economy's path on the demand curve plotted in Part a. Then, draw your own version of Figure 8–7 and 8–8. (You may assume that inflation was initially zero.) From these graphs, does the economy overshoot or converge directly to equilibrium?
  e. Assume now that inflation is given by $\pi = .6\pi_{-1} + 1.2\ [(Y_{-1} - 6{,}000)/6{,}000]$. Compute the path of the economy for the first 5 years, and diagram the economy's path as in Part d. Now is there overshooting?
  f. In Part e, what does the $.6\pi_{-1}$ term in the price-adjustment equation represent? Explain the relationship between this term and overshooting.
2. Again, suppose that the model of the economy is given by

$$Y = 3{,}401 + 2.887M/P$$
$$\pi = .6\pi_{-1} + 1.2\ [(Y_{-1} - 6{,}000)/6{,}000]$$

  a. For what value of M will GDP equal potential? Assuming that $M = \$850$ billion, calculate output, inflation, and the price level for Years 0 through 5.
  b. Using the numerical IS-LM equations given in Chapter 7, find out what happens to the interest rate, consumption, investment, and net exports in each of these years. What is the long-run equilibrium value for each of these variables?
  c. Note that income, consumption, and investment tend to overshoot and undershoot at the same time. Using the IS-LM diagram, explain why this is necessarily so. Why isn't the same true of net exports?

Analytical

1. In view of Okun's law, is it possible for both output and the unemployment rate to increase from one year to the next? Explain.

2. According to the price-adjustment equation (8–2), is inflation a predetermined variable? Explain.

3. Using the expectations-augmented Phillips curve, explain what happens when the unemployment rate decreases for 1 year and then returns to the natural rate. Then describe what happens when the unemployment rate stays below the natural rate year after year.

4. From a position of potential GDP and zero inflation the government increases

defense spending. Describe qualitatively, using words and graphs but no algebra, what happens to GDP, the price level, interest rates, consumption, investment, and net exports. Assume at first that expectations of inflation remain at zero. Then describe how your answers change if expectations of inflation depend on last year's inflation.

5. Suppose that there is a sudden and permanent decline in potential GDP. Describe the behavior of prices, output, interest rates, consumption, investment, and net exports.

6. Suppose that output is below potential output in Year 0. Prices that year are given by P_0. In Year 1 (with the level of potential output unchanged) the Fed stimulates the economy by shifting the aggregate demand curve until it intersects the point (P_0, Y^*).
   a. Sketch the aggregate demand curve for Years 0 and 1. Describe the action taken by the Fed.
   b. Assume that the price-adjustment process is given by Equation 8–2. If inflation in Year 0 was zero, how will prices behave in Year 1? Sketch the price-adjustment curve for Year 1.
   c. Explain why output in Year 1 will be above potential.
   d. In which direction should the Fed have shifted the aggregate demand curve in order to set $Y_1 = Y^*$? Is it possible to say?
   e. Given the Fed's action, is it possible to say whether prices will increase or decrease in Year 2? Why or why not?

7. The Phillips curve originally described a relationship between inflation and unemployment. In this problem we look at some of the properties of the Phillips curve.
   a. Use Okun's law and the price-adjustment equation (8–1) to derive a relationship between inflation and unemployment. Is inflation related to current or past values of unemployment? Sketch a graph of this relationship with inflation on the vertical axis and unemployment on the horizontal axis.
   b. How would a change in Y^* shift the curve? How about a change in U^*?
   c. How would a change in π^e shift the curve?
   d. In view of your answers to Parts b and c, how might the Phillips curve have actually shifted in the 1970s and again in the 1980s? Explain.

8. When thinking about the adjustment process, remember that underlying the aggregate demand curve are the IS and LM curves.
   a. During the adjustment process, is it the IS or LM curve that moves? Why does it move?
   b. Assume that the economy is initially in equilibrium and then the IS curve is shifted out. Using the IS and LM graphs, show the adjustment process (i) for the case when the economy returns directly to equilibrium and (ii) for the overshooting case.
   c. Repeat Part b for the case where the LM curve is initially shifted out.

9. Suppose that at the end of 1991 Y is equal to potential, $P = 1.2$, and $M = \$1,080$ billion. Assume that prices in 1991 have risen by 5 percent. The aggregate demand and price-adjustment equations for the economy are given by:

$$Y = Y_0 + 2.887M/P$$
$$\pi = \pi^e + f[(Y_{-1} - Y^*)/Y^*]$$

a. What is the real money supply? What is the nominal money supply?

b. Suppose the Fed wishes to maintain output at a potential for each of the years 1992 through 1995. If $\pi^e = \pi_{-1}$, what are the required increases in the real and nominal money stocks for each of the four years? Repeat your calculations for $\pi^e = .6\pi_{-1}$.

c. Qualitatively, how would your answers to Part b differ if the Fed expected government spending to increase in each of these years?

MacroSolve Exercises

In this chapter, we continued to use the basic model of aggregate demand. To it, we added consideration of potential output, and price adjustment when output differs from potential output. The price-adjustment schedule that we added has the form

$$\pi = .8 \left[(Y_{-1} - Y^*)/Y^* \right] + \pi^e.$$

1. Suppose, first, that $\pi^e = 0$ (i.e., that there is no expected inflation). This model is available in the Select Model option as "AD/PA zero exp. π." Change government spending by $100 billion and make a table of multipliers (the change in GDP per dollar change in government spending) for each time period. Explain in words why the steady-state (or long-run) multiplier differs from its value in Equation 7–9.

2. Now select the "AD/PA, Closed Econ" model in which inflation expectations are determined in the following manner: $\pi^e = .4\pi_{-1} + .2\pi_{-2}$. Repeat the analysis of Question 1 with this model. Explain why the time taken for the multiplier to settle down to its long-run value differs from the previous case.

3. Is adjustment of the price level to a change in the money supply faster or slower when inflation expectations respond to past inflation (as in Question 2) than when they do not (Question 1)? Explain why.

4. *Policy Decisions 1997.* You have been hired by the Bundesbank—the central bank of Germany. You were hoping to help in the continuing transition of the former East Germany into a market economy. But the president of the Bundesbank finds out you did well in macroeconomics and that you kept your copy of MacroSolve. The last 6 years have seen continued trouble with the budget deficits with constant pressure on the Bundesbank to ease policy. But the Bundesbank has remained tight trying to fight inflation.

a. Use the dynamic model ("AD/PA, Closed Econ") to show what would be predicted to happen to interest rates, output, saving (which you can calculate as the differences between disposable income and consumption), and investment under an expansionary fiscal policy and a tight monetary policy.

b. In order to defend the Bundesbank policies, the president of the Bundesbank asks you to prepare a comparison of the German experience with that of the United States in the years 1981 to 1986. Check the actual data for the U.S. economy during this period by plotting, tabulating, or graphing them to see if the theoretical predictions for these variables actually occurred. Were there any significant deviations from the model's predicted results? If so, give reasons to the Bundesbank president.

CHAPTER 9

Macroeconomic Policy: A First Look

Monetary and fiscal policy have powerful effects on the economy. Changes in the money supply or in government spending have an immediate impact on real GDP and a delayed impact on the price level. An increase in the money supply, for example, will stimulate output and employment in the short run, with inflation rising later, and real GDP eventually returning to normal.

Because monetary and fiscal policies have such powerful effects on the economy, they are constantly being discussed and debated. When the chairman of the Federal Reserve Board testifies in Congress, hoards of news reporters crowd the room. They stampede out of the room to call their newsrooms whenever anything about interest rates is mentioned. Each sentence is dissected for clues about whether the Fed might increase or decrease the interest rate. "Fed Chairman Hints Easier Money Policy" might be the headline in the next morning's *Wall Street Journal*. Guessing right means big profits to those involved with financial markets, but the news has an impact on all of us, as for instance on those of us who are buying or selling a home and are concerned about what happens to mortgage interest rates.

Discussions about fiscal policy usually focus on the deficit. The deficit is probably the most talked about economic statistic in the United States.

Concerns about interest rates and investment are part of the reason. An increase in government spending will obviously increase the deficit if not matched by an increase in taxes. Our analysis shows that an increase in the deficit will increase interest rates, and crowd out some investment even as it stimulates the economy in the short run.

In this chapter we take a systematic look at the formulation and evaluation of macroeconomic policy, that is, monetary and fiscal policy. The fact that monetary and fiscal policy have the potential to affect the economy suggests that these policies might be used to improve macroeconomic performance. We will want to investigate whether this is the case.

Sometimes there are economic **shocks** or **disturbances** to the economy that might call for policy response. We distinguish between two types of disturbances in this chapter: **aggregate demand disturbances** and **price disturbances.** An aggregate demand disturbance is some event other than a change in policy that shifts the aggregate demand curve. A price disturbance is some event that shifts the price-adjustment relationship. The immediate effect of a price disturbance is to change the price level, unless policy acts to offset the disturbance. Another important policy problem is disinflation—getting the inflation rate down after it has been built into the economy. This chapter considers the appropriate policy responses.

We will also consider the issue of how to choose between monetary and fiscal policy. Both types of policies can shift aggregate demand, but they have different effects on investment and net exports.

9.1   SHOCKS AND DISTURBANCES TO THE ECONOMY

Unforeseen or unpredictable events are commonplace in the economy. At the most basic level, many of the relationships we use to describe the economy depend on human behavior, which is frequently erratic. Keynes used the term "animal spirits" to characterize the moods of business people. Other economic relationships depend on technology; the money demand relationship, for example, depends on how technically advanced the financial system is. It seems that, no matter how successful we are in describing the systematic parts of economic behavior, there will always be some room for uncertainty, and thus for shocks and disturbances to our economic relationships. The model we developed in Chapters 4 through 8 would certainly be affected by such shocks.

Shocks to Aggregate Demand

Consider some examples of shocks to the behavioral relationships of the extended model of aggregate demand:

1. Foreign demand suddenly shifts away from U.S. goods. Net export demand falls.

2. A new type of credit card makes it easier to get by with less cash. The money demand schedule shifts inward.

These two examples are illustrated graphically in Figure 9–1. The reduction in the demand for exports shifts net exports inward for each interest rate. The decline in money demand shifts the demand for money inward for each interest rate.

Disturbances can be distinguished according to whether they are temporary or permanent. This distinction is important for policymakers: A temporary disturbance might be ignored because its effects will disappear soon anyway. In practice it is difficult to distinguish between temporary and permanent shocks when they occur. In the following examples we will assume that the disturbances are permanent.

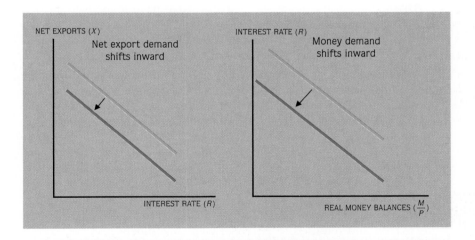

FIGURE 9–1   Shocks: inward shifts in net exports and money demand

On the left, a shift in foreign demand away from U.S. goods shifts the net export schedule inward. On the right, deregulation reduces money demand. The money demand function shifts inward.

Analyzing the Effects of Aggregate Demand Shocks

We will look at the effects of different kinds of disturbances on the aggregate demand curve. Before we start, we need to clarify one point. Monetary and fiscal policies are themselves important determinants of the shape and position of the aggregate demand curve; the curve is not just a property of the economy itself. In order to talk about the effect of a disturbance on the curve, we need to take a position on how monetary and fiscal policy will react to the disturbance. To start the discussion, we will assume that monetary policy keeps the money stock the same no matter what kind of disturbance hits the economy. We will also assume that fiscal policy—taxes and spending—does not respond at all to the disturbance. Both these assumptions are arbitrary. The first was not true of the U.S. economy in the 1980s and early 1990s while the second was generally true. Later we will turn to more realistic assumptions about the Fed's response to disturbances.

Under our assumptions about monetary and fiscal policies, disturbances both to spending and to money demand, the two major components of our model of aggregate demand, shift the aggregate demand curve: The downward shift in net export demand pushes the aggregate demand curve to the left. The downward shift in money demand has the same effect as an increase in the money supply, which we know shifts the aggregate demand curve to the right.

These shifts in the aggregate demand curve have immediate impacts on real GDP, as shown in Figure 9–2.

From the analysis used in Chapter 8 we can trace out the full dynamic movement of the economy in response to the aggregate demand shocks:

1. With real GDP below potential GDP after the drop in net exports, the price level will begin to fall. Firms have found that the demand for their products has fallen off and they will start to cut their prices. This drop in the price level is shown in Figure 9–2 as a movement down and to the right along the aggregate demand (AD) schedule. The lower price level causes the interest rate to fall. With a lower interest rate, investment spending and net exports will increase. The increase in investment and net exports will tend to offset the original decline in net exports. This process of gradual price adjustment will continue as long as real GDP is below potential GDP. By the time that real GDP has again recovered and returned to potential GDP, investment and net exports will have increased by just the amount that net exports fell in the first place. The interest rate will be lower by enough to stimulate this much investment and net exports. In the long run, real GDP will be back to normal, but during the period of gradual price adjustment the economy will have gone through a recession with an increase in unemployment.

2. When the demand for money drops, the aggregate demand curve will

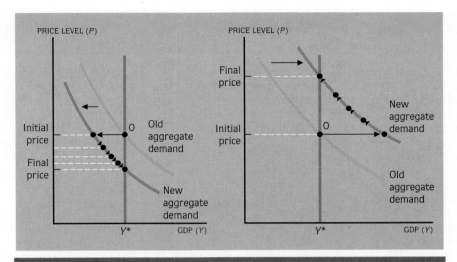

FIGURE 9–2 Disturbances shift the aggregate demand schedule

On the left, aggregate demand has shifted inward because of the decline in the net export schedule. On the right, aggregate demand has shifted outward because of the decline in money demand. On the left, GDP falls at first. Then the economy moves down and to the right along the AD schedule until it reaches equilibrium again at a lower price level. On the right, GDP rises at first. Then the economy moves up and to the left along the AD schedule until it reaches equilibrium again at a higher price level.

shift outward. The interest rate drops; investment, net exports, and consumption rise. But higher GDP will cause prices to rise, and this will tend to raise the interest rate. Through this process of gradual price adjustment the economy will eventually return to normal. In the mean time, however, the economy has experienced a period of inflation and a boom in economic activity.

To summarize the examples, in both cases there is a shock to aggregate demand that temporarily moves the economy away from potential GDP and sends the economy into either a boom or a recession. Through gradual adjustment of the price level, the economy eventually returns to normal.

Shocks to the Price Level

The shocks considered so far had the effect of shifting the aggregate demand curve. Another type of shock occurs when the price level shifts. There are several reasons why this might occur:

1. The price of an input to the economy might suddenly rise; the best example is an increase in the price of oil, such as occurred in the 1970s

Model Validation: Four Oil Price Shocks

The U.S. economy was buffeted by four major oil price shocks in the last 20 years. In 1973, the Arab oil embargo ushered in a huge increase in the price of crude oil and oil products. In 1978, the Iranian revolution and the Iran-Iraq war set off another large increase. At the beginning of 1986, the oil market collapsed. Finally, in 1990, the Iraqi invasion of Kuwait caused a near doubling of crude oil prices.

To measure the size of the shocks themselves, we can look at the retail price of gasoline, as reported in the consumer price index (CPI). The percentage changes in gasoline prices for the four episodes were:

1973–74 Embargo	1978–79 Revolution	1985–86 Collapse	1989–90 Invasion of Kuwait
35	35	−22	14

Oil price shocks are clearly passed along into total inflation. The *increases* in the rate of inflation as measured by the overall CPI were:

1973–74 Embargo	1978–79 Revolution	1985–86 Collapse	1989–90 Invasion of Kuwait
4.8	3.7	− 1.7	0.6

Moreover, as the aggregate demand analysis suggests, the economy moves down along the AD schedule when a price shock occurs. The changes in GDP in the year following the shocks were:

1975	1980	1987	1991
-.8	− .5	3.9	− .7

The effects are quite pronounced and confirm the predictions of the model in all four cases.

and again in 1990. Suppose that there is a cutback in crude oil production and, as a result, an increase in the price of crude oil. This will tend to increase the price of all petroleum-related products. Moreover, prices in other energy industries will also tend to increase. Unless there is a fall in the price of other goods, when the price of crude oil rises there will be an increase in the overall price level.

2. A large group of workers—perhaps during a union negotiation—may get a wage increase that is abnormally high. When firms pass on the wage increase in the form of higher prices, there will be an upward shift in the price level—a price shock.

3. Firms might simply make a mistake and increase their prices, perhaps because they mistakenly expected an increase in inflation.

A price shock is shown in Figure 9–3. If monetary and fiscal policies do not change, then real GDP will fall below potential GDP. After the initial price shock the economy will be operating below its full-employment level

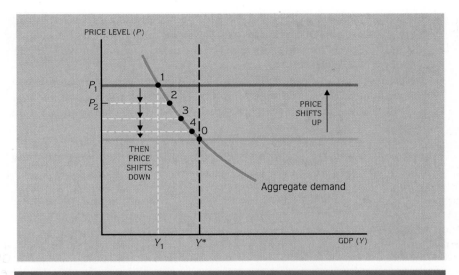

FIGURE 9–3   An upward shock in the price level

Real GDP is reduced when the price level jumps up; the economy moves to point 1, up and to the left along the aggregate demand curve. Then the process of price adjustment causes the economy to return gradually to its original equilibrium as the price level falls.

at Y_1. With no increase in the money supply, this will in turn cause prices to fall as firms try to cut prices to increase sales. The fall in prices corresponds to a downward movement in the price-adjustment curve, which will continue until real GDP is equal to potential GDP. Eventually, therefore, the economy returns to normal operating levels. In the meantime the price shock has caused a recession. The period of recession puts downward pressure on prices and offsets the original price shock.

ECONOMIC SHOCKS

1. There can be unexpected shifts in spending; for example, the amount of investment undertaken by businesses at any given interest rate might rise or fall.
2. There can be unexpected shifts in the money market; for example, the amount of money demanded by the public at any given interest rate might rise or fall.

3. Spending or money market shifts will in turn shift the aggregate demand curve. At first, real GDP will rise or fall. Later, as price adjustment occurs, real GDP will return to equilibrium and the price level will move to a permanently different level.

4. Prices may shift unexpectedly as well. When that occurs, real GDP will change at first. Then price adjustment will return the economy to its original equilibrium. Neither the price level nor GDP will change in the long run.

9.2 RESPONDING TO AGGREGATE DEMAND SHOCKS: STABILIZATION POLICY

In considering appropriate responses to aggregate demand shocks, let us first consider the case of a shift in the aggregate demand curve caused by a shift in the demand for money. A negative shock to money demand occurs because people want to hold less money at every interest rate and income level than they did before. In the early 1990s some economists at the Federal Reserve Board worried that a negative shift to money demand was occurring because people were putting less money into savings accounts at Savings and Loans, as many of these institutions were being shut down. Positive shocks are also possible. For example, increased money demand could be caused by an increase in uncertainty about the future, creating the need for very liquid assets such as cash and demand deposits.

Figure 9–4 shows the effect of an *increase* in money demand. Unless the Federal Reserve takes action to offset such a change in money demand, interest rates will rise and the aggregate demand curve will shift to the left. What action would be appropriate for the Fed? An increase in the money supply to match the increase in money demand would exactly offset any leftward movement in the aggregate demand schedule shown in Figure 9–4. On the other hand, if a negative shock to money demand were occurring in 1990 and 1991, then the appropriate policy for the Fed would be to reduce money growth. In fact, money growth was below the Fed's targets in both 1990 and 1991.

Other types of aggregate demand shock raise many of the same issues for aggregate demand policy. In 1991 there was a sharp decline in consumer confidence, which caused a slump in consumption that pushed the aggregate demand schedule to the left. Without any policy response we know from the discussion above that this will result in a temporary decrease in GDP followed by a period of decrease in the rate of inflation. Pol-

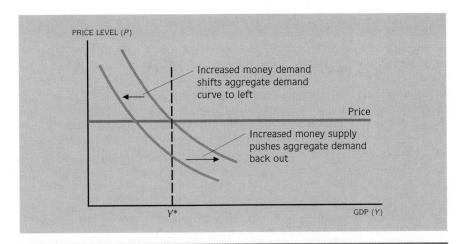

FIGURE 9–4　Increase in money demand

An increase in money demand shifts the aggregate demand schedule to the left; that is, it raises interest rates and reduces real GDP. Timely action by the Fed to increase the money supply could offset the reduction in GDP.

icymakers could avoid this instability by taking some action to increase aggregate demand: The money supply or government spending could be increased or, alternatively, taxes could be cut. Any of these actions would have the effect of bringing the aggregate demand schedule back to the right. In fact, many economists argued that such actions were appropriate in 1991.

The type of aggregate demand policy outlined in these two examples is called **countercyclical stabilization policy,** because it attempts to counter those disturbances to the economy that otherwise would cause cyclical fluctuations in real GDP and the price level. Such a policy is also sometimes called *activist,* because the policymakers are actively manipulating the instruments of monetary and fiscal policies.

When Do Macroeconomists Disagree about Stabilization Policy?

The underlying objective of policy in the above examples is to maintain a steady or stable level of aggregate demand. The importance of a stable aggregate demand has been recognized by most economists since the 1930s. Even economists who normally differ on other issues agree on the principle that it is desirable to maintain a stable growth of aggregate demand.

Keynesians such as the late Walter Heller of the University of Minnesota and James Tobin of Yale University, who served together on President Kennedy's first Council of Economic Advisers, agree with monetarists such as Milton Friedman, new classicals such as Robert Lucas, and new Keynesians such as Edmund Phelps of Columbia University. As we showed in Chapter 2, the U.S. economy has been much more stable in the period following World War II—even if one includes the turbulent 1970s and early 1980s. Many economists feel that this improvement in macroeconomic performance is related to the recognition of the importance of stable aggregate demand growth. The late Arthur Burns, a conservative who was chairman of the Federal Reserve Board, argued persuasively that changes in economic policy that stabilized aggregate demand were responsible for the improvement in performance after World War II.[1]

If macroeconomists agree on such a basic issue as the goal of stable aggregate demand growth, then what is all the highly publicized controversy and disagreement about? Primarily, it is about the means of achieving this goal. Monetarists argue that the most effective way to maintain a steady growth of aggregate demand is to keep the rate of money growth constant. But how does such a view make sense in light of our previous arguments that timely changes in the money supply can be used to offset disturbances to the economy?

Monetarists have no disagreement about the powerful effects that changes in the money supply can have on real GDP in the short run; for example, Milton Friedman has said, "Because prices are sticky, faster or slower monetary growth initially affects output. . . . But these effects wear off. After about two years the main effect is on inflation.[2] However, for a number of reasons, monetarists feel that it is not possible to use monetary policy in the way that we illustrated. Their criticism of activist policy is that the impact of monetary policy occurs with a lag and the length of this lag is uncertain. Because of the lag, monetary stimulus or restraint may come too late. In an attempt to offset a decline in investment, the policy response may come after the recession is over, when the economy is recovering back to potential GDP. This might add to the expansion in economic activity and exacerbate the economic fluctuations. Figure 9–5 illustrates this possibility. Because of the practical difficulties of conducting monetary policy in an uncertain world, monetarists argue that attempts to manipulate monetary policy to offset disturbances to the economy could result in more rather than fewer fluctuations in economic activity.

---

[1]See Arthur Burns, "Progress toward Economic Stability," in his *The Business Cycle in a Changing World,* (New York: Columbia University Press, 1979).
[2]See *Newsweek,* July 12, 1982, p. 64.

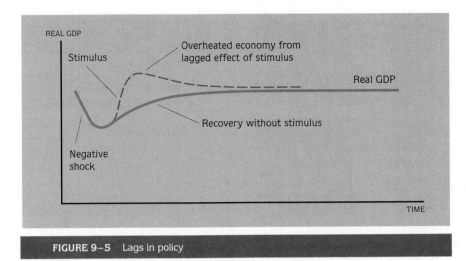

FIGURE 9–5   Lags in policy

A change in a policy instrument that arrives too late might exacerbate the fluctuations in the economy.

A second argument of the monetarists against activist countercyclical policy is that the instruments of policy might be used to overstimulate the economy and bring about higher and higher rates of inflation. In our examples of countercyclical policy we never considered the possibility that policymakers might try to push the economy beyond its potential output Y^*. But clearly this is feasible. With prices temporarily sticky, real GDP can be raised above potential output Y^*. The long-run consequence of such a policy will be a higher price level, but, in the short run, real GDP growth could appear quite attractive. The danger of such an inflationary policy becomes quite serious when policy decisions are made in a political environment, as usually happens in the United States. The long-run disadvantages of such a policy may be overlooked in favor of short-run advantages when election day nears.

A fundamentally different objection to countercyclical policy comes from some new classical and real business cycle economists who view GDP as being close to its potential value in recessions and booms as well as in normal times. Monetary policy just affects the price level in their view; it has no effect on output and employment. They think it would be frivolous to try to use monetary policy to offset a decline in employment in a recession. In the long run fiscal policy can affect employment and output in their model, but its use to offset fluctuations is probably undesirable.

POLICY RESPONSE TO DEMAND SHOCKS

1. When an aggregate demand shock occurs, monetary or fiscal policy can offset the shock. Whatever inward or outward shift of the aggregate demand curve has taken place can be reversed through a policy move in the opposite direction.
2. Though almost all economists agree on the desirability of stable aggregate demand, many believe that active policy might add to the instability rather than offset it. Monetarists generally oppose enacting policy that attempts to act against aggregate demand shifts.
3. Another argument against active policy comes from economists who believe that a systematic policy of offsetting demand disturbances won't have any effect on GDP.

9.3   RESPONDING TO PRICE SHOCKS

The response to a price shock raises more difficult issues than does the response to a demand shock. Even under the best of circumstances—no lags or uncertainty in the conduct of policy—such a shock will inevitably affect either the price level or real GDP.

Suppose, for example, that there is a price shock of the type illustrated in Figure 9–6. As we discussed above, with no policy response, such a price shock tends to reduce real GDP and raise the price level. This is shown in the left-hand panel of Figure 9–6.

Now, suppose that the monetary authorities increase the money supply in response to the price shock. As shown in the right-hand panel of Figure 9–6, this shifts the aggregate demand curve outward and tends to mitigate the downward fluctuation in real GDP. However, the increase in the money supply will accommodate the temporary increase in the price level. If output does not fall much below potential, there will be little downward pressure on the price level. The price level will stay high for a longer time and never return to normal if the money supply is not reduced. As shown in the right-hand panel of Figure 9–6, the price line will remain at a higher level if the aggregate demand curve remains at its new higher position. In the sense that there is less downward pressure on the price level so that it never returns to normal, there is thus less long-run price stability with the policy that tries to offset the fluctuation in real GDP. In other words, with a price shock there is a trade-off between the stability of real GDP and the stability of the price level.

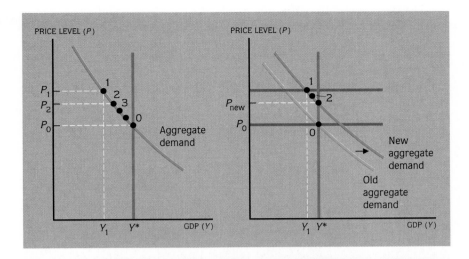

FIGURE 9–6 Monetary response to a price shock

On the left, monetary policy does not respond to the price shock. The shock raises the price level from P_0 to P_1. Output falls from Y^* to Y_1. Then the price-adjustment process starts. In the next year the price level drops to P_2. Eventually prices fall back to normal and output returns to potential output. On the right, monetary policy responds to the price shock. The money supply is increased and the aggregate demand curve moves outward. At the new intersection of the price line (point 1), there is less downward pressure on the price level because output at Y_1 is closer to potential than in the panel on the left. Assuming that the new aggregate demand curve is maintained, eventually the price level falls to the level marked P_{new}.

Policies that increase the money supply in response to positive price shocks are called **accommodative policies.** A policy that holds the money supply constant is called **nonaccommodative.** Figure 9–7 summarizes, for the two policies, the behavior of GDP and the price level after a price shock. The plots show the results of the calculations of GDP and the price level from Figure 9–6. The accommodative policy is better in terms of GDP performance, but worse in terms of price level performance.

POLICY RESPONSE TO PRICE SHOCKS

1. In the absence of a policy response (that is, with a nonaccommodative monetary policy), a positive price shock causes a rise in the price level and a sustained period of economic slack.
2. Price shocks create a serious problem for policy. If policy tries to limit the decline in GDP from a positive price shock, it will make the price level less stable. If it tries to head off the inflation, it will deepen the recession.

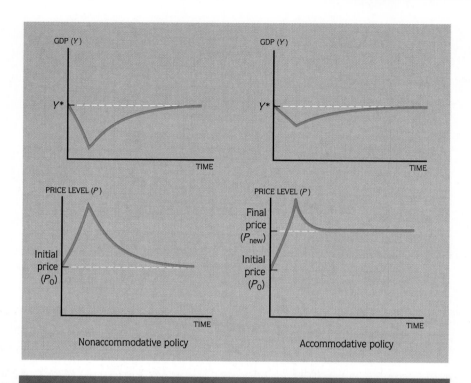

FIGURE 9–7   The response of the price level and GDP to price shocks for accommodative and nonaccommodative policies

These charts summarize the calculations from Figure 9–6. The nonaccommodative policy is shown on the left and the accommodative policy is shown on the right. Output is more stable with the accommodative policy, but the price level is less stable.

MONETARY POLICY AS A RULE: HOW THE FED PICKS THE AGGREGATE DEMAND CURVE

9.4

Our discussion of the appropriate response of monetary policy to price shocks naturally gives rise to the question of whether the money supply is an exogenous variable, as we have been assuming all along. If the money supply responds to the price level, then it no longer can be exogenous for it is determined in the model.

Treating policy variables as exogenous has long been a tradition in macroeconomics. But more recently an alternative view, that they should be treated as endogenous, is becoming more attractive. Endogenous policy is determined according to some behavioral relationship, or what is frequently called a **policy rule.** The most frequently discussed policy rule in macroeconomics is the fixed growth rate rule for the money supply that Milton Friedman and other monetarists have advocated. A fixed growth rate rule is simply to keep the growth rate of the money supply constant. But this is a very special rule in that it involves no response of the money supply to economic events. A more general rule would call for some response.

Even if policymakers do not determine policy according to a mechanical formula, they do respond to economic events much like the firms and consumers in the economy. Their behavior and its impact on the economy are therefore probably more accurately described by a systematic behav-

Okun Gaps and Harberger Triangles

As in the microeconomic analysis of intervention in particular markets, the case for macroeconomic intervention rests on identifying some kind of market failure that can be corrected. Recessions appear to be market failures. The marginal product of labor exceeds the value of workers' time. The basic case for an expansionary intervention is that there is a social gain equal to the difference between marginal product and value of time. The most active debate in macroeconomics concerns the magnitude of that social gain. The late Arthur Okun of the Brookings Institution was a strong advocate of intervention to offset recessions; the social gain from correcting a recession is sometimes called the "Okun gap" as a result. Arnold Harberger of the University of Chicago pioneered the measurement of the social cost of market failure at the microeco-

nomic level by measuring the area of the triangle formed between the supply curve and the demand curve when the quantity produced is below the equilibrium level. James Tobin of Yale University—another ardent proponent of aggressive policies to offset recessions—made the famous remark: "It takes a thousand Harberger triangles to fill an Okun gap." He meant that the social cost of a recession dwarfed the costs of the failures that occur in individual markets.

Other macroeconomists are less convinced of the importance of market failure. For example, Robert Lucas of the University of Chicago has calculated the welfare benefits from a policy of smoothing out the fluctuations of the economy but keeping the same average level of production. He finds the benefits to be tiny.

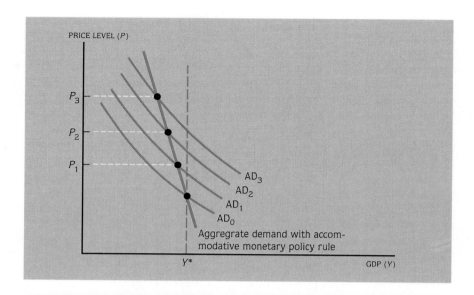

FIGURE 9–8 The aggregate demand schedule with an accommodative policy rule

If the price shock is small, so that the price level is P_1, the Fed sets the money supply so that the AD schedule is AD_1. For larger shocks that raise the price level to P_2 or P_3, the Fed raises the money stock more, so that the corresponding AD schedule is AD_2 or AD_3. The set of intersections traces out a steeper aggregate demand schedule. This schedule includes the monetary response to price shocks.

ioral relationship. If so, we can think of the behavioral relationship as a policy rule.

We saw in Section 9.3 that an accommodative monetary policy was one that reacted to a positive price shock with an increase in the money supply. We showed the effect of this type of policy on the fluctuations of real GDP and the price level, by treating the money supply as exogenous. If the Fed regularly, or systematically, reacted to price disturbances in this way, then we would say that the Fed was following an accommodative policy rule. The money supply would not be an exogenous variable. It would join the list of endogenous variables to be determined in the basic macroeconomic model. As with the other endogenous variables, a behavioral relationship would describe how the monetary authorities determined the money supply. In fact, the policy rule *is* that behavioral relationship.

The derivation of the policy rule and its effects on the economy can be shown graphically. In Figure 9–8 we show how the monetary authorities react to price shocks. There are several different price lines drawn.

Each line represents a price shock of a different magnitude. For each price shock, we show how the Fed reacts by shifting the aggregate demand schedule outward. This accommodative reaction leads to intersections of the aggregate demand curve and the price line at higher levels of real GDP than would otherwise occur, shown by the darker colored line. This line represents the combined effects of the accommodative policy and the price shocks. Note that it is downward sloping—like an aggregate demand curve—but it is steeper than the aggregate demand curve without the influence of policy. In effect, the policy of responding *as a rule* to price shocks leads to a steeper aggregate demand curve. An accommodative monetary policy rule twists the aggregate demand curve clockwise, and makes it steeper. The more accommodative the policy, the steeper the aggregate demand curve.

In Figure 9–9 we have drawn two aggregate demand curves that represent alternatives to the policy rule shown in Figure 9–8. One of the schedules is simply the aggregate demand schedule with a fixed money supply. Note that when there is a price shock, the more accommodative rules translate into a smaller decline in real GDP. However, this also leads

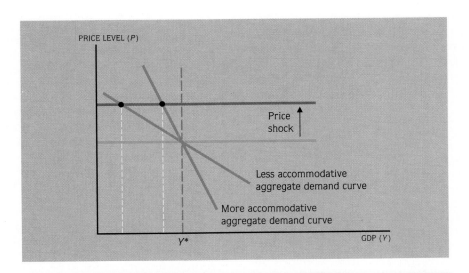

FIGURE 9–9   Aggregate demand schedules with alternative monetary policy rules

More accommodative policy makes the aggregate demand schedule steeper. As a result, the downward shift in output after a price shock is smaller the more accommodative the policy.

NEW RESEARCH IN PRACTICE
The Budget Enforcement Act of 1990

Much recent macroeconomic research has pointed to the importance of setting clear and credible rules for fiscal and monetary policy. Not only do such policy rules reduce uncertainty, they help prevent policy from being time-inconsistent by making it more difficult for policymakers to change policy for short-term economic or political gains. The idea of time inconsistency was first put forth by Edward Prescott of the University of Minnesota, Finn Kydland of Carnegie-Mellon University, and Guillermo Calvo of the International Monetary Fund. The idea has proved to be one of the more lasting contributions of the rational expectations revolution.

Has the research on policy rules had an influence on policymaking in practice? One way to address the question is to look for cases where policy rules have been implemented. The Budget Enforcement Act that was passed into law in 1990 provides one possible case. This case also shows how not so recent—but still very relevant—macroeconomic research on structural deficits and automatic stabilizers is used in practice.

The Budget Enforcement Act was the result of intense negotiations during the summer of 1990 between the Bush administration and Congress. The budget deficit, after declining in the late 1980s, had begun to grow again. The intent of the negotiations was both to reduce the budget deficit and to provide new budget rules that would help prevent the budget from growing in the future. The aim of the deficit reduction was to raise national saving. The aim of the budget rules was to increase credibility about long-term budget deficit reduction and thereby reduce long-term interest rates.

Much of the negotiating took place at the relatively secluded setting of Andrews Air Force Base outside of downtown Washington. The negotiations and the agreement set off tremendous controversy. Soon after starting, the negotiations stalled. To get the negotiations started again President Bush, in June 1990, offered the following statement:

It is clear to me that both the size of the deficit problem and the need for a package that can be enacted require all of the following: entitlement and mandatory program reform; tax revenue increases; growth incentives; discretionary spending reductions; orderly reductions in defense expenditures; and budget process reform—to ensure that any bipartisan agreement is enforceable and that the deficit problem is brought under responsible control. The budget negotiations will resume promptly with a view toward reaching substantive agreement as quickly as possible.*

The second item in this long list—tax revenue increases—attracted the most attention, and the eventual agreement is still remembered by most people for this. However, it is the last item on the list—budget process reform—that we are concerned with here. As part of that budget process reform, several new rules for fiscal policy were legislated. And as of this writing those rules are still in force. These legislated rules appear to put into practice some of the macroeconomic research on the design of policy rules.

The rules distinguished between two types of government spending: (1) discretionary spending, which consists primarily of military purchases, foreign aid, and domestic purchases of goods and services and (2) entitlement spending, which consists largely of transfer payments such as welfare, medicare, medicaid, and unemployment insurance. The rules put explicit dollar limits on discretionary spending for 5 years and require that any *new* entitlement program be matched either by reductions in other entitlement programs or by increases in taxes; this requirement was called the pay-as-you-go rule. Any legislation that violated either the limit rule or the pay-as-you-go rule would bring about an automatic sequester—an automatic across-the-board cut in the category of government spending where the violation occurred. A key feature of these rules is that they would prevent new government pro-

*Statement by the President, The White House, Office of the Press Secretary, June 26, 1990.

grams from increasing the budget deficit in the future.

On the other hand if the budget deficit were to increase because of the automatic stabilizers—then the budget deficit would be allowed to increase with no sequester. For example, if transfer payments were to rise as the economy slowed down, then the deficit would be allowed to increase. But new transfer programs or legislated changes in transfer programs were not allowed unless they could be offset elsewhere in the budget.

In effect, the Budget Enforcement Act attempted both to reduce the structural deficit through the limit and pay-as-you-go rules and simultaneously to allow the automatic stabilizers to increase the bud-

get deficit in a recession. Research on optimal policy rules has shown that such automatic stabilizers are important policy rules for stabilizing the economy.

Although the new budget rules have these attractive features, there are still significant budget problems and considerable room for improvement. Entitlement spending, even on existing programs, is still growing rapidly. Legislative changes will probably be required simply to restrain this growth. In addition, some have argued that the demise of the Soviet Union in 1991 may have reduced the required growth in military spending below the previously set limits.

---

to less downward pressure on prices and thereby less price stability. What is crucial is the slope of the aggregate demand schedule. The more accommodative policies result in more real GDP stability and less price stability. Less accommodative policies tend to increase price stability at the cost of less real GDP stability.[3]

The upshot of our analysis of the response of monetary policy is that the Fed can pick the slope as well as the position of the aggregate demand curve. The Fed can be hawkish and make the curve very flat. In that case, the price level will be stable but recessions and booms in output will be more pronounced. Or the Fed could be dovish and make the curve steep. Then we would have weaker recessions and booms but wider swings in inflation. Either one would be a reasonable policy. The signs of a monetary policy adhering to the principles of our analysis are the following: Money supply growth is fairly irregular. Aggregate demand shifts from instability in the economy itself do not affect output or prices. Positive price shocks raise the price level and lower output in a ratio that depends on how dovish the Fed has decided to be. Prices and output never both move in the same direction.

---

[3]We haven't tried to give an exact definition of *price stability* at this stage. Our concept gives weight to the long run. An accommodative policy that lets individual events have an effect on prices in the indefinite future does not achieve price stability, in our way of thinking. A policy that tried to stabilize the rate of inflation, on the other hand, could be quite accommodative. In Figure 9–7, it is the accommodative policy on the right that avoids a period of deflation following the inflation of a price shock.

Why Focus on Policy Rules?

Aside from the desire to model the economy and the effect of policy as accurately as possible, there are two important reasons why policy analysis in recent years has concentrated on rules rather than on exogenous changes in the policy instruments. These reasons will come up naturally in our later discussions of policy rules, but are worth mentioning briefly now. One reason is the recognition that *expectations* of policy can influence how policy affects the economy. If people anticipate a certain policy then they will act differently than if that policy were unanticipated. By stipulating policy as a rule, policymakers are implicitly stating how policy will react to future contingencies. That the money supply will increase if there is a positive price shock is an example of such a rule.

A second reason for the emphasis on rules is the problem of *time inconsistency*. Unless there is a systematic way for policymakers to commit themselves to operating in a particular way in the future, there will be a temptation to change their plans from what they announce. That is, policymakers will be tempted—in order to stimulate the economy—to do things differently from what they had promised. The advantage of policy rules in such situations is that rules commit policymakers to behaving in a certain predictable way—as long as they do not break the rule! We will come back to the problem of time inconsistency[4] in Chapter 18.

POLICY RULES

1. When macro policy is conducted according to a rule, it means that the policy instruments become endogenous variables; they respond in a known way to changes that occur in the economy.
2. One important example of a rule is the way the Fed responds to a price shock. The Fed can emphasize price stability by not adjusting money growth after a shock, which will worsen unemployment, or it can limit unemployment by adding to inflation through monetary expansion.
3. Many economists favor policy rules because their use may have favorable effects on the economy through expectations and because a binding rule may prevent shortsighted attempts to overstimulate the economy.

[4]The importance of time inconsistency for macroeconomics was first pointed out in Guillermo Calvo, "On the Time Inconsistency of Optimal Policy in a Monetary Economy," *Econometrica,* Vol. 46 (1978), pp. 1141–1428, and in Finn Kydland and Edward Prescott, "Rules Rather than Discretion: The Inconsistency of Optimal Plans," *Journal of Political Economy,* Vol. 85 (1977), pp. 473–491.

9.5   DISINFLATION

The problem of maintaining price stability in the face of price shocks is closely related to another type of price stabilization problem: that of bringing down the rate of inflation when it has become too high and has become incorporated into people's expectations and price-setting behavior. This latter problem is called the problem of **disinflation,** that is, reducing the rate of inflation. This problem requires us to pay close attention to the role of expectations in the Phillips curve.

The Phillips relationship, as we saw in Chapter 8, can be written

$$\pi = \pi^e + f \, \frac{Y_{-1} - Y^*}{Y^*}. \tag{9–1}$$

The most challenging problem of disinflation occurs in the case where the expected rate of inflation equals last period's inflation rate; $\pi^e = \pi_{-1}$. With this expectation of inflation, the only way that inflation can be reduced is by letting actual output Y drop below potential output Y^*. Equation 9–1 states that the *change* in the rate of inflation over its previous level π_{-1} depends on the percentage deviation of GDP from potential GDP.

The Phillips curve tells us that if the inflation rate is viewed by the policymakers as being too high and in need of reduction, then some type of a recession is inevitable. The essential policy questions related to disinflation are how long and how deep the recession should be. In other words, how sharply should the policymakers reduce the policy instruments to bring about a path for real GDP that is consistent with the desired reduction in inflation?

Setting Policy to Hit a Target Level of GDP

To answer this question, we first need to show how the policy instruments, such as the money supply or government spending, can be manipulated to get a desired path for real GDP. Recall that, with the price-adjustment equation, the price level is predetermined during the course of any particular year. Recall also that monetary and fiscal policies shift the aggregate demand curve to the right or left. The intersection of the aggregate demand curve with the price line gives the current value of real GDP. Hence, by changing monetary policy, the Fed can achieve just about any value of real GDP that it wants. Note that this ability of the monetary authorities to pinpoint real GDP perfectly needs to be qualified by the inherent uncertainty and lags in the effect of monetary policy that we discussed above. In addition, we know that aiming for a value of real GDP above potential GDP will

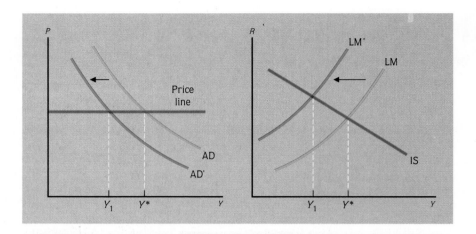

FIGURE 9–10   Aggregate demand in reverse: the money supply is set to hit a GDP target

The left-hand panel shows the situation in the economy. Output is equal to potential output Y^*. The Fed wants to set the money supply so that output is reduced to the level Y_1. To do this it must shift the aggregate demand curve inward from AD to AD'. As shown in the right-hand panel, the Fed thus reduces the money supply by an amount that makes the LM curve shift in and intersect the IS curve at a level of output equal to Y_1.

soon result in an inflationary spiral. But in the policy problem considered here, this latter possibility is not an issue because the aim of policy is to set real GDP below potential GDP in order to put downward pressure on prices and reduce the rate of inflation.

So far we have used the aggregate demand curve to find a level of GDP for a given level of the money supply or government spending. Now we must use the curve in *reverse*. We want to find a level for the money supply for a given target level of GDP. The idea is illustrated in Figure 9–10. The economy is shown to be operating at potential output Y^*. Suppose that the Fed wants to set the money supply to push the economy to a lower target level Y_1. What level of the money supply should it choose? The answer, as shown in the right-hand panel of Figure 9–10, is to reduce the money supply to the level that sets the aggregate demand curve at a point of intersection with the predetermined-price line at the target level of output Y_1.

NUMERICAL EXAMPLE. Suppose that the aggregate demand curve is the one that we studied in Chapter 7, Equation 7–9, namely,

$$Y = 2,015 + 1.155G + 2.887 \frac{M}{P} . \qquad (9\text{–}2)$$

Suppose that Congress has set government spending G at \$1,200 billion and that the predetermined-price level P equals 1. Potential GDP is \$6,000 billion. The Fed now wants to choose a money supply M to bring actual GDP below potential to \$5,900. For $G = 1,200$ and $P = 1$, the aggregate demand curve looks like

$$Y = 3,401 + 2.887M. \tag{9-3}$$

The level of the money supply is found by setting output Y in Equation 9–3 equal to 5,900 and finding M. The answer is

$$M = \frac{5,900 - 3,401}{2.887} = \frac{2,499}{2.887} = 866. \tag{9-4}$$

Note how this calculation is just the reverse of setting M to a value and finding Y, as we did in the numerical example in Chapter 7 (page 193).

Alternative Disinflation Paths

Suppose that the rate of inflation has risen to 10 percent and that the Fed wants to disinflate. Table 9–1 shows three alternative paths for the devia-

TABLE 9–1   Three Paths for Inflation and the GDP Gap

Year	Path 1 GDP Gap	Path 1 Inflation	Path 2 GDP Gap	Path 2 Inflation	Path 3 GDP Gap	Path 3 Inflation
0	0	10	0	10	0	10
1	0	10	-5	10	-10	10
2	0	10	-5	9	-10	8
3	0	10	-5	8	-10	6
4	0	10	-5	7	-10	4
5	0	10	-5	6	0	2
6	0	10	-5	5	0	2
7	0	10	-5	4	0	2
8	0	10	-5	3	0	2
9	0	10	0	2	0	2
10	0	10	0	2	0	2

Note: The GDP gap is the deviation of GDP from potential measured in percent; that is, gap = $(Y - Y^*)/Y^*$ times 100. Inflation is the percentage change in the price level. Each path shows the GDP gap and inflation over a 10-year period. The calculations are made with the Phillips curve of Equation 9–1 with f equal to .2. In the first path, policy holds real GDP at its potential level. Inflation stays at 10 percent. In the second path, real GDP is depressed below potential. Inflation drops steadily to 2 percent. When it reaches 2 percent, policy eases and GDP pulls back up to potential. In the third path, policy is even more contractionary at first; GDP is 10 percent below normal. Inflation drops to 2 percent sooner than in the second path.

tion of GDP from potential GDP, $(Y - Y^*)/Y^*$, and corresponding paths for the inflation rate. Year 0 shows the starting point, with inflation at 10 percent and GDP equal to potential GDP. The Fed begins to take actions to reduce inflation in Year 1. The values in Table 9–1 are obtained directly from the Phillips curve in Equation 9–1. For these calculations, we assume that the coefficient f in Equation 9–1 is .2. Recall also that we assume that the public believes that inflation will persist unless the Fed contracts the economy. The simple model of expected inflation with this property that we use is $\pi^e = \pi_{-1}$. Inflation expected this year is last year's actual inflation.

The three alternatives given in Table 9–1 are all feasible for the Fed to undertake. Clearly, if the Fed can pick any value of output Y it wants in the short run, it can also pick any value for the deviation of output from potential output, $(Y - Y^*)/Y^*$, since potential GDP (Y^*) is exogenous. By setting the money supply so that the aggregate demand curve is in the appropriate place, the Fed can set output and hence the deviations of output from potential output to the desired level.

The three alternatives were selected to indicate the kind of choice that the monetary authorities have to make when faced with excess inflation. Perhaps the most important thing to note about the choices is that none of them is a good one. The latter two involve a recession, as the inflation rate is decreased. The first avoids a recession, but gets no reduction in inflation.

The second two paths are both successful in getting the inflation rate down from 10 to 2 percent. But there are important differences between the two paths. Path 2 involves a longer, but shallower, recession. GDP is just 5 percent below potential for the entire period of the disinflation. However, it takes 8 years to get the inflation rate down to 2 percent. Path 3 involves a shorter recession, but it is quite deep. GDP is 10 percent below potential. In this case the inflation rate is reduced more quickly; it reaches 2 percent in 4 years. Clearly, more extreme possibilities are open to policymakers. Or a compromise between Path 2 and Path 3 is another possibility. The paths we have presented in Table 9–1 are meant to be representative of the choices facing policymakers. We illustrate in Figure 9–11A how Paths 2 and 3 differ.

In comparing these paths, it is important to note their implications for unemployment. Suppose that the natural rate of unemployment that corresponds to potential GDP is 6 percent. Recall from Chapter 3 that Okun's law translates a GDP gap of 1 percent into .3 percentage point of unemployment. Thus, for Path 2, the unemployment rate rises to 7.5 percent for 8 years, and for Path 3, the unemployment rate rises to 9 percent for 4 years. Of course the unemployment rate stays at 6 percent, the natural rate, for all years in Path 1.

Assuming that some reduction in inflation is desired, we must rule out Path 1. The choice is between Path 2 and Path 3. If very high unemploy-

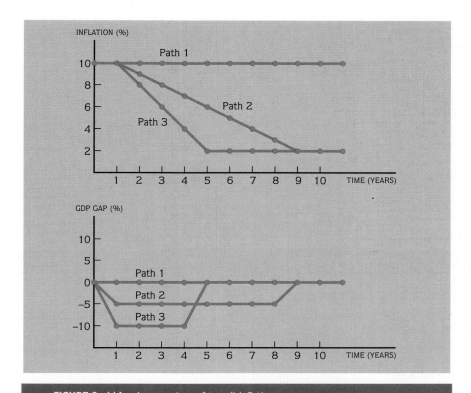

FIGURE 9–11A A comparison of two disinflations

Path 2 shows a long, shallow recession (lower panel) and a slow decline in inflation (upper panel). Path 3 shows a short, deep recession and a speedy decline in inflation. Path 1 has no recession and no disinflation.

ment is to be avoided, then a more gradual approach is appropriate. Moreover, the more gradual approach is better because it gives people more time to adjust their plans.

An illuminating way to compare the two disinflation paths is shown in Figure 9–11B. The rate of inflation is on the vertical axis and the GDP gap is on the horizontal axis. At the start of the disinflation, the inflation rate of 10 percent and the GDP gap of zero are shown by the point labeled "0" in the diagram. The alternative possibilities for inflation and the GDP gap are then shown as two big **C**'s emanating from this initial point and ending up at the final point. The **C** for Path 3 is much more elongated than the **C** for Path 2. This illustrates how Path 3 pushes the economy into a deeper recession than does Path 2.

The alternative possibilities in Figure 9–11B are very similar to the

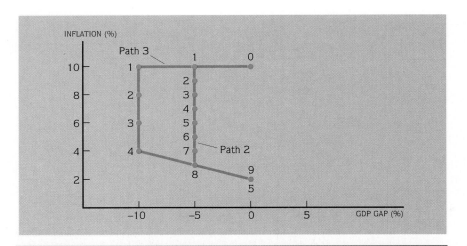

FIGURE 9–11B Inflation and GDP during two disinflations

The inflation rate is on the vertical axis; the GDP gap is on the horizontal axis. Both disinflation paths start at "0" and end at the same point. Path 3 shows a much deeper recession than does Path 2.

choices faced by policymakers in the late 1970s and early 1980s when the rate of inflation in the United States had reached levels near 10 percent. In 1979 President Carter appointed Paul Volcker chairman of the Federal Reserve Board with a clear "go ahead" to reduce inflation. When Ronald Reagan came into office in 1981, he gave the Fed further encouragement to reduce inflation. In President Reagan's report to Congress in February 1981, he listed as a key element of his plan to reduce inflation a "new commitment to a monetary policy that will restore a stable currency and healthy financial markets" and assumed as part of his plan that the growth rate of money would be "steadily reduced from the 1980 levels to one-half those levels by 1986."[5]

Figure 9–12 shows the actual rates of inflation and the GDP gap that occurred starting from 1979. Inflation was very high in 1979 when the GDP gap was above zero. As the Fed tightened its policy, the economy began to slow and GDP fell below potential GDP. Because of the slow reaction of prices to the depressed demand conditions, inflation did not slow for a while (in fact it increased slightly). The Fed continued with a tight policy and the GDP gap got larger, until inflation finally began to give way. There was a considerable reduction in inflation in 1982, and by 1985 inflation had come down to near 4 percent. Inflation began rising slightly as GDP appeared to exceed potential in 1985.

[5]*A Program for Economic Recovery,* The White House, February 18, 1981.

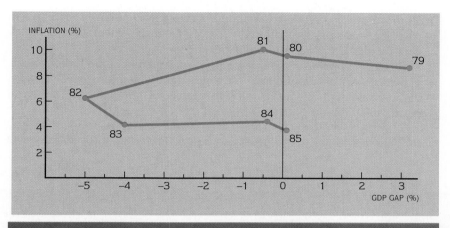

FIGURE 9-12   The 1979–85 disinflation

As money growth was reduced, GDP fell below potential. For a while there was little effect on inflation. The tight monetary policy was continued and eventually inflation came down.
Source: *Economic Report of the President*, 1992, Table B–59.

Comparing the actual experience from 1979 to 1985 with the two alternative paths, Paths 2 and 3, it looks as if Path 3 was chosen by the Fed. GDP fell to about 7 percent below potential in 1982 and the inflation rate came down much more quickly than in the gradual path. This disinflation was brought about mainly by monetary policy. Fiscal policy was in fact stimulative during that period. The beginning of the more contractionary monetary policies began in late 1979 and coincided fairly closely with the beginning of Paul Volcker's term as chairman of the Federal Reserve Board.

It is likely that a more gradual path was actually attempted by the Fed, but that mistakes led to the deeper recession. In retrospect there appears to have been an upward shift in the demand for money, which reduced aggregate demand for the reasons discussed in Section 9.1. But in 1982 it was difficult to tell that money demand was shifting. Because of this uncertainty and because the Fed was concerned about inflation, it was reluctant to offset the money demand shift by increasing money.

DISINFLATION

1. The price-adjustment equation is the key to understanding the problem of disinflation. Unemployment must rise above its natural rate to reduce inflation.

2. Monetary policy can be set to aim for a target level of GDP. Policymakers have a choice of disinflationary paths; the more unemployment they choose, the faster disinflation will occur.

3. From 1979 through 1988, rapid disinflation occurred in the United States, with GDP well below potential and high rates of unemployment. Inflation began rising slightly in 1989 as GDP exceeded potential, but fell again during the downturn of 1990–91.

Other Schools of Thought on Disinflation

Figure 9–12 seems to give strong support to the general view we have expressed in this book: It takes time for prices to adjust, and during that time, there can be large departures of GDP from potential. A negative shock to aggregate demand has the effect of sending the economy into recession.

Other schools of thought do not agree that recession is inevitably the result of a policy to bring down inflation quickly. One of the most influential critics of the view expressed in this book is Thomas Sargent of Stanford University. Sargent has written:

. . . Inflation only *seems* to have a momentum of its own; it is actually the long-term government policy of persistently running large deficits and creating money at high rates which imparts the momentum to the inflation rate. An implication of this view is that inflation can be stopped much more quickly than advocates of the "momentum" view have indicated and that their estimates of the length of time and the costs of stopping inflation in terms of forgone output ($220 billion of GDP for 1 percentage

point in the inflation rate) are erroneous. This is not to say that it would be easy to eradicate inflation. On the contrary, it would require far more than a few temporary restrictive fiscal and monetary actions. It would require a change in the policy regime; there must be an abrupt change in the continuing government policy, or strategy, for setting deficits now and in the future that is sufficiently binding as to be widely believed [emphasis added].*

Sargent examines the experiences of four countries—Austria, Hungary, Germany, and Poland—in the aftermath of World War I to test his theory. In his view, the magnitude of the recession that accompanied huge decreases in the inflation rate in these countries was small in those instances where there was a complete change in government policy and the public believed that highly expansionary fiscal and monetary policy had ended.

*"The Ends of Four Big Inflations," in Robert E. Hall, ed., *Inflation: Causes and Effects*, a National Bureau of Economic Research Project Report (Chicago: University of Chicago Press, 1982), pp. 41–97.

9.6   MONETARY VERSUS FISCAL POLICY

In our discussion of policy in this chapter we did not emphasize the different qualities of monetary and fiscal policy. Either policy can shift the aggregate demand curve and thus affect output and prices. Here we discuss some of the issues that arise in the choice between monetary and fiscal policy.

Fiscal policy is a change in government purchases of goods and services (G), a change in transfer payments (F), or a change in taxes (T). Each of these changes affects aggregate demand. Purchases directly add to demand, and transfers and taxes change income; this changes demand indirectly through the consumption function. A more **expansionary** (or a **looser**) **fiscal policy** is an increase in government purchases, an increase in transfers, or a decrease in taxes. A **contractionary** (or **tighter**) **fiscal policy** is the reverse.

Recall that *monetary* policy is a change in the money supply (M). A more **expansionary,** or looser, **monetary policy** is an increase in the money supply. A **contractionary,** or tighter, **monetary policy** is a decrease in the money supply.

Note that we frequently measure changes in monetary and fiscal policy relative to growing trends in the variables. Thus, a contractionary fiscal policy frequently means a reduction in the growth *rate* of government expenditures (rather than an absolute decline) or an increase in the growth *rate* of taxes (rather than an absolute increase). Similarly, a contractionary monetary policy frequently means a reduction in the growth rate of money.

Recall from our discussion in Chapter 7 that both fiscal and monetary policy are capable of shifting the aggregate demand schedule. A fiscal expansion stimulates spending directly. It causes the interest rate to rise. If the fiscal expansion raises government purchases or stimulates consumption by raising disposable income, then the higher interest rates tend to depress investment and net exports. By contrast, a monetary expansion lowers the interest rate. Investment and net exports grow and consumption responds to that growth through the multiplier.

Even though both policies affect the basic variables of our analysis—output and the price level—in the same way by shifting the aggregate demand schedule, there are important differences in their other effects. These differences are mediated by the interest rate. Monetary expansion favors investment and net exports, whereas fiscal expansion through higher government purchases or tax cuts discourages investment and net exports.

REVIEW AND PRACTICE

Major Points

1. One important type of macroeconomic shock shifts the aggregate demand curve. Such a shock can originate anywhere in the spending and financial parts of the economy.

2. The other important type of shock shifts the price level.

3. In principle, monetary and fiscal policy can be used to offset shifts in aggregate demand, so that the shifts have little effect on GDP or the price level. But some economists question the feasibility or the wisdom of trying to counteract every demand shift.

4. Price shocks create a much more serious problem for policy. Without a policy response, shocks bring lower GDP and higher inflation. Policy can limit the GDP decline only by permanently increasing the price level.

5. It is advantageous to adopt a policy rule and to follow the rule each time a macro shock occurs. Some rules limit variations in unemployment at the cost of long-term variability in the price level. Other rules stabilize prices at the cost of variable unemployment. No rule achieves the ideal of low variation in unemployment and long-term stability of the price level.

6. Another policy issue is how to phase out inflation once it is established. Policy can choose between ending inflation rapidly, with high unemployment, or disinflating gradually, with unemployment closer to the natural rate.

7. The government can put its aggregate demand policy into effect with either monetary or fiscal policy.

Key Terms and Concepts

aggregate demand disturbance	countercyclical stabilization policy	policy rule
price disturbance	activist policy	disinflation
accommodative policy	accommodation of price shock	time inconsistency

Questions for Discussion and Review

1. What are some of the possible reactions of the economy in the short run to an event that causes an aggregate demand shift? A price shock? What about in the long run? What if both types of shocks occur at the same time?

2. Explain how the economy would respond to a negative price shock if there were no policy response.

3. What are the dangers of a vigorous response to a demand shock? What are the benefits?

4. Explain how the Fed can choose the slope of the aggregate demand curve.

5. Explain why an extended period of excess unemployment is needed to bring about disinflation. Do you find your explanation completely convincing?

6. What factors should policymakers consider in deciding whether to use fiscal or monetary policy to shift the aggregate demand curve?

Problems

Numerical

1. Suppose the economy is initially described by the following equations:

$$Y = C + I + G$$
$$C = 220 + .63Y$$
$$I = 1,000 - 2,000R$$
$$X = 525 - .1Y - 500R$$
$$M = .1583Y - 1,000R$$
$$\pi = 1.2 [(Y_{-1} - 6,000)/6,000]$$

The money supply is equal to $900 billion, government spending is $1,200 billion, and output is at its potential level of $6,000 billion with a price level of 1. Then there is a money demand shock. The new money demand equation is given by

$$M = .1583Y - 2,000R.$$

a. In the year of the shock, compute the value of GDP, the price level, interest rates, and the real money supply.

b. Using aggregate demand curves, illustrate the economy's path in the year of the shock and in subsequent years.

c. Calculate the new long-run equilibrium values for income, prices, interest rates, and the real money supply.

d. Could the Fed have done something to avert the adjustment process? If no, why not? If yes, describe exactly what it could have done.

2. Repeat Exercise 1, Parts a to c, assuming now that the shock is to investment. The new investment equation is given by

$$I = 800 - 2,000R.$$

What change in fiscal policy, if any, would have offset the shock?

3. Suppose the economy has the aggregate demand schedule

$$Y = 3,401 + 2.877 \frac{M}{P}$$

and a price-adjustment schedule

$$\pi = .6\pi_{-1} + 1.2[(Y_{-1} - Y^*)/Y^*] + Z,$$

where Z is an exogenous price shock; potential GDP is $Y^* = 6,000$.

a. Graph the aggregate demand schedule for $M = 900$. Graph the price-adjustment schedule. Find the price level for $Z = 0$.

b. Suppose the economy starts with a price level of 1.0 and zero expected inflation. A price shock of 5 percent occurs in the first year ($Z = .05$). No further price shocks occur ($Z = 0$ in all future years). Trace the path of the economy back to potential by computing the values of the price level, GDP, unemployment, and expected inflation in each year for 5 years.

c. Repeat the calculations for the following monetary accommodation: The money supply is 5 percent higher starting in the second year. Compare this new path for inflation and unemployment with the original path.

d. Suppose, instead, that monetary policy tries to limit inflation by contracting the money stock by 5 percent starting in the second year. Repeat the calculations and compare with the original path.

e. Now suppose that there is no price shock ($Z = 0$ in all years), but that the economy starts with expected inflation of 3 percent. Compute the path to potential. How much excess unemployment (over the natural rate of 6 percent) occurs in the process of returning to potential? Use Okun's law.

4. Consider the following closed-economy model of aggregate demand:

$$C = 835 + .56Y_d \qquad \text{(Consumption)}$$
$$I = 640 - 2,000R \qquad \text{(Investment)}$$
$$M = 139.5P/(R + .66) \qquad \text{(Money demand)}$$

Government taxes (T) equal tY where the tax rate t is .29. Government purchases G are constant at 690. Each time period represents 1 year. In addition prices adjust according to

$$\pi = \pi_{-1} + .3[(Y_{-1} - Y^*)/Y^*]. \qquad \text{(Price adjustment)}$$

Suppose that it is January 1997 and that you have just been hired as an adviser to the chairman of the Fed. Because the Fed is trying to put on a low-budget image, the chairman asks you to bring a hand calculator to your new job. History has repeated itself and the rate of inflation in 1996 was 10 percent. That is, the price level increased from .909 in 1995 to 1.0 in 1996. The Fed set the money supply for 1996 at 186, and real output in the economy in 1996 was equal to potential. What was potential output in 1996?

Assume that potential output remains constant at its 1996 value for the rest of the 1990s. What follows pertains to your new Fed job.

a. The chairman asks you what actual output will have to be in 1997, 1998, and 1999 in order for inflation to be reduced to 7 percent in 1998, to 4 percent in 1999, and then held constant at 4 percent for 2000. What is your answer based on the above model?

b. The chairman decides to disinflate the economy according to the path that you calculated in Part a and asks you to give a recommendation to the Federal Open Market Committee (FOMC) about where to aim the money supply in 1997, 1998, and 1999 to achieve this path. What do you say?

c. Suppose the FOMC ignores your recommendation and increases the money supply by 20 percent to 223 in 1997. What will happen to output in 1997, and inflation in 1998?

Analytical

1. Suppose that the economy is initially in equilibrium and that there is a permanent increase in money demand. The following year the money supply is increased so that at the old equilibrium level of prices, income, and interest rates, money supply equals money demand.
   a. Illustrate the shock and the Fed's reaction to it with an aggregate demand graph. Using arrows, as in Figure 9–2, sketch the economy's path.
   b. What happens to prices, income, and interest rates in the year of the shock, the year immediately following the shock, and all subsequent years?
   c. Whose views of countercyclical stabilization policy does this example illustrate?

2. Evaluate the following statement: It is price changes, not higher prices, that bother people so much. Therefore, the best response to a price shock is full accommodation. This will prevent output from falling below potential, as well as avoiding any additional price changes.

3. Explain the following statement: The reason that price shocks pose a dilemma for policymakers is that they cannot directly control the price level. Contrast this situation to the case of aggregate demand shocks.

4. Suppose that the Fed fully accommodates a price shock, shifting out the aggregate demand curve until aggregate demand equals Y^* at the higher price level. The behavior of income and of the price level are given by the following graphs:

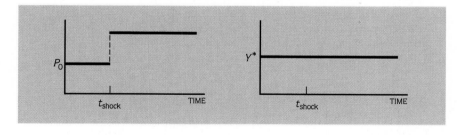

a. Assumming that aggregate demand is given by the usual relationship, which of the following equations must describe the adjustment of prices?

$$\pi = f[(Y_{-1} - Y^*)/Y^*] \qquad \pi = .6\pi_{-1} + f[(Y_{-1} - Y^*)/Y^*]$$

b. Assume now that there is the same policy response, but that prices are governed by the other equation. Describe the path followed by output and prices.

5. Suppose the Fed used monetary policy to keep the interest rate at 7 percent no matter what else happened in the economy.
   a. When would such a policy be inflationary? How would the nominal money stock and output behave in this instance?
   b. When would such a policy be deflationary? How would the nominal money stock and output behave in this instance?
   c. What other policy is available for targeting the interest rate? What are its advantages?

6. "Stagflation" was a term coined in the 1970s to describe a sustained period of high inflation and unemployment. Using graphs, describe how stagflation may come about in the wake of a price shock.

7. The "political business cycle" is said to occur because the administration expands policy in the election year in order to get reelected. How could this be prevented?

8. One example of a monetary policy rule is $Y = Y^*$.
   a. What does the aggregate demand curve look like for such a policy rule?
   b. Explain why the money stock is an endogenous variable under such a rule. How is the money stock affected by price shocks? By aggregate demand shocks?
   c. Explain why $P = P_0$ is not a feasible policy rule.

9. When the Reagan administration came into power in 1981, three of its primary objectives were to reduce inflation, lower taxes, and increase defense spending.
   a. Explain why the achievement of all three goals required an extremely restrictive monetary policy.
   b. Could the same rate of disinflation have been achieved with a less restrictive monetary policy and a more restrictive fiscal policy? If not, why not? If so, explain how the following variables would have been affected during the 1981–84 period: output, inflation, interest rates, consumption, investment, the trade deficit, and the government budget deficit.

10. Suppose that the only source of instability in the economy is disturbances to investment demand and that the administration is considering adopting a rule for government spending that can be expressed as

$$G = G_0 + r(Y - Y^*),$$

where G_0 and r are positive constants. Will a rule of this form reduce the fluctuations in GDP? Why or why not? If not, indicate how you would change the rule to accomplish stabilization.

11. Understanding the source of shocks to the economy is important for determining the appropriate policy response. For each of the following sources of shocks describe the correlations you would expect to observe between real GDP and real interest rates in the short run. (Assume monetary and fiscal policy are exogenous.)
    a. Shocks to investment demand.
    b. Shocks to money demand.

c. Shocks to the price level.

d. Shocks to net exports.

For each of these sources of shocks, describe the combination of monetary and fiscal policy that could offset the disturbance completely and keep real output and the price level unchanged.

12. Assume that the only source of instability in the economy is price shocks. Compare a policy of fixed money supply with each of the following monetary policy rules. Indicate whether the aggregate demand schedule becomes flatter or steeper or if you are uncertain. Justify your answer. (Suppose output initially equals Y^*, $P = 1.0$, and M_0, s, and r are positive constants.)

a. $M = M_0 + s(P - 1.0)$.

b. $M = M_0 + s(Y - Y^*)$.

c. $M = M_0 + s(P - 1.0) - r(Y - Y^*)$.

MacroSolve Exercises

In this chapter we have continued to assume that the aggregate demand side of the economy is given by the IS-LM model, and we have added to our price-adjustment equation the influence of supply shocks. Our price-adjustment equation becomes

$$\pi = \pi^e + .8 \, [(Y_{-1} - Y^*)/Y^*] + Z,$$

where Z represents a price shock. This model is called "AD/PA, Closed Econ."

1. Select a price shock of 5 percent. Assume that government spending and the money supply are kept constant.

   a. How much output is "lost" in the following five periods, where lost output is measured as the sum of the deviation of output from potential output over those years?

   b. Increase the responsiveness of investment to interest rates. Is the output loss greater or smaller than it was with less responsive investment? Explain in words why this is the case; emphasize the role of changes in the interest rate in transmitting price shocks to the real side of the economy.

   c. Reset the interest responsiveness of investment to its default, and make prices less responsive to aggregate demand. Explain why the price shock has a more prolonged depressing effect on GDP when prices are more "sticky."

2. Continue to assume that the 5 percent price shock hits the economy, and reset all parameters to their default values. Compare the output loss over the first 5 years with that in the previous question. Why would a government ever choose not to accommodate a price shock in this manner (i) in the short run or (ii) in the long run?

3. Suppose that instead of changing the money supply, the government increases its own expenditure to keep output constant in the period of the price shock.

   a. Explain how the solution differs from the previous case where the money supply was increased.

b. What variables are significantly different in the last period of the two (monetary and fiscal policy response) simulations? What explains their differences? Why might a policymaker prefer one over the other?

4. *Policy Decision 1997.* The day you arrive at your job at the Fed there is another crisis in the Middle East and the price of oil skyrockets. You have to make a presentation to the board the next day about the problem. The board wants you to find a way to keep GDP from falling if the shock raises the price level 10 percent. Use MacroSolve to find a path for the money supply that meets the board's request.

5. Suppose the Fed adopts a policy to fight inflation. What should it do in response to an increase in government expenditure? Select the "AD/PA, Closed Econ" model and increase government spending by $50 billion.

a. What change in the money supply is required to maintain stability of the price level?

b. Now suppose the economy suffers a 5 percent price shock (as opposed to the increase in government spending). How should you respond according to the inflation-fighting policy? What is the impact of your response on output? Are GDP fluctuations larger or smaller?

PART

2

The Micro Foundations of Aggregate Demand

CHAPTER

10

Consumption Demand

The study of consumer behavior—what, how much, and when individuals consume—has been a lifetime occupation of thousands of economists. This is not surprising for the consumer occupies center stage in economics. A first principle of microeconomics is that consumers choose their consumption plans in order to maximize their satisfaction or utility. And ever since Adam Smith the performance of an economic system has been judged by how efficiently it allocates scarce resources to satisfy the wants of consumers. It is natural, therefore, to start with consumers in our examination of the micro foundations of macroeconomics.

Traditionally, macroeconomists have been concerned with consumption because consumption is such a large and important component of aggregate demand. In Part I we saw that consumption is about two-thirds of all spending and that the response of consumption to changes in income—the consumption function—is a crucial ingredient in macroeconomic analysis. In the first section of this chapter we look at the empirical evidence on consumption. We show that this evidence raises questions about the simple consumption function, and then we show how consumption theory has been reconstructed in light of this empirical evidence. We also examine the response of consumption to interest rates.

10.1   FLUCTUATIONS IN GDP, CONSUMPTION, AND INCOME

As the overall economy grows and fluctuates, so does consumption. Figure 10–1 shows how real GDP and personal consumption expenditures have grown and passed through cycles together during the period 1959 to 1991. Note that, *over the long run, consumption expenditures and GDP grow at about the same rate, but, over short-run business cycles, consumption expenditures fluctuate less than GDP.*[1] The smoother path for consumption expenditures is particularly evident during the period 1980 to 1984 when real GDP fell and rose sharply, while consumption expenditures slowed

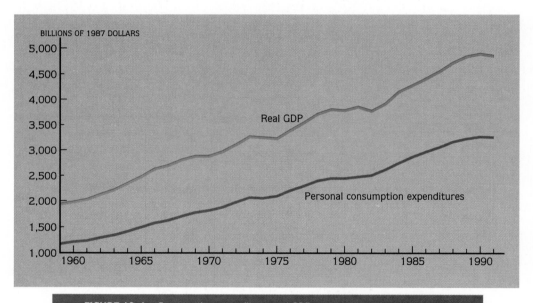

FIGURE 10–1   Consumption expenditures and GDP

Real GDP and real personal consumption expenditures grow at about the same rate over long periods of time so that, on average, consumption expenditures maintain roughly a two-thirds share of GDP. However, over the business cycle, consumption expenditures fluctuate much less than GDP. Consumption expenditure is less volatile than the other components of GDP.
Source: *Economic Report of the President,* 1992, Table B–2.

---

[1]Note that the increasing gap between real GDP and real consumption in Figure 10–1 is not inconsistent with the fact that the *ratio* of real consumption to real GDP remains constant. The gap gets larger as the level of the two series increases.

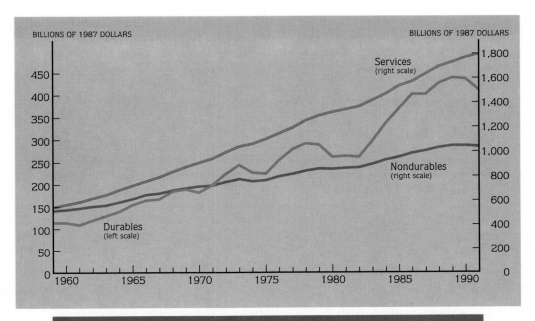

FIGURE 10–2   Fluctuations in the components of real personal consumption expenditures

Expenditures on services grow smoothly with little cyclical fluctuation. Expenditures on durables are the most volatile component of consumption.
Source: *Economic Report of the President,* 1992, Table B–2.

down only slightly before returning to a more normal pace. This relatively smooth behavior of consumption expenditures compared with GDP is one of the most important facts of the business cycle.

The smoothness of consumption differs greatly by type of consumption. Figure 10–2 shows the breakdown of personal consumption expenditures into its three components: durables, nondurables, and services. Note that the relatively smooth behavior of consumption expenditures is most striking for services, which grow steadily regardless of the fluctuations in the economy. Nondurables fluctuate a bit more, but most of the business cycle fluctuations in consumption expenditures are due to durables. When recessions occur, people reduce their purchases of durable items such as furniture and automobiles much more than nondurable items such as food; service items such as medical care hardly fluctuate at all. Note, too, that services now represent the largest and fastest growing component of consumption. As services become more important, we might expect overall consumption expenditures to become less volatile.

Overall consumption behavior would show even smaller fluctuations if we looked at the true economic measure of **consumption** rather than at **consumption expenditures.** The distinction between consumption and consumption expenditures is a subtle one, but takes on special importance in the case of durables. Consider a car, for example. Expenditure on a car occurs at the time that we buy the car and bring it home from the car dealer, even if we finance it by borrowing. Consumption of the car is then spread out over several years as we drive the car and it gradually deteriorates through normal wear and tear. Expenditure occurs when the car is acquired; consumption occurs as the car is used up. Consumption of durables is more spread out over time and is smoother than expenditure on them. For services and nondurable items there is no meaningful distinction between consumption and expenditure: When we purchase a haircut, we consume it at the same time. Because consumption of durables fluctuates less than expenditures on durables, it is clear that total consumption has smaller fluctuations than total consumption expenditures.

GDP and Personal Disposable Income

Why does consumption fluctuate less than GDP? Part of the answer can be found in the behavior of disposable personal income. As we saw in Chapter 6, according to the simplest theory, consumption depends on personal disposable income: When fluctuations in disposable income are small, fluctuations in consumption will be small as well. We stressed in Chapter 2 that GDP is very different from the personal disposable income that is available to consumers for spending. GDP is about 40 percent greater than personal disposable income. Part of GDP is not really income at all because it includes the depreciation of machines, factories, and housing. An important part of GDP is unavailable to consumers because it is paid to the various levels of government in the form of taxes. Still another part is plowed back into corporations in the form of retained earnings rather than being paid out to consumers. On the other hand, some people receive transfers from the government—such as unemployment compensation or social security—that are not related to current production.

Although the difference between GDP and disposable income is large on average, what is more important for our purposes is that the difference shrinks during recessions and expands during booms. Taxes fall during recessions, and transfers increase because more people collect unemployment insurance and social security. Therefore disposable income does not fall as much as GDP. These changes in taxes and transfers are sometimes called **automatic stabilizers** because of their stabilizing effect on disposable income; we will be studying them in more detail in Chapter 13. Retained earnings also fall during recessions, because corporations don't cut

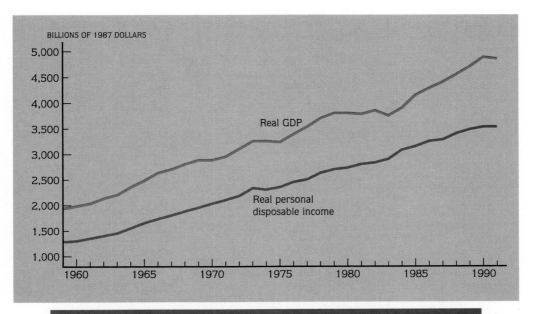

BILLIONS OF 1987 DOLLARS

Real GDP

Real personal
disposable income

FIGURE 10–3   Real GDP and real personal disposable income

Disposable income fluctuates much less than real GDP. The automatic stabilizers—taxes and trans-
fers—as well as the dividend policies of corporations prevent disposable income from falling as far as
GDP during recessions.
Source: *Economic Report of the President*, 1992, Tables B–2 and B–25.

their dividends very much and thus further mitigate the effect on disposable income. The sum of these effects is shown in Figure 10–3, where real
GDP and real personal disposable income are plotted for the years 1959 to
1991.

Figure 10–3 shows that personal disposable income fluctuates less
than GDP. On average, when GDP falls during a recession, disposable income does not fall as much. There are exceptions to this general rule, but,
again, on average, over this period a fall in real GDP of $10 billion reduced
real disposable income by only $4 billion.[2]

[2]The relationship was estimated by comparing real disposable income and real GDP in the
United States each year during the 1959–1991 period. The least-squares relation between the
change in real disposable income and the *change* in real GDP has a slope coefficient of .4.
The least-squares line is the straight line that minimizes the sum of squared vertical distances
between the dots and the line.

The Relation between Real Disposable Income and Consumption

As we have just seen, part of the reason that consumption fluctuates less than real GDP is that disposable income fluctuates less than GDP. But can all of consumption behavior be explained by current personal disposable income as the simplest consumption function would suggest? In Figure 10–4 we examine the relationship between personal consumption expenditures and personal disposal income for the period from 1959 through 1991. Each dot in Figure 10–4 represents real consumption and real disposable income in the United States for 1 year. We can summarize the relationship by drawing a straight line through the dots.[3] The straight line gives

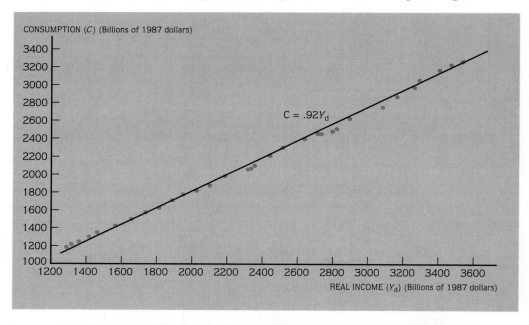

FIGURE 10–4   The relation between real disposable income and real consumption expenditures

The horizontal position of each dot shows real disposable income in that year and the vertical positions shows real consumption in that year. The straight line is a simple consumption function that is fit through the scatter of dots. The vertical distances between the line and the dots measure the error in the consumption function.
Source: *Economic Report of the President*, 1992, Table B–25.

[3]We estimated this relationship by finding the straight line that minimizes the sum of the squared vertical distances between the dots and the line (that is, the least-squares line) for the years 1959 through 1991. This line has a negligible intercept or constant term, which is therefore omitted from Equation 10–1.

the relationship

$$C = .92Y_{d,}$$ (10-1)

which is in the form of the simple consumption function; the **marginal propensity to consume** (MPC) is .92. On average, the U.S. public spends about 92 percent of its disposable income on consumption goods and saves 8 percent. Figure 10-4 indicates that consumption is sometimes less and sometimes greater than predicted by the simple consumption function. The errors are given by

$$\text{Error} = C - .92Y_d$$ (10-2)

and are measured by the vertical distances between the line and the dots in Figure 10-4. The errors appear to be small. The simple consumption function seems to give a surprisingly good description of consumption.

10.2 DEFECTS IN THE SIMPLE KEYNESIAN CONSUMPTION FUNCTION

Unfortunately, Figure 10-4 paints too rosy a picture about the reliability of the simple consumption function. Although the errors in Figure 10-4 appear small to the naked eye, for some purposes—such as forecasting or policy analysis—they are actually quite large. A more revealing picture of the errors is found in Figure 10-5, where the error in the simple consumption function (as calculated in Equation 10-2) is plotted for each year. The vertical scale in Figure 10-5 is much finer than the vertical scale in Figure 10-4. This magnifies the errors much as does an enlargement of a photograph and makes them easier to analyze.

Very large negative errors occurred in 1973 through 1975. People consumed much less than normal given their disposal incomes; they acted as if they distrusted their income figures in those years. Why? Perhaps they were becoming pessimistic about their incomes in the future; the stock market had recently fallen and the price of oil rose dramatically starting in 1973. These uncertainties about the future could have led to caution and increased saving.

At the other extreme, consumption rose well above its normal relationship to disposable income in the 1987-through-1989 period. The economy was on a consumption binge. Surveys confirmed that families were more confident about their own financial positions and the prospects for the economy than they had been ever before. The only comparable buying binge in U.S. history occurred just after World War II, another episode of

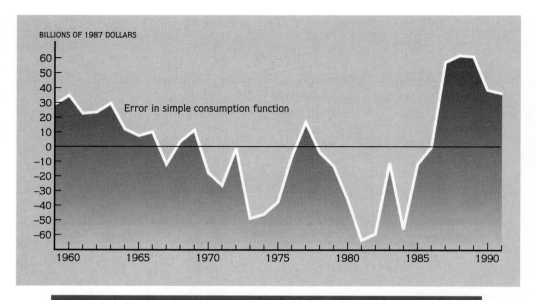

BILLIONS OF 1987 DOLLARS

Error in simple consumption function

FIGURE 10–5   Error analysis in the simple consumption function

This diagram gives a microscopic view of the errors in the simple consumption function that are barely visible in Figure 10–4. It blows up the distances between the actual consumption-income dots and the simple consumption-income line in Figure 10–4. The distances are then plotted each year from 1959 through 1991. Big negative errors are evident in 1973 through 1975, and big positive errors are evident in 1987 through 1991.
Source: The errors are computed from Equation 10–2 with consumption and income data from Figure 10–4.

high confidence about the future. One factor in the high confidence of 1987 to 1989 may have been the Tax Reform Act of 1986, which lowered tax rates for many families. In 1987, consumer confidence was matched by confidence on Wall Street; the stock market reached record levels in relation to corporate earnings. But the crash of the stock market in October 1987 did not mark the end of high consumer confidence or high levels of consumption in relation to disposable income.

Starting in 1990, consumption was closer to its normal relation to disposable income, though still substantially above that relation. Surveys of consumer confidence showed large declines in 1990 and 1991. The fall of consumption from far above its normal relation to income to a more moderate level, still above the normal relation, was one of the factors leading to the recession that started in July 1990. The recession would have been worse if consumption had actually returned to its normal relation to real income. And if consumption had fallen well below that normal relation, as it did in the recession years 1973 to 1975 and 1980 to 1982, the recession would have been much worse than it was.

Note that these informal but plausible explanations of the errors in the simple theory imply a much more sophisticated consumer than the one that simply looks at current income, as the Keynesian model postulates. Expected future income enters the decision. The main contribution of the newer theories of consumption described in the next section is to bring these expectations of the future explicitly into account.

The Effect of Consumption Errors on Forecasting and Policy

Some perspective on the practical importance of these errors in the consumption function can be gained by looking at their effect on economic forecasting and policy. These errors can have significant effects on economic forecasts. For example, the error in the consumption function in 1986 was $58 billion. From 1985 to 1986 real GDP increased by $91 billion. A forecaster who missed the error in the consumption function in 1986 would have underpredicted real GDP growth by more than 100 percent — predicting a GDP growth of about 1 percent rather than the 2.5 percent that actually occurred. By ignoring the negative consumption errors in 1974 and 1975, forecasters would have completely missed the declines in real GDP in those years.

These large forecasting errors can obviously lead to economic policy errors. More fiscal stimulus might have been called for in 1974 and 1975 if the unusually low consumption demand had been correctly forecast in advance. Moreover, if consumers don't automatically spend 92 cents of every dollar of additional disposable income—as the simple model predicts—then a reduction in taxes aimed at stimulating demand might not work as planned; it might generate too little or too much stimulus. More complicated consumer behavior makes policymaking difficult, especially if policymakers don't understand the more complicated behavior.

Short-Run versus Long-Run Marginal Propensity to Consume

There is one systematic feature of the errors in the simple consumption function that is difficult to see in the charts with a naked eye, but which nonetheless has provided a crucial insight and stimulus to advanced research on consumption: *On average, consumption is smoothed out compared with disposable income; consumption fluctuates less than disposable income.* This phenomenon can be detected and illustrated by using the concept of the long-run and short-run marginal propensity to consume. Figure 10–6 shows how the long-run and the short-run marginal propensities to consume differ for total consumption. The **long-run marginal propensity to consume** tells us how much consumption will increase over the long haul when personal disposable income rises. For total con-

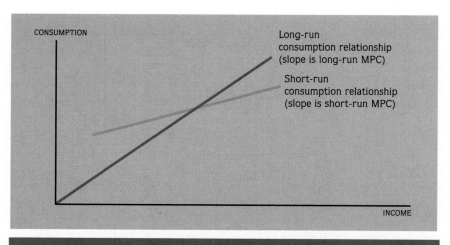

FIGURE 10–6   The marginal propensity to consume in the short run and in the long run

The steeper line shows how consumption rises with income in the long run. Its slope is the long-run marginal propensity to consume (MPC). The flatter line shows how consumption rises with income in the short run. Its slope is the short-run MPC.

sumption the long-run marginal propensity to consume is .92, as we have already seen in Equation 10–1.

The **short-run marginal propensity to consume** tells us how much consumption will rise over the short run—during one year or during one business cycle—when disposable income rises. As Figure 10–6 illustrates, the short-run marginal propensity to consume is less than the long-run marginal propensity to consume.

Table 10–1 shows the actual difference between the short-run and the long-run marginal propensity to consume in the United States from 1959 to 1991 for total consumption and two of its components. The short-run marginal propensity to consume can be calculated statistically by noting how much consumption changes from one year to the next when disposable income changes. For total consumption the short-run MPC is .71, compared with .92 for the long-run MPC. The difference is even more pronounced for consumption of nondurables plus services: Nondurables and services consumption falls by 40 cents in the short run for each dollar decrease in disposable income, but the fall is 78 cents over the long run if that dollar shortfall in income persists. Note that the difference between the long-run and the short-run MPC is reversed for durable expenditures; unlike the

TABLE 10–1 Short-Run and Long-Run Marginal Propensity to Consume 1959–91

	Total Consumption	Nondurables plus Services	Durables
Long-run MPC	.92	.78	.14
Short-run MPC	.71	.40	.31

Note: The long-run MPCs are based on the least-squenes fit of the annual *levels* of real consumption and real disposable income. The short-run MPCs are based on the fit of the year-to-year *changes* in the same two variables.

other components of consumption, durables are more sensitive to income in the short run than in the long run. A complete theory of consumption has to come to grips with these empirical observations.

GDP, CONSUMPTION, AND INCOME

1. Consumption fluctuates much less than GDP. The least stable component of consumption expenditures is durable consumption. Services and non-durable consumption grow more smoothly.
2. The main reason that consumption fluctuates less than GDP is that disposable income fluctuates less than GDP. Consumption is financed out of disposable income.
3. Over the past few decades in the United States, consumption has more or less tracked income according to a simple Keynesian consumption function with a marginal propensity to consume of .92. Of each incremental dollar of disposable income, 92 cents has been spent on consumption goods and 8 cents has been saved.
4. There have been significant deviations from the simple consumption function. Just after World War II, consumers spent more than the simple function predicted. In the mid-1970s, they spent quite a bit less. And in 1987 to 1989 they again consumed much more than the simple function predicted.
5. A systematic feature of consumption behavior is that the short-run marginal propensity to consume is less than the long-run marginal propensity to consume. The change in consumption that results from a change in income is apparently spread over a number of years.

10.3   THE FORWARD-LOOKING THEORY OF CONSUMPTION

A number of different theories of consumption have been developed in response to the deficiencies in the simple consumption function. The most durable and widely accepted today are the **permanent-income theory** developed in the 1950s by Milton Friedman and the **life-cycle theory** developed independently at about the same time by Franco Modigliani of the Massachusetts Institute of Technology.[4] The two theories are closely related, and together they have served as a foundation for most of the rational expectations research on consumption in macroeconomics in the 1970s and 1980s. We will refer to them jointly as the **forward-looking theory of consumption.** The theory embodies the basic idea that individual consumers are forward-looking decision-makers. The life-cycle theory gets its name from its emphasis on a family looking ahead over its entire lifetime. The permanent-income theory is named for its distinction between permanent income, which a family expects to be long-lasting, and transitory income, which a family expects to disappear shortly. In practice the theories differ primarily in the types of equations used to express the basic idea of forward-looking consumers and to implement this idea empirically.

Like the simple consumption function, the forward-looking theory of consumption assumes that families or individuals base their consumption decisions on their disposable incomes. To simplify matters, we will begin by ignoring factors other than disposable income that might also influence consumption, such as interest rates. The forward-looking theories break ranks with the simple consumption function by saying that consumers do not concentrate exclusively on this year's disposable income. Instead, they also look ahead to their likely future disposable income, which will depend on their future earnings from working, on their future income from wealth they have accumulated, and on how high taxes will be in the future. Based on their current income and expected future disposable income they decide how much to consume this year after taking account of their likely consumption in future years as well.

The consumption decision is thus much like a plan; this year's consumption is the first year of a plan that covers perhaps the next 50 years.

---

[4]Friedman published his findings in 1957 in a famous book *A Theory of the Consumption Function* (Princeton University Press); the findings on the life-cycle theory were published in a series of papers, the most important of which are F. Modigliani and R. E. Brumberg, "Utility Analysis and the Consumption Function: An Interpretation of Cross-Section Data," in K. K. Kurihara, ed., *Post-Keynesian Economics* (New Brunswick, N.J.: Rutgers University Press, pp. 388–436), and A. Ando and F. Modigliani, "The 'Life-Cycle' Hypothesis of Saving: Aggregate Implication and Tests," *American Economic Review,* Vol. 53 (March 1963), pp. 55–84.

Next year, the plan will have to be adjusted to take account of all the new information that has become available, but if everything works out as expected the plan will be followed. Although few consumers actually sit down and work out formal forward-looking plans in great detail, it is likely that a significant fraction do some informal planning when they borrow to buy now and plan to pay off the loan later with future anticipated earnings or when they save for retirement. We will talk about a very self-conscious plan, of the sort that an economist might make, but we recognize that most families are much more informal in their planning.

The Intertemporal Budget Constraint

To describe how such a planning process results in a consumption decision, we will focus on a single family. The family could consist of a single individual, but would more typically be a family with parents and children. The first aspect we will look at is the budget constraint the family faces. The budget constraint applies not to one single year, but to many future years taken together. The constraint is more flexible in any one year than it is over time; in any one year a family can consume more than its disposable income by borrowing or by drawing down some of its financial assets. But a family can't go on forever consuming more than its disposable income; eventually it will run out of assets or places to borrow. The family faces an **intertemporal budget constraint** that limits its consumption over the years. In some years, a family will consume less than its income; the excess of income over consumption—saving—is then added to the family's financial assets and can be used for consumption in later years. Consumption this year is thus reduced so that consumption in later years can be increased. The budget constraint incorporates the accumulation of assets that results from savings.

The intertemporal budget constraint can be described in words as follows:

Assets at the beginning of next year
= Assets at the beginning of this year
+ Income on assets this year
+ Income from work this year $\Big\}$ Disposable income
− Taxes paid this year
− Consumption this year $\Bigg\}$ Saving

Assets include items such as bank deposits, bonds, corporate stock, and pension funds. There are two types of income: (1) income on assets, such as interest payments from the bank where the family holds its deposits, and (2) income from work. If a family adds to its assets, then it also adds to its future income on those assets. Hence it is important to distinguish between the two types of income.

Disposable income is, of course, income on assets plus income from work minus taxes. Note that the budget constraint simply states that each year's saving—disposable income less consumption—is added to assets.

To give a clearer picture of the intertemporal budget, we introduce the following symbols:

A_t = Assets at the beginning of Year t
R = Interest rate on assets
E_t = Income from work during Year t
T_t = Taxes during Year t
C_t = Consumption during Year t

The small subscript indicates the year. The interest rate (R) tells us how much income a given amount of assets will earn. For example, if the interest rate is 5 percent and assets A_t equal $1,000 in Year t, then income on assets is $50 in Year t. (The interest rate R is the *real* interest rate, that is, the nominal interest rate less the expected rate of inflation.)

Using these symbols, the intertemporal budget constraint can be written as

$$A_{t+1} = A_t + RA_t + E_t - T_t - C_t. \qquad (10\text{--}3)$$

The six algebraic terms in Equation 10–3 correspond one for one with the six items listed in the budget constraint that we wrote in words above. The subscript $t + 1$ indicates assets at the beginning of Year $t + 1$. (For example, if Year t is 1988, then Year $t + 1$ is 1989.) The budget constraint, Equation 10–3, applies to all years of the family's future—working years and retirement years. By applying this equation year after year, the family can figure out what its asset position will be many years in the future, given expectations about the interest rate, income from work, and taxes. By reducing consumption this year, the family can increase its assets in future years. The increased assets—plus the interest earned on these assets—could be used for consumption on timely items such as the children's education, for retirement, or as a bequest. (The interest rate R is measured in fractions in this formula: If the interest rate is 5 percent, then set R equal to .05 in Equation 10–3. Then R times A, for example, equals $50 if A equals $1,000.)

A consumption plan is feasible if it does not involve an impractical asset position at any time in the future. Any positive amount of assets is practical, since it means the family is lending to others, rather than borrowing. For most people, it is impractical to have their assets drop significantly below zero. Our concept of assets is *net* across all borrowing and ownership of the family; if a family buys a house with a 20 percent down payment and takes on a mortgage for the remaining 80 percent, its net asset position is positive. The value of the house as an asset exceeds the liability of the mortgage. Borrowing from a positive net asset position is perfectly practical—almost everybody does it. But it is difficult to borrow when there is a negative net asset position. An exception might be medical or business school students who can borrow because their expected future incomes are so favorable.

Preferences: Steady Rather than Erratic Consumption

Many different consumption plans are feasible. As long as the family is careful not to consume too much, it has a wide choice about when to schedule its consumption. It could consume very little in the early years and build up significant assets by middle age. Or it could consume as much as possible and keep its assets only barely positive. Which of the feasible plans will the family choose? The forward-looking theory of consumption assumes that *most people prefer to keep their consumption fairly steady from year to year.* Given the choice between consuming $10,000 this year and $10,000 next year, as against $5,000 this year and $15,000 next year, people generally choose the even split. There are exceptions, but it seems that most people prefer not to have ups and downs in their standard of living.

Figure 10–7 shows a typical path for income for a family with a steady consumption plan. Income from employment is low in the early

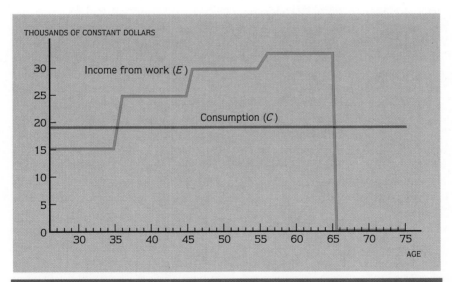

FIGURE 10–7   Illustration of steady consumption compared with income growth and decline

Income from work is assumed to grow as experience and seniority increase and then drop to zero during retirement. Thoughtful forward-looking consumers who prefer a smooth consumption path will tend to borrow during their early years, save in their middle-years, and draw down their assets during retirement.

years and gradually rises until retirement, as job experience and seniority increase. During retirement income from work is zero. Note how consumption is relatively large compared with income in the early years of work; young families tend to borrow when they can in anticipation of greater future income in later years. During the years immediately before retirement, consumption is relatively low as the family saves more in anticipation of retirement. Finally, during retirement consumption is much greater than income as the family draws down its assets.

Preferences: How Large an Inheritance for the Next Generation?

Figure 10–7 illustrates the important features of the typical smooth consumption path. But the assumption that families prefer a smooth consumption path is still not sufficient to pin down one consumption path among those that are feasible. The family can choose a high smooth consumption plan or a low smooth consumption plan. Different smooth paths of consumption will leave the family with different levels of assets at the end of the parents' lifetimes. Figure 10–8 shows the path of assets for the smooth consumption path already shown in Figure 10–7 (Path 2) along with asset paths for higher (Path 1) and lower (Path 3) consumption paths.

A higher consumption path leaves fewer assets at the end of the lifetime. To pin down the consumption path completely, we need to make an assumption about what the parents' preferences are for assets at the end of their lifetimes. How much will they want to leave to the next generation as inheritance? If parents are convinced that their children can make it on their own, they may prefer to consume most of their assets during retirement. Or they might want to reward their children for doing well by giving a large bequest. There is little agreement among economists on what motivates bequests.[5] Fortunately, however, many of the important empirical predictions of the life-cycle and the permanent-income hypotheses hold regardless of what assumption we make about inheritance. We will discuss the effect of alternative assumptions below, where the assumption about inheritance does matter.

The Marginal Propensity to Consume Out of Temporary versus Permanent Changes in Income

It should already be apparent from Figure 10–7 that there is a relation between the family's current assets plus its expectations about future earnings

---

[5]Douglas Bernheim, Andrei Shleifer, and Lawrence Summers argue that parents use bequests to influence their children's actions in "The Strategic Bequest Motive," *Journal of Political Economy,* Vol. 93 (December 1985), pp. 1045–1076.

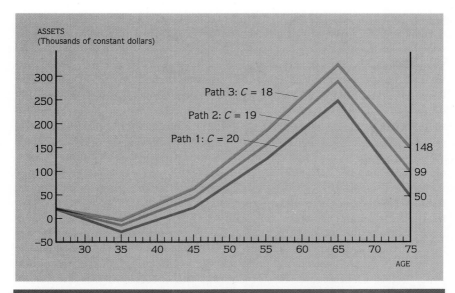

ASSETS
(Thousands of constant dollars)

Path 3: $C = 18$
Path 2: $C = 19$
Path 1: $C = 20$

148
99
50

AGE

FIGURE 10–8 Assets and bequests under smooth consumption paths, starting with $15,000

If consumption follows Path 1 over the family's lifetime, assets will follow the path marked 1, with little left for the next generation. If consumption follows Path 2, sufficiently more assets are accumulated to leave more for the next generation. Along Path 3, consumption is even lower and assets left for inheritance are even higher.

from work and its consumption decision. If news comes along that the family is better off, either because it has higher assets today or because it expects higher earnings in the future, the family will adjust its consumption upward. Moreover, it will adjust its future consumption plans upward by about the same amount. If the family reacted to good news by changing only current consumption and not future planned consumption, it would be planning a consumption path that would not be smooth.

By how much does consumption change when disposable income changes? For forward-looking consumers the answer depends on how long the change in income will last—in particular, whether the change is viewed as *temporary* or *permanent.*

Consider first the case where income increases permanently. An interesting and important example is a permanent cut in taxes, though any other change such as the winning of a state lottery that pays the family a yearly payment for life would serve just as well. Suppose that the family learns that its taxes will be lower by a certain amount, say $1,000, this year, next year, and every year in the future. Disposable income increases in the first year by $1,000, and the increase is viewed as permanent. Assume that the tax cut was unexpected so that the family could not have planned for it in advance. If the family didn't change its consumption plans, future assets would pile up quickly. Next year, assets would be higher by $1,000. In later years, this would grow as interest compounded. But next year, there would be another increment to assets in the amount of $1,000, and in later years this too would earn compound interest. Moreover, if the family raised its consumption, assets would still pile up unless the increase in consumption were equal to the decrease in taxes, $1,000. The family's exact plan would depend on how much of the income improvement it wanted to pass on to the next generation. Assuming the the amount of the improvement passed on is zero, we get a simple conclusion: *The marginal propensity to consume from the increase in disposable income is 1. Consumption rises by the full amount of the increase in income when the increase is viewed as permanent.* If the family wanted to pass on some of the increased income as a bequest, then the marginal propensity to consume would be smaller.

Now consider a temporary tax cut of $1,000 that will last only 1 year; taxes are then expected to return to their normal level in the remaining years. Again assume that the tax cut was unexpected so that the family could not have adjusted its plans in advance. If the family raises its consumption by $1,000 in the year of the tax cut, then it will finish the year with nothing extra saved. At the end of the year it will have to reduce its consumption to the level previously planned; this goes against the rule that consumption should be smooth. The family can achieve a better consumption plan by raising consumption less than the tax cut and accumulating some assets. Hence, the marginal propensity to consume will be less than 1. But how much less?

We can determine the amount by using the forward-looking model. If the family didn't change its consumption plans at all, the $1,000 would be added to the family's assets and would start earning interest at rate R. Suppose that the interest rate is 5 percent. As the years passed, the increment to assets, including compound interest, would become quite large. After 50 years, $1,000 left to compound at 5 percent interest becomes $12,000. But rather than leave this much more for the next generation, the typical family will probably raise its planned consumption. If it raises planned consumption by the amount of the interest, $50 per year, then after 50 years the family will have just the additional $1,000, not the extra $11,000 in compound interest. Thus, one option for the family is to plan to consume an extra $50 per year and leave an extra $1,000 to the next generation. Or, the family could consume just a bit more and leave nothing extra to the next generation. The intertemporal budget constraint, Equation 10–3, can be used to figure out how much more than $50 the increase in consumption would have to be to exhaust the $1,000 windfall after 50 years.

The forward-looking theory predicts the following consumption rule from this planning process: *If a family receives an unexpected temporary increment to its disposable income, it will raise its consumption by the interest earned by the increment, plus a bit more if it does not want to pass the full amount on to the next generation.* If the tax cut is $1,000, then the rise in consumption is $50, or a little more if not all of the $1,000 is passed on. The marginal propensity to consume from the 1-year temporary tax cut, or any other temporary increase in income, is the same as, or a little greater than, the interest rate, or about .05 in this example. It is far, far less than the marginal propensity to consume arising from a permanent increase in income, which is closer to 1. It is also much less than that suggested by the simple consumption function we looked at earlier in the chapter. The difference between the marginal propensity to consume out of a temporary change in income and the marginal propensity to consume out of a permanent change in income is the single most important feature of the newer theories of consumption based on a forward-looking consumer.

Anticipated versus Unanticipated Changes in Income

In each of the above examples we assumed that the change in income was unanticipated. If the change was anticipated, then the family would adjust its plans in advance. How? Suppose, for example, that the family learns about the temporary tax cut of $1,000 one year in advance. Then it would increase its consumption before the tax cut actually took place. Postponing the increase in consumption to the year of the tax cut would mean that the planned consumption path would not be smooth, and this would violate the steady consumption rule. The increase in the consumption path would be slightly less than in the case where the tax cut was unanticipated simply because there is one more year of consumption to spread the improved income over. If the family wanted to leave the full $1,000 to the next generation, then the increase in consumption would be slightly less than the interest rate times the tax cut. If the tax cut occurred with 50 years on the planning horizon, then consumption would be spread over 51 years. The increase in consumption would thus be about $48.

Note that the marginal propensity to consume in the year that the tax cut is anticipated is astronomical. The change in income is zero in that year and consumption increases by about $48. The marginal propensity to consume is literally infinite! But the important point is that with forward-looking consumers the marginal propensity to consume depends not only on whether the change in income is temporary or permanent, but also on whether it is anticipated or unanticipated.

THE FORWARD-LOOKING MODEL

1. The forward-looking model of consumption assumes that households choose current consumption as part of a lifetime consumption plan.

2. The intertemporal budget constraint implies that total planned consumption cannot exceed total household resources (the sum of current wealth and expected future income). If the household plans to leave a bequest, total planned consumption is less than total resources.

3. Although the forward-looking model can accommodate any pattern of preferences, it is typically assumed that households prefer smooth consumption profiles.

4. The theory predicts that the marginal propensity to consume out of permanent changes in income will be close to 1. The marginal propensity to consume out of temporary changes in income will approximately equal the rate of interest.

5. Another important insight that comes from the theory is that current consumption responds not only to changes in current income, but also to changes in expected future income.

10.4 HOW WELL DOES THE FORWARD-LOOKING THEORY WORK?

The key point of the forward-looking theory of consumption is that the marginal propensity to consume from new funds depends on whether the new funds are a one-time increment or will recur in future years. The marginal propensity to consume from temporary increases is low—only a little above the interest rate. The marginal propensity to consume from permanent increases in earnings is high—close to 1.

Consumption in the economy as a whole is the aggregation of the consumption decisions of millions of families. Some tests of the forward-looking model focus on aggregate consumption. Many of the events that matter a great deal for an individual family—births and deaths, promotions, winning big at the racetrack—don't matter at all in the aggregate. The "law of large numbers" guarantees that purely random individual experiences do not influence the total. But some of the influences affecting individual families are common across all families, as, for example, when the economy goes into recession.

The Short-Run and Long-Run MPC: A Rough Check of the Theory

Before looking at the particular methods that Friedman, Modigliani, and other economic researchers have used to test this theory formally, let's see how well it explains the facts of aggregate consumption that we presented in the previous section. The most important statistical regularity that the simple consumption function misses is that the short-run marginal propensity to consume is less than the long-run marginal propensity to consume; that is, consumption does not increase as much with income over short-run business cycle periods as it does over long-run growth periods. If consumers usually expect short-run business cycle fluctuations in their income to be temporary, then the forward-looking consumption theory provides an explanation for this finding. If they expect the drop in income that they experience during a recession to be temporary, then they will not cut their consumption as much as if they thought the drop was more lasting. Similarly, they will not increase their consumption so much during the boom stage of a cycle. Is is plausible that many consumers tend to view recessions and booms as temporary? The experience of much of the last 35 years is that business cycle recessions and booms have in fact been temporary. If consumers can remember this experience, then an expectation that recessions are temporary seems reasonable. Moreover, economic forecasters usually predict a return to a steady growth path following a recession— they at least remember what happened in the last cycle—and their forecasts are covered on television, in newspapers, and in magazines.

There is even an important exception that seems to prove the rule. In the recession that followed 1973 the dramatic increase in the price of oil and other energy sources probably made many consumers feel that the drop in real income they were experiencing was unlike a typical recession and was likely to be more permanent. According to the forward-looking consumption model, consumers therefore would have cut their expenditures by more than the decreased consumption of a typical recession. This is just what happened in 1973 through 1975. (See Figure 10–5, which shows that consumption was well below normal during that period.) Overall the forward-looking theory of consumption seems to pass this rough check pretty well.

Ando and Modigliani: Do Assets Matter for Consumption?

One of the earliest formal statistical tests of the forward-looking theory was done by Albert Ando of the University of Pennsylvania in collaboration with Modigliani. Ando and Modigliani formulated consumption as depending on two factors: (1) current income from work and (2) total assets. In

Why Is the Saving Rate Higher in Japan than in the United States?

Personal saving is personal disposable income less consumption and interest paid by households. The *personal saving rate* is personal saving as a percentage of personal disposable income. For example, in 1991, saving was $222 billion and the saving rate was 5.3 percent [the calculation is (222/4218) x 100 = 5.3]. The 5.3 percent personal saving rate was one of the lowest in the United States since the post-World War II consumption binge of 1947. (In 1987, the saving rate was 4.3 percent.) This low saving rate is just another way to think about the huge errors in the consumption function for 1987 to 1989 shown in Figure 10–5 and discussed in the text (consuming an abnormally high fraction of disposable income is the same thing as saving an abnormally low fraction of disposable income).

A 5.3 percent saving rate is low even by U.S. standards, but saving rates in the United States are always low by Japanese standards. For most of the post–World War II period, the personal saving rate in Japan was almost double that in the United States. In a detailed study of saving behavior in Japan and the United States, Fumio Hayashi of Osaka University showed that Japanese saving rates are higher than U.S. saving rates, even for alternative saving definitions that include business and government saving and after adjustments for several different measurement concepts.

Why is the saving rate higher in Japan? The forward-looking theory of consumption may provide part of the answer. In countries with high growth rates, the young tend to have higher incomes than the old people did when they were young. Since young people tend to save and old people tend to dissave according to forward-looking models, the young people with higher incomes will tend to raise the overall saving rate.

Because Japan has a higher growth rate than the United States, the Japanese saving rate will be higher according to the forward-looking model. Simulations of detailed life-cycle models suggest, however, that the growth differential between Japan and the United States is not the entire explanation of the saving rate differential.

There are other possible explanations. Land and housing prices are very high in Japan. Hence, families need to save more for a down payment to buy a house. Further, there is not as extensive a social security system in Japan; families may feel they have to save more for old age. The tax system in Japan is also thought to favor saving.

There are also some noneconomic explanations. As stated by Hayashi, "If all else fails, there is a cultural explanation. The Japanese are simply different. They are more risk-averse and more patient. If this is true, the long-run implication is that Japan will absorb all the wealth in the world. I refuse to comment on this explanation."*

*Fumio Hayashi, "Why Is Japan's Saving Rate So Apparently High?" in S. Fischer, ed., *Macroeconomics Annual*, Vol. 1, National Bureau of Economic Research, 1986.

their formulation a change in income, given the value of assets, is assumed to be indicative of a permanent change in income (the current level of income would be representative of all future income). Hence, the marginal propensity to consume from a change in income from work—holding constant the level of assets—would be close to 1. The equation would have to be made more complicated if current income is known to be different from likely future income. On the other hand, their formulation assumes that a change in the value of total assets, given the level of income, would tend to be a temporary change—an example would be a one-time increase in the value of corporate stock. Hence, the marginal propensity to consume from a change in the value of total assets would be close to the interest rate. Algebraically, the Ando-Modigliani consumption function takes the form

$$C = b_1 Y_d + b_2 A, \tag{10-4}$$

where Y_d is disposal income, A is assets, and b_1 and b_2 are coefficients. Note that Equation 10-4 is a modification of the simple Keynesian consumption function: Assets have been added as a second factor to income. When Ando and Modigliani fit this simple equation to data in the United States during the period after World War II, they found that b_1 was close to .7 and b_2 was close to .06; this provided striking confirmation for their ideas about consumption. Moreover, the addition of total assets to the equation could eliminate some of the errors in the simple Keynesian consumption function that we noted earlier. For example, the bulge of consumption relative to income in the years just after World War II could be explained by the high level of consumer assets in those years. The decline in consumption starting in 1973 could be explained by the drop in the stock market and other asset valuations. Fluctuations in asset values are not much help in explaining the fluctuations of consumption in recent years, however.

Friedman: Does Past Income Matter for Consumption?

Friedman expressed the ideas about forward-looking consumers in a slightly different way. He simply defined permanent income as that constant level of annual income that has a present value equivalent to the family's assets and expected future income. All other changes in income are then viewed as transitory. Friedman argued that the marginal propensity to consume from permanent income should be close to 1, and the marginal propensity to consume from transitory income should be close to zero. Algebraically, he formulated the consumption function as

$$C = b_p Y_p, \tag{10-5}$$

where Y_p is permanent disposable income and b_p is a coefficient. According to Friedman's formulation b_p should be close to 1.

An important part of Friedman's formulation was his assumption that permanent income is an average of income over the last several years. Thus, if current income suddenly increased, there would be only a small increase in permanent income; income would have to increase for several years in a row before people would expect that permanent income had increased. To test the theory, he thus substituted an average of current income and previous income over the past several years for permanent income in Equation 10–5. Effectively, therefore, consumption should depend on past income as well as on current income. Past income should matter for consumption because it helps people to forecast future income. Although it is an admittedly simple model of people's expectations, Friedman found that his formulation of the consumption function fit the facts better than the simple Keynesian function with current income.

Where Do We Stand Now?

The empirical work of Ando, Modigliani, and Friedman is now more than 35 years old. Economic research in the 1970s and 1980s has led to more revealing tests of the forward-looking theory and has raised puzzling new questions. Three strands of the new research are particularly important: the use of rational expectations to measure future income prospects, the analysis of data on the histories of thousands of individual families, and case studies of particular economic policy "experiments."

RATIONAL EXPECTATIONS. The hypothesis of consumers as forward-looking decision-makers already postulates a considerable degree of rationality to consumers. The hypothesis of rational expectations postulates more, but not necessarily less plausible, rationality. Recall that Ando, Modigliani, and Friedman postulated rather naive assumptions about what people expected about their future income: It would tend to stay where it was recently. The rational expectations approach attempts to look at the actual historical behavior of income and use this to describe statistically how people expect income to behave in the future.

The approach is a statistical formalization and a much finer version of the rough check on the theory that we described at the start of this section. Rather than just saying that people expect business cycles to be temporary, the approach assumes that people act as if they have a little algebraic model of the behavior of income over the business cycle in their heads and that they use this model when guessing their future income. Of course, nobody except perhaps an economist would actually use such a model in their personal family planning: The idea is that by watching television, reading the newspaper, or just talking with friends, people get a view of future economic developments that is not much different from that of the average professional economist who actually uses such a model.

The rational expectations approach is used by many economists engaged in macroeconomic research.[6] The most straightforward version of this approach is to substitute the forecasts of income from such a model into the permanent-income equation (10–5) for consumption. More technical versions substitute forecasts of future income into the intertemporal budget constraint, Equation 10–3, and calculate the optimal plan for consumption directly without the intermediate step of Friedman's permanent-income equation. Using rational expectations this way clearly requires advanced mathematical skills, and understandably the approach has attracted economists who specialize in such skills.

Although much of this research is new, it is already clear that the forward-looking consumption theory does not fare as well when people are assumed to forecast rationally. One problem is that consumption is a bit too responsive to temporary changes in income, although clearly not as responsive as in the simple Keynesian consumption theory. In other words, the forward-looking theory with rational expectations suggests that the short-run marginal propensity to consume should be even smaller than is observed in the United States data summarized in Table 10–1.

INDIVIDUAL FAMILY HISTORIES. One of the most important improvements in our knowledge of the economy in recent years is the availability of data on the economic histories of individuals and families over a span of several years. At the University of Michigan, for example, a survey called the Panel of Study on Income Dynamics has kept tabs on the major economic and personal events of thousands of families since 1969. Such surveys that collect information on individuals over a number of years are typically called **panel** or **longitudinal surveys**. They are useful to macroeconomists because they tell how families experience recessions and booms individually. Aggregate data tell us only about all families in the economy added together. One study has looked at how well the forward-looking consumption model performs in describing the consumption be-

---

[6]The research referred to is found in a series of papers published in the *Journal of Political Economy:* Robert Hall, "Stochastic Implications of the Life Cycle –Permanent Income Hypothesis: Theory and Evidence," *Journal of Political Economy,* Vol. 86 (December 1978), pp. 971–988, and Marjorie Flavin, "The Adjustment of Consumption to Changing Expectations about Future Income," *Journal of Political Economy,* Vol. 89 (October 1981), pp. 974–1009. Lars Peter Hansen and Kenneth Singleton have incorporated rational expectations into the budget constraint in a formal intertemporal planning process in their "Stochastic Consumption, Risk Aversion, and the Temporal Behavior of Asset Returns," *Journal of Political Economy,* Vol. 91 (April 1983), pp. 249–265. All these papers are technically demanding. They are listed here as sources; we suggest them as reading only for the more mathematically inclined students.

NEW RESEARCH IN PRACTICE
How Consumers Deal with Uncertainty and Changes in Their Incomes

Economists have put a huge amount of effort into understanding how families ought to deal with uncertainty about, and fluctuations in, their incomes. Research has also compared the predictions of the theory with the actual behavior of families, as it is reflected both in total consumption in the national income accounts and in data from the longitudinal surveys of individual families, such as the panel study of income dynamics. This research is applied in practice when economists make recommendations about cuts in income taxes during recessions. For example, very few economists who testified to Congress in 1991 about the recession thought that a temporary tax cut would do much to increase demand. A summary of the research explains why.

Current Consumption Is the Best Predictor of Future Consumption

One of the most interesting theoretical propositions to come out of this research is that, for a family or for the whole economy, the current level of consumption is the best predictor of future consumption. Once you look at current consumption, there should not be any other variable that will improve your forecast of consumption. Why? There are two basic elements to the analysis. First, consumers think about all information that is relevant for their present and future consumption decisions when they choose current consumption. Second, consumers want to smooth consumption; they will not normally plan to consume a lot more or a lot less in the future than they are consuming now.

Suppose that a family knew that its income was going to rise next year. Because the family wants to smooth its consumption, it will try to increase its consumption as soon as the news of the higher income comes along. Within the limitations of its knowledge of future income and its ability to finance higher consumption before the income is ac-

tually available, the family will make a consumption choice today that is the same as it expects consumption to be in the future.

Economists have tested this theoretical proposition by seeing if any variables apart from current consumption help to predict future consumption. In aggregate data, the results show two things. First, in line with the theory, current consumption is a terrific predictor of future consumption. As we noted at the beginning of the chapter, consumption is not particularly volatile; it tends to change relatively little from year to year, even when investment and other components of GDP are changing quite a bit. Second, other variables do add a little to our ability to forecast consumption. The facts do not entirely support the theoretical proposition that everything but current consumption is irrelevant. Recent changes in income and in the value of the stock market show up in the best forecasting equation for consumption even when current consumption is included.

One fascinating implication of consumption theory is that there is no systematic business cycle in consumption. When the economy is at its trough, there is no reason to expect higher than normal consumption growth. One of the ways to express the forecasting proposition is that normal growth is the best forecast of consumption growth, independent of the level of consumption or the overall state of the economy.

Random Walks

Another way to express this theoretical property of consumption is that consumption is a random walk. If it is as likely that you will take your next step forward as backward, you are taking a random walk. Your location in 5 minutes is just as likely to be ahead of where you are now as it is to be behind where you are now. Hence, your current position is the best predictor of your future position.

Another economic random walk, derived long before the consumption proposition, is the value of a particular stock in the stock market. The current value of a share in Exxon is the best available predictor of its value in the future. If it were generally known that the share was going to be more valuable tomorrow, then people would try to buy more shares today. In the process, they would bid up the price until it was no longer true that the share price was expected to rise tomorrow.

Qualifications

Both the consumption random walk and the stock market random walk have an important qualification as a matter of theory. Suppose that the real in-terest rate is unusually high. Consumers may choose to depart from consumption smoothing in order to take advantage of the high return to saving. They may deliberately make a plan to consume less now and more later. In principle, the expected real interest rate should have predictive power in the presence of current consumption. We will discuss this point in section 10.5.

The random walk of stock prices also has the same qualification: if the interest rate is high, but a stock is paying a low dividend, the market for the stock will be in equilibrium when the price of the stock is expected to rise enough in the future so that the owner will receive a combination of dividend and capital gain to equal the high interest rate. The higher the interest rate, the higher the predicted increase in the stock price. This qualification has been verified by data from the stock market.

---

havior of about 2,000 families in the Michigan panel data set.[7] The results show an excess sensitivity of consumption to temporary changes in disposable income. The marginal propensity to consume from temporary income was about 30 percent of the marginal propensity to consume from permanent income. This is higher than the 5 to 10 percent ratio that the pure forward-looking model suggests. The results seem to say that about 80 percent of the families behaved according to the forward-looking model, while about 20 percent behaved according to a simple model in which consumption is proportional to disposable income.

POLICY EXPERIMENTS. In 1968 during President Johnson's administration, Congress passed a temporary surcharge on the personal income tax; the surcharge raised taxes by 10 percent. The purpose was to restrict consumption temporarily and thereby reduce aggregate demand in an economy overheated by Vietnam War expenditures. A similar temporary tax change occurred during President Ford's administration, but in the reverse direction. When the economy was in the trough of the 1974–75 recession, a tax rebate and social security bonus of $9.4 billion was paid out in the second quarter of 1975. The hope was to stimulate the economy by increasing aggregate demand. According to the forward-looking theory of

---

[7]Robert Hall and Fredric Mishkin, "The Sensitivity of Consumption to Transitory Income: Estimates from Panel Data on Households," *Econometrica,* Vol. 50 (March 1982), pp. 461–481.

consumption, families who realized that these tax changes were temporary would adjust their consumer expenditures by only a small amount; if so, the policy changes would not have their desired effect of restricting demand in 1968 or stimulating demand in 1975. On the other hand, according to the simple consumption function, these tax changes would be translated into large changes in consumption and thereby in aggregate demand.

Although clearly not conceived as experiments, these two changes in policy gave economists a rare opportunity to test the predictions of the forward-looking theory of consumption. It is probably as close as macroeconomics will ever get to a laboratory experiment. As it turned out, the response of consumption to the change in disposable income seemed to be small in both cases. After the increase in taxes in 1968 consumers simply saved less of their reduced income and thereby reduced their spending only slightly. In the second quarter of 1975 the rate of saving as a fraction of disposable income rose to almost 10 percent from about 6 percent in the first quarter. Almost all the increase in disposable income was saved, evidently because people knew the temporary nature of the income changes. In addition to providing evidence in favor of the forward-looking theory of consumption, the lesson from these two policy experiments has been to make policymakers much more reluctant to use such temporary tax changes to affect aggregate demand. Economists in the Ford administration wrote in the 1977 *Economic Report of the President:* "Consumers normally adjust expenditures to their 'permanent' or long-run income." In 1977 President Carter came into office proposing another rebate to stimulate the economy out of an apparent slowdown in the recovery, but the proposal was criticized by many economists and was not passed by Congress.

Alan Blinder of Princeton University has systematically studied the response of consumer spending to temporary changes in consumer income using a rational expectations approach similar to that described above.[8] His overall finding was that the marginal propensity to consume from a temporary tax change is about half the marginal propensity to consume from a permanent tax change. This ratio is a bit above that found in the Michigan panel data (.3). Blinder's data suggest that the world is split about 50–50 between forward-looking consumers and those who consume a constant proportion of their current disposable income. But Blinder emphasizes that these estimates are not precise. Perhaps the most important lesson from these experiments is that the response of the economy to a temporary income tax change is not the sure, predictable stimulus predicted by the simple consumption function.

---

[8]Alan Blinder, "Temporary Income Taxes and Consumer Spending," *Journal of Political Economy*, Vol. 89 (February 1981), pp. 26–53. The figures on tax rebates and saving mentioned in the previous paragraph are tabulated in Blinder's paper.

Defects in the Forward-Looking Model

Overall the empirical research discussed above indicates that the forward-looking model works fairly well: The marginal propensity to consume from temporary income is always less than the marginal propensity to consume from permanent income, as the theory predicts. But why doesn't it work better? Why does consumption respond as much as it does to temporary income? One reason is that the tests might be incorrectly estimating expectations of future income. In the case of temporary tax changes, for example, families may not be so aware of the machinations of the government. Perhaps they pay no attention to the news about tax changes. If they, like most people, see the benefits of a tax cut in the form of reduced withholding deductions from their paychecks, they may mistakenly assume that this cut in deductions is permanent. Then they will apply their regular marginal propensity to consume from income, which will be, say, .9. Moreover, when they find their deductions back up to the old level, they will reduce consumption accordingly.

Or suppose the family pays close attention to the economic news and believes that a temporary tax cut will accomplish its purpose of stimulating the economy. The family will benefit in the next year or two from the more favorable performance of the economy. According to the life-cycle and permanent-income hypotheses, the family should immediately increase its consumption because of its expected increase in economic well-being. Even though such a family would spend only a little of its tax rebate, it might raise its total consumption level because of the improved national economy.

Another possibility is that consumers cannot borrow as easily as the forward-looking model suggests and that especially during recessions they cannot obtain the funds to maintain their consumption. Economists call such consumers **liquidity constrained.**[9] Such consumers might be described very well by the simple Keynesian model; they would increase their expenditures as they receive more income regardless of whether it is permanent or temporary.

In concluding our discussion of the forward-looking model of consumption, it is important not to lose sight of the central ideas by focusing too much on the particular equations or tests that express the ideas. The basic point is that families are thoughtful about consumption decisions. The way they react to a change in economic circumstances depends on the context of the change. If the change is transitory—if it involves a windfall gain or loss—consumption is likely to respond relatively little. If the change in

---

[9]See Fumio Hayashi, "Tests for Liquidity Constraints: A Critical Survey and Some New Observations," in Truman Bewley, ed., *Advances in Econometrics,* Vol. 2 (Cambridge, England: Cambridge University Press, 1987), pp. 91–120.

income will sustain itself for the foreseeable future, consumption will change almost by the full amount of the change in income.

EMPIRICAL EVIDENCE ON THE FORWARD-LOOKING MODEL OF CONSUMPTION

1. Verification of the forward-looking model with aggregate data confirms its main implications.
2. More detailed tests with data on individual families reveal some shortcomings. Liquidity constraints may help explain the discrepancies between theoretical predictions and actual behavior.

10.5 REAL INTEREST RATES, CONSUMPTION, AND SAVING

Thus far we have assumed that consumers want a steady consumption path. They would like to consume about the same amount this year as next year and every year thereafter. This is a reasonable assumption if the price of future consumption goods is not too low or too high relative to present consumption goods. But suppose that the price of future consumption goods is suddenly expected to fall; suppose, for example, that sales taxes will be repealed starting next year! Clearly people would postpone their consumption expenditures until next year to take advantage of the lower price. They would do this as long as they were not so impatient that they couldn't get along without the goods this year. Consumption today would fall and consumption next year would rise.

The interest rate becomes a factor in consumption because it affects the price of future consumption relative to current consumption. In fact, the *real* interest rate is the relative price between present consumption and future consumption. It thus directly affects the choice of whether to consume more today or tomorrow. Recall that the interest rate quoted in the newspaper, the *nominal* interest rate, does not correct for changes in purchasing power. The real interest rate R equals the nominal interest rate minus the expected rate of inflation π^e. For example, if the nominal interest rate is 11 percent, but prices are expected to rise at 4 percent per year, then the real interest rate is 7 percent. If you postpone 1 unit of consumption this year, you can consume 1.07 units next year by investing at an 11 percent nominal rate and losing 4 percent to inflation.

If the real interest rate is positive, as it generally is, people face an incentive to defer spending. A dollar saved today will buy more than a dollar's worth of goods tomorrow. Hence people will tend to defer consumption unless they are too impatient. Economists have a measure of impatience called the **rate of time preference.** If the real interest rate is higher than the rate of time preference, then people will tend to shift their consumption a bit toward the next year. If the real rate of interest is high, today's consumption will tend to be low. This factor makes consumption negatively related to the real rate of interest. Saving, which is simply the difference between disposable income and consumption, is therefore positively related to the real rate of interest.

Changes in the interest rate do something else in addition to changing tomorrow's price of goods relative to today's. They change income. If interest rates rise, for example, a family can earn a higher real return from its accumulated assets. This makes the family better off. On this account, planned consumption is higher. This increase in consumption might offset the reduced consumption that comes from the incentive to defer consumption from today to tomorrow. Hence, we can't say unambiguously whether consumption in the first year falls or rises; the *income* effect makes it rise while the incentive to make a *substitution* of future consumption for present consumption makes it fall. Similarly, the effect of change in the real interest rate on saving is also ambiguous.[10] Of course, this offsetting tendency of the income effect and the substitution effect is common to many relative price changes in economics, not only to interest rate changes.

It is a controversial matter whether or not consumption is negatively related to the interest rate in the U.S. economy.[11] The most difficult problem in interpreting the data is that consumption depends on disposable income as well as on the interest rate, and during the business cycle income and the interest rate tend to move together. It is difficult to separate out the effect of just the interest rate.

Another complication in examining the relation between real interest and consumption is that the real interest rate is not observed directly. What we observe is the nominal interest rate. To convert it to a real rate, we must subtract the expected rate of inflation. Measuring the expected rate of inflation is difficult.

Effect of Real Interest Rates on Work

There is one last complication in our analysis of consumption. For this whole chapter we have assumed that individuals do not or cannot change

[10]The income and substitution effects are shown graphically in the appendix to this chapter.
[11]One attempt to measure the substitution effect alone is Robert E. Hall, "Intertemporal Substitution in Consumption," *Journal of Political Economy*, Vol. 96 (April 1988), pp. 971–987.

how much they work. Income from work was taken as exogenous. But some people are free to vary how much they work. In particular, if real interest rates rise, the value of income from working today relative to tomorrow rises. People could gain from working harder and longer hours now and taking time off to spend the earnings later. Hence, in principle, income from work is a positive function of the real interest rate. Because saving is the difference between disposable income and consumption, this positive effect or real interest rates on income from working reinforces the negative effect of real interest rates on consumption to make saving positively related to income.

Detecting the effect of real interest rates on work effort has proved even more elusive than detecting the effect of real interest rates on consumption. It appears that most people cannot or do not adjust their work effort very much in response to interest-rate changes. This corresponds with casual observation.

CONSUMPTION, SAVING, AND THE INTEREST RATE

1. The consumption planning process should take the interest rate into account. The real interest rate—the nominal interest rate less the expected rate of inflation—is the trade-off facing the consumer between current and future consumption. When real interest rates are high, future consumption becomes cheaper relative to consumption this year.
2. It is difficult to isolate the effect of interest rates on consumption in actual data. There is no strong empirical confirmation of the theoretical possibility that saving responds positively to real interest rates, at least for the variation in real interest rates observed in the United States.
3. In principle, interest-rate changes may cause people to reallocate labor supply over time. Higher interest rates today increase the return to current labor effort measured in units of future consumption. Evidence suggests this effect is very weak.

10.6   CONSUMPTION AND THE IS CURVE

In Chapter 7 we introduced the IS curve. It shows all the combinations of real GDP and interest rates where spending balance occurs. To find a point on the IS curve, we consider a particular interest rate. Then we find the level of GDP that gives spending balance at the interest rate. The IS curve is downward sloping in the IS-LM diagram with the interest rate R on the vertical axis and output Y on the horizontal axis. The slops of the IS curve and how much it is shifted by fiscal policy are crucial for evaluating the effects of monetary and fiscal policy.

Recall that the simple Keynesian consumption function was used in the derivation of the IS curve in Chapter 7. How is the IS curve affected by the factors considered in this chapter?

The Slope of the IS Curve

Consider first the slope of the IS curve. The smaller the marginal propensity to consume (MPC), the steeper the slope of the IS curve. A small MPC means that the multiplier is small and changes in interest rates thereby have a small effect on output. The results considered in this chapter make us scale down the MPC. In our complete model, departures of output from potential are best thought of as temporary changes in income. Thus, the variation in income along the IS curve is a variation in temporary income, for which the marginal propensity to consume is likely to be quite small. On this account the IS curve is steeper than it seemed in Chapter 7, because output is less sensitive to the interest rate.

However, the interest-rate effects on consumption considered toward the end of this chapter have an opposite effect on the IS curve. If consumption depends negatively on the interest rate, then a higher interest rate will shift the consumption function down, in which case the level of GDP corresponding to spending balance will be lower. On that account the IS curve is flatter than it seemed in Chapter 7, because output is more sensitive to the interest rate.

On balance it is an empirical question whether the true IS curve that incorporates the issues raised in this chapter is flatter or steeper than the IS curve derived in Chapter 7.

Shifts in the IS Curve Due to Tax Changes

The IS curve in Chapter 7 did not distinguish between temporary and permanent changes in taxes. A cut in tax payments of any kind would shift the IS curve to the right by the same amount and thereby stimulate output by the same amount. The forward-looking theory of consumption says that the shift in the IS curve should be much larger if the tax cut is permanent rather than temporary. A purely temporary tax cut—such as the 1975 tax rebate— would have a very small effect on the IS curve.

Because it is sometimes difficult to tell whether people think a tax cut is permanent or temporary, the forward-looking theory points to an element of uncertainty in our ability to determine how much the IS curve will shift in response to tax changes.

Finally, the forward-looking theory says that the IS curve will shift to the right in response to an *expectation* of future tax cuts. Future tax cuts will stimulate consumption today because lifetime disposable income has increased. The strong growth of consumption in 1986, for example, may have been due to the expectation of future tax cuts in 1987 and 1988 that were enacted in 1986.

REVIEW AND PRACTICE

Major Points

1. Consumers finance their consumption from their incomes, and consumption has tracked income reasonably closely in U.S. history.

2. There have been, however, significant deviations from a simple consumption function.

3. The forward-looking consumption theory relates consumption to current and expected future income rather than to just current income.

4. In this view, the marginal propensity to consume from transitory changes in income is much lower than that from permanent changes in income.

5. Tax policy does not operate in a mechanical way through disposable income. Families raise their consumption only if a tax cut makes them feel better off, which may not happen with some types of cuts.

6. The forward-looking model passes empirical tests with aggregate data quite well, but still has some defects, which have been revealed mainly by studies of individual family behavior.

7. Though higher real interest rates ought to stimulate saving by making consumers defer consumption, this hypothesis has not been firmly established by the data.

8. The marginal propensity to consume is one of the determinants of the slope of the IS curve. Because of automatic stabilizers and the low short-run marginal propensity to consume of forward-looking consumers, the IS curve may be steeper than the one derived in Chapter 7.

Key Terms and Concepts

consumption	intertemporal budget constraint	rational expectations tests
disposable income	smooth consumption path	panel data tests
Keynesian consumption function	Friedman permanent-income model	real interest rate
marginal propensity to consume (MPC)	Ando-Modigliani life-cycle model	rate of time preference
		income effect

long-run marginal
    propensity to consume
short-run marginal
    propensity to consume

forward-looking theory
    of consumption
marginal propensity to
    consume out of
    temporary income

marginal propensity to
    to consume out of
    permanent income
substitution effect
automatic stabilizers

Questions for Discussion and Review

1. List some of the reasons that disposable income is less than GDP. What factors tend to raise disposable income even though they are not part of GDP?

2. How can you tell if a simple consumption function governs the relation of consumption and income?

3. What is an estimate of the marginal propensity to consume from the historical relation of consumption to income? Why is this estimate probably an overstatement of the reaction of consumption to a temporary tax cut? What is an estimate of the short-run marginal propensity to consume?

4. Outline the way that a family might plan its consumption. How would it react to learning that tax rates are going to rise in the future?

5. Why is the marginal propensity to consume out of temporary income a bit above the real interest rate?

6. List some of the reasons that a tax cut has an uncertain effect on consumption.

7. Review all the steps involved in constructing the IS curve, including the possibility that consumption responds to the interest rate.

Problems

Numerical

1. Use the intertemporal budget constraint for this problem. To make calculations easy, assume that a family lives for 5 years with 4 years of work and 1 year of retirement. (A more realistic assumption would be a 50-year horizon with 40 years of work and 10 years of retirement.) Consider a family that wishes to consume the same amount each year. Assume earnings of $25,000 per year and an interest rate of 5 percent. Assume initial assets of zero.

   a. Find the level of consumption such that the assets at the end of 5 years are roughly zero, say within $100. What is the level of assets at the beginning of retirement?

   b. Repeat the calculation of consumption, but with initial assets of $1,000. By how much does consumption rise? Compare this with the interest earnings on $1,000 at 5 percent, namely, $50 per year. Would the increase be closer to $50 if the family lived for 50 years?

   c. Repeat the calculation of consumption, with initial assets of zero, but with earnings of $26,000 per year. By how much does consumption rise? Explain why the increase in consumption is larger than in Part b.

2. Suppose that we have a consumption function of the form

$$C = 220 + .9 Y_{\mathrm{p}},$$

where Y_p is permanent disposable income. Suppose that consumers estimate their permanent disposable income by a simple average of disposable income in the present and previous years:

$$Y_p = .5(Y_d + Y_{d-1}),$$

where Y_d is actual disposable income.

a. Suppose that disposable income Y_d is equal to $4,000 in Year 1 and is also equal to $4,000 in Year 2. What is consumption in Year 2?

b. Suppose that disposable income increases to $5,000 in Year 3 and then remains at $5,000 in all future years. What is consumption in Years 3 and 4 and all remaining years? Explain why consumption responds the way it does to an increase in income.

c. What is the short-run marginal propensity to consume? What is the long-run marginal propensity to consume?

d. Explain why this formulation of consumption may provide a more accurate description of consumption than the simple consumption function that depends only on current income.

3. Suppose that consumption is given by the same equation as in Problem 2, but that consumers set their permanent income Y_p equal to the average of their expected income in all future years.

a. Suppose that, as in the previous problem, disposable income was $4,000 in Years 1 and 2, but suppose also that in Year 2 consumers expect that disposable income will be $4,000 in all future years. What is consumption in Year 2?

b. Suppose that in Year 3 disposable income rises to $5,000 and that consumers expect the $5,000 level to remain in all future years. What is consumption in Year 3?

c. Explain why consumption in Year 3 is different from that in Problem 2 even though the disposable income is the same.

4. Suppose again that consumption is given by the same equation as in Problem 2 and that permanent income is estimated in the same way as in Problem 2. Place this consumption function into a simple macro model like the one in Chapter 7. That is, disposable income Y_d is equal to income Y less taxes T, where taxes equal $.3Y$, and the income identity is $Y = C + I + G$.

a. Suppose that in Year 2 investment I is $650 and government spending G is $750. Suppose that disposable income Y_d in Year 1 was $2,800. What are consumption, income, and disposable income in Year 2?

b. Suppose that in Year 3 government spending increases to $800 and then remains at $800 for all future years. What are consumption, income, and disposable income in Year 3? (Make sure to use your calculation from Part a of disposable income in Year 2 when you calculate consumption in Year 3.)

c. Calculate income and consumption for Years 4, 5, and 6. Do you see a pattern developing?

d. Where do you think income will end up after it stops changing? Compare your answer with the simple case where consumption depends on current disposable income only, so that the multiplier formulas of Chapter 6 apply.

5. Suppose that the consumption function is given by

$$C = 270 + .63Y - 1,000R$$

rather than by the consumption function in Chapter 7. Add this consumption function to the other four equations of the macro model:

$$Y = C + I + G + X$$
$$M = (.1583Y - 1,000R)P$$
$$I = 1,000 - 2,000R$$
$$X = 525 - .1Y - 500R$$

Treat the price level as predetermined at 1.0,. and let government spending be $1,200 and the money supply be $900.

a. Derive an algebraic expression for the IS curve for this model and plot it to scale. Compare it with the IS curve in the examples in Chapter 7. Which is steeper? Why?

b. Derive the aggregate demand curve and plot it to scale. How does it compare with the aggregate demand curve in the example of Chapter 7?

c. Calculate the effect of an increase in government spending on GDP. Is the effect larger or smaller than in the case where consumption does not depend on the interest rate? Describe the process of crowding out in this case.

d. Calculate the effect of an increase in the money supply on GDP. Is the impact larger or smaller than in the case where consumption does not depend on the interest rate? Explain.

6. The problem of the family choosing a consumption plan can be analyzed using utility functions from intermediate microeconomics. In fact, this is how the forward-looking theory has been tested in recent research. Consider a very simple 2-year horizon for a family planning consumption. The family wants to determine how much to consume in Year 1 and in Year 2. Let consumption in Year 1 be C_1, and let consumption in Year 2 be C_2. Suppose that the family's satisfaction, or utility, from consuming C_1 and C_2 is given by the function

$$\text{Utility} = \sqrt{C_1} + \frac{1}{1+RT}\sqrt{C_2}$$

where RT is the rate of time preference. Start with the rate of time preference equal to zero.

a. Show that this utility function means that the family prefers smooth consumption to erratic consumption. Which plan for consumption gives the family the greater utility: $3,600 in the first year and $4,900 in the next or $4,250 in both years?

b. Show that when the rate of time preference is high, the family will prefer to consume more in the first period. Do the following comparison: First set RT equal to zero and evaluate the utility of $3,600 in the first year and $3,000 in the second year versus $3,300 in both years; then raise RT to .25 and make the comparison again.

Analytical

1. Which of the following stylized facts are consistent with forward-looking theories of consumption? Which are not? Justify your answer in each case. Where the facts are not consistent with the theory, can you suggest some alternative explanations?
   a. The *marginal* propensity to consume out of current income is less for old people than for middle-aged people.
   b. The *marginal* propensity to consume out of current income is less for farmers than for most other occupations.
   c. Most European countries have both more extensive social welfare systems for older people and higher saving rates than the United States does.
   d. The saving rate for the United States fell in the early 1980s.
   e. The marginal propensity to consume out of temporary tax cuts is around .3 to .5.
   f. Across the population as a whole, people with lower incomes have lower saving rates than people with higher incomes.
   g. The amount of wealth in the economy is far greater than what current wage earners will consume in their retirement.

2. Suppose that actual GDP is below potential GDP, that inflation is low, and that the President and Congress want to cut taxes in order to increase aggregate demand and bring the economy back to potential.
   a. Describe the situation using an IS-LM diagram. Show where you want the IS curve to move in order to reach potential.
   b. In light of the forward-looking theory of consumption, describe some of the problems that might arise with the tax cut plan.

3. Draw a sketch of an IS-LM diagram. Compare two cases, one where the consumption function depends on the interest rate and the other where the consumption function does not depend on the interest rate. Compare the relative effectiveness of monetary and fiscal policy in the two different situations.

4. Explain the following puzzle: Saving depends positively on the interest rate, investment depends negatively on the interest rate, and saving equals investment. How does an increase in the money supply that lowers the interest rate and thereby increases investment also increase saving? It would seem that with the lower interest rate saving would be lower. What's going on?

5. An important implication of the permanent-income hypothesis is that fiscal policy operates with a lag.
   a. Explain why a permanent increase in government spending may cause the IS curve to shift out slowly over time, rather than shift out all at once.
   b. If permanent income is a weighted average of last period's and this period's income, what determines the speed at which the IS curve shifts out over time?

6. Suppose a family wants a smooth consumption profile and does not wish to leave a bequest. Indicate how each of the following factors would affect the magnitude of the marginal propensity to consume out of a temporary change in income.
   a. The size of the temporary income change.

   b. The length of the family's planning horizon.

   c. The rate of interest.

7. Suppose that you know the true magnitudes of the marginal propensities to consume out of temporary and permanent changes in income and that they are stable over time. Explain what can be learned about households' perceptions of the nature of changes in income from observations on the short-run marginal propensity to consume. In particular, what is implied by unusually large changes in consumption relative to income in a given year? What about unusually small changes?

MacroSolve Exercises

1. Provide an explanation that is consistent with the permanent-income hypothesis of the unusual behavior of the ratio of consumption to income in 1972–74 and 1986–88. To see this behavior, either plot or tabulate the quarterly time series of the APC (average propensity to consume) or graph consumption expenditures against disposable income.

2. Using the basic fixed-price model in MacroSolve ("ISLM, Closed Econ"), investigate the implications of changing the marginal propensity to consume. Explain how and why the slope of the IS curve changes when the marginal propensity to consume increases.

3. In the basic AD/PA model, does an increased responsiveness of consumption to current income lead to faster or slower adjustment to equilibrium GDP following a cut in the money supply? Explain in words why this is.

4. Plot the saving rate ("Saving/GDP%") using quarterly data from 1980.1 to 1983.4. What major event during this time period may account for the pattern in the saving rate?

APPENDIX: A Graphical Approach to Consumption Planning

In this appendix we show how a two-period consumption planning problem can be represented graphically. Suppose that the representative family must choose how much to consume this year and next year. Figure 10–9 shows how the family's preferences for consumption in the two periods might look; the vertical axis is consumption next year (Year 2) and the horizontal axis is consumption this year (Year 1). The curved lines are **indifference curves**; they give the alternative values for consumption in the two years between which the family is indifferent. The slope of the line measures how many dollars of consumption next year must be given up when consumption this year rises by 1 dollar for the family to maintain the same level of satisfaction, or utility. This is sometimes called the **marginal rate of substitution** between consumption this year and consumption next year. The family is better off when the indifference curves are farther out and up.

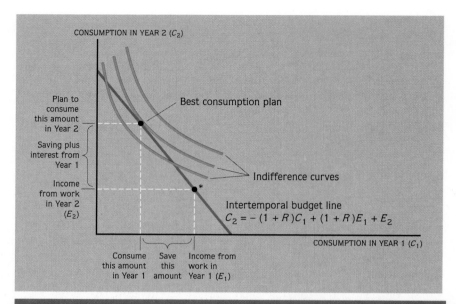

FIGURE 10–9   Indifference curves and the intertemporal budget line for consumption planning

The indifference curve is the combination of consumption in the two years that gives the same level of satisfaction to the family. The straight line is the budget constraint. The family tries to get to the highest indifference curve. This occurs where the indifference curve and the budget line just meet at a point of tangency.

The straight line in Figure 10–9 is simply the intertemporal budget constraint for the two periods. The slope of the line is $-(1 + R)$ because the family will have an additional $(1 + R)$ dollars of consumption next year for each dollar of consumption that is reduced (and thus saved) this year. [The equation for the budget line comes directly from Equation 10–3 with no taxes, no initial assets, and no bequest and is applied for two periods. Then Equation 10–3 is $A_2 = E_1 - C_1$ in Year 1, and $0 = (1 + R)A_2 + E_2 - C_2$ in Year 2. Putting A_2 into the equation for Year 1 gives the equation for the budget line.] The point on the line marked * represents the amount of income from work this year and next year. Moving up the line from * means that the family is saving this year, because income is greater than consumption. Moving down on the line means that the family borrows this year.

The family tries to maximize utility or, in terms of the graph, to get to the highest indifference curve. This occurs at a point of tangency between the budget line and the indifference curve, as shown in the diagram. At this point the slopes are equal so we know that the marginal rate of substitution between consumption next year and consumption this year is equal to 1 plus the interest rate.

Now, suppose that the interest rate increases. This is shown in Figure 10–10. The budget line will then tilt in a steeper direction, pivoting around the point *. A

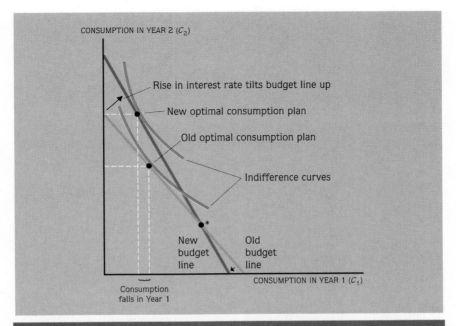

FIGURE 10–10   Increase in the interest rate

As the interest rate increases, the budget line gets steeper. This leads to a higher level of utility. As drawn, the family consumes less this period. But it is uncertain whether the family will consume less if other indifference curves are drawn.

higher level of utility is thereby achieved. As the graph is drawn, less is consumed this year. But note that this depends very much on how the indifference curves are drawn. (Try to draw another for which the reverse occurs). The tilting of the curve represents the substitution effect, which certainly causes consumption this year to fall. But the budget line has also moved out to the right from where it was before on the indifference curve. This is the income effect. It certainly leads to more consumption today.

CHAPTER

11

Investment Demand

Investment is the most volatile component of aggregate demand. While smaller in magnitude than consumption, it fluctuates more. And through the multiplier process its fluctuations lead to fluctuations in total output and income. Keynes argued that investment is the primary driving force in the economy, that it fluctuates erratically because of capricious shifts in business expectations, whereas consumption responds passively according to the simple consumption function.

In looking at the microeconomic underpinnings of investment we will see that Keynes's distinction between investment and consumption is not so pronounced. For one thing, investment, much as consumption, responds to income and output in a systematic way. When investment rises, it may be the result, not the cause, of an increase in spending elsewhere in the economy. Moreover, while investment decisions do depend on business expectations, these expectations are based on calculated estimates of future changes in demand and prices that businesses are likely to face. In making their investment decisions, business firms are at least as forward-looking as the consumers that we described in Chapter 10.

11.1 FLUCTUATIONS IN INVESTMENT SPENDING

We saw in Chapter 2 that investment spending is divided into three categories:

1. Nonresidential fixed investment—business purchases of new plants and equipment.
2. Residential fixed investment—construction of new houses and apartments.
3. Inventory investment—increases in stocks of goods produced but not yet sold.

Nonresidential fixed investment was 10.6 percent of GDP in 1991. Residential investment was 3.6 percent of GDP in the same year. But the shares of the different types of investment in GDP are not a good measure of their importance in economic fluctuations. Although plant and equipment investment is the dominant component of total investment, it is the most stable over time. Since inventory investment is negative as stocks of unsold goods fall and positive when stocks of goods rise, its share of GDP is not a very meaningful statistic. Yet, inventory investment is particularly volatile and has a major role in recessions. Finally, residential investment is important because housing construction drops when mortgage interest rates go up.

Figure 11–1 shows how tightly fixed investment is linked to overall economic activity. When investment falls as it did in the mid-1970s, the early 1980s, and 1990, the economy goes into a recession. The fluctuations of investment are larger in percentage terms than the fluctuations in real GDP. Unlike consumption, investment contributes more than its share to the fluctuations in real GDP. Note that investment slowed down in 1986, although there was no slowdown in real GDP growth in 1986. Sometimes fluctuations in investment occur without fluctuations in GDP, when consumption, government spending, or net exports move in the opposite direction.

The behavior of the two components of fixed investment—business (nonresidential) and residential—is shown in Figure 11–2. In most recessions, residential investment turns down before business investment turns down. This was true of the most recent downturn in 1990. We will show later that rising interest rates have large negative effects on residential investment and that the start of most recessions is accompanied by rising interest rates. Note that in 1986 business fixed investment declined even though residential investment continued to grow. As we will see, this decline may have been due to the increase in taxes on business capital that was passed into law in 1986.

Real GDP and *business* fixed investment move together almost in tandem. We cannot tell from the data whether movements in GDP are inducing movements in business investment or movements in business investment are inducing movements in GDP. Another mechanism to be considered is that both GDP and business investment are responding to the same underlying stimulus, which is causing both to move together.

In the economy as a whole, the volume of investment observed is the joint outcome of three factors: (1) **investment demand,** decisions made by businesses about the amount of investment to undertake; (2) **saving supply,** decisions made by consumers about the amount to save; and (3) **investment supply,** decisions made by producers of investment goods about how much to supply.

This chapter focuses on investment demand. A complete model of the economy that combines saving behavior as described in Chapter 10 and the

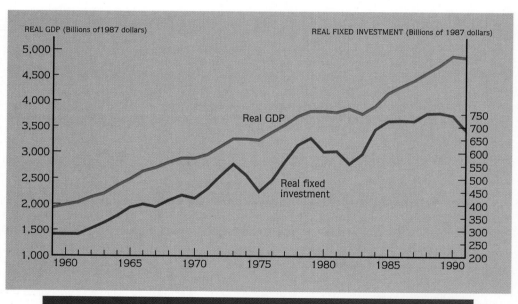

FIGURE 11–1 Fixed investment and GDP

Real fixed investment and real GDP fluctuate together. Investment and GDP rose together in the great expansion of the 1960s, fell together in the recession beginning in 1974, rose again in the late 1970s, fell together in the early 1980s, and fell together again in 1990–91. However, as percentages, the fluctuations in fixed investment are larger than the fluctuations in total GDP.
Source: *Economic Report of the President,* 1992, Table B–2.

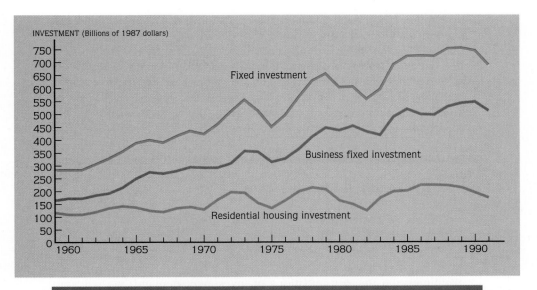

FIGURE 11–2 Housing versus factories and equipment

Separating housing investment from business investment reveals some important timing differences. Both business investment and housing investment fluctuate widely during recessions and booms. But housing investment leads real GDP while business investment moves together with real GDP.
Source: *Economic Report of the President*, 1992, Table B–2.

supply side of the economy is necessary to give a complete picture of investment. But we have already had a preview of the demand-and-supply process in Chapters 4 through 7. The economy reconciles the decisions of the various groups with the interest rate and the price of capital goods. If businesses want to invest more than consumers are willing to lend, the interest rate rises enough to depress investment and stimulate saving to the point of equality. If businesses want to invest more than the producers of investment goods want to produce, the price of capital goods rises. Then investment demand falls and the supply of capital goods rises, again to the point of equality.

INVESTMENT ANALYSIS

1. Investment is the flow of newly produced capital goods. It consists of plant and equipment investment, residential investment, and inventory investment.

2. Investment is much more volatile than consumption. Declines in business fixed investment are closely timed with declines in the overall economy. Declines in housing investment lead the declines in the overall economy.

3. The overall level of investment depends on three elements: the investment demand of firms and households, the funds available for investment, and the amount of investment goods produced. Interest rates and the prices of investment goods move to equate the three elements. In this chapter we focus on investment demand.

HOW A BUSINESS LOOKS AT THE INVESTMENT DECISION

In examining the micro foundations of investment demand, we will start with business fixed investment and look at the decision process of a typical business firm. From a firm's perspective there are really two decisions that can be distinguished. The first thing for the managers to decide is how many factories and machines they want. That is, what is the firm's desired **capital stock**? The second question is how fast to build the factories and when to order the machines that they want. That is, what is the **flow of investment**? The simple investment function that we introduced in Chapter 7 focuses on the flow of investment while ignoring the desired capital stock. Here we start with the question of the desired capital stock, and derive the flow demand subsequently.

It is helpful to pose the typical firm's problem in the following rather abstract way: Suppose a firm has already figured out how much output it plans to produce during the upcoming period, say a year. Further, suppose that, whatever capital it will use, it will *rent* from another firm in the equipment rental business. For example, a firm in the business of offering typing services to its customers would rent word-processing equipment from a computer-leasing firm. (Many firms own most of their capital, but we will look at that case a little later.) The idea of thinking about a firm's investment decision as a choice about how much capital to rent was developed by Dale Jorgenson of Harvard University. He developed such models of investment starting in the early 1960s.[1] It is a useful abstraction because it makes the capital decision much like the decision to employ other factors used in production, such as labor and raw materials.

How much capital will the firm choose to rent? Microeconomics tells us the answer: the amount that equates the marginal benefit to the marginal

[1]Dale Jorgenson, "Capital Theory and Investment Behavior," *American Economic Review*, Vol. 53 (May 1963), pp. 247–259.

cost. The **marginal benefit** is the amount of dollars saved by using fewer of the other factors of production when more capital is employed. A firm with more capital will need fewer workers, less energy, or fewer materials to produce the same amount of output. For example, with a word processor, a firm offering typing services might require fewer hours from proofreaders and typists, and perhaps fewer correction materials (like Liquid Paper). Note that the firm must look ahead to determine the marginal benefit of employing more capital during the period that it will rent the capital. Firms are thus assumed to be *forward-looking* in this theory of investment.

The **marginal cost** of capital is just the rental cost charged by the renting firm. For example, it is the amount that the computer-leasing firm charges each year for word-processing equipment.

The firm's decision can be illustrated graphically. The most important input to production is labor, so consider the case where the input displaced by capital is labor. The production function relating labor input to output produced is shown in Figure 11–3. When there is more labor input, there is more output. For example, for the typing services firm, when typists and proofreaders work more hours, more typed pages are produced. When there is more capital in the firm, the production function relating labor input to output produced is shifted upward, as shown in Figure 11–3. In this case fewer hours worked by typists and proofreaders result in the same number of typed pages. In Figure 11–3, *N* is the level of employment needed to produce planned output with the existing capital stock, and *N'* is the reduced level of employment needed to produce planned output if

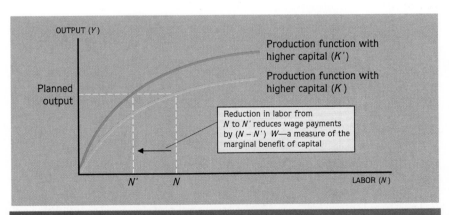

FIGURE 11–3 The production function and the marginal benefit of capital

The production function shows the amount of output produced from different amounts of labor. The lower production function describes the situation with the existing capital of the firm. In order to produce the planned output, the firm will have to employ *N* workers. The upper production function applies if the firm decides to rent some extra capital. In that case, to produce the planned output, only *N'* workers need to be employed. The marginal benefit of capital is the reduced wage payments. (*N* − *N'*) *W*.

extra capital is rented. If the wage per worker is W, the marginal benefit of the extra capital is $(N - N')W$.

We assume that capital has a **diminishing marginal product,** which means that the amount of the upward shift in the production function and the corresponding decrease in labor requirements decline as the amount of capital grows. For example, if the typing services firm began with one full-time typist and one half-time proofreader, the first word processor would result in more labor saved than a second word processor. The third and fourth word processors would displace essentially no labor. We can describe the relationship between capital and the marginal benefit of additional capital in a **marginal benefit of capital** schedule, as shown in Figure 11–4.

The marginal benefit of capital schedule is the firm's **demand curve for rented capital** as well. To choose its level of capital, the firm simply finds the amount of capital that equates the marginal benefit of capital to the marginal cost of capital, which is the rental price. We call the rental price of capital R^K. The superscript K is a mnemonic for capital. Figure 11–5 illustrates the process.

What happens if the firm decides to produce more output? Looking back at Figure 11–3, you can see that producing more output with the same capital stock will require more labor. That, in turn, raises the marginal benefit of capital. To equate the marginal benefit to an unchanged rental price of capital, the firm will have to rent more capital. Figure 11–6 shows how the firm responds to an increase in output.

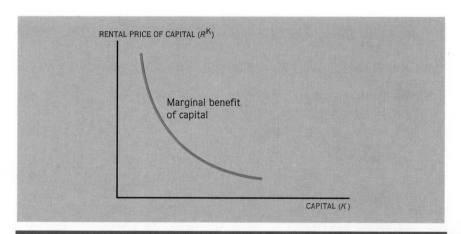

RENTAL PRICE OF CAPITAL (R^K)

Marginal benefit
of capital

CAPITAL (K)

FIGURE   11–4 The marginal benefit of capital schedule

The marginal benefit of capital is a declining function of the amount of capital because of the diminishing marginal product of capital. The position of the schedule depends on the level of planned output and on the wage rate.

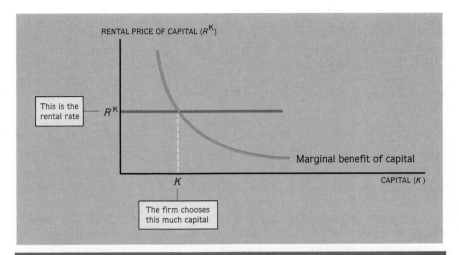

FIGURE 11–5 Choosing the capital stock

The marginal benefit of capital schedule is the firm's demand function for rented capital. The firm chooses its capital stock by equating the marginal benefit of capital to its rental price. With planned output and the wage rate held constant, the firm will choose to rent more capital and employ less labor if the rental price falls.

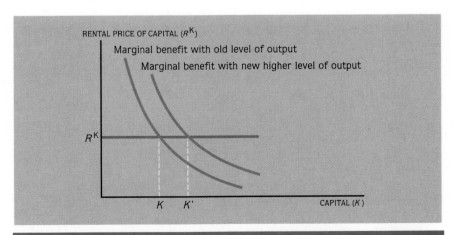

FIGURE 11–6 Effect of higher output

When planned output rises and the rental price of capital and the wage remain the same, the firm's demand for capital rises. Higher planned output shifts the marginal benefit for capital schedule to the right. The firm's demand for rented capital rises from K to K'.

We have not said anything yet about investment, only about the firm's decision to rent capital. A firm could rent more capital without bringing about any investment in the economy as a whole. The firm might just rent some existing capital that another firm had decided not to rent anymore. The relation between the decisions of individual firms and total investment in new capital goods is the subject of Section 11.3.

Determination of the Rental Price of Capital

How would the market set the rental price of capital? We can answer this by looking at the costs faced by a rental firm—like a computer-leasing firm—that is in the business of owning machines and renting them out. We will make use of the following terms and assumptions:

P^K is the price for purchasing a new machine from a producer of machines. The price is assumed to be unchanging for now. The price is measured in "real" terms, that is, relative to the price of other noncapital goods, like haircuts or typing services.

R is the real interest rate.

d is the rate of depreciation. At the end of each year, the rental firm has to spend an amount d times the original amount spent on the machine P^K in order to make up for wear and tear on the machine.

R^K is the rental price of the equipment. This is the amount received by the rental firm for renting out the machine for 1 year.

First, consider the cost side of the rental operation. Suppose the rental firm decides to sell the machine after 1 year in the rental market. At the beginning of the year it borrows P^K to buy the machine at an interest rate of R and incurs an interest cost of RP^K. It has to pay dP^K to make up for depreciation. Total rental costs are therefore

$$(R + d)P^K. \qquad (11\text{--}1)$$

In words, Equation 11–1 states:

> The cost of renting out one machine for 1 year
> = (The rate of interest + The rate of depreciation)
> × The price of a new machine.

For example, if the price of a word processor is $10,000, the interest rate R = .05, and the depreciation rate d = .15, then the rental price is $2,000 per year.

What will be the market rental price? If the renter does not have a monopoly in the rental market, the market rental price will exactly equal the cost of renting. If it were any higher, new firms would enter the rental business and bid down the rent. If the rent were below cost, some rental firms would go out of business and rents would rise. Thus, the rental price of a machine for a year is just as spelled out above—the interest rate plus the rate of depreciation times the price of a new machine. Algebraically, we have

$$R^K = (R + d)P^K.$$ (11–2)

Now we can go back to Figure 11–5 and relate the demand for capital by the firm that uses capital to the underlying determinants of the rental price of capital. Remember that the firm's demand for capital is a declining function of the rental price, so that the demand for capital is a declining function of the price of new equipment and a declining function of the real interest rate.

DEMAND FOR CAPITAL AND RENTAL PRICE

1. The demand for capital declines if the rental price of capital rises. The rental price will rise if the price of new equipment rises or if the interest rate rises.
2. The demand for capital rises if planned output rises.
3. The demand for capital rises if the wage rises.

The Rental Price and the Decision to Buy New Capital Goods

A good deal of the capital equipment in U.S. industry is in fact rented, so the analysis we have just presented is more than an abstraction. But the bulk of capital is owned by the firm that uses it in production. Moreover, the 1-year perspective we used to solve for the rental price of capital is not representative. Most firms purchase capital for the long run. Their concern is not just with the payoff in the first year, but with the financial success of the project over a decade or more. They must look ahead and estimate the benefits of a new capital project under the assumption that it will operate for quite a number of years.

The attraction of Jorgenson's rental price approach is that it gives the same answer to the question of what should be the desired capital stock as the more realistic approach in which the firm buys the capital and uses it for a number of years. Firms are constantly formulating and evaluating investment projects. An investment project that consistently earns more than the rental price of capital is worth undertaking. The project is a winner because the firm earns more than it would have to pay to borrow money to finance the project plus pay to cover the depreciation of the capital required for the project. Similarly, an investment project that consistently earns less than the rental price of capital is not worth undertaking. It is a loser.

Because of the diminishing marginal product of capital, as the winning projects are put into effect, they will depress the earnings of future projects. Eventually, the last winning project will earn just the borderline revenue, namely, the rental price of the capital. On the margin, the firm taking a long-term view and purchasing its own capital will reach just the same point it would if it chose to rent capital and made a year-by-year decision about the amount of capital to use. Both the capital budgeting approach and the rental approach arrive at the same conclusion: *The firm makes use of capital up to the point where the marginal benefit of capital equals the rental price of capital.*

Not all investment decisions fit neatly into this analysis. If the firm's technology requires that investment take place in large lumps—like building blast furnaces or power plants—it may not be able to find a combination of projects with the property that the marginal benefit of investment in each year is just equal to the rental price of capital. It may have to settle for a situation where the marginal benefit is higher in some years and lower in others. The basic criterion for selecting winning investment projects remains the same for these lumpy investments. On the average, the marginal benefit of capital will be equated to the rental price even in those cases. An investment theory based on the equality of marginal benefit and rental price seems a reasonable approximation by which to deal with the aggregate economy, even when some of the thousands of firms in the aggregate are making decisions about lumpy investments.

Expected Changes in the Future Price of Capital

So far we have assumed that the relative price of capital, P^K, does not change, and is therefore not expected to change. What happens if the relative price of capital goods is expected to change? The forward-looking aspects of the firm's investment decision now become important. Consider first the rental firm. Suppose that the price of capital is *expected* to *decrease* during that period that the capital equipment is rented out. On this account the rental firm stands to take a loss. It purchased the capital for P^K, and the capital will be worth less than that, say P^K_1, next year when the equipment is returned. The rental firm expects to lose $P^K-P^K_1$. Recall that a competitive firm in the rental market must break even in equilibrium. Thus, the rental rate must increase. For example, if the price is expected to fall from $P^K = \$1,000$ to $P^K_1 = \$950$ next year, then it would increase the rental price by $50. Conversely, if the rental firm expected an increase in the price of capital, it would stand to gain. It could cover its costs by charging a lower rental price. In general the rental price is decreased by the amount of the *expected* increase in the price of capital, ΔP^K.

With capital goods prices expected to change, the formula for the rental price becomes the old formula in Equation 11–1 less the expected change in the price of capital equipment:

$$R^K = (R + d)P^K - \Delta P^K.$$

The same thing can be written a bit more compactly as

$$R^K = (R - \pi^K + d)P^K,$$

where π^K is the expected percentage change in the relative price of capital equipment: $\pi^K = \Delta P^K / P^K$.

This modification of the earlier rental price formula becomes very important when the price of capital is expected to change by a large amount relative to the price of other goods. As we will see below, for example, changes in taxes can alter the effective price of capital. If these changes in taxes are *anticipated* by firms, then the rental price of capital will change. Since firms increase their desired capital stock when the rental rate falls, a decline in the rental rate due to an expected change in taxes will increase capital spending.

 ## 11.3   THE INVESTMENT FUNCTION

To keep things simple in our derivation of the investment function, we will assume that firms purchase all their capital. As we have just seen, the rental price of capital is the central economic variable for investment decisions.

The firm's **investment demand function** tells how much capital equipment the firm will purchase given its planned level of output and the rental price of capital. If the firm has been in business for a while, it will have an existing stock of capital at the beginning of the year. After examining the planned level of output and the rental price of capital, it will decide on a level of capital to use during the year. Finally, it will purchase enough new capital to make up the difference. In a nutshell, this is the theory of investment.

Earlier we showed that the firm chooses the amount of capital it uses by equating the marginal benefit of capital to the rental price of capital. When the amount of capital is high, the marginal benefit of further capital is low. By adjusting the amount of capital, the marginal benefit can be brought into equality with the rental price. The result of this process is the firm's **desired capital stock,** which we call K^*.

An example of an algebraic formula describing the desired capital is

$$K^* = .5(W/R^K)Y. \tag{11–3}$$

In this formula, W is the wage rate, Y is the firm's level of output, and R^K is the rental price of capital. The formula says that the desired capital stock equals .5 times the ratio of the wage to the rental price of capital, times the level of output. Hence, the firm will want to increase its use of capital whenever the wage to rental price ratio rises. When labor becomes more expensive relative to capital, the firm substitutes toward capital. Whenever planned output Y rises, the firm will also want to use more capital.

Now consider how the **actual capital stock** changes. Suppose that the firm finishes the last year with a capital stock of K_{-1} (the subscript "–1" means last year) that is not equal to the desired capital stock for this year, K^*. If there is no depreciation, then the level of investment will increase the capital stock by the amount of the investment. That is, investment equals the change in the capital stock:

$$I = K - K_{-1}. \tag{11–4}$$

If the firm wants its capital stock K to equal the desired capital stock K^*, then its investment demand I during the year is obtained by substituting $K = K^*$ into Equation 11–4. That is,

$$I = K^* - K_{-1}. \tag{11–5}$$

This much investment added to its existing capital will give the firm its desired level of capital for this year. This formula is the firm's **investment function.** The investment function for the example formula for the desired capital stock K^* in Equation 11–3 can be written out as

$$I = .5(W/R^K)Y - K_{-1}. \tag{11–6}$$

Then it is apparent that *investment depends positively on the wage rate, negatively on the rental price of capital, and positively on output.*

The effect of output on investment is called the **accelerator.** To simplify the notation, set $.5(W/R^K)$ equal to the simple expression v. Then, Equation 11–3 states that $K^* = vY$. If the firm always adjusts its capital stock each year so that it is equal to the desired stock, then

$$K = vY \quad \text{and} \quad K_{-1} = vY_{-1}. \tag{11–7}$$

$\underbrace{}_{\text{This year}} \qquad \underbrace{\phantom{K_{-1} = vY_{-1}}}_{\text{Last year}}$

Investment, which is the change in the capital stock, must therefore be given by the difference between the two expressions in Equation 11–7. That is,

$$I = vY - vY_{-1} = v\Delta Y. \tag{11–8}$$

In words, the *level* of investment I depends on the *change* of output ΔY. When output accelerates, that is, when its change gets bigger, investment is stimulated. A rise in output from one level to another causes a burst of investment, but if output remains at its higher level, investment subsides. This accelerator process seems to explain a large fraction of the movements in investment.[2] It certainly is part of the reason for the close association between investment and GDP that we noted at the beginning of the chapter.

Depreciation and Gross Investment

If the capital stock depreciates, as of course it does in reality, then the investment equations we have derived so far are only for net investment; recall that net investment is the change in the capital stock. A gross investment equation can be easily derived by adding a term to Equation 11–6 that measures the part of investment that goes for replacing worn-out capital. One assumption is that a constant fraction d of the existing capital stock wears out each period.[3] Then d times K_{-1} is added to Equation 11–6 and to all the related forms of the investment demand function in this chapter. Depreciation accounts for a very large part of gross investment. In 1990, for example, gross private domestic investment was $744 billion, while depreciation was $550 billion. Net investment was therefore $194 billion.

PROPERTIES OF THE INVESTMENT FUNCTION

1. When the growth of output Y is high, investment is high.
2. When the rental price of capital (R^K) is high, investment is low. In particular:
   a. When the real interest rate is high, investment is low.
   b. When the price of new capital goods is high, investment is low.
3. When wages are high, investment is high.
4. The amount of replacement investment due to depreciation is a large fraction of investment in a typical year. This large fraction of investment is closely related to the level of the capital stock and thus to the level of output.

---

[2]See Peter K. Clark, "Investment in the 1970s: Theory, Performance and Prediction," *Brookings Papers on Economic Activity,* Vol. 1 (1979), pp. 73–113.

[3]There has been relatively little research on replacement investment. A good but somewhat mathematical discussion is in Martin S. Feldstein and Michael Rothschild, "Towards an Economic Theory of Replacement Investment," *Econometrica,* Vol. 42 (March 1974), pp. 393–423.

Lags in the Investment Process

A somewhat unrealistic element in the investment function we just derived is that the capital stock is adjusted to its desired level immediately. The investment function in Equation 11–6 assumes that the firm puts new capital in place as soon as it becomes aware that the level of output, the rental price of capital, and the wage warrant the new capital. For some kinds of equipment, this assumption is reasonable. But for many projects, there is a **lag** of several years between the firm's realization that new capital is needed and the completion of the capital installation. To put it another way, much of the investment occurring this year is the result of decisions made last year, the year before, and even the year before that. The decisions were governed by the expectations prevailing in those years about economic conditions this year. New information about this year's conditions that became available after the launching of the projects cannot affect this year's investment in those projects. Much of this year's investment was predetermined by earlier decisions.

To set down an algebraic expression of lags in the investment process, we will assume that firms invest so that their capital stock is adjusted *slowly* toward the desired capital stock. Suppose that firms change their capital stock by a fraction s of the difference between the desired capital stock and the capital stock at the end of the last year. That is,

$$I = s(K^* - K_{-1}). \qquad (11\text{–}9)$$

Comparing this equation with Equation 11–5, we see how the investment function is modified to take account of lags in the investment process. The investment demand function in Equation 11–9 has all the properties of the original investment demand function plus one more: The more slowly the capital stock is adjusted (the smaller is s), the weaker will be the reaction of investment demand to any of its determinants—planned output, the rental price of capital, or the wage rate.

Economic researchers have reached the conclusion that the responsiveness of investment to its determinants is very much attenuated by lags.[4] No more than a third of investment can take place in the year that economic changes make it apparent to firms that more capital is needed. Investment in this category includes tools, trucks, office equipment, and other portable items that are not produced to order. Major investments like whole plants or new custom-made equipment take 1 or more years to put in place.

---

[4]See Peter K. Clark, "Investment in the 1970s: Theory, Performance and Prediction," *Brookings Papers on Economic Activity,* Vol. 1 (1979), pp. 73–113.

The Aggregate Investment Demand Function

Our discussion has looked at investment in the firm. We need to go from the firm to the economy as a whole. We will assume that total investment in plants and equipment is governed by Equation 11–9, with the wage to rental ratio taken as an economywide average and output taken as total real GDP. Of course, going from the firm to the total economy involves an element of approximation, because the firms we are adding together do not all have the same investment functions. Still, an aggregate investment demand function is a reasonable approximation. Even if firms are diverse, the basic properties of the investment process still hold: Investment responds positively to planned output and negatively to the rental price of capital. The strength of the response depends on how quickly investment plans can be carried out.

THE INVESTMENT FUNCTION

1. The firm's investment demand function tells how much investment it needs to make this year in order to raise its capital stock to the desired level. Investment demand depends negatively on the rental price of capital and positively on the planned increase in output and on the wage.
2. Lags in putting new investment in place limit the response of investment to changes in its determinants. Between one-tenth and one-third of the total amount of investment occurs in the first year.

11.4 TAXES AND INVESTMENT

Taxation of capital tends to discourage investment by reducing the earnings the firm receives from its investment. This effect of taxation can readily be incorporated into the rental price formula.[5] We first consider the effect of permanent tax changes.

---

[5]This method of incorporating taxes into the rental price of capital is based on the work of Robert E. Hall and Dale W. Jorgenson, "Tax Policy and Investment Behavior," *American Economic Review*, Vol. 57 (June 1967), pp. 391–414.

Permanent Tax Changes

Consider again our derivation of the rental price of capital. Suppose the rental firm has to pay a tax rate of u on rental income. In addition, suppose the rental firm receives a payment of z dollars as an investment incentive from the government for each dollar of capital purchased. We derived the formula for the rental price by equating the rental income of the rental firm to the costs of renting. We can modify that analysis to take account of taxes by equating the after-tax rental income to the after-tax costs of renting. After-tax rental income is $(1 - u)R^K$. The effect of the investment incentives is to make the cost of purchasing a machine equal to $(1 - z)P^K$. Equating after-tax rental income to after-tax costs gives

$$(1 - u)R^K = (R + d)(1 - z)P^K. \qquad (11-10)$$

Dividing by $1 - u$ gives

$$R^K = \frac{(R + d)\ (1 - z)P^K}{1 - u}. \qquad (11-11)$$

The net effect of taxation and investment incentives is to multiply the rental cost by $(1 - z)/(1 - u)$.

For example, suppose the marginal tax rate applied to the revenue from capital is 50 percent. That is, $u = .5$. This by itself would double the rental price of capital; if rental firms lose half their revenue to taxation, they have to double their earnings to cover the costs of holding capital.

Suppose further that there is an investment incentive of 10 percent and that tax deductions for depreciation on investment are worth 30 cents of current benefits for each dollar of investment. The combined effect of the two makes z equal .4. In this example, the tax multiplier in the rental price of capital, $(1 - z)/(1 - u)$, is .6/.5, or 1.2. The tax system adds 20 percent to the rental price of capital.

For investments that are financed by issuing debt or taking on mortgages, the tax system gives further incentives to invest because firms can deduct their interest costs as well. Suppose that borrowing adds another 20 cents in current tax benefits for each dollar of investment. In that case, z would be .6 and the tax multiplier would be .4/.5, or .8. Tax incentives then outweigh the direct effect of taxes, and the net effect of the tax system is to subsidize investment.

Changes in taxes and tax incentives for investment are powerful tools for changing investment spending. The Tax Reform Act of 1986 raised the rental price of capital by as much as 10 percent. A reduction in the corporate tax rate from 46 to 34 percent tended to lower the rental price, but an elimination of the investment tax credit, a lower depreciation allowance, and a reduction in the value of deductions for interest payments (due to the lower tax) tended to raise it by a larger amount.

Suppose the desired capital stock falls by .75 percent for each percentage point that the rental price of capital is increased (that is, the elasticity is −.75). Then the desired capital stock would fall by 7.5 percent as a result of this legislation. If the capital stock of plants and equipment in the United States is about $4,000 billion, then this reduction would amount to a fall in investment of $300 billion. Even if it were spread over 10 years, the effect on aggregate demand in each year could be substantial.

Anticipated Tax Changes

The above calculations assume that the tax rates are always in effect and that tax changes are not anticipated by firms. If firms are forward-looking, as we have argued they are, then anticipations of future tax changes can also affect investment. The effects are tricky to calculate, and can go in a direction opposite from unanticipated changes.

Suppose, for example, that U.S. firms anticipated in 1985 that the 10 percent investment tax credit would be repealed starting in 1986. In fact, this is a very realistic example, because such a repeal was proposed by the Reagan administration and widely discussed in 1985. The repeal occurred as part of the Tax Reform Act of 1986. And the repeal was made effective on January 1, 1986.

Firms that anticipated such a change would realize that they would have to pay 10 percent more for capital goods starting in January 1986 than in 1985. Accordingly they would want to buy capital in 1985 before the effective price rise. If possible, they would shift their purchases of equipment from 1986 to 1985.

Rental firms would also cut their rental price in 1985 in anticipation of the repeal of the investment tax credit. With the effective price of capital goods expected to increase, rental firms could charge less for rent because of the expected capital gain on the capital that they owned. With a decrease in the rental price there would be more investment in 1985. Hence, an *anticipated* elimination of the investment tax credit would increase investment in the year that the elimination was anticipated.

The behavior of investment in the United States in 1985 and 1986 provides dramatic confirmation of this forward-looking anticipatory behavior of firms. Investment in business equipment grew by 19 percent at an annual rate in the last quarter of 1985 and then fell by about the same amount in the first quarter of 1986. Evidently firms bunched their capital purchases in the last months of 1985 right before the effective date of the repeal. Investment remained rather low throughout 1986 as we have discussed previously.

Investment is the component of spending that usually falls the most in recessions. The changes in the components of GDP from 1990 to 1991 show that the most recent recession was no exception:

Change in consumption	Down 5.9 billion 1987 dollars
Fixed investment	Down 56.5
Inventory investment	Down 15.3
Net exports	Up 33.7
Government purchases	Up 7.6
Total change in GDP	Down 36.5 billion 1987 dollars

Not surprisingly, recessions create the desire for compensatory policies to restore investment to normal levels. Modern economic analysis has quite a bit to say about the effects of different proinvestment policies.

The Investment Tax Credit

The investment tax credit first came into being in 1962, just after the recession of 1960–61. The credit is essentially a percentage subsidy on investment. As it applied in the United States from 1962 through 1986, it subsidized investment in equipment only. The investment tax credit is part of the variable z in Equation 11–11 for the rental price of capital; a 10 percent investment credit adds .1 to z. A permanent investment credit creates an incentive for a permanently higher capital stock, so it stimulates a burst of net investment as the economy makes the transition to the higher stock. In that respect, raising the investment credit is a desirable move in a recession, because its short-run effect is greater than its long-run effect. And the investment credit has an even larger short-run effect if it is known to be temporary. For example, a credit in effect for only a single year in the trough of a recession would make businesses speed up investment to take advantage of the credit.

But there are pitfalls in the systematic use of changes in the investment credit to stabilize the economy. If firms anticipate that an investment tax credit will be enacted during a recession, then a forecast of a recession could lead firms to hold back on investment and help bring on the recession. These are the findings of Lawrence Christiano of Northwestern University, whose work shows that the anticipation of changes in the investment tax credit can actually increase the volatility of investment (see "A Re-examination of the Theory of Automatic Stabilizers," Carnegie-Rochester Conference Series on Public Policy, 1984, Volume 20). Anticipated tax changes are discussed further in Section 11.4.

Write-offs

A permanent feature of U.S. and all other tax laws is write-offs (depreciation deductions) for fixed investment. The present discounted value of these write-offs is another factor increasing the variable z in Equation 11–11. When write-offs can be made faster (accelerated depreciation), their present discounted value is higher and the rental price of capital is lower. Faster investment write-offs were also part of the investment stimulus package in 1962, in response to a recession. Even faster write-offs were put into effect in the 1981 tax bill, though not just in response to a recession. Write-offs were dramatically slowed down in the 1986 tax bill, which passed during a period of strength in the economy. The recession of 1990 brought forth proposals for speeding up write-offs as one of the ways to get investment moving again.

Capital Gains Taxes

It stands to reason that lower capital gains taxes should stimulate investment. Essentially, the capital gains tax rate is one of the determinants of the interest rate R, which appears in Equation 11–11. If a company borrows to finance investment, R is the interest rate it pays the lender, and the tax that matters is the tax on the interest. But many firms invest their shareholders' funds—most commonly by keeping the funds within the firm rather than paying them out as dividends. The tax rate that matters in that case is the tax that the shareholders will have to pay when the investment generates added profit for the firm. Part of the tax is the personal income tax on dividends and the other part is the personal income tax on capital gains. A lower capital gains rate will lower the return that the firm has to generate in order to put a given amount of after-tax income in the hands of its shareholders. Thus a lower capital gains rate will stimulate investment. By the same token, a lower tax rate on interest and dividends will also stimulate investment. Proposals to lower capital gains rates and raise taxes on interest and dividends may not stimulate investment at all. Investment is sensitive to other taxes besides capital gains taxes.

Residential Subsidies

Almost half of the decline in fixed investment between 1990 and 1991 was in residential invest-ment. Construction of new houses and apartment buildings fell dramatically in the recession, as construction has in most earlier recessions. Some type of tax stimulus to residential construction could offset these declines. For houses owned by the families living in them, none of the other tax stimuli discussed here have any significant effect—there has never been an investment credit for any residential investment, there is no tax write-off, and there is little effect from capital gains taxation. In 1992, the Bush administration proposed a tax credit for house purchases by families who had never owned houses before. A more potent stimulus could come from a broader credit available to any purchaser of a newly built house. Again, the effectiveness of such a measure to counteract a recession would be greater if it were announced from the start to be temporary.

These same anticipatory effects can work in the opposite direction. If firms anticipated a reenactment of the investment tax credit, perhaps because of a prolonged economic slump, then the rental price of capital would increase at the time of anticipation, and investment would actually fall.[6]

TAX INCENTIVES

1. The government can influence the level of investment through tax policy. Heavier taxation raises the rental price of capital and discourages investment.
2. Tax incentives such as investment tax credits and depreciation deductions lower the rental price of capital and stimulate investment.
3. Anticipated increases in tax incentives can reduce investment today, because firms will postpone their capital purchases until they can take advantage of the incentives.

[6]For rational expectations approaches to consequences of anticipated changes in investment incentives, see Lawrence H. Summers, "Taxation and Corporate Investment: A q-Theory Approach," *Brookings Papers on Economic Activity*, Vol. 1 (1981), pp. 67–140, and John B. Taylor, "The Swedish Investment System as a Stabilization Policy Rule," *Brookings Papers on Economic Activity*, Vol. 1 (1982), pp. 57–97.

11.5   RESIDENTIAL INVESTMENT

The economic theory of residential investment can be approached in much the same way as the theory of business investment. We can start again with the concept of the *rental price*. Because a significant amount of housing of all kinds is rented in the open market, there is nothing unfamiliar about the idea of a rental price of housing. Even though many American families own their houses rather than rent them, we can examine their decision about how large a house to own by looking at the rental price they pay implicitly when they own. Let R^H represent the rental price for houses. As before, the rental price is the interest rate plus a rate of depreciation times the price of houses (P^H):

$$R^H = (R + d)P^H. \tag{11–12}$$

An important quantitative difference is the rate of depreciation, d. The equipment that makes up the bulk of business investment depreciates at around 10 percent per year, so d is .10 in the formula for R^K. Houses hardly depreciate at all. A reasonable value for d in the formula for R^H is .02. Consequently, the real interest rate is a much larger fraction of the rental cost of housing than it is of the rental cost of business investment. As we will see, residential investment is much more sensitive to interest rates than is business investment.

The public has a demand function for housing just as it has a demand function for any good. When the rental price of housing is high, the public demands less rental housing. We can find the public's **desired stock of housing** by finding where the rental price of housing intersects the demand curve, as in Figure 11–7.

Lags in housing construction are not nearly as long as in business investment. It is reasonable to suppose that the bulk of housing can be put in place within a year after a change in demand. The investment demand function for housing is just

$$I = H^* - H_{-1}, \tag{11–13}$$

where H_{-1} is the stock of houses in the previous year and H^* is the desired stock of houses.

The accelerator principle operates for housing investment as well as for business investment. The stock of housing is related to the level of real

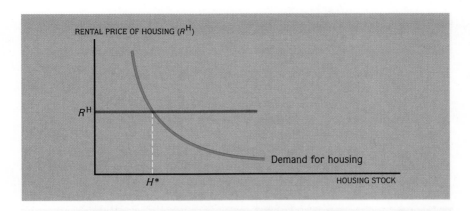

FIGURE 11–7 Determination of the desired housing stock

The desired stock of housing, H^*, is found at the point on the demand curve for housing where the rental price of housing, R^H, has the value determined by the real interest rate and the price of houses.

income. Thus investment, which is the change in the stock, is related to the change in real income.

Housing Investment and Monetary Policy

Of all the components of aggregate demand, housing investment is the most sensitive to real interest rates. We have already noted one reason for the sensitivity: Because housing depreciates at a low rate, the real interest rate is the dominant element in the rental price of housing. Most of what you pay your landlord is compensation for the capital tied up in your apartment. If you own a house, most of your annual cost is mortgage interest. Therefore, when a monetary contraction or other influences raise interest rates, housing investment declines the most. The substantial drop in housing construction from 1979 to 1982 seems clearly attributable to the high interest rates prevailing during those years. Mortgage interest rates in 1982 were over 15 percent. On the other hand, housing construction reached a peak in 1986 as mortgage interest rates dropped below 10 percent. As the economy slowed in 1990, residential investment fell even more sharply. The Fed acted to lower interest rates, with mortgage rates falling below 9 percent for the first time since the early 1970s, in the hope that residential investment could lead the economy out of recession.

HOUSING INVESTMENT

1. Housing investment is negatively related to the interest rate R. A higher interest rate makes housing more expensive by raising the rental price. A higher rental price depresses investment demand.
2. Housing investment is positively related to real GDP. Higher incomes raise the demand for housing and so raise investment demand.
3. Housing is the component of investment most sensitive to monetary and fiscal policies through interest rates. Because housing depreciates so slowly, its rental price is dominated by interest cost.

11.6 INVENTORY INVESTMENT

Inventories are stocks of goods in the process of production and also finished goods waiting to be sold. In 1990, total inventories were about $985 billion. Gross domestic product was about $4,885 billion, so about 20 cents' worth of inventories were held for each dollar in annual GDP. To put it another way, inventories were about 2.4 months of GDP. A significant amount of capital is tied up in inventories in the U.S. economy.

Inventories fit into the general framework for analyzing investment set up at the beginning of this chapter. Inventories have a rental price, equal to the real interest rate times the price of goods held in inventory.

Firms choose a desired level of inventories by equating the marginal benefit of inventories to the rental price. What benefits do inventories provide the firm? We can distinguish two basic functions. First, and quantitatively most important, inventories are an intrinsic part of the physical production process. We will call this the **pipeline function** of inventories. In the oil industry, large amounts of oil are unavoidably in transit in pipelines at any moment. The pipeline function also includes goods in process. Inside an auto plant, you will always find stocks of parts ready to be made into cars together with a large number of cars partway through the assembly process. It would be costly to the auto manufacturer to coordinate the flow of parts and speed up the assembly process in order to cut down on the volume of inventories. The manufacturer has made a basic decision about the design of the production process that balances the advantages of inventories against their holding cost. About two-thirds of all inventories seem to be held because of the pipeline function.

The other third of inventories are finished goods. Auto plants have cars sitting in parking lots ready for shipment to dealers. The dealers themselves also keep quite a number of cars in their lots and showrooms. As a general matter, substantial inventories of finished goods ready for sale are held at the wholesale and retail level. One of the reasons for holding these inventories is to maintain a **buffer stock** to accommodate unexpected changes in demand. The buffer stock is the second major function of inventories. The grocery store keeps dozens of bottles of ketchup on the shelves because there is always a chance that an unusual number of people will buy ketchup on any given day.

Buffer-stock inventories are held at a certain average level that equates the marginal benefit to the rental cost. When sales surge, the inventories decline to below the desired stock. The firm then adjusts its purchases to replenish the stock. When sales fall short of expectations, inventories build up. The firm then decreases its purchases to run inventories down to their desired level.

Occasionally, unintended disinvestment and investment in buffer-stock inventories show up in the aggregate amount of inventory investment throughout the economy. For example, in the last quarter of 1989, aggregate final sales of goods in the U.S. economy stalled. The production of goods continued to rise rapidly despite unchanged sales. As a result, inventory investment bulged. At annual rates inventory investment was 30 billion 1987 dollars in the last quarter of 1989.

We can get an idea of the relative importance of the pipeline and buffer-stock influences on inventory investment by looking at the relationship between the *change* in real GDP and the *level* of inventory investment in the U.S. economy. Figure 11–8 shows this relationship for the years 1959 to 1991.

We can draw two important conclusions about inventory investment from Figure 11–8. First, inventory investment tends to be closely related to changes in production. When higher levels of output are being produced, there are more goods in the pipeline. Filling up the pipeline to the higher level requires more inventory investment. Consequently, years of rapid GDP growth tend to be years of high inventory investment. This is the third important place where the accelerator principle is in operation. The accelerator effect is particularly strong for inventory investment, because lags are less important for inventories than for any other component of investment.

Second, there are occasional episodes when businesses are caught by surprise and inventories pile up or are depleted unintentionally. In these episodes, inventory investment departs from its usual relation to the change in real GDP. In Figure 11–8, the small number of dots away from the pre-

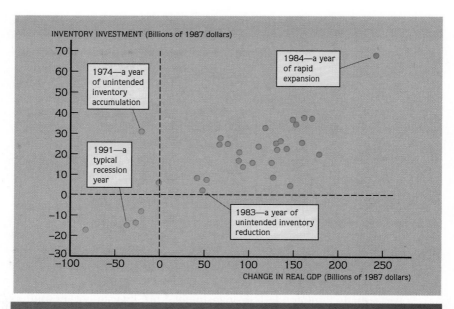

FIGURE 11-8 Inventory investment and the change in GDP

The amount of inventory investment tends to be closely related to the change in real GDP. Each dot corresponds to a year in the period from 1960 through 1991. The horizontal axis shows the change in real GDP and the vertical axis shows the real amount of inventory investment. As a rule, inventory investment is high when real GDP is growing and low when it is contracting. There are two large exceptions—1974 and 1983—that prove the rule. The dot in the upper left is for 1974, when real GDP fell but inventory investment was high. In 1974, there was probably substantial unwanted inventory accumulation. The dot to the right and below the general trend is for 1983, when real GDP grew rapidly but inventory investment was negative. In 1983, there was probably unintended reduction of buffer stocks because sales were unexpectedly high. As a general matter, intended changes in inventory stocks dominate unintended changes. Years of high GDP growth are years of high inventory investment and vice versa.

vailing upward-sloping line are years when unintended accumulation or depletion of inventories occurred. There is no systematic tendency for buffer stocks to absorb every change in real GDP. Instead, big movements of buffer stocks are a rare surprise. Research on inventory behavior has confirmed the general proposition that relatively few important movements of inventories can be traced to surprises in sales.[7]

---

[7]See Albert A. Hirsch and Michael Lovell, *Sales Anticipations and Inventory Behavior* (New York: John Wiley & Sons, 1969). For a formal treatment of the pipeline function of inventories see Valerie A. Ramey, "Inventories as Factors of Production and Economic Fluctuations," *American Economic Review*, Vol. 79 (June 1989), pp. 338–354.

INVENTORY INVESTMENT

1. Inventories provide two benefits to firms. The production process involves a pipeline of partly produced goods. When the level of output is high the stock of goods in the pipeline is high. Inventories of finished goods also function as a buffer stock against unexpected changes in sales.
2. The pipeline function of inventories dominates inventory investment in most years, but occasionally economywide surprises in sales are large enough for changes in buffer stocks to contribute an important component to inventory investment.
3. The increase in pipeline inventories when output rises is a major part of the accelerator in the short run.

THE INVESTMENT FUNCTION AND THE IS CURVE

Total investment is the sum of investment in plants and equipment, residential housing, and inventory. We can summarize the ideas of this chapter in an overall investment function. Investment depends positively on real GDP and negatively on the interest rate R.

The accelerator principle is important in investment. Higher output requires firms to invest in new plants and equipment, it causes families to want to increase their stock of housing, and it calls for higher pipeline stocks of inventories. For all three reasons, an increase in GDP stimulates added investment. However, the stimulus is stronger in the short run than in the long run. If the economy moves once and for all to a higher level of GDP, there will be a bulge of investment as the economy moves to the new, higher stock of plants, equipment, housing, and inventories desired at the new level of GDP. Once the new stock is reached, investment will subside to normal levels.

Investment depends negatively on the real interest rate. When the real rental cost of plants and equipment rises, firms substitute toward other inputs, especially labor. When the real rental price of housing rises, families substitute toward other forms of consumption. When the real cost of holding inventories rises, firms reduce their stocks of inventories, though this effect appears to be small. But the influence of higher real interest rates in depressing total investment is unmistakable.

Investment is central to the IS curve—in fact, as we mentioned in Chapter 7 the "I" in IS stands for investment. The IS curve can be defined as the set of combinations of real GDP and the interest rate where investment and saving are equal.

As a general matter, the IS curve slopes downward because it takes a lower interest rate to stimulate spending enough to achieve spending balance at a higher level of GDP. The investment function is a key part of that process. Lower interest rates stimulate investment—the effect is most important for housing and least important for inventories. The interest sensitivity of investment is an important determinant of the slope of the IS curve. If investment is highly responsive to the interest rate, the IS curve is flat; small changes in the interest rate cause large changes in investment and thus large changes in the level of GDP. If investment is not very responsive to interest rates, and other components are also unresponsive, the IS curve will be steep. Because investment and other categories of spending are unable to respond in the very short run (say one month) to changes in interest rates, the IS curve is close to vertical in the short run.

REVIEW AND PRACTICE

Major Points

1. There are three types of investment: business purchases of new plants and equipment, construction of new housing, and addition to inventories.

2. A business determines its desired capital stock by equating the marginal benefit of capital to the rental price of capital. A household determines its desired stock of housing in the same way.

3. The desired capital stock falls if the rental price of capital rises. It also rises if output or income rises. A business's desired capital stock rises if the wage rises, because it will substitute away from labor and toward capital.

4. The rental price of capital depends on the real interest rate and the price of capital goods.

5. The investment function tells how much investment will occur in a given year depending on conditions in that year. Although firms would like to invest up to the point where actual capital equals desired capital, they generally cannot do so. Only a fraction of the move to the new level can occur in the first year.

6. Because of the lag in investment, a large fraction of the investment that occurs in one year is actually the result of investment projects initiated in earlier years. This part of investment is predetermined in the current year and does not respond to current economic conditions.

7. For plants and equipment, it is a good approximation to say that suppliers will supply whatever amount of new investment goods businesses demand.

8. Tax incentives, including depreciation deductions and interest deductions, have an important influence on investment. A higher investment credit lowers the rental price of capital and stimulates investment.

9. Inventory investment contributes an important part of the fluctuations in total investment. The stock of inventories tends to be proportional to real GDP, so an increase in GDP is accompanied by a period of inventory investment.

10. Overall, investment responds positively to both the level of and the change in real GDP. The relationship with the level of GDP is due to replacement investment. The relationship with the change in GDP, called the accelerator, is due to the need to increase the capital stock in order to maintain output at higher levels and because desired inventories will grow when output increases.

11. Investment is negatively related to the interest rate since the interest rate is an important determinant of the cost of inventories. If the relationship is strong, the IS curve will be relatively flat.

Key Terms and Concepts

investment	marginal benefit of capital	depreciation deductions
nonresidential fixed investment	rental price of capital	desired stock of housing
plant and equipment investment	demand for capital	final-goods inventories
	rate of depreciation	unfinished-goods inventories
residential investment	desired capital stock	buffer-stock function of inventories
inventory investment	investment demand function	pipeline function of inventories
investment demand	accelerator tax incentives	

Questions for Discussion and Review

1. What variables adjust so that the level of investment chosen by firms and households is equal to the amount of funds available for investment?

2. Why do investment and GDP move so closely together?

3. Suppose that a firm can reduce its energy bill by adding some capital. How does this enter the marginal benefit of capital schedule?

4. Why does the marginal benefit of capital schedule shift upward when output rises?

5. Explain the various predetermined elements in the investment function.

6. What are the effects of tax policy on investment in the long run?

7. Why is housing especially important in the economy's response to a high-interest-rate policy?

8. Explain exactly what happens to the three categories of investment as you move down the IS curve.

9. Explain how announcements of future changes in tax policy can affect current investment demand.

Problems

Numerical

1. Suppose that the demand for investment is given by the model

$$I = s(K^* - K_{-1}),$$

where K* is the desired stock of capital given by

$$K^* = .1\,Y/R,$$

where Y is output and R is the interest rate. Assume that there is no depreciation and that $R = .05$. Let $s = .25$ to start.

   a. Calculate the desired capital stock in Year 1 if output is 200. Calculate the level of investment in the first year if the capital stock was 400 at the beginning of the first year.

   b. Suppose now that output rises from 200 to 250 in Year 2 and then remains at this new level forever. Calculate the level of investment and the capital stock in Years 2, 3, and 4. What are the new long-run levels of investment and capital? Explain why investment reacts with a lag to the increase in output.

   c. Repeat the calculations in Parts a and b for $s = 1$ and comment on the difference between your answers.

2. Repeat Problem 1 for the case where investment is given by

$$I = s(K^* - K_{-1}) + .1K_{-1}.$$

The last term on the right is replacement investment. Explain the reason for the differences between the answers to Questions 1 and 2.

3. Suppose that the investment function is given by

$$I = 400 - 2,000R + .1Y$$

rather than by the investment function given in Chapter 7. Add this investment function to the other four equations of the IS-LM model:

$$Y = C + I + G + X$$
$$C = 220 + .63\,Y$$
$$X = 525 - .1\,Y - 500R$$
$$M = (.1583\,Y - 1,000R)P$$

Treat the price level as predetermined at 1.0, and let government spending be 1,200 and the money supply be 900.

   a. Derive an algebraic expression for the IS curve for this model and plot it to scale. Compare it with the IS curve in the examples of Chapter 7. Which is steeper? Why?

   b. Derive the aggregate demand curve and plot it to scale. How does it compare with the aggregate demand curve in the example of Chapter 7?

   c. Calculate the effect of an increase in government spending on GDP. Is the effect larger or smaller than in the case where investment does not depend on output Y? Describe what is going on.

d. Calculate the effect of an increase in the money supply on GDP. How does the impact compare with the situation where investment does not depend on output?

4. Multiplier-accelerator interaction: Consider a macro model that has both a consumption function that depends on lagged income (like Friedman's permanent-income equation) and an investment equation that depends, with a lag, on changes in income. Ignore interest-rate effects. In particular assume that the following equations describe the economy:

$$Y = C + I + G$$
$$C = 220 + .63 Y_p, \text{ with } Y_p = .5(Y + Y_{-1})$$
$$I = 900 + .2(Y_{-1} - Y_{-2})$$
$$G = 1,200$$

a. By algebraic substitution of C and I into the income identity, obtain a single expression for output Y in terms of output in the previous years (Y_{-1} and Y_{-2}).

b. Calculate the constant level of output Y that satisfies all the relationships in the model. (Hint: Set $Y_{-1} = Y$ and $Y_{-2} = Y$ in the equation from Part a and solve for Y using algebra.)

c. Suppose that Y has been equal to the value that you calculated in Part b for the past 2 years (Years 1 and 2). But now suppose that government spending increases by $50 billion (in Year 3). Calculate the effect on output in Year 3. Calculate the effect on output in Years 4 through 10. Be sure to use the relationship that you derived in Part a, and substitute the values for Y_{-1} and Y_{-2} that you calculated in the previous two steps.

d. Plot the values of Y on a diagram with the years on the horizontal axis. Do you notice any cyclical behavior in Y? Explain what is going on. (This algebraic model was originally developed by Paul Samuelson of M.I.T. while he was a student at Harvard in the 1930s.)

5. (This problem refers to the material in Appendix A.) Consider the case where the price of capital goods P^K and the revenues from investment J are the same each year. Work with the equation for the financial position V:

$$V_t = (1 + R)V_{t-1} - dP^K + J.$$

Always start with $V_0 = -P^K$. In the last period of the project the firm sells the capital good for P^K.

a. Show that, regardless of the length of the project, V is zero if the revenues from investment $J = (R + d)P^K$.

b. Calculate the financial position for each year of a 10-year project that costs $100,000 and earns a revenue of $16,000 per year. Use an interest rate of 5 percent and a depreciation rate of 10 percent. Is the project a winner or a loser?

c. Repeat the above calculation for an interest rate of 10 percent. Is the project a winner or a loser? Explain the difference between this answer and the answer to Part b.

Analytical

1. What theory of inventory investment predicts that inventory investment is negative when GDP suddenly rises? What theory predicts the opposite? For both theories explain what happens at firms during a sudden *decline* in GDP.

2. Consider a firm whose capital stock is initially equal to its desired capital stock, where $R = .05$, $d = .1$, $P^K = 100$, and P^K is initially not expected to change in the future.
   a. Suppose P^K suddenly rises to 110. Ignoring taxes, what must the firm expect P^K to be next year in order for its desired capital stock to remain unchanged?
   b. Suppose now that P^K is expected to return to 100 the following year and to remain at 100 in all future years. Assume that this is in fact what happens. Describe the behavior of investment in the year of the price increase and in all future years. Consider both the case where the capital stock adjusts immediately to its desired level and the case where it adjusts with a lag.

3. In this problem we consider an economy in which the price of *new* capital goods never changes. It is always equal to 100.
   a. Assuming $R = .05$, $d = .1$, and the corporate income tax is 50 percent, what is the rental cost of capital?
   b. The government is considering an investment tax credit (ITC) where 10 percent of the purchase price of a new capital good can be subtracted from a firm's taxes. Under such a proposal, what will the rental cost of capital be? Assuming that the ITC is unanticipated, describe the behavior of I and K^* in the year that it is implemented.
   c. Assuming that the old capital goods are perfect substitutes in production for new capital goods, what will the price of old capital goods be under the ITC? If the value of a firm's capital stock changes in the year the ITC is implemented, will this change directly affect the firm's investment decision?
   d. Assume now that such a proposal is announced a year ahead of time. What will the rental cost of capital be in the year in which firms learn about the ITC? Compare your answer with the rental cost calculated in Parts a and b. Explain any differences.
   e. Compare the level of investment in the year in which the ITC is announced with what it would be without the ITC. Compare the level of investment in the following year when the ITC is implemented with what it would be if the ITC was implemented *unannounced* that year.

4. How sensitive would you expect automobile production to be to the interest rate? In answering this question, consider (i) the sensitivity of the desired stock of automobiles to the interest rate, (ii) the lags in the adjustment of the automobile stock to its desired level, and (iii) the impact of changes in final automobile sales on inventory investment in automobile manufacturing.

5. *Paradox of Thrift.* Assume a closed-economy model with $Y = C + I + G$. Suppose that investment demand depends on the level of income but not on the interest rate, according to the formula

$$I = e + dY$$

and that consumption also depends on income according to the consumption function

$$C = a + b(1 - t)Y.$$

a. Sketch the spending line for the economy that shows how total spending increases with income Y. (Put spending on the vertical axis and income on the horizontal axis.) Draw a 45-degree line and indicate where spending balance is.

b. Suppose that consumers decide to be more thrifty, to save more. They do this by reducing a once and for all. Show the new point of balance in the diagram.

c. What happens to investment as a result of consumers' attempts to save more? Explain.

d. Explain the paradox of thrift, that the attempt to save more may result in a reduction in private saving. What happens to total saving?

e. Explain why the paradox of thrift is a short-run phenomenon. Introduce interest rates into the investment function, and add a money demand function and price-adjustment equation to the model. If the economy is operating at potential GDP before the reduction in a, will it eventually return to potential after the reduction in a? What happens to saving and investment when prices have fully adjusted?

6. Suppose the desired capital stock is given by the expression

$$K^* = vY/R^K$$

where v is a constant and R^K is the rental cost of capital.

a. Assuming that output in the economy is fixed at Y^*, will a permanent increase in the interest rate have a permanent or temporary effect on the level of investment?

b. Is your answer to Part a consistent with the investment function incorporated in the IS curve?

c. Suppose now that output in the economy is growing each period so that $\Delta Y = g$. Assuming that the actual capital stock adjusts immediately to its desired level, answer Part a.

7. Sketch an IS-LM diagram. Compare two cases: one in which the investment demand function depends on income and the other in which it is independent of income. In which case are both monetary and fiscal policy more effective? Explain.

8. Suppose that GDP is below potential GDP, and that inflation is low. The President and Congress are talking about reducing taxes on investment in order to get the economy back to potential.

a. Sketch the situation on an IS-LM diagram. Show where you want to move the IS curve to get back to potential.

b. In light of lags in the investment process and the forward-looking nature of firms' investment decisions, describe some of the problems that the policymakers need to worry about in enacting the tax legislation.

9. The 1986 Tax Reform Act called for an increase in taxes on businesses and a decrease in taxes on consumers, with total revenue remaining about the same. Describe the effects of the tax on *investment demand*. Be explicit: Are these effects likely to occur immediately, or will they occur with a lag? Distinguish between the effects that work through the rental rate on capital and the effects that work through the accelerator. Which of these two effects is likely to be larger in the long run?

10. In Chapter 10 we argued that forward-looking consumers with rational expectations are likely to have consumption patterns that evolve like a random walk. If firms are forward-looking and have rational expectations, will investment also behave like a random walk? Why or why not?

11. Countercyclical policy in recent recessions has typically involved increases in incentives for investment, often through increases in the investment tax-credit. How might firms' behavior at the beginning of future recessions be affected by beliefs that government may take actions to reduce the cost of investment? What effect would this have on the behavior of real GDP?

MacroSolve Exercises

1. Graph the ratio of investment to GDP against the real interest rate for both annual and quarterly data.
   a. Describe the relationship that you see. Is it compatible with the theoretical model in the chapter?
   b. Why might the relationship between investment and the real interest rate be obscured in the graph?
   c. How might you be able to distinguish whether the movements in the real interest rate caused by other factors are causing the changes in investment, or shocks to investment are shifting the IS curve and causing interest rates to change?

2. Compare the behavior of the ratio of investment to GDP and the growth rate of GDP for both annual and quarterly data. (Hint: Try graphing one series against the other and plotting both of the time series on the same screen.) Is this relationship consistent with the theoretical model in the chapter? Would you expect to see a closer relation between investment and the GDP gap or between investment and the growth of GDP?

3. How does the interest elasticity of investment affect the size of the government spending multiplier in the fixed-price IS-LM model? Use the model "ISLM, Closed Econ" to illustrate your answer.

4. a How does the interest elasticity of investment affect the size and time pattern of the government spending multiplier in the dynamic AD/PA model? Explain why.
   b. Why does the interest elasticity of investment have no effect on the long-run government spending multiplier?
   c. Is the output cost of reducing the price level by cutting the money supply higher or lower the more responsive investment is to interest rates? Explain why.

APPENDIX A: Capital Budgeting and the Rental Price of Capital

In this appendix we show that Jorgenson's rental price approach gives the correct answer to the question of what should be the desired capital stock for a firm that *buys* capital. As discussed in the text the key result is that investment projects that earn more than the rental price will be undertaken and those that earn less than the rental price will not be undertaken. We use a capital budgeting formulation to describe the firms's investment decision.

Suppose that a firm is considering buying some capital equipment that will contribute an amount J_t to revenue in each future year t. The year of the decision is $t = 0$. The equipment costs P^K.

The firm keeps track of its financial position—benefits less costs—for this capital project using an intertemporal budgeting process in the following way. Let V_t be the financial position in Year t. The firm starts in the hole by the cost of the capital equipment P^K. That is, the financial position in Year 0 is

$$V_0 = -\text{The price of the capital equipment} = -P^K. \qquad (11\text{–}14)$$

For example, if the capital equipment cost \$1,000, then $V_0 = -\$1,000$. In the next year, the firm may be even deeper in the hole because it pays interest at rate R on the funds it used to pay for the project last year plus the additional spending it made at the end of last year to make up for wear and tear, or depreciation. For example, for the \$1,000 equipment, if the interest rate were 5 percent ($R = .05$) and 10 percent of the equipment needed to be replaced because of wear and tear ($d = .10$), then the financial position would be reduced by another \$50 + \$100 = \$150. On the other hand, the project contributed an amount J_0 to revenue in its first year. For example, if the revenue is \$200, the position in the project at the beginning of the second year is

$$V_1 = -\$1,000 - \$50 - \$100 + \$200 = -\$950. \qquad (11\text{–}15)$$

The same process repeats each year. In words:

> Position at the beginning of next year
> = Position at the beginning of this year
> + Interest owed this year
> − Depreciation this year
> + Revenue from the project this year.

The general algebraic form is

$$V_t = V_{t-1} + RV_{t-1} - dP^K + J_{t-1}. \qquad (11\text{–}16)$$

Note that this equation is like the intertemporal budget constraint from the forward-looking consumers in Chapter 10. It is essentially the firm's intertemporal budget for the project in question. At the end of the project, the firm will be able to sell the capital equipment. If the firm has been paying for all the wear and tear each year, so that the equipment is like new, then the firm will be able to sell the equipment for what it paid for it. The firm will sell the equipment for P^K, and the firm's financial position will be increased by P^K at the end of the project. (Recall that we assume that the price of new equipment is unchanging.)

With the repeated application of Equation 11–16, the firm can figure out its financial position in the project as long as the project is still in existence. The firm's projects will fall into two categories: **winners,** for whom the position becomes positive (the initial investment pays itself back) and then becomes more and more positive, and **losers**, for whom the position is always negative and the project never pays for itself. A reasonable theory of investment is that the firm goes with the winners and rejects the losers. This is equivalent to the capital budgeting recommendation, which says that projects that have a positive present discounted value should be undertaken and those with a negative present discounted value should be rejected. The present discounted value of a project is simply the financial position V_t as we have defined it divided by $(1 + R)^t$. When the financial position is positive, so is the present discounted value. When the financial position is negative, so is the present discounted value.

Now, to prove that the rental approach gives the same answer as the capital budgeting approach we need to show that *an investment project that consistently earns more than the rental price is a winner and a project that consistently earns less than the rental price is a loser.*

Suppose a project earns exactly the rental price each year; that is,

$$J_t = (R + d)P^K. \tag{11–17}$$

As we noted, the financial position in year 0 is

$$V_0 = -P^K. \tag{11–18}$$

In the next period the financial position is

$$V_1 = -(1 + R)P^K - dP^K + J_0, \tag{11–19}$$

where we have used the budget equation (11–16) Substituting $J_0 = (R + d)P^K$ into Equation 11–19, we get

$$V_1 = -(1 + R)P^K - dP^K + (R + d)P^K, \tag{11–20}$$

which, after canceling out terms on the right-hand side, simply equals $-P^K$. If you repeat this procedure to obtain the financial position after 2 years V_2, 3 years V_3, and so forth, you will find that the firm's financial position is always equal to *minus the current price of a machine.* At the end of the project the firm sells the machine. Because the firm receives the current price of the machine P^K, the financial position at the end of the project is exactly zero. That is, the investment is just on the borderline between being a loser and being a winner.

If the investment earned a little more than the rental price each year, the firm's financial position would end up positive. The investment would be a clear winner. If the investment earned a little less than the rental price each year, the financial position would turn out negative. The firm would reject it. Hence, the rental price is the key factor in the investment decision, even though the firm is buying the capital.

APPENDIX B: Tobin's *q* and the Rental Price of Capital

We saw in Section 11.3 that investment takes place with a lag. This lag has implications for the observed relationship between investment, the rental price of capital, and a related variable called Tobin's *q*. To understand this relationship, suppose that the rental price R^K suddenly falls below the marginal benefit *J* of capital. The situation is illustrated in Figure 11–9, which is a replica of Figure 11–5. The firm will want to raise its capital stock until the marginal benefit of new capital is reduced to the new rental price. But if the firm must adjust its capital slowly, the marginal benefit of capital will remain above the rental price during the adjustment period when the firm is investing in new capital. Only when the adjustment is complete and the

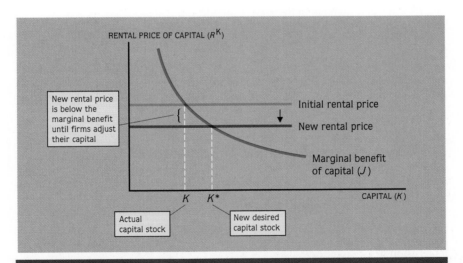

FIGURE 11–9 Desired capital greater than actual capital

When the rental rate on capital falls, firms do not immediately adjust their capital to the new desired level. The adjustment takes place with a lag. Until the capital stock is adjusted, the rental price of capital R^K is below the marginal benefit of capital *J*.

actual capital stock equals the new desired level will the marginal benefit of capital equal the rental price. In the meantime, the greater is the difference between the desired capital stock and the actual capital stock, the greater is the difference between the rental price and the marginal revenue of capital. Investment is positively related to this difference between J and R^K.

Alternatively stated, investment will be a positive function of the ratio of the marginal benefit of new capital J to the rental price of capital R^K. When this ratio (J/R^K) is greater than 1, the rental price is below the marginal benefit of capital and the firm is investing in new capital. When the ratio is less than 1, the firm wants to reduce its capital stock and thus does not invest at all.

The ratio J/R^K of the marginal benefit of capital to the rental price of capital has an interesting interpretation. Suppose that the firm issues shares that can be bought or sold on a stock market, such as the New York Stock Exchange. If the interest rate on bonds is R, then the market value (MV) of the firm's shares should be such that the return on the shares J/MV—the ratio of the marginal benefit of capital (J) to the value of the shares (MV) that represent ownership of that capital—is equal to the interest rate R. Then the return on holding the firm's shares is the same as the return on bonds. In other words, the market value MV of the firm's shares is directly related to the marginal benefit J of capital by the formula $MV{\times}R = J$. For example, if J = \$10 per share and R = .05, then the market value MV of shares should equal \$200.

There is a similar relation between the price of capital at the firm P^K and the rental rate R^K. Ignoring depreciation, the formula for the rental price of capital says that $P^K \times R = R^K$. Combining these two formulas, we get

$$\frac{J}{R^K} = \frac{MV \times R}{P \times R} = \frac{MV}{P^K} = q.$$

The ratio on the far right (MV/P^K), the market value of the firm divided by the price of the firm's capital, is called Tobin's q, after James Tobin of Yale University, who emphasized the importance of the ratio for investment.[8] It is clear from our discussion thus far that investment should be positively related to q.

Tobin's q provides a very useful way to formulate investment functions because it is relatively easy to measure. Data on a firm's share price can usually be obtained from a stock exchange, and the price indexes for capital are tabulated as part of the national income and product accounts (NIPA). For this reason, Tobin's q is a useful gauge of the climate for investment. For example, in 1983 when investment was booming in the United States, Tobin's q was quite large, even though the measured real interest rate and the rental price of capital suggested an unfavorable climate for investment. The microeconomics of investment that underlie Tobin's q approach to investment are really no different from the rental price approach that we focus on in this chapter.

---

[8]See James Tobin and William Brainard, "Asset Markets and the Cost of Capital," in Bela Balassa and Richard Nelson, eds., *Economic Progress, Private Values and Public Policy: Essays in Honor of William Fellner* (New York: North-Holland, 1977), for more details about q.

Foreign Trade and the Exchange Rate

Foreign trade is a central issue in U.S. economic policy. For example, in early 1992, President Bush visited Japan with the heads of major U.S. corporations to discuss trade issues with the Japanese government. As was pointed out in Chapter 4, international trade is essential for strong, long-term economic growth. And the 1990–91 recession would have been worse were it not for the strong U.S. export performance. In the early 1990s, the United States continued to import far more goods and services than it exported, although the trade deficit had diminished from the record highs of the 1980s. As the deficit continued, foreigners acquired claims on U.S. government and business. The federal government borrowed substantial amounts from foreigners. European and Japanese investors bought landmark buildings in many major U.S. cities. Foreigners acquired U.S. corporations and gained big positions in the U.S. stock market.

The ups and downs of foreign trade are important in the U.S. economy as well. Trade has a powerful influence on aggregate demand. For example, when consumers decide to purchase Japanese or German cars rather than American cars, the demand for U.S.-made goods declines. The immediate effect is a decline in GDP and employment in the United States.

The international value of the dollar affects foreign trade and thereby influences aggregate demand, GDP, and employment. Fluctuations in the dollar were common in the 1980s. Against other major currencies, the dollar rose to extreme heights in the first half of the decade, fell sharply, and rose and fell again going into the 1990s. Some of these movements were very extreme; for example, the dollar lost almost half its value relative to the German deutsche mark between 1985 and 1989.

Many commentators have called for policies to reduce the trade deficit. Some think that restrictions on imports from Japan and other countries with trade surpluses would be appropriate. Others call for a correction of the fiscal budget deficit in order to reduce borrowing from foreigners. Some economists feel that the volatility of the value of the dollar in relation to other currencies needs to be controlled by intervention in the foreign exchange market or even by pegging exchange rates at fixed levels. Proposals for policy intervention are founded on the belief that there is something wrong with a trade deficit or a volatile currency. A contrary view, held by many economists, is that the trade deficit and the value of the dollar should be set in international markets, free from intervention by the United States or other governments. In this chapter, we will study the determinants of net exports and exchange rates. We will look at the ways that changes in trade affect the domestic economy and how policy can respond. We will also look at policies aimed at influencing the trade deficit and the international value of the dollar.

12.1   FOREIGN TRADE AND AGGREGATE DEMAND

Figure 12–1 shows what happened to the flows of goods and services into and out of the United States between 1959 and 1991. Generally, imports and exports have been about equal, but in some years, especially most recently, there have been important swings. The huge excess of imports over exports since the mid-1980s will be a particularly important subject of this chapter.

The quantity of goods and services flowing into and out of the United States is not the only important dimension of trade. It matters how much we have to pay for imports and how much we can get for our exports. In this respect, the nominal or dollar flows are important in foreign trade, whereas it is the real flows that concern us in considering domestic production. If imports become more expensive, it is costly to the United States even if net exports in real terms do not change. The **terms of trade** is the ratio of the price of exports to the price of imports. When the prices of imports rise, we say there has been an adverse shift in the terms of trade.

When the value of American imports exceeds the value of exports, either because of a high quantity of imports or because of the high price of

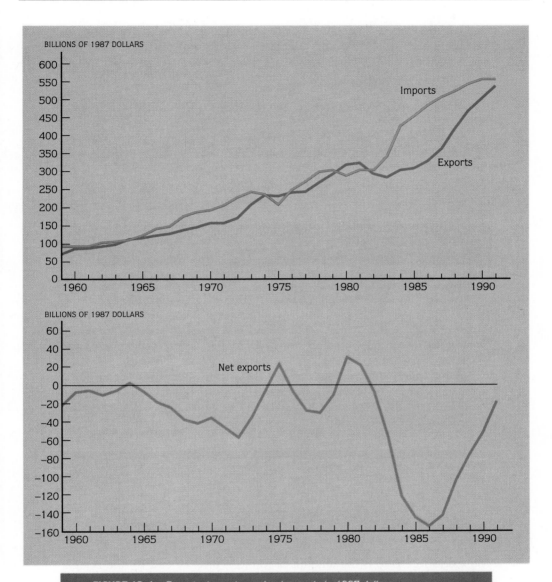

FIGURE 12–1 Exports, imports, and net exports in 1987 dollars

The top panel shows the quantities of goods exported out of and imported into the United States in constant 1987 dollars. The difference between the two is net exports, shown separately in the bottom panel. Imports grew very rapidly in the early and mid-1980s while exports were roughly constant. Net exports turned sharply negative.
Source: *Economic Report of the President,* 1992, Table B–2.

imports, the United States must borrow enough from foreigners to pay for the difference. As we saw in Chapter 2, U.S. borrowing from abroad is called a capital inflow. For example, in 1990 net exports were –$75 billion; the United States had to borrow $75 billion in order to finance the excess of imports over exports. Actually, total borrowing was even larger because the United States also paid transfers to people outside the country of about $22 billion.

The capital inflows since the mid-1980s have been large by historical standards. They brought the United States from a net creditor position with the rest of the world to a net debtor position. In other words, by 1991 Americans owed more to foreigners than foreigners owed to Americans.

FOREIGN TRADE AND AGGREGATE DEMAND

1. **Foreign trade influences U.S. aggregate demand in two ways. First, Americans can purchase their goods from abroad instead of from U.S. producers. When they do, their imports contribute to aggregate demand in the rest of the world instead of to U.S. aggregate demand. Second, foreigners can purchase goods produced in the United States. These exports enter U.S. aggregate demand.**
2. **When exports are less than imports, Americans must finance the difference plus any other expenditures abroad by borrowing. This borrowing— or, equivalently, investment by foreigners in the United States—is called capital inflow from abroad.**

 12.2   THE EXCHANGE RATE

The **exchange rate** is the amount of foreign currency that can be bought with one U.S. dollar. For example, on February 28, 1985, the exchange rate between the West German mark and the dollar was 3.1 marks per dollar. If you went to a bank with $100 on that day you could have obtained 310 marks. Like other prices the exchange rate can change: On March 13, 1991, the exchange rate between the mark and the dollar was 1.7 marks per dollar. The exchange rates between the dollar and foreign currencies are listed in the financial pages of most newspapers.

The exchange rate is determined in the **foreign exchange market** where dollars and other currencies are traded freely. The foreign exchange market is not in one location; it is a global market. Banks all over the world

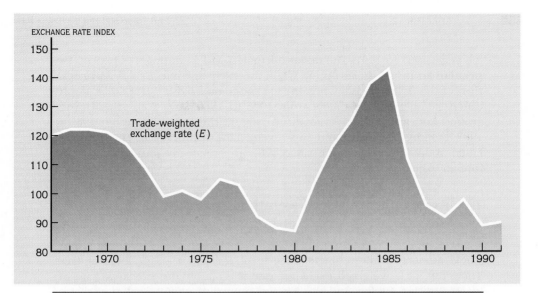

EXCHANGE RATE INDEX

Trade-weighted
exchange rate (E)

FIGURE 12–2   The trade-weighted exchange rate

The trade-weighted exchange rate is the best overall measure of the dollar exchange rate. It is an average of exchange rates with many different currencies, including the Canadian dollar, the French franc, the West German mark, the Japanese yen, and the British pound. The exchange rate fluctuates by large amounts. It was very high in the early 1970s and in the early 1980s. The dollar was low in the late 1970s.
Source: *Economic Report of the President*, 1992, Table B–107.

actively buy and sell dollars and other foreign currencies for their customers. The banks are linked by a network of telecommunications that allows instantaneous contact around the globe. Because of different time zones, the foreign exchange market is open 24 hours a day.

In today's monetary system the dollar exchange rate is allowed to **float** against the currencies of other large countries. For this reason the system is called a floating or **flexible exchange-rate system.** The United States and other major Western countries permit a free market in foreign exchange. Neither the United States nor other major countries try to fix the exchange rate with the dollar within narrow bands as they did prior to the early 1970s. This does not mean that the United States is powerless to affect the exchange rate or must ignore the exchange rate when it sets macro policy. As we will see, changes in monetary and fiscal policy have strong influences on the exchange rate, and these influences must be considered when setting macro policy.

Since there are many countries in the world, there are many exchange rates for the dollar. A convenient single measure of the dollar exchange rate is the **trade-weighted exchange rate,** which we will denote by the symbol E. This is an average of several different exchange rates, each one weighted according to the amount of trade with the United States. Figure 12–2 shows the trade-weighted exchange rate E for the United States for the years 1967 to 1991. The dollar fluctuated widely during this period. **Depreciation** of the dollar occurs when the exchange rate E falls. **Appreciation** of the dollar occurs when the exchange rate E rises. The dollar depreciated steadily by 17 percent from 1976 to 1980. The dollar then turned around and appreciated by over 60 percent through 1985. From 1985 to 1987 it fell by 50 percent and thus reversed the appreciation. The dollar has fallen about 7 percent more since 1987 in a relatively tranquil period for foreign exchange markets.

The Exchange Rate and Relative Prices

In our discussion of the role of the exchange rate in foreign trade, we will speak of the rest of the world (ROW) as if it were a single country with a single monetary unit, a single price level P_W, and a single level of GDP. Then, the trade-weighted exchange rate E is simply the exchange rate between the U.S. dollar and the foreign monetary unit. Like the exchange rate, the price level in the rest of the world P_W is measured by taking an average of the price levels in the countries that trade with the United States.

The **real exchange rate** is a measure of the exchange rate that is adjusted for differences in price levels between the United States and the ROW. It is a measure of the relative price of goods produced in the United States compared with goods produced in the ROW. If P is the U.S. price level, the real exchange rate can be written in symbols as

$$\text{Real exchange rate} = \frac{\text{Foreign price of U.S. goods}}{\text{Foreign price of ROW goods}} = \frac{E \times P}{P_W}.$$

When the real exchange rate is high, foreigners have to pay more for goods produced in the United States compared with the price of goods produced in the rest of the world. For example, when the mark-dollar exchange rate rises from 1.8 to 2.0 marks per dollar, the price of a $1,000 Apple computer produced in the United States rises from 1,800 marks to 2,000 marks in West Germany. Note that the exchange rate for the individual item is multiplied by its price in the United States to get the price outside the United States; similarly, we multiply E times P in the numerator of the real exchange rate to get a measure of the average price of U.S. goods in the ROW.

Recall our basic assumption that prices set by U.S. producers are fixed in the short run. Aggregate demand in this period, domestic or foreign, will not influence the dollar price level P in this period. We make the same assumption about the ROW. The price level P_W set by ROW producers is fixed in the short run.

The exchange rate E, on the other hand, varies minute by minute. Thus the real exchange rate (EP/P_W) varies minute by minute. The price of U.S. products in the ROW is flexible in the short run because the exchange rate is flexible. By the same token, the dollar price of ROW products is flexible in the short run.

When the dollar appreciates, ROW products become cheaper to Americans. At the same time, U.S. products become more expensive in the ROW. If the United States and the ROW produced identical, readily transportable products, the exchange rate would not fluctuate in the short run. We would always buy from the cheapest producer. The exchange rate would always have the single value that equated the dollar prices of U.S. and ROW products. The real exchange rate would never change. If the United States and the ROW produced all the same products, the exchange rate could not fluctuate in the short run and would change in the longer run only by as much as prices in the ROW rose by more than prices in the United States. This theory of exchange-rate fluctuations is called **purchasing power parity.** The theory does not work for short-run fluctuations. Exchange rates fluctuate far more than the theory predicts. We can see this easily. According to the theory, the *real* exchange rate ought to be constant over time. The real exchange rate between the U.S. dollar and the currencies of the rest of the world is shown in Figure 12–3. The real exchange rate is not at all constant.

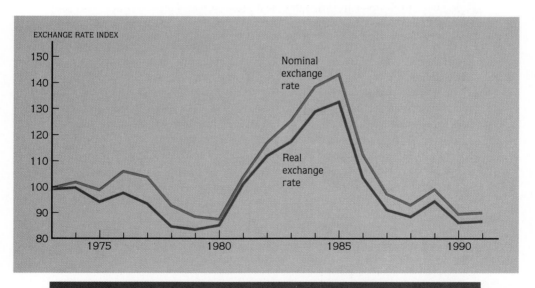

FIGURE 12–3   The real trade-weighted exchange rate

The real exchange rate between the United States and the ROW is the nominal exchange rate adjusted for changes in the domestic purchasing power of the dollar and the currencies of the ROW. When the real exchange rate falls, it means that Americans find foreign goods more expensive. Through much of the 1970s, the real exchange rate fell. The price of American goods relative to foreign goods fell from .99 in 1974 to .83 in 1979. In the early 1980s, the relative price of American goods rose dramatically; then it fell sharply in 1986. Since 1986, the relative price has been stable.
Source: *Economic Report of the President*, 1992, Table B–107.

Clearly, purchasing power parity is not a good theory of the determination of the exchange rate in the short run. On the other hand, the theory has a powerful economic logic. How can we reconcile the fact of wide variations in the real exchange rate with the principle that people buy at the lowest possible price?

One answer is that different countries produce different products. Japanese cars are not identical to American cars, for example. When the dollar appreciates, Japanese cars become cheaper, but the U.S. public does not stop buying American cars altogether. Instead, the new price advantage of Japanese cars raises Japanese sales in the United States somewhat and depresses sales of American cars somewhat. The same thing occurs in hundreds of other markets. Appreciation of the dollar makes it more difficult for U.S. producers to sell their output, but it does not wipe them out. The exchange rate has room to vary. It is not locked in place by purchasing power parity.

THE EXCHANGE RATE AND PURCHASING POWER PARITY

1. The nominal exchange rate is the number of units of foreign currency that a dollar is worth. An increase in the exchange rate is an appreciation of the dollar.
2. The real exchange rate measures the relative purchasing power of the dollar by adjusting the nominal exchange rate by the price levels in the respective countries. When the real exchange rate is high, U.S. goods are expensive for foreigners and foreign goods are inexpensive for U.S. buyers.
3. Purchasing power parity asserts that the nominal exchange rate must equate the prices of tradable goods across countries. This implies a constant real exchange rate, which is inconsistent with the empirical evidence. Nonetheless, purchasing power parity exerts some influence on the exchange rate.

12.3   THE DETERMINANTS OF NET EXPORTS

The Effect of the Exchange Rate

As we have just seen, fluctuations in the exchange rate change the relative price of U.S. and ROW goods and thereby affect the demand for imports and exports. Imports depend positively on the exchange rate. If the dollar is strong, it buys a lot of foreign currency, and the goods sold by the ROW are correspondingly cheaper. When the dollar appreciated in the early 1980s, many U.S. industries, especially autos and steel, suffered from the reduced price of their foreign competitors. The same thing is true in all sectors, though the effect is less severe for products of which the ROW does not produce close substitutes. And for services, utilities, and many other important components of GDP, imports are difficult or impossible. Overall, the effect of a higher exchange rate is to divert some aggregate demand to the ROW.

Exports, too, are sensitive to the exchange rate. A strong dollar—that is, a high exchange rate—makes U.S. goods more expensive in the ROW. In the period of the strong dollar in the early 1980s, U.S. export industries like construction equipment suffered from the increase in their prices as perceived by the ROW, even though dollar price increases were moderate.

The Effect of Income

In Chapter 6, we noted that net exports depend on U.S. GDP. Higher incomes make consumers spend more on imported products; this relation is particularly sensitive because many types of products that consumers spend extra income on, such as electronics and cars, are frequently imported. In addition, some investment goods are imported, such as machine tools from Germany. When GDP rises and investment strengthens, part of the increase in investment goods come from overseas. Thus, in general, imports respond positively to GDP. On the other hand, there is little connection between U.S. exports and U.S. GDP. Hence net exports depend negatively on GDP.

The Net Export Function

As we have seen, we can combine imports and exports into a single measure, net exports X, defined as exports less imports. Our conclusions about the determinants of net exports are:

1. Net exports depend negatively on the real exchange rate. When the dollar is strong, exports are lower and imports are higher. Net exports are lower on both counts.
2. Net exports depend negatively on real income in the United States. This dependence comes from subtracting imports, which depend positively on real income.

We can summarize these ideas in a simple algebraic formula:

$$X = g - mY - n\frac{EP}{P_W}.$$ The Net Export Function (12–1)

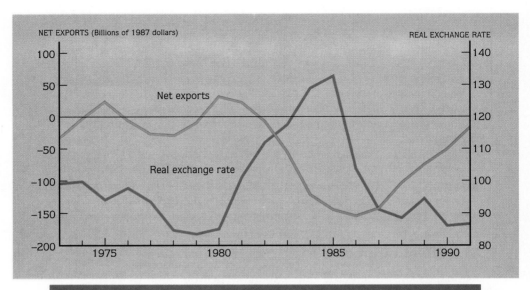

FIGURE 12–4   Net exports and the real exchange rate

The real exchange rate and net exports move at the same time, but in opposite directions. When the real exchange rate rises, net exports fall; conversely, when the real exchange rate falls, net exports rise.
Source: *Economic Report of the President*, 1992, Tables B–2 and B–107.

Equation 12–1 is the net export function. It says that net exports equal a constant *g* minus a coefficient *m* times income *Y*, minus a coefficient *n* times the real exchange rate. The net export function summarizes how net exports depend negatively on both income *Y* and the real exchange rate (EP/P_w).

How well does the net export function work? Figure 12–4 shows the relation between net exports and the exchange rate since 1973. The negative relation is quite evident; note especially that the increase in the dollar exchange rate in the mid-1980s was accompanied by a decline in net exports. Net exports rose in the late 1980s and early 1990s after the decline in the exchange rate. The effect of the other determinant of net exports—real income in the United States—is not so evident in Figure 12–4 because exports rose as income in the ROW increased in this period. However, in the early 1980s the economy of the United States grew more rapidly than those of many European countries and this added to the trade deficit. The weakening of the dollar in the late 1980s was the dominant factor in the increase in net exports.

EXAMPLE. A numerical example of the net export function can be written

$$X = 600 - .1Y - 100\frac{EP}{P_W}.$$

Numerical Example of the
Net Export Function (12–2)

Suppose that the price level in the United States and the price level in the ROW are both predetermined at the value of 1.0. If output Y is $5,000 billion and the exchange rate E is 1.0, then net exports X equal zero. If output Y rises by $100 billion, then net exports fall by $10 billion because imports rise by this amount. If the exchange rate rises from 1.0 to 1.3, about as much as it did from 1980 to 1984, then net exports would fall by $30 billion.

Net exports is an endogenous variable that depends on the exchange rate. To complete our theory, we therefore need to explain what determines the exchange rate. As we have just seen, purchasing power parity doesn't work very well. We now develop a theory that relates the exchange rate to the interest rate.

12.4 THE EXCHANGE RATE AND THE INTEREST RATE

Fluctuations in the exchange rate are closely related to interest rates in the United States and the ROW. In particular, policies in the United States that raise interest rates tend to cause the dollar to appreciate. The appreciation of the dollar in the early 1980s, for example, was related to the monetary and fiscal policies that brought extraordinarily high interest rates. Why are interest rates and the exchange rate positively related?

The financial markets of the major developed countries are closely linked. Investors are constantly comparing the returns they make by investing in Germany (in stocks and bonds that pay in marks), in Japan, in Britain, and in many other countries. There are billions of dollars and marks and trillions of yen of "hot money" that will migrate almost instantly to the place where it will earn the highest return.

As we stressed in Chapter 2, when the dust settles, trade flows and capital flows have to equal each other, except for measurement error. The net exports of the United States must be equal to the amount of U.S. capital flowing to the rest of the world less the amount of foreign capital coming into the United States. It is not possible for there to be a large U.S. trade deficit at the same time that large amounts of capital are flowing out of the United States to seek a higher return in other countries. The exchange rate and interest rates fluctuate minute by minute to keep trade flows and capital flows equal to each other.

When the U.S. interest rate is high in comparison with foreign interest rates, capital will be attracted to the United States.[1] Even a fraction of a percentage point of extra return could bring hundreds of billions of dollars of wealth to be invested in the United States. In order to prevent such a large flow, something else must happen at the same time that the U.S. interest rate rises in order to deter the huge capital flow. What happens is an appreciation of the dollar. When foreign investors see the combination of attractive U.S. interest rates and a strong dollar, they reason in the following way: On the one hand, I like the high return I can earn in dollars. But, on the other hand, I am not so sure that the return I will earn in my own currency is any better than at home. The dollar is strong today, but it is likely to come back to normal over the next year or two, as it always has in the past. As the dollar depreciates, I will lose some of my capital when I convert it back to my own currency.

The more the dollar rises when the U.S. interest rate rises, the more powerful will be the second part of that logic. Hence, there is some degree of appreciation of the dollar that will block the huge capital inflow that would otherwise accompany a higher U.S. interest rate. Figure 12–5 shows the relation between the U.S. interest rate and the exchange rate that is needed to stave off the capital inflow.

In algebra, we can express the positive relation between the real exchange rate and the U.S. interest rate as

$$\frac{EP}{P_W} = q + vR, \qquad (12\text{–}3)$$

where R is the U.S. interest rate and q and v are constants. Recall that it is the rise in the U.S. interest rate relative to foreign interest rates that brings about the rise in the exchange rate. In Equation 12–3 we suppress the foreign interest rate under the assumption that it does not move as much as the U.S. interest rate. More details on the relation between the exchange rate and the U.S. interest rate appear in the appendix to this chapter.

EXAMPLE. If prices are measured in such a way that the real exchange rate EP/P_W is equal to 1 when purchasing power parity holds, then the relation between the U.S. interest rate and the real exchange rate might be

$$\frac{EP}{P_W} = .75 + 5R. \quad \text{\small Numerical Example of the Exchange-Rate/Interest-Rate Relation} \qquad (12\text{–}4)$$

---

[1]Just as in the case of consumption and investment, the interest rate that matters for the foreign exchange market is the real interest rate. If the U.S. nominal interest rate is high only because expected U.S. inflation is high, foreigners will not be attracted to U.S. investments. They will anticipate that the value of the dollar and so the value of dollar-denominated bonds will decline in the future at the expected rate of inflation.

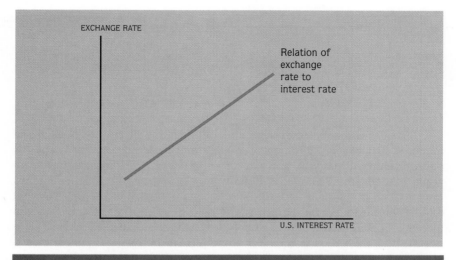

FIGURE 12–5   Relation between the U.S. interest rate and the exchange rate

A higher U.S. interest rate requires a stronger dollar. If not, huge capital inflows would occur, which would be inconsistent with trade flows. The stronger dollar discourages the capital inflow that would otherwise occur by creating expectations of a subsequent depreciation of the dollar, which would off-set the advantage of the higher U.S. interest rate.

When the net export function, Equation 12–2, is combined with this rela-tion, we get the numerical example of the net export relation we used in Chapter 7:

$$X = 525 - .1Y - 500R.$$

THE INTEREST RATE AND THE EXCHANGE RATE

1. The exchange rate and the interest rate are positively related. When the real interest rate rises, say because of an increase in government spend-ing, the exchange rate also rises.
2. The relationship between the interest rate and the exchange rate comes about as investors shift their funds between different countries to obtain the best return. When the interest rate rises in the United States, investors buy dollar-denominated bonds and this drives up the exchange rate.
3. When U.S. interest rates are high relative to the rest of the world, it must be the case that investors expect the dollar to depreciate at an annual rate equal to the interest-rate differential. Expectations of future depreciation require a strong dollar today. Thus, there is a positive relation between the interest rate and the exchange rate.

THE IS CURVE AND ECONOMIC POLICY IN AN OPEN ECONOMY

12.5

Recall that the IS curve describes the combinations of interest rates R and incomes Y that satisfy the income identity and the equations for spending: consumption, investment, and net exports. *Without* net exports in the income identity, the IS curve is downward sloping because higher interest rates reduce investment and, through the multiplier, reduce GDP. *With* net exports, more things happen to spending when the interest rate rises. An increase in the interest rate raises the exchange rate and thereby reduces net exports; this tends to augment the effect of the interest rate on investment and makes the IS curve flatter than it would be in a closed economy. Not only do high interest rates cause firms to invest less, they also cause Americans to meet their needs with imported goods and foreigners to divert their demand away from U.S. products.

But the presence of net exports also reduces the size of the multiplier, and this tends to make the IS curve steeper. Net exports depend negatively on GDP. As GDP rises, part of the increase in spending goes overseas and does not enter domestic aggregate demand. This spillover abroad is sometimes called **leakage** and it reduces the size of the multiplier.

In Chapter 7, we derived the open-economy IS curve graphically and algebraically. The next section adds some more details in the process of deriving it algebraically.

Algebraic Derivation of the Open-Economy IS Curve

The IS curve is derived algebraically by substituting the functions for consumption C, investment I, and net exports X into the income identity. That is,

$$Y = \underbrace{a + b(1 - t)Y}_{C} + \underbrace{e - dR}_{I} + \underbrace{G + g - mY - n(EP/P_W)}_{X}. \qquad (12\text{–}5)$$

Putting the interest rate on the left-hand side gives

$$R = \frac{a + e + g}{d} - \frac{1 - b(1 - t) + m}{d}\,Y - \frac{n}{d}\,\frac{EP}{P_W} + \frac{1}{d}\,G. \qquad (12\text{–}6)$$

This equation relates the interest rate R to output Y, the real exchange rate EP/P_W, and government spending G. It shows that the interest rate is negatively related to the real exchange rate. Appreciation of the dollar shifts the IS curve downward; depreciation raises the curve. To get the IS curve, substitute Equation 12–3 into Equation 12–6 in order to eliminate the real exchange rate:

$$R = \frac{a + e + g - ng}{d + nv} - \frac{1 - b(1 - t) + m}{d + nv} \, Y + \frac{1}{d + nv} \, G. \qquad (12\text{–}7)$$

The coefficient on Y shows that the IS curve slopes downward for two reasons: the negative response of investment to the interest rate, described by d, and the negative response of net exports, described by nv.

The IS curve of Equation 12–7 is the one we discussed in Chapter 7.

Effects of Monetary and Fiscal Policy on Trade in the Short Run

Monetary and fiscal policy have important effects on trade and the exchange rate. Suppose that the Fed increases the money supply. This shifts the LM curve to the right; that is, it lowers interest rates and stimulates investment. The decline in interest rates depreciates the exchange rate; net exports rise. Because of the rise in investment and net exports, GDP rises. However, the increase in GDP tends to decrease net exports because imports rise. There are thus two offsetting effects of an increase in the money supply on net exports. Exports definitely rise, but imports might rise by a greater amount. In any case, interest rates fall, the dollar depreciates, and GDP rises. Conversely, when the money supply is decreased, interest rates rise, the dollar appreciates, and GDP falls.

Now suppose that government spending is increased. The IS curve is pushed to the right, and interest rates rise. The rise in interest rates reduces investment spending, but also causes the exchange rate to appreciate. The higher exchange rate reduces exports as U.S. goods become relatively expensive compared with foreign goods. Hence, the increase in government spending crowds out export industries as well as investment. Imports also rise because of the increase in the dollar and because GDP has increased. Thus an increase in government spending increases the trade deficit or reduces the trade surplus, as it stimulates the economy.

Price Adjustment

What happens in these alternative policy scenarios when firms begin to adjust their prices? If output was equal to potential output in the case of the increase in the money supply, the price level would begin to rise because output increases above potential. The increase in prices will lower real money balances and the interest rate will begin to rise. As it does, the real exchange rate will begin to rise. These adjustments will continue until the

The Budget Deficit and the Trade Deficit

What happens to the trade deficit when the government runs a fiscal budget deficit? Suppose the budget deficit comes from a large tax cut that puts much more disposable income in the hands of consumers. There is no corresponding reduction in government spending, and consumers choose to spend most of the increase in disposable income. Then the IS curve shifts outward. The interest rate rises. The dollar appreciates and net exports decline. Thus a budget deficit causes a trade deficit.

The accounting identity we studied in Chapter 2 suggests that there should be a relation between budget and trade deficits. Funds available for investment in the United States are private saving less the government deficit plus the capital inflow from abroad (the trade deficit). Unless an increase in the budget deficit depresses investment significantly, it will have to cause a capital inflow.

U.S. experience in the 1980s demonstrated this principle on a grand scale. The following chart shows how the decline in tax receipts relative to the growth of expenditures brought about a gigantic budget deficit. The chart shows the deficit of all levels of government—federal, state, and local. From trade surpluses at the beginning of the decade, very large trade deficits emerged starting in 1984. The trade deficit peaked in 1987 and then declined to a low level by 1991.

The budget deficit causes an accumulation of government debt. In a closed economy, the nation owes the debt to itself. But when the budget deficit is financed through a capital inflow, the borrowing is from the rest of the world. In effect, the United States owes the part of the national debt accumulated since 1981 to Japan and the other countries that have financed the U.S. trade deficit by running trade surpluses.

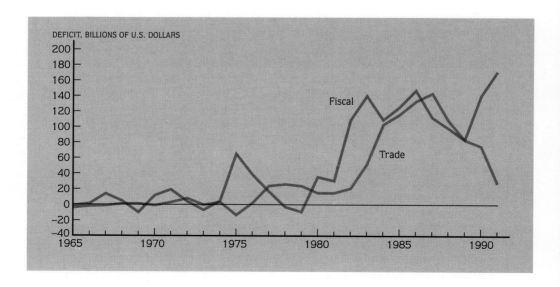

Trade deficits are not the inevitable result of budget deficits.[*] The U.S. trade deficit fell substantially from 1987 to 1991, while the budget deficit reached an all time high in 1991. Similarly, in the mid-1980s, Japan had a budget deficit even larger than the one in the United States, but Japan had a trade surplus. The explanation is the remarkably high rate of saving of the Japanese. Private saving in Japan is enough to finance a large volume of investment, a huge government deficit, and leave enough left over to make large investments in U.S. government debt and other forms of lending to the United States.

[*]See Martin Feldstein, *"The Budget and Trade Deficits Aren't Really Twins"* Working Paper 3966, National Bureau of Economic Research, January 1992.

---

economy has returned to potential. Eventually the price level will have increased by the amount of the original increase in the money supply. The real exchange rate will have returned to normal so that the nominal exchange rate E will have depreciated by the amount of the increase in the price level. In the long run money is neutral.

An increase in government spending will also eventually bring about an upward adjustment in prices. The reduction in real balances will raise interest rates and further reduce investment and net exports. Eventually, output will return to potential output, and the sum of investment and net exports will have declined by exactly the amount of the increase in government spending. The real exchange rate and the interest rate will be permanently higher after the process is complete.

OPEN-ECONOMY IS CURVE AND POLICY

1. The downward slope of the IS curve in an open economy comes in part from the positive relation between the interest rates and the exchange rate. Net exports decline when the interest rate rises.
2. The offset to fiscal expansion through crowding out is stronger in an open economy. Fiscal expansion raises the interest rate and depresses net exports.
3. Monetary policy has an enhanced effect through the interest rate in an open economy. A monetary expansion lowers the interest rate and stimulates net exports as well as investment in the short run.
4. In the long run, money remains neutral with respect to all real variables. The price level increases and the nominal exchange rate depreciates in proportion to the increase in the money supply.

12.6   THE EXCHANGE RATE AND THE PRICE LEVEL

One of the macroeconomic principles we have stressed in this book is that the price level is very unresponsive to most economic events in the short run. For example, a sudden contraction in monetary policy does not seem to have any measurable impact on the price level within the first year, even though its eventual effect is to lower prices considerably. One important exception is that prices respond quickly to changes in costs of imports such as oil. The dramatic price rises of 1974–75, 1979–80, and 1990 and the sudden slowing of inflation in 1986 can be linked directly to events in the world oil market. To a certain extent, fluctuations in the exchange rate can influence the price level in a similar way. A rise in the dollar is like a decline in world oil prices; it makes imports cheaper. A collapse of the dollar, as in 1986–87, is an adverse price shock.

In a small economy, the domestic price level is closely tied to the exchange rate. Many consumption and investment goods are imported; those that are not compete with imports. A small country's exports trade in large world markets and are usually constrained to sell at home for essentially the world price. Hence, changes in a small country's exchange rate bring immediate and important changes in that country's price level.

In the large U.S. economy, the situation is quite the reverse. For Japanese cars, for example, the U.S. market is over half the total market worldwide. The setting of the U.S. dollar price for foreign products is a major business decision for the makers of those products. Frequently, the outcome of that decision is to keep the dollar price of foreign products unchanged in the United States, even though the exchange rate has risen or fallen sharply. For example, when the dollar rose dramatically against the German mark in 1983, German auto companies raised the mark price of cars in order to stabilize their dollar prices in the United States. They might have chosen to let the dollar price fall in order to sell more cars. Similarly, when the dollar fell sharply relative to the mark after 1985, the mark price of cars shipped to the United States fell. Again, the dollar price was stable. German car makers maintained a stable share of the U.S. market and kept their cars at stable prices relative to other cars in the market. Many other foreign sellers of products with well-known brands in the United States behaved in the same way.

From its peak in early 1985 until late 1986, the real exchange rate declined by over 15 percent. The real price of imports to the United States rose by only about 1 percent over the same period. All the rest of the change in the exchange rate was absorbed by a decline in profit margins by importers. For Japan, the numbers are particularly striking; Stated in yen, the cost of producing products in Japan rose by about 6 percent from the beginning of 1985 to the middle of 1986. But the number of yen received by the Japanese for their typical exported product declined by 23 percent over the same period.[2] Costs and profit margins of U.S. exporters appear to be much less sensitive to exchange-rate fluctuations. Dollar prices of U.S. exports are largely unaffected by exchange-rate changes; this implies that foreign currency prices of U.S. goods change roughly in proportion to the exchange rate.[3]

Because importers tend not to adjust their U.S. prices quickly in response to changes in the exchange rate, large movements in the exchange rate do not create price shocks in the U.S. economy. The price-adjustment process we described in Chapter 8 applies reasonably well to the prices of imported goods as well as those made in the United States. We will not stress the immediate impact of the exchange rate on the U.S. price level. That impact would be large in a small, highly open economy, but appears to be quite small in the U.S. economy.

12.7 PROTECTIONISM VERSUS FREE TRADE

All industries in the United States that produce products that can be shipped from one country to another face foreign competition. These industries make up the tradables sector. Only industries like services communications, and utilities are insulated from that competition. If foreign competition could be eliminated or discouraged, domestic producers would enjoy increased profits. The losers would be U.S. consumers, who would pay higher prices as a result of lessened competition.

Industries in the tradables sector push constantly in favor of protectionist measures. These measures include:

1. Tariffs, which are a tax on imports.
2. Quotas, which limit the quantity of imports.
3. Outright bans of certain imports.

The incentive to seek protection exists all the time. However, the likelihood of convincing Congress to enact protectionist legislation rises dramatically when imports are high and domestic industries are suffering from diminished sales and high unemployment.

[2]The data are from Paul Krugman and Richard Baldwin, "The Persistence of the U.S. Trade Deficit," *Brookings Papers on Economic Activity,* Vol. 1 (1987), pp. 1–43.
[3]See the comparative study by Michael Knetter, "Price Discrimination by U.S. and German Exporters," *American Economic Review,* Vol. 79, No. 1 (March 1989), pp. 198–210.

Dumping and Predatory Pricing

Countries with trade deficits often accuse their major trading partners of competing unfairly by pricing below cost, a practice called **dumping.** The United States has an important agency—the International Trade Commission (ITC)—which hears numerous complaints of this kind. In 1989, the ITC found that Asian producers of business telephones were dumping their products in the United States. The U.S. government imposed countervailing duties to offset the adverse effects of Asian telephone makers on AT&T and other U.S. competitors. When there is good evidence that a foreign seller is trying to drive U.S. makers permanently out of the market, countervailing duties may be a good remedy. Critics of the ITC say that it is just trying to make life easier for domestic producers with the effect of denying bargains to U.S. consumers.

Recently the U.S. Supreme Court decided an antitrust case involving the question of whether the low price of Japanese color TV manufacturers was a predatory strategy aimed at driving out U.S. manufacturers. The Court noted that low Japanese prices had prevailed for 17 years and showed no signs of rising, even though Japan now dominates the U.S. TV market. It denied the U.S. industry any relief on the grounds that Japan showed no signs of jacking up prices in an assertion of monopoly power once the domestic industry was eliminated. Instead, the Court reasoned, Japan was permanently committed to providing U.S. customers with bargains [*Matsushita v. Zenith Radio,* 106 S. Ct. 1348 (1986)].

U.S. policy on dumping is on divergent paths. It has become easier to get the ITC to act against foreign sellers who set low prices, while it has become more difficult to persuade the courts that a seller, foreign or domestic, has violated antitrust law by setting a lower price with the intention of eliminating a competitor. But the two issues are the same and ought to be resolved with the same standards.

The history of protection in the United States can be characterized in the following way. In normal times, under the leadership of the President, trade barriers are gradually reduced. Consumer interests predominate in the long run; purchasers in the United States are generally free to take advantage of bargains that foreigners make available. But in times of recession or large trade deficits, strong pressures develop for protectionist legislation. Tariffs and quotas are tightened in those times. When the emergency is over, protectionism lingers for some years, but eventually is reduced.

In 1992, even after a number of years of intensive pressure for protection, tariffs were still generally only a few percent on the great majority of imports. Some special protectionist steps were in effect, however, including:

1. Voluntary quotas enforced by Japan on its exports of cars to the United States. Robert Crandall of the Brookings Institution has estimated that

these quotas raised the price of the typical Japanese car to a U.S. purchaser by between $2,000 and $3,000.[4]
2. Voluntary restrictions on steel exports to the United States by a number of foreign steel makers. Crandall finds that these restrictions have had relatively little effect on the U.S. price of steel.
3. The Multifiber Agreement, which restricts international trade in a large number of textile and apparel items.
4. Special duties on rubber shoes and Canadian lumber.

An independent government agency, the International Trade Commission (ITC), has the power to impose protectionist measures even without special congressional action. The President must approve each measure recommended by the ITC, and this has substantially limited the scope of ITC action. Both the voluntary restraints in steel and the semiconductor agreement were the results of requests from domestic industries for ITC action. If those agreements were to fail, the ITC could use its power to impose special tariffs on imports.

Macroeconomic Effects of Protectionism

A tariff or quota has the effect of shifting the net exports schedule in the direction of higher net exports given the exchange rate. That shift enters the spending process just as any other shift in a spending schedule or an increase in government purchases. The IS curve shifts to the right. The interest rate and GDP increase along the LM curve, which remains unchanged. All the usual accompaniments to a spending stimulus occur. In particular, the higher interest rate makes the dollar appreciate.

Because protectionism makes the dollar appreciate, the actual effect on prices and trade is smaller than it might appear at first. Although a tariff makes imports more expensive, a stronger dollar offsets this to some extent. In other words, the exporting country pays part of the tariff, rather than the U.S. consumer. Moreover, to the extent that the exporter tends to stabilize its dollar price in the United States, as we discussed in the previous section, it is even more true that the exporter, not the consumer, pays the tariff. At the same time, the macroeconomic stimulus becomes smaller, because if U.S. consumers see no price change, they will not cut their imports. Note that this effect cannot apply to quotas. If a quota forces the quantity of imports to decline, it must cause an increase in the prices paid by U.S. purchasers.

Our analysis assumes foreign countries do not respond to trade restrictions with similar sanctions against U.S. products. Retaliation would

---

[4]Robert Crandall, "The Effects of U.S. Trade Protection for Autos and Steel," *Brookings Papers on Economic Activity,* Vol. 1 (1987), pp. 271–288.

certainly undo whatever short-run benefits protection might bring. In fact, the infamous Smoot-Hawley tariff touched off a trade war in the 1930s that contributed to the Great Depression.

PROTECTIONISM

1. Protectionist policies lessen foreign competition facing domestic producers. They generally help domestic producers and hurt domestic consumers. They include tariffs on imports, quotas on the quantities of imports, and bans on some imports.
2. Protectionist measures stimulate net exports. They shift the IS curve outward, raise the interest rate, and raise GDP.
3. Protectionism raises the exchange rate; this discourages net exports and offsets some of the effects of protection.
4. Protection runs the risk of retaliation by our trading partners. A trade war would certainly undo any temporary benefits protectionism might bring and would reduce the welfare of the nations involved.

12.8   STABILIZING THE EXCHANGE RATE

The wild swings in the exchange rate shown in Figure 12–2 have been of concern to both Americans and foreigners. When the dollar was strong, U.S. producers of tradables suffered, while U.S. purchasers of imports had the advantage of bargains. The collapse of the dollar in the mid-1980s reversed the situation. Many observers have suggested that the world would have been better off with more stable exchange rates, though there is no detailed analysis that has tried to add up the benefits and costs of both consumers and producers. Most discussions consider only the interests of producers and fail to give weight to the benefits that consumers receive when the rest of the world is making bargains available to the United States.

How might U.S. policy be changed to stabilize the exchange rate? Recall that there is a simple relation between the exchange rate and the U.S. interest rate, holding constant economic conditions in the rest of the world. When the rest of the world is quiescent, the United States would have to hold its own interest rate constant in order to keep the exchange rate constant. Figure 12–6A illustrates the necessary policy in terms of the LM curve. A commitment on the part of the Fed to keep the interest rate constant means that the LM curve is perfectly flat. A shock in spending—say unexpectedly strong investment—would shift the IS curve to the right, as

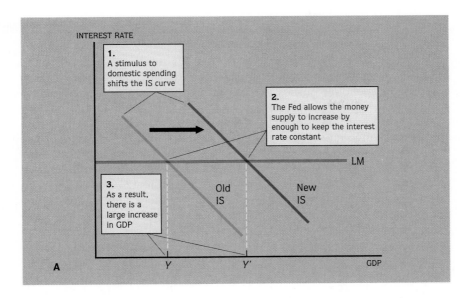

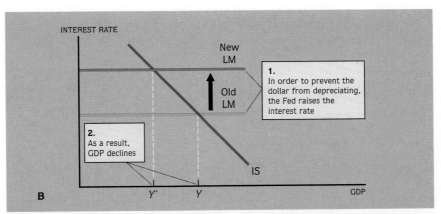

FIGURE 12–6 Effect of a spending shock and a foreign shock under exchange-rate stabilization

(A) When the Fed is operating monetary policy under the principle of keeping the exchange rate stable, it must keep the interest rate constant. That is, the LM curve is a horizontal line. When the IS curve shifts, it causes large changes in output. (B) When a change occurs in the rest of the world, such as a monetary contraction in a major foreign country, the Fed must raise the interest rate to prevent depreciation of the dollar if it has a policy of stabilizing the exchange rate. Such a move contracts output in the United States.

shown in the figure. GDP would rise by the full amount of the spending shift together with the resulting multiplier effects. The normal offset from higher interest rates would not occur. Thus GDP would be highly vulnerable to spending disturbances under a policy that kept the exchange rate constant.

Note that the flat LM curve also indicates that fiscal policy is more powerful when the central bank stabilizes the exchange rate. An increase in government spending pushes the IS curve to the right. With floating exchange rates, we saw that the increase in government spending partially crowds out private investment *and* net exports because interest rates rise and the exchange rate appreciates. With the exchange rate stabilized there is no appreciation of the currency and the interest rate does not rise. Hence, there is no crowding out. Production increases by the full amount of the shift in the IS curve. This is illustrated in Figure 12–6A.

Figure 12–6B shows what would happen if there were a shock in the rest of the world that would normally have made the dollar depreciate (such as an increase in interest rates on other countries). The Fed has to shift the LM curve upward by enough to prevent the depreciation. As a result of the higher interest rate, the level of GDP would fall, as the economy moved up and to the left along the IS curve. When the Fed takes an action like this—deliberately contracting the economy to raise the dollar—it is called "defending the dollar." It sacrifices stability of employment and output in the United States in order to stabilize the exchange rate.

The important point is that making monetary policy responsible for stabilizing the exchange rate prevents monetary policy from achieving other goals, such as stability of employment or prices. We cannot ask the Fed to prevent fluctuations in the purchasing power of the dollar without recognizing that it must sacrifice the stability of other variables, which may be more important.

STABILIZING THE EXCHANGE RATE

1. To stabilize the exchange rate, the Fed would have to set a horizontal LM curve.
2. With a stable exchange rate, a domestic spending shock would have a large effect on GDP. The normal cushioning through interest-rate fluctuations would not occur, because it would cause exchange-rate fluctuations.
3. With a stable exchange rate, the Fed would have to change the U.S. interest rate in response to each foreign shock. It could not insulate GDP and employment from those shocks as it could with a floating rate.

REVIEW AND PRACTICE

Major Points

1. The long-run value of the exchange rate is determined by purchasing power parity. In the short run, expectations and conditions in financial markets create large deviations from purchasing power parity.

2. The interest-rate differential between two countries is equal to the expected rate of depreciation.

3. When the U.S. interest rate is relatively high, the exchange rate must be high also so that interest-rate parity holds in the short run and purchasing power parity holds in the long run.

4. The net export function depends negatively on income and on the real exchange rate.

5. The multiplier is smaller in an open economy than in a closed economy. This makes the IS curve steeper.

6. In an open economy, an increase in the interest rate has a larger first-round effect on spending because it reduces net exports as well as investment. This makes the IS curve flatter.

7. An expansionary monetary policy lowers the interest rate and the exchange rate. Investment and exports are stimulated in the short run. In the long run, money is neutral.

8. An expansionary fiscal policy raises the interest rate and the exchange rate. The policy crowds out investment industries and export industries.

9. Changes in the exchange rate do not have large immediate effects on the price level. The U.S. price of imported products is sticky.

10. Protectionist policies such as tariffs and quotas will reduce the trade deficit and stimulate GDP in the short run. They also tend to make the dollar appreciate, which offsets some of their effects. Protectionism is harmful to consumers because it raises prices of foreign products and is likely to lead to retaliation by foreign governments.

11. If the Fed sets a policy of stabilizing the exchange rate, it must give up other goals, such as employment stability. When the exchange rate is being held constant, domestic spending shocks have large effects on GDP. In addition, the policy makes GDP vulnerable to shocks occurring in foreign countries.

Key Terms and Concepts

purchasing power parity	real exchange rate	tariffs
interest-rate parity	net export function	quotas
interest-rate differential	flexible exchange rate	protectionism
exchange rate	marginal propensity to import	exchange-rate stabilization

Questions for Discussion and Review

1. Explain how you would compare the return on a Japanese bond with the return on a U.S. bond.

2. What happens to the exchange rate between the U.S. dollar and the Italian lira when chronic inflation in Italy is well above inflation in the United States?

3. Why is it rational for investors to expect that the exchange rate will depreciate when it is above normal? Under what circumstances would it not be rational to expect this?

4. Summarize the steps and assumptions that link the exchange rate and the interest rate. What would happen to the relationship if the ROW decided to use a more expansionary policy?

5. Describe what happens to consumption, investment, and net exports when you move down the IS curve.

6. What happens to net exports, investment, and consumption when government spending is decreased? Distinguish the long run from the short run.

7. What happens to net exports, investment, and consumption when the money supply is decreased? Why is monetary policy neutral in the long run, but not in the short run?

8. Describe the changes to the U.S. price of Japanese cars when the yen appreciates, in the short and medium runs.

9. What would happen to the interest rate, GDP, exchange rate, and trade deficit if a uniform 10 percent tariff were placed on all imports? What would happen to these variables if foreign countries retaliated with an equal tariff on U.S. goods?

10. What must the Fed do to keep the exchange rate constant if interest rates in Europe rise because of monetary contraction there?

Problems

Numerical

1. Consider a macro model consisting of the following relationships:

$$Y = C + I + G + X$$
$$C = 220 + .63Y$$
$$I = 400 - 2{,}000R + .1Y$$
$$M = (.1583Y - 1{,}000R)P$$
$$X = 600 - .1Y - 100\ EP/P_{\mathrm{w}}$$
$$EP/P_{\mathrm{w}} = .75 + 5R$$

where government spending G equals 1,200 and the money supply M equals 900. Suppose that the ROW price level P_{w} is always equal to 1.0 and that the U.S. price level is predetermined at 1.0.

a. Which are the endogenous variables and which are the exogenous variables in this relationship?

b. Find the values of Y, R, C, I, X, and E that are predicted by the model.

c. Derive an algebraic expression for the aggregate demand curve in which the money supply M, government spending G, and price level P explicitly appear. For $M = 900$ and $G = 1,200$ draw the aggregate demand curve accurately to scale.

d. Keeping the price level P at 1.0, calculate the effect a decrease in government spending of $10 billion will have on output, the interest rate, consumption, investment, net exports, and the exchange rate. Do the same thing for an increase in the money supply of $20 billion.

2. Using the same numerical example as in Problem 1, calculate private saving, the government budget surplus, and the capital inflow from abroad for the case where $G = 1,200$ and $M = 900$. Show that the sum of these three equals investment. Repeat your calculation for $G = 1,190$ and $M = 920$. Comment on what happens to the three components of saving.

3. For the same numerical example as in Problem 1, calculate a change in the mix of monetary and fiscal policy that will leave output equal to the level it is when $M = 900$ and $G = 1,200$, but in which the interest rate is 3 percent rather than 5 percent. Describe what happens to the value of the dollar, net exports, the government budget deficit, and investment for this change in policy.

4. Now assume that prices adjust according to the price-adjustment equation

$$\pi = 1.2(Y_{-1} - Y^*)/Y^*,$$

where π is the rate of inflation and potential output Y^* is equal to $6,000 billion. Continuing where you left off in Problem 1d, calculate the effect on the endogenous variables in the second, third, and fourth years after the increase in the money supply of $20 billion. Do the same for the decline in government spending of $10 billion. Describe the economy after prices have fully adjusted.

5. Consider a small economy that is much more open than the one in the previous examples. Its net export function is

$$X = 900 - .1Y - 400EP/P_{\mathrm{W}}$$

and the relationship between the interest rate and the exchange rate is

$$EP/P_{\mathrm{W}} = 10R + .5.$$

The other equations are the same.

a. Explain why this economy is more open.

b. Calculate what happens in the first year and in the long run when the money supply increases by $10 billion. Calculate what happens when government spending increases by $10 billion.

Analytical

1. Suppose it was agreed that the United States would spend less on defense and that Japan would spend more.

    a. How would a reduction in defense spending affect the U.S. trade balance?

    b. How would an increase in Japan's defense spending affect the U.S. trade balance?

    c. To the extent that the United States and Japan purchase defense goods from each other, how will this affect your answer?

2. Purchasing power parity (PPP) is a theory of exchange-rate behavior as described in Section 12.2.

    a. Explain why the real exchange rate never changes under the theory of purchasing power parity.

    b. What governs the behavior of nominal exchange rates under PPP? Under what conditions are nominal exchange rates sticky?

    c. Suppose that inflation in the United States is 4 percent while in the rest of the world it is 7 percent. Under PPP, how does E change over time? Does the dollar appreciate or depreciate?

    d. PPP clearly doesn't hold up in the short run; see Figure 12–3, where the real exchange rate is calculated using the GDP deflators for the United States and the ROW. If the real exchange rate were instead calculated using price indexes for manufactured goods, would you expect it to vary by more or less than it does in Figure 12–3?

3. On any given day, interest rates will differ from country to country. For example, U.S. government securities may pay 10 percent interest while comparable Japanese securities are paying 5 percent interest.

    a. Assume Japanese investors have access to U.S. securities. Why would any of them invest in Japanese securities when they could earn a higher interest rate on U.S. securities? Be specific.

    b. Is it likely that any American investors would want to hold the Japanese securities?

    c. Suppose that PPP (see Question 2) holds exactly, that interest rates in the United States and Japan are 10 percent and 5 percent respectively, and that the U.S. inflation rate is 5 percent. If international investors are to be indifferent between holding U.S. and Japanese securities, what must the Japanese inflation rate be?

4. Given the net export function developed in this chapter, explain why the effect of fiscal policy on the trade balance is unambiguous, whereas the effect of monetary policy is ambiguous.

5. The topic box in Section 12.5 summarizes the relationship between trade deficits and budget deficits.

    a. Are *increases* in the trade deficit an inevitable result of *increases* in the budget deficit?

    b. Consider the cases where investment is very sensitive to the interest rate and where it is very insensitive. Compare the effect that an increase in the budget deficit will have on the interest rate, the exchange rate, investment, and the trade deficit for each case.

6. In Chapter 7 we developed a model in which net exports were a function of the interest rate. In this chapter we have described in more detail why net exports depend on the interest rate.

a. What factors determine the sensitivity of net exports to the interest rate?

b. Consider the cases where net exports are very sensitive to the interest rate and where they are very insensitive. Compare the effect that an increase in the money supply will have on output, the interest rate, investment, and the trade balance for each case.

c. Suppose foreign manufacturers maintain a fixed dollar price for their goods regardless of the exchange rate. Will this result in net exports being more or less sensitive to the interest rate?

d. Given this behavior, explain why the only way the monetary authorities could act to reduce the trade deficit is by inducing a recession.

7. Suppose that the economy is at potential, but that the trade deficit is thought to be too large and the dollar is overvalued. Describe a change in monetary and fiscal policy that will keep the economy at potential, but will lower both the dollar and the trade deficit. Explain intuitively how the change in policy will bring about the desired results. Illustrate your answer using an IS-LM diagram.

8. Suppose that the economy is operating at potential but that inflation is thought to be too high. Macro policy will therefore have to turn contractionary, in order to reduce inflation. Describe the pros and cons of using monetary policy or fiscal policy to bring about the contraction, paying attention to the international factors.

MacroSolve Exercises

1. Graph the ratio of net exports to GDP against the exchange rate using quarterly data. Why would it not be valid to conclude from recent experience that a high exchange rate necessarily leads to low net exports?

2. *Policy Decision 1997.* It is early 1997 and you have been hired by the Federal Reserve Board. After the 1996 election, the new administration and Congress are planning to pass a massive government spending package to build more roads, bridges, telecommunications channels, and so on. It is a $1,000 billion program spread evenly over 5 years. You bring your MacroSolve computer program to work. Using the flexible-rate IS-LM model, analyze the effects of these policies.

a. Describe what happens to interest rates, exchange rates, net exports, and output under two Fed policies: a fixed money growth and an increase in money growth.

b. Repeat the analysis for the comparable dynamic models. (Hint: You may find it helpful to use the Change Display option to show the time paths of these variables on the screen.)

c. The Fed is being pressured to keep the dollar and interest rates from rising. What do you recommend?

3. a. Select the closed-economy dynamic model and increase government spending by $50 billion. Calculate for the first 2 years of the policy the increase in the budget deficit, the change in investment, and the change in savings. Is the budget deficit primarily financed by a reduction in investment or an in

crease in saving? Do the same for the final simulation period. Is the financing of the deficit generally the same as in the previous periods?

    b. Repeat for the open-economy dynamic model with a flexible exchange rate. Calculate the changes in the government deficit, investment, saving, and net exports in the first two periods and the last. Explain why the pattern of financing changes in this model. What variables account for this change?

4. Suppose as Fed chairman you want to keep the exchange rate fixed. What must you stabilize in order to keep the exchange rate constant? Select the "ISLM, Open, Flex E" model and increase government spending by $50 billion. Next, increase the money supply by $20 billion. What happens to the exchange rate? How are output, consumption, investment, and net exports affected? What happens to the relative strength of fiscal policy?

APPENDIX: The Interest Rate and the Exchange Rate under Rational Expectations

The purpose of this appendix is to derive the relationship between the real exchange rate and the real interest rate—Equation 12–3 and the example in Equation 12–4. The derivation requires that we consider expectations of exchange-rate movements.

Interest-Rate Parity

The bond markets of the United States and the ROW are closely linked. Investors are constantly comparing the returns they can make from holding their funds in the United States in dollar-denominated form with the returns they can make in the ROW in German marks, Japanese yen, British pounds, etc. A key consideration is the comparison of the returns they can earn in these markets.

    Suppose that an investor is comparing the return for holding a dollar-denominated bond in the United States with the return for holding a mark-denominated bond in Germany. An investor comparing a U.S. bond with a German bond has to do more than compare the interest rates paid on the two bonds. The dollar earnings of the mark bond could be different from the interest rate because the dollar might appreciate or depreciate. Suppose that the German bond pays 10 percent interest and that the exchange rate is 2.0 marks per dollar. Then a United States investor with 100 dollars could obtain 200 marks, buy a mark bond, and get back 220 marks at the end of the year (interest plus principal). But suppose that the dollar depreciated by 2 percent over the year so that the exchange rate is 1.96 marks per dollar at the end of the year. Then the 220 marks could be exchanged back into about 112 dollars (220/1.96 = 112.2). The net return on the German bond, measured in dollars, is 12 percent, more than the stated interest of 10 percent on the bond in Germany. The depreciation of the dollar makes the difference.

    Investors will compare the dollar interest rate with the mark interest rate plus the expected rate of depreciation of the dollar. Suppose the dollar interest rate is 10 percent, the mark interest rate is 5 percent, and the expected rate of depreciation of the dollar is zero. Then the comparison made by investors will strongly favor U.S.

bonds and no investor would want to hold the mark-denominated bonds.

What conditions would make investors willing to hold the mark-denominated bonds? One answer, obviously, would be for the United States interest rate to fall to 5 percent, and another, for the German interest rate to rise to 10 percent. But even if interest rates remain different, the expected appreciation or depreciation of the dollar can bring the expected return on the two bonds into equality. When we observe that the dollar interest rate is 10 percent and the German interest rate is 5 percent, we can reasonably guess that markets are expecting around a 5 percent annual depreciation of the dollar.

Of course the same relationship holds for bonds denominated in any foreign monetary unit. In general, *the interest-rate differential between dollar bonds and bonds denominated in the foreign monetary unit is equal to the expected rate of depreciation of the dollar in terms of the foreign monetary unit.* More formally,

$$R - R_\mathrm{w} = \text{Expected rate of depreciation of the dollar,} \qquad (12\text{--}8)$$

where R is the dollar interest rate and R_w is the interest rate in the rest of the world. For example, if $R = .05$ and $R_\mathrm{w} = .10$, the expected rate of depreciation of the dollar is $-.05$. In other words, the dollar is expected to appreciate by 5 percent. This relationship between the interest-rate differential and the expected depreciation is called **interest-rate parity.** The relationship is shown graphically in Figure 12–7.

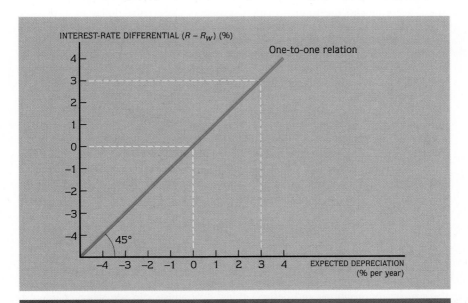

FIGURE 12–7   Expected depreciation and the interest-rate differential

There is a one-to-one relationship between the interest-rate differential and the expected depreciation of the dollar. If dollar bonds are yielding a higher interest rate compared with foreign bonds, investors must be expecting that the dollar will depreciate in the future. As the dollar depreciates, it will reward the holders of foreign bonds by enough to make up for the lower interest rate paid on the bonds.

The expected depreciation of the dollar is shown on the horizontal axis and the interest-rate differential is shown on the vertical axis. The slope of the line is equal to 1. When the interest-rate differential increases by 1 percentage point, the expected depreciation of the dollar increases by 1 percentage point.[5]

Testing Interest-Rate Parity Using Futures Markets

We saw that purchasing power parity does not work in the short run. How well does interest-rate parity work? To test the relationship, we need a measure of investors' *expected* rate of depreciation of the currency. An easy way to find out what people expect about future exchange-rate movements is to look at the **forward** or **futures markets** for foreign exchange. In a futures market for marks, for example, one can buy marks for delivery in the future, say a year from now. Futures markets reveal at what prices investors are willing to buy and sell foreign exchange in the future. The prices on forward or futures markets are found in the financial pages of most newspapers. Prices on forward markets are found along with other exchange-rate quotes. Futures markets for foreign exchange are usually listed with wheat or soybean futures.

Suppose that the exchange rate for marks for delivery one year from now is 2.1 marks per dollar. Suppose that today's exchange rate is 2.0 marks per dollar. Then, according to the futures market, investors expect the dollar to appreciate against the mark by 5 percent. If interest-rate parity holds, then the U.S. interest rate should be 5 percent below the German interest rate. In practice, the percentage difference between the futures exchange rate and the current exchange rate—the measure of expected depreciation—is almost exactly equal to the interest-rate differential for any currency that can be freely traded. Interest-rate parity seems to work fairly well.

This is not a complete test of interest-rate parity, however. By using the futures market, an investor covers the risk associated with changes in the exchange rate. A futures market locks in the yield by guaranteeing the exchange rate in the future. For this reason equality of the percentage difference between the future and current exchange rates, and the interest-rate differential, is called **covered interest-rate parity.** Without using the futures market, the investor takes a chance that the exchange rate will be different from what was expected. The investor is exposed to the risk of a currency change.

An alternative test of (uncovered) interest-rate parity that takes risk into account is based on the rational expectations method of estimating the expected future exchange rate. This approach supposes that investors predict the exchange rate based on how it has behaved in the past. Essentially investors are assumed to have a model of the exchange rate. By guessing what this model is and using it to project the size of appreciations and depreciations, economists can see whether interest-rate parity holds. Such tests indicate that interest-rate parity is a good approxima-

---

[5]If the interest rates in the interest-rate parity condition are *real* rates, then the exchange rate should be the real exchange rate. If the interest rates are nominal, then the exchange rate should be the nominal exchange rate. In this book we generally interpret interest rates as real interest rates, and we do so here.

tion. Takatoshi Ito of the University of Minnesota, for example, has found that uncovered interest-rate parity holds for the dollar-yen exchange rate. Most of the discrepancies can be attributed to restrictions on the purchase and sale of foreign bonds. Other discrepancies have been noted by other researchers.[6]

The Exchange Rate and Its Expected Depreciation

Thus far we have related the interest-rate differential to the expected rate of depreciation of the dollar. Our next step is to discuss how markets form expectations of the rate of depreciation of the dollar. We base our analysis on the idea of rational expectations.

Although not accurate in the short run, purchasing power parity is a reasonable guide for the tendency of the exchange rate in the long run. It appears that the exchange rate has generally fluctuated around purchasing power parity, sometimes above and sometimes below. For example, when the dollar exchange rate rose high above purchasing power parity in the late 1960s, it eventually fell back toward purchasing power parity. When the dollar was very low in the late seventies, it eventually rose again. Similarly, in 1984 when the dollar zoomed above purchasing power parity, it eventually fell again. Historical experience suggests that the movements of the dollar back toward purchasing power parity are larger when the dollar is far away from purchasing power parity than when it is close to parity.

Investors are likely to be aware of these general movements of the dollar. They therefore expect that when the dollar is high, the exchange rate will ultimately depreciate down to its normal level as set by purchasing power parity. Similarly, when the dollar plunges below the level of parity, investors expect the dollar to appreciate over the future, to restore parity in the long run. In general, there is a relationship between the expected rate of depreciation and the level of the exchange rate: *The higher the exchange rate, the larger the expected depreciation of the exchange rate; conversely, the lower the exchange rate, the larger the expected appreciation of the exchange rate.*

If the exchange rate returns to normal at a speed of 10 percent per year, then the relationship says

$$\text{Expected depreciation of the dollar} = .10 \ (\text{Exchange rate} - \text{Parity}), \quad (12\text{–}9)$$

where "parity" stands for the level of purchasing power parity. For example, if the exchange rate is 1.3 and purchasing power parity is 1.0, then expected depreciation is .03, or 3 percent per year. A graphical representation of the relation between the

---

[6]Takatoshi Ito shows how the interest-rate parity between the dollar and the yen became more and more accurate as restrictions on Japanese investments were relaxed. The results are reported by Takatoshi Ito, "The Use of Vector Autoregressions to Test Uncovered Interest Parity," *The Review of Economics and Statistics*, Vol. 50, No. 2 (May 1988), pp. 296–305. Discrepancies have been detected by Lars P. Hansen and Robert Hodrick, "Forward Exchange Rates as Optimal Predictors of Future Spot Prices: An Econometric Analysis," *Journal of Political Economy*, Vol. 88 (October 1980), pp. 829–853.

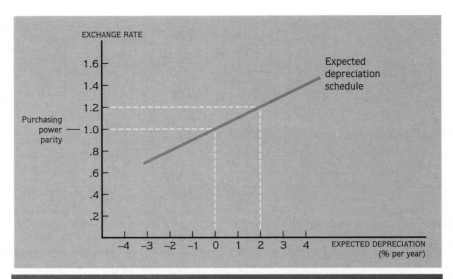

FIGURE 12–8 Expected depreciation and the level of the exchange rate

On the basis of past experience, investors expect the exchange rate to return to the level of purchasing power parity at a fairly slow rate. If the exchange rate is above the parity level, investors expect depreciation. If it is below, investors expect appreciation. There is an upward-sloping relation between the level of the exchange rate and the expected depreciation of the dollar.

expected rate of depreciation and the level of the exchange rate is shown in Figure 12–8.

It is important to distinguish between the rational, expected future behavior of the exchange rate as given by Equation 12–9 or Figure 12–8, on the one hand, and the actual behavior of the exchange rate, on the other. The expected behavior is smooth and slow; the exchange rate moves back to parity at a rate of at most 10 percent per year.[7] The actual behavior is jerky, with possible movements of 10 percent in a single week. The foreign exchange market is like the stock market. It undergoes large, completely unexpected movements in response to surprising economic news. According to the rational expectations view, participants in the market have expectations of small movements in the exchange rate—sometimes up, sometimes down—even though large movements are the rule. The small movements give the best forecast on the average, given the information available to investors. Even the most informed expert cannot guess in advance all the movements that will occur.

Recall that we are deriving a relation between the dollar interest rate and the exchange rate. So far, we have two separate relations, summarized in Equations

---

[7]This is a very rough estimate and is meant to suggest the slow expected movement.

12–8 and 12–9. One is between the interest-rate differential and expected depreciation (Equation 12–8). The other is between the level of the exchange rate and expected depreciation (Equation 12–9). We can combine the two to get a relation between the interest-rate differential and the level of the exchange rate:

$$\underbrace{R - R_{\text{w}}}_{\substack{\text{Equals expected}\\ \text{depreciation}\\ \text{from Equation 12–8}}} = \underbrace{.10 \text{ (Exchange rate − Parity)}}_{\substack{\text{Equals expected}\\ \text{depreciation}\\ \text{from Equation 12–9}}}. \tag{12–10}$$

That is, when the dollar interest rate is high relative to the foreign interest rate, the exchange rate is high relative to parity. But this is not exactly what we are looking for. We want to say something about the dollar interest rate itself, not the interest-rate differential.

The Interest-Rate Differential and the U.S. Interest Rate

Interest rates in the United States are determined by the various ingredients that we discussed in Chapters 4 through 7, including monetary and fiscal policy. Interest rates in the ROW are determined in the same way, again with ROW monetary and fiscal policy. If conditions and policies in the ROW are opposite to those in the United States, the interest-rate differential is large. If they are similar, the differential is small.

The United States is a major force in the world economy. When its conditions and policies change, it exerts a significant influence on interest rates in the ROW. For example, when the United States adopted a policy of monetary contraction starting in late 1979, not only did the dollar interest rate rise, but so did interest rates in most other countries.

In order to create a complete model of foreign interest rates, we would need to build a complete macro model of the ROW. Instead, we will make use of a simple summary of what such a model would tell us about the relation between the interest rates in the United States and in the ROW. United States interest rates influence ROW rates, but by less than point for point. When monetary contraction in the United States raises dollar interest rates by one point, the ROW interest rate rises by a fraction of a point. For example, suppose that the fraction is .5. Then, algebraically our model of foreign interest rates might be

$$R_{\text{w}} = .025 + .5R. \tag{12–11}$$

In this example, when the United States interest rate is 5 percent ($R = .05$), the ROW interest rate is also 5 percent ($R_{\text{w}} = .05$). When the dollar interest rate rises to 10 percent ($R = .10$), the ROW interest rate rises to 7.5 percent ($R_{\text{w}} = .075$). This relationship can be written in terms of the interest-rate differential by subtracting both sides of Equation 12–11 from the interest rate R. That is,

$$R - R_{\text{w}} = .5R - .025. \tag{12–12}$$

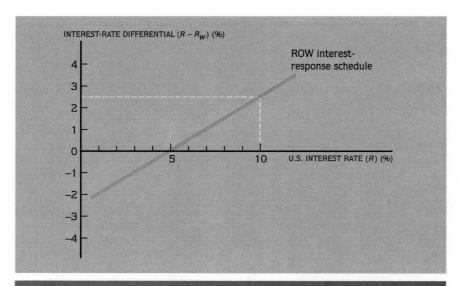

FIGURE 12–9   The relationship between the U.S. interest rate and the interest-rate differential

The interest rate in the ROW will react to the interest rate in the United States. A policy generating higher interest rates in the United States will generally be partly matched in the ROW. As a result, there is an upward-sloping relation between the dollar interest rate and the differential between the U.S. interest rate and the ROW interest rate. On the average, the interest-rate differential rises when the dollar interest rate rises by 1 point.

In words, when the U.S. interest rate is high, the interest-rate differential is high. The relationship between the interest-rate differential and the U.S. interest rate is shown in Figure 12–9.

Now we have everything we need to derive the relation between the U.S. interest rate and the exchange rate. We first proceed using the algebraic examples. The interest-rate differential is related to the U.S. interest rate in Equation 12–12. The interest-rate differential is also related to the exchange rate in Equation 12–10. By substituting the interest-rate differential in Equation 12–12 for the interest-rate differential in Equation 12–10, we get

$$\text{Exchange rate} = \text{Parity} + 5R - .25. \tag{12–13}$$

In this example, if the U.S. interest rate is 5 percent ($R = .05$), then the exchange rate equals purchasing power parity. If purchasing power parity is 1.0, an increase in the U.S. interest rate from 5 to 6 percent will appreciate the dollar from 1 to 1.05, or by 5 percent. Note that if purchasing power parity is 1.0, Equation 12–13 is identical to Equation 12–4 in the main text of this chapter.

Figure 12–10 shows how all the relationships fit together graphically. It puts the three graphs in Figures 12–7, 12–8, and 12–9 together. Starting from an arbitrary interest rate, the interest-rate differential is calculated on the lower left. The expected depreciation must match this differential, as shown on the lower right. The expected depreciation relation tells what the exchange rate must be, as shown on the upper right. The result is one point on the exchange-rate/interest-rate curve, shown on the upper left. This curve appeared earlier in the chapter as Figure 12–5.

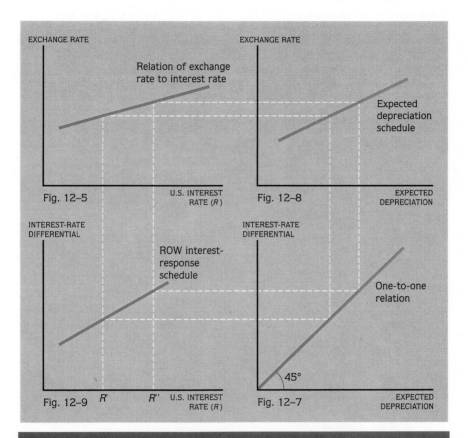

FIGURE 12–10   Derivation of the interest-rate/exchange-rate relation

Pick an interest rate, say R'. From Figure 12–9, reproduced at the lower left, the interest-rate differential can be found. Then from Figure 12–7, reproduced at the lower right, the expected rate of depreciation can be found. From Figure 12–8, reproduced at the upper right, the exchange rate can be found. Now pick a higher interest rate, say R'', and you will get another point on the relation with a higher exchange rate.

You may find the story behind the interest-rate/exchange-rate relationship a little indirect. It says that the dollar appreciates when dollar interest rates rise because higher interest rates fit into the world economy only if the dollar is expected to depreciate, and, in order to be expected to depreciate, the dollar must appreciate first.

What is going on in the economy to bring about these changes in the exchange rate? Suppose that the U.S. interest rate rises, both absolutely and relative to the ROW interest rate. U.S. and ROW investors will now find dollar securities more attractive. They will try to sell their foreign-denominated bonds and buy dollar-denominated bonds. At some point in this process, they will be trying to buy dollars and sell foreign exchange. Consequently, the price of dollars relative to foreign exchange—the exchange rate—must rise to clear the market. Thus the higher interest rate brings about an increase in the exchange rate. As the process proceeds, the higher exchange rate brings expectations of greater depreciation, until investors no longer find dollar bonds more attractive, even though dollar interest rates are still higher.

13

The Government's Budget Deficit and Aggregate Demand

For its fiscal year starting in October 1991, the U.S. government projected a budget deficit of $415 billion, or about 7 percent of GDP. Even by the more favorable standard of the national income accounts measure, the federal deficit in 1991 was huge—$201 billion. The large budget deficit occurred in spite of two major rounds of budget discipline legislation, the Gramm-Rudman-Hollings bill in 1986 and the Budget Accord between the President and Congress in 1990. Two major factors caused the federal government to spend much more than it took in as revenue: the recession starting in 1990 and the savings and loan bailout. The recession had the double effect of cutting revenue and raising spending, especially for income supplement programs.

How does the budget deficit affect the economy? First, government purchases contribute directly to demand. Second, transfer payments such as social security or unemployment compensation augment income. Third, interest paid on the national debt also augments income. Fourth, personal and business income taxes reduce income. In the last three cases demand is indirectly influenced because incomes change. The effect of the budget deficit is best analyzed in terms of these components of the deficit: *purchases* plus *transfers* plus *interest on the national debt* less *taxes*. In this chapter we will examine in detail the effects of these components on the economy.

Traditionally in macroeconomics government purchases have been considered exogenous—not explained in the model. This was so, for example, in the long-run growth model of Part I where government purchases G were taken as an exogenous variable. Empirically speaking, however, the government sector reacts to the state of the economy—partly because of conscious attempts to affect the economy. Transfers and taxes react to the state of the economy even more than purchases do.

One of the most significant recent developments in macroeconomics is the effort to describe the government's reaction to economic fluctuations and to build this behavior into the model. The equation describing government behavior is typically called a **reaction function.** Sometimes it is called a **policy rule** because, as we saw in Chapter 9, government actions are policy in one way or another, and if the behavior is systematic, it is like a rule. For example, generally, taxes decline in recessions.

There are two ways to look at economic policy—from the **normative** perspective and from the **positive** perspective. Normative policy analysis asks what is the best policy and how one policy is better than another. For instance, normative analysis might study what policy can give the lowest rate of unemployment consistent with a prescribed rate of inflation. Positive analysis tries to describe policy actions without inquiring whether or not they are good for the country. In Chapter 9 we took the normative perspective and will do the same in Chapter 18. In this chapter, on the other hand, most of our discussion will be positive and descriptive.

13.1   GOVERNMENT BUDGETS

Because the United States has a federal system of government, we need to distinguish between the different types of government: federal, state, and local. In 1991 federal government purchases were 41 percent of total purchases, and state and local purchases were 59 percent.

The Federal Government Budget and Deficit

The best place to start looking at the budget deficit's effect on the economy is with the federal **budget.** The federal government budget summarizes all three of the types of effects on aggregate demand: purchases, transfers, and taxes. The overall budget totals do not distinguish between purchases and transfers. Rather, purchases of goods and services and transfers are lumped together as government **outlays.** The federal government's budget for 1991 is shown in Table 13–1.

Government outlays consist of purchases and transfers. Purchases involve the use of goods and services by the government, whereas transfers

TABLE 13–1 The 1991 Budget of the United States Government
(billions of dollars during the calendar year)

RECEIPTS	1,119
Individual income taxes	470
Corporate income taxes	102
Social security taxes	468
Other taxes and receipts	79
OUTLAYS	1,320
Purchases	
National defense	323
Other purchases	122
Transfer payment	512
Grants to local governments	152
Interest on the debt	188
Subsidies less enterprise profits	22
DEFICIT	201

Source: *Economic Report of the President,* 1992, Table B–79.

move funds to people outside the government. Less than a third of federal outlays take the form of purchases of goods and services. National defense accounts for about three-quarters of federal purchases. Federal purchases in 1991 were $445 billion, out of which $323 billion went for defense. Clearly, a major direct contribution of the government to aggregate demand is military spending. Purchases for other purposes were about 9 percent of the budget. In 1991 total federal purchases of goods and services were about 7.8 percent of GDP.

Note that a substantial part of the government's expenditures is interest on the debt. As the debt has risen with high deficits in recent years, these interest payments have also risen. In 1991 interest payments on the debt represented about $1,500 for each person in the labor force on average. There is little that the government can do to change interest payments in a given year. The payments depend on past deficits and on the interest rate on past borrowing.

Aside from national defense the major role of the federal government is to take in funds through taxes and pay them out as transfers. Most of the transfer takes the form of taxing families through the personal income tax and the social security tax and then paying out the proceeds as family benefits. The great bulk of these benefits are social security payments for retirement, disability, and medical needs.

The $201 billion deficit at the bottom of Table 13–1 is simply expenditures less tax receipts. After declining from 1986 to 1989, deficits are once again on the rise in the federal budget.

State and Local Government Budgets

One of the major developments in government policy during the Reagan and Bush administrations was to shift responsibility away from the federal government to the local level, especially state governments. If this decentralization process continues, the state and local governments will play an increasingly important role in the economy in the future.

Table 13–2 shows the receipts and outlay figures in 1991 for all state and local governments combined in the United States. Compared with the federal government, a much larger percentage of state and local government outlays are purchases of goods and services that add directly to demand. Transfers are about 25 percent of total outlays. The largest single purchase item for state and local governments is education—about one-third of total purchases. Much as defense dominates federal government purchases, education dominates state and local government purchases.

In marked contrast to the federal government, the state and local government ran a combined budget surplus in 1991. A combined budget surplus at the state and local level has been typical in recent years. This state and local surplus tends to offset the federal government deficit. Many municipal governments have laws that prevent their operating budgets from going into large deficits. In recent years balanced budget laws have been enacted in many states. Of course, some local governments do run serious deficits even though there is a general surplus. In 1975, for example, when the city of New York ran such a large deficit that it essentially went bankrupt, all state and local governments combined ran a surplus of $5.5 billion.

TABLE 13–2 The 1991 Combined Budgets of State and Local Governments (billions of dollars)

RECEIPTS	771
Personal tax	146
Corporate tax	21
Sales and property taxes	392
Payroll tax	59
Grants from federal government	152
OUTLAYS	741
Purchases (goods and services)	642
Transfer payments	187
Net interest paid	-66
Subsidies less enterprise profits	-21
SURPLUS	30

Source: *Economic Report of the President*, 1992, Table B–80.

A large percentage of state and local government receipts—about 51 percent—comes from property taxes and sales taxes. The federal government raises only a negligible part of its revenues from these sources. This means that the economy will have different effects on state and local governments' budgets than it has on the federal government's budget.

13.2   FLUCTUATIONS IN THE DEFICIT: PURCHASES, TRANSFERS, AND TAXES

From the point of view of macroeconomic *fluctuations*, what matters most about the government budget deficit is not its average level, but the way the budget responds to conditions in the economy. How large is this response? How do the fluctuations in the government deficit compare with the fluctuations in the economy as a whole? We will try to answer these questions separately for purchases, transfers, and taxes. We do not consider charges in the fourth component of the deficit, interest on the national debt, because the federal government has no separate control over that component. The amount of debt was determined by past deficits, and the interest rate is determined by monetary and fiscal policy and by non-policy factors.

First, federal purchases of goods and services do not seem to change much as real activity in the private economy fluctuates. This is shown in Figure 13–1. During the post-World War II period, federal spending has fluctuated mostly because of defense spending. Federal spending rose during the Vietnam War, when unemployment was low, and during the defense buildup of the early 1980s. Except possibly for the early 1980s when defense spending increased as the Fed tightened monetary policy and there was a recession, federal spending has not increased during recessions. Federal purchases were flat during the recession starting in 1990.

Every recession brings programs to raise spending and provide added government employment. In fact, however, spending programs have been small and have taken several years to get into gear. Programs launched in the depths of a recession frequently do not generate a significant contribution to aggregate demand until several years later. By then, the economy might be approaching boom conditions. This is another example of the lags in the effect of policy that we mentioned in Chapter 9.

On the other hand, the federal government's transfers usually do fluctuate in the right direction and offset other movements in the economy. Government transfers rise when unemployment rises, as can be seen clearly in Figure 13–2.

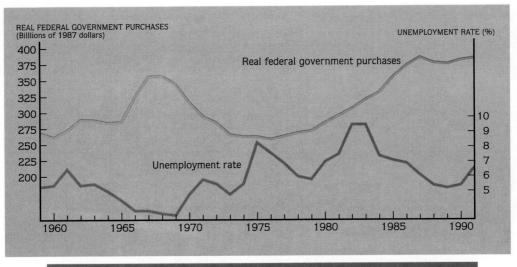

FIGURE 13–1 Real federal government purchases and unemployment

Federal purchases of goods and services have not responded in any systematic way to the state of the economy, as measured by the unemployment rate. There was a big increase in federal spending in the late 1960s and again in the early 1980s. Except possibly for the 1980s, spending has not cranked up the economy during recessions by increasing relative to aggregate demand.
Source: *Economic Report of the President*, 1992, Tables B–2 and B–37.

TABLE 13–3 Automatic Stabilizers: Government Transfer Programs That Respond to the State of the Economy

Program	Description
Unemployment insurance	A combined federal-state program that pays benefits to workers who have lost their jobs.
Food stamps	A federal program that pays benefits to any family with an income below a certain threshold; in recessions, additional families become eligible.
Welfare programs	A combined federal-state program that pays benefits to poor families with dependent children; as incomes fall during recessions, payments increase.
Medicaid	A combined federal-state program that assists poor families with medical benefits; the number drawing these benefits rises during recessions.
Social security	A federal program that supports people in retirement; some people who are eligible for benefits choose to work instead, but their number declines in a recession and the volume of benefits rises.

Government transfers rise in recessions and fall in booms largely through the normal operation of benefit programs. No discretionary intervention on the part of government officials is required. When unemployment rises and incomes fall, a number of government programs automatically increase their income transfers to families. For this reason they sometimes are called **automatic stabilizers.** These programs are listed in Table 13–3.

Taxes also rise and fall with the level of economic activity. The data are summarized in Figure 13–3. In each recession since 1959 federal government tax receipts dropped sharply. This behavior is particularly dramatic in the 1969–70, the 1974–75, and the 1981–82 recessions. On the other hand, the decline in the 1990–91 recession was small. The drop in tax receipts in these periods was larger in percentage terms than the drop in real GDP. The **elasticity** of year-to-year changes in real tax receipts with respect to changes in real GDP was above 1 (an elasticity is the percentage change in one variable induced by a 1 percent change in another variable).

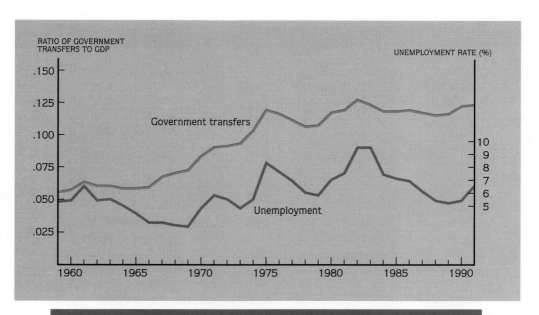

FIGURE 13–2   Government transfers and unemployment

Government transfer payments tend to rise in years of high unemployment and fall in years of low unemployment. This has been especially true in recent years. The synchronization has been achieved mainly through unemployment insurance and other programs that make the rise in transfers during recessions automatic.
Source: *Economic Report of the President*, 1992, Tables B–1, B–37, and B–78.

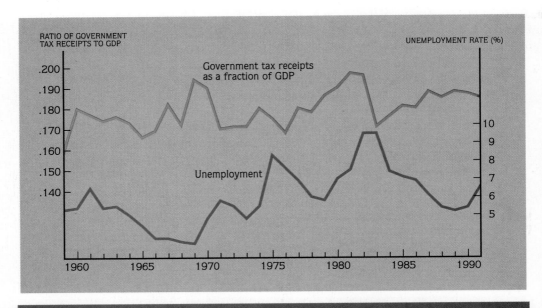

FIGURE 13–3   Government tax receipts and unemployment

As the economy fluctuates in and out of recessions and booms, government tax receipts also fluctuate. Tax receipts tend to fall in years of high unemployment and rise in years of low unemployment. The decline in tax receipts mitigates the drop in demand and helps stabilize the economy.
Source: *Economic Report of the President*, 1991, Tables B–1, B–37, and B–74.

This can be seen directly in Figure 13–3 as a decline in the tax receipt/GDP ratio in each recession.

One reason that tax receipts fall by more than real GDP—why the elasticity is greater than 1—is that the items that are not taxed do not fluctuate much compared with the items that are taxed. Depreciation, which is not taxed, hardly fluctuates at all. Corporate profits, on the other hand, fluctuate widely. Another reason that the elasticity is greater than 1 is that average tax *rates* rise and fall with income. Some of the fluctuations in tax rates occur automatically because of the progressive tax system in the United States. As incomes fall in a recession some people fall into lower tax brackets, or even fall into the region in which no taxes are paid. Hence, the proportion of their income that is paid in taxes goes down as income falls. Conversely, the proportion goes up as income rises. (With the new tax system, there is a small drop in the tax rate for high income earners, but the effect on total tax revenue of this drop is very small.)

Some of the reductions in tax rates in recessions have occurred because the tax law was changed by Congress in order to mitigate the drop in aggregate demand. These are **discretionary changes** rather than automatic changes, but they have been fairly regular and should be included as part of our behavioral description of the reaction of government to the economy. Proposals to cut taxes to stimulate the economy out of a recession in the early 1960s were made by President Kennedy, and most of these changes were enacted into law by Congress. Proposals to cut taxes were made by President Reagan during the depressed economic conditions of the early 1980s. Although the rationale for these tax cuts was not the conventional countercyclical one—some in the Reagan administration argued that the tax cuts would greatly increase supply, others argued that they were necessary to offset the effect that inflation had on tax rates—in retrospect they fit right in to the general story that tax rates are usually cut during periods of high unemployment. Other examples are the temporary tax surcharge of 1968 and the tax rebate of 1975. Discretionary policies are summarized in Table 13–4. Although there were proposals for tax cuts to offset the 1990–91 recession, none were enacted.

In Chapter 6 we wrote tax receipts T as a constant proportion of income Y:

$$T = tY \qquad\qquad (13\text{--}1)$$

TABLE 13–4 Discretionary Stabilization Measures: Ways the Federal Government Can Affect Demand through Fiscal Policy

Measure	Description
Temporary income tax change	A temporary cut in personal income taxes will stimulate consumption and offset a recession; a temporary surcharge will discourage consumption and cool off a boom.
Investment tax credit	A subsidy to investment through the tax system will stimulate investment for the period when the credit is in effect and discourage investment before it takes effect and after it is removed.
Home purchase credit	A subsidy for home purchases by individuals has the same effect as an investment credit, but on residential investment.
Public works	An increase or speedup in highway construction and other government purchases adds directly to demand.

where t is the constant tax rate. The discussion of the previous two paragraphs means that it is incorrect to treat the tax rate t as a constant. The tax rate t actually falls when income Y falls, and rises when income rises.

Much of the overall impact of the government's influence through taxes and transfers eventually shows up in personal disposable income. Recall that in Chapter 10 we looked at the relation between disposable income and GDP and found that the fluctuations in disposable income were much smaller (look back to Figure 10–3 for a review). Disposable income changes by only about 40 percent as much as total income. Consumers see only about 40 percent of the total loss in the economy's income when a recession hits. Automatic stabilizers and discretionary changes in taxes and transfers soak up much of the other 60 percent. (Recall that a bit of the 60 percent is due to the fact that corporations try to maintain their dividend payouts when corporate profits fall during recessions.)

Note that the effect of such countercyclical movements in taxes and transfers is to reduce the multiplier of the IS-LM model. When there is an increase in investment spending, for example, the increase in GDP leads to a smaller increase in disposable income and hence a smaller effect on consumption. The multiplier effect is smaller due to the automatic stabilizers.

THE EFFECTS OF THE GOVERNMENT DEFICIT

13.3

The budget deficit of the federal government is constantly in the limelight. Two Republican presidents were elected in the face of large deficits run up by Republican administrations, even though criticism of deficits is a traditional Republican political tactic.

Why is the government deficit so controversial and mysterious? Part of the reason is that the deficit is just a summary statistic that reflects the behavior of many other variables. It is really just the tip of an iceberg. We emphasized that the budget deficit is simply the difference between government *expenditures* (purchases and transfers) and *receipts*. Moreover, from the government accounting identity discussed in Chapter 2, we know that deficits must be financed by issuing *bonds* or *money* to the public. The overall impact of the budget on the economy can thus be pieced together by looking at the effects of receipts, expenditures, bonds, and money.

In this section we address some of the questions raised about the deficit in the 1980s by examining the cyclical behavior of the deficit, the empirical relation between deficits and interest rates, and the implications of the simple fact that the government must borrow to finance its deficits.

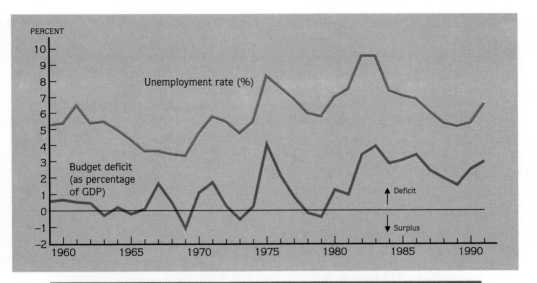

FIGURE 13–4   The cyclical behavior of the deficit

The chart shows the budget deficit, as a percentage of GDP, and the unemployment rate. The latter is a measure of the state of the economic cycle. The deficit is strongly cyclical.
Source: *Economic Report of the President*, 1991, Tables, B–1, B–37, and B–77.

Cyclical versus Structural Deficits

The government budget deficit always goes deep in the red during recessions. We know the reasons for this from the last section: Expenditures rise and receipts fall during recessions. The automatic stabilizers exacerbate the swing of the deficit during a recession.

Figure 13–4 shows the relationship between the deficit and the cyclical fluctuations in unemployment for the years 1959 to 1991. When the economy is below potential, the budget deficit is large. When the economy is above potential, the budget is in surplus, or at least less in the red. Economists have developed the concept of the **full-employment deficit** to adjust for cyclical effects.[1] The full-employment deficit is the deficit that would occur if the economy were at full employment. The full-employment deficit takes out the cyclical effects on the deficit. This is done by estimating reaction functions for expenditures and receipts and calculating what expenditures and receipts would occur at potential GDP and full employment.

[1]The idea of the full-employment deficit was used by E. Cary Brown, "Fiscal Policy in the Thirties: A Reappraisal," *American Economic Review*, Vol. 46 (December 1956), pp. 857–879. He showed that the actual deficits observed in the early 1930s were large surpluses in the full-employment deficit.

In more recent years the concept of the full-employment deficit has usually been discussed by distinguishing between the structural and cyclical parts of the deficit. The **structural deficit** is the same thing as the full-employment deficit, and the **cyclical deficit** is the difference between the actual deficit and the structural deficit.

Have Deficits Been Related to Interest Rates in Recent U.S. History?

The relation between the deficit and interest rates is one of the most important issues with respect to the government's role in aggregate demand. In Chapters 6 and 7 we showed that an increase in the government's budget deficit, brought about by either an increase in expenditures or a cut in taxes, would raise interest rates and expand output by shifting the IS curve to the right. How does that theory fit the facts? Here we look at some of the relevant facts. Figure 13–5 shows the historical relation between a measure

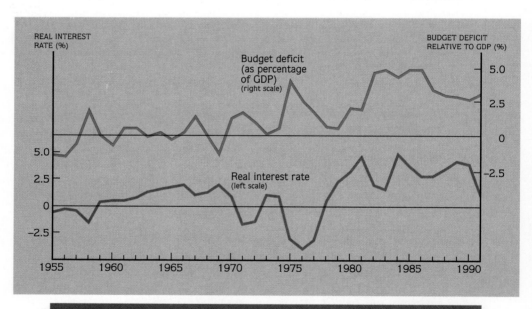

FIGURE 13–5   Budget deficits and real interest rates

During much of the past 35 years interest rates have fallen during periods when the federal government was running a deficit. However, this does not mean that deficits cause lower interest rates. Falling interest rates and deficits are both largely the result of recessions. The 1980s was one of the few periods when high budget deficits and high interest rates occurred at the same time. Note: The real interest rate is the 3-month Treasury bill less the average of the rate of change in the GDP deflator during the previous 3 years.
Source: *Economic Report of the President*, 1991, Tables B–1, B–3, B–69, and B–77.

of the real interest rate and the budget deficit. Two things are important from the chart.

First, over short-run periods and for much of the last 35 years, it appears that the real interest rate falls when the government budget goes into the red. Deficits do not appear to cause high real interest rates. Before you jump to any conclusions, recall the previous discussion that pointed to the cyclical behavior of the deficit. Deficits occur when the economy is in a slump. Now, there are many reasons for interest rates to be low during a slump: the demand for money is low and investment demand is low. It is thus likely that much of the relation between interest rates and the deficit during the last 35 years is due to other factors in the economy.

Second, what evidence there is indicates a positive relation between the budget deficit and interest rates during the 1982–90 period. Real interest rates were higher than normal rates during this period and the budget deficit reached a high-water mark as well. Perhaps the very large deficits— and prospects for future deficits—raised interest rates. This would be the prediction of both the long-run and short-run models we have developed. But real interest rates fell in 1991 and 1992 even though massive deficits continued.

The Deficit and the Explosion of Government Debt

When the government runs a deficit, it must borrow from the public. The top panel of Figure 13–6 shows how budget deficits have led to an explosion of outstanding national debt in recent years, especially since the start of the Reagan administration in 1981. Most of the debt consists of interest-bearing bonds, but part is non-interest-bearing money. As we will see in the next chapter, the Federal Reserve System **monetizes** part of the government debt when it purchases it and issues currency and non-interest-bearing deposits. In the United States the Fed has monetized only a small amount of the debt. It monetizes the debt primarily to provide sufficient money for the economy to work efficiently, rather than to raise revenues.

During World War II the government also ran a large deficit, as is typical of most wars. Government expenditures were, of course, abnormally high in the war years; rather than raise taxes temporarily to pay for the war the government borrowed the money. This shifted some of the burden of the war to future generations who would have to pay the interest on the borrowings. After the war years the federal government ran a surplus in its budget with some exceptions during recessions. The debt fell slightly during the surplus years, but was relatively unchanged compared with the increase during World War II.

Scaling the debt by nominal GDP gives a better perspective of the importance of the debt for the whole economy as shown in the lower panel of Figure 13–6. At the end of World War II the government debt relative to

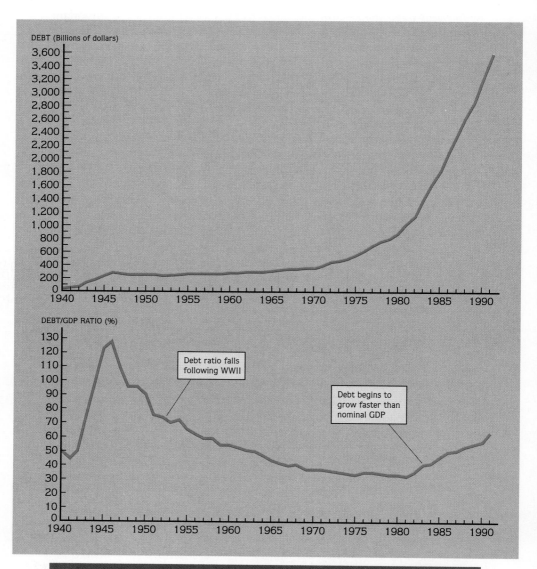

The national debt has had two big periods of rapid growth: during the war years in the 1940s and from 1981 onward. In between, the debt dropped as a ratio of GDP and stayed fairly constant.
Source: *Economic Report of the President,* 1991, Tables B–1 and B–74.

GDP reached an all-time high of a bit over 100 percent. Since World War II the public debt divided by GDP fell steadily until the mid-1970s. Then the stock of outstanding debt began to grow relative to GDP as we had a big deficit in the recession of 1974–75 and even bigger deficits in the 1980s and early 1990s. The ratio of the debt to GDP is still below the levels reached at the end of World War II, but the ratio is growing rapidly, and continued large deficits will raise the public debt to levels about which we know relatively little empirically.

We can express the relation between the deficit and the accumulation of debt formally as

Debt at the start of next year
   = Debt at the start of this year
   + Purchases this year
   + Transfers this year   Deficit
   + Interest on the debt this year
   − Receipts this year.

Using the notation D for debt, G for purchases, F for transfers, T for receipts, and R for the interest rate, we can write this as

$$D_{t+1} = D_t + G_t + F_t + RD_t - T_t. \qquad (13\text{–}2)$$

Each of the terms in Equation 13–2 corresponds with the verbal description of the relation between the deficit and debt accumulation. Note that Equation 13–2 is nothing more than an **intertemporal government budget constraint** faced by government officials. It corresponds exactly to the intertemporal budget constraint for the households in our analysis of forward-looking consumption (Chapter 10). The only difference is that the government is usually a net debtor; hence we call its outstanding financial stock D. The household's asset stock was simply called A; we assumed that the household was usually a net lender.[2]

Problems in Measuring the Federal Budget Deficit

Some economists, such as Robert Eisner of Northwestern University, argue that traditional measurement techniques overstate the magnitude of the budget deficit and thereby sound false alarms that could misguide policy.[3]

---

[2]Note that the government budget is balanced when the stock of government debt is not growing. The stock of government debt is usually stated in nominal terms. A reasonable alternative is to measure the stock in real terms. If there is inflation, then the nominal budget is in deficit when the *real deficit* is balanced. The real deficit is simply the change in the real debt.
[3]For example, Robert Eisner, "Budget Deficits: Rhetoric and Reality," *Journal of Economic Perspectives,* Vol. 3 (Spring 1989), pp. 73–93.

The biggest problem in measuring the deficit is the treatment of all government purchases as consumption. When the government builds a highway, the entire expenditure adds to the deficit the year the highway is built. When businesses reckon their profits or losses, they do not count investment spending as a cost. Only the depreciation of capital is a cost. The same approach would give a clearer picture of where the revenues of the federal government stand in relation to the cost of the services the government provides. Changing to formal capital accounts would have two effects on the deficit. First, current investment spending would be removed from the spending side. The deficit would decline as a result. Second, the depreciation of government capital would be added to the spending capital. The deficit would then rise. The net overall effect of the change would be to lower the deficit in a year when the government's investment exceeded the depreciation of the existing capital.

In 1988 the Office of Management and Budget classified $207 billion of federal government outlays as investment. Removing this much from the spending side of the budget would have more than eliminated the deficit in 1988. However, depreciation on the huge existing stock of roads and other types of federally supported capital or infrastructure was probably in the hundreds of billions of dollars as well. It is not clear which way the shift between generations would come out after careful calculations.

Although the calculations may be straightforward for some types of government spending, others are problematical. If we consider the government's education spending a form of investment, how do we compute the depreciation on the stock of education? Some hawks would argue that the huge military buildup of the 1980s was a prime causal factor in the dramatic shift in world politics at the beginning of the 1990s. Should we call this an investment? There are no good answers to these questions. They illustrate the ambiguity inherent in the concept of the deficit.

Economic Significance of the National Debt

The growth of the U.S. national debt has attracted a lot of attention from economists and other commentators. The debt exists because the federal government sold bonds in order to finance spending in excess of current revenue. Historically, the U.S. debt has grown mainly in wartime. The decline in the debt to GDP ratio through 1974 shown in Figure 13–6 is typical of earlier U.S. experience except during major wars and is also typical of the peacetime experience of other countries. The massive accumulation of debt since 1981 is an unusual event. Similar buildups occurred in a few other advanced industrial countries (Canada and Belgium, for example) during the same period.

In the United States since the early 1980s, there was a political consensus favoring a reduced role for the government in the economy. Deregulation of air travel and trucking was one outcome of that consensus. Aggressive reductions in tax rates in 1981 and 1986 were another. Though politicians of both parties favored spending reductions as part of the overall plan for lowering the burden of government on the private economy, these proved difficult to achieve. The three areas of greatest spending growth in the 1980s were military spending, income maintenance, and interest on the national debt. These areas were exempt in the 1980s from the political consensus favoring smaller government. To a great extent the large amount of debt issued in the 1980s was the result of sustaining spending in these areas after revenue declined early in the decade. In the 1990s, military spending has shrunk, but income maintenance and interest payments have risen even faster.

Interest on the debt is now a major factor in federal spending. In 1991, interest was $195 billion out of total outlays of $1,323 billion. Were it not for the legacy of past spending in excess of revenue, the budget would have been almost in balance in 1991. The federal debt appears to be an important element in the political process for making spending decisions. When there is relatively little debt outstanding, spending on goods and services and income maintenance tends to rise above revenue. Those in Congress have trouble saying no to their constituents' spending demands when the budget is in balance or close to it. A deficit develops and debt builds up. Rising interest on the debt adds to spending growth. As the deficit grows, political opposition to spending rises. The economy reaches a sustainable path where spending growth is held down to the rate of growth of the economy. Debt also grows at the rate of growth of the economy, so the path can be sustained year after year. The economy may have reached this equilibrium in 1990.

Economists are divided on the question of the purely economic significance of the national debt. A good way to think about the issue is to ask how the 1980s and early 1990s would have been different if the government had spent the same amount but had not financed any of the spending by borrowing. There are two differences between what actually happened and the hypothetical zero-deficit case. First, consumers had more disposable income because they paid lower taxes. Borrowing made up for the taxes that would have been levied in the zero-deficit case. Families felt better off and consumed more than they would have in the hypothetical case. Second, taxpayers are worse off because they now have to pay higher future taxes to finance the interest on the debt. Their consumption is lower than in the zero-deficit case because of this factor.

Which effect is larger? Economists have usually emphasized the first effect. The increase in current disposable income is immediate and concrete; the increase in future taxes is distant and theoretical. Deficit spending makes families think they are better off than they really are. They consume too much and the economy has fewer resources for investment. There is a *burden of the national debt.* Debt displaces productive capital in portfolios.[4] But one analysis reaches the conclusion that the two effects offset each other precisely; it asserts that there is no burden of the debt. This analysis—called **Ricardian equivalence**—was put forward in its modern form by Robert Barro, currently at Harvard University.[5]

Ricardian equivalence holds if consumption is independent of the timing of taxation. When the government defers taxation by building up debt, as it did in the 1980s and early 1990s, consumption is just the same as it would have been with the same amount of government spending financed by current taxes. Moreover, it is through consumption that income taxes affect other macro variables. Looking at the IS-LM model of Chapter 7 or the underlying long-run growth model of Chapter 4, we can see that a change in income taxes that has no effect on consumption will have no effect on interest rates, investment, trade, GDP, or inflation. On the other hand, if there is a burden of the debt—if deficit spending encourages consumption—all variables will be affected. Higher consumption will mean a higher real interest rate, less investment, a larger trade deficit, and lower potential GDP in the longer run. Figure 13–5 shows the evidence on the real interest rate. Although there is little overall relation between deficits and real interest rates, the large recent deficits have coincided with very high real rates.

Two assumptions are critical to Ricardian equivalence. First is that families think about the future when they make consumption plans. The forward-looking theory of consumption, based on the idea of rational expectations and rational behavior, supports this assumption. Second is that families look as far into the future as the taxes will be levied. If the government never pays off the debt from the 1980s, but simply continues paying interest on it forever, then strict Ricardian equivalence would require that families look into the indefinite future. One of Barro's important contributions to the theory of Ricardian equivalence was to point out that families may look into the indefinite future even though individual lifetimes are limited. Families may be linked across generations through gifts and bequests. When the government defers taxes to future generations, the current generation may respond by saving more in order to make gifts to future generations. These gifts spread the burden of taxation evenly across generations.

Ricardian equivalence takes the path of government spending as exogenous. If, on the contrary, spending responds to the conditions of the budget, the analysis becomes more complex. Some of the supporters of the 1981 tax cuts saw lower revenue as a way to force down government spending. They considered most government spending as wasteful. To

[4]See Peter Diamond, "National Debt in a Neoclassical Growth Model," *American Economic Review,* Vol. 32 (June 1965), pp. 161–168.
[5]See Robert Barro, "Are Government Bonds Net Wealth?" *Journal of Political Economy,* Vol. 82 (November–December 1974), pp. 1095–1117.

them, the buildup of debt in the 1980s was just part of the process of scaling back government. On the other hand, lower revenue may cut into government investment. Then the burden of the debt includes the displacement of public as well as private capital.

Although the business press accepts the burden of the debt as absolute economic truth, with the support of many prominent economists (such as Martin Feldstein of Harvard University), the burden has been hard to quantify. The bulge of consumption during the 1980s may have been a response to artificially high disposable income, or it may have been the result of great consumer optimism. High real interest rates in the 1980s may have been the result of huge amounts of federal borrowing, or they may just have reflected the combined effect of optimistic consumers, strong government purchases of goods and services, and favorable investment opportunities in the United States in comparison with the rest of the world. There is no strong consensus among macroeconomists that the federal debt has either a large or a small burden.

13.4 THE GOVERNMENT AND THE IS CURVE

Fiscal policy can shift the IS curve in two ways. First, government purchases of goods and services G enters spending directly. In Chapters 6 and 7 we looked at how changes in G shift the IS curve through the multiplier process. We noted in this chapter that over the last 35 years the federal government rarely offset the fluctuations in aggregate demand by altering its purchases of goods and services. Historically, government purchases do not appear to be an effective instrument to control aggregate demand but rather another shock or disturbance to aggregate demand. Recent experience with large deficits does not indicate that this situation is likely to change soon.

Second, policies on taxes and transfers can influence consumption. A tax cut increases income and stimulates consumption and so shifts the IS curve to the right. However, the magnitude of this shift is highly uncertain because of people's uncertainty about how permanent the tax cut will be. Moreover, there is a possibility that some people may increase their saving because they figure that taxes will rise in the future in order to pay the interest on the increased government debt.

Fiscal policy also influences the *slope* of the IS curve. We noted in this chapter that the automatic stabilizers operating through taxes and transfers reduce the multiplier. Because of the automatic stabilizers an increase in interest rates along the IS curve brings about a smaller decline in consumption and GDP. Therefore the IS curve is steeper as a result of the automatic stabilizers.

REVIEW AND PRACTICE

Major Points

1. Government purchases, transfers, and receipts are not exogenous. They respond to the state of the economy.

2. Expenditures rise and receipts fall in recessions. Real tax receipts fall by a greater percentage than real GDP during recessions. This is mainly because of the progressive tax system.

3. The deficit fluctuates countercyclically with GDP.

4. The structural or full-employment deficit has had these cyclical effects removed.

5. The government budget constraint relates the deficit to the public debt.

6. The debt has declined relative to GDP for most of the period since World War II. It has increased since the early 1980s, however.

7. Higher government purchases of goods and services shift the IS curve to the right, though the federal government has not used this policy instrument to try to stabilize the economy in the past few decades.

8. Taxes influence both the position and the slope of the IS curve. A tax cut shifts the IS curve to the right, though the magnitude of the shift is uncertain. Automatic stabilizers make the IS curve steeper.

Key Terms and Concepts

outlays	full-employment deficit	government budget constraint
purchases	elasticity of tax revenues	government debt
policy rule	progressive taxes	defense expenditures
reaction function	automatic stabilizers	Ricardian equivalence

Questions for Discussion and Review

1. Explain the difference between government purchases and government transfers. Which is larger for the federal government? For state and local governments? Which fluctuates more with the business cycle? In which direction?

2. What are the major automatic stabilizers? What is their significance for economic fluctuations?

3. Why is the budget typically in deficit during periods when the unemployment rate is high? What is the full-employment budget deficit? Does the full-employment deficit fluctuate with the state of the economy?

4. Explain why a progressive tax structure leads to an increase in the tax revenue/GDP ratio when the economy is growing rapidly in a boom.

5. Why has the deficit usually been large when interest rates have been low? Does this mean that the deficit does not cause interest rates to rise as predicted by the IS-LM model?

6. Describe the behavior of the government debt since World War II. Why did the debt decline as a fraction of GDP until 1981?

Problems

Numerical

1. Use the following example of a progressive tax schedule to compute what happens to average tax rates in the economy during a typical recession.

Income Bracket	Marginal Tax Rate
0–9,999	0
10,000–29,999	.2
30,000–49,999	.4
50,000 and above	.6

To make it easy, suppose that there are just three income groups of taxpayers. Just before the recession there are 200,000 taxpayers making $20,000, 700,000 making $40,000, and 100,000 making $60,000.

a. Compute the average tax rate for the whole economy before and just after the recession if everybody's income drops by $10,000 during the recession. Has anyone moved to a different tax bracket?

b. What happens to the average tax rate if everybody's income is reduced by $20,000?

c. Suppose that the government introduces a "flat tax" whereby everyone making equal to or more than $10,000 pays the same proportional tax of 25 percent. For this new tax system recalculate your answers to Parts a and b.

d. Comment on the effect on stabilization policy of a move from a progressive tax rate system to a flat tax rate system.

2. Suppose that federal tax receipts, transfers, and purchases are given by T = .25YP, F = .15YP, and G = 400, all in billions of current dollars. Suppose that at the start of 1984 the federal debt D was $800 billion, the interest rate R was 9.5 percent, real GDP was $3,500 billion, and the price level P was 1.08.

a. Calculate the actual and full-employment budget deficit for 1984 in current dollars assuming that real potential output is $3,700 billion. Include interest payments in your calculation of the deficit using Equation 13–2.

b. Two forecasts made in early 1985 (the Reagan administration's and an average of three private forecasters: DRI, Chase Econometrics, and Wharton) for real GDP growth, the rate of inflation $(P - P_{-1})/P_{-1}$, and the interest rate for 1985 through 1988 are given below:

	Real GDP Growth		Inflation		Interest Rate	
	Admin.	*Priv.*	*Admin.*	*Priv.*	*Admin.*	*Priv.*
1985	3.9	3.6	3.8	3.6	8.1	8.2
1986	4.0	2.8	4.4	3.9	7.9	8.9
1987	4.0	3.4	4.2	4.4	7.2	9.4
1988	4.0	3.6	3.9	4.8	5.9	8.4

Assuming that G increases at 5 percent per year, calculate the deficit for 1985 through 1988 for the two sets of forecasts. Start with the 1984 figures in Part a. Be sure to use Equation 13–2 to calculate the change in federal debt.

3. Assume that government outlays and taxes are initially zero, as is the stock of government debt. In Year 1 the government begins to spend $50 billion per year, in real terms, on environmental protection. Each year the government issues enough debt to finance this program, as well as to repay the interest on the previous stock of debt. The stock of government debt and the deficit, measured in current dollars, obey the equations

$$D_t = (D_{t-1} + G_{t-1})(1 + R)$$
$$DEF_{t-1} = D_t - D_{t-1}$$

where G is measured in current dollars. The initial price level is 1.

a. For an interest rate of 5 percent and an inflation rate of zero, calculate the real and nominal values of government debt and the deficit for each of the first 5 years.

b. Now suppose prices rise at an annual rate of 5 percent. Assuming that the interest rate remains at 5 percent, repeat your calculations for Part a.

c. Finally, assume an inflation rate of 5 percent and an interest rate of 10.25 percent. Again, repeat your calculations for Part a.

d. Compare the paths of real debt under Parts a, b, and c. Explain any differences.

e. Comparing Parts a and c, you should find that the real debt stock is the same for Part c, but that the real deficit each year is higher. Why doesn't a higher deficit lead to a higher stock of debt?

f. In which case was inflation anticipated by financial markets? Explain your answer.

4. Suppose that instead of G being exogenous, it is given by the formula

$$G = 1{,}200 - .1(Y - Y^*),$$

where Y^* is potential GDP and is equal to $6,000 billion. Suppose that the other relationships in the economy are given by the example considered in Chapter 7:

$$C = 220 + .63Y$$
$$I = 1{,}000 - 2{,}000R$$
$$M = (.1583Y - 1{,}000R)P$$
$$X = 525 - .1Y - 500R$$

where the price level is predetermined at $P = 1$ and the money supply is 900.

a. Derive an algebraic expression for the IS curve for this model. Plot it to scale. Compare it with the IS curve of Chapter 7 in which government purchases are exogenous. Which is steeper? Why?

b. Derive the aggregate demand curve and plot it to scale. How does it compare with the aggregate demand curve when government spending is exogenous?

c. Calculate the effect on GDP of an increase in the money supply of $10 billion. Is the effect larger or smaller than the case where government spending is exogenous? Explain in words what is going on.

d. Is this equation an accurate description of government purchases in the United States? If not, what other components of the government budget act as automatic stabilizers? How is the impact of aggregate demand and price shocks affected by such stabilizers?

5. (Simple proof of the Ricardian equivalence.) Consider the intertemporal budget constraint for families that we introduced in Chapter 10 and the intertemporal budget constraint for the government that we introduced in this chapter. Suppose that taxes are cut by $1,000 in Year 1 and the government debt increases.

a. If the interest rate is 5 percent, by how much will taxes have to increase next year if the government debt is to come back to normal by the end of next year?

b. What is the effect of this decrease and subsequent increase in taxes on the intertemporal budget constraint for consumers? How would you expect this change to affect consumption?

Analytical

1. The President is required by law to submit each year projections of budget deficits for the next 5 years. In discussing this law about budget projections, President Reagan said in 1985, "Frankly, I pay no attention to [the budget projections]. . . . There isn't any economist in the world who can do that and accurately tell you what you're going to need down the road." He then proposed that the law be abolished (*New York Times,* January 12, 1985).

a. Obtain a copy of a recent Economic Report of the President and evaluate whose forecasts in Numerical Problem 2 have proven more accurate: those of the Reagan administration or those of the private forecasters.

b. In light of the relation between economy and the budget (again, see Numerical Problem 2), comment on the proposal made by Reagan.

2. Suppose our model of the economy is the simple spending balance model of Chapter 6. The equations of the model are

$$Y = C + I + G + X$$
$$C = 100 + .9Y_d$$
$$Y_d = Y + F$$

where $I = 750$, $X = 0$, and F stands for government transfer payments.

a. You are told that government outlays equal 500, and there are no taxes. With this information can you calculate the point of spending balance?

b. What is the maximum value of income for which there could be spending balance? What is the minimum value?

c. Explain why government transfers and spending affect aggregate demand differently. Be specific.

3. Explain why imports act as automatic stabilizers. Compare the case in which imports consist mainly of necessities with the case in which they consist mainly of luxury goods.

4. Suppose it is 1997, and the newly elected President, in order to win, promised (i) not to raise taxes, (ii) not to tamper with social security and other transfer programs, and (iii) not to cut defense. At 6 percent unemployment, output is very close to potential. There still, however, are the two nagging problems of the government budget deficit and the trade deficit.

   a. In the short run, how can the administration reduce the budget deficit without breaking any of its campaign promises? Be specific about the policy. What effect will the policy have on output and interest rates? How will this policy reduce the budget deficit? Describe the effect of this policy on the trade deficit. Is it unambiguous?

   b. Will this policy reduce the budget deficit in the long run? Again, be specific. What are its long-run effects on the trade deficit?

   c. What will the effects of such a policy be, in the short run and in the long run, on the real value of government debt outstanding?

   d. Recall the relationship between nominal interest rates and expected inflation discussed in Chapter 7. How might the expectations of such a policy affect long-term nominal interest rates in the 1980s?

   e. By comparing nominal interest rates with the actual rate of inflation, it has been suggested that real interest rates in the mid-1980s were at nearly an all-time high. How would the preceding analysis affect such a judgment?

5. Suppose that government spending is increased when the economy is below potential GDP. Why doesn't the decrease in government saving lead to an equal decline in total saving and investment?

6. Sketch an IS-LM diagram. Compare two cases, one in which government spending is exogenous, and the other in which government spending declines when the economy rises above potential GDP and increases when the economy is below potential GDP. Which curve is steeper? For which curve is monetary policy more powerful?

7. Suppose that the President and the Congress agreed to raise personal income taxes by $100 billion per year starting in 1994 in an attempt to reduce the budget deficit by 1996. However, the legislation actually increased taxes only until 1996; starting in 1997, taxes would automatically be lowered back down by $100 billion. What would be the effect of this tax increase on *consumption demand*? Use the forward-looking theory of consumption to explain what the impact of the tax increase would be.

8. Consider once again the simple spending balance model of Chapter 6. Suppose now that the model is

$$Y = C + I + G + X$$
$$C = 100 + .9Y_d$$
$$Y_d = Y + F - T$$

where $I = 750$, $X = 0$, and G, T, and F are initially zero.

   a. Calculate the initial point of spending balance.

   b. Suppose that the country goes to war for a year—requiring government expenditures of 100—and that taxes are temporarily raised to 100 in that same year. Calculate consumption and the point of spending balance in the war year and all future years.

c. Now suppose that the government issues war bonds instead of raising taxes. The war bonds are 5 percent consoles. Consoles are bonds on which interest is paid forever and the principal is never repaid. Again, calculate consumption and the point of spending balance in the war year and in all future years.

d. What is the net effect of the government running a deficit in the war year instead of raising taxes? Is your result consistent with the idea of Ricardian equivalence? If not, how can you explain the difference?

9. In deriving the aggregate demand curve, we have implicitly assumed that the government announces a budget in real terms. In practice, the budget is announced in nominal terms for the coming fiscal year before the price level is known with certainty. This practice of not indexing public expenditure plans to the price level has implications for the shape of the aggregate demand schedule. Relative to an aggregate demand schedule with constant real government expenditures, will a schedule with constant nominal government expenditures be flatter or steeper? Is the policy rule of "nominal budgeting" stabilizing or destabilizing with respect to GDP in the presence of unanticipated price shocks?

10. In an attempt to stimulate the economy, the government announces that it will drastically reduce taxes for one year with no change in government spending. Describe the effect of the temporary tax cut on output, consumption, investment, and net exports for each of the following assumptions about household consumption behavior:

a. Households obey the simple Keynesian consumption function.

b. Households are forward-looking but do not anticipate future tax increases to offset the current reduction.

c. Households are forward-looking and anticipate future tax increases to offset the current reduction.

MacroSolve Exercises

1. Plot the government deficit as a percentage of GDP against time using annual data. Graph the real interest rate against the government deficit since 1970. On the basis of this, could you agree with the current public sentiment that high deficits cause high interest rates? Why might the statement not make sense in any case? (Hint: Consider what is exogenous and what is endogenous in macroeconomic models.)

2. Plot the quarterly values of the ratios of net exports and the government deficit to GDP for the period 1981.1 to 1983.4. Do you see a positive or negative relationship between the two? (You may also want to graph one series against the other for the same period to help you answer the question.) Does your finding suggest that high government deficits cause high trade deficits? Repeat the analysis for the period 1967.1 to 1980.4. Why do your findings change in this period?

3. Select the "ISLM, Closed Econ" model.

a. Increase government spending by $50 billion. What happens to the interest rate and the government deficit?

b. Reset the change in government spending to zero. Decrease the money supply by $20 billion. What happens to the interest rate and to the government deficit?

c. Do your answers to Parts a and b imply that "deficits cause high interest rates"? Explain your answer.

4. Select the "AD/PA, Closed Econ" model. Increase government expenditure by $100 billion.

a. Explain why the government deficit increases by less than $100 billion increase in the second period.

b. Explain why the government deficit tends toward a $100 billion increase in subsequent periods (becoming exactly $100 billion at the end of the simulation period). How is this consistent with your answer to Part a?

c. Compute the change in investment and saving to show "how the deficit is financed" in the second and last periods. Explain why the pattern of financing changes between the periods.

5. *Policy Decisions 1997.* The Congressional Budget Office has hired you to help give economic advice to the new Congress. A bill to slash defense spending, which would lower government spending by $100 billion in 1997, is pending. Analyze the macroeconomic impact of the legislation.

CHAPTER

14

The Monetary System

A monetary system is an arrangement through which people express economic values and carry out transactions with each other. A well-developed monetary system is essential to a smoothly operating economy. History has shown that poorly developed monetary systems have been responsible for severe recessions and inflations. But even normal, everyday economic life is greatly facilitated by an efficient monetary system.

The monetary system is just one of many social arrangements that exist in any civilization. Language is another. Weights and measures are a third. Some of these arrangements have evolved without formal or conscious social agreements; others have been the result of organized planning and formal agreement. Although monetary systems originally evolved informally in primitive cultures, in modern times most countries have enacted laws and institutions that define their monetary systems. One of the concerns of macroeconomics is whether certain revisions to these laws and institutions might improve macroeconomic performance.

The monetary system takes on a central role in aggregate demand because prices and wages do not move quickly enough to offset shifts in money supply or money demand. As we saw in Chapter 7, shifts in the LM curve—the curve for which money supply equals money demand—first result in changes in GDP, and later in changes in inflation. In this chapter we look at the microeconomic foundations of *money supply* and *money demand.* In doing so, we will see that the monetary system is an intrinsically interesting part of the economy and a subject worthy of study even without its role in macroeconomics.

14.1   THE ELEMENTS OF A MONETARY SYSTEM

A monetary system must specify two things: first, the way that payments are to be made; second, the meaning of the numbers that merchants put on goods and the numbers that appear in contracts. The first is called the **means of payment,** and the second the **unit of account.**

In most monetary systems one item is designated as a universally acceptable means of payment. Traditionally, it was a precious metal, gold or silver. With gold or silver serving as the means of payment, it was natural for merchants to price their goods with numbers that corresponded to units of these precious metals; horse traders would find it natural to charge a certain number of gold pieces for a horse. Hence, designated amounts of precious metals became units of account as well as a means of payment. For example, in England at the time of William the Conqueror, silver was the universally accepted means of payment and the pound of silver became the unit of account. Ever since, the English unit of account has been called the pound, though its purchasing power has become much less than the value of a pound of silver.

As financial systems developed, means of payment came into use that were different from the underlying unit of account. For example, in the United States before the Civil War, the unit of account was .04838 of an ounce of gold, but the most common means of payment was paper money issued by private banks. A dollar bill from a bank carried a promise that it could be redeemed for gold at any time.

In the twentieth century, governments became more involved in the monetary system. In the United States, banks are not allowed to issue dollar bills; only the Federal Reserve has that power. Moreover, the unit of account no longer has anything to do with gold. Instead, it is the government's dollar bill. Though dollar bills are widely used as means of payment, other means of payment are even more important, such as checks and credit cards.

Although there is no law in the United States that requires prices to be quoted in dollars, nobody would choose to quote prices in another unit, such as French francs. The public is familiar with dollar prices and reluctant to think in any other terms. Even if you are good at doing arithmetic in your head, it is a lot more convenient to do all your financial thinking in one set of units.

Together, the government's paper money and coins are called **currency.** Until the nineteenth century, currency was virtually the only means of payment. As monetary systems evolved during the nineteenth and twentieth centuries, currency began to be replaced by other means of payment in the great majority of transactions. Nevertheless, all transactions continue to be denominated in the units of the government's currency. By law, if you owe somebody a dollar debt, that person can require you to pay in currency. For larger debts, this right is rarely exercised. Instead, the person's right to receive currency sets up a situation where the two of you agree on some alternative, more convenient way to settle the debt. The other person may agree to accept a personal check from you. A check is an instruction to the banking system to make accounting entries to transfer wealth from you to the other person.

A great many customs exist about what means of payment are acceptable besides currency. In prisoner-of-war camps during the Second World War, prisoners used cigarettes as a means of payment. In modern times, credit cards are frequently an acceptable means of payment. Stores that accept credit cards let you know with a little sign in the window. Credit cards are another way to issue instructions to the banking system to transfer funds from one person to another. Like accepting checks, the acceptance of a credit card in place of currency is voluntary. When you buy a house, neither a personal check nor a credit card is likely to be accepted. You will be expected to present a bank check, which is a promise by the bank itself to pay from its own funds and a guarantee that the funds actually exist. Customs differ by country as well. In Greece today, for example, currency rather than a personal check is a much more common means of payment than it is in the United States.

Monetary economists have attempted to pin down exactly what things should be counted as the means of payment.[1] Unfortunately, this is a very difficult task. Many techniques are available for conveying purchasing power. Currency and checking accounts certainly should be counted as a means of payment. But what about the funds in savings accounts that can be electronically transferred in an instant to checking whenever a payment is desired? Some means of payment, like credit cards, do not involve an asset at all. Despite these problems, the fact that there are means of payment other than currency is crucially important for monetary economics.

As discussed in Chapter 5, we use the term **money** to mean currency plus the deposits in checking accounts. Checking accounts are usually held at banks, but sometimes at other financial institutions, such as savings and

---

[1]The research discussed in D. Patinkin, *Money, Interest, and Prices,* covers much of the work on the various definitions of money.

loan associations. Some checking accounts pay interest, but usually at rates below market interest rates. The Federal Reserve monitors the sum of currency and checking accounts in the United States, which they call M_1. In 1990, M_1 was $825 billion, of which $246 billion, or 30 percent, was currency. M_1 is one of three major monetary aggregates that are tabulated and regularly published by the Fed; the other two are M_2 and M_3. The items included in M_1 most certainly can serve as a means of payment in transactions. But as we mentioned above, there are many other means of payment. Other types of deposits, such as savings deposits or small-time deposits against which checks cannot be directly written, are not included in the M_1 definition of money; these are included in M_2 (M_2 includes everything that is in M_1 as well). Money market mutual funds and money market deposit accounts at banks that can be used for checking are also included in M_2. In 1990 M_2 was $3,328 billion. Items that are even less likely to be used for transactions purposes—such as time deposits over $100,000—are included in M_3, which was $4,111 billion in 1990 ($M_3$ includes everything in M_2 as well).

The difficulty in determining exactly what should be counted as the means of payment indicates the difficulty in deciding which of the definitions of money one should look at. Currency and checking deposits are not quantitatively the most important part of transactions. Far more dollars' worth of transactions are made by credit card than with currency. Nevertheless, M_1 and M_2 are significant primarily because currency and deposits are closely related to the operations of the Federal Reserve. But because there are other means of payment besides currency and deposits, a careful examination of changes in the monetary system is a necessary part of interpreting the behavior of M_1 and M_2.

THE MONETARY SYSTEM

1. A monetary system includes a unit of account and various means of payment. Usually, one of the means of payment (the dollar bill in the United States) defines the unit of account.
2. Various means of payment make up the money stock. The stock includes the means that are close substitutes for currency. These are primarily balances in checking accounts.

14.2 MONEY SUPPLY: HOW THE FED CONTROLS IT

We now consider how the Fed controls the money supply. The money supply consists of currency (CU) and checking deposits (D) that individuals and firms hold at banks. We will not distinguish at this point between M_1 and M_2 by distinguishing between different types of deposits. Rather we let the symbol D represent all deposits at banks (or private financial institutions more generally) and let M be the resulting money supply. The money supply M is thus defined as

$$M = CU + D. \qquad (14\text{--}1)$$

Because deposits at banks are part of the money supply, we must consider how the Fed's actions affect these deposits. Table 14–1 shows a set of balance sheets for four sectors of the economy: the private nonfinancial sector (consumers and businesses), the banks, the Federal Reserve, and the government. This balance sheet shows how the sectors are related financially.

In the balance sheet assets are shown on the left and liabilities on the right. Assets are the things owned by the individual or organization, and liabilities are the amounts owed to others. For example, loans are assets for banks and liabilities for borrowers. Note that all the things listed in these accounts appear at least twice; once in somebody's assets and again in somebody else's liabilities.

TABLE 14–1 Financial Relationships (Balance Sheets) between the Banks, the Fed, the Government, and the Private Sector

| Private Nonfinancial | | Banks | | Fed | | Government | |
Assets	Liabilities	Assets	Liabilities	Assets	Liabilities	Assets	Liabilities
Currency (CU)					Currency (CU)		
Deposits (D)			Deposits (D)				
Bonds (B)		Bonds (B)		Bonds (B)			Bonds (B)
		Reserves (RE)			Reserves (RE)		
	Loans	Loans					

The "banks" column of the balance sheet includes all depository institutions that accept checking deposits and that hold reserves at the Fed. Thus "banks" include not only commercial banks, but also those savings and loan associations and mutual savings banks that provide checking services to their customers. The "Fed" column of the balance sheet includes the assets and liabilities of all 12 district banks of the Federal Reserve System.[2]

Note where the major assets and liabilities appear on the balance sheets of each sector:

CURRENCY (CU) AND DEPOSITS (D). The private sector holds currency that is issued by the Fed.[3] As we discuss below, it is the Fed's job to supply the currency that the private sector demands even though the government prints and mints currency at the Treasury Department. The private sector also holds deposits at the banks. These are assets of the account-holders and liabilities of the banks.

GOVERNMENT BONDS (B). Government bonds are shown as a liability of the government. The private sector, the banks, and the Fed hold bonds as assets.

RESERVES (RE). These are what the banks hold on deposit at the Fed. The Fed acts as a banker's bank by accepting deposits from banks. These reserves must be held by law at a fixed fraction of the private nonfinancial sector deposits that the banks have as liabilities.

LOANS (L). The last line in the balance sheet shows the loans of the banks to the private sector. One of the main reasons that banks are in business is to issue loans to their customers. They take deposits from some individuals and make loans to others. This is the **intermediation role** of the banks. They intermediate between individuals. But banks are important in macroeconomics because their liabilities (deposits) are part of the money supply.

The Fed controls the money supply by selling bonds to, or by purchasing bonds from, the banks and the public. These purchases or sales of government bonds by the Fed are called **open-market operations.** To see how these open-market operations affect the money supply, we first define

---

[2]The 12 District Federal Reserve Banks are in Atlanta, Boston, Chicago, Cleveland, Dallas, Kansas City, Minneapolis, New York, Philadelphia, Richmond, St. Louis, and San Francisco. The San Francisco Fed has the largest amount of reserve assets. Open-market operations take place at the New York Fed.

[3]Part of the reserves held by the banks is in the form of paper money in the vaults of the bank. The term "currency" in the text always means paper money and coin *outside* banks. Vault cash is essentially equivalent to bank reserves held on deposit at the Fed.

the **monetary base** (M_B). The monetary base is defined as currency plus reserves.[4] That is,

$$M_B = CU + RE. \qquad (14\text{–}2)$$

The Fed does not try to exercise separate control of reserves and currency. Instead the Fed controls only the total of the two. The Fed lets the banks and the private sector decide how much of the monetary base is currency and how much is reserves. Any bank can withdraw currency from its reserve account whenever it wants, and any bank can put currency into its reserve account and receive credit dollar for dollar. For example, when legalized gambling started in Atlantic City, the banks in the Philadelphia Federal Reserve District found that their customers were using a lot more cash. The banks therefore withdrew currency from their reserve accounts and made it available to their customers.

Using open-market operations the Fed can add to or subtract from the total amount of bank reserves plus currency whenever it chooses. An open-market operation to expand the monetary base involves a purchase by the Fed of government bonds from the banks. Look again at the balance sheet in Table 14–1. When a bank sells a bond to the Fed, the bank receives a credit in its reserve account that adds to the total amount of reserves. The simple fact that assets must equal liabilities in the Fed's balance sheet indicates that any purchase of bonds must lead to an increase in the sum of currency and reserves, that is, an increase in the monetary base. Whenever a bank transfers funds to another bank, nothing happens to total reserves; one bank's reserves rise by the exact amount that the other bank's fall. But a purchase of bonds by the Fed must raise the monetary base. Similarly, a sale of bonds by the Fed must reduce the monetary base.

The effects of the Fed's open-market operation on the monetary base over the last 20 years are shown in Table 14–2. The monetary base increased fourfold during this period. Note that the amount of currency is much larger than the amount of reserves. About three-quarters of the monetary base is currency.

There is a direct relationship between the monetary base and the money supply, and this is how the Fed achieves its control of the money supply. The relationship between the monetary base and the money supply is due to two factors:

1. *Reserve requirements:* Banks are required to hold a certain ratio of their checking deposits on reserve at the Fed. This ratio is called the **reserve**

---

[4]Phillip Cagan of Columbia University has done much of the research on the determination of the monetary base and its relation to the money supply in the United States. See his *The Determinants and Effects of Changes in the Stock of Money, 1875–1960* (New York: Columbia University Press, 1965). Cagan refers to the monetary base as high-powered money.

TABLE 14–2 Currency, Reserves, and the Monetary Base
(billions of dollars)

	Dec. 1970	Dec. 1980	Dec. 1990
Currency	49	115	246
Reserves	17	26	49
Monetary base	66	141	295

Source: *Economic Report of the President*, 1992, Tables B–66 and B–67.

ratio (r). For example, r might equal .1 (or 10 percent). Reserves (RE) are then given by the formula

$$RE = rD. \tag{14–3}$$

2. *Currency demand:* Most people want to hold some of their money in the form of currency. We will discuss the determinants of currency demand in Section 14.3. For now we can describe this demand in terms of a simple ratio. The **currency deposit ratio** (c) measures how much currency people want to hold as a ratio of their deposits. For example, the currency deposit ratio c might equal .2. Currency demand is thus given by

$$CU = cD. \tag{14–4}$$

Now we can derive the relationship between the monetary base and the money supply. From the definition of the money supply,

$$M = CU + D = cD + D = (1 + c)D,$$
$$M_B = CU + RE = cD + rD = (c + r)D.$$

Dividing M by M_B, we get

$$M = \frac{1 + c}{r + c} M_B. \tag{14–5}$$

The coefficient that multiplies M_B is called **monetary base multiplier,** which we will call m. If $r = .1$ and $c = .2$, then the monetary base multiplier is 4. Open-market operations that increase the monetary base by \$1 billion would then increase M by \$4 billion. Because of this multiplier, the monetary base is sometimes called **high-powered money.** Here the reserve ratio and the currency ratio are assumed to be fixed, so the Fed can control the money supply as accurately as it wants by controlling the monetary base. In reality, as we will show in Section 14.3, the currency ratio can vary, so control of the money supply is not so simple.

Required Reserves and Excess Reserves

In the United States, the reserve requirement for banks is now 10 percent. Banks are penalized if they fall below their requirements, and for this reason they always keep some **excess reserves** over and above their **required reserves.** This is illustrated in Table 14–3, which is a more detailed version of Table 14–1, focusing only on the banks and the Fed. The amount of excess reserves is small because banks do not receive any interest on their reserve balances at the Fed. They prefer to keep reserves close to the minimum required amount and invest the rest of their funds in loans or bonds. Excess reserves were only 1.5 percent of total reserves in 1984. Excess reserves rose to 2.3 percent of total reserves by 1985 as interest rates fell, but the amount was still small. In the mid-1960s, when interest rates were very low, excess reserves were higher but still fairly small, ranging up to 4 percent of total reserves. In recent years it is a good approximation to say that all bank reserves are required reserves.

Would banks hold reserves if they were not required to hold them? Reserve requirements were initially enacted into law in order to make sure that banks would have enough funds on hand if their depositors wanted to cash in their deposits. Even without reserve requirements, banks would hold some reserves for this purpose, but probably much less than 10 percent. Holding assets in interest-bearing short-term government securities is almost as safe as holding assets in reserves. Government securities can be

TABLE 14–3 Reserves: Required, Borrowed, and Excess

	Banks		Fed	
Assets	Liabilities		Assets	Liabilities
				Currency
	Deposits			
Bonds			Bonds	
Loans				
Required reserves				Required reserves
Excess reserves				Excess reserves
	Borrowed reserves		Borrowed reserves	

readily sold if there is a need for cash. But reserves are also used to carry out the instructions of a bank's depositors to transfer reserves from one account to another and from one bank to another. A large bank executes several million transfer instructions from checks, credit cards, and electronic requests every day. In the process, it will be holding positive amounts of reserves as a normal part of its business. Someone in the melon business always owns a certain amount of melons at any one time even though they turn over constantly. Similarly, someone in the reserve business is likely to own reserves. Again, however, the amount of reserves necessary to carry out the business of a bank is probably much less than its required reserves.

Borrowed Reserves and the Discount Rate

An important addition to this simple story of how the Fed and the banking system determine the money supply is that reserves at the banks can increase even if there is no open-market operation. One of the traditional functions of the Fed has been to provide loans to troubled banks. This tradition developed because of the frequent bank failures and bank panics in the late nineteenth and early twentieth centuries. The Fed was created to serve as "lender of last resort" to the banks. In recent years this role of the Fed has become apparent again. When several large loans at Continental Illinois Bank in Chicago went bad in the early 1980s, there were not enough funds to pay off the depositors. The small depositors were insured by the Federal Deposit Insurance Corporation (FDIC), a federal agency set up in the 1930s to insure bank deposits. But the many depositors holding amounts well over $100,000 were not insured. In this case the bank received loans so that even the large depositors obtained their funds.

The Fed usually makes loans to banks at the borrowing "window" of one of the 12 District Federal Reserve Banks. As shown in Table 14–3, the bank borrowings are a liability of the banks and an asset of the Fed. The interest rate on the borrowings is called the **discount rate.** In the past changes in the discount rate have signaled movements in the Fed's monetary policy. In recent years the discount rate has been adjusted to follow market interest rates, though usually with a time lag. When market interest rates are above the discount rate, the banks prefer to borrow at the discount window and make profits by lending out at a higher rate. Hence borrowings increase with market interest rates. There is a limit on this, however, because the Fed refuses to lend very much to banks without good reason.

What happens when a bank borrows reserves from the Fed? Looking at Table 14–3, you can see that the bank's assets will rise by the amount of the borrowed reserves. A new item will appear in the bank's liabilities, borrowings from the Fed. And the Fed's liabilities will rise by the amount of the reserves it has issued to the bank. Finally, the Fed's assets will contain a new item, a loan to the bank.

Thus *an increase in borrowed reserves increases the monetary base just as an open-market operation does.* However, if the Fed wants to insulate the monetary base from changes due to an increase in borrowings, then all it needs to do is make an offsetting open-market sale. Even when banks are borrowing heavily at the discount window, the Fed can set the monetary base at any level it chooses. Hence, the existence of borrowed reserves does not change the basic principle of money supply analysis that the Fed can control the monetary base. In discussing monetary policy, money market economists and financial columnists sometimes find it convenient to refer to reserves or the monetary base net of borrowings. Total reserves less borrowed reserves are called **nonborrowed reserves.** The monetary base less borrowings is called the **net base.**

The Federal Open Market Committee

Decisions about monetary policy in the United States are made by the Federal Open Market Committee (FOMC). Its voting members consist of those on the Federal Reserve Board and some of the presidents of the District Federal Reserve Banks. The FOMC meets about 8 to 10 times each year. The main job of the FOMC is to tell the New York trading desk, which actually carries out the open-market operations, what to do from week to week. The details of how the FOMC states its instructions to the trading desk change quite frequently. At the end of the 1980s under Alan Greenspan, chairman of the Federal Reserve Board, the operating instructions dealt primarily with short-term interest rates. Between meetings of the FOMC, the Fed maintains a horizontal LM curve by buying and selling bonds from its portfolio as needed to keep interest rates constant. At each meeting, the FOMC considers changes in the interest-rate target as needed to meet the objectives of monetary policy. One of the objectives is to keep the growth of monetary aggregates such as M_2 on target. More important in recent years has been the real GDP growth and inflation. The FOMC lowers the interest-rate target when real growth drops below normal and raises the target when inflation threatens to rise.

Distinguishing between Monetary and Fiscal Policies

Our analysis of the money supply and the monetary base raises some definitional questions about monetary and fiscal policy. The government budget identity implies a relationship between the monetary base, government bonds, and government expenditures that must be kept in mind when distinguishing between monetary and fiscal policies. The monetary base, gov-

Financing Government through the Printing Press

How much does the United States resort to the printing press to raise revenues to pay for government expenditures? The monetary base gives a good measure of this. Suppose, for example, that Congress passes a bill authorizing the navy to build new ships for an amount of $2 billion. But Congress does not raise taxes to pay for the ships. In order to pay for the ship construction, the government issues bonds. But rather than selling the bonds to the public, it sells the bonds to the Fed in exchange for currency, which it then pays out to the workers and firms that build the ships. In effect, the increase in government expenditures was financed by the printing of more currency. Note that the monetary base increased by $2 billion.

Just as in this example, the increase in the monetary base is a measure of the amount of government revenue that is raised each year through the printing press rather than through taxes or borrowing. In 1990 the monetary base in-

creased by about $25 billion. Compared with the $1,270 billion of government expenditures during 1990 this is a trivial amount: Less than 2 percent of government expenditures were financed by the printing press in 1990. This small percentage is typical in recent U.S. history. Hence, the printing presses are not a very important source of revenue for the United States in modern times. But this was not always true. About 80 percent of American Revolutionary War expenditures were financed by printing paper money called "continentals." So much money was printed that a serious inflation occurred: Prices rose by over 300 percent from 1776 to 1778 and by 1,000 percent from 1778 to 1780. Hence the phrase "not worth a continental." The printing press set off even worse inflations in Germany and several other European countries in the 1920s and in Argentina, Brazil, and other South American countries in the 1970s and 1980s.

ernment bonds, and the deficit are related to each other by the following government budget identity:

$$G + F + N - T = \Delta M_B + \Delta B, \qquad (14-6)$$

where ΔM_B is the change in the monetary base and ΔB is the change in government bonds. (See equations 2–2 and 2–5 in Chapter 2.) Equation 14–6 says that the government budget deficit is financed by increasing either the monetary base or government bonds. Note that the base as well as government expenditures and taxes appear in this expression, so that there is a link between monetary policy and fiscal policy.

To separate monetary policy changes from fiscal policy changes, we therefore need to specify what is happening to budget financing.

Fiscal policy is defined as **bond-financed changes** in government expenditures and taxes. That is, the monetary base and the money supply remain unchanged, and bonds are issued if government spending increases or taxes are reduced.

Monetary policy is defined as an increase in the monetary base matched by a reduction in government bonds. This exchange of money for bonds is an open-market operation. Note that open-market operations do not affect government purchases (G), transfers (F), interest payments (N), or taxes (T). Thus open-market operations do not affect fiscal policy.

THE MONETARY SYSTEM AND THE FED

1. The monetary system in the United States is based on the dollar, which is the unit of account and a means of payment.
2. The institutions most prominent in providing the means of payment are the Federal Reserve System and banks. The liabilities of the Fed—currency and reserves—make up the monetary base.
3. The money supply consists of currency and deposits at banks and other financial intermediaries. The supply of money is directly related to the monetary base.
4. The Fed controls the monetary base by buying and selling bonds. In doing so it controls the supply of money. The control over the supply of base money is the fundamental source of the Fed's leverage in the economy.

14.3

THE DEMAND FOR MONEY: CURRENCY AND CHECKING DEPOSITS

The alternative operating procedures for the Fed, outlined in Section 14.2, have significant macroeconomic implications. But before we can discuss them, we must examine the determinants of the demand for money.

Families and businesses constantly face decisions about how to conduct their financial affairs. They face big issues, such as how to finance the purchase of a house or a major capital investment, or how to hold wealth for retirement. They also face much smaller issues, such as whether to buy things with currency, checks, or credit cards or by special credit arrangements or electronic transfers of funds. Their choices depend on their income, wealth, volume of transactions, and the relative prices of all the different financial services available in the market. There is no clean separation between specifically monetary decisions and more general economic decisions. The blurring of choices between transactions and between bigger financial issues has increased in the past decade as deregulation of financial institutions has proceeded.

At the most general level, we could look at the demands for currency and checking deposits—or what we call money—as just parts of a large set of demand functions for financial instruments and services. Modern finance theory has sought a way to set up these demand functions, taking into account the central role of economic uncertainty. Our approach is less general. Among the many demand functions, the demand for currency and checking deposits is particularly important for macro issues.

James Tobin of Yale University, who was awarded the Nobel Prize in economics for developing modern portfolio theory, first applied his portfolio ideas to the same money demand functions that we consider here.[5] Tobin was interested in developing a microeconomic foundation for the demand for money that Keynes had originally introduced in *The General Theory*. Keynes referred to the demand for money as **liquidity preference,** a term which is still used quite frequently, and which has permanently left the "L" in the LM curve (the "M" refers to the money stock). The term **liquid,** when applied to a financial instrument, means that it can be sold readily; money is the most liquid of all assets. The originator of many ideas about money demand, Keynes was responsible for stressing the importance of money demand in macroeconomic fluctuations.

Keynes distinguished among three motives in people's demands for money: a **transactions** motive, a **precautionary** motive, and a **speculative** motive. More recent research—such as Tobin's—has refined these categories, and Keynes's classification scheme has been revised somewhat. However, our discussion of money demand will touch on all three of these elements.

What Are the Opportunity Costs of Holding Funds as Money?

When you put funds in a checking account, you are giving the bank the use of the funds. The bank earns the interest you would have earned if you had invested it. In exchange, the bank may pay you some interest, but less than what the bank is earning. In addition, if you have a sufficiently high balance, the bank may excuse you from service charges you would other-

---

[5]See James Tobin, "Liquidity Preference as Behavior Toward Risk," *Review of Economic Studies,* Vol. 25 (February 1958), pp. 65–86.

wise have to pay. Your opportunity cost per dollar in your checking account is the interest you forgo (the rate you might have received elsewhere less the amount you receive from the bank) less the avoided service charges. As usual in microeconomics, what matters precisely is the *marginal* opportunity cost—the interest forgone on the last amount added to your balance less the reduction in service charges if you took it out. For example, suppose you would earn 9 percent elsewhere and your bank pays 5 percent interest on checking accounts. Suppose that, over the year, it will excuse you from $2 in service charges if you raise your average balance by $100, so you earn 2 percent on the $100. Then your opportunity cost for the $100 of funds placed in your checking account is

$$9\% - 5\% - 2\% = 2\%.$$

We call the opportunity cost of holding money R_o, the subscript "o" standing for "opportunity." When you think about the added convenience of having another $100 in your account on the average over the year, you will keep in mind that you are sacrificing 2 percentage points of annual return on the funds.

Whatever complicated system the bank has for paying you interest on the one hand and charging you for services on the other, you can boil it down to an annual net opportunity cost of the account. This is the price we have in mind for checking deposits as one of the many financial services available to you.

For currency, the computation of the opportunity cost is easy. There are no service charges at all. Currency pays no interest. Therefore, the cost of holding currency is just the forgone interest. If you are contemplating meeting your needs by holding an average amount of currency of $500 and you could earn 9 percent on the funds elsewhere, then the cost is just 9 percent of $500, or $45 per year.

Another hypothetical way of handling your finances might avoid money altogether. You could open a special savings account and obtain a credit card. The savings account would allow you to write three checks a month, one of which could pay for your credit card charges. You would pay for everything with the credit card. Suppose the special savings account pays you 8 percent interest (1 percent less than the 9 percent that you could get outside the bank) and the credit card has no finance charges if you pay the bill on time. If you keep an average balance of $2,500 in the account, your only cost would be the opportunity cost of 1 percent of $2,500, or $25 per year.

By now it should be clear that each type of financial service has its own opportunity cost. But consumers do not simply pick the cheapest service on the market. Different services have different characteristics. Choosing among them is like choosing laundry detergent at the grocery store.

The Transactions Demand for Money: An Inventory Theory

One of the reasons that families and businesses hold currency and keep funds in their checking accounts is the same as the reason stores keep inventories of goods for sale. Because income is received periodically and expenditures occur every day, it is necessary to hold a stock of currency and checking deposits. This inventory theory of the demand for money falls into Keynes's category of **transactions motive.**[6]

We first illustrate the inventory theory of money demand with a simple case. Suppose a family earns an amount W every month. The family consumes W over the month, in equal amounts each day. If the family draws down its money to zero just before being paid, then its money balance starts at W and declines smoothly to zero over the month. Figure 14–1A illustrates how the family's money holdings decline smoothly each day during the month. Its average level of money balances M is $W/2$. This family has a demand for money ($W/2$) that is proportional to its income W and does not respond to the prices of financial services. For one reason or another, the family has rejected ways other than money to hold its funds.

Next, take the same family with one additional financial option. It can have its paychecks deposited for free in a savings account. It can transfer any amount of funds to its checking account. The cost of each transfer is k. The cost k includes the value of the time of the family members who make the transfer—it might involve a trip to the bank. The checking account has an opportunity cost R_O. The family chooses an average balance to hold in its checking account. The higher the average balance, the fewer transfers have to be made from the savings account. But the higher the average balance, the larger is the opportunity cost. The family wants to balance one cost against the other. For example, if the family makes one transfer at the beginning of the month, its money balance is the same as in Figure 14–1A. If the family makes two transfers to checking, one at the start of the month and one halfway through, as in Figure 14–1B, the average money balance is half as much as when it makes one transfer. If three transfers are made, as in Figure 14–1C, the average money holdings are lower still.

In general, the average money balance M is half the amount transferred from savings to checking on each transfer. The total number of transfers is the size of each transfer, 2 times M, divided into the total amount of consumption planned over the month, W. That is, the family will make $W/2M$ transfers during the month. The total cost of the transfers is k times $W/2M$ (remember that k is the cost of one transfer). The opportunity cost

---

[6]The inventory theory of the demand for money was first worked out by William Baumol, "The Transactions Demand for Cash: An Inventory Theoretic Approach," *Quarterly Journal of Economics,* Vol. 56 (November 1952), pp. 545–556, and James Tobin, "The Interest Rate Elasticity of the Transactions Demand for Cash," *Review of Economics and Statistics,* Vol. 38 (September 1956), pp. 241–247.

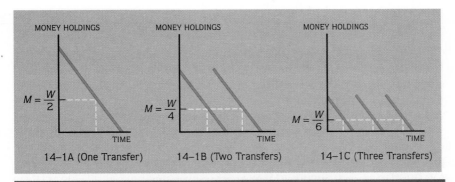

FIGURE 14–1A, B, AND C Three alternative money management strategies

In A, the family puts all its money into its checking account at the start of the month. Average money holdings are large. In B, the family leaves half its income in a savings account at the start of the month and withdraws the rest at the middle of the month. Average money holdings are less than in A. In C, the family makes three withdrawals and money holdings are even lower. Hence, when there are more withdrawals, the family's average money balance is lower.

over the month is just R_o times the average balance, that is, $R_o M$. The family wants to choose its average balance to minimize the sum of the two costs. Algebraically it wants to find M to minimize total cost:

$$\frac{kW}{2M} + R_o M. \tag{14–7}$$

A famous theorem from management theory is the **square-root rule** for inventories. The square-root rule says that stores should hold inventories proportional to the square root of sales. The same square-root rule applies to the demand for money. Specifically, the theorem says that the value of the average checking balance M that minimizes total cost is given by [7]

$$M = \sqrt{\frac{kW}{2R_O}}. \tag{14–8}$$

[7]Calculus is not necessary to derive the square-root rule. Rather, one can use a "complete the square" approach as follows. The total cost is

$$\begin{aligned} kW/2M + R_o M &= \sqrt{(kW/2M + R_o M)^2} \\ &= \sqrt{(kW/2M)^2 + kWR_o + (R_o M)^2} \\ &= \sqrt{(kW/2M)^2 - kWR_o + (R_o M)^2 + 2kWR_o} \\ &= \sqrt{(kW/2M - R_o M)^2 + 2kWR_o}. \end{aligned}$$

The second term under the last square-root sign does not depend on M. Thus costs are minimized when the first term under the square-root sign is at its smallest value, which is zero. This term is equal to zero when

$$M = \sqrt{kW/2R_o},$$

which is the square-root rule. Alternatively, if you have had calculus you can differentiate Equation 14–7 with respect to M.

The square-root rule gives the family's transactions demand for cash. Note that the formula would be the same if they chose to keep their transactions balance in the form of currency instead of in a checking account. In that case, because currency earns no interest, the opportunity cost of currency would be the interest rate paid on their savings account.

According to the square-root rule, the family holds less money if the opportunity cost R_o of holding money increases. The services of money are just like anything else the family consumes; they make do with less when the price rises. The square-root rule also says something about the relation between total spending and income W and the family's demand for money: Demand depends on the square root of total income. In comparing two families, one with double the income of the other, we should find that the second family has a transactions balance only 41 percent higher (the square root of 2 is 1.41).

Money as a Store of Wealth

Some families hold their wealth in the form of money; if they completely distrust all financial institutions, they might accumulate dollar bills under a mattress. Criminal activities generate wealth that is held as currency to avoid detection. People who are not thinking very hard about their affairs sometimes leave large amounts idle in their checking accounts at zero or low interest rates.

Hoards of inactive large-denomination paper money are apparently a large fraction of the total demand for currency. Almost half the total value of currency outstanding is in the form of $100 bills. The records of the Fed show that $100 bills last for quite a number of years, whereas the usual life of a $1 bill is only about 18 months. Apparently, the large bills do not change hands very often. The sheer volume of currency is surprising: There are about 120 million families in the United States; if the $246 billion in currency were distributed evenly among them, each would have $2,050 in currency at any one time. Very few families hold anything like this much. It is unlikely that businesses, which try to get their currency into the bank as quickly as possible, can account for much of the extra currency outstanding. Therefore, a few people must have extremely large hoards. Many of them are probably outside the country. In politically unstable nations, U.S. currency is one of the safer ways to hold wealth.

Keynes's notions of precautionary and speculative demand for money fit into this store-of-wealth category. Under the precautionary motive individuals save some wealth in the form of money in case of an emergency need for funds. Since currency and checking deposits are the easiest funds to obtain, it might seem natural to hold money in this form. However, in the United States, other interest-bearing assets serve the precautionary demand perfectly well. In politically unstable countries or in countries without a well-developed financial system, this motive for holding money would be more important.

Keynes's speculative motive captures the idea that changes in market interest rates will change the value of bonds. For individuals, bonds paying fixed interest rates are one of the main alternatives to holding the money in financial institutions. But, when interest rates rise, the price of these bonds falls.[8] Keynes argued that when interest rates were high, more people would expect them to fall or, equivalently, would expect bond prices to rise and would therefore want to hold bonds and less money. Thus, the demand for money declines as interest rates rise. Changes in bond prices also add risk to holding bonds. It was this risk that James Tobin formalized in his portfolio theory. People are assumed to be averse to risk; hence, they do not put all their wealth in a risky asset. Some of their wealth will be held as relatively riskless money. Unless they are unwilling to take on any risk, they will balance their wealth between money and bonds. This balancing gives rise to a demand for money as an aversion to risk.

The Demand for Checking Deposits to Pay for Banking Services

An important motive for holding checking account balances is to pay the bank for the services it provides. With most checking accounts, you can eliminate service charges by keeping a high enough balance. Instead of paying you interest and then charging you for the services you use, the bank offsets one against the other. In effect, you are earning a reasonable return on your wealth, but the return is paid in banking services rather than in cash.

The custom of offsetting interest and service charges had its origin in restrictions on the amount of interest banks could pay on checking accounts. Starting in the 1930s, the federal government prohibited the payment of interest on checking accounts. Only since 1980 have these limitations been lifted. However, the practice by banks of encouraging depositors to keep larger balances by forgoing their service charges will continue. If interest is paid explicitly, it is taxable; if it is paid as banking services, it is not taxed. As long as this feature of the tax system continues, there is an incentive to conceal interest by paying it as services.

For business customers, banks have traditionally linked loans and deposits. A business is more likely to get a loan if it has kept large deposits with a bank. Some loans require explicitly that part of the proceeds be kept

---

[8]Interest rates and prices of existing bonds have an inverse relation. When the interest rate falls, the market price of a bond issued earlier rises. The bond continues to pay its interest payments, but new bonds have smaller payments. Hence, the old bond has a higher market price.

as "compensating balances," which are inactive, non-interest-bearing balances in checking accounts. Again, the bank is charging for its services by paying its depositors less than market interest rates on their deposits.

As deregulation of financial markets proceeds, banks are shifting in the direction of paying closer to market interest on deposits and charging more explicitly for their services. We will have more to say about the implications of this shift later in the chapter.

Demand Functions for Money

We do not have any firm basis for dividing up the total demand for checking account balances or currency into the categories just listed—transactions demand, store of wealth, and payment for banking services. We can offer a few rough guesses. First, the transactions demand for both forms of money appears to be a fairly small fraction of total demand. An upper-bound estimate of the amount of money the typical family should hold, on the average, for transactions purposes is $1,000. Then total transactions demand should not exceed $1,000 times 120 million, or $120 billion. In 1990, currency alone was $246 billion and checking accounts were more than twice as much.

Nobody holds currency to compensate a bank for services. Hence, the rest of the demand for currency presumably comes from people who want the anonymity it provides. For checking accounts, probably much of the demand comes from the motive of compensating banks for services.

Because the transactions demand is a small fraction of total demand, the square-root rule cannot be sufficient to explain the total demand for money. Empirical studies of the demand for money indicate that money holdings have not grown quite as fast as income, but they have grown much more than the square root of income.[9]

The response of the demand for money to the price of holding money—the opportunity cost—is much more uncertain. For checking accounts, it is hard to measure the price in the first place, because it involves both forgone interest and forgone service charges. We do not have any systematic information about the reduction in service charges that the typical bank customer can obtain by holding a larger checking balance, but we can look at the relation between interest rates and cash holdings.

Currency holdings have declined gradually relative to GDP since 1959. This is shown in Figure 14–2. The most interesting finding about currency in circulation is the weakness of its downward trend. Even though credit cards are much more widely used today and checking accounts have more favorable terms than they used to, the public has decreased only

[9]See Stephen Goldfeld, "The Demand for Money Revisited," *Brookings Papers on Economic Activity,* No. 3 (1973), pp. 577–683.

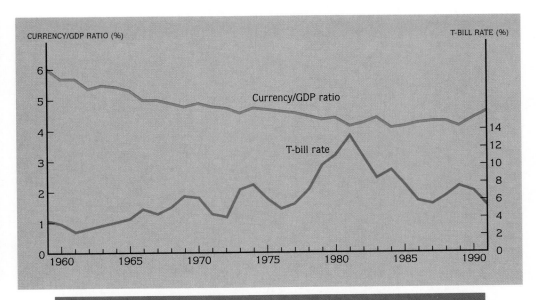

FIGURE 14–2   Currency divided by GDP

Holdings of currency have declined slowly in recent decades. The upper line is the total amount of currency in circulation, divided by nominal GDP—a measure of nominal demand. The interest rate as measured by the return on T-bills is also shown in the diagram. Higher interest rates are associated with less currency as a percentage of GDP.
Source: *Economic Report of the President*, 1992, Tables B–1, B–66, and B–69.

slightly the amount of currency it holds per dollar of production. In order to explain the sustained level of demand for currency some economists have inferred that the "underground economy"—activities not reported to the Internal Revenue Service and not part of GDP, such as "under-the-table" wages or illicit drug sales—is growing rapidly. But many other forces could be at work as well.

We would expect that periods of low income and high interest rates would be periods of low holdings of currency, but the evidence suggests that this tendency is weak. Currency holdings (in real terms) do drop a little during recessions, but not so much during periods of high interest rates. With the extremely high interest rates of 1981, however, currency fell quite a bit.

The behavior of checking deposits is shown in Figure 14–3. There is a long-standing trend away from checking deposits, presumably related to the growth of credit cards and other means of payment, as well as the growth of new types of accounts in banks and elsewhere offering conve-

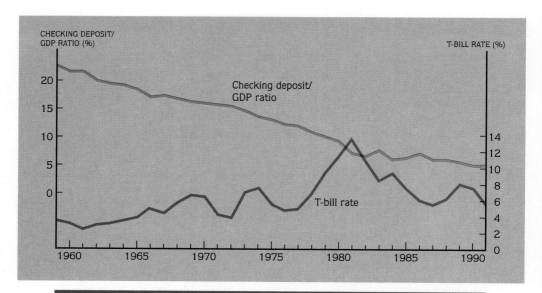

FIGURE 14–3   Checking deposits divided by GDP

Checking deposits have declined steadily when divided by nominal GDP, a measure of nominal demand. The interest rate as measured by the return on T-bills is also shown in the diagram. Higher interest rates are associated with lower checking deposits.
Source: Economic Report of the President, 1991, Tables B–1, B–66, and B–69.

nient transfer and bill-paying arrangements. Checking balances tend to rise when real GDP rises. Also, they tend to fall when the interest rate rises. The negative response to the interest rate is not absolutely obvious to the naked eye but is revealed in Figure 14–3 by the increase in deposits as a fraction of GDP as interest rates fell from 1981 to 1986 and again in 1991 and by the decrease when interest rates rose at the end of the 1980s. The negative relationship is confirmed with statistical methods.[10]

We can summarize the previous discussion about the demand for currency and checking deposits in two demand functions,

$$CU = CU(R, PY) \tag{14–9}$$

$$D = D(R_0, PY), \tag{14–10}$$

where CU is currency and D is checking deposits. The first equation shows that the demand for currency is a function of the market interest rate R and nominal income PY (the price level P times real income Y). The second

[10]See Stephen Goldfeld, "The Demand for Money Revisited," *Brookings Papers on Economic Activity*, No. 3 (1973), pp. 577–683.

equation shows that the demand for checking deposits is a function of the opportunity cost of checking deposits R_o and nominal income. Total money demand is the sum of these two demands. Our discussion implies the following characteristics for total money demand:

1. Demand depends negatively on the costs of holding currency and checking balances. In the case of currency, the cost is just the interest rate R. In the case of checking deposits, the cost is the difference between the market interest rate and the rate on checking deposits, less the reduction in service charges obtained by having a larger balance. We have called this cost R_o.
2. Demand is positively related to the price level P.
3. Demand is positively related to real income or output Y.

Note that in our discussion of money supply in the previous section, we defined $c = CU/D$, the ratio of currency to deposits. Our discussion in this section shows that this ratio is not a simple constant. Rather it depends on movements in R and R_o.

How does the opportunity cost of checking balances R_o depend on the interest rate R? Since 1980, banks have been free to pay interest on checking deposits. Checking balances do not automatically become more expensive when interest rates rise, because banks can pay higher interest on checking accounts. However, the account-holder does not get the full benefit of an increase in interest rates. For one thing, the bank has to hold 10 percent of the account-holder's funds as reserves at the Fed, and these reserves do not pay any interest. The bank therefore cannot be expected to pass along any more than 90 percent of any increase in interest rates. Hence the most the account-holder could ever hope for would be to earn interest on 90 percent of the account's balance. Another reason that the opportunity cost of checking balances rises with interest rates is that the rate that banks pay on checking accounts has proven to be quite sticky. The rate may stay at 4 percent per year as the market rate rises from 7 to 10 percent. In that case, the opportunity cost rises by the full 3 percentage points of the increase in the market rate.

Knowing that the opportunity cost of checking balances depends on the market interest rate, we can rewrite the demand function for checking balances as

$$D = D(R, PY). \qquad (14\text{--}11)$$

When the interest rate R rises, it raises the opportunity cost of checking balances and so depresses the demand for checking balances. The strength of this effect is greater if checking account interest rates are sticky and if account-holders conserve aggressively on balances when the opportunity cost rises.

THE DEMAND FOR MONEY

1. The demand for currency depends negatively on the interest rate and positively on income and the price level.
2. The demand for checking deposits depends negatively on the difference between the market interest rate and the rate on checking deposits and positively on income and the price level.

14.4

THE LM CURVE AND THE FED'S POLICY RULE FOR THE MONETARY BASE

We saw in Section 14.2 how the Fed can use open-market operations to change the monetary base and thereby change the money supply. The central question of monetary policy is how the Fed decides on the level of the monetary base. Consider three alternative instructions for open-market operations that the FOMC can give bond traders at the open-market desk in New York:

1. *Target the Level of* M_1. The bond traders are to keep the total amount of checking balances and currency (M_1) at a prescribed target level. If M_1 goes above target, they are to sell bonds and so reduce the monetary base and M_1. If M_1 goes below target, the traders are to buy bonds and so increase the monetary base and M_1.

2. *Target the Interest Rate.* The bond traders are to keep an eye on the short-term interest rate and maintain it at a prescribed target level. If the rate goes over the target, they are to buy bonds. This lowers the interest rate. If the rate goes below the target, they are to sell bonds. This reduces the monetary base and raises the interest rate back to the target.

3. *Target the Level of GDP.* The bond traders are to keep GDP at a prescribed target level. If GDP goes above target, they are to sell bonds; this will raise interest rates, contract the economy in general, and lower GDP. If GDP goes below target, they are to buy bonds; this will expand the economy and raise GDP.

We will look at each of these three policies in turn, to see what are the implications of each policy for the relations between the interest rate and the level of output.

Money Supply (M_1) Target

The first policy for setting the monetary base is to adjust it as necessary to keep the sum of checking balances and currency—the money supply M_1—at a prescribed level. What kind of adjustments of the monetary base are likely to be required? Recall that the relationship between M_1 and the monetary base M_B can be written.

$$M_1 = m M_B, \qquad (14–12)$$

where m is the money multiplier. The money multiplier depends on the ratios of reserves to deposits (r) and on the ratio of currency to demand deposits (c)—the *currency deposit ratio*. Recall that the exact formula is $m = (1 + c)/(r + c)$. When the reserve ratio (r) is high, the base multiplier is low. When the currency deposit ratio (c) is high, the base multiplier is low. (For example, suppose that r is .12. Then when $c = .2$, the money multiplier is about 3.8, and when $c = .4$, the money multiplier is about 2.3.) The reserve ratio and the currency deposit ratio will depend on the interest rate and consumer preferences.

As a close approximation, the ratio of reserves to deposits is equal to the *required* reserve ratio .10 and will therefore not change by much as long as reserve requirements are not changed. Suppose also that the currency deposit ratio is constant, independent of the interest rate. In that case, the relation between the monetary base and M_1 is one of strict proportionality. The multiplier m is constant. To hold M_1 at a prescribed level, all the Fed has to do is keep the base at the corresponding level. The money stock cannot shift when the base is held constant.

For two reasons, however, the money multiplier is not constant and is likely to be affected by interest rates.

First, recall that some reserves are held in excess of required reserves. These excess reserves decline when interest rates rise because reserves do not pay interest. Hence, r declines when interest rates rise. On this account, the money multiplier m increases when interest rates rise. Conversely, the money multiplier will decline when interest rates fall. Although this effect is probably small, it means that the Fed will have to decrease the base when interest rates rise in order to keep M_1 on a fixed target.

Second, the currency deposit ratio will also depend on the interest rate. The demand for checking balances is probably more sensitive to interest rates than is the demand for currency. High interest rates make the public economize on checking balances relative to paper money. Thus, when interest rates rise, the currency deposit ratio increases and the multiplier decreases. The Fed has to raise the base in order to keep M_1 at its prescribed level.

The LM curve for a money supply target is simply an upward-sloping line, shown in Figure 14–4, the same line we derived in Chapter 7. We will

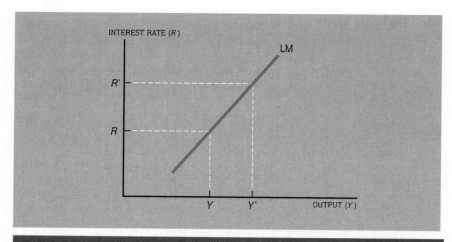

FIGURE 14–4   LM curve with a money supply (M_1) target

This LM curve is identical to the one derived in Chapter 7. The LM curve shows all the possible combinations of GDP and the interest rate when the price level is held constant. Because the Fed is holding the money supply constant, a higher level of GDP requires a higher interest rate. When GDP rises from Y to Y', the interest rate rises from R to R'. The LM curve could look very different if the Fed were using a different policy rule.

want to compare the slope of this line with the other two policies: the interest-rate target and the GDP target.

Interest-Rate Target

Under the second policy the Fed is to keep the interest rate at a prescribed level. This is a very different policy. Under this policy, the base would change every day as necessary to keep interest rates at the target. If the demand schedule for money as a function of the interest rate shifted upward because of a higher level of GDP, the supply of the monetary base would rise by enough to intersect the monetary base demand curve at the same interest rate. Thus, the LM curve is a horizontal line at the prescribed interest rate, as shown in Figure 14–5.

GDP Target

The third policy is for the Fed to keep GDP at a prescribed level. The Fed's operating policy rule is to expand and contract the base as necessary to keep GDP on target. Under this policy, the LM curve is simply a *vertical* line. If an event elsewhere in the economy causes interest rates to rise, the

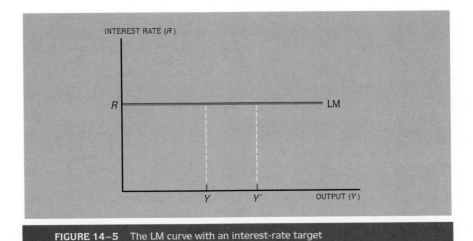

FIGURE 14–5   The LM curve with an interest-rate target

When the Fed is keeping the interest rate at the prescribed level *R*, the LM curve is a horizontal line at that interest rate. When GDP rises from *Y* to *Y'*, the interest rate does not change.

Fed's operating rule would call for it to lower the base as needed to keep real GDP on target. The event would stimulate GDP if the Fed were pegging the money supply, but, instead, the Fed is "leaning against the wind" to keep GDP constant. Note that targeting GDP may be more difficult for the trading desk than targeting interest rates because GDP is observed with a lag. In Chapter 18 we will discuss how the Fed could choose a GDP target.

HOW THE FED'S RULE DETERMINES THE EFFECT OF FISCAL POLICY

Suppose that the Fed holds the money supply constant, so that the LM curve is upward-sloping—neither perfectly vertical nor perfectly horizontal. Now consider a fiscal stimulus that increases aggregate demand so that GDP rises. At a higher level of GDP, with no change in interest rates, consumption and investment will be higher. This increase will be partly offset by higher imports. But if GDP rises and interest rates remain the same, the money market will be out of balance. Higher interest rates are needed to offset the higher money demand that goes with higher GDP. Higher interest rates depress investment and possibly consumption. They also cause the dollar to appreciate and so depress net exports. Consequently, the rise in GDP is dampened. The IS-LM analysis sorts out all of these considerations and finds the point where both GDP and the interest rate have risen by just the right amount to restore expenditure balance and equality of demand and supply for the monetary base.

Diminished private spending in response to higher government spending is called **crowding out.** Since the Fed can control the slope of the LM curve, it can control crowding out in the short run. But crowding out also depends on the interest-rate sensitivity of the demand for money. If account-holders can benefit from higher interest rates by leaving funds in their checking accounts rather than shifting to other investments, the LM curve will be steeper.

Consider how the other two policy rules for the Fed can influence the effect of fiscal policy. Suppose that the Fed tries to keep the interest rate constant. Under this policy, the Fed eliminates the feedback effects of interest rates that normally limit the ramifications of fiscal policy. Investment, consumption, and net exports are not held back by a rise in the interest rate. GDP rises by the full amount of the rightward shift in the IS curve. A monetary policy that keeps interest rates constant when fiscal policy changes is said to **accommodate** the fiscal policy. This is illustrated in Figure 14–6.

At the other extreme, suppose the Fed adjusts the monetary base as necessary to keep GDP constant. In this case, the negative feedback effect

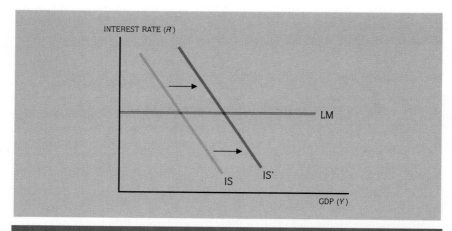

FIGURE 14–6   Fiscal expansion with a horizontal LM curve

When the Fed conducts monetary policy by holding the interest rate at a prescribed level, the LM curve is a horizontal line. When the IS curve shifts to the right due to a fiscal stimulus, the result is a large increase in GDP and no change in the interest rate.

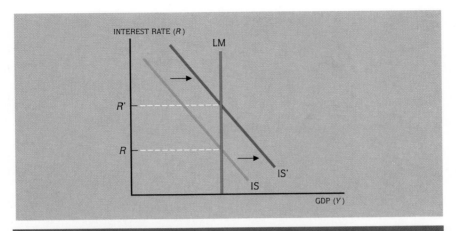

FIGURE 14–7　Fiscal expansion with a vertical LM curve

When the Fed conducts monetary policy so as to keep GDP constant, the LM curve is vertical. A shift in the IS curve has no effect on GDP; it only changes the interest rate.

through the interest rate is complete. Fiscal policy raises the interest rate without altering GDP. However, the composition of GDP may well be changed. If the fiscal stimulus takes the form of higher government purchases of goods and services, consumption, investment, and net exports must fall if GDP is to remain the same. The interest rate rises by enough to depress these categories of spending just enough to offset the increase in government purchases. Similarly, if the fiscal stimulus comes from higher transfers and lower taxes, higher interest rates depress investment and net exports by enough to offset the increase in consumption. Then the LM curve is a vertical line and fiscal policy does not affect GDP at all, as shown in Figure 14–7. Monetary policy is reacting in a manner that gives long-run results in the short run.

UNAVOIDABLE SHOCKS TO THE IS CURVE AND LM CURVE

One of the factors that enter into the choice of policy rule for the Fed—that is, how steep an LM curve should it establish—is the likelihood of unanticipated and unavoidable shifts in these curves. Suppose, for example, that

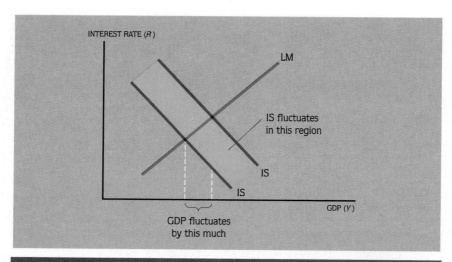

FIGURE 14–8   Random shifts in the IS curve

The band around the IS curve illustrates the random shifts. A steep LM curve insulates real GDP from such shifts.

the IS curve shifts around a lot because of erratic investment demand. The situation is illustrated in Figure 14–8. Then the best thing for the Fed to do is maintain a steep LM curve. Any drop in investment thereby brings a drop in interest rates, which mitigates the decline in investment.

But suppose that the LM curve shifts repeatedly, perhaps because of changes in financial technology or changes in the public's desire to hold currency. Then the steep LM curve is not a good idea. A flat LM curve would result in fewer of these financial shocks affecting aggregate demand. From Figure 14–9, you can see that GDP would be affected less by LM shifts if the LM curve were flat.[11]

As we mentioned earlier in this chapter, the Fed has placed less emphasis on the money supply and more emphasis on interest rates in recent years. In fact, it apparently abandoned M_1 targets in early 1987. One of the rationales for this shift is given by the analysis of this section: Shocks to the

---

[11]The idea that random shocks are important for deciding how steep the LM curve should be was first shown by William Poole, "The Optimal Choice of Monetary Policy in a Simple Stochastic Macro Model," *Quarterly Journal of Economics,* Vol. 84 (May 1970), pp. 197–216.

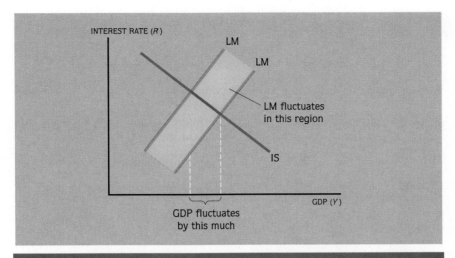

FIGURE 14–9 Random shifts in the LM curve

Now it is better for the Fed to maintain a flat LM curve. Interest-rate pegging would be a good idea.

LM curve have become more serious in the last few years. With more uncertainty about the LM curve, interest-rate rather than money targeting is the appropriate policy rule for the Fed.

THE EFFECT OF POLICY RULES ON FLUCTUATIONS

1. The policy rule chosen by the Fed effectively determines the slope of the LM curve. The slope of the LM curve determines the short-run effectiveness of fiscal policy.
2. The policy rule that is best at reducing fluctuations in real output depends on the source of instability in the economy.
3. An interest-rate target will tend to stabilize real GDP if most disturbances originate with money demand.
4. A money supply target will tend to stabilize real GDP if most disturbances originate with spending demand.

14.7 LAGS IN THE EFFECT OF MONETARY POLICY

Monetary policy does not control the demand for goods and services directly. There is usually a lag in its effect. There are two principal channels of monetary policy and both act through interest rates: the response of investment and the response of net exports through the depreciation of the dollar.

In Chapter 11, we stressed the lags in the investment process. Businesses take months to get almost any investment plan into effect; those involving the construction of new plants or the ordering of special equipment can take years. Housing investment takes 6 months or a year to respond strongly to a change in the interest rate.

Less is known about the lags in the response of net exports to dollar depreciation. Exchange rates respond immediately to changes in the interest rate. But buyers in the United States and overseas do not switch their purchases immediately when U.S. goods become cheaper. Americans who have learned that Japanese cars offer good value do not immediately reconsider U.S.-produced alternatives when the value of the dollar declines and causes the dollar price of Japanese cars to rise. It takes time for foreigners to discover the advantage of American products as well.

The peak effect of monetary expansion on GDP probably occurs between 1 and 2 years after the expansion. At first, a monetary expansion drives down the interest rate without much effect on GDP. The money market handles the monetary expansion through lower interest rates instead of higher GDP. After a year or so, the response of spending to the interest rate is stronger and GDP expands.

The lag in the economy's response to monetary expansion greatly complicates the conduct of monetary policy. As we have mentioned before, recessions generally hit the economy by surprise. The Fed learns that the economy is headed for trouble only a few months before the trouble is at its worst. It can step on the gas to try to head off the recession, but the peak effect of the stimulus will occur well after the worst part of the recession. In fact, if the recession is brief and is followed by a brisk recovery, the monetary stimulus may hit hardest when it is least needed; in the worst case, it can worsen the boom that follows the recession.

Because the main effect of monetary expansion occurs in the year after the expansion is launched, when formulating monetary policy, the Fed must always think about the likely conditions in the economy a year in the future. Even if the economy is in bad shape this year, the Fed will not expand if it anticipates that the economy will recover on its own by next year. There is little the Fed can do to help the economy this year; any stimulus it adds now will only create problems next year.

The Fed never knows with any confidence what will happen in the future. Even if it does not know confidently that the economy will be in good shape on its own next year, the Fed will not take vigorous action this year. If it is 50 percent likely that the economy will be below potential next year and 50 percent likely that it will be above potential, the best action for the Fed is to do nothing. As a general matter, the more uncertain the Fed is about conditions next year, the more cautious it will be about policy actions this year.

LAGS IN MONETARY POLICY

1. Monetary policy operates through interest rates. Consequently, there is a lag before the policy influences GDP.
2. The evidence suggests that the peak effect of monetary policy on GDP occurs after a lag of between 1 and 2 years.
3. Today's monetary policy has to be formulated with the state of the economy a year from now in mind. Even if GDP is well below potential, it may not be desirable to launch a monetary expansion.
4. Uncertainty about the future state of the economy adds to the caution of monetary policymakers.
5. The net effect is to limit the monetary policy to much smaller adjustments than would be used if the effect of the policy occurred instantly.

REVIEW AND PRACTICE

Major Points

1. A monetary system is an agreement on the way to quote prices and convey purchasing power.
2. In the United States the Fed issues currency and also reserves. Reserves are accounts at the Fed equivalent to currency. The sum of currency and reserves is the monetary base.

3. The Fed's policy rule determines the LM curve. A policy of targeting M_1 gives a steep but not vertical LM curve. A policy of targeting the interest rate gives a horizontal LM curve. A policy of targeting GDP gives a vertical LM curve.

4. The effects of a fiscal stimulus depend on the Fed's policy rule. If the Fed chooses a horizontal LM curve by targeting the interest rate, fiscal stimulus raises GDP strongly. If the Fed chooses a vertical or near-vertical LM curve by targeting GDP, then fiscal stimulus raises interest rates but has little or no effect on GDP.

5. An interest-rate target for monetary policy cushions the economy against the effects of shifts in money demand, while a money supply target provides greater stability against shifts in spending.

6. Monetary policy influences GDP with a lag. The immediate effect of monetary stimulus is to lower interest rates. After the lags in investment and foreign trade work themselves out, the stimulus raises GDP. Because of the lag and because of the Fed's uncertainty about the future, monetary policy needs to be used with caution.

7. Fiscal and monetary policy can be used in tandem to achieve any desired combination of GDP and the interest rate. Fiscal and monetary expansion together can raise GDP without changing the interest rate. Fiscal expansion and monetary contraction can raise the interest rate without changing GDP. Monetary expansion and fiscal contraction can lower the interest rate without changing GDP.

8. Monetary policy influences the exchange rate and net exports. Monetary expansion makes the dollar depreciate but has an ambiguous effect on the trade deficit.

Key Terms and Concepts

means of payment	financial intermediaries	compensating balances
unit of account	monetary base	open-market operation
currency	reserve requirements	discount rate
reserves	transactions motive	interest-rate target
checking deposits	precautionary motive	M_1 target
money supply	speculative motive	GDP target
	store of wealth	

Questions for Discussion and Review

1. Why is the dollar the unit of account and the medium of exchange in the United States?

2. In what sense do commercial banks play a role as financial intermediaries? What other role do they play in determining the nation's money supply?

3. Why doesn't the Fed have separate control over the quantities of both reserves and currency?

4. Why do some banks borrow reserves from the Fed? How does the Fed decide on the discount rate on these borrowings?

5. How does the Fed control the monetary base? What types of open-market operations increase the monetary base?

6. Why do banks require businesses to maintain compensating balances on deposits at the banks rather than simply charging them a service charge?

7. Does the demand for currency depend on the real rate of interest or on the nominal rate of interest?

8. How does the Fed choose the slope of the LM curve?

9. Why might the Fed choose a vertical LM curve? A horizontal one?

10. What happens when monetary policy is contractionary and fiscal policy is expansionary?

Problems

Numerical

1. Suppose that money demand is given by an expression similar to Equation 14–8,

$$M = \sqrt{\frac{kY}{2R_o}}$$

where Y is income, the opportunity cost of holding money is given by

$$R_o = q_1 R - q_0,$$

and the transaction cost k is equal to 2.

a. Assuming $q_1 = 1$ and $q_0 = .06$, what is the level of money demand at $Y = 2,500$ and $R = .08$? Suppose the money supply is set equal to this value. Find the interest rate at which money supply equals money demand for $Y = 1,000$ and for $Y = 4,000$. Plot the points to scale on a graph.

b. Now let $q_1 = .25$ and $q_0 = 0$. Find the level of money demand at $Y = 2,500$ and $R = .08$. Again, supposing that the money supply is set equal to this value, find the interest rate at which money supply equals money demand for the values of Y given in Part a. Plot these points on the same graph.

c. Suppose the Fed's policy rule is to target M. For which values of q_0 and q_1 given above will the LM curve be steeper? Give a brief economic interpretation of your result.

d. How does the change in the parameters given in this problem parallel recent economic history? What events have triggered this change? Given this change, are spending shocks more or less destabilizing to output than they were before?

2. In this problem we consider the relationship between monetary policy and the financing of the deficit.

a. Suppose that the reserve ratio r is equal to .1, and the currency ratio c is equal to .2. Assume that $G - T + F = \$200$ billion. By how much would the money supply, monetary base, currency, and bank reserves have to change if the Fed were to finance the entire budget deficit?

b. Suppose now that the money supply is initially equal to $600 billion with output equal to potential. Suppose further that potential output is increasing by 2 percent per year, prices are expected to grow by 3 percent, and monetary velocity ($V = PY/M$) is expected to remain constant. If the Fed wishes to keep output at potential, what percentage of the deficit will it have to finance?

3. Suppose that the required reserve ratio is .12 for deposits and that there are no excess reserves. Suppose also that the total demand for currency is equal to .3 times deposits.
   a. If total reserves are $40 billion, what is the level of the money supply?
   b. By how much does the money supply change if the Fed increases the required reserve ratio to .20? Assume that total reserves are unchanged at $40 billion.
   c. By how much does the money supply change if the Fed purchases $1 billion of government bonds in the open market? (Keep the required reserve ratio at .12.)

Analytical

1. Suppose that as a result of recent tax cuts, the amount of activity in the underground economy was significantly reduced.
   a. What effect would this have on the demand for currency?
   b. Explain why such a change would have an expansionary effect on the economy (holding the Fed's open-market operations fixed).
   c. Describe the Fed's response to such a change under each of the three policy rules discussed in Section 14.4.

2. Use Equation 14–8 to write an expression for real money demand as a function of real income and real transactions costs. Assuming that nominal income and nominal transactions costs increase proportionately with changes in the price level, describe how real money demand is affected by a change in prices. How is the nominal demand for money affected?

3. Consider the following cash management problem. A college student earns $400 a month which she uses to meet personal expenses. All expenses are paid for in cash. She maintains a savings account at a local bank which pays 1 percent per month (12 percent annually) in interest. At the beginning of each month she deposits her $400 paycheck in her savings account and makes periodic cash withdrawals throughout the month. Cash withdrawals are made through an automatic teller at a service charge of 25 cents each.
   a. Calculate the student's average currency holdings and the number of withdrawals made each month.
   b. Suppose it's observed that the student always withdraws $40. There are several possible explanations. Perhaps she doesn't wish to risk losing larger amounts of cash. Protection against such loss is one of the benefits of a savings account. In addition, she may wish to avoid the temptation of spending more money than she can really afford. Call this the "piggy bank" value of savings accounts. What must the value of such benefits be, expressed as a rate of return, in order for her withdrawals of $40 to be optimal?

4. Suppose that competition in the credit card industry drives down the cost of using credit cards.
   a. How is that likely to affect money demand? Illustrate the macroeconomic impact using an IS-LM diagram.
   b. If the Fed is aware of such a trend, but cannot be certain of its timing, what kind of policy rule should it use?

5. Explain the effect that a lowering of the discount rate has on the money supply. In particular, consider the effect of such a change on the money multiplier and the monetary base.

6. Suppose that banks began both to pay market rates of interest on all checking accounts and to charge the full costs of providing such accounts. These costs would not be waived, regardless of one's average balance. Describe the possible effects of such a change on money demand.

7. The velocity of money V is defined by the expression

$$V = PY/M.$$

A policy rule frequently used by the Fed can be described as follows. First, it is assumed that the velocity of money remains roughly constant from year to year. Next, the Fed forecasts this year's rate of inflation (which is viewed as being predetermined and thus beyond its control). Finally, the Fed chooses its target rate of growth for real output. This results in a target rate of growth for the money stock.
   a. Suppose that inflation for the current year is forecasted to be 5 percent and that the Fed's target rate of growth for output is 2 percent. By how much should it increase the money stock this year?
   b. Suppose now that money demand is given by the expression

$$M/P = kY - hR.$$

   Derive an expression for the velocity of money V. On what does V depend?
   c. What kinds of changes in the economy could affect V? Consider both the cases where $h > 0$ and $h = 0$.
   d. Explain why the policy rule described above is only useful when money demand is not very sensitive to interest rates.

8. Suppose that the U.S. government budget deficit is reduced through a cut in government purchases.
   a. First assume that the Fed targets the *money supply* and does not change the target when the budget deficit is reduced. What happens to the exchange rate, net exports, and private saving? Use an IS-LM diagram and an aggregate demand curve with a price line to illustrate your answer. Be sure to distinguish between the short-run and the long-run effects, and describe in words how the economy adjusts over time as prices adjust.
   b. Now assume that the Fed targets the *interest rate* and does not change the target when the budget deficit is reduced. Answer the questions in Part a for this alternative Fed policy. Explain your answer using diagrams.

9. Monetary policy is one of the most hotly debated issues in macroeconomics. Yet, the policy implications of the IS-LM model would seem to be rather clear:

Assuming that the Fed wishes to maintain output at potential, simply set the LM curve to intersect the IS curve at Y^*. Provide a brief explanation of why monetary policy isn't so simple a matter.

10. There is reason to believe that money demand may be more closely related to consumption than to total output. Suppose this is indeed the case. The money demand function takes the form

$$M = (sC - bR)P \qquad s > 0$$

where the rest of the economy is described by the usual spending equations:

$$C = a + b(Y - T)$$
$$I = e - dR$$
$$X = g - mY - nR$$

a. What is the slope of the LM curve for this model?

b. Suppose taxes T are lump-sum rather than proportional to income. Show the short-run effect of a tax cut in this modified model using an IS-LM diagram. Comment on the qualitative effect on interest rates and income in relation to the model in which money demand depends on income rather than on consumption.

11. A 1989 proposal by Representative Stephen Neal endorsed a zero-inflation goal for the Fed as being favorable for long-run economic growth. Describe how price level stability might promote growth in potential GDP relative to a policy regime in which there is no commitment to any particular price level. Could a policy that commits to 4 percent inflation accomplish the same thing as one that commits to 0 percent inflation?

MacroSolve Exercises

1. Velocity is the ratio of nominal GDP to the money supply. Plot the behavior of the velocity of M_1 using quarterly data. Is velocity procyclical or countercyclical? Why do you think this is? Do you find the same result using annual data?

2. Velocity used to be thought of as a constant. If nominal GDP increases, the money supply would increase, keeping velocity relatively stable. Plot velocity, nominal growth in GDP, and the money growth rate against time using annual data from 1930 to 1987 to confirm this theory. Now plot the same variables using quarterly data from 1979.1 to 1987.4. What happened to the relationship? What other variable might be affecting velocity? (Hint: Graph velocity against the short-term interest rate.)

3. Graph velocity against the short-term interest rate using quarterly data. What relation do you see between them?

a. Is this relationship consistent with the money demand theory that you have learned?

b. Do you see the same relationship in the annual data?

c. Will this type of velocity movement make the effects of monetary policy on GDP greater or smaller than they would be if velocity were constant? Explain why.

d. Will this type of velocity movement make the effects of fiscal policy on GDP greater or smaller than if velocity were constant? Explain why.

4. *Policy Decisions 1997.* Suppose you have been hired to be an economic analyst for the new treasury secretary. After the first meeting with finance ministers from several other large countries, the treasury secretary wonders whether pegging the exchange rate to that in the other countries by targeting U.S. interest rates would work. In particular, you are asked about the effects of such a policy of maintaining a constant real interest rate of 5 percent. Using the "IS-LM, Closed Econ" model, show how this policy affects the potency of fiscal policy, compared with a policy of fixing the money supply.

The Micro Foundations of Output Determination and Price Adjustment

The Labor Market and Flexible-Price Theories of Fluctuations

Ever since Chapter 6, we have been looking at the behavior of real GDP, the interest rate, and the price level, without saying much about the labor market. An important and controversial feature of the complete model developed in Chapters 6 through 8 is that employment may differ temporarily from the point where labor supply and labor demand intersect. When employment is either above or below that point, firms can profit and workers can gain as well by moves that would help the labor market return to the intersection point. Because economists are reluctant to say that buyers and sellers in a market fail to pursue self-interest, they have asked whether these temporary departures from labor market equilibrium are really essential in understanding economic fluctuations. If so, what forces prevent firms and workers from taking immediate advantage of the gains from trade that exist whenever employment moves away from the point of intersection of labor supply and demand?

To answer these important questions, we need to develop the analysis of labor supply and labor demand in more detail, which we do in the first two sections of the chapter. Then we tackle the first of our questions by examing two flexible-price models where shifts in labor supply explain the ups and downs of employment. Employment is always at the intersection of supply and demand. Movements in the real interest rate turn out to be key in these flexible-price models. Our discussion follows up the discussion in Chapter 4 on the real business cycle model.

In Chapter 16, we will tackle the second question by taking a closer look at the labor market in the sticky-price model. Economists who believe in that model must be able to identify the market failure that makes employment depart from the point of intersection of supply and demand. We look at both theoretical explanations of, and facts about, wage and price setting in the U.S. economy.

In this chapter, we also examine an important theory that incorporates *informational problems* into a flexible-price model. These informational problems provide another flexible-price explanation for the departures of GDP from potential.

15.1   LABOR SUPPLY

The labor supply schedule of an individual worker shows the amount of time the worker chooses to work at alternative real wage rates. A higher real wage increases the incentive to work. Choosing to work an additional hour is choosing to forgo the next best alternative—an hour of time relaxing at home, an hour cooking or fixing up the house, or an hour at the movies. The return from working is the real wage, and microeconomic principles tell us that the real wage must be greater than (or at least equal to) the value of the alternative activity in order to induce somebody to work another hour. The labor supply schedule thus shows, for each level of employment, the value to the worker of time spent in alternative activities.

Long-Run versus Short-Run Labor Supply

It is useful to distinguish between the short-run labor supply schedule and the long-run supply schedule. Long-run labor supply shows the amount of time a worker chooses to work over a long period of time—perhaps the worker's entire life or at least 5 years—for a given real wage over that same period of time. Short-run labor supply looks at a worker's decision to work during the next day or week or at most a year for a given real wage for that day, week, or year.

A good deal of empirical evidence (see footnote 3 in Chapter 4, page 96) suggests that the long-run labor supply schedule is quite steep (as in Chapter 4, the real wage is on the vertical axis and the amount of work is on the horizontal axis). In other words, long-run labor supply is not very sensitive to the real wage. Real wages have risen dramatically over the past 40 years, but people are working just about the same amount as they did in 1950, on the average. Economists infer that a permanent increase in the real wage over a worker's lifetime has little effect on the number of hours per week or weeks per year an individual is willing to work on average

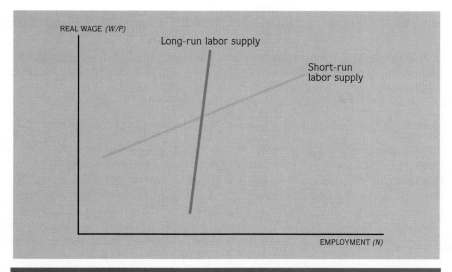

FIGURE 15–1 Long-run and short-run labor supply

The long-run labor supply schedule is approximately vertical. Workers' marginal value of time, measured by the real wage on the vertical axis, falls a large amount for a small permanent reduction in the amount of work. The short-run supply schedule is flatter. The marginal value of time falls less during a temporary decline in the amount of work than during a prolonged decline.

throughout a lifetime. In the long run, the income and substitution effects, discussed earlier in Chapter 4, come close to canceling each other out. The *income effect* of a permanent, or long-run, increase in the real wage makes a worker better off and stimulates consumption of almost all goods, including leisure time. The result is a reduction in labor supply. The *substitution effect* means that there is a greater incentive to work—the price of time away from work (the opportunity cost of work) is higher when the real wage is higher. The result is an increase in labor supply. The net effect is that the labor supply schedule is nearly vertical for permanent changes in the real wage. To put it differently, even a small permanent reduction in the amount of work supplied by workers would lower the marginal value of time away from work by quite a bit.

What about the short-run labor supply schedule? Is it also vertical? To answer this question, we must consider temporary changes in the amount of work. Does the value of workers' time away from work fall dramatically during the temporary lull in work during a recession? If so, it would appear that there would be mutually advantageous opportunities for workers with low value of time to supply more work to firms with normal levels of the marginal product of labor. The recession would quickly end as workers and firms took advantage of these opportunities. Some macroeconomists argue, however, that the short-run labor supply schedule is fairly flat. With flat supply, a temporary reduction in work does not lead to much of a reduction in the value of time. Figure 15–1 illustrates this difference between the long-run and short-run labor supply schedules. Two of the reasons for flatness in the short run are the alternative activities available to workers and fixed costs of going to work.

Alternative Activities during Recessions

When people are working less, they are spending more time in other activities. Real business cycle economists emphasize that these alternative activities include more recreation and more time at home. Alternative activities also include some kinds of investment; home improvements and education are probably the most important examples. If workers have been putting in long hours during a boom, they may welcome the time off they get during a recession. The alternative activities that workers find in recessions are far from valueless. Ski areas in Michigan do a booming business during recessions when many auto workers are on layoff. School attendance rises in recessions. Higher-paid workers who lose jobs or are on layoff do not frequently take low-paying service jobs or become self-employed, though both opportunities are widespread even during recessions.

Real business cycle economists have considered two factors that determine how much the value of a worker's time away from work drops during a recession. First is the size of the backlog of alternative activities that exists at the beginning of the typical recession. If the backlog is enough to allow the worker to make good use of the time that is freed up by the recession, then it is likely that the marginal value of time away from work remains fairly high and labor supply is flat.[1] Second is the need for time off to take a rest from past hard work. If several boom years create a desire for an easy year, then the value of time does not fall very much during a recession year. On the other hand, if one weekend of rest makes up for the hardest five days of previous work, then the idea that a recession provides a valuable stretch of lower work effort is incorrect.[2]

The suggestions that real business cycle economists have made about why the labor supply schedule may be quite flat may appear implausible when we think about the unemployed who remain out of work for many months or even a year. To be sure, however, we need to keep in mind some facts about the distribution of unemployment among workers. When a recession strikes, unemployment rises. But the majority of extra unemployment in a recession takes the form of one or two stretches of 1 to 10

---

[1]Jess Benhabib, Richard Rogerson, and Randall Wright, "Homework in Macroeconomics," unpublished, New York University, 1989.
[2]Finn Kydland and Edward Prescott, "Time to Build and Aggregate Fluctuations," *Econometrica,* Vol. 50 (November 1982), pp. 1345–1371.

weeks of time off the job during the year, spread across many workers. Thus, the question of flat labor supply does not pertain solely to whether workers can make good use of a whole year of time off the job. For some workers, the question is whether they find productive or enjoyable activities to fill in the extra weeks of time off the job.

Fixed Costs of Going to Work

Richard Rogerson of the University of Minnesota has developed an alternative model that explains a flat labor supply. He starts from the assumption that workers face a fixed cost of going to work each day.[3] The cost includes the time and expense of commuting, the time needed to pack a lunch and put on work clothes, and the time needed to get set up after arriving at work. Because of the cost, firms and workers organize work schedules to conserve on the number of days at work. Conservation of days of work has led to the custom of the 5-day workweek, holidays that last all day, and vacations that come in consecutive weeks. On family farms, where commuting costs and other fixed costs are small, work tends to spread over all the days of the year. In the presence of fixed costs, workers concentrate work in about 230 out of the 365 days of the year (52 five-day weeks less 30 days for vacations and holidays). When the process of conserving fixed costs by cutting days is at its optimum, there is nothing to gain or lose by adding or subtracting a day from the work schedule; the value of the worker's time plus the cost of going to work just equals the worker's daily earnings. The number of hours in the workday is determined by setting the marginal value of an hour of time to the hourly wage. For most workers, the resulting length of the workday is around 8 hours. If the work schedule lengthens by a few days, but the number of hours of work each day remains unchanged, nothing changes in either of these equations. Hence the wage that the worker has to receive to make going to work worthwhile is the same no matter how many weeks per year the worker is employed. The labor supply schedule is perfectly flat. In the U.S. economy, variations in weeks of work are a more important source, in percentage terms, of variations in total employment than are variations in hours per day. But there are some variations in hours per day, so it is an unresolved research question whether Rogerson's model explains highly elastic labor supply.

---

[3]Richard Rogerson, "Indivisible Labor, Lotteries, and Equilibrium," *Journal of Monetary Economics,* Vol. 21 (January 1988), pp. 3–16.

LABOR SUPPLY

1. The labor supply schedule reflects the value of workers' time for alternative amounts of work. Empirical evidence shows that the long-run labor supply schedule is close to vertical.
2. Real business cycle economists argue that short-run labor supply is quite flat, so that small short-run changes in the real wage will result in large changes in labor supply. In this view, there are important alternatives to work in the short run. Also, workers may be indifferent to adding more days to their annual work schedules.

15.2   LABOR DEMAND

The labor demand schedule shows the **marginal product of labor** at alternative levels of employment. It is important for real business cycle theories of macroeconomic fluctuations that labor demand be fairly flat, as in Figure 15–2. If the marginal product of labor is substantially higher during a recession when employment is low, firms have a larger incentive to raise employment. Moreover, if labor demand is flat, shifts in labor supply cause large changes in employment with little change in the real wage.

As a general matter, economic analysis presumes some degree of diminishing marginal product of labor—downward-sloping labor demand. As workers are added to a plant to increase output, they will begin to interfere with one another and to have to wait in line at work stations. Once a plant or office reaches a certain point of crowding, adding more workers will do nothing to add output, and the marginal product of labor will reach zero.

There are three main reasons to believe, however, that for short-run variations in employment most firms are not in a region of diminishing marginal product of labor:

1. *Unused Capacity.* If a firm has idle plants or unused work stations, then new workers can be equipped with the same amount of capital as existing workers, and there is no reason to expect a diminishing marginal product. The evidence suggests that unused capacity is common even when the economy is at potential GDP. Surveys of firms ask them to compare their

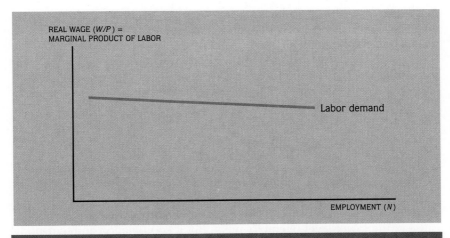

FIGURE 15–2   A flat labor demand schedule

The labor demand schedule shows the marginal product of labor at alternative levels of employment. The economic principle of diminishing marginal product says that the labor demand schedule slopes downward. However, the slope may be quite small, as shown here. With a flat labor demand schedule, the marginal product of labor does not rise very much in a recession, so there is not a large increase in the firm's incentive to hire workers.

actual output with the practical upper limit on output. The surveys show that, on the average, about 83 percent of capacity is in use. Even in very strong periods, capacity utilization rarely exceeds 90 percent. The cyclical behavior of productivity also suggests that there is unused capacity much of the time. Output per worker is high when output and employment are high. Productivity would not be procyclical if there were an important tendency for diminishing marginal product of labor.[4]

2. *Unused Shifts.* Most plants and offices are used only during the day. When demand is unusually high, more workers can be added in the evening or on weekends. Again, there is no crowding of workers relative to facilities, so there is no reason to expect diminishing marginal product.[5]

---

[4]See Robert Hall, "Invariance Properties of Solow's Productivity Residual," in Peter Diamond, ed., *Productivity/Inflation/Unemployment: Essays to Celebrate Bob Solow's Birthday* (Cambridge, Mass.: M.I.T. Press, 1990), pp. 71–112.

[5]See Robert Lucas, "Capacity, Overtime, and Empirical Production Functions," *American Economic Review Papers and Proceedings,* Vol. 60 (May 1970), pp. 23–27, and Thomas Sargent and Neil Wallace, "The Elasticity of Substitution and Cyclical Behavior of Productivity, Wages, and Labor's Share," *American Economic Review Papers and Proceedings,* Vol. 64 (May 1974), pp. 257–263.

3. *Complementarities.* In some situations, higher levels of activity raise productivity. For example, delivery services are more efficient when they are making large volumes of deliveries to customers who are near one another. When their customers are less close or receive fewer packages, the cost of delivering each package rises. Some economists have proposed that complementarities across firms are widespread and are an important reason why the marginal product of labor does not fall when employment rises. The examples of complementarities usually involve transportation and coordination more than the actual physical production of goods. The fact that there are far more workers in those types of activities—handling paperwork and moving goods—than there are workers producing goods supports the importance of complementarities.[6] A different way to put the idea is to consider what happens in a recession. With diminishing marginal produce of labor, workers should become more productive in a recession because of the lower level of employment. But if coordination and transportation costs per unit rise, then the increase in productivity in recession will be offset by the loss of the benefits of the complementarities.

LABOR DEMAND

1. The standard assumption of microeconomics is a downward-sloping labor demand schedule due to the diminishing marginal product of labor. However, the standard analysis does not take account of certain other factors.
2. Firms with unused capacity are less likely to have downward-sloping labor demand. The same holds for firms capable of expanding by adding a new shift at a different time of day. Complementarities across firms may also result in a flat industry or aggregate labor demand schedule.

15.3

MODELS WITH AN EFFECT OF REAL INTEREST RATES ON LABOR SUPPLY

As shown in Figure 15–3, in the real business cycle model, an adverse shock to productivity causes employment and output to fall; the labor de-

---

[6]For an argument that the cyclical movement of productivity is mainly the result of complementarities, see Ricardo Caballero and Richard Lyons, "The Role of External Economies in U.S. Manufacturing," Discussion Paper 431, Department of Economics, Columbia University, May 1989.

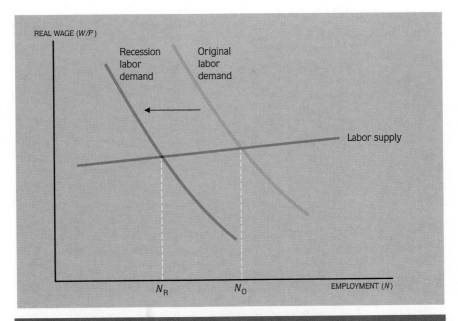

REAL WAGE (*W/P*)

Recession
labor
demand

Original
labor
demand

Labor supply

N$_R$ *N*$_O$ EMPLOYMENT (*N*)

FIGURE 15–3   The real business cycle model

In the real business cycle model, prices are flexible and the level of employment is always at the intersection of labor supply and labor demand. A recession occurs when the labor demand schedule shifts
inward. The inward shift occurs because of an adverse productivity shock. Fairly flat labor supply is an
important part of the model.

mand curve shifts inward and the labor supply curve is fairly flat. With
large enough productivity shocks and flat enough labor supply, the real
business cycle model can generate large changes in employment with little
change in the real wage. As discussed in Chapter 4 and Section 15.1, a
problem with the real business cycle model is whether labor supply is flat
enough.

However, employment fluctuations can also occur through shifts of
labor supply, that is, changes in labor supply due to some factor other than
the real wage. Figure 15–4 shows the basic analysis. If some outside factor
discourages people from working, then the economy will move to the left
as the labor supply schedule shifts. The factor of this kind that has been
featured in flexible-price models is the real interest rate. One source of
shifts of labor supply, then, is a change in the real interest rate. Recall that
we discussed the effects of real interest rates on labor supply during our
analysis of consumption in Chapter 10.

A higher real interest rate stimulates labor supply by making it attractive to work now and consume later. With a high real rate, an hour of work

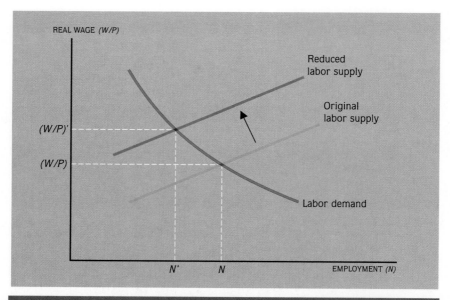

FIGURE 15–4 Decline in labor supply

A fall in the real interest rate shifts labor supply to the left. Employment falls and the real wage rises.

today buys more consumption goods next year than it would with a lower real rate. The effect of the real rate on labor supply is similar to the effect of the real wage; a higher real interest rate improves the trade-off between hours of work and consumption of goods.

For a shift in labor supply to have its largest effect on employment and not have an unrealistically large effect on the real wage, labor demand needs to be flat. The factors we listed in Section 15.2 that are favorable to flat labor demand are helpful to the view that interest-rate effects on labor supply are important in explaining fluctuations. One of the ideas—the use of added shifts to accommodate more workers without diminishing the marginal product of labor—was put forward by two of the leading proponents of flexible-price models, Robert Lucas and Thomas Sargent.

Robert Barro, currently of Harvard University, has emphasized the effects of the real interest rate on labor supply in a flexible-price model. The interest-rate effect on labor supply has some important implications. Suppose that the government purchases more output. In the full-employment model discussed in Chapter 5, output is unaffected by the increase in demand; labor supply and hence output supply are completely inelastic. The interest rate rises to choke back investment and net exports by the full amount of the increase in government purchases. However, when interest rates affect labor supply, the increase in government purchases raises real interest rates and thereby stimulates labor supply. Output rises. Because the real interest rate rises, there is a decline in investment and net exports. But because output rises, government purchases do not come entirely at the expense of investment and net exports. Part of the increase in government use of output comes from the increase in total output.

The addition of the interest-rate effect on labor supply to the flexible-price model makes the flexible-price model give predictions about fiscal policy that are similar to those of the sticky-price model. Tax cuts or spending increases that raise the real interest rate will stimulate output, just as they do in the IS-LM model. Some economists (including Barro) feel that this explanation embodies superior economic logic and still explains the same facts as does the sticky-price model. Other economists (including your authors) question the strength of real interest effect on labor supply and are skeptical of the ability of this theory to make sense out of the ups and downs of the economy.

Note that even with real-interest-rate effects on labor supply monetary events do not affect the level of output or employment. Neither the supply curve nor the demand curve in Figure 15–4 is shifted by a monetary expansion. Figure 5–3 (page 136) continues to describe the effects of monetary changes on the price level, with the understanding that potential GDP depends on government purchases and other determinants of output demand to the extent that they influence labor supply. According to the flexible-price view, the government cannot (and should not try to) influence booms and recessions through monetary policy. Instead, monetary policy should be devoted single-mindedly to objectives related to the price level.

INTEREST RATES AND LABOR SUPPLY

1. The results of the standard full-employment flexible-price model change dramatically when one adds a positive interest-rate effect on labor supply.
2. With these interest-rate effects, an increase in government purchases or some other component of output demand raises the real interest rate, and this raises employment and output.
3. Critics of this explanation of the effects of government purchases question the assumption that labor supply responds significantly to the real interest rate.

15.4   IMPERFECT INFORMATION: THE MISPERCEPTIONS MODEL

The **misperceptions model** is an attempt to come to grips with the influence of monetary policy on employment and output without departing from flexible-price principles. Most other flexible-price models have the property of monetary neutrality; monetary policy affects only the price level in those models. The misperceptions model rests on the idea that workers sometimes think the real interest rate is high when actually it is not. When workers make that mistake, they work harder, because of the effect of the real interest rate on labor supply. Monetary expansion may create misperceptions about the real interest rate. The original research on the misperceptions model was done by Robert Lucas of the University of Chicago.[7] In the model, a monetary expansion raises both output and the price level along an upward-sloping curve. This curve is usually called the **Lucas supply curve.**

The role of information is very important in Lucas's model. As in other flexible-price models, the labor supply decision is key. Workers consider relative prices when they decide how much to work. During times when they think that the return from working is unusually high, workers will supply more labor. When is the return from working unusually high? It is when the wage is high relative to the cost of future consumption, with allowances for the difference in the interest that the worker will earn between working now and consuming later. A boom is a time when perceived relative prices favor large amounts of work, and a recession is a time when perceived relative prices favor activities other than work. Note our emphasis on *relative* prices. When the *general* price level rises, as it does in booms, there is not necessarily any change in relative prices. Hence, labor supply should not be greater than normal. So how do we explain the boom that usually occurs when the general price level rises? To put the question differently, how do we explain that a monetary expansion makes people work harder, even though in the flexible-price model monetary policy does not affect relative prices?

Something must be added to the model to generate the upward-sloping price-output relation that we know is an important characteristic of the U.S. economy and similar economies. The addition is an assumption about

[7]Robert Lucas: "Expectations and the Neutrality of Money," *Journal of Economic Theory,* Vol. 4 (April 1972), pp. 103–124. "Some International Evidence of Output-Inflation Tradeoffs," *American Economic Review,* Vol. 63 (1973), pp. 326–334; and "Understanding Business Cycles," in Karl Brunner and Allan Meltzer, eds., *Stabilization of the Domestic and International Economy,* supplement to the *Journal of Monetary Economics,* 1977, pp. 7–29.

the information available to different workers. This information assumption provides a connection between general price movements and the supply decisions of workers. Lucas refers to the model as being "rigged" by these information assumptions.[8]

In Lucas's model, workers cannot get information about the price level or the interest rate in the economy as a whole. In fact, the only information available to a worker is the current nominal wage. The most important decision facing workers is how much to work now in order to support retirement consumption. The model has no capital; one unit of labor produces one unit of goods. Competition ensures that the price of goods always equals the wage. Hence, the relative price that matters is the real interest rate, the number of units of future consumption that can be achieved by working 1 unit today.

Workers have to try to figure out the real interest rate from their limited information. There are two types of disturbances in Lucas's economy. First, the central bank expands the money stock by a random, unpredictable amount each period. The monetary expansion raises the wage level. Second, there may be unusually good conditions for workers in the local labor market. Again, this will raise the nominal wage. Workers would benefit from knowing which type of disturbance is responsible for a high wage when it occurs. If a monetary expansion is the source of the high wage, there is no reason to work harder. The wage is high now, but the price of goods will be just as high in the future, and there has been no change in relative prices favorable to harder work and more deferred consumption. If the good situation in the labor market is the source of the high wage, then extra work is justified. In the future, the worker will usually be consuming goods whose prices are unaffected by conditions in the local labor market, and the current increase in the wage will bring an increase in the real interest rate.

Under Lucas's assumptions, when the nominal wage rises, workers cannot figure out which disturbance is responsible. Consequently, they cannot make the best labor supply decision—work a normal amount if there is a monetary expansion and work hard if there are good local conditions. Instead, as Lucas shows through a rigorous analysis, workers have to split the difference. When the wage jumps up, workers should increase their work effort, but not by as much as they would if they knew that the wage signaled a true increase in the real interest rate. The increase in work effort occurs whenever the wage rises. In particular, if the only thing that happens is a monetary expansion, work effort rises and the economy is in a boom. Lucas shows that purely monetary events have effects on employment and output in an economy where misperceptions occur.

---

[8]Robert Lucas, "Tobin and Monetarism: A Review Article," *Journal of Economic Literature,* Vol. 19 (1982), pp. 558–567.

We can write a Lucas supply function based on this logic:

$$Y_t = b(P_t - P_{t-1}) + Y^*.$$

Output is its normal or potential level Y^* plus an amount that depends on the increase in the price level over its previous level. The slope of the relationship is controlled by the coefficient b. The coefficient depends on the random environment perceived by workers. If most wage changes in their own markets come from changes in local conditions, then b will be large; workers will be fooled by occasional monetary expansions into working harder, because most of the time a higher wage is a correct signal for harder work. On the other hand, if most wage changes come from monetary expansions, b will be small. Workers will choose to ignore changes in local conditions in order to avoid being fooled into undesirable changes in work effort from purely monetary sources.

As Lucas is the first to admit, the assumptions in his model about information limitations are stark and unrealistic. In particular, workers are likely to have some information about the overall economy beyond the current and lagged wage-price levels. Remember that workers would like to adjust their hours of work to the best available measure of the incentive to work; they would like to purge as much noise as possible that comes from monetary expansions that do not affect relative prices. A more general Lucas supply curve is

$$Y_t = b\,(P_t - P_t^e) + Y^*. \tag{15-1}$$

Here P_t^e is the best inference of the purely monetary effect on the price level based on information available to individual workers. It is usually called the **expected price level** because the information that goes into it becomes available with a lag. The difference $P_t - P_t^e$ is the collective error made by workers as a result of monetary influences. When the difference is positive, workers in general think that conditions are better than usual in their own local markets, when in fact what has really happened is that there has been an unexpected, unperceived general monetary expansion.

Another way to write the Lucas supply curve is to reverse the variables:

$$P_t = \tfrac{1}{b}(Y_t - Y^*) + P_t^e. \tag{15-2}$$

Then we can subtract P_{t-1} from each side to get

$$P_t - P_{t-1} = \tfrac{1}{b}\,(Y_t - Y^*) + P_t^e - P_{t-1} \tag{15-3}$$

or

$$\pi_t = \tfrac{1}{b}(Y_t - Y^*) + \pi_t^e. \tag{15-4}$$

Where we approximate the change in the price level $P_t - P_{t-1}$ by the inflation rate π_t, actual inflation π depends on the difference between actual and potential output $Y_t - Y^*$, and is shifted upward by the amount of expected inflation π_t^e. Lucas's model provides an explanation of the price-adjustment equation we introduced in Chapter 8. We will say more about price adjustment in Chapter 17.

Lucas's supply curve continues to have an important influence on macroeconomic thinking. Robert Barro claimed empirical support for the basic idea of Lucas's model in U.S. data.[9] Barro constructed a measure of unexpected monetary expansions and contractions. He found that his measure was strongly associated with movements in employment and output.

Policy Implications of the Misperceptions Model

Thomas Sargent of Stanford University and the University of Chicago and Neil Wallace of the University of Minnesota pointed out an important policy implication of the misperceptions model.[10] The implication is an application of rational expectations. In fact, it is probably the best-known and most controversial idea to emerge from rational expectations, so much so that some economists virtually equate it with rational expectations.

Recall that monetary policy cannot influence employment and output at all in the full-employment flexible-price model. Using a monetary expansion to try to offset a recession is futile. In the misperceptions variant of the flexible-price model, on the other hand, a sudden burst of money creation by the central bank will stimulate the economy. Does Lucas's analysis support the idea that the Fed should use a deliberate countercyclical policy? The answer is not nearly as obvious as in the full-employment model. But Sargent and Wallace showed that the answer is the same: a systematic countercyclical policy can do nothing to counter fluctuations in the misperceptions model. This famous **monetary policy ineffectiveness theorem** was an important turning point in the development of macroeconomists' thinking about monetary policy.

Prior to Sargent and Wallace's work, almost all economists had taken for granted that countercyclical policy could affect output. The full-employment flexible-price model had few adherents in the 1970s. Even economists such as Milton Friedman, who crusaded against active countercyclical policy, did not dispute its influence on employment in the short run. Friedman's concern was the likelihood that monetary policy was too powerful and would be misused.

---

[9]Robert Barro, "Unanticipated Money Growth and Unemployment in the U.S.," *American Economic Review*, Vol. 67 (March 1977), pp. 101–115.

[10]Thomas Sargent and Neil Wallace, "Rational Expectations, the Optimal Monetary Instrument, and the Optimal Money Supply Rule," *Journal of Political Economy*, Vol. 83 (1975), pp. 241–254.

Sargent and Wallace's starting point was the premise that the central bank has essentially the same information about the economy as workers have. If the Fed uses information—say about the unemployment rate—to make monetary policy, then workers will use the same information to take account of the Fed's policy when forming their expectation P_t^e. The Fed can affect employment only by surprising workers. But it can't surprise workers by expanding the money stock every time unemployment rises, because workers know the unemployment rate. Put differently, workers with rational expectations cannot be surprised by systematic policy. *Policy rules* based on the same information available to workers cannot influence output fluctuations. Even though surprise monetary expansions have an important influence on the employment, systematic expansions based on observed conditions affect only the price level. This astute observation has profoundly influenced economists and has even had an impact on thinking in the government and the Federal Reserve. Coming into the 1990s, the Fed is much more careful to state its objectives in terms of price stability rather than claiming that it can offset fluctuations in employment.

Critique of the Misperceptions Model

The idea that monetary misperceptions are an important driving force in fluctuations receives less attention today than in past decades. First, the main assumption of the model—that the public cannot find out what is happening to the money stock—is not at all realistic. The *Wall Street Journal* publishes detailed information about Federal Reserve activities each week. Armed with this information, nobody should be making the mistakes that form the basis of Lucas's theory. Second, Barro's evidence supporting the theory is now seen as missing the point. Barro interpreted Lucas's idea of misperceptions about money as surprises about money. But it is not at all the same thing to be unaware of something (Lucas's theory) as it is to be surprised by something (Barro's interpretation). It turns out that Barro's evidence shows only that monetary changes precede employment and output fluctuations. It does not show that misperceptions, rather than some other channel of influence, are at work. Third, recent evidence casts doubt on the importance of monetary shocks compared with other types of shocks in macro fluctuations. Monetary variables explain only a tiny fraction of the total variability of real GDP once interest rates are included. The profession has moved to the more general view that a variety of forces—financial shocks, technological shocks, and changes in preferences—are at least as important as monetary developments. The diminishing importance of monetary shocks is partly a reflection of the stability of monetary policy in the United States and other major economies from 1982 to the present.

THE MISPERCEPTIONS MODEL

1. In Lucas's misperceptions/flexible-price model, markets always clear. Workers adjust their employment to the perceived level of the real interest rate.
2. Workers have limited information, which makes them think that the real interest rate rises when there is a monetary expansion, As a result, monetary expansion stimulates output. The Lucas supply curve which summarizes this relationship can also be stated as a price-adjustment equation.
3. Even though monetary surprises can stimulate employment, no systematic policy based on stimulating the economy when employment is low can have any effect in the model. This is the monetary policy ineffectiveness theorem of Sargent and Wallace.

REVIEW AND PRACTICE

Major Points

1. The labor supply schedule shows the marginal value of workers' time, measured by the real wage, at various levels of employment. Empirical evidence suggests that permanent changes in the real wage have little effect on the willingness to supply labor; the long-run labor supply schedule is quite steep.

2. It is possible that short-run labor supply is relatively flat. Temporary increases in the real wage may elicit a large response in labor supply if workers attempt to bunch effort in periods in which the returns are greatest. Alternatively, workers may value nonlabor activities enough that small temporary reductions in the real wage lead to large reductions in the willingness to work.

3. Flat labor supply tends to make real business cycle models more plausible; it would enable large shifts in labor demand to cause large swings in employment with little change in the real wage.

4. The demand for labor shows the marginal product of labor, measured in terms of the real wage, at alternative levels of employment.

5. The presence of fixed inputs and the resulting congestion that occurs as more workers are added to production lead economists to conclude that labor demand slopes downward.

6. The fact that we frequently observe unused capacity suggests that labor demand may be nearly flat. Complementarities that arise in distribution reinforce this tendency.

7. One class of flexible-price models identifies the source of economic fluctuations to be shifts in labor supply that arise due to (perceived) changes in the real interest rate. High real interest rates make current wages worth more goods in the future and thereby stimulate labor supply.

8. Some economists believe that potential GDP is positively related to the real interest rate. In their flexible-price models, fiscal policy can change real GDP by changing the real interest rate.

9. The misperceptions model assumes that workers are unaware of the nature of changes in the nominal wage rate, which may represent relative wage increases or pure inflation. If some probability is attached to each possibility, workers will alter labor supply when the nominal wage changes.

10. In the misperceptions model, unobserved changes in the money supply can affect real output. If workers can rationally anticipate the behavior of the Fed and thus the money supply, then money has no effect on output. This is known as the monetary policy ineffectiveness proposition.

Key Terms and Concepts

long-run labor supply
short-run labor supply
marginal product of labor
interest rates
labor demand
unused capacity

unused shifts
complementarities
flexible-price
  model with
  interest-rate
  effects

misperceptions model
Lucas supply curve
monetary policy
  ineffectiveness

Questions for Discussion and Review

1. Which of the flexible-price theories of fluctuations require flat labor supply in order to generate movements in employment and real wage that are consistent with the typical business cycle?

2. Which of the flexible-price theories require flat labor demand to be consistent with empirical evidence?

3. Are the slopes of labor supply and labor demand of any consequence for sticky-price models? Why or why not?

4. Explain why temporary changes in the real wage affect labor supply much like changes in the real interest rate.

5. What are the main criticisms of the flexible-price models that rely on real-interest-rate effects in labor supply?

6. Do you think persistent large fiscal deficits could permanently boost real output?

7. Which assumption of the misperceptions model is essential to generate a Phillips curve relationship?

8. Suppose the money supply evolves according to policy rule that is known by all firms and households. Would you expect movements in the money stock to have any correlation with output?

Problems

Numerical

1. Suppose the following relationships hold in the economy:

$$
\begin{aligned}
Y^* &= 2{,}000 + 1{,}000R \\
Y^* &= C + I + G + X \\
C &= 80 + .75(Y + T) \\
I &= 400 - 1{,}000R \\
X &= 200 - .1Y - 500R \\
M/P &= .3Y - 2{,}300R
\end{aligned}
$$

The government budget is balanced initially, with purchases equal to lump-sum taxes at 450. The money supply is 500.

   a. Find the equilibrium levels of real output, the real interest rate, consumption investment, net exports, and the price level.

   b. What is the effect on real GDP of an increase in government spending of 50?

   c. What is the effect on real GDP of an increase in government spending and taxes of 50?

2. The labor supply schedule is $100 + 2W/P$. The labor demand schedule is $200 - 8W/P$. Find the levels of the real wage and employment in equilibrium. Now suppose that demand falls, so that the demand schedule is $190 - 8W/P$. By how much does the wage fall? By how much does employment fall? Explain why the wage falls by a larger percentage than does employment.

3. Suppose that the Lucas supply curve is

$$
Y = h(P - P^e) + Y^*,
$$

with $h = 20{,}000$ and $Y^* = 4{,}000$ (billions of dollars). For example, when the price level P is 1.01 and the expected price P^e is 1.0, output Y is 4,200, or 5 percent above potential output $Y^* = 4{,}000$. Suppose that the aggregate demand curve is

$$
Y = 1{,}101 + 1.288\,G + 3.221M/P
$$

   a. Suppose that the economy has been at rest for some period with output at potential and that no changes in policy are expected for the near future. The money supply M is 600 and the government spending G is 750. What is the price level? (Hint: If there are no surprises, the actual and the expected price levels will be the same.)

   b. Now suppose that the Fed announces that it will increase the money supply from 600 to 620. What are the new levels of output and price level?

   c. Now suppose that the Fed announces that it will increase the money supply from 600 to 620 but actually increases it to 670. What are the new levels of output and price level?

4. Suppose that automatic stabilizers cause government purchases to rise when GDP is below potential and to fall when GDP is above potential. Algebraically we might represent this as

$$G = 750 - g(Y - Y^*),$$

where potential output Y^* is 4,000. The coefficient g measures the strength of the automatic stabilizer.

a. Substitute this expression for G in the aggregate demand function in Problem 3, and solve for output Y in terms of P (M is held fixed at 600). This is the aggregate demand curve incorporating the automatic stabilizer. Describe how the slope of the aggregate demand curve depends on the coefficient g.

b. For three different values of g (0, .01, and .1) describe the effect on output of an unanticipated increase in money like the one in Problem 3c. Assume that people know the value of g in each case. Do the effects on output depend on the value of the coefficient g? If so, then does it appear that even well-understood automatic stabilizers are effective in that they influence output? Explain your results intuitively. Why might automatic government spending stabilizers affect output while anticipated changes in money do not? [See B.T. McCallum and J.K. Whitaker, "The Effectiveness of Fiscal Feedback Rules and Automatic Stabilizers under Rational Expectations," *Journal of Monetary Economics*, Vol. 5 (1979), pp. 171–186, for a further discussion of this type of policy problem.]

Analytical

1. Consider an economy in which prices are flexible, but in which supply varies positively with the interest rate. Recall that this may be the case if labor supply shifts to the right with increases in the interest rate. Aggregate demand continues to be described by spending balance and money market equilibrium conditions. The economy is described by the following three equations:

$$
\begin{aligned}
Y &= a_0 - a_1 R & \text{(IS curve)} \\
M/P &= kY - bR & \text{(LM curve)} \\
Y &= c_0 + c_1 R & \text{(Supply with interest rate)}
\end{aligned}
$$

a. Describe how output, interest rates, and the price level are determined in this economy. Depict the situation graphically.

b. Describe the effects of an increase in the money supply on output, interest rates, price level, consumption, investment, and net exports. Does monetary neutrality hold in this model?

c. Describe the effects of an increase in government spending on output, interest rates, the price level, consumption, investment, and net exports.

d. From Part c, is an increase in government spending necessarily inflationary, deflationary, or ambiguous? If it is ambiguous, on what does it depend?

2. If the Lucas supply function is written with output on the right and price surprises on the left, it looks like a Phillips curve. Explain what happens to this Phillips curve when (i) price changes are mostly due to changes in the local conditions and relative prices, and (ii) when price changes are mostly due to changes in the supply of money.

3. Assume that workers know the true model of the economy, which is given by

an aggregate demand curve and a Lucas supply curve. They may or may not, however, know the true value of the money supply.

   a. On the same graph, draw two aggregate demand curves, one for $M = M_0$ and one for $M = M_1 > M_0$.

   b. On the same graph, draw a Lucas supply curve assuming workers believe that $M = M_0$. Explain how you know where to position this graph.

   c. Assume now that M is actually equal to M_1. Depict the equilibrium price level, given the assumption of Part b.

   d. Now assume that workers know that M equals M_1. Again, depict the equilibrium price level. For which equilibrium is the price level higher? Explain your result.

   e. Compare the levels of Y, C, X, and I across the equilibria of Parts c and d.

4. Suppose our model of the economy is given by

$$Y = k_0 + k_1(M/P) \qquad \text{(Aggregate demand)}$$
$$Y = b\,(P - P^e) + Y^* \qquad \text{(Lucas supply)}$$

Assume further that workers have complete information about the model of the economy, including the value of the money supply. Potential output is equal to 4,000. The aggregate demand curve goes through the point (4,000, 1.5).

   a. Consider three possible Lucas supply curves going through the points (4,000, 1), (4,000, 1.5), and (4,000, 2). What is the value of P^e for each of these curves?

   b. Which of the three curves in Part a is the rational expectations Lucas supply curve? In what sense would the other two curves not satisfy rational expectations?

5. In Chapters 8 and 9 we saw that output could deviate from potential in the short run, but that output would always return to potential in the long run after prices had time to adjust. In this chapter we also saw how output could deviate from potential. What defines the "long run" in this model? That is, what must happen in order for output to return to potential? Is this likely to take a very long time?

6. On a graph (3 to 4 inches square) sketch an aggregate demand curve and a Lucas supply curve. Label their intersection point as Y^* and P^*. Now draw two aggregate demand curves, each one 1/4 inch to either side of your initial curve. Label the intersection points with the Lucas supply curve $Y+$, $P+$ and $Y-$, $P-$. Finally, draw two more aggregate demand curves, 3/4 inch or so to either side of the original curve, and label the intersection points as Ys and Ps with ++ and --.

   a. What kinds of shocks can cause the aggregate demand curve to vary in the way shown on your graph? What is the relationship between the magnitude of those shocks and the variability in Y and P?

   b. Suppose initially that shocks to the money supply cause the aggregate demand curve to vary within the narrow region. Assume that the Lucas supply curve shown in your graph is the appropriate curve given the magnitude of these shocks. In what sense is the curve "appropriate"?

   c. Now suppose that shocks to the money supply cause the aggregate demand curve to vary within the wider region. How will the new Lucas supply curve appropriate to these shocks compare with your initial Lucas supply curve?

Sketch the new curve. How do the swings in output and price level compare with $P--$, $P++$ and $Y--$, $Y++$?

d. Use these results to explain why output may not deviate much from potential in periods of either highly stable or highly variable prices, but that it may deviate considerably from potential in the transition period from stable to variable prices. Relate your analysis to the experience of the U.S. economy in the late 1960s.

7. Suppose that the misperceptions model were an accurate description of the economy. How could you rationalize the fact that workers and firms enter into long-term nominal contracts in such a world? What sort of behavior by the Fed would be required in order for nominal contracting to be a reasonable practice?

MacroSolve Exercises

1. Plot the real interest rate and employment from 1950 to 1990. Are the comovements in data consistent with real interest rates stimulating labor supply?

2. Plot the same data for 1978 to 1990. Does the same pattern exist?

CHAPTER

16

The Firm and the Labor Market with Price and Wage Rigidities

We studied flexible-price models including the real business cycle model in Chapters 4 and 5, and we considered the inner workings of those flexible-price models in Chapter 15. Our attention to flexible-price models reflects the belief among a substantial number of economists that standard economic models with flexible prices are a good way to think about macro fluctuations.

Still, many macroeconomists find that sticky prices and wages are features of the economy that should appear in a realistic macroeconomic model. The high levels of unemployment present during recessions raise questions about flexible-price models. The historical correlations between inflation and the business cycle are difficult to explain without wage and price rigidities. In this chapter we will study reasons why wages and prices may not always be perfectly flexible. We also consider some basic microeconomic problems that arise in sticky-wage and sticky-price analysis.

Research is active at the beginning of the 1990s on new kinds of flexible-price models as well as new kinds of sticky-price models. This research may overcome some of the problems with both of these models. For many economists, the jury is still out on the verdict of which type of model is most appropriate.

16.1   REAL WAGE AND PRICE RIGIDITY

We begin our discussion of wage and price rigidities by focusing on *relative* prices and *real* wages as in the first part of Chapter 15. We then go on to nominal price issues analogous to the Lucas misperceptions model.

The conclusions reached in the last chapter are important for theories based on real wage and price rigidities. As we noted there, a gap between actual employment and the intersection between supply and demand makes much more microeconomic sense in a market with flat labor demand and flat labor supply. Before considering some additional aspects of that analysis, we will discuss one more reason for flat labor supply. We did not include it in Chapter 15 because it is not part of the standard microeconomic analysis of labor supply. The reason—called **real wage rigidity**— has been studied by macroeconomists in order to understand what happens in labor markets in booms and recessions.

The basic idea behind real wage rigidity is that arrangements in the labor market make the real wage paid by employers remain high even when the actual value of workers' time has declined in a recession. Under this hypothesis, there are unemployed workers who would willingly work at or below the current real wage but who cannot find jobs. Figure 16–1 illustrates the real wage-rigidity view. There is a horizontal line at the rigid real wage. Firms can choose whatever level of employment they want as long as they pay the wage. Firms see the rigid-wage line as the labor supply schedule, even if the perfectly flat line does not reflect the actual preferences of workers. Because the actual value of workers' time rises with employment, the rigid real wage understates the value of time in booms and overstates the value of time in recessions.

Why would firms be constrained to pay a predetermined real wage, when the value of workers' time rises in booms and drops in recessions? The answers to this question are highly controversial. A number of economists accept real wage rigidity as a reasonably accurate statement about how the world works, without finding themselves convinced by any single explanation. The most convincing answer to date, however, is that employment arrangements have to deal with many issues besides national fluctuations. In particular, the sales of each firm fluctuate widely even when the national economy is stable. Real wage rigidity is a desirable way to deal with employment adjustments when demand changes for just one firm and conditions remain normal in the labor market in general. If the wage is set at the level of earnings that workers could expect to find at other firms, then workers should move away from a particular firm that has suffered a decline in demand. Their economic contribution will be greater if they

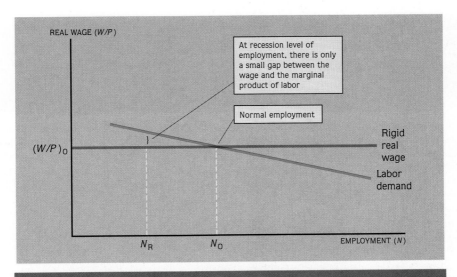

FIGURE 16–1 The real wage-rigidity view

Initially, employment is at N_0 and the real wage is $(W/P)_0$. In a recession, employment falls to N_R. Because the real wage employers are required to pay workers remains at $(W/P)_0$, there is only a small incentive to restore employment to N_0. That incentive is the vertical distance between the labor demand schedule (the marginal product of labor) and the horizontal rigid-wage line.

leave the firm with low demand and join a firm with normal demand. A simple way for this to come about is for workers to be laid off. The employer makes the layoff decision because the employer knows about the decline in demand. If the firm lays workers off whenever the marginal product of labor at the firm drops below a given fixed wage (equal to the wage paid elsewhere in the economy), the allocation of labor will be economically efficient. There is a strong economic case for real wage rigidity under these conditions.[1]

Because the wage that should be rigid for one firm is equal to the actual wage in the rest of the economy, wages should be responsive to overall conditions in the economy. Wages in one firm are rigid and unresponsive to developments at that firm, but, in principle, are responsive to what is happening in the rest of the economy. But that is asking a great deal of wage policy. It appears that the importance of making the wage unresponsive to the firm's situation is the dominant influence. Firms pay wages that hardly respond to any determinants in the short run. Hence the assumption of real wage rigidity makes sense.

[1]See Robert E. Hall and Edward P. Lazear, "The Excess Sensitivity of Quits and Layoffs to Demand," *Journal of Labor Economics*, Vol. 2 (April 1982), pp. 233–257.

NEW RESEARCH IN PRACTICE
Why Does the Employer Choose the Level of Employment? Why Does the Customer Choose the Quantity Sold?

One of the most important ideas in the literature on price and wage rigidity is that the customer chooses the quantity. In the employment setting, the employer chooses the level of employment, given the wage. For products, the customer—either another business or the final consumer—chooses the quantity given the price. This fact about daily economic life seems so obvious as not to require analysis. But building a theory to explain such an obvious fact has had some payoffs in the development of the economic analysis of labor and output markets.

In a perfectly competitive auction market, there is no asymmetry in the determination of quantity. The supplier—worker or firm—consults the market price and decides how much to deliver to the market. The demander consults the market price and decides how much to take from the market. The market price fluctuates to make the choices consistent. The two sides have equal roles in determining quantity.

The asymmetric determination of quantity arises in cases, like the labor market, where buyers and sellers deal with each other as individuals. The two sides need to have a contract, or at least an understanding, that determines how the quantity of work or product will be determined. Analysis of these explicit or implicit contracts has had an important role in a number of branches of economic theory.

The Labor Contract

Both explicit and implicit contracts or understandings between workers and employers generally have the following character: There is a wage rate set in advance; often the wage rises over time according to a predetermined path or according to a fixed relation to the cost of living. The employer decides how much work will be done. When demand is strong, everybody works at least full time and may work overtime as well (at a premium wage). When demand is weak, hours are shorter and some

or all workers may be on layoff, meaning that they have kept their jobs but are not actually working.

One could imagine alternative arrangements. In particular, suppose that management had the right to reduce wages when demand was weak. The problem is that only management knows the actual state of demand. If management had the right to change wages unilaterally, it would be tempted to offer a high wage to attract workers and then, after the workers were settled into their jobs, cut their wages on the excuse that demand had fallen. To the extent that workers are locked into their jobs by having moved to live near the plant, by having cut off relations with other prospective employers, and by having invested in the particular skills need by this employer, they are the potential victims of this kind of opportunism.

Because workers don't know the actual level of demand facing their employers, they will reject any employment arrangement that employers can exploit by making false claims that demand has fallen. But employers need to be able to respond flexibly to changes in demand. The answer is simply to let employers choose the level of employment but to pay for that employment according to a prescribed wage schedule. The schedule may specify things like the overtime premium and supplemental unemployment pay as well as the wage itself.

If the only uncertainty in the employment relationship is the demand facing the employer, and the wage schedule traces out the actual labor supply schedule of workers, then the contract that lets the employer choose the level of employment acts just like the market. The employer will choose the level of employment that equates the marginal revenue product of labor to the wage, which also equals the marginal value of workers' time.

In the real world, neither of these conditions holds precisely. But the prevalence of employment arrangements where the employer decides on the level of employment unilaterally suggests that this arrangement is the most workable one.

The Product Contract

Final consumers face the same situation for some of their product purchases as employers do in the labor market. For example, your relation with your electric company has the same features; your demand for electricity depends on factors only you know about, but the electric company has to make a substantial investment to serve you. If you had the power to choose the price, you would set a lower price after you were hooked up than you seemed to promise when you arranged for service. An agreement in advance on the price of electricity not just this year, but for many years in advance, is needed to make the relationship function well. Here, the economy tends to depend on regulation. A regulatory board sets the price you will pay, and you rely on their ability to keep the price at a reasonable level in the future.

Most markets for final consumption do not have this character. Instead, you have a free choice about where to buy groceries, gasoline, and most other products. Hence there is not much general application of the principle that the buyer sets the quantity subject to a prior arrangement on price. Rather, prices are set by the principles of the open market.

For transactions among businesses, however, the situation is much more like the labor market. A retailer of Whirlpool washing machines needs to be able to rely on prescribed terms under which it gets its machines at wholesale. Here again, the explicit or implicit arrangement is the same as in the labor market: the retailer chooses the quantity given a prescribed price or price schedule from the manufacturer. In some business-to-business transactions, such as those between a coal mine and a steel maker, the issue is so centrally important that contracts lasting 20 years or more are written. These contracts give the steel maker the power to choose the amount of coal subject to very carefully drafted provisions for setting the price of coal.

In the labor market and in business-to-business transactions, the employer or the purchaser often has the right to choose the quantity. Economic research has been successful in showing why: the practice arises from the information that the employer or purchaser has about the usefulness of the labor or product being bought.

An important principle for the sticky real wage hypothesis is the following: A firm with a flat labor demand, facing a flat labor supply curve or rigid-wage line, is almost indifferent to alternative levels of output and employment. Figure 16–2 shows why profit is almost the same over a range of levels of employment. The gap between demand and supply is the amount of profit a firm could earn by adding one more worker. The gap measures the slope of profit (on the vertical axis) against employment (on the horizontal axis), as in the bottom part of Figure 16–2. Flat supply and demand schedules imply that little profit is at stake when the firm decides to raise employment to the exact intersection of supply and demand (the very top of the profit curve) from a point below the intersection.

Price Determination

Next we look at reasons for unresponsive prices. Microeconomic theory instructs us that the firm maximizes its profit when its marginal revenue MR equals its marginal cost MC:

$$MR = MC. \qquad (16\text{--}1)$$

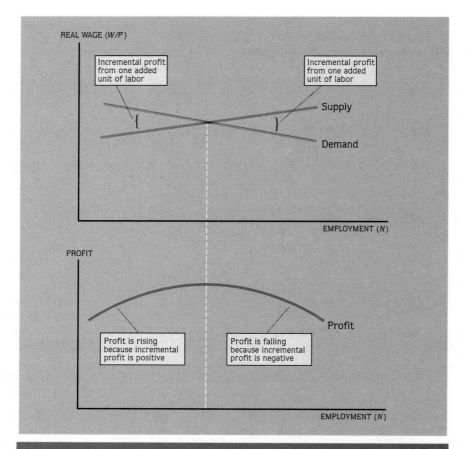

FIGURE 16–2   When labor supply and labor demand are nearly flat, profit is insensitive to employment

Profit rises when the demand curve for labor (the marginal product of labor) is above the supply curve (the marginal cost of labor to the firm). Profit falls when supply is above demand. Profit is perfectly flat when demand and supply are equal. If both supply and demand curves are flat, incremental profit will be small and the profit curve will be extremely flat. Firms are almost indifferent among levels of employment not too far from the intersection.

Let s be the slope of the demand schedule; $s = 0$ for the flat demand curve facing a firm under competition and s is positive for a firm with market power able to influence price by changing quantity. Another important fact from the microeconomic theory of the firm is that marginal revenue depends on price and on the slope of the demand curve:

$$MR = P - sQ. \tag{16–2}$$

Here Q is the quantity sold. A competitive firm, with $s = 0$, has marginal revenue equal to price. If a firm has market power, with s greater than zero, then marginal revenue is less than price; one additional unit of output reduces the price on all the units sold (sQ), as well as selling for the price P.

Yet another idea from the microeconomic theory of the firm is that it is convenient to talk about marginal revenue in terms of the elasticity of demand e. The elasticity is defined by

$$e = \frac{P}{Q} \frac{1}{s}. \tag{16-3}$$

The elasticity is infinite for a competitive firm; the lower the elasticity, the greater is the market power of the firm. Equation 16–3 allows us to express sQ in terms of the price and the elasticity of demand. We can eliminate sQ from Equation 16–2 and simplify to get

$$MR = P \left(1 - \frac{1}{e} \right)$$
$$= \frac{e-1}{e} P. \tag{16-4}$$

When the firm maximizes profit, it sets marginal revenue equal to marginal cost:

$$\frac{e-1}{e} P = MC. \tag{16-5}$$

We can solve for the price given marginal cost:

$$P = \frac{e}{e-1} MC. \tag{16-6}$$

Price is a multiple of marginal cost. The multiple, $e/(e-1)$, is at least 1. It is called the **markup ratio.** Under competition, where e is infinity, the markup ratio is 1; price equals marginal cost. A firm with market power has a markup ratio greater than 1. The less elastic is demand, the higher is the markup ratio.

From Equation 16–6, we can see that there are two factors that determine the response of the price to a rise in demand. The first is that the elasticity of demand e may change at the same time that the demand curve is shifting to the right. Although we can think of special circumstances where elasticity might change in this way, there is no reason to believe it happens very often. The second reason for a price response is that marginal cost can rise with output.

Marginal cost can rise with output because of the diminishing marginal product of labor that results from crowding more workers onto the same facilities. Marginal cost rises with output precisely to the same extent that the marginal product of labor declines with employment. Marginal cost will be flat under the same conditions that the labor demand curve is flat. We already discussed these conditions and the evidence about flatness of labor demand in Section 2 of Chapter 15. The various considerations listed there point toward flat labor demand and flat marginal cost.

Another determinant of the slope of marginal cost is how much the wage changes when a firm hires more labor. The issue here is the slope of labor supply. If it takes a wage premium to get people to work harder or to attract more workers, then marginal cost will rise to the extent of that premium. If labor supply is very flat, so the firm can get as much extra work as it wants at essentially the same wage, then marginal cost will tend not to rise when output rises. Overall, we reach a simple conclusion: *The firm's marginal cost schedule is flat if the firm has a flat labor demand curve and if the firm faces a flat labor supply curve.*

Looking back at Equation 16–6, we can see that nothing much happens to the firm's price when demand changes. The change in demand probably does not change the elasticity of demand nor does it change marginal cost. Marginal cost changes only when the wage changes. The ratio of the price to the wage is a constant, unaffected by the level of demand.

Direct observation of many markets supports the hypothesis that output can vary widely without appreciable movement in the price-cost markup ratio. For example, consider what happened to steel prices and demand from the mid-1950s to the mid-1970s. Figure 16–3 shows that steel demand seems to have little effect on price compared to cost.

The steel industry is not exceptional in having prices that are stable relative to costs in the face of wide fluctuations in demand. The same is true of most manufactured goods and services. On the other hand, many raw materials, especially agricultural products, have prices that fluctuate a great deal in response to changes in demand.

Figure 16–4 shows the *ratio* of the average wage W to the price level P for the U.S. economy over the last 25 years. Recall that this ratio is just the real wage. If prices were determined just by costs for the economy as a whole, then this ratio would be stable over business cycles. On the other hand, if demand were important in pricing decisions, then the ratio would fall when demand was strong as prices would be bid up relative to wage costs. As is evident in Figure 16–4, there is no tendency for the real wage to fall during booms or to rise during slumps. There is a general upward movement in the real wage due to increases in labor productivity, but there is no noticeable cyclical movement that might be related to demand. If anything, the real wage appeared to fall during the most recent recessions.

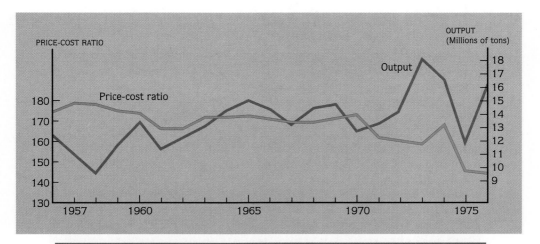

FIGURE 16–3   Output and the price-cost ratio in the steel industry

Steel is a cyclical industry and output has varied sharply, mainly due to shifts in the demand schedule for steel. The ratio of the price of steel to an index of costs of production remained quite constant over the period except for the last few years. The price did not move up and down the marginal cost schedule of the steel industry.
Source: Robert W. Crandall, *The U.S. Steel Industry in Recurrent Crisis: Policy Options in a Competitive World* (Washington, D.C.: The Brookings Institution, 1981), Appendix A.

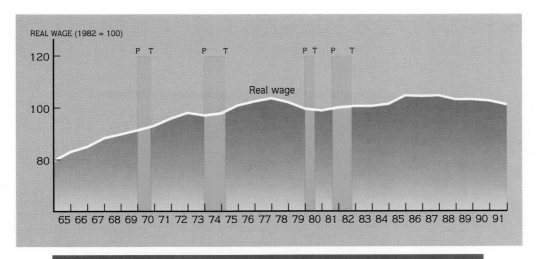

FIGURE 16–4   The real wage during recessions and booms

The diagram shows real wage, in particular, average hourly compensation for all private nonfarm employees in the United States divided by the price level. Recessions are marked on the diagram. The real wage is very stable during recessions and booms. There is no tendency for the real wage to increase during recessions. If anything, the real wage appears to fall slightly, but the fixed markup equation appears to be a good approximation.
Source: *Economic Report of the President,* 1992, Table B–44.

One of the important implications of the stable relationship between prices and costs is that a jump in costs very quickly results in a jump in prices. We can express this algebraically as

$$\pi = \text{Wage-cost contribution} + Z, \qquad (16\text{--}7)$$

where π is the rate of inflation (rate of growth of prices from one year to the next) and Z is the change in an index of costs of production other than wage costs.

EMPLOYMENT AND REAL WAGES

1. Real wage rigidity is a plausible arrangement when demand disturbances are sector specific rather than economywide.
2. If labor supply and labor demand are relatively flat, then profit is insensitive to the level of employment. Consequently, firms may have weak incentives to choose precisely the level of employment that generates the most profit.
3. The same conditions that make profit insensitive to employment also tend to make marginal cost flat. If marginal cost is flat and the elasticity of demand does not change much, price is insensitive to the level of output.
4. Much empirical evidence suggests that price-cost margins are stable in relation to the level of output.

16.2   NOMINAL WAGE AND PRICE RIGIDITY

So far, our discussion in this and the previous chapter has dealt with relative prices and real quantities, not nominal prices or the money stock. The only exception was Lucas's misperceptions model, where the money stock influenced output through information limitations. Now we will consider the possibility that *nominal* prices are rigid because of limited incentives. The consequence is a theory of real effects of monetary policy that tries to explain the same association of booms and monetary expansions that Lucas's model tackles. We already laid out the theory in Chapters 6 to 8, without giving much of an explanation for the key assumption of rigid dollar prices.

Firms' prices are sticky and they are set in dollars. The result is to make the Fed's policy on the volume of dollars outstanding a tremendously important one for output and employment. We could imagine a world where prices were sticky, but not in nominal terms. For example, firms could set their prices relative to the price of some standard commodity. Instead of setting the price of a six-pack of Coke at $2.50, Coca-Cola bottlers could set the price at the level of 6 pounds of sugar. Someone buying a six-pack would have to find out how much a pound of sugar currently costs in order to know how much they would have to pay. Under the hypothetical sugar reference point for prices, there would be rigidity in the relative prices of goods compared with sugar, but not in their dollar prices. Sugar policy would be an important determinant of overall economic activity, whereas monetary policy would have little impact on output and employment. It is important for macroeconomists to explain why price rigidity takes the particular form of setting prices rigidly in dollars rather than rigidly in sugar or some other relative price.

Not every economy follows the price-setting conventions that are familiar in the United States. In countries with histories of extreme inflation, prices are sometimes set in terms other than those countries' monetary units. For example, in Chile, there is a unit called the *Unidad de Fomento* or UF. Chile also has a standard monetary unit called the peso. The peso has suffered a great deal of inflation in the past and still continues to have declining purchasing power. The UF has a constant purchasing power, as defined by the cost-of-living index. The number of pesos making up a UF gradually rises in order to keep the UF's purchasing power constant. For example, if the UF is 200 pesos in one month, and the peso price level rises by 1 percent the next month, the new UF is worth 202 pesos. Many prices and values are quoted in UFs rather than in pesos, including rents for apartments and balances in savings accounts. Macroeconomic analysis for Chile cannot make the same type of sticky-price assumptions that are appropriate for the United States. Other countries have found other alternatives to their own monetary units for quoting prices. One of the most common is to use the U.S. dollar. In countries where this "dollarization" has reached an advanced stage, domestic monetary policy has less impact and U.S. monetary policy is correspondingly more important.

In the United States and other countries that have avoided extreme inflation, prices are almost invariably set in terms of the country's own currency unit, not in commodity units, units like the UF, or in another country's currency unit. For this reason, the assumption that prices are sticky in terms of the nominal currency unit makes sense in the U.S. economy and in similar economies.

Studies of nominal stickiness have found enormous variations in the length of time over which prices remain the same in nominal terms. Stickiness tends to be most extreme in cases where there are significant hardware costs for change in the price; pay telephone calls cost a dime for decades before jumping to 25¢. Magazine prices remain the same for several years and then jump up by 25¢.[2] A study by Dennis Carlton of the University of Chicago showed that businesses tend to keep the same price for a given customer for a year or more even when they have set new prices for new customers.[3]

Prices printed in catalogs, on price sheets, and on menus can be sticky simply because it is costly to print new versions with new prices. These **menu costs** are a possible contributor to overall price stickiness, though it is not known what fraction of total transactions occur under this type of pricing.[4]

Not every price is sticky. Many agricultural and industrial commodities trade in open markets where prices change every few seconds. In addition, many prices paid in transactions between businesses are linked to these open-market prices. Among businesses, and, to a lesser extent, between businesses and consumers, many prices are set on the spot by negotiations. There is no reason to expect stickiness of negotiated prices. However, if the retailer pays a sticky price at wholesale, stickiness will be passed on at retail. Even though you negotiate a price for a car from a dealer, the result of that negotiation will be sticky if the car manufacturer sets a dollar price in advance that the dealer pays at wholesale.

Sticky Nominal Wages

We have already discussed why real wages may be predetermined and not vary as employment changes. Our discussion dealt exclusively with relative prices; our diagram, Figure 16–1, has a relative price, the real wage, on the vertical axis. But one of the most important principles of sticky wage-price macroeconomics, dating back to Keynes, is that *the wage bargain is made in money terms*. Wages are not set in pounds of sugar, UFs, or foreign currency units. Even though the importance of the fact that wages are set in dollars has been evident to macroeconomists for over 50 years, the reasons for nominal wage stickiness are still imperfectly understood and controversial. Many economists feel that we should simply accept the fact that wages

---

[2]Stephen G. Cechetti, "The Frequency of Price Adjustment," *Journal of Econometrics*, Vol. 20 (April 1986), pp. 255–274.

[3]Dennis Carlton, "The Rigidity of Prices," *American Economic Review*, Vol. 76 (September 1986), pp. 637–658.

[4]N. Gregory Mankiw, "Small Menu Costs and Large Business Cycles: A Macroeconomic Model of Monopoly," *Quarterly Journal of Economics*, Vol. 100 (May 1985), pp. 529–539.

are predetermined in money terms and build it into our macro models. In the next section we will discuss more of the institutional detail about how wages are set in the U.S. labor market. All the details support the basic idea of nominal wage stickiness.

We explained the logic of predetermined wages earlier in this section. The logic is not specific about how this predetermination is to take place; it certainly did not dictate that wages be predetermined in dollars. Efficient labor market arrangements would make the cost of labor to one firm approximate the wage elsewhere in the labor market. In that case, the wage should be predetermined to be some kind of average or index of wages in the labor market as a whole. As we will see in the next section, many wage-setting institutions do link wages at one firm to the general level of wages. But it is difficult to measure wages in general and complicated to update wages at one firm based on whatever measures are available. Keeping wages on a predetermined nominal track between occasional rebargaining seems to be a workable approximation of the goal of setting wages at one firm in line with wages elsewhere in the economy. And many of the reasons we have discussed earlier for the use of the currency unit rather than other units of purchasing power in the case of price setting apply equally to wage setting.

The Relation of Wage Stickiness to Price Stickiness

Equation 16–6 shows that prices tend to be a fixed markup over marginal cost. Marginal cost depends on the wage and on the prices of inputs the firm buys. If the wage and input prices are sticky in nominal terms, then the firm's price will be sticky in nominal terms as well. This conclusion holds even if the firm carefully sets its price and output at exactly the optimum. And this leads to an important conclusion: *Prices can be sticky in nominal terms because firms have limited incentives to set their prices at the exact optimum and they find it convenient to stay with existing prices. A second, independent cause of sticky nominal prices is that wages are sticky in nominal terms, and this makes prices sticky even if firms price at the exact optimum.*

Research has not succeeded in determining which source of nominal price rigidity is the more important. For pay telephone calls, magazines, and many other goods and services, straight price rigidity is probably the most important factor. For basic industrial goods sold by businesses to one another, price rigidity probably derives mainly from wage rigidity. And, of course, for some products (such as precious metals or commodities) price rigidity is not a significant factor at all.

NOMINAL PRICE AND WAGE RIGIDITY

1. "Price rigidity" is a general term that refers to the apparent insensitivity of prices to shifts in demand or other market factors.
2. The exact nature of price rigidity depends on the economic environment. In the United States and in other countries with relatively low inflation, prices tend to be rigid in terms of the domestic currency unit. In inflation-prone economies, prices are rigid in terms of some other unit that has stable purchasing power.
3. Nominal price rigidity can arise in a number of ways. If profits are insensitive to price, then firms have little incentive to change their prices when conditions change. If wages are sticky in nominal terms, prices will be rigid because costs are rigid.

16.3 HOW WAGES ARE SET IN THE U.S. ECONOMY

The most comprehensive information about wage determination in the United States pertains to the formal contracts of workers who are members of large labor unions. We will consider this group of workers first and then go on to discuss the nonunion sector.

Wage Determination in the Large Union Sector

Of the 20 percent of U.S. workers who are unionized, about half are involved in collective-bargaining situations that are regularly tracked by the Bureau of Labor Statistics. In total, this group consists of about 10 million workers. Although only 10 percent of the labor force, this group receives enormous attention in the media and in public policy discussions. The unions that make up this group almost personify big labor, and the industries they negotiate with, big business. They include the steel, trucking, automobile, aerospace, airline, tobacco, aluminum, coal, rubber, and electrical industries. Some economists, such as John Dunlop of Harvard and Lester Thurow of M.I.T., have argued that this group establishes wage patterns that other union and nonunion workers imitate, although recent empirical studies on the subject indicate that the evidence is mixed.[5]

In most of these industries, contracts last 3 years. Unless there is an early reopening or a delay in negotiating a new contract, the workers signing 3-year contracts will do so every 3 years. For example, the electrical workers negotiated contracts in 1976, 1979, 1982, and so on. About 80 percent of the workers under major collective-bargaining agreements are under 3-year contracts, 15 percent are under 2-year contracts, and only 5 percent are under 1-year contracts.

Not all workers sign contracts at the same time. Contracts are unsynchronized. Wage negotiations are staggered over the 36 months of the basic contract cycle. At any one time, only a small fraction of the workers are signing contracts; the remaining workers either have recently signed their contracts or will sign their contracts in the future. The period in which one contract is in force overlaps the period in which other contracts are in force.

An example will be helpful to illustrate the characteristics of a typical long-term contract. The United Mine Workers signed a contract with the bituminous coal operators in May 1981. The contract affected about 160,000 workers, lasted 40 months, and expired in September 1984. The contract stipulated wage increases that averaged 11 percent per year. The wage increases were $1.20 per hour in the first year, $1.10 in the second year, $1.00 in the third year, and $.30 in the last quarter. This pattern is illustrated in Figure 16–5. These contracted wage increases were made through September 1984. A new contract was negotiated and signed on October 1, 1984.

Part of the wage increase in the 1981–84 agreement was deferred to the second and third years of the contract. These deferred increases indicate that management and labor had expectations of continued high inflation. It would have been possible to **index** the contract to inflation. In an indexed contract, wages automatically increase if there is inflation. But there were no indexing provisions in the coal contract; these increases would—and did—occur regardless of economic conditions and indicate the extent of the nominal rigidity that such contracts impose on the economy. The contract signed in 1984 called for much smaller wage increases (about 3 percent per year), and it was not indexed either. The 1984 contract expired in January 1988 (another 40-month contract). During the 1984–87 period much smaller nominal wage increases were locked in by contracts like this.

Thus far we have seen that most workers in large labor unions change their contracts about once every 3 years. What are the factors that

[5]See Daniel J. B. Mitchell, *Union Wages and Inflation* (Washington D.C.: Brookings Institution, 1980), p. 171, or Richard B. Freeman and James L. Medoff, *What Do Unions Do?* (New York: Basic Books, 1984), Chapter 3.

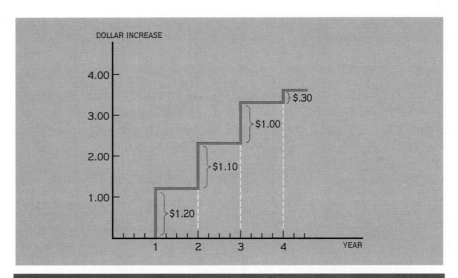

FIGURE 16–5   Current and deferred wage increases in the 1981–84 coal contract

The largest percentage increase occurred in the first year, but a significant part of the increase was deferred to the second and third years. An inflation rate of about 11 percent was built in to the contract; there was no indexing. The 1984–87 coal contract that followed had a much smaller inflation rate built in to the contract.

determine the size of the wage adjustment when it does occur? Wage and salary decisions are made in collective-bargaining meetings for which both management and labor leaders spend extensive time preparing. While the outcome of any one bargaining situation cannot be predicted with much certainty, a number of factors clearly influence the outcome in particular directions.

The first and perhaps most important is the state of the labor market. If unemployment is high, then labor will be in a relatively weak bargaining position. Conversely, if unemployment is low, then workers will be able to bargain for larger wage increases. The threat of a strike is more credible in good times than in bad. Moreover, firms are likely to settle for larger wage increases in tight market conditions, because they will be better able to pass on their costs in the form of higher prices.

A second factor influencing wage bargaining is the wage paid to comparable workers in other industries. Because not all contract negotiations are synchronized, there are two components of this comparison wage: the wage settlements of workers who have recently signed contracts, and the expected wage settlements of workers who will be signing their contracts in the near future. Looking back at the wage settlements in recently signed contracts makes sense in a current negotiation because those settlements will be in force during part of the contract period under consideration. This backward-looking behavior tends to give some built-in inertia to the wage-determination process. If one union group gets a big increase, then the next group of workers in the wage-determination cycle will also tend to get a big increase. Lester Thurow describes the process as follows: "Suppose that this year the machinists' union is negotiating a new three year contract. Last year the auto workers negotiated a three-year contract for a 10% rise per year. No leader of the machinists can settle for less than 10% and still remain in office. And in two years' time the auto leader will be similarly imprisoned by what the machinists negotiate today."[6] But looking forward to future settlements also makes sense, because the current contract will be in force when these changes take place. In other words, wage determination generally combines elements of forward-looking and backward-looking behavior.[7]

A third factor that will influence wage decisions is the expected rate of inflation. If inflation is expected to be high, then workers will ask for larger wage increases and management will be willing to pay them because their own prices are expected to rise. As with the effect of comparable wage increases, the effect of expected inflation will have both a backward-looking element and a forward-looking element.

Wage Determination in the Nonunion Sector

It is very common for workers who are not in unions to receive wage and salary adjustments once each year. Although there is no formal contract involved, it is unlikely that this wage decision will be changed before the next scheduled adjustment period. Hence, the nominal wage rigidity is very similar to that in the union contracts. One difference is that the entire wage adjustment usually occurs at one time rather than part being deferred as in the second and third years of the large union contracts. This is probably due to the shorter time between wage adjustments.

For example, our university adjusts our salaries once each year. We get a letter from the dean in July giving our salary for the 12-month period beginning September 1. This nominal wage rate is rarely changed before the next salary-adjustment period the following year. This type of annual wage setting is common in many sectors of the economy.

In preparation for a wage adjustment, the management of nonunion firms must obtain information very similar to that obtained by the manage-

[6]Lester Thurow, "Thurow's Third Way," *The Economist*, January 23–29, 1982.
[7]The implication of staggered wage setting combined with rational expectations of future wage, price, and unemployment is discussed in more detail in John B. Taylor, "Staggered Wage Setting in a Macro Model," *American Economic Review*, Vol. 69 (May 1979), pp. 108–113.

ment of unionized firms preparing for a collective-bargaining meeting. In a large nonunion firm there are usually specialists called wage and salary administrators who must make a wage decision. They obtain information about the current labor market situation. They conduct wage surveys or subscribe to a wage survey performed by an outside group. They also attempt to forecast the rate of inflation.

Although the wage decision will usually be made under more competitive conditions than exist in a collective-bargaining situation, the same factors—the state of the labor market and wage and price inflation—will influence the final outcome in similar directions. If unemployment is very low and is expected to remain low for the next year, then management will try to pay a relatively high wage compared with other firms employing similarly skilled workers. An attractive wage will prevent workers from quitting and help to lure workers from other firms if necessary for expansion. On the other hand, if unemployment is high, there will be less of a worry that workers will quit to look for jobs elsewhere. Moreover, if the year is expected to be bad for sales, an expansion of production requiring more workers would be unlikely.

If wages are expected to be relatively high at other firms—either because of recent wage decisions of these firms or because of expected wage increases at other firms—then the wage will necessarily be higher. Information about both recent wage decisions and intended wage decisions in the near future can be obtained from wage surveys.[8]

Although there is little direct evidence on when most nonunion firms have their scheduled wage increases, it is unlikely that they all occur at the same time. Hence, there is a type of nonsynchronization that we observe for the union sector. Figure 16–6 illustrates the simple situation where there are four wage-adjustment periods through the year: January 1, April 1, July 1, and October 1. It is clear from this illustration that staggered wage setting gives rise to an overlapping of wage decisions.

Why Are Wages Set for Long Periods with Few Contingencies?

We have just seen that unionized workers generally have their wages predetermined in 3-year contracts. Only a fraction of these contracts are contingent on the cost of living, and none, to our knowledge, is contingent on

---

[8]Recently some formal theories have been developed to explain this relative wage setting. See Janet Yellen, "Efficiency Wage Models of Unemployment," *American Economic Review*, Vol. 74 (May 1984), pp. 200–205. Or see Lawrence F. Katz, "Efficiency Wage Theories: A Partial Evaluation," in S. Fischer, ed., *Macroeconomics Annual*, Vol. 1 (National Bureau of Economic Research, 1986), pp. 235–289. The term "efficiency wage" theory is used for these explanations because paying a wage close to the going wage for similar work is usually supposed to increase efficiency by reducing turnover or by making the workers feel better.

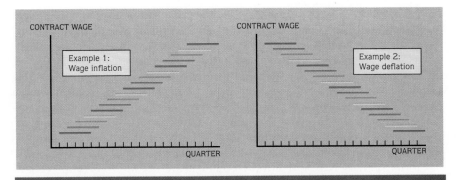

FIGURE 16–6 Staggered annual wage setting with four wage-adjustment periods throughout the year

There are four groups of workers in each example. The contract wage of each worker group is denoted by a different color shade from very dark to very light. Because wages are not all set at the same time (that is, they are not synchronized), the contract wage of one group overlaps that of all the other groups. This is shown in the diagram as flat contract wage lines on top or below each other. In the left panel, there is a general inflation: Each group attempts to get above the previous group. In the right panel, there is a general deflation: Each group tries to get below the previous group.

any other economic variable. Furthermore, wage setting in nonunion firms seems to operate in much the same way, though wages are reconsidered annually instead of every 3 years.

ADJUSTMENT COSTS.   The costs of adjusting wages and salaries may be high. Consider the situation where wage rates are determined in collective-bargaining negotiations between large corporations and labor unions. In preparation for these negotiations management spends months surveying wages in other industries, estimating changes in labor productivity, forecasting changes in the firm's own profits, and obtaining estimates of the general inflation during the upcoming contract period. To be adequately informed during the collective-bargaining sessions, labor leaders must be equally and independently prepared; hence, they must also spend months preparing for negotiations. Moreover, there is a threat of a strike in almost every collective-bargaining situation. An actual strike is obviously costly for both sides, but the mere preparation for a possible strike is also costly. The firm must accumulate and finance additional inventories to be used if a strike occurs. Hence, production will be abnormally high before negotiations and abnormally low after negotiations as firms draw down inventories when a strike does not occur. These swings in production raise average costs to the firm. Given these high costs, it is understandable that many collective-bargaining negotiations occur only once every 3 years.

INDEXING.   Why aren't the contracts that are negotiated contingent on events that may occur before the next renewal? We have noted that some of the contracts in recent years have included cost-of-living adjustments whereby the wage is indexed to the consumer price level. However, these clauses rarely involve 100 percent protection from cost-of-living changes, and many contracts (about 60 percent) do not have any such clauses. Moreover, cost-of-living clauses represent only one of many possible contingency clauses. For example, the contracts could be directly linked to the unemployment rate, GDP, or more local measures of the performance of the economy and the value of workers' time.

The primary reason that more contracts are not indexed to the cost of living is that such indexing can be harmful if there are import price or technology shocks. Suppose that the marginal productivity of labor is reduced because of a shift in the production function. Recalling the flexible-price model of Chapter 4, we know that such a shift will eventually require a reduction of the real wage; that is, W/P must decline so that it is equal to the marginal productivity of labor. But a 100 percent indexed contract will prevent such a decline. The escalator clause will call for an increase in W in the same proportion as the increase in P. Hence, W/P remains constant and too high. It is understandable that many firms and workers are reluctant to institute an arrangement that rules out any adjustments in the real wage if prices should rise suddenly during the contract period. Of course, if the reason for the increase in prices is a general monetary-induced inflation, then there will be no need for a reduction in the real wage. Unfortunately there is usually no way to tell in advance whether the price rise is due to monetary effects or to shifts in the production process.

Why not index wages to unemployment, GDP, or other indexes that might indicate whether the shocks are to money or to productivity? Part of an answer is similar to the reason we gave for caution in indexing to the cost of living. For instance, some of the shifts in overall unemployment are not relevant for the productivity of a particular group of workers. When a special event, not a recession, makes unemployment zoom for auto workers, the unemployment rate may not reveal much about the jobs available to computer workers.

A final reason that contracts do not have many indexing clauses is that they add complexity. There are good reasons to have a straightforward contract that the rank and file can easily understand and vote on. Similarly, contingency clauses appear to add uncertainty about the wage that the workers will actually get. Many workers would object to this added uncertainty, even though the economic theorist may argue that the uncertainty makes the worker better off.

Although we have focused on labor union contracts, the same arguments pertain to the more informal wage-setting procedures used by firms employing nonunion workers. A review of each worker's performance is costly, and obtaining survey information about wages paid elsewhere and forecasts of inflation requires time and expense. To make such an adjustment more than once a year is probably prohibitive for many firms. The arguments stated above against extensive contingency clauses also apply to this type of wage setting. Moreover, indexing would do little to improve the workings of annual wage-setting arrangements; waiting less than a year to make an adjustment after the fact is usually adequate.

Why Is Wage Setting Staggered?

In a decentralized economy like that of the United States, firms and workers decide by themselves when their wages and salaries are adjusted. The fact that these decisions are not synchronized therefore seems natural; one would be surprised to see a coordinated wage (or price) adjustment without some centralized orchestration of such a move. Historical accident would be enough to explain why the auto workers always negotiate just before the machinists.

It is important to know, however, whether the lack of synchronization in the United States serves any microeconomic purpose. If it does not, then proposals for reforming the economic system to bring about more synchronization would be innocuous for microeconomic welfare but could have some macroeconomic advantages.

Imagine what would happen if all wages and prices were set at the same time and without a central planner to tell workers and firms what to do. A firm that thought that a relative wage increase was appropriate for its workers would have a difficult time knowing what other wages would be in order to achieve that relative increase. A wage survey would tell only about current wages in other firms, not the direction in which they were heading.

Staggered wage setting provides information to firms and workers about wages and prices elsewhere. Even though other wages will be adjusted before the current contract expires, there will be some period of time when the desired relative wage is in force. Nonsynchronized wage and price setting thus seems desirable in a decentralized economy.[9]

Moreover, staggered wage setting adds some stability to wages. Without staggering, all wages and prices would be up for grabs each period; there would be no base for setting each wage. Tremendous variability would be introduced into the price system.

---

[9]See Gary Fethke and Andrew Policano, "Will Wage Setters Ever Stagger Decisions?" *Quarterly Journal of Economics*, Vol. 101 (November 1986), for further discussion of the rationale for nonsynchronized wage setting.

The situation is different in some other countries, especially in those where the government plays an active role in wage setting. For instance, a significant number of wage decisions are synchronized in Japan, where each spring there is a *shunto* or simultaneous wage adjustment for the large companies. However, the government is actively involved in the *shunto*. Prior to the *shunto*, extensive deliberations take place to determine the appropriate wage adjustment for that year, and the government is a player in the deliberations. Some economists feel that such a system would be desirable for the United States.

TEMPORARY WAGE RIGIDITY

1. Union wage contracts in the United States last as long as 3 years. The contracts are not synchronized with one another. There is some indexing to inflation, but it is less than 100 percent and appears in only about half the contracts.
2. Nonunion workers typically have wage adjustments about once per year. These adjustments are staggered over time, much as the union contracts. Since the wage is rarely changed within the year, this wage-setting process creates rigidities much as formal contracts do.
3. Wages are set for long periods because collective bargaining, threats of strikes, or simply careful reviews of worker performance make adjusting the wage costly. Wages are rarely indexed in the U.S. because supply shocks as well as demand shocks occur. With indexing, the real wage does not adjust enough after supply shocks. Moreover, extensive contingency clauses add complexity and apparent uncertainty to wage contracts.

16.4   A SIMPLE MODEL OF STAGGERED WAGE SETTING

A simple stylized algebraic model of staggered wage setting and price determination brings together most of the facts about wage and price setting discussed in this chapter and illustrates their macroeconomic implications in a simple way. Wage setting is nonsynchronized, prices are given by a markup over costs, and expectations are rational.

Suppose that all wage contracts last 2 years, that all wage adjustments occur at the beginning of each year, and that there is no indexing. Half the

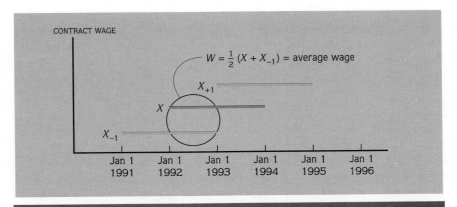

FIGURE 16–7 Configuration of wage setting in the simple model

There are two groups of workers in the economy. One group has a wage adjustment January 1 of the even years and the other group has a wage adjustment January 1 of the odd years. The average wage W is shown to be equal to the average of this period's contract wage X and last period's contract wage X_{-1}. In the picture the average wage for 1992 is shown. It is the average of the contract wage set in 1991 and the contract wage set in 1992.

workers sign contracts at the start of even-numbered years and half at the start of odd-numbered years. This configuration of assumptions is shown in Figure 16–7, where X represents the contract wage and W the average wage. Since we need to distinguish between past and future variables, let the subscript "–1" represent the *previous* year and let the subscript "+1" represent the *next* year. Of course, events in the next year are not known; people must form expectations of them. The average is given by

$$W = \frac{1}{2}(X + X_{-1}). \tag{16–8}$$

In words, the wage W this year is the simple average of the contract wage signed last year X_{-1}, which is still outstanding, and the contract wage signed this year X. For example, suppose that the contract wage is 10 in 1991 and 8 in 1992. Then the average wage is 9 in 1992 (the wage of 8 set in 1991 is still outstanding in 1992).

An algebraic relationship that describes how the contract wage is set each period might be given by

$$X = \underbrace{\frac{1}{2}(W + W_{+1})}_{\substack{\text{Effect of expected} \\ \text{average wage}}} - \underbrace{\frac{c}{2}[(U - U^*) + (U_{+1} - U^*)]}_{\substack{\text{Effect of current and future} \\ \text{unemployment}}}, \tag{16–9}$$

where U is the unemployment rate, U^* is the natural rate of unemployment, and c is a coefficient describing the response of wages to unemployment.

Equation 16–9 leads to an interesting observation. Rewrite Equation 16–9 with W and W_{+1} replaced by the expressions in Equation 16–8. That is,

$$X = \frac{1}{2}[\underbrace{\frac{1}{2}(X + X_{-1})}_{\substack{W \text{ from Equation} \\ 16-8}} + \underbrace{\frac{1}{2}(X_{+1} + X)}_{\substack{W_{+1} \text{ from Equation} \\ 16-8}}] - \frac{c}{2}[(U - U^*) + (U_{+1} - U^*)]. \qquad (16\text{–}10)$$

Now gather together the X terms (without the subscripts) and put them on the left-hand side of the equation. After some cancellation (you can work it out in the margin), we get the simpler expression:

$$X = \frac{1}{2}(\underbrace{X_{-1}}_{} + \underbrace{X_{+1}}_{}) - c[(U - U^*) + \underbrace{(U_{+1}}_{} - U^*)]. \qquad (16\text{–}11)$$

Backward-looking   Forward-looking   Expected future unemployment
component   component   is also a factor

Equation 16–11 shows how wage determination has a backward-looking component X_{-1} and a forward-looking component X_{+1}. The backward-looking component, which we discussed in words above, is what makes inflation persist from year to year. Workers base their wage decisions partly on what previous wage decisions were. The forward-looking component, also discussed previously in words, is what makes expectations of the future so important. Expectations of moderate wage settlements next year will tend to moderate wage settlements this year. For example, if wage settlements next year are expected to be 10 percent lower, then, according to Equation 16–11, actual settlements this year will be 5 percent lower. The coefficient on X_{+1} is $1/2$.

Equation 16–11 also shows how expected future unemployment conditions next year can affect wage settlements this year. If the unemployment rate is expected to rise next year by 2 percent, then wage settlements this year will be 2 times c percent lower. For example, if c equals .5, then wage settlements this year will be 1 percent lower. The expectation of a slump in the future with its accompanying increase in unemployment has a simple effect: It decreases wage inflation today.

With prices given by a constant markup over costs, all these effects on wages will be passed through to prices. The policy implications are therefore clear. Expectations of a monetary policy that is noninflationary in the future and that will let unemployment rise if necessary in the future, should inflation rise, will have favorable effects on inflation today. These favorable effects on inflation can actually work with little or no adverse effects on unemployment. The expectation of a credible stance against inflation in the future should therefore have a favorable effect on the trade-off between inflation and unemployment.

Consider, finally, the operations of the model in a steady inflation. Say the contract wage X increases by the same amount each year. For example, let the amount of increase be 10. In a steady inflation the *change* in the contract wage this year, $X - X_{-1}$, and the change in the contract wage next year, $X_{+1} - X$, will be the same, namely 10. Equation 16–11 can then be written as

$$\underbrace{\frac{1}{2}(X - X_{-1})}_{5} = \underbrace{\frac{1}{2}(X_{+1} - X)}_{5} - \underbrace{c\,[(U - U^*) + (U_{+1} - U^*)]}_{0}. \quad (16\text{–}12)$$

Notice that there is a $10/2 = 5$ on the left-hand side and a $10/2 = 5$ on the right-hand side. The two cancel out. The term involving unemployment must equal zero. This implies that $U = U^*$ and that $U_{+1} = U^*$. In other words, the unemployment rate is always equal to the natural rate. The same result holds, of course, for any steady change in prices, not just 10. Regardless of the rate of inflation, as long as it is steady and anticipated, there is no trade-off between inflation and unemployment in the long run.

The simple model consisting of Equations 16–8, 16–9, and 16–10 can be viewed as an alternative, more microeconomic-based representation of the price-adjustment equation that we introduced in Chapter 8, Equation 8–2. As such, it can be combined with a model of aggregate demand that tells how the money supply and government spending shift demand when prices are predetermined. Simulating such a model requires a large computer and sophisticated computer programs. Fortunately, most of the results can be conveyed in a more intuitive and less complex way by introducing some simple approximations to capture the essence of forward-looking and rational expectations behavior. We turn to this in the next chapter.

STAGGERED WAGE CONTRACTS

1. Wage determination will have backward-looking and forward-looking elements when contract negotiations are staggered over time.
2. The backward-looking component reflects the influence of last year's contracts on this year's prices. This influence of the past on the present gives inflation persistence.
3. The forward-looking component reflects the impact of next year's contracts on this year's prices. This influence of the future on the present makes expectations about policy important. The more accommodative policy has been to price shocks in the past, the more inflation may be expected in the future.

16.5   POLICY IMPLICATIONS

Two important policy implications can be drawn from the theoretical and factual background of this chapter. The first concerns the problem of *disinflation*, that is, bringing the rate of inflation down from a level that is thought to be too high. The second concerns the *effectiveness of monetary policy when expectations are rational.*

Disinflation and the Real Effects of Monetary Policy

These issues are best understood by first considering an extreme case. In Section 16.3 we mentioned the May 1981 coal contract which called for annual wage increases of approximately 11 percent for 3 years. Suppose, for illustrative purposes, that *all* workers in the U.S. economy sign the same 11 percent 3-year wage contract, but starting May 1994. All wages in the economy would be locked into 11 percent increases for 3 years. According to Equation 16–7, the markup pricing equation, prices would also be locked into 11 percent increases for 3 years. General inflation would be 11 percent. If real GDP were at potential and growing at 3 percent per year, then we know from our study of long-run growth in the flexible-price model in Chapter 5 that the money stock would be increasing by 14 percent per year. With no shifts in the demand for money, real GDP growth plus inflation equals money growth.

With this economic situation in mind, imagine now that in June 1994 the chairman of the Federal Reserve Board decides that inflation is too high and at the June meeting of the Federal Open Market Committee (FOMC) proposes to end inflation—to disinflate—by cutting money growth from 14 to 3 percent. The FOMC goes along and instructs the open-market desk in New York to sell government securities at a sufficient rate to reduce reserve growth and hence money growth from 14 to 3 percent *immediately.*

The results of this hypothetical policy action should now be clear. With an 11 percent inflation built into the economy, the only possibility is that real GDP growth is reduced substantially, probably to a negative rate. (The amount of the reduction depends on the slope of the aggregate demand schedule.) The economy is thrown into a deep recession. As sales begin to fall, firms lay off workers and unemployment rises. Unless contracts are reopened, the recession will last 3 years—until the scheduled end of the labor contracts. Only then might we expect an end to the inflationary wage increases, a subsequent decline in inflation, and eventually an economic recovery as the 3 percent money growth permits 3 percent real GDP growth with zero inflation.

The fact that monetary policy can affect real output and employment, even if expectations are rational, is also demonstrated by this example. Everyone in the economy could be perfectly aware of the new policy action by the Fed. But as long as everyone is locked into contracts, the contractionary effect occurs. Note also that the Fed could have brought about a boom starting in June 1994 by increasing the rate of monetary expansion from 14 percent to some higher number. Policy that is anticipated in advance can have an effect with rational expectations, as long as knowledge of the policy change comes after the contracts are set.

In such a situation, a sharp decline in money growth is certainly costly. A far better approach would be for the Fed to *announce* its disinflation plans before the contracts are set. For example, in April 1994 the Fed could announce that it will reduce money growth from 14 to 3 percent in May 1994 when the labor contracts expire. This would give management and labor the chance to adjust their new contracts to incorporate the new anti-inflationary monetary policy; if the policy announcement were credible—this is a big if—then the recession could be entirely avoided. Disinflation without recession would be a reality.

Of course, we already know that the actual U.S. economy is not like the hypothetical economy in this extreme example. Contract signing is not synchronized in the major union sector and most nonunion workers are employed under wage-setting arrangements in which the wage is set for 1 year. Hence, a sharp decline in money growth would begin to have some immediate effect on inflation as those workers signing new contracts see the rise in unemployment. Again, it would be better to announce the program in advance so that newly negotiated contracts could take account of the lower anticipated rate of inflation.

But the decline in inflation will be more gradual than the sharp 11 percent decline in money growth because only a small fraction of wages could be adjusted at first. A gradual decline in the rate of money growth would be better in that it would permit a gradual decline in inflation consistent with the configuration of contracts in the economy. An announced gradual reduction in money growth would be the least costly way to reduce inflation. Rather than an immediate reduction of 11 percent, recent studies suggest a reduction of about 1 percent in the first year, 2 percent in the second year, 6 percent in the third year, and 2 percent in the fourth year.[10] If such a policy could be announced in advance and be believed, it would minimize the harmful side effects of a monetary disinflation. The alternative paths for a monetary disinflation are illustrated in Figure 16–8 for the hypothetical 1994–98 example.

The important role of contracts during a disinflation is recognized by economists of differing persuasions. Arthur Okun, who was happy to be

[10]See John B. Taylor, "Union Wage Settlements during a Disinflation," *American Economic Review*, Vol. 73 (December 1983), pp. 981–993.

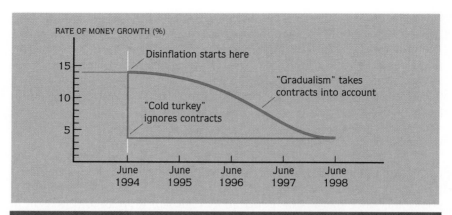

FIGURE 16–8   Alternative disinflation paths for the money supply

The least costly policy is one that is gradual and announced. The largest deceleration should occur near the third year because of the 3-year contracts that expire at that time. Suppose that inflation has risen to 14 percent by mid-1994. The Fed wants to reduce it. An immediate short reduction in money growth—"cold turkey"—would probably cause a big recession like that in the early 1980s.

identified as a Keynesian, emphasized contracts in much of his writings.[11] In their best-selling book *Free to Choose*, Milton Friedman and Rose Friedman argued:

> The most important device for mitigating the side effects is to slow inflation *gradually but steadily* by a policy announced in advance and adhered to so it becomes credible. The reason for the gradualness and advance announcement is to give people time to readjust their arrangements—and to induce them to do so. Many people have entered into long-term contracts . . . on the basis of anticipations about the likely rate of inflation. These long-term contracts make it difficult to reduce inflation rapidly and mean that trying to do so will impose heavy costs on many people. Given time these contracts will be completed or renewed or renegotiated, and can then be adjusted to the new situation.[12]

What about reforming the wage-determination process in the United States so that contracts are shorter and more synchronized? If all contracts were 1 year in length and synchronized, then the above example indicates that it would be possible to have a sharper reduction in inflation in a shorter period of time. But it would still be important to announce the policy in advance and to make it as credible as possible. The disadvantages of

[11]A comprehensive discussion of Okun's view is found in *Prices and Quantities: A Macroeconomic Analysis* (Washington, D.C.: Brookings Institution, 1980).
[12]Milton Friedman and Rose Friedman, *Free to Choose* (Avon Books, 1980), p. 273.

such a change would be the increased negotiating costs and the likely increased volatility of relative wages and prices, as we discussed above.

Another reform that has been suggested by Milton Friedman and others would be to induce the private sector to use more wage indexing. This would in effect make changes more flexible because they could adjust before the contract expires. The problem with indexing, as we have already pointed out, is that it prevents real wage adjustments when these are needed because of changes in labor productivity.[13]

16.6 SUMMARY AND APPRAISAL

Macroeconomists have been active in the past decade in trying to understand how the decisions made by individual firms and workers influence macroeconomic events. They have also studied the institutional arrangements—such as labor contracts—that have evolved to guide employment and wage determination. These investigations have generally supported an idea, discussed in this chapter, that Keynes introduced to macroeconomics: Wages tend to be set a year or more in advance in dollar terms. Employers choose the level of employment subject to paying workers a predetermined wage. Some prices may have their own inertia in nominal terms. Many prices are set as markups over labor costs, so wage stickiness leads to downstream price stickiness. As a result, a model in which prices are sticky in the short run is realistic and appropriate for studying fluctuations.

In the wage-price rigidity model, the level of employment departs from the intersection of supply and demand during recessions or booms. When a negative shock hits the economy, output and employment fall below their potential values. In response to the incentives pointing toward restoration of equilibrium, workers gradually accept lower wages and firms set lower prices. The economy moves along the aggregate demand curve until GDP reaches potential. This process takes several years.

Because the wage-price rigidity model says that the level of employment can differ from the intersection of labor supply and labor demand in the short run, the model departs from regular microeconomic principles. For this reason, some macroeconomists remain unconvinced or skeptical of

[13]Stanley Fischer, "Wage Indexation and Macroeconomic Stability," in Karl Brunner and Allan Meltzer, eds., *Stabilization of the Domestic and International Economy*, Carnegie-Rochester Conference Series in Public Policy (New York: North-Holland, 1977), pp. 107–148, and Jo Anna Gray, "Wage Indexation: A Macroeconomic Approach," *Journal of Monetary Economics*, Vol. 2 (1976), pp. 221–236, have explored these effects of indexing on macroeconomic fluctuations.

the theories.[14] The most important dividing issue among macroeconomists is the influence of monetary policy on output and employment. Under the assumption of flexible prices and wages, it has proven impossible so far to create a convincing model where monetary policy has much effect on output and employment. Yet, every day, the *Wall Street Journal* tells us how important the Fed's next step is for the economic outlook. In flexible-price models, the Fed does not have any important influence over employment and output.

The ideas discussed in this chapter help make the sticky-price view more acceptable to economists who depart only reluctantly from the principles of flexible prices and wages. When labor demand and labor supply are both quite flat, the incentive to restore employment to the intersection of the two schedules is weaker than when one or both are steep. The transmission of wage stickiness to price stickiness is also more direct under these conditions. However, the root idea of wage-price rigidity—that some prices and many wages are predetermined in dollar terms—is by no means firmly established and universally accepted. We expect to see much more published on this subject in the next decade.

REVIEW AND PRACTICE

Major Points

1. The wage-rigidity model accepts the possibility that the levels of employment and the real wage in the short run may differ from the levels consistent with the intersection of labor demand and labor supply.

2. This hypothesis is more easily justified when labor demand and labor supply are relatively flat. Under those circumstances, the benefits to the firm of moving to potential employment are small.

3. The same conditions that make profit insensitive to employment also tend to make profit insensitive to price.

4. The situation in which prices are infrequently adjusted is known as nominal price rigidity. In inflation-prone countries, price rigidity may exist with respect to a unit with stable purchasing power.

5. Nominal price rigidity may result from nominal wage rigidity. Much empirical

---

[14]See, for example, Robert E. Lucas, Jr., "Methods and Problems in Business Cycle Research," in Robert E. Lucas, Jr., ed., *Studies in Business Cycle Theory* (Cambridge, Mass.: M.I.T. Press, 1981), pp. 271–296, or Robert E. Lucas, Jr., and Thomas Sargent, "After Keynesian Economics," in Robert E. Lucas, Jr., and Thomas J. Sargent, eds., *Rational Expectations and Economic Practice* (Minneapolis: University of Minnesota Press, 1981), pp. 295–319.

evidence suggests that price-cost margins are quite stable over time. This observation supports the belief that nominal wage rigidity explains a good deal of observed price rigidity.

6. Most detailed information about wage setting in the United States comes from the large labor union sector. About 20 percent of all workers in the United States belong to labor unions. About 80 percent of the contracts signed by large unions last 3 years.

7. Workers who are not in a labor union typically have their wages adjusted about once each year. The size of the wage adjustment is influenced by expectations of inflation, expectations of the wages paid to other workers, and the level of unemployment.

8. Wage setting is staggered. Not all workers obtain wage adjustments at the same time. This staggering adds to the inertia of wage rigidities.

9. Wage and price rigidities arising from overlapping contracts and other sources make the process of disinflation slow and painful.

10. A specific model of wage adjustment with overlapping contracts confirms that an unvarying unemployment rate is consistent with any chronic rate of inflation.

Key Terms and Concepts

real wage rigidity	long-term concepts	policy effectiveness
flat profit function	unionization	with rational
flat marginal cost	bargaining costs	expectations
markup pricing	indexation	long-run trade-off
nominal price rigidity	staggered contracts	between inflation
Unidad de Fomento	relative wage setting	and unemployment
menu costs	disinflation	credibility
nominal wage rigidity		gradualism

Questions for Discussion and Review

1. Explain why real wage rigidity may be efficient if most disturbances are relative shifts in demand at the firm level rather than economywide shifts in aggregate demand.

2. What conditions tend to make profit insensitive to employment? To price?

3. Under what conditions will nominal price rigidity exist?

4. What kinds of rigidities exist in high-inflation countries?

5. What factors contribute to nominal price rigidity in the United States?

6. Describe the typical long-term union wage contract in the United States. What is indexing? Are many contracts indexed? Why?

7. What is staggered wage setting? Why does it occur?

8. Describe the typical wage adjustment for workers who are not in unions. Are these wage-setting dates staggered? Why aren't wages adjusted more frequently?

9. Explain how markup pricing might be the result of information limitations at firms concerning what is going on in the economy.

10. Is monetary policy effective when expectations are rational? Why? Do any wages adjust when expectations of future monetary policy change?

11. When disinflating, is it better to be gradual or to be quick in reducing money growth?

12. What are the forward-looking and the backward-looking components of wage determination? What is their significance?

13. Why is there no long-run trade-off between inflation and unemployment, even though there is a short-run trade-off?

14. What good does it do for the Fed to maintain its own credibility about its promise not to tolerate inflation in the future?

Problems

Numerical

1. A worker has a contract with an employer. The worker will work as many hours as the employer chooses and will be paid $10 for each hour. The marginal product of the worker is $25 - .125H$ dollars per hour when the worker is working H hours. The marginal value of the worker's time is $.5H - 50$ dollars per hour when he is working H hours. How many hours will the employer ask the worker to work? Is this the efficient level? What if the marginal product schedule is $30 - .125H$? How can you measure the inefficiency of this amount of work?

2. Using tight monetary policy, the Fed is able to bring about a deceleration of prices, so that inflation falls from 10 percent to zero. The time path of the price level is as follows:

Year	Price Level
1	1.000
2	1.100
3	1.188
4	1.259
5	1.310
6 and later	1.336

There are two groups of workers, those whose wages are set in odd years and those whose wages are set in even years. When the wage is set, it is equal to 10 times the price level in the preceding year, raised by the amount of inflation that occurred in that year relative to the year before; that is, $W = 10P_{-1}(1 + \pi_{-1})$ and $\pi = (P - P_{-1})/P_{-1}$. In the second year of the contract, the wage is increased in proportion to the inflation that occurred in the first year relative to the year before; that is, $W_{+1} = W(1 + \pi)$. Compute the wages paid to the two groups and the average wage across the two groups starting in Year 2. Compute the rate of wage inflation and the real wage. Comment on the problems that disinflation creates when there are lags in wage setting, using the numbers from this example.

3. A firm enjoys a monopoly; its average revenue schedule is $15 - .25Y$ and its marginal revenue schedule is $15 - .5Y$ (Y is its amount of output). Its marginal cost schedule is $(Z + W)(.3 + .01Y)$. Z and W are the price of materials and the wage rate, respectively. For $Z = 2$ and $W = 8$, find the price and amount of output that maximize the monopolist's profit. Now suppose that the intercept in marginal and average revenues rises from 15 to 21 because demand rises. Find the price and level of output. Compare these with the case of markup pricing, where $P = (Z + W)m$ and the markup m exceeds 1 and does not change when demand rises. Now go back to the original average revenue and marginal revenue schedules and compute price and output when Z rises to 3. Again, compare these with the case of markup pricing. Conclude by comparing the general nature of markup and monopoly pricing, using your calculations as examples.

Analytical

1. Suppose that initially the economy is in equilibrium with unemployment equal to the natural rate and inflation equal to 10 percent. The Fed would like to reduce inflation down to 0. Listed below are several different descriptions of the way in which wages and prices are set. For each of them, indicate a desirable strategy for disinflating, and explain in each case the short-run consequences of such a strategy.
   a. Wages and prices are perfectly flexible, as in the long-run growth model of Chapters 4 and 5.
   b. Wages are governed by 3-year contracts, while firms use markup pricing. All wage contracts in the economy are renegotiated at the same time.
   c. Wages and prices are set as in Part b except that wage contracts are staggered. One-third are renegotiated each year.
   d. Wages are set annually. They are a function of the prior year's wage, the prior year's inflation rate, and the prior year's unemployment rate. Prices are set as a markup over cost.

2. Discuss the relationship between Lucas's misperceptions model and the overlapping-contracts model in terms of correlation between output and the price level.

3. In an economy in which the monetary authority fully accommodated shocks that increased the price level, how do you think the wage-setting process might be affected? In particular, what might happen to the length of contracts and the extent of indexation to price level changes? Would this type of change in the behavior of the money supply and its resulting impact on wage setting increase or decrease the ability of monetary policy to influence output? What about the ability to reduce inflation?

4. Suppose that the government encouraged unions to moderate their wage increases in exchange for a promise of tax cuts if inflation should exceed wage increases. Such a proposal was actually made by the Carter administration in the late 1970s. Explain why such a policy might be useful in an economy with staggered wage setting and markup pricing.

5. In what way does an economy in which prices are determined by the condition that marginal revenue equal marginal cost respond differently to an aggregate

demand shock than an economy in which prices are set as a markup over cost? Does it matter how wages are set in the latter case? How does each type of economy respond to a price shock?

6. Suppose that wage contracts last for 3 years. Each year, one-third of the economy's wage contracts are renegotiated. Contract wages are set according to

$$X = \frac{1}{3}(W + W_{+1} + W_{+2}) - \frac{c}{3}[(U - U^*) + (U_{+1} - U^*) + (U_{+2} - U^*)].$$

a. Provide an expression for the average wage rate W.
b. Derive an expression analogous to Equation 16–11. How far backward- and forward-looking is the wage-determination process? What determines the responsiveness of contract wages to *current* labor market conditions?

7. In this chapter we developed a model in which contract wages change in response to *current and expected future* conditions in the labor market. How does such a model provide the underpinnings for our price-adjustment equation of Chapter 8, where prices respond to output *with a lag?*

8. Evaluate the following statement: Synchronized wage contracts offer the best prospect for "cold turkey" disinflation. But they also provide the Fed with the greatest temptation to cheat. Moreover, if the Fed loses credibility, disinflation with synchronized contracts can be very painful. Therefore, it is probably better that contracts are staggered.

9. If expectations are rational, monetary policy has no effect on output, and disinflation without recession is possible. Is this statement true or false? Explain your answer calling on both models with the Lucas supply function and models with wage contracts and sticky prices.

MacroSolve Exercises

1. Compare real GDP growth and money growth. Do the two series move closely together? Does one appear to lead the other?

2. Compare inflation and money growth. Do the two series move together? Does one appear to lead the other?

3. Do your answers to Questions 1 and 2 provide any basis for choosing between sticky-price and flexible-price models?

Aggregate Dynamics and Price Adjustment

In this chapter we develop a model of price adjustment that brings together the theories of price-wage rigidities and rational expectations. It thus responds to the important issues raised in the previous chapter, yet it is simple enough that we can incorporate it in our complete model of the economy. In fact, the algebra and graphs that we use to analyze the price-adjustment model are very similar to those that we used to study the price-adjustment relationships in Chapter 8. Here, however, we examine *changes in the coefficients* of the model of price adjustment and of expected inflation that occur when macro policy or the economic environment changes. We also examine with more practical examples the *dynamic response of inflation and output to disturbances* that was presented in Chapter 9. Finally, we study *empirical tests of the model* using the actual macroeconomic data of the United States, Germany, and the United Kingdom.

 17.1 THE WAGE-PRICE PROCESS AS A WHOLE

In Chapter 8 we introduced the *expectations-augmented Phillips curve* as our basic model of price adjustment: According to the Phillips curve, inflation rises when demand conditions are tight, when expectations of inflation rise, or when there are price shocks. The Phillips curve can be written

$$\pi = f\underbrace{\left(\frac{Y_{-1} - Y^*}{Y^*} \right)}_{\substack{\text{Market conditions} \\ \text{(slack or tight)}}} + \underbrace{\pi^e}_{\substack{\text{Expectations} \\ \text{of inflation}}} + \underbrace{Z.}_{\text{Price shocks}} \qquad (17\text{--}1)$$

$$\underbrace{\hspace{5cm}}_{\text{Determinants of wage inflation}}$$

The last term (Z), representing price shocks, was not made explicit in the discussion of Chapter 8; it represents the upward shift in the price-wage relationship that we discussed in Chapter 16.

One of the most important properties of Equation 17–1 is that there is no long-run trade-off between inflation and the level of GDP. A country with a high average inflation rate that is generally expected to continue will not have any higher output than a country with a low inflation rate that is generally expected to continue. This is easily seen from Equation 17–1: On average, the effect of price shocks will be zero ($Z = 0$), and expected inflation π^e will equal actual inflation π in the long run regardless of the level of actual inflation. Hence, according to Equation 17–1, the market conditions term ($Y_{-1} - Y^*)/Y^*$ equals zero, or, equivalently, actual output equals potential output. As we saw in Chapter 8, the proposition that there is no long-run trade-off between output and inflation is sometimes called the *natural rate property* because the unemployment rate is equal to the natural rate regardless of the rate of inflation; it is also sometimes called the *accelerationist property* because attempts to keep output above normal result in accelerating prices.

Three specific aspects of the theory of wage and price rigidities of Chapter 16 provide a simple interpretation of Equation 17–1:

1. *Prices are set as a markup over the costs of production,* including wage costs and the cost of materials, such as crude oil, iron ore, and timber. Because of markup pricing, if there are no changes in the price of crude materials, then the rate of change in prices π will equal the rate of change in wages. The first two terms on the right-hand side of Equation 17–1 reflect influences on the rate of change in wages—market conditions and expectations of inflation—as we will see in the next two paragraphs. The last term Z reflects changes in the price of raw materials. According to this interpretation, the primary reason for the price shock Z is changes in the price of raw materials. Major examples of this type of shock were the increases in the price of oil in 1973, 1979, and 1990.

2. *Wages respond with a lag to unemployment.* When unemployment is high and the labor market is slack, currently negotiated wages fall, or

rise by less than they would under favorable conditions. The average wage thus moves in the direction needed to bring the labor market into balance, but it moves only a fraction of the way each period because only a fraction of the wages are changed each period. As we have seen, there is a close relationship—Okun's law—between the unemployment rate and the departures of GDP from potential: When the unemployment rate is above normal, GDP is below normal, and vice versa. Because Okun's law is so accurate, we can represent the pressure of labor market conditions on wage inflation by the output gap $(Y_{-1} - Y^*)/Y^*$. The subscript "−1" indicates that current wage change is related to market pressure in the previous period, reflecting the lags in wage adjustment.

3. *Wages respond to expected inflation.* When workers expect prices and other workers' wages to rise by 8 or 10 percent per year, they will start off their negotiations by asking for this much of an increase. One of the reasons that workers might expect inflation in the future is that other workers have recently signed 3-year contracts with 8 to 10 percent increases in the second and third years. This is the reason for the expectations term π^e on the right-hand side of Equation 17–1. The price-adjustment equation says that the combined effect of a 1 percentage point increase in expected inflation is to raise wage inflation by 1 percentage point.

CHANGES IN THE COEFFICIENTS OF THE PRICE-ADJUSTMENT MODEL

The theory of wage and price rigidities underlying the price-adjustment relationship suggests that it would change if economic conditions or policies change. In particular, the sensitivity of inflation to recent market conditions (f) is likely to change when the economic environment changes. Here we consider two important examples of changes in the economic environment: an increase in the amount of indexing and a reduction in the size and length of business cycles.

The Effect of Wage Indexing

As we saw in Chapter 16, there is some indexing in the United States of union labor contracts (cost-of-living adjustment provisions). Indexing is more prevalent in other countries; a good example is Italy. With indexing, each time the price level rises by 1 percent, wages rise by a fraction of a percent *a,* automatically. How would indexing affect the price-adjustment relationship? Indexing means that the wage will respond to the *current* rate of inflation as well as to the lagged rate of inflation. The effect of this is to speed up the overall response (f) of inflation to changes in unemployment. To see this, suppose there is an increase in output that initially increases wage inflation by 1 percent. Through markup pricing, this will quickly have an upward influence of 1 percent on prices. But, if wages are indexed, the upward adjustment of price inflation will mean a further upward adjustment of wage inflation of the amount a. This in turn will increase price inflation by a, through the markup process. Again indexing will raise wage inflation, now by an amount a times a, or a^2. And the process will continue for a third round, where inflation will increase by another multiple of a (a^3). The whole process is called a **wage-price spiral.** As long as indexing is less than 100 percent, the process will eventually settle down, but the end result has been to make wages adjust more to the increase in output than if there had not been any indexing. The total effect is

$$1 + a + a^2 + a^3 + \cdots = \frac{1}{1 - a},$$

using the formula for the geometric series. Note that the total effect is much like the formula for the multiplier. For example, if a equals .5, then the effect of market conditions on inflation is doubled: $1/(1 - .5) = 2$. In general, *indexing makes nominal wages more responsive to market conditions,* as represented by a higher value for the coefficient f in Equation 17–1.

For the same reasons, indexing also increases the response of inflation to price shocks Z. When the cost of materials rises, firms increase their price. But because of indexing, this price increase will raise wages. In turn, the increase in wages increases prices again. The wage-price spiral thus multiplies the effect of a raw materials price on inflation. If there is no indexing, so that the wage does not respond at all to prices, other costs would go directly into prices with a coefficient of 1. But because wages rise when prices rise, there is a feedback effect—the wage-price spiral. The feedback effect more than doubles the impact of a price shock.

Length and Severity of Business Cycles

In Chapter 16 we saw that long-term contracts are set in a forward-looking manner: Workers and firms look ahead to future labor market conditions and to price and wage inflation. If workers expect a recession to be short, then they will be more reluctant to accept lower wages than if they expect the recession to last for a number of years. In the price-adjustment equation, the market conditions term ($Y_{-1} - Y^*)/Y^*$ partially represents how recent excess supply or demand is indicative of future excess supply or demand. Usually business cycles last for a number of years, so, if output is below potential this year, that is an indication that output will probably be below normal for a few more years.

But suppose that departures of output from potential become less persistent; for example, suppose that the average length of business cycles is reduced from 4 to 2 years. Then if GDP is below potential today, there is no implication that GDP will be below potential 2 years from now. The best guess is that GDP will be back to potential 2 years from now. As a result inflation will be less responsive to recessions. Algebraically, the coefficient f in Equation 17–1 will be smaller when recessions are expected to be less prolonged.

Robert Solow of M.I.T. has argued that this type of coefficient change has occurred in the period since the Second World War in the United States.[1] Since business cycles have become shorter, the downward response of wages to high unemployment has been reduced. Phillip Cagan of Columbia University and Jeffrey Sachs of Harvard University have also found evidence of this.[2]

17.3 MODELS OF THE EXPECTED INFLATION TERM

One of the most difficult issues in the price-adjustment equation is how to determine the measure of expected inflation π^e. There are two important factors to consider:

1. *Forward-looking forecasts.* When wages are set, the fact that prices and other wages are expected to rise in the future influences the wage that emerges from whatever process the worker and the employer use to determine wages. For example, when a 3-year contract is negotiated, the built-in wage increases in the second and third years are larger if inflation is expected to continue during the contract. The amount of inflation that is forecast to occur in the future is therefore part of the expected inflation term. If workers and unions are informed about the economy, then these forward-looking forecasts will match rational expectations theory.

2. *Staggered contracts and backward-looking wage behavior.* The influence of today's expectations on the expected inflation term is only part of the

---

[1] See Robert M. Solow, "The Intelligent Citizen's Guide to Inflation," *The Public Interest,* Vol. 38 (1975), pp. 30–66.

[2] Phillip Cagan, "Changes in the Cyclical Behavior of Prices," in his *The Persistence of Inflation* (New York: Columbia University Press, 1979), pp. 69–94, and Jeffrey Sachs, "The Changing Cyclical Behavior of Wages and Prices," *American Economic Review,* Vol. 70 (March 1980), pp. 78–90.

story, however. Because of wage contracts and staggered wage setting, the expectations term involves inertia that cannot be changed overnight. Workers and firms must take account of the wages that will be paid to other workers in the economy. Since wage setting is staggered over time, some wages must be set by looking back at the previous wage decisions of other workers; once these wages are set, they are not changed during the contract period unless economic conditions change drastically. Wage inflation has a momentum due to contracts and relative wage setting. The expectations term must take account of this momentum as well as of the pure expectational influence.[3]

There is no reason to choose between these explanations. Both are part of the simple algebraic model of staggered contracts with rational expectations discussed in Chapter 16.

Changes in the Model of Expected Inflation

For macroeconomic policy the particular model of the expected inflation term is crucial. Any reasonable model of expectations will give the long-run result that there is no long-run trade-off between the levels of inflation and output. But much of macroeconomic policy is concerned about the short run, and here different models of expected inflation make quite a difference.

Any *model* of expected inflation must be consistent with the *actual behavior* of inflation as observed over a number of years. If inflation typically tends to have momentum, then the public's model of expected inflation will also have momentum. But if inflation tends to be temporary, because of a policy to stabilize prices, for example, then people's view of expected inflation will incorporate the belief that a burst of inflation will probably not be followed by continued inflation.

For the above reasons, any model of expected inflation is therefore itself endogenous to the type of economy or type of policy that is in operation. If policy changes, the model of expected inflation should change.[4] Consider some examples:

---

[3]For more detail on this point and a contrast with other texts that emphasize only pure expectational effects, see John B. Taylor, "Staggered Wage Setting in a Macro Model," *American Economic Review,* Vol. 69 (May 1979), pp. 108–113.

[4]Robert Lucas made this point forcefully in his critique of macroeconomic models as they existed in the early 1970s. Lucas pointed out that these models failed to consider that rational individuals would change their behavior when policy rules change. Fixed models of expected inflation in the Phillips curve were a particular target of Lucas's criticism. See Robert Lucas, "Econometric Policy Evaluation: A Critique," in Karl Brunner and Allan Meltzer, eds., *The Phillips Curve and Labor Markets,* Carnegie-Rochester Conference Series, Vol. 1 (Amsterdam: North-Holland, 1976), pp. 19–46.

1. *Changes in monetary policy.* When the Fed announces that it is switching to a new policy that puts more weight on controlling inflation, and the public believes it, the model of expected inflation will change.

2. *Introduction of specific policies for wage restraint.* The federal government has experimented with a variety of mandatory and voluntary programs for cutting wage inflation. Typically, these involve the announcement of a national wage norm and some method for punishing or exposing employers that exceed the norm. Economists have proposed alternative policies based on tax penalties for excessive wage increases. If the public believes that a policy of this type is working, the model of expected inflation will change.

If people are highly skeptical about promised changes in government programs, then they may well take the view that the only convincing evidence that expected inflation has changed is for actual inflation to change. If so, a simple backward-looking model of the expected inflation term is closer to the truth—at least for the period of time that it takes the government to convince people that it means business.

In what follows we will work through some of the implications of a particular example of a model of expected inflation and examine how the process might change.

A simple model says that this year's expected inflation depends on actual inflation last year and the year before:

$$\pi^e = .4\pi_{-1} + .2\pi_{-2}. \tag{17-2}$$

This equation is more complicated than the model of the expectations term that we considered in Chapter 8, but conceptually the same ideas are at work. In Chapter 8 we assumed that expected inflation depended only on the rate of inflation last year π_{-1}. In Equation 17–2, expected inflation also depends on inflation 2 years ago. To illustrate the implications of this model of the expected inflation term, we will look at four examples of how prices adjust to different disturbances.

Example 1: Effect of a 1-Year Stimulus

The economy starts with zero expected inflation. Policymakers choose to push output above normal by 3 percentage points for one full year. From then on, output is kept at its normal level. Throughout the period, there is no contribution to inflation from materials prices (Z is zero). What happens to the price level?

In order to answer this question, we need to know the numerical value of the coefficient f that governs the unemployment effect in Equation 17–1. A reasonable value, inferred from the last few decades of experience, is $f = .25$. That is, if real GDP is 1 percent above potential in a particular year, inflation is .25 percentage point higher on that account.

In the first year, the output gap is above normal by 3 percent, which adds .75 percent to inflation in the second year through the first term in the price equation. Materials prices and expected inflation are both zero, so inflation π in Year 2 is .75. In the second year, output is back to normal, so there is no contribution from the first term. However, expected inflation is up because of the actual inflation the year before. Because last year has a coefficient of .4, expected inflation is .3. This is the only term affecting inflation, so inflation is .3 in Year 3. In the fourth year, again only expected inflation is contributing to actual inflation, so expected inflation is .4 times last year's inflation of .3 plus .2 times the .75 inflation of 2 years ago. The sum is .27. Thus, inflation in Year 4 is .27. In the fifth year, expected inflation is .4 times last year's rate of .27 plus .2 times the .3 inflation of the year before. That is, inflation in Year 5 is .17. This process continues year after year. If you keep computing in this way, you will get results that gradually approach zero. But the measurable effects of the 1 year of stimulus continue for quite a few years. The results are summarized in Table 17–1.

This example illustrates the *dynamic* nature of the trade-off between output and inflation in an economy where expected inflation responds to actual inflation, on the one hand, and then gets built into actual inflation, on the other hand. A 1-year period of lower unemployment brings a sustained increase in the inflation rate. The effect is dynamic because an action in one year has an effect that lasts for many years.

The intuitive reason that a temporary period of higher output prompts a sustained increase in inflation is that higher output raises actual inflation. In the next year, expected inflation must be higher. Once expected inflation is up, it tends to remain up, because expected inflation feeds point for point into actual inflation. In our simple model, expected inflation gradually dies out if there is no further inflationary stimulus from lower unemployment or higher materials prices.

TABLE 17–1   Inflation Effects of a One-Time Stimulus to Output

Year	Inflation (%)	Output Gap (%)
1	0	3
2	.75	0
3	.30	0
4	.27	0
5	.17	0
.	.	.
.	.	.
.	.	.
∞	.0	0

TABLE 17-2 Effect on Inflation of a Materials Price Shock When Output Is Held at Potential

Year	Inflation (%)	Output Gap (%)
1	2.50	0
2	1.00	0
3	.90	0
4	.56	0
.	.	.
.	.	.
.	.	.
∞	0	0

Example 2: Effect of a Materials Price Shock

The full story of the response of the economy to an increase in materials prices involves the aggregate demand side of the economy. But, even without the demand side, we can answer the question: What would happen to inflation if aggregate demand policy were manipulated in such a way that output remained at its normal level at the time of the materials price shock and during its aftermath?

Suppose that the rise in the price of materials is 1 percent for 1 year and then is zero in future years. Because of indexing, the contribution to the price-adjustment equation Z is 2.5 percent. Output is held at its normal level in every year. Expected inflation starts at zero. In the year of the shock, materials prices are the only contributor to inflation, so the immediate impact is to give 2.5 percentage points of inflation: Inflation π in Year 1 is 2.5. In the year after the shock, neither output nor materials prices are contributing to inflation, but expected inflation is up because of the actual inflation in the previous year. It gets a weight of .4, so expected inflation in the second year is 1.0, and that is the actual inflation rate as well: Inflation is 1.0 in Year 2. In the second year after the shock, expected inflation is .2 times actual inflation in Year 1 plus .4 times actual inflation in Year 2, or .9 percent: Inflation in Year 3 is .9. This process continues until inflation gradually reaches zero. The results are summarized in Table 17–2.

Example 3: Effect of Extended High Output

Finally, suppose that aggregate demand policy provides whatever stimulus is needed to keep output 3 percentage points above normal for every year starting with Year 1. What will happen to the rate of inflation?

We already know that an attempted policy of permanent stimulus will break down sooner or later, because expected inflation will respond to the policy and will move up to anticipate its effects. What happens in our simple model of expected inflation? It turns out that the simple model does not obey this accelerationist proposition. Even if the simple model worked fairly well in describing expected inflation over the last 35 years of U.S. experience, when inflation ebbed and flowed several times, it would change under different conditions of extended periods of high inflation.

If we trace through the operation of the simple model under sustained stimulus, we get the following: The first year is exactly the same as the policy that kept output above normal just for the first year. Actual inflation is .75 percent in the second year. In the third year, expected inflation is .30 percent. In addition, because output is still 3 percentage points above normal, the first term of the price equation contributes another .75 percent. Actual inflation is 1.05 percent in Year 3. In the fourth year, expected inflation is $(.4)(1.05) + (.2)(.75) = .57$. Output remains 3 percentage points above normal and contributes its usual .75 percent. The sum is 1.32 percent: Inflation in Year 4 is 1.32. In the fifth year, expected inflation is .74 percent and actual inflation is 1.49. The process continues indefinitely, with actual inflation rising each year. Ultimately, inflation stabilizes at 1.88 percent per year.

The behavior we have just described is a complete violation of the natural rate-accelerationist proposition. The output gap is permanently 3 percentage points above normal, whereas the natural rate proposition says that output must be equal to potential, on the average. Inflation reaches a constant level of 1.88 percent per year, instead of rising to unlimited levels as predicted by the accelerationist proposition. The problem is that we are not allowing our simple model of expected inflation to adjust to a fundamental change in the economic environment. If policymakers decide to introduce permanent inflation, then the simple model of expected inflation no longer makes sense.[5]

To see the problem, note that, if inflation reaches the constant level of 1.88 percent, we can substitute 1.88 for π_{-1} and π_{-2} in Equation 17–2. Expected inflation is $\pi^e = 1.13$ percent per year. Expected inflation is chronically well below actual inflation. The government has tricked wage setters into thinking that inflation is less than it really is.

In the long run, people will not fall into this trap. They will revise expected inflation to the full level of actual inflation, and the natural rate–accelerationist proposition will hold. Our simple model of expected inflation will not work under sustained constant inflation. Instead, it is a model suited to a world where inflation is not sustained, but comes in occasional bursts that then subside.

It is likely that the model of expected inflation will change to something like

$$\pi^e = .5\pi_{-1} + .5\pi_{-2}.$$

[5]Our simple model is subject to the Lucas critique discussed in Footnote 4.

TABLE 17–3 Increase in Inflation with Permanent High Output

Year	Inflation (%)	Output Gap (%)
1	0	3
2	.750	3
3	1.125	3
4	1.688	3
5	2.156	3
6	2.672	3
.	.	.
.	.	.
.	.	.
∞	∞	3

Note: The expectations term is given by Equation 17–2 with a .5 coefficient on last year's inflation, and .5 on the previous year's inflation.

This formula has the property that expected inflation becomes equal to actual inflation if the actual inflation is sustained for 2 years. If you go back over our calculations of the effect of a policy of keeping output 3 percent above normal permanently, you will find that the alternative model predicts that inflation will rise each year and become greater without limit. The amount of the increase is shown in Table 17–3. Eventually, the process settles down to a constant amount of increase in inflation of .5 percentage point each year.

The last example seems to show the accelerationist proposition at work. When policymakers hold output above normal year after year, inflation gets worse each year. If output is 3 percentage points above normal, inflation eventually worsens by .5 percentage point each year.

The alternative model of expected inflation is far from satisfactory, however. Although the *level* of expected inflation becomes equal to the level of actual inflation, the rate of increase of expected inflation constantly lags behind the rate of increase of actual inflation. Even though the game policymakers are playing must eventually become evident to everybody in the economy, expected inflation constantly lags behind actual inflation. In reality, a policy that added .5 percentage point to inflation each year would probably not keep output above normal indefinitely.

We could look at more complicated models of expected inflation that try to keep up with the rate of change of inflation as well as its level, but the main ideas should already be clear. There is a very general point at work here: *No mechanical model of expected inflation is universally applicable.* If the public has a particular way of arriving at expected inflation, the government can design a policy that fools the public and makes actual inflation continually exceed expected inflation. But then the public will revise its method of calculating expected inflation so that it will no longer be fooled.

If the government uses a policy that does not attempt to fool the public by making actual inflation exceed expected inflation, then there can be a stable way that the public arrives at expected inflation. In particular, if the government aims at a noninflationary economy and acts to offset occasional bursts of inflation from materials prices and elsewhere, then our simple model of expected inflation is a reasonable description of the process. Inflation does persist after it develops, but a point of past inflation does not contribute a full point to expected inflation.

A policy that attempts to keep output above normal permanently will fail. Eventually the public will catch on to the policy and revise expected inflation by a method that makes it keep up with actual inflation.

With any given method for determining expected inflation, the government can figure out an expansionary policy that keeps unemployment below normal permanently. For example, with our simple model of expected inflation, a policy of continued inflation will keep unemployment below normal. The model of expected inflation would not apply with such a policy.

17.4 THE COMBINED OPERATION OF PRICE ADJUSTMENT AND AGGREGATE DEMAND

We now integrate the price formulations, Equations 17–1 and 17–2, into a model of aggregate demand, working in terms of a numerical example. A simple form of the aggregate demand function is

$$Y = 3{,}143 + 3.175 \, \frac{M}{P}. \tag{17–3}$$

Note that monetary policy is more powerful in this example than in the aggregate demand function in Chapter 7, which did not include the effect of interest on consumption goods such as automobiles. Fiscal policy and other exogenous spending variables determine the level of the constant 3,143. Government spending is assumed to be fixed at $1,200 billion. The starting value for the money supply M is $900 billion. Potential output is assumed to be $6,000 billion.

Consider the case where the Fed targets M_1. Note that a higher price level means a lower level of aggregate demand. Recall the mechanism lying behind this conclusion:

1. If the price level is higher relative to the money stock, the LM curve is farther to the left in the IS-LM diagram.
2. The intersection with the IS curve occurs at a lower level of real GDP and a higher interest rate.
3. Investment is lower because the interest rate is higher.
4. Net exports are lower because the interest rate and thus the exchange rate are higher and output is lower.
5. Consumption is lower because real income is lower and interest rates are higher.

The second major element of the complete model is the price-adjustment equation, Equation 17–1. The third is the model of expected inflation.

THE FOUR RELATIONSHIPS OF THE NUMERICAL EXAMPLE

Aggregate demand	$Y = 3{,}143 + 3.175M/P$
Price adjustment	$\pi = .25(Y_{-1} - Y^*)/Y^* + \pi^e + Z$
Expected inflation	$\pi^e = .4\pi_{-1} + .2\pi_{-2}$
Price level	$P = (1 + \pi)P_{-1}$

To analyze the three equations we can proceed graphically, as we did in Chapter 8, or algebraically. The graphical approach would use an aggregate demand diagram with price adjustment (see Figure 8–7). Each year we would treat the price level as predetermined and determine output at the intersection of aggregate demand and the flat price line; then we would calculate the price level for the next year using the price-adjustment diagram.

Here we proceed algebraically using the numerical example, but the analysis is equivalent: Take the price level as predetermined each year, and use the aggregate demand curve to determine output. Then use the model of the expectations term and the price-adjustment equation to determine the price level for the next year. At the new price level determine output in the next year and so on. We use this approach to look at the following four different examples: (1) recovery from a demand-deficient recession, (2) recovery from stagflation, (3) a boom, and (4) an oil price shock. In the first two examples we start the economy off from a position below full employment without asking how the economy got there. In the second two examples we start the economy at full employment and then push it away from full employment with a shock.

Example 1: Recovery from a Demand-Deficient Recession

Suppose the economy starts out at a position below full employment. Suppose, as well, that expected inflation at the outset is zero. How does the economy get back to equilibrium with full employment and stable prices?

In the first year, output is determined by the aggregate demand function given the initial price level and the money stock. This level of output is below potential. Consequently, the first term of the price-adjustment equation pushes the price level downward. Materials prices and expected inflation contribute nothing at this point. Inflation is negative. The price level falls slightly.

In the second year, the process continues. Output is still below potential, so the $(Y_{-1} - Y^*)/Y^*$ term in the price-adjustment equation pushes the price level down some more. But actual deflation in the previous year makes expected inflation negative in the second year. The result is a larger decline in the price level in the second year than in the first year.

In the third year, there is even more deflation, because the negative contribution from expected inflation is even larger. In the fourth year, deflation is about the same as in the third year. Expected inflation is making a somewhat larger negative contribution. But output has been improving steadily. As the price level falls, output rises, according to the aggregate demand function. Consequently, the negative contribution from the $(Y_{-1} - Y^*)/Y^*$ term is not as large as it was in earlier years.

In the fifth year, the price level falls some more, but not by as much as in the fourth year. The rate of inflation rises, in the sense that the rate of deflation is no longer as high. However, prices are still falling, and output rises some more.

By the seventh year, we find that the price level has fallen far enough to restore full employment. However, the rate of inflation is still negative, because expected inflation is negative. The price level continues to fall and the economy enters a period that is slightly above full employment.

Some years later, the price level is again at equilibrium and output is at its potential level. But now expected inflation is very slightly positive. The economy overshoots a little and enters a period of less than full employment. By this time, the economy is so close to equilibrium that the rest of the process of cycling to equilibrium is almost invisible.

We now introduce a convenient diagram (Figure 17–1) to look at the movements of output and inflation. This diagram shows the rate of inflation on the vertical axis and the level of output on the horizontal axis.

The basic mechanism of a recovery is simple. From a point of deficient aggregate demand, the economy gets back to full employment by moving to a lower price level. As the price level falls, the LM curve shifts to the right, the interest rate falls, investment and net export demand rise, and output rises.

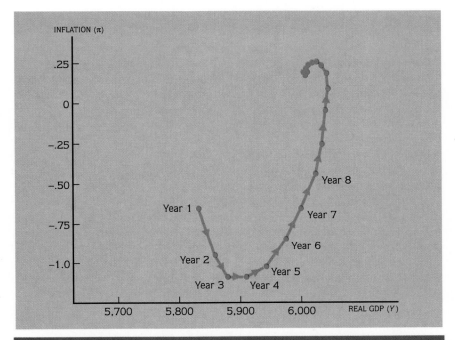

FIGURE 17–1   Economic recovery (Example 1)

In the first year, real GDP is far below potential. In the next year inflation falls. In the year after that, inflation becomes even more negative because expected inflation becomes negative. Throughout the first 10 years, the price level is falling, so aggregate demand rises and output approaches potential. Because of the momentum of deflation, the price level continues to fall after Year 7 and the economy enters a period with GDP above potential. The economy makes a spiral approach to equilibrium, where output equals potential and inflation is zero.

The complete model describes this process. The most critical feature of the model is the response of the price level to output. In our portrayal of the complete model, a 1-year period in which output is 1 percent below potential lowers the price level by .25 percent below what it would have been if output had been at potential. It takes 8 years to restore full employment from a starting point below potential, with zero initial expected inflation and no disturbances from materials prices throughout the recovery.

If the price level is significantly more sensitive to output, then the recovery would take place much faster. For example, if the coefficient in the price-adjustment equation is 1.00 point instead of .25 point of deflation per point of departure from potential, it takes only about 3 years to get back to full employment from a starting point below full employment.

Example 2: Recovery from Stagflation

The case we just studied started with deficient aggregate demand but zero expected inflation. An even unluckier economy might start with both deficient demand and positive expected inflation—the condition Nobel laureate Paul Samuelson of M.I.T. has called **stagflation.**[6] An economy recently hit by a serious materials price shock might be in this condition.

At the beginning of a recovery from stagflation, two terms in the price-adjustment equation are fighting against each other. Expected inflation is positive, but the $(Y_{-1} - Y^*)/Y^*$ term is negative. Either one could win. In the case shown in Figure 17–2, expected inflation wins in the first year, and inflation is positive.

Because inflation won in the first year, the price level is a bit higher in the second year and the level of real GDP actually falls some more. Then expected inflation declines but still dominates. The price level rises slightly going into Year 3 and output falls a bit. In Years 4 through 9, the price level finally begins to fall and the recovery proceeds. The output gap is exerting more influence than expected inflation. By Year 10, output is back up to potential but, because expected inflation is negative in that year, the economy overshoots a little. Output remains slightly above potential for a number of years.

If you compare Figures 17–1 and 17–2, you will see that the main effect of starting from a point of positive expected inflation is to delay the recovery for about 2 years. During these 2 years, the economy of Figure 17–2 is working off expected inflation and suffering from little growth of real output, while the economy of Figure 17–1 is getting started on its recovery. Again, falling prices are the key to recovery. In the years when expected inflation is working against falling prices, the stagflation economy of Figure 17–2 cannot expand.

Example 3: A Boom

What happens in the short, medium, and long runs when an outward shift in aggregate demand sets off a boom? At first, higher aggregate demand raises output, in the way described by the IS-LM model. But higher output means inflation. After inflation gets started, expected inflation begins to catch up with it. As the price level rises, aggregate demand falls. Eventually, the economy gets back to equilibrium, with output equal to potential and inflation at zero. In the new equilibrium, the only effect of the increase in

---

[6]Paul Samuelson, "Worldwide Stagflation," in Hiroaki Nagatani and Kate Crowley, eds., *The Collected Scientific Papers of Paul Samuelson,* Vol. 4 (Cambridge, Mass.: M.I.T. Press, 1975), pp. 801–807.

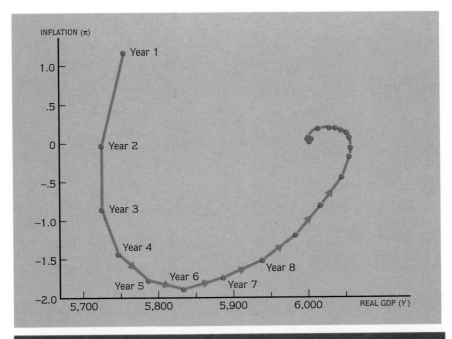

FIGURE 17–2 Recovery from stafglation (Example 2)

In the first year, inflation remains positive because of expected inflation. In the second year, real GDP is even lower because the price level has risen. From then on, the recovery is similar to the one in Figure 17–1, which started from zero expected inflation. The economy approaches equilibrium in a spiral.

aggregate demand is to raise the price level. The path of the economy in response to an increase in aggregate demand is shown in the inflation-output diagram of Figure 17–3.

The path starts at equilibrium in Year 1. There is no inflation and output is at potential. In Year 2, the outward shift in aggregate demand raises output sharply. Because the price level does not respond immediately, output increases by the full amount of the shift in aggregate demand. For the next 9 years, a series of increases in the price level depresses aggregate demand. At first, through Year 5, inflation gets worse each year, as expected inflation catches up with actual inflation. From then on, inflation gradually dissipates because output is less and less above potential. In Year 15, output is back to its potential level. However, expected inflation is still positive. Further price increases depress aggregate demand below potential, and the economy enters a very slight recession. The spiral approaches equilibrium rapidly thereafter.

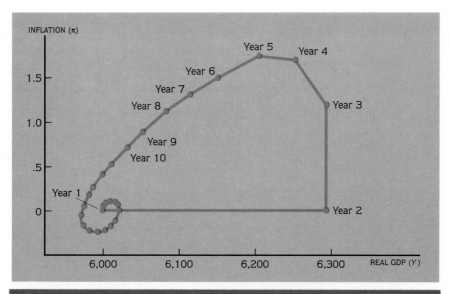

FIGURE 17–3   A boom (Example 3)

The economy starts in equilibrium in Year 1, with output equal to potential and zero inflation. In Year 2 the aggregate demand curve shifts outward. Real GDP shifts upward immediately. Inflation starts in Year 3. As the price level rises, aggregate demand falls and output begins to recede toward equilibrium. In 15 years, output is back to equilibrium but the economy overshoots because expected inflation is positive at that point. The approach to equilibrium is again a spiral.

Example 4: An Oil Price Shock

In the 1970s and in 1990, the U.S. economy was battered by large and sudden increases in oil prices. These shocks sent the economy into periods of stagflation. We can trace out the reaction of the complete model to a one-time increase in materials prices Z. Suppose Z is 2.5 percent in Year 2 and returns to zero for the indefinite future. The path of inflation and output is shown in Figure 17–4.

In Year 2, inflation jumps up to 2.5 percent from the contribution of oil prices to total costs and from the feedback through wages. The higher price level depresses output; the economy is in a state of stagflation. The recovery from stagflation proceeds as in Figure 17–2. At first, expected inflation dominates the deflation that is associated with output that is below potential. The price level rises some more and output falls even further below potential. As expected inflation subsides and deflation from low output dominates, aggregate demand begins to recover. The recovery overshoots a little and the economy experiences a little boom on the way to equilibrium.

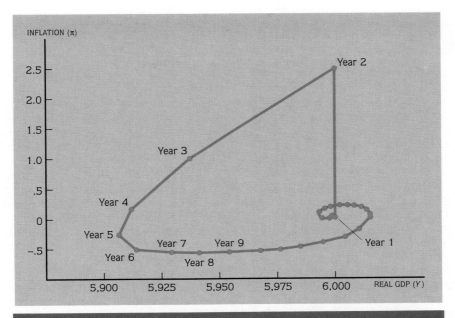

FIGURE 17–4   An oil price shock (Example 4)

The economy starts at equilibrium in Year 1. In Year 2, inflation jumps up to 2.5 percent because of the 1 percent increase in total costs from the higher oil price. In Year 3, the level of output is much lower because the price level is higher. In Years 4 and 5, the price level is even higher and output even lower because of expected inflation. Starting in Year 7, a recovery takes place because the price level begins to fall. Around Year 17, output is back to potential. The economy overshoots slightly on its way back to equilibrium.

INFLATION-OUTPUT LOOPS IN THE UNITED STATES, GERMANY, AND THE UNITED KINGDOM

How well does this model work as an explanation of the record of inflation and output fluctuations in modern economies? Before proceeding with policy analysis in the next chapter, it is important to check whether the theory is consistent with experience.

The four inflation-output diagrams of the previous section (Figures 17–1 to 17–4) provide a fascinating and reasonably accurate way for us to confront the theory with the facts. In all the cases we considered—(1) recovery from a demand-deficient recession, (2) recovery from stagflation, (3)

Why Are Output Fluctuations in Japan So Small?

During the last 18 years fluctuations in real output in Japan have been much smaller than in the United States and the other countries discussed in this chapter. As illustrated in the figure below, real GDP fluctuations in Japan are so small compared with those in the United States that actual GDP in Japan behaves much like smoothly trending potential GDP for the United States. Compared with the United States economy, the Japanese economy completely avoided the boom in GDP for the late 1970s as well as the bust of the early 1980s. It is not yet clear, but it appears Japan will avoid the recession of the early 1990s as well.

What might explain this difference? The theory of aggregate demand and price adjustment described in this chapter offers one possible explanation. If prices and wages adjust very quickly to demand,

that is, if the coefficient f in the price-adjustment equation is large, then relatively small fluctuations in output will be capable of stabilizing inflation. For example, if the response (f) of prices and wages is high, then the effect of a price shock like that in Example 4 and Figure 17–4 would result in only a small drop in output. Similarly, a boom resulting from a monetary expansion like that in Example 3 and Figure 17–3 would be relatively small.

In Japan, wages and prices do seem to be more sensitive to demand conditions than in the United States. One reason is that a significant fraction of wage payments comes in the form of bonuses that can be easily adjusted. Another reason for the greater sensitivity of wages is that most wage changes are synchronized in the spring quarter.

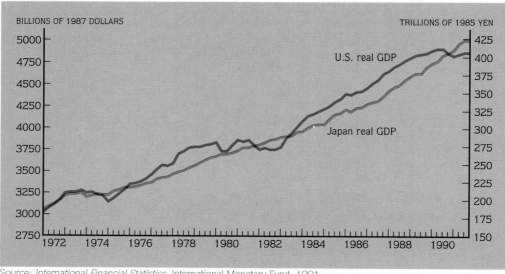

Source: *International Financial Statistics*, International Monetary Fund, 1991.

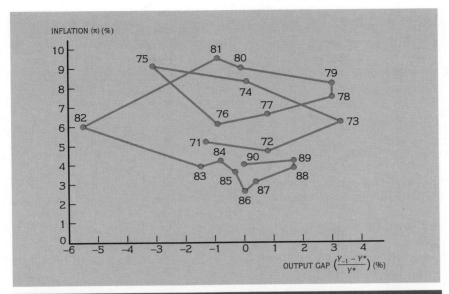

FIGURE 17–5   Inflation-output loops in the United States, 1971–90

During the 1971–90 period there were two big loops in the United States. The second loop started from a higher rate of expected inflation.
Source: *Economic Report of the President*, 1990, Tables B–2 and B–3.

a boom, and (4) an oil price shock—the model economy was displaced from its long-run potential. In each case the return path to potential displays a striking characteristic that is clear in the diagrams: The path is a **counterclockwise loop** because the economy tends to spiral back to potential in a counterclockwise fashion.

Do inflation and output actually behave this way? Since real-world economies are constantly being shocked by many events, it is difficult to separate out isolated episodes like the special shocks in the model economy. Nevertheless, inflation and output fluctuations do display such counterclockwise loops. They are not so smooth and circular as in the model economy, but they are there nonetheless.

In Figure 17–5 we show inflation and output pairs in the United States for each of the years from 1971 through 1991. Three loops are evident: one from 1971 through 1976, another from 1976 through 1986, and a third from 1987 to 1990. The first loop involves the monetary-induced boom of 1971–72, the oil price shock of 1974, and the recession of 1975. The second loop occurred under very similar circumstances: a boom in 1977–78 followed by another oil shock in 1979—this time related to the revolution in Iran, a major oil producer—and a subsequent large recession in the early

1980s. In both cases expected inflation first rose and then fell. Note that the second loop started at a higher rate of expected inflation. The third loop started from the lowest level of expected inflation and had the smallest movement of GDP above potential.

This type of output and inflation fluctuation is not unique to the U.S. economy. Figure 17–6 shows the data for a similar period in Germany. There are two and a half loops. Germany showed no signs of completing the overshoot phase of its last loop as of 1990.

The same picture is shown in Figure 17–7 for the United Kingdom. Here again two loops are evident. The first loop involved a very large increase in inflation and a small drop in output following the 1973 oil shock. Hence, the loop was standing up and skinny, though leaning slightly to the left. The second loop started with the 1979 oil shock. It was followed by an extended period of low GDP and falling inflation. GDP then recovered to potential in 1986, overshot in 1988 and 1989 with rising inflation, and then declined starting in 1990. (Note the vertical scale is compressed for the United Kingdom compared with that for the United States and especially with that for Germany.)

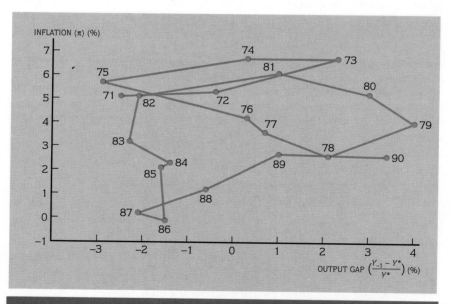

FIGURE 17–6   Inflation-output loops in Germany, 1971–90

In Germany there were two loops during the 1971–90 period, and they appear flatter than those for the United States.
Source: *International Financial Statistics*, International Monetary Fund, various issues.

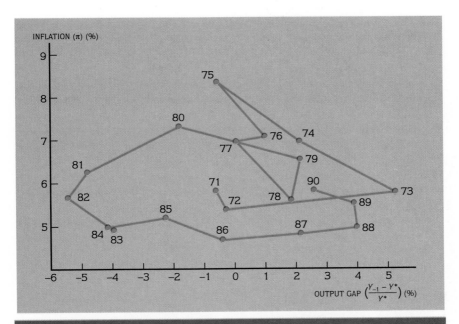

FIGURE 17–7 Inflation-output loops in the United Kingdom, 1971–90

There are two loops here too, but they are much less evident and seem to have changed their orientation. Both were skinny, but the first was leaning up and the second was lying down.
Source: *International Financial Statistics*, International Monetary Fund, various issues.

Overall, the model is consistent with the dynamic movements of inflation and output. While these graphical tests focusing on loops may appear overly simplistic, they are confirmed by more accurate statistical techniques, and we believe they capture the essence of the theory and the facts.

REVIEW AND PRACTICE

Major Points

1. A model of price adjustment must incorporate the response of wages to excess demand and to expected inflation.

2. Expected inflation has forward-looking features and backward-looking features. Expectations and contracts are both part of the micro underpinnings of the expected inflation term.

3. A simple model of price adjustment can be derived by combining wage adjustment with markup pricing behavior. The model of price adjustment is the same as in the model of Chapter 8 except that the coefficients of the model can change.

4. No simple mechanical formula is satisfactory as a model of expected inflation. Any such model would be inconsistent with actual inflation behavior if policy or the economic environment changed.

5. The accelerationist or natural rate hypothesis holds that, in the long run, unemployment will equal the natural rate regardless of how high inflation is, as long as inflation is steady.

6. A model that combines aggregate demand with price adjustment implies that inflation and output will fluctuate or spiral as the economy returns to potential after a shock.

7. From the 1970s to the present the United States and other countries went through economic fluctuations that displayed such spirals of counterclockwise loops.

Key Terms and Concepts

expected inflation	stagflation	oil shock to price
accelerationist hypothesis	inflation-output loops	setting
indexing	markup pricing	wage-price spiral
expectations of future	consistent model of	Lucas critique
labor market conditions	expected inflation	

Questions for Discussion and Review

1. What are the three elements included in the price-adjustment equation?

2. How is expected inflation related to forward-looking behavior? To staggered wage setting?

3. Why might the total effect of an increase in materials prices be greater than the effect portrayed in the markup equation?

4. How can you determine potential output from the price-adjustment equation?

5. Why does a 1-year stimulus cause inflation to remain higher for many years?

6. Trace out the effects over time of an increase in materials prices, assuming that output is held constant.

7. What happens if policy tries to hold output above the natural rate for an extended period?

8. What are the three relationships that make up the unified model that shows how the economy moves over time?

9. Explain why the economy approaches equilibrium in a spiral in the inflation–real GDP diagram.

Problems

Numerical

1. Example 1 of Section 17.3 looked at the inflation effects of a one-time stimulus to output. In this problem we show how such effects vary with different models of inflationary expectations. Consider the following alternatives to Equation 17–2: (i) $\pi^e = \pi_{-1}$; (ii) $\pi^e = .9\pi_{-1}$; (iii) $\pi^e = .5\pi_{-1} + .5\pi_{-2}$; (iv) $\pi^e = .33\pi_{-1} + .33\pi_{-2} + .33\pi_{-3}$.

   a. For each of these expressions find the inflation effects of a one-time 3 percent stimulus to output. Calculate the inflation rate for Years 1 through 10.

   b. Estimate the long-run rate of inflation in each case.

   c. On the basis of your calculations and the calculations shown in Table 17–1, explain how inflation varies with (i) the sum of the coefficients in the expression for π^e and (ii) the weight given to recent inflation compared with more distant inflation in the expression for π^e.

   d. Do any of the expressions for inflationary expectations given above lead to systematic errors in forecasting inflation? If so, which ones? If not, explain the relationship between expected and actual inflation when fiscal and monetary policy are used to keep output at potential. Is one expression for expected inflation more likely to prevail than another?

2. In this problem we consider the behavior of the economy following a demand-deficient recession. We look at how the recovery is influenced by the model used for inflationary expectations. Suppose the economy starts off with output at potential ($Y = Y^* = 6,000$), $\pi = 0$, and $P = 1$. Aggregate demand is given by Equation 17–3; price adjustment is given by Equation 17–1 with $f = .25$. In Year 1 the money supply is reduced from 900 to 855; this creates a recession.

   a. Calculate the path of inflation, the price level, and output for Years 1 through 6 assuming (i) $\pi^e = .4\pi_{-1} + .2\pi_{-2}$ and (ii) $\pi^e = \pi_{-1}$. In performing your calculations, compute P as $(1 + \pi)P_{-1}$.

   b. For which model of expectations does the return to potential output take longer? For which model will there be more overshooting?

   c. We assumed here that the value taken by f in the price-adjustment equation was the same for both models in inflationary expectations. Explain why in reality the value of f might differ from one model to the other.

3. In this problem we look at how the recovery from an oil price shock is affected by the model used for inflationary expectations. Let the model of the economy and its initial conditions be the same as in Problem 2. Note that the money supply will remain at 900. In Year 1 let $Z = .025$.

   a. Calculate the path of inflation, the price level, and output in Years 1 through 6 under each of the models for π^e given in Part a of Problem 2.

   b. In each case, how long does it take inflation to first return to zero? Analyze the factors that cause inflation to fall in each case.

   c. In which case is the fall in output greater? How do you explain this result?

4. Reconsider the oil price shock of Problem 3, only now suppose that the aim of policymakers is to keep inflation equal to zero in every year possible. This is achieved by manipulating the money stock.

a. Assuming that the oil price shock was unexpected, can anything be done about the rate of inflation in Year 1? Why or why not?

b. Suppose π^e is always equal to zero. Find the values of M chosen by policy-makers each year during and following the oil shock.

c. Now assume that π^e is given alternately by π_{-1} and $.5\pi_{-1} + .5\pi_{-2}$. Repeat the calculations from Part b for each case.

d. Is $\pi^e = 0$ reasonable given the goals of policy? Use this example to explain how important it is for policymakers to maintain their credibility.

Analytical

1. Explain why the inflation-output loops in Section 17.4 are vertical at the point where inflation equals zero. Would the same be true if the money supply was increasing each year?

2. In this problem we consider the policy actions underlying Example 1 of Section 17.3.

a. Assuming that the natural rate of unemployment is 6 percent, what is the un-employment rate in Year 1 and in Year 2 onward?

b. Diagram the actions taken by policymakers in Year 1 and in Year 2 onward on an aggregate demand graph.

c. Again, diagram the actions of policymakers each year on an IS-LM graph as-suming that (i) all policy actions consist of fiscal policy and (ii) all policy ac-tions consist of monetary policy. Explain why your diagram in Part b does not depend on the nature of the policy action taken.

3. Describe the behavior of investment and interest rates during the boom de-scribed in Example 3 of Section 17.4 assuming that the boom was created by an exogenous increase in investment. How do interest rates and investment be-have during and following an oil price shock?

4. What is the correlation between output and interest rates implied by the infla-tion-output loops of Section 17.4? What assumption is made about monetary policy in constructing these loops? Are the predictions of the model consistent with the data presented in Chapter 1?

5. Suppose that agents use all available information to make unbiased, but not error-free, forecasts of inflation. In that case, we can say that

$$\pi_t = \pi_t^e + e_t,$$

where e_t is a forecast error whose average value is zero.

a. What does this relationship between π and π^e imply about the average value of the output gap? (Hint: Use the price-adjustment equation.)

b. Suppose now that π^e was formed so that π^e always differed from π by a constant, e. Using the price-adjustment equation, show that the accelera-tionist hypothesis doesn't hold.

MacroSolve Exercises

1. Using annual data, graph the GDP gap on the horizontal axis against the infla-tion rate on the vertical axis. You will get inflation-output loops such as those

shown in the text. The loop between 1930 and 1935 is clockwise, while most of the postwar loops observed in the data are counterclockwise. (It will be easier to see this if you slow down the display; remember that you can then stop the display by pressing any key.) What might explain the difference in the directions of the loops in the different periods?

2. If prices were very flexible, would you expect to see flatter or steeper inflation-output loops following an increase in demand? Would the same be true for the loops following a price shock?

3. a. Simulate the "AD/PA, Closed Econ" model in response to a 10 percent price shock. Tabulate the results, and draw on a sheet of paper the implied inflation-output loop. (Hint: Calculate the inflation rate as the percentage growth rate of the price index, and the GDP gap as the difference between GDP and 6,000.)

   b. Do the same for the "AD/PA zero exp π" case (where the expected inflation rate is zero). Is the inflation-output loop flatter or steeper than in Part a? Explain both why this is and the policy implications of the changed slope.

   c. Do the loops become flatter or steeper when the responsiveness of prices to output increases?

PART

4

Macroeconomic Policy

CHAPTER

18

Designing and Maintaining a Good Macro Policy

As we have seen, modern macroeconomic theory incorporates new ideas about rational expectations and price adjustment into traditional Keynesian and monetarist frameworks. What are the policy implications of this theory? This chapter begins with a review of the principal features. After examining the problem of matching policy instruments to targets and the problem of uncertainty in implementing policy, we go on to apply these principles to macroeconomic policy problems in the United States. In the next chapter we extend this analysis to the world economy.

18.1   GENERAL PRINCIPLES OF MACRO POLICY ANALYSIS

Much of our discussion of the recent developments in macroeconomics—rational expectations, policy rules, time inconsistency, theories of wage and price rigidities, the nature of economic fluctuations—has been technical. It is important not to lose sight of the central ideas by focusing too much on the technical details. The central ideas are summarized in the following five propositions.[1]

1. *When making decisions, people think about the future, and their expectations of the future can be modeled by assuming that they have a sense of economic fluctuations and use their information to make unbiased (but not error-free) forecasts.*

The notion that people make the most of the information available to them when forecasting the future was originally proposed by John Muth in 1960 for use in microeconomic applications, such as the demand and supply for agricultural commodities.[2] Farmers need to predict future prices in order to know how much to grow. Muth suggested that we model a farmer's expectations by simply assuming that the supply-and-demand model was known to the farmer.

Whatever its value in agricultural economics, the idea seems reasonable for macroeconomic applications. Many features of economic fluctuations are recurrent from one business cycle to another; there are established statistical regularities. We have documented many of these regularities. Since business cycles have been observed for hundreds of years, it makes sense to assume that people have become familiar with them. Of course, in the face of new, unprecedented events, people will make significant errors in trying to look forward.

2. *Macroeconomic policy can be usefully described and evaluated as a policy rule, rather than by treating the instruments as exogenous and looking only at one-time changes in these instruments.*

Because people are forward-looking, their expectations of future policy actions affect their current behavior and the state of the economy. Hence, in order to evaluate the effect of policy on the economy, we need to specify not only current policy changes but also future policy changes. In other words, we need to specify a contingency plan that describes how policy will react to future events. Such a contingency is nothing more than a rule for policy. The contingency plan could be as specific as a constant growth rate rule for the money supply, but more generally it establishes a range of reactions depending on the state of the economy.

The rational expectations approach almost forces a macroeconomic

---

[1]This discussion is related to that in John B. Taylor, "An Appeal for Rationality in the Policy Activism Debate," in R. W. Hafer, ed., *The Monetary and Fiscal Policy Debate: Lessons from Two Decades* (Totowa, N.J.: Allanheld, 1986).

[2]John Muth, "Rational Expectations and the Theory of Price Movements," *Econometrica*, Vol. 29 (1960), pp. 315–335.

analyst to think about policy as a rule or a strategy. Once you are working with a rational expectations model, you soon realize that you have little choice but to specify policy as a rule. We will see in our policy evaluation study in the latter part of this chapter that it is natural and convenient to specify policy as a rule.

Note that the focus on rules does not mean that the effect of one-shot changes in policy should never be calculated; such a calculation can be a useful exercise to help understand the workings of the model. We did this in the previous chapter to see if our model was consistent with the facts.

In his famous critique of traditional policy evaluation, Robert Lucas of the University of Chicago argued in the early 1970s that traditional macro models, like the model of Chapter 8, could give incorrect answers to policy evaluation questions if expectations were forward-looking and there was a change in the policy rule.[3] Since these traditional models were based on adaptive backward-looking expectations, their parameters would change when the policy rule changed. This was the negative part of the critique, and it has clearly made policy analysts wary of using the traditional models. But there was also a positive side. The critique provided a general framework for modifying the traditional models; stipulating policy as a rule, it is possible to calculate by how much the parameters of the traditional models would change. An example of this was discussed in Chapter 17, where we showed how the sensitivity of inflation to recessions would diminish if business cycles became less prolonged, due, perhaps, to a change in policy. Similarly, the model of the expected inflation term in the price-adjustment equation (Equation 17–1) would change if monetary policy changed.

Some macroeconomists, such as Christopher Sims of Yale University, have argued that the focus on policy rules is irrelevant.[4] Sims argues that we rarely get big changes in rules anyway, so we might as well use conventional models for policy. Indeed there is a utopian flavor to the "policy rules" approach. The search is for big policy reforms that would improve economic welfare over a long period of time. The reforms would probably require changes in the policymaking institutions or the creation of new institutions. Such reforms are by their very nature rare. But they do occur. The creation of the Federal Reserve System, the departure from the gold standard, and the shift to floating exchange rates are all examples. These reforms seem to have had substantial effects on the economy. A careful analysis of the effects of future policy reforms therefore seems quite relevant.

---

[3]Robert E. Lucas, "Econometric Policy Evaluation: A Critique," in Karl Brunner and Allan Meltzer, eds., *The Phillips Curve and Labor Markets,* Carnegie-Rochester Conference Series, Vol. 1 (Amsterdam: North-Holland, 1976), pp. 19–46.

[4]Christopher Sims, "Policy Analysis with Econometric Models," *Brookings Papers on Economic Activity,* Vol. 1 (1982), pp. 107–164.

3. *In order for a particular policy rule to work well, it is necessary to establish a commitment to that rule.*

We briefly discussed the problem of time inconsistency in Chapter 9. The possibility that policymakers will find it tempting to change their plans in the future—be time inconsistent—is a reason for maintaining a commitment to a stated rule. The problem of time inconsistency was first pointed out in macroeconomics by Finn Kydland of Carnegie-Mellon University and Edward Prescott of the University of Minnesota and by Guillermo Calvo of the University of Pennsylvania.[5]

In attempting to find optimal policies for economies where people are forward-looking, these researchers found that once policymakers began an optimal policy, there was incentive in future periods for the policymakers to change the plan—to be inconsistent. Policymakers could make things better by being inconsistent. This was true even if the policymakers had the interests of the public in mind. One example close at hand is that of a teacher giving an examination. It is tempting to call off an examination after the students have studied and learned the material in a course in anticipation of the exam. Then the students do not have to sweat through the exam, and the teacher does not have to grade the exam papers. The government's patent laws provide a similar problem of inconsistency. Patent laws confer a temporary monopoly as a reward for inventions. Hence, they spur inventiveness. But the monopoly is undesirable: It would be tempting to remove patents when an invention is completed, so that the new product would be produced and marketed competitively. Another example from the government sphere is the construction of dams for flood plains. The government tells people not to build houses on a dangerous flood plain, because there will be no dams for flood control built. But when people move in anyway, the government will find it desirable to build the flood control project in order to protect them.

However, by being inconsistent the policymakers are likely to lose credibility; people would begin to assume that the policymakers will change the rules and this would lead to a new policymaking equilibrium that was generally inferior to the original policy plan of the policymakers. If the students began to expect that the exam would be called off, they probably would not study for it. The implication is that, to prevent this inferior outcome, it is better to maintain a firm commitment to a policy rule.

---

[5]Finn Kydland and Edward Prescott, "Rules Rather than Discretion: The Inconsistency of Optimal Plans," *Journal of Political Economy,* Vol. 85 (1977), pp. 473–491, and Guillermo Calvo, "On the Time Inconsistency of Optimal Policy in a Monetary Economy," *Econometrica,* Vol. 46 (1979), pp. 1411–1428. Also see Stanley Fischer, "Dynamic Inconsistency, Cooperation, and the Benevolent Dissembling Government," *Journal of Economic Dynamics and Control,* Vol. 2 (1980), pp. 93–107.

Returning to the patent example, a policymaker who had the discretion to award patents each year would indeed be tempted not to do so. By holding back the patent, the economic inefficiencies of a monopoly are avoided. Fortunately, reneging on patent promises does not occur in practice because it is so clear that future inventive activity would suffer. Instead, we have patent laws that limit such discretion. The time inconsistency research suggests that discretion should be limited for similar reasons in macroeconomic policy.

It is important to distinguish between **activist policy rules** and **discretionary policy.** Activist policy rules involve *feedback* from the state of the economy to the policy instruments, but the feedback is part of the rule. Sometimes the term **passive policy rule** is used to refer to special rules without feedback, like the fixed growth rate rule for the money supply. An example of an activist policy rule is the following: If the unemployment rate rises by a certain amount next year, then the money supply will increase by a certain stated amount. Discretionary policy is formulated on a case-by-case and year-by-year basis with no attempt to commit to or even talk about future policy decisions in advance. Those in favor of discretionary policy disagree with the whole concept of a rules-of-the-game approach, whether the rule is a feedback rule or a constant setting for the policy instruments. Activist and constant-growth-rate policy rules have much more in common with each other than do activist policy rules and discretionary policy. Both types of policy rules involve commitments and lead to the type of policy analysis suggested by the rational expectations approach.

4. *The economy is basically stable; after a shock the economy will eventually return to its normal trend paths of output and employment. However, because of rigidities in the economy, this return could be slow.*

The macro models we have looked at are *dynamic* systems continually disturbed by *shocks*. After each shock the economy has a tendency to return to the normal or natural growing level of output and employment, although there may be overshooting or a temporary cumulative movement away from normal. A smooth return is never observed in practice, however, because new shocks are always hitting the system. Since the economy is viewed as always being buffeted around by shocks, the equilibrium is really a random or stochastic equilibrium. The combination of the shocks and the dynamics of the model is capable of mimicking the actual behavior of business cycles surprisingly well, as we saw in the previous chapter. The properties of the random equilibrium are much like the actual behavior of business cycles.

The shocks can be due to many factors, but usually have been money shocks, demand shocks, or price shocks. The dynamics are due to many possible rigidities in the economy, but price-wage rigidities and slow adjustment of capital (including inventories) have been the most important empirically.

Because of these rigidities the impact of a shock to the economy takes time to sort itself out. Suppose, for example, that there is a shift in money demand with people wanting to hold more money at any level of income and interest rates. Eventually the price level will fall so that the real supply of money is effectively increased. But if there are wage and price rigidities, this adjustment will take time: First the increase in money demand will cause an increase in interest rates; the higher level of interest rates will in turn depress the demand for durables and have repercussions throughout the economy; depressed demand conditions will then begin to put downward pressure on prices; and the fall in prices will begin to raise the real supply of money—this process will continue until the economy is back to its natural level of output and employment. The whole process could take more than a year.

Combined with these structural rigidities is the supposition that expectations are not restrained by similar rigidities. A shock can change expectations of inflation, exchange rates, and other variables overnight even though there are rigidities that cause the economy to take additional time to adjust fully to the shock. The expectations take account of the structural rigidities since these are part of the model. The combination of rigidities in the economy with perfectly flexible expectations is an essential feature of most rational expectations models.

There has been a tendency to get expectations assumptions mixed up with assumptions about how markets work. Hence, the comment that expectations might be rational in flexible auction markets but not in sticky wage-labor markets is frequently heard. But there is no reason why expectations are not rational in both areas. Labor union staffs may spend more time predicting future wage and price inflation than the staffs of brokerage firms. When workers and firms set wages and prices, they look ahead to the period during which the prices or wages will be in effect—to demand conditions, to the wages of other workers, and so on. This means that expectations of future policy actions will affect wage and price decisions, a property that is quite unlike models of wage and price rigidities with purely backward-looking expectations. The view that the economy will eventually return to normal—however slowly—after a shock is also inconsistent with the view that the economy stagnates permanently below potential.

5. *The objective of macroeconomic policy is to reduce the size (or the duration) of the fluctuations in output, employment, and inflation from normal levels after shocks hit the economy. The objective is to be achieved over a long period of time, which will in general include a larger number of business cycle experiences. Future business cycle fluctuations are not viewed as less important than the current one.*

By responding to economic shocks in a systematic fashion, economic policy can offset their impact or influence the speed at which the economy returns to normal. It thus can change the size of the fluctuations. How this should be done is a main area of disagreement among proponents of different policy rules.

From a technical viewpoint the disagreement can be addressed by inserting alternative policy rules into a rational expectations model and calculating how each rule affects the variability of output, employment, and inflation in the moving equilibrium that describes the business cycle fluctuations. We want to choose a policy that provides the best economic performance. One simple criterion is the minimization of the size of the fluctuations in output and inflation. Since in many models with price and wage rigidities there will be a trade-off between the reduction of output and inflation variability, it will usually be necessary to stipulate a welfare or loss function that reflects certain value judgments. Frequently one policy will so dominate another that the particular welfare weights do not matter much, however. This approach to policy will be featured later in this chapter.

The average rate of inflation can obviously be influenced by monetary policy, and it is important to choose a target rate that maximizes economic welfare. The objective of macroeconomic policy, however, is to keep the inflation rate close to this target rate, that is, to minimize fluctuations around the target, regardless of what the actual value of the target is. Alternatively, if a zero inflation target is appropriate, the objective of policy is to keep the price level near some target; the specific target value itself is much less important.

18.2 INSTRUMENTS AND TARGETS

Generally stated, the macro policy problem is one of choosing policy rules that describe how the *instruments* of policy should respond to economic conditions in order to improve the performance of the *target* variables. The instruments of macro policy are things like the monetary base or tax rates, or, more generally, monetary policy and fiscal policy. The targets of policy are the endogenous economic variables that we care about: inflation, unemployment, capital formation, and economic growth. Sometimes it is useful to distinguish between *intermediate* targets and *final* targets. For example, for the Fed, the money supply is an intermediate target while its instrument to control that target is the monetary base. The final targets for the Fed are real output and inflation.

To describe our objectives for the target variables, it is necessary to define a **social welfare function** that summarizes the costs of having the target variables deviate from their desired levels. Such a social welfare function should reflect the tastes of individuals in society. If people do not like inflation, then deviations of inflation from zero should register as a loss of welfare in the social welfare function. In practice, it is very difficult to determine what the social welfare function actually is. Since people are different, we cannot just choose policy to improve the welfare of some representative individual.

Once a social welfare function has been specified, we can view the macro policy problem much as any other economic problem: We want to choose policy rules for the instruments to maximize the social welfare function. Analogously, in a consumption problem the consumer chooses a contingency plan for consumption—a decision rule—to maximize utility.

In most macro problems we are faced with the typical economic problem of scarcity. Whenever there is scarcity in economics we are faced with a *trade-off* between competing goals. In fact, scarcity is the most fundamental problem in economics. An important principle of optimal macro policy is that whenever there is a scarcity of instruments—that is, the number of instruments is less than the number of target variables—there is a trade-off between the different target variables. Jan Tinbergen, the Dutch economist who won the Nobel Prize for his work on macro modeling and on techniques for macro policy evaluation, established this important principle relating the number of instruments to the number of targets.[6] As long as the number of instruments is less than the number of targets, society is faced with a cruel choice between meeting one goal or another. The choice between inflation and unemployment is the best example of this type of cruel choice in macroeconomics, and we will consider it in detail later in this chapter. Another example that we will consider is the trade-off between money supply instability and interest-rate instability.

It is very important to note that equality between the number of instruments and the number of targets is not sufficient for avoiding a cruel choice. In many cases the different instruments are not independent enough in their effects on the target variables. Again, the best example of this is the inflation-unemployment trade-off. A simple counting of instruments and targets could lead to the following type of incorrect reasoning: "We have two instruments, monetary policy and fiscal policy, and we have two target variables, inflation and unemployment. Thus there is no cruel trade-off. We can use monetary policy to control inflation and fiscal policy to control unemployment." This reasoning is wrong because it assumes that monetary and fiscal policies affect inflation and output in different and in-

---

[6]Jan Tinbergen, *On the Theory of Economic Policy* (Amsterdam: North-Holland, 1952).

dependent ways. In fact, we already know from our macro model that monetary and fiscal policies affect output and inflation in the same way—by shifting the aggregate demand curve. Unless one instrument can directly affect inflation without going through aggregate demand, we are left with a trade-off. For example, if monetary policy had a separate effect on expected inflation or if tax policy could affect price setting, then there would be a separate channel by which one or the other policy could affect inflation.

UNCERTAINTY AND TIMING CONSIDERATIONS

In practice, the target-instrument approach described above is too simple. It ignores the inherent uncertainty that exists in our understanding of the economy. If there is uncertainty about the effect of an instrument of policy on the economy, then we must be careful not to exploit that relationship too much. Very active use of an uncertain instrument can be risky. This is one of the central reasons for using less active policies in practice.

When there are many instruments and uncertainty, the theory of economic policy tells us to use a mix of the instruments in a way that minimizes the risk. William Brainard of Yale University showed how the choice of instruments under uncertainty is much like the problem of choosing an optimal portfolio of common stocks.[7] Just as an individual should attempt to diversify a portfolio of stocks—"don't put all of your eggs in one basket"—policymakers should diversify their instruments in order to reduce risk.

Another reason that macroeconomic policymaking is difficult is that its benefits do not occur at the same time as its costs. An expansionary monetary or fiscal policy, for example, involves balancing the short-term benefits of a stimulative move against the long-term costs of inflation the move will bring. Conversely, the costs of a contractionary policy occur in the short run and the benefits occur later and are perhaps drawn out over many years. We will start with a look at the benefits and costs. Then we will set up a framework within which policymakers can make an intelligent choice between expansion and contraction.

---

[7]William Brainard, "Uncertainty and the Effectiveness of Policy," *American Economic Review, Papers and Proceedings,* Vol. 57 (1967), pp. 411–425.

18.4 THE BENEFITS OF FULL EMPLOYMENT AND PRICE STABILITY

Macro policymakers should try to achieve the best combination of employment and inflation. The Employment Act of 1946 and the Humphrey-Hawkins Act of 1978 legislated this requirement, though without an enforcement provision. Chapter 17 showed the difficulties that policymakers face in dealing with unemployment and inflation. No policy can give the ideal of low unemployment and zero inflation year after year. A policy that concentrates on low unemployment will permit a good deal of price instability; one that keeps prices on target will bring serious recessions and booms. Policymakers face a trade-off between unemployment stability and price stability.

Economic analysis deals with trade-offs of many types. For example, consider a consumer who cannot afford an expensive car and an expensive home; to buy a better car, the consumer will have to settle for a more modest home, and vice versa. Micro theory describes the consumer's preferences in terms of indifference curves. The consumer chooses the combination of car and house on the best indifference curve within the consumer's budget. The combination is at a point of tangency of an indifference curve and the line showing all the different combinations of car and house the consumer can afford.

We can look at the nation's choice between employment and price stability in the same way. Preferences give a set of indifference curves. The behavior of the economy, as described by the model of Chapter 17, gives the set of different combinations of employment and price stability that can be achieved. We call the curve showing those combinations the **policy frontier.** The optimal policy is at the point of tangency of an indifference curve and the policy frontier.

The starting point for the analysis is to choose the two axes for the indifference curves and for the policy frontier. One axis has something to do with price stability and the other something to do with unemployment. For inflation, it seems clear that the desirable level is near zero. Large departures above zero have been the big problem in recent decades. Departures below zero were the problem in the depression of the 1930s and in some earlier contractions. There is no good reason to think that the cost of a positive error is any different from the cost of a negative error. In addition, it seems reasonable to suppose that *the marginal cost of an inflation or deflation error rises with the magnitude of the error.* A simple measure of the loss associated with these properties is the **squared error.**

This suggests that a good general summary of the economic loss caused by inflation is the average of the squared deviation of the inflation rate from its target, near zero. We will call this the **inflation loss.** If every-thing else is held the same, the ideal macro policy will keep the inflation loss at zero. In real life, the inflation rate cannot be kept exactly at zero, and the average inflation loss will be positive.

For the output-employment-unemployment side of the economy, the situation is a little different. For a number of reasons, the *natural* unem-ployment rate is probably not the *optimal* unemployment rate. Because of taxes and unemployment compensation that make the social cost of unem-ployment exceed the private cost and because of monopoly power, it is likely that social welfare rises whenever unemployment drops below the natural rate. But, in the last chapter, we stressed that macro policy cannot influence the average rate of unemployment. It can only influence the fluc-tuations of unemployment around the natural rate. Consequently, macro policymakers should do what they can do: limit the fluctuations of unem-ployment about the natural rate. Based on this logic, we define the **unem-ployment loss** as the average squared departure of unemployment from the natural rate.

Social preferences about inflation and unemployment can be dis-played in a family of indifference curves as shown in Figure 18–1. Note that the indifference curves bend in the opposite direction from the usual ones for the theory of the consumer. Consumer theory deals with things people like. Inflation and unemployment losses are things the public does not like,

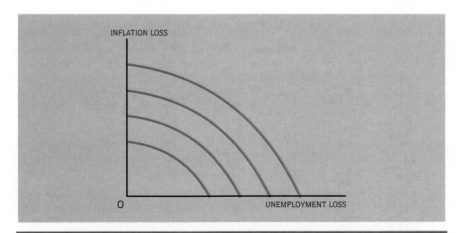

FIGURE 18–1 Social preferences about inflation and unemployment

Each indifference curve shows the locus of combinations of average inflation loss and average unem-ployment loss that the public finds equally acceptable. The curve that is farthest from the origin is the worst one. The public prefers curves that are closer to the origin.

so the indifference curves have the opposite curvature. At the upper left end of each curve, the public is willing to trade quite a bit of added unemployment loss to reduce their inflation loss a little from its high level. At the lower end, they will accept only a small added amount of unemployment loss to reduce their inflation loss quite a bit. Curves closer to the origin are socially preferred because they involve lower amounts of both unemployment and inflation loss.

Why Is Inflation Undesirable?

The American public has made it abundantly clear that inflation is unpopular. In 1976 and 1980, two Presidents—Ford and Carter—were denied re-election soon after large bursts of inflation. Stringent anti-inflation policies in the early 1980s seem to have been politically acceptable, even though they brought on a pair of recessions. Whenever inflation rises above 10 percent per year, public opinion polls show that inflation is the number-one economic problem, even when unemployment is high.

Though some specific economic costs of inflation have been identified, it is hard to quantify and assess them. The areas of economic costs include the following:

1. *"Shoe-Leather Costs" of Holding Money.* When inflation is high, currency and non-interest-bearing checking accounts are undesirable because they are constantly declining in purchasing power. People will make extra trips to the bank to avoid holding much money. These trips involve genuine economic costs, and these costs would be avoided with stable prices. One response to inflation has been the development of checking accounts that pay interest closer to market interest rates. This change in banking has reduced the cost of inflation because people do not have to spend so much time and effort transferring money between accounts.

2. *Tax Distortions.* Until recently the U.S. tax system was written entirely in current dollars. In 1985 the brackets for the personal income tax were indexed, as we discussed in Chapter 13, and they will rise with the consumer price index. Bracket creep due to inflation has been eliminated. But many other parts of the tax system are not indexed; the presumption is that the purchasing power of the dollar is stable from one year to the next. For example, businesses take depreciation deductions that are based on the original dollar cost of plant and equipment investments. When inflation rages, the actual value of these deductions is much less than it should be, thanks to the declining purchasing power of the dollar. But this problem has been offset by speeding up the deductions. Even better, the tax law could be changed so that the deductions automatically rise along with the cost of living.

3. *Unfair Gains and Losses.* When inflation hits, some people gain and some lose. Retired people whose pensions are fixed in dollar terms lose. Homeowners gain because they can pay off their mortgages in less valuable dollars. In total, losses equal gains. In each transaction set in dollars, when inflation is high, there is somebody who wins and somebody who loses exactly the same amount. The social loss occurs because inflation makes long-term transactions more unreliable. There seems to be no clear tendency for inflation to favor the rich over the poor or the poor over the rich. Gains and losses from inflation are more or less randomly distributed in this respect.

4. *Nonadapting Economic Institutions.* Certain standard economic practices have not adapted readily to inflation, and the public has suffered as a result. The most important is private retirement arrangements. The typical private pension plan pays its retirees a certain number of dollars per month when they retire. The number of dollars is based on their earnings in the last few years of work. In this respect, the pension keeps up with inflation. But once retirement starts, the amount of the pension is fixed in dollars. A pension that starts out at a generous level may dwindle to inadequacy as a result of inflation. One way retirement plans could adapt would be to build in an allowance for, say, 5 percent inflation. Payments would rise by 5 percent every year. They would start at a lower level than they do now, but keep up better with inflation.

Many of these costs are avoidable by apparently simple means. Shoe-leather costs have been cut by permitting banks to pay market interest rates on checking accounts. Changing the tax system to avoid distortions from inflation is not too difficult and would be even easier if some other highly desirable tax reforms were instituted. Gains and losses could be avoided completely by linking payments and receipts to government price indexes, as many businesses do today in their transactions with other businesses. Better pension plans with cost-of-living indexation have been designed and put forward by a number of economists.

The public's negative view of inflation seems to come from sources other than these identifiable economic costs. One is the notion that the dollar is supposed to be a unit of purchasing power just as the yard is a unit of length. If the government decreased the length of the yard randomly by 5 or 10 percent each year, the public would be upset in a way that would also be out of proportion to the technical costs a changing unit of length would impose on us. It is a sign that the government is doing its job when its units of weights, measures, or purchasing power are reliable. Inflation is historically associated with the breakdown of government.

Perhaps another reason some people may be upset about inflation is that they do not take the same broad view as an economist, who sees inflation as a general rise in all prices and dollar incomes. Recall that, in a general inflation, wages and prices increase by the same amount. If wages increase less rapidly than prices, then something else in addition to inflation—like a drop in productivity—is affecting the economy. Someone who does not think about the economy in that way will not associate an increase in income with the increase in prices that goes with it. Such a person may imagine that the increase in income would have occurred even without the inflation. In that case, the inflation appears to diminish the purchasing power of the income and so to be a loss. To put it another way, some people may not realize that both their incomes and the prices they pay will not rise as fast under an anti-inflation policy.

COSTS OF INFLATION

1. There are some specific economic costs of inflation, but they are hard to quantify. These include:
   • Shoe-leather costs of conserving money holdings.
   • Distortions because much of the tax system is not indexed.
   • Capricious losses suffered by holders of dollar claims, though offset by surprise gains enjoyed by those paying fixed dollar debts.
   • Problems caused by the failure of retirement plans and other institutions to adapt to declining purchasing power.
2. People see inflation as a breakdown of the basic government responsibility to provide a stable unit of purchasing power.
3. Some people may not understand the relation between their own incomes and rising prices. To them, higher prices represent diminished real income.

Costs of Output Loss and Unemployment

There is less mystery about output and unemployment losses, especially on the downside. As we noted in Chapter 13, when real GDP falls by a billion dollars, people see about $400 million immediately in the form of reduced disposable income. Reduced corporate retained earnings account for part of the reduction. The remainder, hundreds of millions of dollars, takes the form of reduced tax revenues for federal, state, and local governments. The public suffers from this reduction as well, either in the form of cuts in government services or in the form of future higher taxes.

In addition to the obvious economic costs of lost output, there are other serious costs of a period of low output and high unemployment.

Young workers are particularly likely to become unemployed. Many of them are working in low-wage jobs where part of the benefit is the training they are receiving. When they stop work, the loss includes not just what they were producing, which is included in GDP, but also the value of the training, which is not included in GDP. The experience of unemployment itself may have social costs beyond reduced GDP. Unemployed people may be more likely to turn to crime or to become physically or mentally ill.

The direct costs of lost GDP are overwhelming. In a typical recession, GDP falls below potential by around 5 percent for about 2 years. Total lost GDP is about 10 percent of 1 year's GDP, or almost $600 billion at 1991 levels. There are about 100 million families in the United States, so the loss is about $6,000 per family. Some recessions are much deeper and involve even larger losses.

In order to get a full picture of the net social impact of a recession, we have to look at the benefits as well. Here our discussion of short-run labor supply in Chapter 15 becomes significant. If workers have a backlog of useful activities other than work in the market, or if they can store up memories of the leisure they enjoy during a recession, then there is a large offset to the lost output during a recession. In fact, with a completely flat labor supply schedule and no complications from taxes, the offset is exact. The value of the increased leisure and other nonmarket activities during a recession just equals the value of the output forgone. Data do show that people make some good uses of their extra time during recessions. For example, school and college attendance rises in recessions.

Taxes are one important reason to think that the offset is far from complete. Because work in the market is taxed but leisure and most other nonmarket uses of time are not taxed, there is a bias in the economy against market work. The social value of market work exceeds the worker's private earnings by the amount of payroll and income taxes. Any perturbation in the economy, such as a recession, that moves people from market work to nonmarket activities has a social cost even if it does not have a private cost.

The other important reason for less than full offset from the value of nonmarket activities is wage rigidity. If employers face a flat labor supply schedule because contracts and customs require it, but workers actually have steep labor supply schedules, then workers gain little from the extra time that becomes available during a recession. The marginal value of their time drops sharply in a recession because they quickly use up the backlog of valuable uses of time other than work in the market. With wage rigidity, there is a gap between the social value of work and the value of time to workers. As a result, recessions are socially costly.

Economists have thought less about the costs of episodes when GDP is above potential. The microeconomic argument supporting the idea that the costs are important is the following: The extra work effort needed to push GDP above potential is worth more than is the extra GDP. Instead of working as many hours as they do during a boom and consuming and investing the extra output, the public would be better off with less output and more time to spend with their children, on their houses, and in recreation. Again, because of high taxes, the private value of time is well below the social value of work, so there is at least a range where a boom is socially beneficial even though it is privately costly to workers to be working longer hours.

In terms of unemployment, there is little disagreement that the marginal social costs of unemployment are higher at higher rates of unemployment. Remember that it is not the overall level of the marginal social cost that matters, but the extent to which the marginal social cost of unemployment is higher in recessions than in booms. The value of the extra time at home that becomes available with higher unemployment is much lower for people who are already partly idle because of a recession than it is for people who are busy because of a boom. Consequently, keeping the variability of unemployment low is an important social goal.

COSTS OF OUTPUT FLUCTUATIONS AND UNEMPLOYMENT

1. The marginal social cost of unemployment is higher when unemployment is high.
2. If labor supply is inelastic, the marginal value of time in other uses falls if employment falls, and rises if employment rises above normal.
3. Because of these considerations, the economy is better off with stable output at its full-employment level, as against fluctuating output and employment.

THE POLICY FRONTIER BETWEEN INFLATION LOSS AND UNEMPLOYMENT LOSS
18.5

In Chapter 9 we saw that, when aggregate demand shifts for some reason not related to macro policy, the shift can be offset through a policy that moves aggregate demand back to its original position. Then output and inflation will be back at their original levels as well. There is no need for aggregate demand shifts to cause either inflation losses or output-unemployment losses. Both can be avoided by a simple reversal of an aggregate demand shift.

In general, the best way to set up policy is to establish fixed rules for dealing with the foreseeable contingencies. One good fixed rule is to offset completely each aggregate demand disturbance. Another is to decide in advance how to deal with a shock that affects the price level. The choice of such a rule is a more complicated issue.

The price-adjustment equation from Chapter 17 is

$$\pi = f \frac{Y_{-1} - Y^*}{Y^*} + \pi_{-1} + Z. \qquad (18-1)$$

Here we use the assumption that the expectations term is simply the lagged value of inflation, $\pi^e = \pi_{-1}$. But recall that alternative models of the expectations term may be more appropriate depending on the type of policy that is used. The last term in Equation 18–1, Z, represents price shocks, like increases in the price of oil.

In Figure 18–2 we show how policy might handle a price shock. The diagram shows the price-adjustment equation (18–1). Output is the horizontal axis and inflation is the vertical axis. Policy can try to offset the price shock by lowering output, or policy can keep output at potential and ignore the increase in inflation. Keeping output at potential is a policy that is

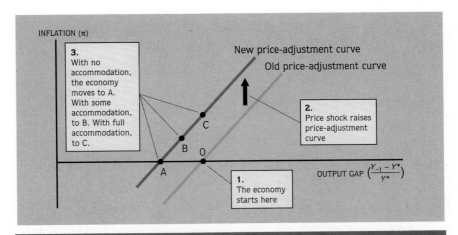

FIGURE 18-2   Alternative responses to a positive price shock

The economy starts in equilibrium with output at potential and inflation at zero. A positive price shock occurs and shifts the price-adjustment schedule upward. Policy can keep inflation at zero with a decrease in output, as at point A. Or, it can tolerate an increase in inflation together with a smaller decrease in output, as at point B. A third alternative is to keep output at potential and let the shock raise inflation, as at point C.

fully accommodative to inflation. The more policy lowers output below potential, the *less accommodative to inflation* is the policy. Because of Okun's
law, the policy that lowers output below potential raises unemployment
above the natural rate. When output stays at potential, unemployment stays
at the natural rate. Policy cannot keep both unemployment and prices stable.

We can characterize the policy alternatives in terms of a coefficient of
response g. If g is zero, the policy response keeps output at potential (and
unemployment at the natural rate) and permits every shift of the price-adjustment schedule to translate into the same amount of inflation. With g
equal to zero, there is no attempt to control inflation. Point C in Figure
18–2 is the one chosen for $g = 0$. If g is greater than zero, the policy response always lowers output and raises unemployment in order to stabilize
inflation. The larger g is, the larger the reduction in output when an inflation shock occurs. In Figure 18–2, point A represents a very large value of
g and point B represents an intermediate value. The coefficient g measures
how accommodative policy is to inflation. For $g = 0$, policy is fully accommodative to inflation. Larger values of g represent less accommodative policies.

In mathematical form, the coefficient of response g is part of the policy response function. Thus:

$$\frac{Y - Y^*}{Y^*} = -g\pi. \qquad (18–2)$$

In words, the output gap is reduced below zero if inflation rises above
zero.

We can use the price-adjustment equation to find out how much inflation will be reduced by different choices of the response coefficient g. If
we substitute the policy rule, Equation 18–2, into the price-adjustment
equation, we get

$$\pi = (1 - fg)\pi_{-1} + Z. \qquad (18–3)$$

When g is large, past inflation affects future inflation less, and the effects of
a single price shock are more quickly withdrawn from inflation. Define k as
$1 - fg$. The coefficient k measures how long and how much a price shock
affects inflation. If g is zero (a fully accommodative policy), so that $k =
(1 - fg) = 1$, then the price shock permanently raises the inflation rate by Z;
in this situation the effects of the price shock are never withdrawn from inflation. If inflation was zero before the price shock, it will be permanently
above zero after the price shock. If, at the other extreme, $k = 0$, then the effect of the price shock disappears after only one year. If k is in the intermediate range, between 0 and 1, then the effect of the price shock *gradually*
disappears: Inflation is k times the price shock in the year after the shock,

k^2 times the price shock in the second year, k^3 in the third year, and so on, eventually back to zero inflation. For example, if k is .8 and inflation is initially raised from zero to 10 percent because of the price shock, then inflation is 8 percent in the next year, 6.4 percent in the third year, 5.1 percent in the fourth year, 4.1 percent in the fifth year, and so on, eventually getting to zero inflation.

A policy that aggressively counters price shocks (with g large and k near zero) will result in large fluctuations in output and unemployment. This is clear from Equation 18–2. For example, suppose that the sensitivity of inflation f to output is .2 Then, to achieve a value of k equal to .8, we set g equal to 1. With these coefficients, suppose that a positive shock initially raises inflation by 10 percent. With $g = 1$, according to the policy rule in Equation 18–2, this will reduce output below potential by 10 percent in the period right after the shock. Eventually output will come back to potential as inflation declines. When g is large, the drop in output is large and, because of Okun's law, the rise in unemployment is large. On the other side, a negative shock that lowers inflation by 10 percent will require output to rise by 10 percentage points above potential if g is 1. According to Okun's law, unemployment falls in this case. A policy that rolls completely with price shocks (g equal to zero) will have a completely stable level of output and employment.

The implications of the choice of the coefficient k for inflation and unemployment losses are shown in Figure 18–3. Because the inflation loss

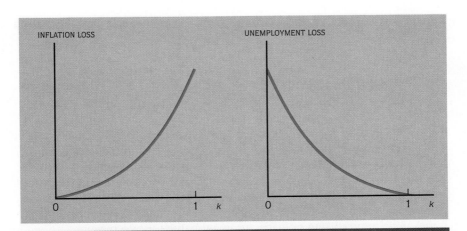

FIGURE 18–3   Average inflation and unemployment losses for alternative policies

For $k = 0$, policy changes unemployment enough to make price shocks disappear from inflation after only one year. The average inflation loss is small, but the unemployment loss is substantial. At $k = 1$, policy keeps unemployment at the natural rate and lets the price shock influence actual inflation fully. Unemployment loss is at a minimum but inflation loss is high.

and unemployment loss are related to the squared deviations from normal, the two curves sag as k is raised from zero.

There is another way we can depict the same trade-off. In Figure 18–4, we draw a curve representing the policy frontier in a diagram where average unemployment loss is the horizontal axis and average inflation loss is the vertical axis.[8]

THE INFLATION-UNEMPLOYMENT POLICY FRONTIER

1. The optimal policy for dealing with a shift in aggregate demand is to reverse the shift through a compensating change in aggregate demand policy. In that case, the shift does not cause either an inflation loss or an unemployment loss.
2. A general policy for dealing with price-adjustment shocks is to let the actual amount of inflation be a fraction k of the amount of the shock. The rest of the shock is canceled through aggregate demand policy.
3. An aggressive anti-inflation policy has a value of k close to 0.
4. There is a policy frontier defined by different values of k from 0 to 1. The frontier shows the available combinations of average inflation loss and average unemployment loss. The frontier curves toward the origin.

18.6   THE OPTIMAL POLICY FOR DEALING WITH PRICE SHOCKS

The policy frontier of Figure 18–4 shows the alternative combinations of inflation and unemployment loss that are available using different policies. The best policy will achieve a compromise between the two types of losses. Remember that the best policy is the one closest to the origin, that is, the one that achieves low values of both unemployment and inflation losses. Uncompromising policies are unattractive for two reasons:

---

[8]The idea of constructing policy frontiers in terms of the squared deviations of output and inflation and choosing alternative policy rules to get to the best point on such a frontier was described in John B. Taylor, "Estimation and Control of a Macroeconomic Model with Rational Expectations," *Econometrica,* Vol. 47 (September 1979), pp. 1267–1286; the model used in that paper corresponds closely with that discussed in the text.

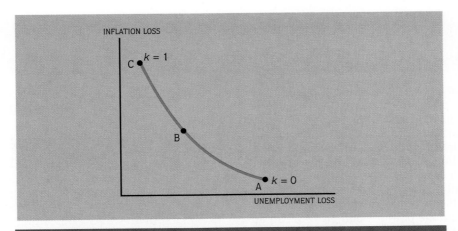

FIGURE 18–4 The policy frontier for unemployment and inflation losses

Every point on the frontier can be achieved by a policy that lets unemployment respond to inflation. At the upper left is the point of minimal unemployment loss and maximal inflation loss, corresponding to $k = 1$. At the lower right is the point of low inflation loss and high unemployment loss, corresponding to the other extreme, $k = 0$. The points marked A, B, and C are the same as in Figure 18–2.

1. A policy of strict price stability ($k = 0$, the point at the lower right-hand end of the policy frontier) involves a large amount of unemployment loss. It takes large movements of unemployment to keep inflation exactly at zero in the face of oil price shocks and other shifts in the process.

2. A policy of strict unemployment stability ($k = 1$, the point at the upper left-hand end of the policy frontier) involves a large amount of inflation loss. When an inflationary shock occurs, the policy does nothing to offset the shock. Not only does inflation jump upward in the year of the shock, but inflation is higher in future years as well, because the shock raises expected inflation.

Uncompromising policies are unsuitable because, in both cases, the trade-off set by the policy frontier strongly favors making at least a small compromise. From strict inflation stability, a small move toward the middle of the frontier gives a large payoff in reduced unemployment loss with only a small sacrifice of inflation loss. From strict unemployment stability, a small move to the middle gives a large payoff in reduced inflation loss with only a small sacrifice of unemployment loss.

To find the optimal compromise, we superimpose the policy frontier of Figure 18–4 on the family of social indifference curves from Figure 18–1.

What Would an Optimal Policy Have Been in 1979 to 1991?

In the late 1970s inflation was high. A large price shock had hit the U.S. economy in 1978 and 1979, when a revolution in Iran overthrew the Shah early in 1979 and Iraq invaded Iran. The result was a substantial fall in world oil production and a dramatic increase in oil prices. The inflation shock was several percentage points and actual inflation rose about 2 percentage points. Then, in 1982, an adverse aggregate demand shock occurred.

With the policy actually pursued, the response of the economy to these two shocks is shown in the diagram. Nominal growth remained at a high level in 1979 but fell substantially in 1980. It resumed in 1981 and then fell drastically in 1982. A vigorous recovery then followed in 1983 and 1984, with more modest growth in 1985 and 1986. Growth was higher in 1987 to 1990, but fell to a very low level in 1991.

What would an optimal policy have looked like? A reasonable set of targets for nominal GDP starting in 1979 is shown by the black line in the diagram.

The decline is in accord with the optimal policy rule of $k = .9$, with underlying real growth.

Nominal GDP growth was 1.4 percentage points above this target in 1979; an error of this magnitude is reasonable and would not have represented a failure of monetary policy. In 1980, nominal growth was almost exactly on target. In 1981, nominal growth was 3.1 percentage points above target. Such an error is outside the bounds of normal variation. In 1982, nominal GDP growth was 4.2 percent below target. Such an excessive contraction is clearly below the targets of the nominal GDP-based policy. Growth in 1983 was close to target, but growth in 1984 again exceeded the target. Some of this later fast growth was appropriate because of the mistake in 1982 which dropped real output too far below potential. Growth in 1985 and 1986 was close to target.

Judged by the nominal GDP targets, the policy for handling inflation and the oil price shock in 1979–80 was appropriate.

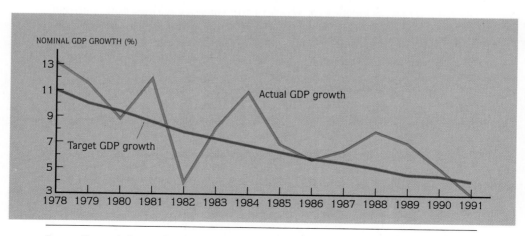

Source: *Economic Report of the President, 1992,* Table B–1.

This meant suffering; unemployment jumped and real GDP slumped. But any macro policy to reduce inflation would require some extra unemployment.

On the other hand, there was a policy error in 1982. Real output fell, unemployment rose, and inflation dropped faster than a smooth decline in nominal GDP growth would have implied. Keeping nominal GDP growth at 8 percent for 1982 would have offset the demand shock. The Fed's reaction appeared to be late. Not until late 1982 did the Fed ease policy. The reasons for the Fed's policy mistake are not clear. Possibly Chairman Paul Volcker and the rest of the FOMC were still very concerned about a resurgence of inflation, or were not sure that money demand was shifting.

Starting in 1987 and continuing through 1989, nominal GDP growth leveled out at around 7 percent per year, instead of declining according to our hypothetical target. The reasons that nominal GDP growth did not decline are not clear. Perhaps the economy grew more rapidly in 1988 than the Fed anticipated. Unlike some other variables, the Fed cannot control nominal GDP exactly. In the recession year 1991, GDP growth finally dropped below target again. All told, policy has followed the path recommended in this box reasonably closely on the average.

The best point on the frontier is the one tangent to the indifference curve closest to the origin, as shown in Figure 18–5.

In Chapter 17 we looked at the macro performance of the United States, Germany, and the United Kingdom from the 1970s to the present in

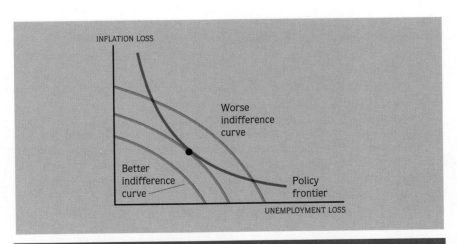

FIGURE 18–5 The optimal policy for responding to price shocks

The colored line shows the policy frontier. At the upper left are policies that stabilize unemployment at the cost of higher average inflation loss. At the lower right are policies that stabilize inflation at the cost of higher average unemployment loss. The optimal policy is in the middle, where the frontier is tangent to the indifference curve that is closest to the origin of all the indifference curves that touch the policy frontier.

terms of output-inflation loops (Figures 17–5 to 17–7). In these diagrams inflation is on the vertical axis and output is on the horizontal axis. Recall that the flat loops represented large output fluctuations and small inflation fluctuations, performance corresponding to values of k near zero. The steep (standing-up) loops represented the reverse—large inflation fluctuations and small unemployment fluctuations, performance corresponding to values of k near 1. Therefore, according to this empirical evidence, Germany, with its flat loops during this period, followed a less accommodative policy: Output fluctuations were relatively large and inflation fluctuations were relatively small. The United Kingdom evidently changed its policy in a less accommodative direction in the late 1970s. The orientation of its loops changed around the time that Margaret Thatcher became prime minister. The United States has had a policy that falls between the others: more accommodative than Germany's and less accommodative than the United Kingdom's before Thatcher. There is not much evidence that the overall accommodative stance of U.S. policy changed during this period.

The Message for Policymakers

It is not an easy matter to conduct macro policy in an optimal way. Our analysis has reached two conclusions about the appropriate response to shocks in the economy:

1. If the shock affects only aggregate demand, then a compensating change in aggregate demand policy (monetary or fiscal) will eliminate both the inflation loss and the unemployment loss.
2. If the shock affects the price-adjustment schedule, then the best policy divides its effects between reducing inflation and unemployment according to the rule that the actual amount of inflation declines by a fraction k each year.

In general, to develop policy within our model, the policymaker needs to be able to separate shocks into their aggregate demand and price-adjustment components and then figure out the magnitude of the response needed to offset fully the aggregate demand shock and to offset partially the price-adjustment shock. Clearly some technical analysis is necessary to do this.

Nominal GDP Targeting: A Reasonable Way to Express Policy?

There is another less technical way to express the optimal policy. The alternative begins with the observation that the optimal policy tends to stabilize nominal GDP. Suppose in some year a positive aggregate demand shock raises real GDP without much effect on prices. It shows up as above-normal growth of nominal GDP. A rule that calls for steady GDP would automatically offset aggregate demand shocks, just as our optimal policy recommends.

When a positive price-adjustment shock strikes, the optimal policy is to let part of the shock raise prices and part of the shock reduce output and raise unemployment. Keeping nominal GDP on a prescribed growth track does exactly that. Nominal GDP is the product of the price level and real GDP. If the price level jumps, real GDP must fall to keep nominal GDP growth at a prescribed rate. Keeping nominal GDP growth at a prescribed rate is a compromise policy of the type we just derived as optimal.

NEW RESEARCH IN PRACTICE
Using Indicators to Guide Policy

Monetary policymakers, and the economists who advise them, have long sought the ideal indicator of the state of the economy. A recent book by Wendy Dobson of the University of Toronto discusses the practical use of different indicators based on her experiences as Canada's representative to the G–7 meetings in the late 1980s. (See *Economic Policy Coordination: Requiem or Prologue?*, Institute for International Economics, 1991.) Some of the indicators considered have been the consumer price index, prices of sensitive commodities, exchange rates, measures of the money stock, interest rates, unemployment, real GDP, and nominal GDP. If there were a single best indicator, then monetary policy might be executed simply by adjusting the Fed's holdings of government securities as needed to keep the indicator at a target level.

Current Fed policy uses a short-term interest rate, the federal funds rate, as the main indicator of monetary policy. The traders at the New York Fed are instructed to buy and sell securities as needed to keep the federal funds rate on target. However, the target needs to be changed frequently, because merely keeping that interest rate at a particular target level does not follow through on the Fed's duty to stabilize the economy and prevent long-run inflation. In the late 1940s, when the Fed just stuck doggedly to an interest-rate target, inflation was briefly out of control. Today, the Fed looks at a variety of indicators such as real GDP, prices, and exchange rates in deciding on the federal funds target. There is no explicit single indicator and no announced target.

Many other countries rely on an explicit exchange-rate target. In particular, most European countries dedicate their monetary policies to keeping their currencies at prescribed exchange rates with the German deutsche mark (DM).

How to Choose an Indicator

An ideal indicator has two characteristics: It is closely related to the fundamental goals of monetary policy, and it is highly responsive to changes in monetary policy. For example, if it were agreed that the single goal of monetary policy was to keep inflation at zero and the price level responded within a day or two to a change in the Fed's holdings of government securities, then the Consumer Price Index would be a good indicator. We could just tell the New York Fed traders to keep the CPI at a particular target, and monetary policy would be taken care of. Or, if keeping nominal GDP on a smooth target path were the accepted goal of monetary policy and nominal GDP responded quickly to monetary policy, we could instruct the traders to keep nominal GDP on the path.

Thus a good indicator must be *relevant* and it must be *responsive*. In a modern economy, relevant means that keeping the indicator on target will keep inflation in a narrow band, say 0 to 4 percent. Relevant also means that the indicator will register recessions, so that monetary policy can help offset them. Responsive means that a change in the Fed's holdings of securities has an effect on the indicator with a very short lag. If the Fed doesn't get quick feedback, it cannot hope to keep the indicator on target. Using a sluggish indicator is like steering a car when it takes several minutes for the car to respond to your turning the wheel.

How Good Are the Existing Indicators?

The Consumer Price Index

The CPI scores well in relevance—stabilizing the price level is the most widely accepted goal of monetary policy—but very low in responsiveness. The CPI is only measured once a month, and little effect of monetary changes is apparent in the CPI until at least a year has gone by.

Prices of Sensitive Commodities

Sensitive commodities include gold and other precious metals and other standardized products such as cocoa, lumber, and grain traded on organized exchanges. Commodities score very low in relevance. There is no single commodity, or package of commodities, whose price is much related to the cost of living or nominal income. Prices of sensitive commodities are adequately responsive, but pegging them at a target level would highly unstabilize the overall economy.

Exchange Rates

For a European country (other than Germany), the exchange rate with the DM is both relevant and responsive. Monetary policy works well if it keeps the exchange rate on target. But for the three mega-economies—the United States, Germany, and Japan—relevance fails. In the first place, one of the three countries has to have a policy other than fixing an exchange rate, so that the other two could fix their exchange rates to it. But even then, for the

United States, for example, to dedicate its monetary policy to keeping the dollar in a fixed relation to the DM would probably not stabilize the U.S. economy.

Measures of the Money Stock

The use of money stock measures to guide monetary policy over the long run can be effective, but in the short run these measures can fail as indicators. The demand for broad money measures such as M2 is sufficiently stable that holding them on target over the long term can considerably stabilize output and prices. Short-run fluctuations in velocity make narrow money targetting on a month-to-month basis de-stabilizing, however.

Interest Rates

Interest rates have a crucial role in current policymaking in the United States, Germany, and Japan. But interest rates are largely irrelevant to the basic long-run goals of monetary policy. There is no magic level of any interest rate that will bring stable output and prices. Interest rates are the quintessentially responsive indicator, on the other hand. The federal funds market responds within seconds to trades made by the Fed.

Unemployment and Real GDP

Okun's law means that we can think of unemployment and real GDP as alternative indicators of the state of employment and output. Most economists would agree on the relevance of the real side of the economy for monetary policy, though only in the shorter run. But real variables are not nearly responsive enough to qualify as the sole indicators of monetary policy. It takes several months for such variables to respond to monetary change.

Nominal GDP

There is growing consensus among economists about the relevance of nominal income for monetary policy. Nominal GDP combines the price and output dimensions that should concern policy. But nominal GDP responds to policy with a lag, just as do its factors, real output and prices.

Looking for New Indicators: Forecasts of Nominal GDP?

There are at least 50 respected and successful forecasts published regularly for the major macro variables in the United States. Forecasts of relevant variables for the next 1 to 3 years may be the ideal indicators for monetary policy. Consider the use of a forecast of nominal GDP 18 months hence as the central indicator for monetary policy. If it is a good forecast, it is obviously relevant. Although nominal GDP is not nearly responsive enough to serve as an indicator, forecasts of its level 18 months forward are highly responsive. When the Fed expands monetary policy by purchasing more government securities, the fact is immediately known to forecasters because it registers the federal funds interest rate. The forecasters then process this information to determine the likely impact on prices and output in the economy in the future. Within a day or two of a policy change, they update their forecasts (many of the forecasts are distributed by computer and can be in the hands of subscribers in a matter of hours). So a forecast of nominal GDP appears to be a very responsive indicator.

Whose forecast should be used? There is an informal consensus among producers and users of forecasts for the U.S. economy about what they are saying as a group. There is even a newsletter, *Blue Chip Economics*, that publishes the average of the forecasts. So using the average forecast of nominal GDP would seem to be the natural answer

The degree of compromise in a policy that stabilizes nominal GDP seems to favor unemployment stability over price stability. The value of the coefficient of response g for a nominal GDP policy is 1. As we showed above, when $g = 1$, the value of k is .8 for the numerical example of price adjustment used here. Eighty percent of a price-adjustment shock is tolerated as a continued increase in inflation the year after it occurs. Twenty percent is extinguished by permitting output to fall. Thereafter, 20 percent of inflation is offset each year, by keeping output below normal.

Suppose the initial inflation impact from a shock is 10 percent. Under the fixed nominal GDP policy, real GDP falls by 10 percent, and inflation in the following year is reduced to 8 percent. From Okun's law, this means that unemployment rises by 3 percent in the first year.

If the public is so opposed to inflation that the optimal value of k is well below .8, then nominal GDP targeting is inappropriate; it gives excessive inflation losses that will not be made up, in the public's view, by the lower unemployment losses it will bring. Or, if the public cares less about inflation, nominal GDP targeting will bring excessive unemployment losses that will not be made up by its favorable influence on inflation losses. In either case it would be possible to change the policy goal and let nominal GDP respond to the price shock. If $k = .8$ is too large, then nominal GDP should be reduced when price shocks occur. If $k = .8$ is too small, then nominal GDP could be allowed to grow a bit when a price shock occurs. But the simplicity of a fixed nominal GDP may outweigh the benefits of modifying the path of nominal GDP in this way.[9]

If nominal GDP targeting were used explicitly in practice, the process might work in the following way: Each year the Fed and the administration would announce a target rate of growth of nominal GDP for the next 2 or 3 years. The announcement dates could occur at the same time as the Fed's money aggregate targets now occur, once in July with an update the following February (see Chapter 14). Then each month, as new information became available about the growth of nominal GDP, the Fed and the administration could adjust monetary and fiscal policy to eliminate errors. If growth were above target, for example, the Fed would contract the monetary base. The FOMC would instruct the open-market desk to sell government securities; this would reduce the monetary base and raise interest rates. If growth were below target, the Fed would expand the monetary base by buying bonds, thus lowering interest rates.

Nominal GDP targeting should not be viewed as an alternative to the optimal policies described above. Rather, it is an easy and convenient way to talk about policy procedures and goals. For example, if there is a policy mistake that brings about a very high unemployment rate, then the optimal policy is to bring the economy back to normal quickly. There is no reason to hold output Y below potential Y^* if inflation is low. Holding nominal GDP growth to a fixed level might not allow the economy to catch up and bring Y back to Y^*. But even in this case the policymakers should announce their intentions for nominal GDP growth.

18.7 CHANGING THE POLICY FRONTIER

The policy we described in the previous section is optimal in the sense that it tells policymakers how to make the best of a bad situation. But the policy does not make the situation good. We should spend at least as much effort thinking about how to move the policy frontier toward the origin as we spend thinking about choosing the best point on the frontier. If the frontier were closer to the origin, both inflation loss and unemployment loss would be lower.

---

[9]See Robert E. Hall, "Macroeconomic Policy under Structural Change," in *Industrial Change and Public Policy* (Federal Reserve Bank of Kansas City, 1983), pp. 85–111, and James Tobin, "Commentary," in *Industrial Change and Public Policy*, pp. 113–122. A review of the alternative proposals is found in John B. Taylor, "What Would Nominal GNP Targeting Do to the Business Cycle?" *Carnegie-Rochester Conference Series on Public Policy*, Vol. 22 (1985), pp. 61–84.

Streamline the Labor Market

The policy frontier lies far from the origin because wages do not respond quickly and vigorously to the situation in the labor market. When an inflation shock strikes, policy has to raise unemployment to get inflation back down. When wages are less responsive, a larger rise in unemployment is necessary. If wages could be made to adjust rapidly to surpluses and shortages of labor, then the average unemployment loss needed to keep inflation loss at a given level would be lower. The policy frontier would be closer to the origin.

Because the reasons for sluggish adjustment of wages are not well understood, it is not obvious what types of new policies would speed up the process. Some proposals include:

1. *Better Job Matching*. In the highly decentralized labor market of the United States, employers have trouble getting in touch with potential workers. There may be a large number of qualified people ready to work at a particular job at a low wage. If the employer cannot let them know about the job, it may be necessary to hire a nearby worker at a higher wage. Some kind of electronic job listing might make it possible to draw from a larger number of potential workers. Or, if there were better information available about the number of qualified job seekers, firms would be in a better position to tailor wage offers to the state of the market. Federal and state employment agencies have tried to perform this service for many years, however, and have found that employers are reluctant to list most types of jobs. Employers fear having to deal with thousands of unqualified applicants if they list jobs publicly. Instead, they seem to prefer to look at smaller numbers of candidates located privately. There seems to be no basis to hope that the labor market could be significantly improved by expansion of public job listings.

2. *Eliminate Government Price and Wage Fixing*. Hundreds of government regulations have the effect of either fixing prices and wages directly or limiting the flexibility of businesses in setting prices and wages. The Davis-Bacon Act, for example, prevents contractors from cutting construction costs by taking advantage of slack conditions in markets for construction workers. Local governments regulate bus and taxi fares, so they cannot fall to accommodate the increased supply of drivers in times of higher unemployment. Many government regulations that limited price and wage flexibility have been abolished, however. Airlines are now free to adjust fares whenever market conditions change. Most restrictions on professionals publicizing their prices have been lifted. The scope for further reform in this area is limited however.

3. *Reform Unemployment Compensation*. Unemployed workers receive unemployment benefits for up to 6 months after a job loss. Conse-

quently, their incentives to look for new work and to accept new jobs at lower wages are reduced. Unemployment compensation serves a vital purpose and should not be abolished, but certain types of reforms could improve incentives without making the unemployed suffer. The most important is to make employers pay more for benefits whenever possible. If an employer had to pay for benefits during a layoff, the employer might prefer to keep the worker at work and cut prices as necessary to sell output. Publicly financed benefits create incentives to lay off a worker, produce less, and maintain a higher price when demand falls.

Improve Indexation

In Chapter 17 we saw that when wages are linked directly to prices through cost-of-living indexation the impact of outside price shocks is amplified; a price shock goes immediately into wages, then into costs, and finally into prices again, all within the same year. Although indexation prevents workers from being left behind by general inflation, it is harmful to the economy when wages rise in response to oil or other outside price shocks.

The ideal method of cost-of-living escalation would omit price increases that arise from imports and other materials costs. Though economists have suggested price indexes that would perform better than the CPI for wage indexation, nobody has started to use them for actual wage setting. It is not easy to persuade a skeptical employer or labor union that a new price index is superior to the tried and true consumer price index. Proposals to make much smaller changes in the indexes used for wage indexation have encountered stiff resistance. There are no grounds for optimism that wage setters will voluntarily adopt new indexation methods. Nor is it clear that the government can or should try to force changes in this area.

Avoid Government Price Shocks

Sometimes the government itself creates a shock in the price-adjustment process. An important example occurred in Britain in 1979. The government cut income taxes and substituted a value-added tax to raise the same revenue. Because the value-added tax is imposed on firms, it adds to costs just as does an increase in the price of a material input. The VAT is much like a sales tax. In terms of the price-adjustment model of Chapter 17, the value-added tax adds an inflationary impetus Z in the year that it goes into effect.

In Britain, the value-added tax shock and the oil price shock occurred simultaneously. The British economy suffered from more inflation and a larger reduction in output than did the U.S. economy, which suffered only from the oil price shock. If self-inflicted government price shocks can be kept to a minimum, the policy frontier will be closer to the origin.

Avoiding government price shocks need not prevent tax reform or other useful changes in the government's influence on the economy. For example, a value-added tax can be changed in a simple way that does not change its favorable properties as a tax; it could be instituted so that the cost falls on workers rather than on businesses. Then the switch to the tax will not create a price shock. Changes in all types of economic policies need to be designed with the harmful effects of macro price shocks in mind.

Controls and Incentives

The reason the policy frontier is so far from the origin is that the government influences inflation only indirectly through its control of demand. If the government could simply dictate the price level, then there would be no need for either inflation losses or unemployment losses. Moreover, there need not be shortages or excess supplies in such an economy. The government could set the price level and the position of the aggregate demand schedule so as to have them intersect exactly at full employment.

Only once has the U.S. government tried to set prices and wages directly in peacetime. In the early 1970s, high inflation inherited from expansionary policies of the 1960s (partly related to the war in Vietnam) created a political uproar. From the summer of 1971 until the spring of 1974, a succession of price-wage control schemes were tried out under the Nixon administration. The professed goal was exactly what we just stated—to keep the economy at a point of full employment and low inflation.

The only point of agreement in evaluating our experience under price controls is that they involved a signficant bureaucracy and a great deal of strife. Firms were supposed to follow government rules in setting prices. If their customers thought the rules were being violated, they could complain in Washington. Every wage change could also be reviewed in Washington. The result was a great accumulation of cases to be studied and ruled upon by the Cost of Living Council which was set up to administer the price and wage control program. Handling the wage cases was particularly important because the labor unions involved were politically powerful and because they could threaten to strike if the wage increases they had won were not approved.

Economists are still unsettled as to whether the Nixon controls had any important effect on inflation. Opponents of controls point to examples of shortages and other distortions from the controls. Proponents say that the Nixon program was exactly the wrong way to run controls and that a good system would work much better. Quite apart from the economic merit of controls, it does seem questionable whether the American political system can operate a system of controls for a sustained period. Just as wartime controls collapsed at the ends of World Wars I and II, growing political opposition brought a fairly speedy end to the Nixon controls.

Economists looking for a permanent policy to shift the inflation-unemployment policy frontier toward the origin have proposed systems based on incentives rather than controls. **Tax-based incomes policies** would reward businesses and workers who followed government guidelines for price and wage increases. Businesses would lose tax deductions for cost increases beyond the guideline rates and would pay extra taxes on revenue attributable to excess price increases. In the aftermath of a price shock, policy could get inflation back down by setting a low guideline for wage and price increases. The disincentive cost to taxpayers would be less than the cost of the unemployment that would result from achieving the same degree of disinflation through higher unemployment.

Since we do not have any practical experience with incentives, it is hard to know how well they would work. Any incentive program would have to be designed with great care. In 1978, President Carter submitted an incentive plan to Congress. In addition to specific incentives for individual price and wage setters, it offered workers a general assurance that the program could not hurt them. Labor had been concerned that they might be required to moderate their wage growth while businesses did nothing to cut price inflation. Carter's program included real wage insurance. In the event that prices did rise more than wages, workers would have received income tax cuts large enough to make up their loss in real wages.

Only a few months after the real wage insurance proposal was made, real wages fell by several percentage points, thanks to an event that had nothing to do with the anti-inflation program. World oil prices almost tripled. That event was never contemplated in designing real wage insurance. Had real wage insurance gone into effect in 1978, huge tax cuts would have occurred quite accidentally in 1979 and 1980, when the federal budget was already in deficit. Fortunately, real wage insurance died in Congress and this accident never took place.

Trade Policy

One of the ways the government affects the variability of inflation is through trade policy. Generally, policies that restrict imports will raise inflation when they are imposed and lower inflation when they are removed. As we noted in Chapter 12, different protectionist policies can have very different effects on U.S. prices. Quotas have a strong and immediate effect on prices. Tariffs have a strong effect if they are not absorbed by foreign sellers. For example, an oil tariff would immediately raise the U.S. price of oil, because it is unlikely that OPEC would choose to lower its price to U.S. purchasers in response to the tariff. On the other hand, a tariff on Japanese cars might well be absorbed by Japanese auto makers, just as they absorbed most of the impact of the appreciating yen in the 1985–88 period.

Each time a protectionist measure is imposed or tightened, it gives a one-time shock to inflation. If a tariff is on a single important product, such as oil, it can cause a perceptible shock to total inflation. An equal but negative shock will occur if the tariff is taken off. Stabilization policy would be significantly more difficult and less successful if protectionist measures were imposed and removed in order to satisfy other goals, such as protecting ailing domestic industries, fostering energy conservation, or reducing the trade deficit.

IMPROVING THE POLICY FRONTIER

1. Policies for streamlining the labor market could push the inflation-unemployment frontier toward the origin. The same amount of inflation loss would be achieved with less unemployment loss if inflation responded more vigorously to unemployment.
2. Public job placement has not been very successful. Reduced government price and wage fixing might be a small help. Reform in unemployment compensation would also improve the frontier a little.
3. Controls on prices and wages are another option, but in practice they have been difficult to administer and have not had a lasting impact on inflation.
4. The government should be careful not to create unnecessary price shocks.

REVIEW AND PRACTICE

Major Points

1. The general policy implication of recent research in macroeconomics is that policy should be formulated as a rule or contingency plan.
2. Macroeconomic policy can be logically formulated and evaluated using the target and instrument framework. A social welfare function could be used to represent goals for the target variables.
3. Much as in most areas of economics, trade-offs are widespread in macroeconomics. As long as the number of instruments is scarce we will face a tough trade-off between the goals of the target variables.
4. Uncertainty in the models leads to less active use of the policy instruments.
5. High inflation is bad because it causes people to hold too little money. It is also difficult to adjust the tax system to be neutral to inflation. Inflation also some-

times brings higher uncertainty, which can interfere with efficient resource allocation. Deflation is undesirable for similar reasons.

6. Variations in unemployment are undesirable because the social costs of periods of high unemployment outweigh the benefits of periods of low unemployment.

7. Indifference curves between inflation loss and unemployment loss curve away from the origin. Higher indifference curves represent poorer macroeconomic performance.

8. Policy rules describe how accommodative the monetary policymakers are to inflation. More accommodative policy results in better output performance, but worse inflation performance.

9. A rule of keeping nominal GDP constant is a good way to characterize an optimal macroeconomic policy.

10. The only type of policy move that could improve both inflation and unemployment performance would be an inward shift of the policy frontier, but unfortunately the prospects seem limited for this type of policy.

Key Terms and Concepts

social welfare function	scarcity of instruments	inflation loss
time inconsistency	policy trade-offs	unemployment loss
model uncertainty	activist policy	social indifference curve
commitment to	discretionary policy	policy frontier
a policy	shoe-leather cost of inflation	policy rule
final targets	marginal social cost	accommodation of inflation shock
intermediate targets	of unemployment	nominal GDP target

Questions for Discussion and Review

1. If the purpose of the final exam is to motivate students to study, why will the instructor not cancel the final at the last minute, after all studying has occurred, in order to save everybody's time and effort?

2. What is the basic argument against discretionary policy?

3. If the effect of a policy instrument is uncertain, will policymakers be more or less aggressive in the use of the instrument than they would be under certainty?

4. Give some of the reasons that both inflation and deflation are undesirable.

5. Explain why both high and variable unemployment are undesirable. Why does the policy frontier deal just with the variability and not with the level of unemployment?

6. Explain the consequences for unemployment and inflation if policymakers fully accommodate a price shock. Repeat for zero accommodation and for 50 percent accommodation.

7. Describe the axes of the policy frontier diagram and how to find points on the frontier.

8. How should policymakers choose the best point on the frontier?

9. How much accommodation of price shocks occurs if nominal GDP targets are followed?

10. List some of the proposals that have been made to shift the policy frontier inward.

11. Trace out the effects of a restrictive quota on auto imports.

Problems

Numerical

1. Calculate the value of k that corresponds to the policy of keeping nominal GDP at a given level in the year that a price shock occurs. Assume that f equals 1. Assume that the economy starts in equilibrium, with $Y = Y^*$, $\pi = 0$, and $P = 1$. Then an inflationary shock of 10 percent, $Z = .1$, occurs. Compute the change in the price level, using Equation 18–1. Compute the change in output from Equation 18–2. Show that the percentage change in real GDP plus the percentage change in the price level equals zero, the percentage change in nominal GDP.

2. An economy has an aggregate demand schedule $Y = 2,067 + 3.221M/P$. It starts at potential ($Y = Y^* = 4,000$) with a money stock of 600. Then it is hit by an inflation shock of $Z = .1$. Policy uses a value of k of .9. Assume that $f = .25$. Compute the change in the money stock necessary to achieve the policy. Also compute the changes in P and Y. Repeat the calculations for $k = .1$. Explain the differences.

3. The purpose of this exercise is to illustrate the trade-off between inflation and unemployment. However, we focus on the output gap rather than on unemployment because the two are so closely related due to Okun's law. Suppose that the policy rule

$$(Y - Y^*)/Y^* = -g\pi \qquad \text{(Policy Rule)}$$

is substituted into the price-adjustment equation to get

$$\pi = (1 - .2g)\pi_{-1} + Z. \qquad \text{(Inflation)}$$

a. Starting from $Y = Y^*$ and $\pi = 0$ (zero percent inflation), use the second equation to calculate the effect on inflation for Years 1 through 10 of a price shock $Z = .1$ (a 10 percent shock to the price level). Set $g = .5$.

b. Using the values of inflation that you calculated in Part a, calculate the value of the GDP gap, $(Y - Y^*)/Y^*$, for all 10 years using the policy rule.

c. Plot the values of inflation and the output gap for all 10 years on two time series diagrams (put the variable on the vertical axis and the year on the horizontal axis).

d. Plot the values of the output gap and inflation on a diagram with inflation on the vertical axis and the output gap on the horizontal axis (like Figure 17–5).

e. Calculate the average squared loss for inflation. That is, square each value of inflation (π^2) for all 10 years, sum up the squares, and divide by 10. Calculate the average squared loss for the output gap in the same way. Now repeat the calculations in Parts a through d and the inflation loss and output loss for $g = .1$ and $g = .9$. You should now have three pairs of inflation loss and output loss, one for each of the three values of the policy rule (g). Plot the three pairs on a diagram with average inflation loss on the vertical axis and average output loss (output gap) on the horizontal axis. Comment on the position of the three points. Is a trade-off between inflation loss and output loss evident? Compare your diagram with that of Figure 18–4. (Note that the output gap loss and the unemployment loss will occupy similar relative positions because of Okun's law.)

4. This exercise shows how a stochastic dynamic model with shocks can lead to business cycle fluctuations. Suppose that the income identity is

$$Y = C + I + G,$$

where $G = 750$. Consumption is equal to

$$C = 80 + .63 Y_{-1},$$

and investment is a random variable given by

$$I = 650 + (7 - \text{Number from a roll of a pair of dice}) + 93.$$

a. Roll a pair of dice 20 times, and record the number for each roll. Use the investment function to calculate investment for each roll. This gives 20 years of stochastic investment. Investment in Year 1 is the first roll and investment in Year 20 is the last roll. Plot the values of investment on a time series chart with investment on the vertical axis and the year on the horizontal axis. The values should look random, with investment fluctuating around 650.

b. Now use the values of investment for the 20 years to calculate income Y. Substitute the consumption function into the income identity. Start with Y_{-1} equal to 4,000 and with investment equal to the value that you calculated for Year 1. Then calculate the second year's income by substituting in income for the first year for Y_{-1} and investment in the second year. Do the same thing for the third year and so on through Year 20.

c. Plot the resulting values of income Y for the 20 years with the year on the horizontal axis. The average value should be near 4,000, but you should see some prolonged fluctutations around this average value that look like business cycles. Compare the prolonged fluctuations of Y with the random but less prolonged fluctuations of investment I. Calculate the average time between peaks for each series. Unless your dice are loaded, the average time between peaks for income will be longer than that for investment. Try to explain why.

5. Suppose that price-adjustment and inflationary expectations are given by Equations 17–1 and 17–2, respectively. Policy is given by Equation 18–2 with $g = 0$. Initially there is an oil price shock of 2.5 percent ($Z = .025$).

a. Calculate inflation and expected inflation for Years 1 through 4. Are expectations rational?

b. Is the monetary authority using a constant money stock target, a constant nominal GDP target, or neither? Explain your answer.

Analytical

1. Derive the aggregate demand schedule for the case where the Fed maintains nominal GDP at a given target level.

2. Given the discussion of optimal policy in this chapter, comment on the validity of the criticism that the Fed was too tight in 1979 and 1990.

3. In Chapter 14 we showed how monetary policy affects the economy with a lag. What are the implications of these lags for our suggestions about optimal policy in this chapter? What do lags in the effect of money imply for nominal GDP targeting?

4. Compare monetary aggregate targeting by the Fed (as described in Chapter 14) with targeting nominal GDP. Prepare a brief argument in favor of each type of targeting; list advantages and disadvantages.

5. Using the IS-LM method, show what the Fed must do to the money supply to reduce output by a certain percentage when there is a price shock. Could the same actions be undertaken by fiscal policy? Why might a mix of monetary and fiscal policies be used to reduce output after a price shock?

6. Suppose that in response to a large and unexpected oil price shock the Fed acts to keep output at potential. Inflationary expectations are given by the expression $\pi^e = .9\pi_{-1}$. Prices are sticky and price adjustment is given by an equation like Equation 17–1. The changes in the money stock, prices, and output for the first 4 years are:

Year	%ΔM	%ΔP	%ΔY
1	10	10	0
2	9	9	0
3	8.1	8.1	0
4	7.3	7.3	0

   a. How large was the oil price shock?
   b. An economist writing for a popular newsweekly comments: "The Fed is up to its old tricks again, fueling inflation with money stock growth." The economist goes on to note that every time the Fed increases the money supply by x percent it leads to an increase in prices of x percent, just as predicted by the classical model. Is this economist right; that is, has inflation over the last 4 years been caused by increases in the money stock?
   c. The economist finishes with an admonition to the Fed to stick to a constant money stock rule. This, the economist asserts, will give us noninflationary full employment. If the Fed had held the money stock constant over the last 4 years, would output have remained constant? Diagram the path the economy would have followed using an output-inflation loop.

7. Suppose that as a result of the Fed's policy rule, inflation is given by Equation 18–3, where the parameter k lies between 0 and 1. Sketch the output-inflation loop for the case of an oil price shock. Is there overshooting as in the output-inflation loops of Chapter 17? Why or why not?

8. In the June 4, 1979, issue of *Fortune*, an article by Herbert Stein, a former chairman of the Council of Economic Advisers, appeared that argued, "The idea that we need to get beyond the day-to-day, or even year-to-year, management of economic policy has been gaining more and more recognition. . . . The idea still has no operational effect on policy, however. Someone in authority has to take a step. The President and the Chairman of the Federal Reserve Board could describe what they regard as the desirable path of GDP for, say, the next five years. They could declare their intention, insofar as it lies within their power, to manage fiscal and monetary policy to stay on that path, and return to it if the economy strayed off. . . . Such an initiative would not prevent anyone from changing his mind. I am not proposing a constitutional amendment." Write a short essay evaluating Stein's proposal. Why would policymakers want to change their minds? What good is the proposal if they probably will? Why is Stein reluctant to propose a constitutional amendment?

MacroSolve Exercises

1. *Policy Decision 1997.* You have been hired to work for the President's Council of Economic Advisers. After 2 days on the job there is a major increase in the price of oil because of a crisis in the Middle East. You are asked to provide answers to a series of questions. Suppose you feel that a reasonable welfare function is the sum over 5 years of the square of the inflation rate and the square of the GDP gap (the percentage deviation of real GDP from 6,000). Use the "AD/PA, Closed Econ" model. Assume that there is a price shock of 10 percent.
   a. What happens if neither the money supply nor government spending is changed? What is the value of your welfare function?
   b. What happens if the money supply is increased by $90 billion? What is the value of the welfare function now? By this criterion, is the economy better off or worse off after this policy of accommodation?
   c. What happens if, instead, the government follows an extinguishing policy of decreasing the money supply by $90 billion? Is this policy preferred by the welfare criterion to the policy of accommodation?

2. An alternative index of welfare that is often discussed during presidential elections is the so-called misery index, the sum of the inflation rate and the unemployment rate. Recall that the unemployment rate is related to the GDP gap by Okun's law (Chapter 3). If the natural unemployment rate is 6 percent, then the unemployment rate is generated by the following equation:

$$U = 6 - \text{GDP gap}/3.$$

Use this equation to calculate the misery index corresponding to the situations in Parts a, b, and c of Question 1. Comment on the differences between the relative desirability of the alternative policies between the two welfare functions.

CHAPTER

19

The World Economy

Total world trade, measured by the dollar value of imports to all countries, was over $3.4 trillion in 1990—more than a tenfold increase since 1960. During this same period U.S. exports as a percentage of GDP doubled, from about 5 percent to 10 percent; in Britain exports are now over 25 percent of GDP. Each day, throughout the world, several hundred billion dollars in financial assets are traded in the interbank foreign exchange market. These large international trade and financial movements indicate how closely the world's economies—including the U.S. economy—are now linked together.

We saw in Chapter 12 that changes in U.S. macroeconomic policy can have significant effects on foreign trade and on the exchange rate. An expansionary fiscal policy, for example, increases demand for imports from abroad and thereby increases aggregate demand in other countries as well as in the United States. An expansionary fiscal policy also raises interest rates in the United States, and this causes the dollar to appreciate. An appreciated dollar reduces demand for U.S. exports and induces U.S. consumers and firms to import goods from abroad, rather than purchase goods produced at home. This further stimulates aggregate demand in other countries, while it reduces the stimulus to the U.S. economy. Hence, an expansionary fiscal policy crowds out spending not only in interest-sensitive capital goods industries, but also in export industries and in import-competing industries.

This chapter extends our analysis of international macroeconomic issues in a number of ways. First, we look at the international monetary and financial system from a world perspective rather than just considering the role of the United States in the system. In addition to describing the system as it exists in the early 1990s, we describe the history of the system. Then we examine how national macroeconomic policy operates within the modern world economy and especially how concern about exchange rates affects policy. Next we consider the worldwide credit market and international capital-trade flows. We consider policies that try to influence these flows by changing saving and investment, on the one hand, or imports and exports on the other hand. Finally, we study the idea of monetary union, the ultimate stopping point of moves toward fixed exchange rates. Monetary union is a major issue in Europe today, just as it was among the 13 colonies after the American Revolution.

19.1   THE INTERNATIONAL FINANCIAL AND MONETARY SYSTEM

Within the United States, the financial and monetary system has a seamless quality. It is almost as easy to make a payment or borrow 3,000 miles away, over many state borders, as it is in your own state or city. The world economy is not as seamless. With relatively minor exceptions, U.S. currency cannot be spent directly in other countries. Borrowing in another country is possible only for larger corporations and then only in a few countries with advanced, open capital markets. In some countries, such as the People's Republic of China and the Republic of South Africa, there are detailed controls on the movement of currency and securities across the border in both directions. In many countries, the government tries to push up the price at which foreigners can trade dollars and other currencies for the domestic currency. The result is a black market or a curb market where the traveler gets a better deal, but may run into trouble with the law. Currency black markets flourished in the former Soviet Union as law enforcement weakened, but artificially high exchange rates were maintained for the ruble.

There is a strong trend toward making the world economy more integrated. For example, the nations of western Europe are almost completely integrating their financial markets, so that it is as easy for a European business to borrow or lend in another European country as it is for an American business to borrow or lend in another state. Later in the 1990s, some of the nations are planning to use a single monetary unit, which will put them close to the United States in monetary integration as well. At the same time, there will be a continuing trend toward free movement of currency and financial securities across the borders of countries that have previously controlled those flows.

In the 1990s, the world financial and monetary system can be summarized in the following way: There are four large economies with sophisticated, integrated financial markets—the United States, Japan, Germany, and Britain. These countries have large, active markets in stocks, bonds, options, and other financial instruments. They permit foreigners to trade in their markets on essentially an equal footing with their own citizens, and they do not interfere with their citizens' transactions in foreign markets. There are no inhibitions to completely free markets in their currencies and central bank reserves. Holders of checking accounts in any of the four countries can move central bank reserves from one country to another by writing checks, just as account-holders in the United States can move them from one bank to another. The four currencies (dollar, yen, deutsche mark, and pound) exchange for each other at rates set in extremely fluid, free markets.

Although the four major governments do not control the financial markets directly, the governments influence the behavior of the markets by trading. The four central banks (the Federal Reserve, the Bank of Japan, the Bundesbank, and the Bank of England) hold large portfolios of short-term government securities. Each bank usually has large holdings of securities issued by each of the four major governments. There are two basic dimensions of central bank policy. One is standard monetary policy, as we discussed in Chapter 14. If the Bundesbank buys more German government securities and expands its reserves correspondingly, that is an expansionary move that lowers the German interest rate and stimulates the German economy. The second dimension is the split of the central bank's portfolio between domestic and foreign securities. The Bank of Japan could sell Japanese government securities and use the proceeds to buy U.S. Treasury bills, for example. This move is called a **foreign exchange market intervention** and is often called "selling yen and buying dollars." However, a more detailed description is "selling yen-dominated securities and buying dollar-denominated securities." The effect of the intervention is to raise the exchange rate of the dollar relative to the yen. The magnitude of the exchange-rate effect per billion dollars of intervention may be very small because the securities markets where the intervention occurs are enormous.

On the next step down the ladder of countries by financial sophistication are the countries with few restrictions on currency and financial transactions. All of them have central banks that influence markets by trading in government securities. The countries include all the remaining countries of western Europe, Canada and other members of the British Commonwealth, and a number of Asian Pacific rim countries. Some of these countries have chosen to run their central bank policies with the single-minded effect of keeping one exchange rate at a constant level. A growing number of European countries belong to the **European Monetary System (EMS)**, including Germany, Britain, France, Belgium, the Netherlands, Italy, Ireland, Denmark, and Luxembourg. Members of the **EMS** keep their currencies at fixed values relative to the deutsche mark. Monetary policy for the **EMS** is made primarily by the Bundesbank as a result. Other countries—such as Canada—pursue independent monetary policies and let their exchange rates fluctuate over time.

The remaining nations of the world maintain some degree of insulation from the world financial and monetary system. The most common form of separation is controls on the movement of capital. The governments of these countries require permits for financial transactions across their borders. Often the intention is to trap economic activity within the country's borders. Other times it is to limit foreign entrepreneurs from undertaking profitable activities that might otherwise go to citizens. The People's Republic of China, for example, limits outsiders to less than a 50 percent interest in most investments. Controls on the movement of goods are also common. Many countries require permits for some or all types of imports. Finally, some countries try to suppress free-market transactions in their currencies. These currencies are **inconvertible,** meaning that they cannot be bought and sold in open markets.

All around the world, there is a powerful trend toward joining the world financial and monetary system. The system operates on strict free-market principles, and the four dominant players in the system are largely free-market economies. Many of the countries most interested in joining the system were previously centrally controlled: eastern European countries emerging from their earlier status as Soviet satellites, the republics of the former Soviet Union, and the People's Republic of China.

The specific steps that a country needs to take to join the world financial and monetary system are:

1. *Open up currency transactions.* Permit anyone inside or outside the country to exchange the country's currency for any other currency at a market-determined price.

2. *Open up capital movements.* Permit anyone in the country to purchase stocks, bonds, or other financial instruments from other countries or to raise funds by selling instruments in other markets. Permit foreigners to buy or sell securities in the country's markets and to borrow or lend to businesses or individuals.

3. *Open up movements of goods.* Permit anyone in the country to buy goods and services anywhere else in the world and permit foreigners to buy and sell goods and services in the country.

It is worth noting that the list requires new freedoms, not new government institutions. It is not important that a country have a central bank operating on the same principles as the Federal Reserve Bank. A country need not accumulate foreign reserves (foreign securities owned by the central bank) in order to function within the world system. But all the major players in the current world system have conventional central banks.

How a Central Bank Carries Out Its Exchange-Rate Policy

Central banks buy and sell government securities in order to affect exchange rates, interest rates, and ultimately the domestic price level. In Chapter 14 we studied the way that the Fed sets the monetary base in the United States. Central banks in other countries operate in almost exactly the same way. The only important difference across countries in central banking is that not all countries have reserve requirements. But all central banks issue reserves as well as currency. Here we will extend the discussion of the central bank to consider foreign reserves as well as domestic assets.

Table 19–1 shows the balance sheet of a central bank. On the asset side of the balance sheet are securities that the central bank has purchased. A similar balance sheet for the Fed was presented in Chapter 14. Here, there are two types of securities: domestic and foreign. Domestic securities are denominated in domestic currency; these may be government bonds or even loans to private firms. The value of domestic securities held by a central bank is frequently called **domestic credit.** Domestic credit is the total credit that the central bank has extended to the home economy, whether to the government or to the private sector. Foreign securities are denominated in foreign currency. Most frequently these are bonds issued by foreign governments. Foreign securities are **foreign reserves.**

Recall that the monetary base is defined as currency plus bank reserves. Because assets must equal liabilities, we know that domestic credit

TABLE 19–1 Balance Sheet of a Central Bank with Foreign Reserves

Assets	Liabilities
Domestic credit	Currency
Foreign reserves	Bank reserves

plus foreign credit equals the monetary base. That is,

$$\text{Monetary base} = \text{Domestic credit} + \text{Foreign reserves.} \qquad (19\text{--}1)$$

Suppose that the central bank wants to increase the money supply in order to stimulate the economy. It purchases government bonds in the open market—an open-market purchase; this causes domestic credit to rise. This means that the monetary base and the money supply will tend to increase. The increase in the money supply will lower the interest rate. Capital will flow out of the country, and the currency will start to depreciate as soon as the interest rate begins to fall below the world interest rate.

What if the central bank wants to prevent depreciation? As foreign-denominated bonds begin to look more attractive relative to domestic bonds, the central bank must provide the increased demand for foreign exchange by selling foreign reserves in order to prevent the exchange rate from depreciating. It does this by entering the foreign exchange market and selling its foreign reserves for domestic currency. Foreign reserves decrease. The decrease in foreign reserves lowers the monetary base and offsets the previous effect of the open-market operation. In fact, since the interest rate does not fall, we know that the decrease in foreign reserves must be exactly equal to the increase in domestic credit. This keep the money supply from increasing.

In the case of an open-market sale, the same channels keep the money supply from falling. The upward pressure on interest rates leads the central bank to buy foreign reserves; this increases the money supply. If the bank wants to maintain the exchange rate at parity, it cannot change the money supply. Monetary policy cannot be used both for domestic purposes and to stabilize the exchange rate.

Now suppose that there is an expansionary fiscal policy—an increase in government spending. This increase in government spending does not increase the interest rate if the central bank is fixing the exchange rate, because the money supply automatically increases.

Sterilized Intervention

A central bank can offset a potential depreciation of its currency by selling foreign reserves. Then the money supply contracts, the interest rate rises, and the potential depreciation is offset. However, it is possible for the central bank to sell foreign reserves and buy domestic credit at the same time in the same amount. Such a move is called a **sterilized foreign exchange intervention.** From Table 19–1, it is apparent that a sterilized intervention has no effect on the assets of the central bank. Thus it has no effect on the monetary base and no effect on the domestic economy.

Under modern conditions with highly integrated capital markets, it is unlikely that a sterilized intervention has much effect. A central bank would have to sell a huge volume of foreign reserves to defend its currency against a threatened depreciation. Its ability to make such a move is limited by its stock of foreign reserves. After the stock is exhausted, the bank would have to revert to normal monetary contraction.

Capital or Exchange Controls

Capital controls, such as restrictions on the amount of foreign currency that domestic residents can purchase, would permit the domestic interest rate to be different from the world rate. In fact, capital controls are still being used in many small countries for exactly this reason. Although they would enable monetary policy to be more effective, capital controls have the disadvantage that they reduce the efficiency of international capital markets. Economic efficiency requires that different types of capital be allocated according to their after-tax rate of return. Although there are already many taxes in the world that distort the allocation of capital, adding additional taxes would probably distort the allocation even further.

EXCHANGE-RATE POLICY

1. With high capital mobility and no expected change in the exchange rate, the domestic interest rate will be the same as the world interest rate.
2. Under fixed rates, the central bank must act to keep the domestic interest rate equal to the world rate.
3. Fixed exchange rates can also be achieved with capital controls, but these interfere with the efficient allocation of capital.

19.2   HISTORY OF THE WORLD FINANCIAL AND MONETARY SYSTEM

Until early in the twentieth century, almost all countries defined their monetary units in terms of gold or silver. Among all the countries on the gold standard, there was no room for variation in exchange rates. The dollar and the pound had a relative value of about $5 per pound because the pound was defined as 5 times as much gold as the dollar. Under the gold standard, convertibility was not an issue. Further, the prevailing standards of thinking about the role of government in the nineteenth century limited government restrictions on flows of capital and goods. In particular, very large flows of capital from Britain to the United States and other rapidly growing countries helped speed the process of economic development.

After World War I and the Great Depression in the 1930s, currencies began to lose their connection with gold. Even though the United States did not formally leave the gold standard until 1971, the Federal Reserve stopped redeeming dollar bills for gold in 1933. Similar changes occurred in other countries. Ever since the 1930s, each country's monetary unit has been defined as its paper currency or reserves, not gold or silver. The type of monetary system we described in Chapter 14 has been almost universal. As a result, there has been no automatic determination of exchange rates as there was under the gold standard. During the Great Depression, the world financial and monetary system virtually broke down.

Near the end of World War II, in 1944, representatives of major economies (including John Maynard Keynes for Britain) met in Bretton Woods, New Hampshire, to design a new world financial and monetary system to replace the gold standard. Because large fluctuations in exchange rates in the 1920s and 1930s seemed to be undesirable in contrast to the fixed rates guaranteed under the gold standard, the Bretton Woods System proposed to keep exchange rates almost constant. The dollar was to be the reference point of the system, replacing gold. Other countries adopted dollar values for their currencies (called **par values**), such as $2.80 per British pound. Each central bank agreed to keep its own currency within plus or minus 1 percent of the par value.

Under the Bretton Woods System, central banks held substantial amounts of dollar securities, mostly U.S. Treasury bills. When a country's currency rose a little above par, its central bank would purchase dollar securities and sell securities denominated in its own currency and thus depress the value of its own currency. When the currency dropped a little below par, the bank would sell dollar securities and buy securities in its own currency. In addition, the central bank might tighten its overall monetary policy by reducing its total holdings of securities (an open-market operation, as we described in detail in Chapter 14).

The dollar securities of foreign central banks under the Bretton Woods System constituted their foreign *reserves*. When a central bank was preventing an appreciation of its currency by purchasing dollar securities, there was a *reserve inflow* or *balance of payments surplus*. This was generally considered a favorable sign for that economy. When the central bank was defending its currency by selling dollar securities, there was a *reserve outflow* or a *balance of payments deficit*. A deficit could last only as long as the central bank had a stock of reserves of dollar securities. After the stock ran out, the bank would have to turn to other restrictive measures, or cease its policy of stabilizing the exchange rate. Balance of payments deficits were a matter of great publicity and concern under the Bretton Woods System.

The Bretton Woods System had a built-in instability that ultimately led to its collapse. Its architects did not completely eliminate the possibility of changes in par values. Once a central bank ran out of dollar securities, it would defend its own currency through monetary contraction or it could **devalue**—reduce the par value of its currency. Monetary contraction is a painful process with adverse political consequences most of the time. But if traders in the exchange market perceive that a devaluation is likely, they push down the market rate immediately. The result is an exchange-rate crisis. The British pound went through a crisis in 1967. The market perceived that British monetary policy was letting the purchasing power of the pound drop below its earlier relation to the dollar and that a reversal of policy was politically unlikely under a Labour government. The Bank of England sold all its dollar securities and borrowed extensively in order to sell even more. But the market saw that the par value of the pound of $2.80 exceeded the value that monetary policy would achieve. Traders started selling pound securities and buying dollar and other securities. The Bank of England lacked the power to keep the exchange rate at par. Finally, in November 1967, the British government validated the traders' judgment by lowering the par value to $2.40.

A second problem with the Bretton Woods System was its vulnerability to mistakes in U.S. monetary policy. In order to maintain fixed exchange rates, other countries had to keep their inflation rates in line with the U.S. inflation rate. High U.S. inflation in the late 1960s made it difficult for most other countries in the system to keep their currencies from rising above par. They bought huge volumes of U.S. government securities to keep their currencies down, but, as in the pound sterling crisis, this type of intervention was not enough. Either the other countries had to expand their monetary policies and match U.S. inflation, or they had to revalue their currencies.

Various stopgap measures were enacted during the 1960s to remedy the situation. An interest equalization tax was enacted to make it more costly to invest in foreign securities. A program to discourage firms from making direct investments abroad was run by the United States Department of Commerce. Export industries were given support by the Export-Import Bank, which made low-interest loans to foreigners who bought U.S. products. But despite all these efforts the current-account deficits of the United States continued. The competitive position of U.S. industries remained unfavorable. By almost all calculations the dollar was overvalued and would remain so unless the United States introduced severe contractionary policies to reduce inflation or the rest of the world enacted expansionary policies to increase inflation.

The Devaluation of the Dollar and the Collapse of Bretton Woods

The Bretton Woods System broke down in the early 1970s. On August 15, 1971, at the same time that wage and price controls came into force, the Nixon administration launched a series of moves that effectively ended the system. First, the United States ended its commitment to sell gold to other governments for $35 per ounce. Though few governments had used their right to buy gold at this price, the U.S. move made it clear that the United States was not prepared to make a permanent commitment to a fixed purchasing power for the dollar. Second, the United States used the club of a special tariff to force negotiations at the Smithsonian Institution in Washington, D.C., in December 1971 to revalue most of the currencies in the Bretton Woods System. The general revaluation was another sign that the United States was not committed to a sufficiently stable purchasing power for the dollar to make the Bundesbank and other European central banks link their currencies permanently to the dollar.

World events had more to do with how the system evolved after 1971 than did any formal reform effort. In 1973–74 the price of oil increased fourfold and inflation accelerated. The acceleration was worse for some countries than for others, as shown in Figure 19–1. With widely different inflation rates in different countries, the Smithsonian parities were soon abandoned as countries found it increasingly difficult to maintain them. The 1974–75 recession, which hit all countries, put additional pressure on existing parities.

The desire of different countries to choose their own macroeconomic policies in response to the 1974–75 recession meant that exchange rates would have to shift further. Eventually most currencies began to float with no set parities, although there were considerable interventions aimed at preventing large movements. The world had emerged from the 1973–74 inflation and the 1974–75 recession with an essentially floating exchange-rate system. It was not until January 1976 at an international conference in Jamaica that previous agreements were changed to reflect the reality of the floating exchange-rate system. At that time the countries also agreed to abandon gold as a part of the international monetary system.

Current Exchange-Rate Policies Around the World

The central banks of the countries that are closely linked to the world financial and monetary system use a number of different strategies. All of them have the two basic policy instruments available to them: changes in the size of their portfolios (standard monetary policy) and changes in the composition of their assets (sterilized intervention).

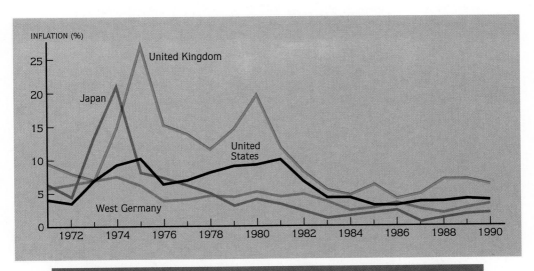

FIGURE 19–1   Inflation rates, 1971–90

The inflation rate increased in most countries in 1973–74. The increase was larger in Japan and the United Kingdom than in the United States and West Germany. The timing of the increase was also differnet in different countries. These discrepancies put additional pressures on existing exchange-rate parities.
Source: *International Financial Statistics Yearbook*, International Monetary Fund, 1991, various tables.

The Federal Reserve Bank and the U.S. Treasury are jointly responsible for U.S. exchange-rate policy. The Fed has complete control over the size of its portfolio and therefore the size of the monetary base, but the Treasury can order the Fed to exchange dollar-denominated securities for securities of other governments. Though concerns about the value of the dollar in relation to other currencies have been an influence on both dimensions of central bank policy, the United States has not had a systematic exchange-rate policy. It has permitted the dollar to float in relation to other currencies, with occasional interventions when the dollar has reached extreme high or lows. In 1985, when the dollar was extraordinarily high, the United States, Germany, Japan, Britain, and France agreed to intervene to bring the dollar down. Subsequently, the dollar fell by a great deal, more than 50 percent relative to the yen. There have been sporadic interventions to counteract large movements in the value of the dollar in both directions since 1985, but the United States has had far from stable exchange rates.

Japan is the other major economy that has not made any specific policy commitment with respect to exchange rates. It permits substantial fluctuations in the value of its currency relative to the dollar and other major currencies, but it considers exchange rates when making central bank policy.

The European countries that belong to the EMS maintain fixed exchange rates among themselves. The EMS was created in 1979 and operates today more or less along the lines of the Bretton Woods System, with the deutsche mark playing the role of the dollar. The Bundesbank has followed policies that keep the purchasing power of the DM stable. The other members of the EMS are committed to equally stable monetary policies, so that there is much less strain within the system than there was in the last years of Bretton Woods. Figure 19–2 shows that the exchange rates in the EMS relative to the DM have been stable and that there has been relatively little inflation in any of the EMS countries since 1979.

Some smaller countries, such as Canada, the Philippines, and Uruguay, have independent monetary policies and floating exchange rates. Again, exchange rates influence policy, but there is no commitment to keeping exchange-rate fluctuations within a particular band around any other currency. Some countries that are not fully connected to the world financial and monetary system—the Pacific rim countries, India, Korea, Mexico, and Yugoslavia are examples—have partly floating exchange rates even though the governments are sometimes directly involved in exchange transactions. Many smaller countries subordinate monetary policy by using it to achieve a fixed or gradually changing exchange rate relative to the dollar or the French franc or to a package of currencies.

THE INTERNATIONAL MONETARY SYSTEM

1. From the late 1940s to the early 1970s, the major economies operated under the Bretton Woods System, with fixed exchange rates. Each central bank aimed to keep the value of its currency within a narrow band around its dollar exchange rate.
2. When inflation rates vary across countries, a system of fixed exchange rates ultimately breaks down. The Bretton Woods System was abandoned in 1971 after inflation worsened in the United States.
3. Under the current system, the dollar floats freely; U.S. policy does little to control its movements. The major European currencies are fixed relative to each other but float relative to the dollar.

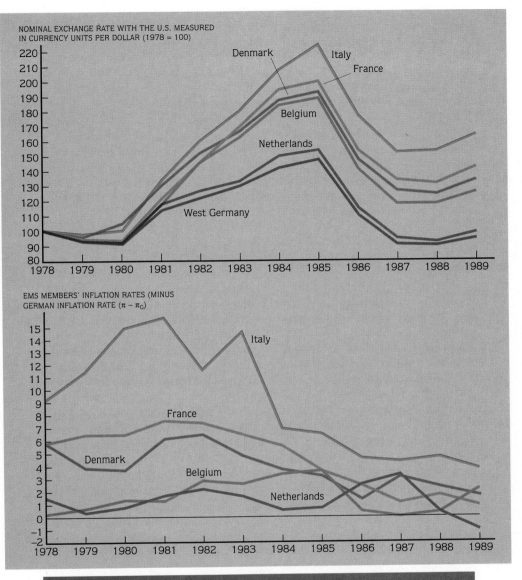

FIGURE 19–2 Exchange rates and inflation rates in selected EMS countries

The European Monetary System (EMS) is a group of countries that maintain stable exchange rates with the German deutsche mark. The top graph shows how the exchange rates of five of the countries have varied against the U.S. dollar since 1978. The countries have achieved relatively stable exchange rates vis-a´-vis each other by following monetary policies similar to those of the German central bank, the Bundesbank. Those countries whose rates of inflation have been similar to German rates, as shown in the bottom graph, have maintained the most stable exchange rates with the deutsche mark.
Source: *International Financial Statistics Yearbook*, International Monetary Fund, 1991, various tables.

19.3 MACROECONOMIC POLICY, EXCHANGE RATES, AND INFLATION

In this section, we will consider international policy issues that arise in the economy as described in Chapter 17. The economy could be the United States, with a substantial amount of trade and a generally floating exchange rate. Alternatively, it could be Britain, with even more trade relative to GDP, or France, both members of the EMS with firm commitments to keeping exchange rates fixed in relation to the deutsche mark.

Policy with Floating Rates

Even though a country that has chosen not to stabilize its exchange rate is free to conduct monetary and fiscal policy with domestic goals in mind, exchange and trade issues figure prominently in policy discussions. The situation of Britain at the end of 1989 is a good illustration of the dilemma that can arise from considerations of the exchange rate. Coming into 1989, the British economy seemed to be in good shape. Output was close to potential. Inflation was less than 5 percent. Forecasts called for continued moderate growth and low inflation. The pound, at $1.80, was about normal in real terms. British interest rates were slightly above U.S. interest rates. But during the year, the situation deteriorated. The Conservative government lost several important mid-term Parliamentary elections. The pound dropped to about $1.60; commentators blamed the anticipation of the election of a Labour government for the depreciation of the pound. The foreign exchange market may have anticipated that a Labour government would follow a more inflationary policy.

As we emphasized in Chapter 18, governments always face the choice between an anti-inflationary policy that may raise unemployment and a pro-employment policy that may raise inflation. The Conservative government faced an unusually adverse choice of this type. The decline in the pound was immediately inflationary; a lower exchange rate meant higher prices for imported products. Because the British economy is smaller and more open than the U.S. economy, the transmission is more complete and widespread in Britain. The Bank of England chose to offset some of the forces depreciating the pound by tightening monetary policy and raising interest rates. However, monetary tightening slowed the economy down. Growth of output slowed by the end of 1989, and the British economy stalled in the early 1990s.

The Bank of England compromised during 1989. It could have been even more contractionary and raised interest rates high enough to keep the pound at $1.80 and avoid a worsening of inflation. Then the economy would probably have been in recession by the end of the year. Or, the Bank could have kept unemployment and real growth at their earlier levels and allowed a greater depreciation of the pound. Then inflation would have risen even more. The change that gave rise to this adverse policy choice was the original downward force on the value of the pound in relation to other currencies, which had a political origin. The effect of the negative political shock is quite similar to the effect of the oil price increase we analyzed in Chapters 17 and 18. Both an oil price increase and a politically driven decline in the currency send the economy into stagflation; unemployment and inflation both rise. We can add exogenous changes in exchange rates from political or other factors apart from economic policy to the list of shocks that create a policy frontier that is uncomfortably far from the origin. An economy that is buffeted by exchange-rate shocks, favorable and unfavorable, will have more variability of both prices and unemployment than will an economy that is free of these shocks.

Exchange-rate shocks are less important in the United States than in economies that are smaller and more open. Because the United States is such a large part of the world market for many goods, foreign suppliers often absorb exchange-rate changes in their own prices rather than keeping the prices in their own currencies constant and letting the dollar prices change. The U.S. price of Japanese cars did not come close to doubling between 1985 and 1987, even though the purchasing power of the dollar in terms of the yen did fall by half. Even so, changes in exchange rates are a source of price-adjustment shocks in the United States. Some economists feel that the unusually good performance of the U.S. economy from 1983 to 1985 was the result of a favorable foreign exchange movement. The sharp appreciation of the dollar over the period may have come in part from perceptions about political developments. By helping inflation fall, the appreciation of the dollar made it possible for the Fed to expand so that output grew rapidly and unemployment fell. The story of the United States from 1983 to 1985 may be exactly the story of Britain in 1989 in reverse.

In recent years, many economists have suggested that the United States may be vulnerable to a collapse of the dollar along the same lines as the decline in the pound in 1989. If a wave of pessimism about the U.S. economy passed through world markets, the dollar could depreciate against other currencies and the Fed would be in the same situation as the Bank of England in 1989. More expensive imports would make the cost of living rise, and the Fed would have to choose between price stability and output-unemployment stability. This problem did not arise in the 1980s, partly because a favorable oil price shock in 1986 offset the decline of the dollar. A run on the dollar cannot be ruled out in the future as one of the kinds of price-adjustment shocks that knock the economy out of equilibrium.

Policy with a Fixed Exchange Rate

The countries in the EMS, together with numerous other countries all around the world, have chosen to commit policy to maintain one particular exchange rate at close to a constant level. A country in the EMS keeps a close watch on its exchange rate with the DM. When the rate dips slightly, the central bank has two options. It can sell securities to lower the money supply and raise the domestic interest rate to halt the incipient depreciation. Alternatively, it can sell DMs or other foreign securities and buy domestic securities at the same time. This will leave the money supply unchanged but will add to the supply of foreign securities and reduce the supply of domestic securities in the world market. The result will be an upward force on the domestic currency to offset the incipient depreciation. And, of course, the bank sometimes uses a combination of monetary contraction and portfolio shift. Then the bank's currency appreciates and the domestic interest rate rises. The economy cools off a little. If the original depreciation was the result of expectations of inflation above the German rate, the slacker economy helps drive the expected rate of inflation back down and removes the original impetus for depreciation.

The rules of the EMS and other fixed-rate regimes eliminate discretionary monetary policy. A fixed exchange rate is one of the ways of putting monetary policy on autopilot. Within the EMS, monetary policy for the entire group of countries is made, in effect, by the Bundesbank. In turn, the Bundesbank must conduct a smooth, noninflationary policy in order to continue to play the role of the central bank for most of continental Europe. Because the nations of the EMS now have considerable faith in the Bundesbank, the EMS has been a successful institution.

What about fiscal policy? Changes in taxes and spending remain important open choices for an economy that has chosen to fix its exchange rate with monetary policy. Tax cuts or spending increases can stimulate employment and output. Figure 14–6 (page 436) applies to the case of fixed exchange rates. Under fixed rates, the central bank has to keep the interest rate constant. As a result, the LM curve is horizontal. Fiscal policies that shift the IS curve do not change the interest rate, so output changes by the full amount of the horizontal shift of the IS curve, as illustrated in Figure 14–6. Although fiscal policy has bigger effects in an economy where the central bank is fixing the exchange rate than in the same economy with a floating rate, the countries in the EMS tend not to rely on fiscal policy for stabilization. In part, their reluctance to change taxes and spending derives from the general problems of fiscal stabilization we discussed in Chapter 13. In addition, the EMS economies are extremely open. When French consumers spend more, much of the increase is on imported goods, for example. The amount of the horizontal shift of the IS curve from a given tax cut or spending increase in an open economy is fairly small. As a result, fiscal stabilization is no more often used in EMS countries than in the United States.

Equilibrium Analysis of Fixed- and Floating-Rate Policies

Recall that an analysis of the economy in equilibrium is useful in thinking about longer-run trends, even though most economies seem to move around equilibrium in the short run. Everything important about exchange rates, price levels, and monetary policy can be stated in one simple equation for an economy in the long run:

$$PE = P_{\mathrm{w}}. \qquad (19\text{--}2)$$

That is, the domestic price level P times the exchange rate E equals the foreign or world price P_{w}. In an EMS country, for example, the exchange rate would be the number of DMS needed to buy 1 unit of the country's currency and the world price would be the DM price level. Equation 19–2 says that purchasing power parity holds in the longer run. In Chapter 12, we noted that purchasing power parity is not a reliable principle in the short run, but that there are good theoretical reasons for it to hold in equilibrium.

Recall from Chapter 5 that the price level P is simply proportional to the money supply in the long-run model. Given an exchange-rate target E, we can solve Equation 19–2 for the price level needed to achieve that exchange rate:

$$P = P_{\mathrm{w}}/E. \qquad (19\text{--}3)$$

Thus, to fix the exchange rate E, the money supply has to be held proportional to the level P_{w}/E. If the world price rises by 50 percent over a decade, the money stock must also rise by 50 percent. A fixed exchange rate locks monetary policy to the price level in the country whose currency is the basis for the fixed rate. Again, in the EMS, the German price level, as determined by the Bundesbank's monetary policy, dictates monetary policies in the other EMS countries.

With a floating exchange rate, Equation 19–2 has a different interpretation. We can solve it for the exchange rate:

$$E = P_{\mathrm{w}}/P. \qquad (19\text{--}4)$$

Monetary policy uses whatever principles it wants to set the money supply and thus set the domestic price level P. If the central bank chooses to raise the price level by expanding the money supply, it will lower the exchange rate in the same proportion.

World Inflation with Floating Exchange Rates

Yet another use of Equation 19–2 is to study rates of change in prices and exchange rates over time periods of a decade or longer. Stated in terms of rates of change, Equation 19–2 says

$$\pi + \frac{\Delta E}{E} = \pi_w. \tag{19-5}$$

The domestic rate of inflation π plus the rate of appreciation $\Delta E/E$ equals the foreign rate of inflation π_w. Another way to express the same relationship is to observe that the excess of the foreign rate of inflation over the domestic rate of inflation is equal to the rate of appreciation of the domestic currency:

$$\pi_w - \pi = \frac{\Delta E}{E}. \tag{19-6}$$

How accurate is this equation as a description of the long-run behavior? In Figure 19–3 the inflation differentials and exchange-rate appreciations between six economies and the United States are shown for the 17-year period from 1973 to 1989. The difference between inflation in each country (π_w) and inflation in the United States (π) is shown on the vertical axis. The rate of appreciation ($\Delta E/E$) of the dollar against each of the corresponding currencies is on the horizontal axis. The 45-degree line is then the relation between inflation differentials and exchange-rate depreciation implied by Equation 19–6. The actual inflation rates and exchange-rate behavior come very close to the theoretical prediction. Germany has had the strongest currency and the lowest inflation rate compared with the United States. Italy is at the other extreme, with a comparatively weak currency and a high inflation rate compared with the United States. This relation between inflation and exchange-rate behavior is even more striking for countries with very high inflation rates. For example, during this same 17-year period, the difference between the inflation rate in Argentina and that in the United States was about 50 percent per year. The Argentine peso depreciated by nearly 50 percent per year against the dollar during that period.

The freedom that a floating exchange rate gives to countries in determining their own inflation rates is a mixed blessing according to some economists. They feel that discipline rather than freedom is needed because of the tendency for many countries' political systems to generate too much inflation. For a small country it might be better to peg its currency to one of its trading partners that has a relatively low inflation rate. As long as the exchange rate is maintained, the small country will then eventually also have a low inflation rate.

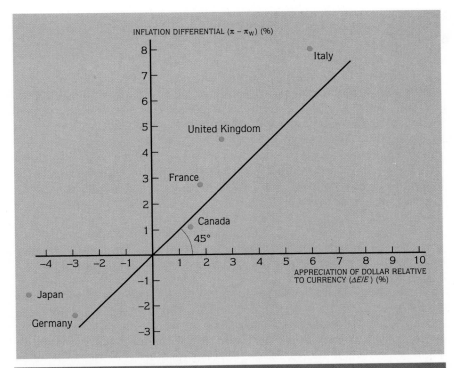

FIGURE 19–3 Inflation differentials and appreciation of the dollar relative to six countries, 1973–89

The inflation rates are measured by the consumer price index in each country. The rates of inflation and appreciation are annual averages for the 17-year period. When the inflation differential is high, appreciation of the dollar against that country's currency is high.
Source: *International Financial Statistics Yearbook,* International Monetary Fund, 1991, various tables.

MACRO POLICY AND EXCHANGE RATES

1. Under a fixed-rate regime, the central bank must keep the domestic price level in step with the price level of the center country. The center country thus establishes monetary policy for the group.
2. Under floating rates, each country is free to choose its own inflation rate. Inflation differentials then determine the long-run behavior of exchange rates.

19.4 INTERNATIONAL MACRO POLICY COORDINATION

We have examined the effects of macroeconomic policy in a number of circumstances relevant to the conditions of the international monetary system today. Monetary policy cannot be used for domestic stabilization purposes in an economy with a fixed exchange rate. If capital is mobile, as it is in advanced countries without exchange controls, the central bank will forgo control over the money supply if it must support a fixed exchange rate. Moreover, a small country with a fixed exchange rate automatically adopts price stability goals that are identical to the country that it pegs its currency to.

Floating exchange rates offer much more freedom to use monetary policy for domestic stabilization purposes. That freedom can be a mixed blessing if the country's political system requires external discipline when it comes to monetary policy.

Floating exchange rates, however, do not insulate one economy from the effects of macroeconomic policies in other countries. In principle, therefore, international coordination of macro policies might be useful. The optimal macro policy that we discussed for the United States in Chapter 18 might be different if the effects of U.S. policy on other countries were taken into account or if the effects of other countries' policies on the United States were taken into account.

Macro policymaking in the world economy can be thought of as a game. Each country is a player in the game. The objective of policymakers in each country might be the same as those we discussed in Chapter 18. Each country has a social welfare function that includes output stability and price stability. Policymakers choose their instruments to minimize a combination of each type of loss (see Figure 18–1). But if there is an interaction among countries, then the choice of a policy rule in one country will affect the social welfare function in the other country. Country 1 might improve its macroeconomic performance by worsening Country 2's macroeconomic performance. But if Country 1 does so, Country 2 might retaliate, or at least watch out for itself, with harmful side effects for Country 1. This would be a **noncooperative policy choice**. A **cooperative policy choice**, on the other hand, is one in which each country agrees to use a policy rule that doesn't have an adverse effect on the other country in exchange for getting the same treatment from the other country. Some international coordination or discussion about policies, like that at Bretton Woods after World War II, would probably be necessary for this cooperative outcome.

In recent years there has been an annual international summit meeting among the leaders of seven industrial countries that interact with each other: Canada, France, Germany, Italy, Japan, the United Kingdom, and the

United States. One of the stated purposes of these summit meetings is to discuss macro policy. The amount of actual international coordination that goes on varies from meeting to meeting. Under the Carter administration there was much effort by the United States to get other countries to expand. In the first term of the Reagan administration, when contractionary policies were enacted in the United States to reduce inflation, these types of coordination efforts were abandoned. However, during President Reagan's second term there was more discussion about coordination. That discussion continued during the Bush administration. For example, in 1992 there was considerable discussion of problems caused by the rising budget deficit in Germany.

Are the gains from coordination large? How different would optimal policies look if countries cooperated, rather than acting independently? For example, should countries be less or more accommodative to inflation than calculations like those in Chapter 18 indicated?[1] Or perhaps countries should use their monetary policies to reduce the size of the fluctuations in the exchange rate as well as in the inflation rate and the unemployment rate.[2]

We saw in Chapter 12 that changes in the U.S. money supply have effects on the exchange rate. A monetary contraction raises the exchange rate and a monetary expansion lowers the exchange rate. What are the effects of these changes abroad? What might foreign macro policymakers do about these changes? Consider the case of a dollar appreciation associated with a tight U.S. monetary policy or a loose U.S. fiscal policy. Obviously, an appreciation of the dollar is a depreciation of other currencies. A depreciation in the rest of the world has two effects that must be considered by policymakers.

First, the depreciation increases aggregate demand in the rest of the world. The depreciation is like an aggregate demand shock that increases net exports in the rest of the world; the aggregate demand curve shifts to the right. According to our optimal policy analysis, the appropriate response of policymakers in the rest of the world is to offset this shift by effecting tighter fiscal or monetary policy. Policies should be coordinated to get this result, but since the effect of the U.S. policy can be offset by the appropriate choice of policies abroad, there is no loss in world welfare on this account.

---

[1]See Koichi Hamada, "Macroeconomic Strategy and Coordination under Flexible Exchange Rates," in Rudiger Dornbusch and Jacob A. Frenkel, eds., *International Economic Policy: Theory and Evidence* (Baltimore: Johns Hopkins Press, 1979), pp. 292–324; Gilles Oudiz and Jeffrey Sachs, "Macroeconomic Policy Coordination among the Industrialized Countries," *Brookings Papers on Economic Activity*, No. 1 (1984), pp. 1–64; and John B. Taylor, "International Coordination in the Design of Macroeconomic Policy Rules," *European Economic Review*, Vol. 26 (1985), pp. 53–81.
[2]See Ronald I. McKinnon, *An International Standard for Monetary Stabilization* (The Institute for International Economics, distributed by M.I.T. Press, 1984).

The second effect cannot be offset so easily, however. *The depreciation of the foreign currency will raise the price of imported products in the rest of the world.* Recall that the price shock term (Z) in the inflation equation (17–1) was due to changes in the price of inputs to production, such as oil. If the exchange rate depreciates, then the price that firms pay for these products rises. For example, Japan Airlines will have to pay 2.5 billion more yen for a $50 million Boeing 747 jet made in Seattle if the yen depreciates from 150 yen per dollar to 200 yen per dollar. The second effect of the U.S. monetary policy is thus to create a price shock in the rest of the world.

As we already know, a price shock presents a cruel choice to policymakers: Inflation must rise, unemployment must rise, or both must rise. The magnitude of the increase in inflation or unemployment depends on how much accommodation is built into policy in the rest of the world. Some loss, however, is inevitable. This effect of the U.S. policy, therefore, does result in a loss in welfare in the rest of the world and opens the possibility of cooperation. A cooperative policy would be one in which both the United States and other countries are more accommodative to inflation than they otherwise would be. This would make monetary policy less contractionary in the face of a price shock at home and would therefore have smaller harmful effects abroad. Although it is clear that optimal cooperative policies should be more accommodative than noncooperative policies, the difference could be small. Since our historical experience with flexible exchange rates is still fairly short, there is unfortunately little empirical evidence about the size of the difference between the policies.

19.5 MONETARY UNION

The nations of continental Europe have already achieved a substantial amount of cooperation through the EMS. Based on the historical record of the Bundesbank in setting a stable, noninflationary monetary policy, other countries have committed themselves to monetary policies that will keep their own currencies at fixed parities with the DM. However, the commitment is not irrevocable. On the one hand, the ability to adopt a different policy in the future gives protection against the possibility of significant error by the Bundesbank. On the other hand, because politicians have the power to revoke fixed rates, there remains the danger of an exchange-rate crisis. If the market guesses, rightly or wrongly, that a devaluation relative to the DM is about to occur, it presents an EMS member with the unpleasant choice of sharp increases in interest rates to head off the speculative attack or capitulation to the attack by devaluing even if that was never planned before the attack.

The cost of the market's belief that devaluation may occur at some time in the future is not just a political headache. Members of the EMS such as Italy, with histories of inflation well above German levels, have had to pay substantially higher interest rates than does Germany. Even though the Bank of Italy is committed to keeping the lira at a fixed parity relative to the DM, the bond market is sufficiently convinced that a devaluation will occur in the future that it requires a higher interest rate for lira bonds.

The next step in the evolution of the monetary system of continental Europe is monetary union. Members of a monetary union make a permanent, irrevocable commitment not to change the value of their own monetary unit relative to the unit prescribed by the union. The best way to express that commitment is to abolish the existing domestic unit and use the union's monetary unit internally. If Italy eliminates the lira and uses a European unit internally, it is much more credible that Italy will not devalue its monetary unit.

The EMS has already created a monetary unit of its own, the European Currency Unit, or ecu ("*ecu*" is the French word for "crown," a traditional European name for a monetary unit). The ecu is defined as a basket of the currencies of the members of the EMS. As long as the members stick to fixed exchange rates with the DM, the ecu and the DM are essentially the same unit. If an EMS member devalues, the ecu depreciates slightly relative to the DM. The ecu is seeing increasing use; a growing fraction of bonds are denominated in ecus, some families hold savings accounts in ecus, and some accounting statements of multinational companies are reckoned in ecus. The ecu is a parallel, subordinate unit like the Chilean *Unidad de Fomento* (UF), which we discussed in Chapter 16. However, the ecu has a purchasing power that tends to decline over time, whereas the UF is guaranteed to have the same purchasing power. Hence, the ecu has had less success than the UF. Some economists have proposed that the ecu be defined like the UF to have constant purchasing power, but the idea has not caught on.

With the European commitment to virtually full financial union, the goal of complete monetary union has been adopted in principle. The idea is to replace the existing monetary units of the EMS members with a single unit. The new unit would be issued by a European central bank. All EMS countries would use the new paper currency and all banks would hold reserves at the new central bank. The Bundesbank and all the other central banks would go out of business. Although Germany would probably dominate decision-making at the European central bank, the smaller members of the EMS generally support the idea. It would relieve them of the burden of higher interest payments and eliminate political squabbles over monetary and exchange-rate policy. Most commentators see monetary union as helping to seal the true economic unification of the European countries. With exchange rates off the political agenda, there is less likelihood of future government interference with trade and capital flows.

NEW RESEARCH IN PRACTICE
Does Western Europe Need a Central Bank? Does Russia?

Europe and the former Soviet Union are in the process of creating new central banks. The nations of western Europe are planning a single currency, while the Commonwealth of Independent States (CIS) is planning separate currencies. Does the creation of a new currency require a corresponding new central bank? A recent study by Oleh Haverlyshyn of George Washington University and John Williamson of the Institute for International Economics in Washington applies recent research on monetary economics to these issues. See *From Soviet Disunion to Eastern Economic Community?*, Institute for International Economics, 1991. A program of assistance to the Commonwealth of Independent States announced by President Bush in 1992 was aimed partly at the establishment of a new monetary system.

Alternative 1. No Government Involvement

The government does not have to sponsor a monetary unit or a currency. One answer, proposed by Friedrich Hayek and actively advocated by some economists today for the CIS, is to let the available nongovernment alternatives compete. Here it is important to distinguish between the unit of value and medium of exchange roles. If there are competing units of value, there will be no national consensus on how to interpret the numbers that merchants put on goods. If Ukraine has no standard monetary unit, and as a result some merchants quote prices in Russian rubles, some in deutsche marks, some in dollars, and some in private units sponsored by Ukrainian banks, there will be confusion and inefficiency compared with a system where there is agreement on how to quote prices. The confusion and inefficiency would be comparable to what would happen if there were no agreement on how to measure fluid volume. If some gas stations sold gas by the U.S. gallon, some by the imperial gallon,

some by the liter, and some by their own measure, the motorist would be at a disadvantage relative to a system where all stations quoted in the same unit. It appears that setting uniform standards of weight, measure, and value is one of the most useful things a government can do and that zero government involvement in the monetary system is undesirable.

Alternative 2. Government Sponsors Use of Existing Foreign Unit

Europe or the CIS could announce that the monetary unit was the U.S. dollar (or the yen or any other foreign unit). The purchasing power of the unit would be stable if the Federal Reserve kept it stable. There would be complete agreement about the unit of value and the interpretation of the numbers that merchants put on goods. No European or CIS government would have to be involved in the monetary system beyond the determination of the unit of value. There would not be a central bank and the government would not issue currency. U.S. dollars might circulate, or bank notes repayable in dollars might be issued by local banks. Bank accounts, bonds, mortgages, and other financial instruments would be denominated in dollars. This system would achieve the minimum sensible degree of government involvement. However, it would be politically unacceptable, for it would permanently forgo monetary independence as well as a source of government revenue that is still essential in the CIS and of some importance in Europe—government revenue from the issuance of currency and reserves. A conventional central bank borrows interest-free from the public; this saves the government from paying the corresponding interest on part of the national debt. Governments are reluctant to part with the central bank as a profit center.

Alternative 3. Government Sponsors Foreign Unit but Captures Central Bank Profit

Either of two minor variants of Alternative 2 solves the problem of forgone profit. The government could prohibit private currency and be the sole issuer of currency, denominated in dollars. This currency board system was widely used by British colonies earlier in this century. Until 1972, Hong Kong had a monetary unit that was defined to be one British pound sterling. A currency board issued currency and held British government securities equal to its issue of currency. The profit earned by the board was simply the interest earnings from the securities.

Another, even easier way to accomplish the same purpose would be for the government to write a contract with the Federal Reserve in which the government would permit only dollar bills to circulate as currency in exchange for a remission of the Fed's profit from the added currency to the government. The Fed negotiated on exactly this arrangement with the government of Israel a number of years ago, though it never came into being.

Alternative 4. Government Issues Self-Stabilizing Money

Because Europe is very unlikely to make the dollar its monetary unit, it might want to consider a system that creates a purely domestic unit with constant purchasing power, without the cost of having a central bank. The idea is to issue a particular type of debt, called a reserve, which is defined to be the monetary unit. The reserve pays interest. Its interest rate is indexed to the price level. If prices are above target, the reserve pays higher interest than other types of government debt, so demand is strong. This puts downward pressure on the price level. Similarly, if prices are below target, the interest rate falls and there is upward pressure on the price level. To capture the profit from currency, the government would issue currency denominated in the reserve. This is an example of a monetary policy rule under which the interest rate is automatically raised when the price level indicator rises above its target. Some of the advantages and disadvantages of price level indicators are discussed in the insert to Chapter 17, "Using Indicators to Guide Policy." If the price level indicator worked effectively, there would be no need to have an expensive central bank with bond traders.

Europeans are conscious of the advantages of the greatest monetary union in the world, the United States. The process of replacing a dozen monetary units with a single European unit, the ecu, is the same as the process of replacing the 13 monetary units of the American colonies with the U.S. dollar. When it was created in 1792, the dollar was a brand-new unit, just as the ecu may be sometime in the 1990s. The fact that the states of the U.S. do not have monetary policies and exchange rates has supported the growth of the country as a unified economy. Europeans have concluded that a "United States of Europe" would have some substantial advantages, even though it would require a transfer of political power to a European government from existing national governments.

MONETARY UNION

1. Monetary union is the last step of financial integration. The countries in a union use a common monetary unit and do not have domestic currency units.

2. Monetary union is a stronger commitment than fixed exchange rates, because it eliminates the possibility of devaluation.

REVIEW AND PRACTICE

Major Points

1. Financial and commercial integration of national economies has been an important phenomenon in recent years. Free trade in goods and assets is a characteristic of an integrated global economy.

2. In an open economy, central bank policy takes two forms: monetary policy and foreign exchange market intervention. Monetary policy refers to measures that change the total liabilities of the central bank. Exchange-rate policy refers to measures that alter the mix of foreign and domestic assets in the central bank's portfolio.

3. Under a fixed exchange-rate system the central bank must use monetary policy to keep the domestic interest rate equal to the world rate. Other goals cannot be pursued.

4. Fixed exchange-rate systems require the nations involved to have similar rates of domestic inflation. The Bretton Woods System failed in the early 1970s when U.S. inflation increased above the rate other members of the system considered acceptable.

5. Under floating exchange rates each country is free to determine its own rate of inflation. Inflation differentials then determine the long-run behavior of nominal exchange rates.

6. The European Monetary System ties the currencies of nine continental European countries to the deutsche mark. The final step in the financial integration of the group is monetary union.

7. Monetary union is a stronger commitment than fixed exchange rates because it rules out periodic devaluations of currencies that occur under fixed rates. This may help to lower the cost of capital for EMS members that frequently devalued their currency in the past.

Key Terms and Concepts

open economy
floating exchange rate
fixed exchange rate
Bretton Woods System

devaluation and revaluation
inconvertible currency
foreign exchange intervention
European Monetary System

capital and exchange controls
sterilized intervention
policy coordination
monetary union

Questions for Discussion and Review

1. Compare the Bretton Woods System with the European Monetary System.
2. How has Japanese monetary policy changed since the collapse of the Bretton Woods System?
3. Why is it important to distinguish between large and small economies in discussing the international aspects of economic policy?
4. Why does high capital mobility cause equalization of interest rates under fixed exchange rates?
5. Explain why monetary policy cannot be used for domestic goals when the exchange rate is fixed. Consider fixed, fully flexible, and gradually adjusting prices.
6. Why is the response of GDP to government purchases higher under a policy of a fixed rather than a floating exchange rate?
7. What determines the price level in a small country with completely flexible prices and a fixed exchange rate?
8. How did the Vietnam War raise the German price level?
9. What determines the price level in a country with completely flexible prices and a floating exchange rate?

Problems

Numerical

1. Consider a macro model of a small open economy consisting of the following equations:

$$Y = C + I + G + X$$
$$C = 80 + .63Y$$
$$I = 750 - 2,000R$$
$$M = (.1625Y - 1,000R)P$$
$$X = 500 - .1Y - 100EP/P_w,$$

where government spending G equals 750. Suppose that the exchange rate is *fixed* at $E = 1$, that the world interest rate $R_w = .05$, and that both price levels P and P_w are predetermined at 1.0. (Note that the domestic interest rate R must equal .05.)

a. Explain why M rather than R is an endogenous variable in this model in contrast to the macro model in Chapters 7 and 12.

b. Find the values of Y, C, I, X, and M that are predicted by the model.

c. Suppose that government spending G increases by $50 billion. Calculate what happens to the endogenous variables Y, C, I, X, and M. What mechanism brings about the change in the money supply? Is there any crowding out of investment or net exports by the fiscal policy expansion? Why or why not?

2. Suppose that prices in the small open economy in Problem 1 are determined by

$$\pi = 2\left(\frac{Y_{-1} - Y^*}{Y^*}\right)$$

where $Y^* = \$4,000$ billion is potential GDP and $\pi = (P - P_{-1})/P_{-1}$ is the rate of inflation. Suppose that $G = 750$, $E = 1$, $R = R_w = .05$, and $P_w = 1.0$. As in Problem 1, start out with a price level $P = 1.0$, but now let prices adjust after the first period.

a. Calculate the responses of Y, C, I, X, M, and P to a permanent increase in G of $10 billion. Give the numerical values in the first 4 years. Plot accurately the values for each variable against time for the first 4 years and then sketch what happens after the fourth year.

b. Is there any crowding out of investment or net exports after the first year? Why or why not?

3. Suppose now that the equations in Problem 1 refer to a small classical open economy in which the price level P is perfectly flexible, Y is always equal to potential output, and $Y^* = \$4,000$ billion. Calculate what happens when government spending G increases by $10 billion. How do your results compare with the long-run results in Problem 2?

4. Consider a model of a world economy consisting of only two countries:

$$Y = C + I + G + X \qquad\qquad Y_w = C_w + I_w + G_w + X_w$$
$$C = 80 + .63Y \qquad\qquad C_w = 80 + .63Y_w$$
$$I = 750 - 2,000R \qquad\qquad I_w = 750 - 2,000R_w$$
$$M = (.1625Y - 1,000R)P \qquad\qquad M_w = (.1625Y_w - 1,000R_w)P_w$$
$$R = R_w$$
$$X = -X_w = 100 - .1(Y - Y_w) - 100EP/P_w$$

The notation is the same as that used in the text except that the subscript "w" means the other country (the world). (Note that net exports from one country must equal the negative of net exports of the other country.) Suppose that the price levels P and P_w are both predetermined at 1.0 and that the exchange rate E is fixed at 1.0.

a. Calculate the values of output, investment, consumption, net exports, and the money supply M_w if $G = 750$, $G_w = 750$, and $M = 600$.

b. Calculate what happens to these same variables if M increases by $50 billion, to $650 billion. Explain why the money supply M_w in the other country changes.

   c. Calculate what happens to these same variables if G increases by $50 billion but M and G_w do not change.

   d. Find a policy for the home country to follow to keep Y unchanged when G_w increases by $10 billion.

Analytical

1. Consider a small open economy with sticky prices under a fixed exchange rate. Explain why the aggregate demand curve is vertical. What determines the level of output at which the curve is vertical?

2. Consider again the economy just described in Question 1. Explain why an increase in government spending will increase output by the same amount as in the simple spending balance model of Chapter 6.

3. In a small open economy with a fixed exchange rate, suppose that actual GDP is below potential GDP. Inflation is low, and the objective is to bring the economy back to potential.

   a. Illustrate this situation with an IS-LM diagram.

   b. Describe a policy that can bring about the desired objectives. Would the policy be any different if investment were very sensitive to the interest rate?

4. Describe what happens in a small classical open economy with a fixed exchange rate when the price level abroad falls. Illustrate your answer with an IS-LM diagram.

5. Explain why aggregate demand shocks need not lead to a policy conflict between countries while a price shock might. (Hint: Take account of the effect of the exchange rate on prices.)

6. Explain why a depreciation of the exchange rate could have an inflationary impact in one country and a deflationary impact in other countries.

7. It is often argued that zero, or at least constant, inflation should be an objective of monetary policy since it makes long-term contracts necessary for capital formation much less risky. If one accepts this line of reasoning, is there any similar case that could be made for fixed exchange rates? Explain.

APPENDIX: Introduction to MacroSolve

MacroSolve has been written to make learning macroeconomics easier. Many questions in macroeconomics require either the manipulation of economic time series or the algebraic solution of equations describing the economy. It is important that you know how to do both these things. But it is also useful to be able to avoid excessive hand calculations when you are first learning the subject. MacroSolve relieves you of this drudgery and so enables you to concentrate on understanding macroeconomic concepts.

This program is separated into four main sections: data, plotting, graphing, and modeling. The data options allow you to generate new series as functions of the more than 30 annual and quarterly time series that the program contains. The plotting options enable you to plot simultaneously up to three of the series against time, either annually (1930–present) or quarterly (1967–present). Graphing also uses historical data, but instead of plotting the variables against time, they are graphed against each other (one on the y-axis the other on the x-axis). Finally, the modeling section of MacroSolve allows you to display either graphically or numerically the effects of a wide variety of fluctuations in economic variables on various economic models.

The software has been designed with both novice and experienced users in mind. For the novice, it is important to realize that there is nothing you can enter at the keyboard that will harm the computer or the program. If you make a mistake when entering something into the program, simply try it again. All mistakes are easily remedied in this manner. For the experienced user, the menu structure has been designed to enable you to achieve quickly the results that you want, without forcing you to wade through a maze of irrelevant menus.

Now that you have a general understanding of the basic purpose of the program, you should read the instructions for either the IBM PC or Macintosh version below, depending on which one you have purchased. If you are already familiar with one version and now wish to learn the other, keep in mind that the menus, models, and theory behind the programs are identical. You will find that the only true differences are the specifics of the various selection routines and how information is presented on the screen.

INSTRUCTIONS FOR THE IBM PC VERSION OF MACROSOLVE

Equipment Required

The IBM version requires that you have an IBM Personal Computer (PC, XT, AT, PS-2, Portable, or Convertible) or a compatible PC ("clone") with at least 384K of free memory and a graphics board. Currently, all standard IBM monochrome and color equipment is supported. The software will work with the IBM CGA, EGA, and VGA displays, the Compaq monochrome display, and the Hercules or Hercules Plus high-resolution monochrome graphics boards.

Installing MacroSolve

You may make one copy of the diskette you have purchased, and we recommend that you do so for your personal use and keep the original as a backup. Making such a copy, either to a hard disk or to a floppy diskette, is quite straightforward and is described below.

Copying to a hard disk: To copy to a hard disk, put your MacroSolve diskette in drive A, and type A: followed by ENTER (or Return). At the A> prompt, type IN-STALL followed by your hard disk's drive letter (generally C) and the name of a subdirectory into which you wish to install MacroSolve, for example, MACRO. If that subdirectory already exists, MacroSolve will be copied to it; if it does not, the installation program will copy MacroSolve to a new subdirectory with that name.

For example, to install MacroSolve onto drive C, creating a subdirectory named MACRO, you should type

INSTALL C MACRO

followed by ENTER.

Copying to a floppy diskette: To install MacroSolve onto a floppy diskette, you will first need a formatted blank diskette. To format a new diskette, put your DOS distribution diskette into drive A, and a blank diskette into drive B. At the A> prompt, type

FORMAT B: /S

followed by ENTER. This command will copy the COMMAND.COM file to your disk in addition to formatting the disk, so that you will not need a separate start-up disk to run the program.

To install the program on this new diskette, replace the DOS diskette in drive A with the MacroSolve diskette, and type INSTALL B followed by ENTER. When the process is complete, you will be able to run MacroSolve from the new diskette by simply typing MACRO. MacroSolve will start automatically if this newly installed diskette is in the A drive when you turn on your computer.

Starting MacroSolve

Put the MacroSolve diskette into drive A of your computer, and at the A> or C> prompt, type Macro (or MACRO; the computer does not distinguish upper- from lowercase entries). From there on, simply follow the instructions that the program gives you.

Colors: The program attempts to discern whether your computer's monitor is color or monochrome (Green or Amber display on a black background). The color scheme used depends on this choice. If the screen display is hard to read, you probably need to force the output to be in monochrome or color. This is done by typing MACRO followed by either color or mono; that is, at the A> prompt from DOS, type MACRO MONO or MACRO COLOR. You can also change the colors within MacroSolve.

Printing Output

MacroSolve is intended to be used by the student interactively. Occasionally you may wish to print the output, and there are three ways in which you may be able to. One is to use the internal printing option of MacroSolve; the second is to use a DOS graphics screen print; and the third is to use a window screen print.

1. *Printing from within MacroSolve:* If your computer is connected to either an Epson printer or a Hewlett-Packard LaserJet printer, you may be able to print from within MacroSolve. To do this, simply press F-9 (function key 9) and follow the instructions. Note, however, that printing graphics is entirely dependent on the particular hardware combinations of your computer. There can be no guarantee that printing will be possible for all combinations of graphics boards and printers.

2. *Graphics Screen Print:* If you have an Epson/IBM graphics compatible printer attached to your computer and if you have run the DOS program GRAPHICS.COM before running MacroSolve, then graphics displays (plots, graphs, and model displays) can be printed by pressing the Shift and PrtSc keys simultaneously. If there is no printer attached, this command will be ignored. However, if there is an incompatible printer attached, you should be warned that it will print a seemingly random selection of characters. The best action that you can take at that stage is to turn off the printer. After a short wait, you can return to MacroSolve with no further ill effects.

3. *Window Screen Print:* Users running MacroSolve under Windows 3.1 can always print the screen for the Windows clipboard by pressing the Alt and Print Screen keys simultaneously. The screen can be printed by pasting the contents of the clipboard into a Windows application, and printing from within that program.

MacroSolve Commands

Macrosolve commands for the IBM PC version are almost all entered from the keyboard using 1 of 12 keys.

↑	Up Arrow	Moves the cursor (highlighted rectangle on the screen) upward.
↓	Down Arrow	Moves the cursor downward.
←	Left Arrow	Moves the cursor to the left or decreases a numeric value displayed in a menu.
→	Right Arrow	Moves the cursor to the right or increases a numeric value displayed in a menu.
↵	Enter	Selects a menu entry or an option (the Space Bar may also be used for this operation, if your prefer).
	Space Bar	Selects an item from a choice box.
	Pg Up	Scrolls screen displays backward.
	Pg Dn	Scrolls screen displays forward.
	Esc	Exits an option.
	F-1	Shows a help screen to remind you what the various menu options do.
	F-9	Prints the screen to a compatible graphics printer.
	F-10	Brings up a calculator on the screen.

Menus and Options for the IBM PC

Help Menu

This option allows you to obtain help on how to use this program. Help can also be obtained by pressing F-1 at any time.

Exit Menu

To exit the program, move the cursor to the **Exit** position, select **Exit to DOS,** and press **Enter.** Notice that this is the only way to exit the program other than turning the power off or rebooting. It is the only guaranteed safe manner in which to exit the program.

Data Menu

This option allows you to create, delete, and review your own data series. **Create Series** prompts you to enter an equation that defines a new series as a transformation of any of the more than 30 annual and quarterly series distributed with MacroSolve. New series are created using equations with the new series name to the left of the equals sign and an expression involving existing series names to the right of the equals sign. The most common mathematical operations are available: + (add), − (subtract), ∗ (multiply), / (divide), and ∧ (power). The unlimited nesting of parentheses controls the order of evaluation. Transformations are carried out on the entire data series, and lags of other variables are accessed by using square brackets. For example, a formula to compute the growth rate of GDP could be entered as follows:

$$\text{GROWTH} = ((\text{GDP} - \text{GDP}[-1])/\text{GDP} [-1]) * 100.$$

Delete Series is used to delete series that you have defined from the data file and would, for example, be used if you wanted to create a new series with an existing name. **Show Description** is used to show the formula that you used to generate a new series or the description of a series distributed with MacroSolve.

Plot Menu

This option allows you to plot on the screen up to three macroeconomic time series. The time series are selected from the choices in the **Select Series** option. Once you have entered this option, you select the series by pointing at them with the cursor (which now appears inside the box with the series names in it) and pressing Space Bar when each desired series is highlighted. Pressing Space Bar again will unselect the chosen series. Press Enter when you have selected all the series that you want to plot. A quick way to unselect all previously selected series is to press the Home key. **Annual** and **Quarterly** options switch between annual data for the period of 1930 to the present and quarterly data for 1967 to the present. You can change the sample for which data are displayed by choosing the **Select Dates** option. The selected series can be displayed numerically using the **Tabulate & Plot** option, or graphically, plotted with time on the horizontal axis, using the **Begin Plot** option. **Statistics** provides statistics on the selected series.

Graph Menu

This option allows you to graph one series on the vertical axis against a second on the horizontal axis. The graph series are selected using the **Select Series** option, exactly as in the **Plot** menu. Annual and quarterly data are similarly chosen using the **Annual** and **Quarterly** options. You can choose the sample for which the data are graphed by using the **Select Dates** option. The screen display is affected by the **Connect** and **Points** options, which toggle between displaying the graph using points only and connecting the adjacent observations with a line. The speed with which the graph is displayed on the screen is changed by the **Fast Speed** or **Slow Speed** options. To get an overall picture of the data, use the fast option. The slow option will help you see more clearly what is happening in particular periods. In the slow mode, you can stop the screen display at any time by pressing any key. To see the graph on the screen, use the **Begin Graph** option. To tabulate and graph the data, select the **Tabulate & Graph** option. **Statistics** provides statistics on the selected series.

Model Menu

There are a total of seven models built into the program: three static IS-LM (fixed-price) models and four AD/PA (aggregate demand/price-adjustment) models. The equations for these models can be viewed with the **Display Equations** option. To select a particular model, use the **Select Model** option. This works exactly as the **Select Series** option in the **Plot** and **Graph** menus. You can change the exogenous variable (the level or growth rate of the money supply, government spending, a price shock, potential GDP, or the tax rate) in the **Change Exogenous Vars** (Change Exogenous Variables) option, using the cursor keys to increase or decrease these variables. You can also change some of the key model parameters in the **Set Parameters** or **Set Exact Parameters** options. The results for the model can be displayed in one of two ways: graphically, using the **Graph Model** option or numerically using the **Tabulate Model** option.

For an AD/PA model, results are displayed in a four-quadrant diagram. The IS, LM, AD, and P curves are displayed on the left side of the screen. **Set Display** enables you to choose which variables are displayed in the two right-side windows of the screen. Series are selected in exactly the same way as in the **Plot** and **Graph** menus. **Set Num of Periods** changes the number of simulation periods between 2 and 30. IS-LM models automatically change this to 2 periods, whereas AD/PA models default to at least 10 periods. **Simultaneous** and **Individual** options toggle between displaying all windows simultaneously and concentrating on one at a time.

INSTRUCTIONS FOR THE MACINTOSH VERSION OF MACROSOLVE

Equipment Required

MacroSolve will run on any Macintosh computer with at least 512K of memory. Also recommended, but not required, is Version 6.0 or higher of the System Folder. It can be found on the Macintosh disk supplied with this textbook.

Running MacroSolve from the Diskette

You may make one copy of the diskette you purchased, and we recommend that you do so. The procedure for copying MacroSolve is discussed below under "Installing MacroSolve."

To run MacroSolve from the Macintosh disk, simply turn the machine on and insert the disk. A double-click with the mouse on the MacroSolve icon (shown below) puts you into the program, though you'll have to wait a few seconds. You'll

MacroSolve

see the title screen for a moment, and then the screen will display the available menu options: "file," "edit," "data," "plot," "graph," "model," and "options." These correspond to the IBM PC menus, but are described again below.

Menus and Options for the Macintosh

MacroSolve Help: If you need help when running MacroSolve, you have only to click on the first (Apple) menu. You can ask for help at any time during the program's execution. **Help MacroSolve** is the second entry of the Apple menu. After the help window appears, you will see that a list of help topics is on the left while the actual text referring to the current topic is on the right. To select a new topic, click the mouse directly on the item for which you would like more information. To scan through all topics, use the "Prev" and "Next" buttons at the bottom of the window (the current topic will change automatically). Click on the "Exit" button to remove the help window from the screen when you are finished.

Data Menu

This option allows you to create, delete, and review your own data series. **Create Series** prompts you to enter an equation that defines a new series as a transformation of any of the more than 30 annual and quarterly series distributed with Macro-Solve. New series are created using equations with the new series name to the left of the equals sign and an expression involving existing series names to the right of the equals sign. The most common mathematical operations are available + (add), − (subtract), * (multiply), / (divide), and ∧ (power). The unlimited nesting of parentheses controls the order of evaluation. Transformations are carried out on the entire data series, and lags of other variables are accessed by using square brackets. For example, a formula to compute the growth rate of GDP could be entered as follows:

$$\text{GROWTH} = ((\text{GDP} - \text{GDP} [-1])/\text{GDP} [-1]) * 100.$$

Delete Series is used to delete series that you have defined from the data file and would, for example, be used if you wanted to create a new series with an existing name. **Show Equation** is used to show the formula that you used to generate a new series.

Plot Menu

This menu allows you to tabulate or plot on the screen up to three macroeconomic time series. The time series are selected from the choices in the **Select Series** option. Once you have entered this option, you select a series (up to three of them) by clicking on the box to its left. When you have checked off the series you want, click **ok,** which returns you to the main menu. If you selected **Auto Apply** for either plot or tabulate, MacroSolve will next automatically plot and/or tabulate the series that you selected. A quick way to unselect all previously selected series is to click on the **unselect** box here.

Back in the plot menu, you have the option of selecting annual data, which give you the broad sweep back to 1930, or quarterly data, which give you a more detailed look at the record since 1967. Click on the option you want.

Your machine is now ready to display the data. For a time-series diagram, click on the **start plot** command. To see the actual numbers, you click on **tabulate data,** and when the table comes up, you can scroll through the entire series. **Statistics** provides statistics on the selected series.

The last option available to you in the plot menu is **select sample.** Here you can narrow the time period for the series. For instance, if you want to focus on inflation and unemployment in the 1960s, you can enter this menu and select a sample restricted to that decade.

Graph Menu

This menu allows you to graph one of the data series against another, rather than against time. You select one series for the horizontal axis and another for the vertical axis. As with the plot menu, the first step is to select the desired series. The same data series are available to you as were presented in the plot menu, but you'll have to scroll through the list to see all of them. When you see the one you want, simply click on it. A black bar will appear to indicate that this series has been selected.

Once you have selected two series, you click on **ok** to return to the main menu. Alternatively, by clicking on the box next to **graph window,** your machine will go straight to the graph when you click **ok.**

Back in the main menu, you have a number of options for your graph. Clicking on **annual** or **quarterly** selects whether the graph will trace all the way back to 1930 or will produce a detailed look at the record since 1967. As with the plot menu, you can use the **set sample** option to focus on a shorter period of time than that specified in the data bank. The choice between **points** and **connect** tells MacroSolve how you want your graph displayed: as a scatter of points or with lines connecting them chronologically. Finally, you can select a **fast** or **slow** speed for the display, depending on how closely you want to study the chronological display. **Statistics** provides statistics on the selected series.

Model Menu

The MacroSolve "model" menu group extends into the "options" group and offers many alternatives. You'll learn all of them with experience, but you'll find it easiest at first if you let MacroSolve make most of the choices for you. All you have to do is to change one of the variables that affect the economy. Go into the **Set exogenous** option and make a change in money supply or government spending, or simulate a price shock (or any combination of the three). Then click **ok** to return to the main menu.

To see the result, click on **display model,** and MacroSolve will give you a four-window display of the analysis: IS-LM diagram, AD/PA diagram, and a time series of each of two variables. Alternatively, you can look at the numbers themselves by selecting the **tabulate model** option.

When you get more familiar with MacroSolve, you'll want to use some of the other model options. Under **select model** you'll find a choice among seven versions of the model: three static IS-LM (fixed-price) models and four AD/PA (aggregate demand/price-adjustment) models. To select a particular model, use the **select model** option and click on the one you want. Under **change parameters,** you'll find six behavioral factors that affect the model's outcome; by clicking on the buttons there, you can change the assumptions behind the model.

Under the option **select display** you can specify the two variables that you want the model to display. With **set speed,** you can increase the speed with which MacroSolve carries out the display and select whether the program should pause between each period. You can control the number of periods, between 2 and 20, over which MacroSolve will carry out the analysis by selecting the **set # periods** menu. Finally, by clicking on **simultaneous** or **individual,** you can tell MacroSolve to proceed through the analysis with all four screens at once or to take it one screen at a time.

To Exit

When you are finished with your session on MacroSolve, you can get out of the program by selecting **quit** under the **file** menu.

Transporting MacroSolve Data and Graphs to Other Programs

Transporting either data or graphs from MacroSolve into another Macintosh program is feasible via the **Edit** menu. When you have the information on the screen that you would like to export, simply choose **Copy Data** or **Copy Graph,** depending on the composition of what you are transferring. This information will now reside in the **Clipboard,** which is incorporated into most applications. Since it cannot hold more than one graph or set of data, however, all subsequent calls to the **Copy** command will simply overwrite whatever was previously copied. To finish the process, exit MacroSolve, open the desired destination program for the contents of the Clipboard, and then select the **Paste** command from the **Edit** menu. The screen will now contain a picture of the last MacroSolve window that was copied.

There are three alternative ways to obtain a hard copy of your screen. The simplest way to print the screen is to select **Print** from the File menu. If you have an Apple Imagewriter attached to your Mac, you can also print the screen by pressing the **Shift, Option,** and **3** keys simultaneously. The printer should then print everything that you see on your screen. Of, if you want to obtain a printout on an Apple Laserwriter, you should press the **Shift, Option,** and **4** keys simultaneously. The first time that you do this, your Macintosh will copy the screen into a MacPaint file called **Screen0**; the next time it will copy to a file called **Screen1**; etc. These screen files can then be printed or edited by using MacPaint.

Window Manipulation

A window, like the one shown below, is simply an area on the screen created to hold and display a particular set of information. One advantage of the Macintosh over the IBM PC is that you can put more than one window on the screen at once; this allows quick alternation between windows by simply clicking inside the window itself. For example, if more than one window is currently on the screen but one is partially obscured by the others, you can click on the visible portion of the obscured window to place it and its contents in front of the other windows. Further manipulation of these windows is possible by clicking on one of the command areas we have labeled and described below the illustration.

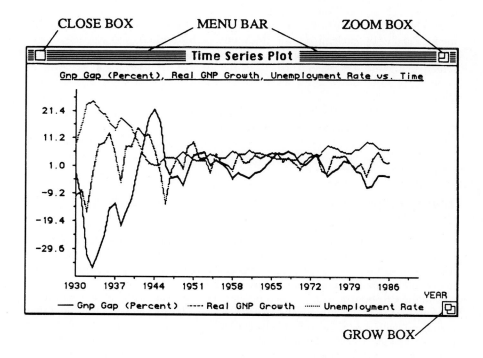

CLOSE BOX: Removes the top (or active) window from the screen; this makes the next window below it the active window.

ZOOM BOX: Revises the active window so that it becomes the full size of the screen. Clicking again will return the window to its former size. As with resizing the window below, the contents of all windows containing graphics will be rescaled to utilize the area available best while still forcing information to fit in the window.

MENU BAR: By clicking anywhere in the menu bar except in the close and zoom boxes, the window can be physically dragged around the screen by moving the mouse itself. The window will be redrawn at the new location when the mouse button is released.

GROW BOX: Serves to resize a window while being anchored in the top left corner. Click and hold down the mouse button while in the box, move the mouse until the desired size is reached, and release. Again, all graphic windows will be redrawn to conform to the new window configuration.

Menu Toggles

In the **Plot, Graph,** and **Options** menus, toggles are used so that simple selections between two items can be made in one easy step. The two choices in any one toggle are separated from the other menu choices by dashed lines. The current selection will always have a check mark immediately to its left. To change a selection, simply select the other option from the menu. If you view the menu again, you will notice that the check mark now appears adjacent to the newly selected item. Selecting an item that already has a check mark next to it has no effect.

Installing MacroSolve

To install MacroSolve on a hard disk, put the MacroSolve disk into your disk drive and drag the disk icon into your hard disk. This will copy all the program files into a folder called MacroSolve.

Index

Abraham, Katherine, 76
accelerationist property, 216
accelerator:
  defined, 320
  for housing, 328
  investment and, 300, 303, 320
accommodative policies, 241, 245–45, 248, 436
accounting identity, 32
accumulation of debt, 395–97
activist economic policy, 237
  constant growth policy rules and, 541
  discretionary vs., 541
advertising, help-wanted, 76
aggregate demand:
  balance of income and spending in, 154–71
  budget deficit and, 383–401
  currents of thought and, 22
  defined, 17, 151
  depreciation and, 595
  financial markets and, 176–208
  foreign trade and, 345, 346–48
  IS-LM approach and, see IS-LM approach
  microeconomic foundations of, 265–447
  output determined by, 148, 149, 210–12
  price adjustment and, 219–24, 518–25
  price level and, 200, 201–2
  in reverse, 250
  in short-run model, 147–54
  spending balance and, 149–54
aggregate demand curve, 17, 147
  accommodative policy rule and, 244–45
  derivation of, 200–202
  fiscal policy and, 200, 202–3, 250–51
  GDP and, 250
  monetary policy and, 201–3, 248, 250–51
  money demand and, 236–37
  price adjustment and , 219
  price disturbances and, 240–41
  real GDP and, 212–13, 232–33
  shifts in, 232–33, 236–37
  slope of, 200
aggregate demand disturbances, 230–49
  analyzing effects of, 231–36
  offsetting of, 552–56
  price adjustment and, 232–35
  recession and, 232–33
  responding to, 232-33, 236–40
  stabilization policy and, 236–40
aggregate investment demand function, 323
American Economic Association, 216–17
Ando, Albert, 278n, 287, 289, 290
Ando-Modigliani consumption function, 287, 289
animal spirits, 230
anti-inflation policies, 548–50
appreciation of U.S. dollar, 350, 575, 592

Argentina, 592
Arrow, Kenneth, 110
Ashenfelter, Orley, 96n
assets:
  in balance sheet, 413
  consumption and, 287, 289
  liquid, 236, 422
  negative, 280
  saving and investment and, 54–55
AT&T, 364
Atlantic City, N.J., 415
auction markets, 542
automatic stabilizers:
  defined, 270, 389
  government transfers as, 388–89
  IS curve and, 401
automobile industry, 153–54

baby boom, 5, 88, 90
backward-looking wage behavior, 488–89
  expected inflation and, 511–12
bailout spending, 193
Balanced Budget and Emergency Control Act (1985), 383
balanced growth:
  conditions for, 100–101
  saving and, 98–103
balanced growth path, 99–103
  defined, 99
balance of payments deficit, 582
balance of payments surplus, 582
balance sheets, 413–14, 579
Balassa, Bela, 344n
Baldwin, Richard, 110, 363n
Bank of England, 577, 583, 588–89
Bank of Italy, 597
Bank of Japan, 577
banks:
  currency deposit ratio of, 433
  deregulation of, 428
  as financial intermediaries, 415
  in foreign exchange market, 348–49
  interest and service charges offset by, 427–28
  intermediation role of, 414
  reserve ratio of, 415–16
Barro, Robert, 400, 460, 465, 466
Baumol, William, 424n
BEA (Bureau of Economic Analysis), 32
Benhabib, Jess, 454n
Bernheim, Douglas, 282n
Blanchard, Olivier, 22
Blinder, Alan, 294
BLS (Bureau of Labor Statistics), 67–69, 70, 73, 77, 80, 99, 486
Blue Chip Economics, 563
bond-financed changes, defined, 421

bonds:
    government, 50, 54–55, 414, 580
    interest rate and, 427
booms, 17, 248, 474, 481
    consumption in, 287
    price adjustment and aggregate demand
        in, 522–24
borrowed reserves:
    discount rate and, 418–19
    monetary base and, 418
borrowing:
    capital inflow, 52, 348
    defined, 50
    from positive vs. negative asset positions,
        280–81
Brainard, William, 344n, 545
Bretton Woods System, 582–83, 586, 594
    balance of payments in, 582
    collapse of, 583–84
    devaluation in, 583
Bronfenbrenner, Martin, 23
Brown, E. Cary, 393n
Brumberg, R. E., 278n
Budget Accord (1990), 383
budget constraint, intertemporal, 279–81,
    286, 397
budget deficit, 383–401
    aggregate demand and, 383–401
    components of, 383
    defined, 51
    in Germany, 595
    measurement of, 397–98
    trade deficit and, 126, 129, 138, 360–61
    see also deficits
Budget Enforcement Act (1990), 246–47
budget process reform, 246–47
budget surplus, defined, 51
buffer stock inventories, 331
Bundesbank, 577, 578, 584, 590, 591, 596,
    597
Bureau of Economic Analysis (BEA), 32
Bureau of Labor Statistics (BLS), 67–69, 70,
    73, 77, 80, 99, 486
Bureau of the Census, 70
Burns, Arthur, 238
Bush, George, 199, 246, 345
Bush administration, 595
business investment, see nonresidential fixed
    investment

Caballero, Ricardo, 458n
Cagan, Phillip, 415n, 511
Calvo, Guillermo, 246, 248n, 540
capital:
    changes in price of, 318–19
    controlled movement of, 578
    defined, 88
    diminishing marginal product of, 314

growth of, 107–8
    marginal cost of, 313–14, 480
    relative price of, 318–19
    renting of, see rented capital
    stimulating formation of, 107–8
    see also money
capital account, 56
capital budgeting:
    rented capital and, 317–18, 341–43
    winner vs. loser positions in, 342
capital controls, 581
capital gains taxes, 326–27
capital inflow, 52, 348
capital-outflow ratio, 100–101
capital stock, 312
    actual, 320, 343–44
    choosing of, 315
    desired, 319–20, 343–44
    fixed investment and, 33–34
    investment demand and, 322
    net investment and, 91
    slow adjustment of, 322
Carlton, Dennis, 484
Carter, Jimmy, 255, 294, 548, 568
Carter administration, 595
Cechetti, Stephen G., 484n
central banks, 577–79, 598–99
    balance sheets of, 579
    domestic credit in, 580
    exchange-rate policies of, 579–80
    foreign reserves of, 579, 583
    sterilized intervention by, 580–81, 584
    T-bills in 582
checking accounts, 411
    opportunity cost for funds in, 422–23
Chevron, 38
Chile, 483
China, People's Republic of, 576
Christiano, Lawrence, 326
CIS (Commonwealth of Independent States),
    598
Clark, Kim, 89n
Clark, Peter K., 321n, 322n
classical dichotomy, 136, 139–40
classical macroeconomics, 21–22
coefficients, defined, 155
COLA (cost-of-living adjustment), 68–69,
    490, 492, 509
collective bargaining, 68–69, 486–89, 491
commodities, as price indicator, 562
Commonwealth of Independent States (CIS),
    598
compensating balances, defined, 428
complementaries, 458
complete model, 19–21, 26–27, 209–28
    aggregate demand in, 219–24
    fluctuations and, 19–21
    long-run growth model vs., 88

price adjustment and, 214–23
Congress, U.S., 20, 122, 192, 199, 229, 255, 293, 363, 383, 390, 391, 568
constant growth rate policy rules, 541
consumer behavior, 267
  backward-looking, 488–89, 511-12
  forward-looking, *see* forward-looking theory of consumption
  liquidity-constrained, 295
  rate of time preference in, 297
  see also rational expectations
consumer price index (CPI), 67–70, 561, 562
consumption:
  assets and, 287, 289
  in booms vs. recessions, 287
  consumption expenditures vs., 270
  current vs. future, 292
  defined, 33
  disposable income compared to, 275
  of durable goods, 270
  fluctuations in, 268–73
  forward-looking theory of, *see* forward-looking theory of consumption
  as function of income, 155–58
  interest-rate sensitivity of, 125–26, 127, 296–98
  IS curve and, 298–99
  life-cycle theory of, 278
  in 1990, 38
  past income and, 287, 289
  permanent-income theory of, 278
  random walk of, 292–93
  real disposable income and, 272–73
  in recessions, 274, 287
  retirement and, 282
  smoothness of, 275
  steady vs. erratic, 281–82
  and temporary changes in income, 292–93
consumption deflator, 69
consumption demand, 267–307
consumption expenditure:
  consumption vs., 270
  durables and, 270
  nondurables and, 270
  services and, 270
consumption function, 155–57
  Ando-Modigliani, 287, 289
  disposable income and, 155–57
  error analysis in, 273–75
  forward-looking theory of consumption vs., 278
  Keynesian, 273–77, 289, 291
  MPC in, 272–73, 275–77
  simple, 273
consumption planning, graphical approach to, 305–7
consumption substitution, 297
Continental Illinois Bank, 418

contingency clauses, union contract, 490–93
contractionary fiscal policy, 257
contractionary monetary policy, 257, 596
contracts:
  indexing of, 487, 489, 492–93, 509–10, 566
  labor, 476, 484, 487
  for products, 476, 477
  union, *see* union contracts
contributions for social insurance, 48
cooperative policy choice, defined, 594
cost-of-living adjustment (COLA), 68–69, 490, 492, 509
Cost of Living Council, 567
counterclockwise loop, 527
countercyclical stabilization policy, 237–39
  effects of, 392
  inflation and, 239
covered interst-rate parity, defined, 376
CPI (consumer price index), 67–70, 561, 562
CPI basket, 67
Crandall, Robert, 364–65
credit cards, 411
crowding out, 129
  defined, 192, 436
  expansionary fiscal policy and, 575–76
  Fed control of, 436
currency, 421–22, 426
  on balance sheet, 414
  defined, 411
  depreciation of, *see* depreciation
  inconvertible, 578
  intervention, 583
  vault cash vs., 414n
currency deposit ratio, 416, 433
current account, 56–58
Current Population Survey, 70–71, 72
curves:
  aggregate demand, *see* aggregate demand curve
  expectations-augmented Phillips, *see* expectations-augmented Phillips curve
  IS, *see* IS curves
  labor supply, 109, 477–78
  LM, *see* LM curve
  Phillips, *see* Phillips curve
cyclical deficits, structural deficits vs., 393–94

Davis-Bacon Act, 565
debt, government:
  deficit and, 395–97
  economic significance of, 398–401
defense spending, 18
deficits:
  accumulation of debt and, 395–97
  balance of payments, 582
  current account, 56–58

deficits (*continued*)
  cyclical vs. structural, 393–94
  fluctuation in, 387–92
  full-employment, 393
  interest rate and, 394–95
  merchandise, 56
  monetization of, 395
  in World War II, 395–97
  see also budget deficit; trade deficit
deflators, 67, 69–70
demand:
  aggregate, *see* aggregate demand
  consumption, 267–307
  elasticity of, 479
  firm and, 209–10
  for housing, 328
  for imports, 575
  interest rate and, 17
  for labor, 94, 114, 456–58
  money, *see* money demand
  price adjustment and, 152–53
  price level vs. level of output and, 17
  in recession, 17
demand curve, macroeconomic, *see* aggre-
      gate demand curve
demand curve, microeconomic, for rented
      capital, 314
demand-deficient recession, 520–21
Denison, Edward, 104
deposits, 414
depreciation:
  aggregate demand and, 595
  defined, 34
  devaluation vs., 583
  exchange rate and expected rate of,
      377–79
  investment and, 321
  of U.S. dollar, 350
  write-offs of, 326
Depression, Great, 8, 22, 25, 582
deregulation, in financial markets, 428
desired capital stock:
  actual capital stock and, 320, 343–44
  defined, 319
desired stock of housing, defined, 328–29
devaluation, 583–84
  depreciation vs., 583
Diamond, Peter, 400
diminishing marginal product, 314
discount rate:
  borrowed reserves and, 418–19
  defined, 418
discretionary changes in tax rates, 390–91
discretionary policy rules, 541
disinflation, 249–57, 498–501
  alternative paths for, 251–57, 500
  avoiding of, 566–67
  defined, 249

GDP and, 251–57
  monetary policy and, 250–57, 498–502
  Phillips curve and, 249
  recession and, 498
  unemployment and, 254, 257
disposable income, 47, 155, 157
  consumption compared to, 275
  consumption fluctuation and, 270–73
  consumption function and, 155–57
  GDP and, 270–72
  government taxes and transfers and, 392
  intertemporal budget constraint on, 280
  real, 271–73
District Federal Reserve Banks, 414n, 415,
      418, 419, 421
disturbances, 230–49
  aggregate demand, *see* aggregate demand
      disturbances
  to money demand, 231, 236, 237
  price, *see* price disturbances
  temporary vs. permanent, 231
Dobson, Wendy, 561
dollar, U.S.:
  appreciation of, 350, 575, 592
  Bretton Woods System and, 582–84
  creation of, 599
  depreciation of, 350
  deutsche mark vs., 346
  devaluation of, 584
  fluctuations in, 345–46
  international value of, 346
  price of, 58
  for quoting prices, 483
  yen vs., 58–59
domestic credit, 579–80
dumping, 364
Dunlop, John, 486
durable goods, 33
  consumption expenditures and, 270
  consumption of, 270
  long-run MPC and, 276–77
  short-run MPC and, 276–77
dynamic model:
  defined, 212
  see also price-adjustment model
dynamic multiplier, 166n

economic fluctuations, *see* fluctuations
economic growth, *see* growth
economic growth theory, 24
Economic Report of the President (1977), 294
Economic Report of the President (1987), 111
ecu (European Currency Unit), 597, 599
efficiency wage theory, 490n
Eisner, Robert, 397
elasticity:
  defined, 389
  of demand, 479

of labor supply, 477–79
employment, 9–10
    full, *see* full employment
    inflation and, 66–86
    measuring of, 70–81
    population and, 73
    production and, 9
    productivity and, 79–81
    real GDP and, 9–10
    real wage and, 477–82
    recession and, 9, 70–71, 113
    see also labor supply; unemployment
EMS (European Monetary System), 578, 586,
        588, 590–91, 596–97
endogenous growth theory, 24, 110–11
endogenous policy, *see* policy rule
endogenous variables, 158
    expected inflation as, 512–13
    money supply as, 243
    net exports as, 355
    predetermined vs., 181–82
equilibrium, 146–49
    analysis of fixed-exchange rate policies,
        591
    analysis of floating–exchange rate poli-
        cies, 591
    labor market and, 97, 144–46
    in money market, 135–37
    price adjustment and, 214–19
    stochastic, 541
    unemployment and, 89, 90, 97
Europe, financial union in, 576–77, 596–97,
        598–99
European Currency Unit (ecu), 597, 599
European Monetary System (EMS), 578, 586,
        588, 590–91, 596–97
excess reserves, defined, 417
exchange rate, 58–59, 345–82, 581, 584–93
    appreciation of, inflation differentials and,
        592–93
    balance of payments accounts and, 58–59
    central banks and, 579–80
    defined, 55, 348
    between deutsche mark and U.S. dollar,
        346
    devaluation vs. revaluation of, 584
    expected depreciation and, 377–79
    fixed, *see* fixed exchange rate
    floating, *see* floating exchange rate
    fluctuations in, 350–52, 582
    foreign exchange market and, 348
    foreign trade and, 348–57
    interest rate and, 355–57, 374–76
    IS curve and, 368
    LM curves and, 368
    money supply and, 595
    net exports and, 352–53, 354
    price adjustment and, 359, 361
    as price indicator, 562
    price level and, 362–63
    purchasing power parity and, 351–52,
        377–79
    real, 350
    relative price and, 350–52
    stabilization of, 366–68
    trade-weighted, 58, 349, 351
    between yen and U.S. dollar, 58–59, 585–86
exogenous variables, 158, 181–82
    money supply as, 242–43
expansionary fiscal policy, 257
    appreciated U.S. dollar and, 575
    central banks and, 580
    crowding out and, 575–76
    and demand for imports, 575
    interest rate and, 575
    short-term benefits vs. long-term costs in,
        545
expansionary monetary policy, 257
    short-term benefits vs. long-term costs in,
        545
expectations, *see* rational expectations
expectations-augmented Phillips curve,
        507–9
    disinflation and, 249
expectations of policy, 248
expected inflation:
    actual behavior and, 512
    backward-looking wage behavior and,
        511–12
    and changes in monetary policy, 513
    determination of, 218–19
    as endogenous variable, 512–13
    extended high output and, 515–18
    forward-looking forecasts and, 510, 511
    materials price shock and, 515
    one-year stimulus and, 513–14
    term of, 511–18
    wage determination and, 218–19, 489,
        511–13, 542
expected price level, 464
Export-Import Bank, 583
exports, 36–37, 168–71
    defined, 36
    GDP and, 36–37, 353
    net, *see* net exports
    see also foreign trade

factor income, 46
family histories, 290–91, 293
Fed, *see* Federal Reserve System
Federal Deposit Insurance Corporation
        (FDIC), 418
Federal Open Market Committee (FOMC),
        419, 432
Federal Reserve Board, 11, 20, 40, 229, 236,
        238, 255, 256, 419

Federal Reserve System (Fed), 122, 132, 134, 135, 136, 137, 244, 245, 247–49, 465, 466, 499, 561, 577, 585
 crowding out controlled by, 436
 functions of, 412
 interest rate and, 24
 in IS-LM approach, 181, 194
 loans to banks from, 418
 monetary policy controlled by, 199, 250, 252
 in monetizing government debt, 395
 money supply controlled by, 413–21; see also Fed policy rule
 open-market operations by, 415, 432
 policy rule of, see Fed policy rule
 Reagan and, 255–57
 real GDP and, 252
 reserve balances in, 417
Fed policy rule, 432–37
 fiscal policy effect and, 435–37
 lags in, 440–41
 LM curve and, 432–35, 439
 M_1 target policy in, 432, 433–34, 438
Feldstein, Martin S., 321n, 401
Fethke, Gary, 493n
final goods, 38
final sales, 35
final targets, 543
financial markets:
 aggregate demand and, 176–208
 volatility of, 24
Financial Markets and Financial Crises (Hubbard), 24
financial variables, 176–208
firms:
 capital budgeting by, see capital budgeting
 and changes in demand, 209–10
 as forward-looking, 312–13
 information and behavior of, 462–65
 inventory investment by, see inventory investment
 investment function of, see investment function
 and labor markets with price and wage rigidities, 473–506
 nonresidential investment by, see nonresidential fixed investment
 price adjustments by, 214–23
 residential investment by, see residential fixed investment
 sticky prices of, 483
 unused capacity of, 456–57
 wage setting by, see wage determination
 see also price adjustment
fiscal expansion:
 monetary expansions vs., 257
 vertical LM curve and, 437
 see also expansionary fiscal policy

fiscal policy:
 aggregate demand curves and, 200, 202–3, 250–51
 changes in, 129
 Congress and, 199
 contractionary, 257
 defined, 122, 257
 expansionary, see expansionary fiscal policy
 Fed policy rule and effect of, 435–37
 GDP and, 435–37
 IS-LM approach and, 192–94, 195–96, 198
 long-term growth and, 121–43
 monetary policy coordination with, 359
 monetary policy vs., 257–58, 419–21
 output and, 132
 strong, 196
 weak, 195–96
 see also Federal Reserve System; Fed policy rule; policy rule
Fischer, Stanley, 501n
Fisher, Irving, 67
fixed costs of going to work, 455
fixed exchange rate, 590–91
 equilibrium analysis of, 591
 see also fiscal policy
fixed growth rate, 243
fixed investment, 309–11, 312
 capital stock and, 33–34
 defined, 33
 write-offs for, 326
 see also nonresidential fixed investment; residential fixed investment
flat tax system, 111
Flavin, Marjorie, 291n
flexible-price model, 16–17, 19
 information problems in, 452, 462–65
 sticky-price model vs., 16
 theories of fluctuation and labor market in, 451–72
floating (flexible) exchange rate, 349, 584
 equilibrium analysis of, 591
 in international macro policy coordination, 594–96
 in macroeconomic policy, 588–89, 592–93
 world, 584–87, 588–89
 world inflation with, 592–93
flow of investment, 312
fluctuations, 3–30
 in deficits, 387–92
 in exchange rate, 350–52, 582
 in flexible-price model, 451–72
 in GDP, see GDP fluctuation
 government spending and, 387–88
 growth and, 3–4
 in income, 270–73
 inflation and, 10–11

in investments, 166
in investment spending, 309–11
policy recommendations for, 242
policy rules and, 439
real business cycle explanations of,
    112–16
in short-run model, 144–75
short-term, 4
in U.S. dollar, 345–46
see also disturbances
FOMC (Federal Open Market Committee),
    419, 432
Ford, Gerald R., 548
Ford administration, 293–94
forecasting, consumption function error and,
    275
foreign exchange market:
    banks in, 348–49
    exchange rate and, 348
foreign exchange market intervention, 577
foreign investment:
    by U.S., 52
    in U.S., 345
foreign reserves, 582, 583
    defined, 579
    sterilized intervention and, 580–81
foreign trade, 5, 6, 345–82
    aggregate demand and, 345, 346–48
    exchange rate and, 348–57
    monetary and fiscal policy in, 359
    open-economy macro model and, *see*
        open-economy macroeconomics
    price adjustment and, 359, 361
    spending balance and, 168–71
    see also exports; imports; net exports
45-degree line, spending balance and,
    158–59
forward-looking theory of consumption,
    278–96, 538, 540
    analysis of, 286
    anticipated vs. unanticipated changes in
        income, and, 285–86
    consumption function vs., 278
    defects in, 295–96
    expected inflation in, 510, 511
    intertemporal budget constraint in, 279–81
    preferences in, 281–82
    rational expectations in, 290–91
    in short vs. long run, 287
    temporary vs. permanent changes in in-
        come and, 282–85
    testing predictions of, 295–96
    see also rational expectations
Freeman, Richard B., 487*n*
free-market economies, 578
Free to Choose (Friedman and Friedman),
    500
free trade, protectionism vs., 363–66

frictional unemployment, 76–77, 89, 97
Friedman, Milton, 22, 26, 216–17, 238, 242,
    278, 287, 289–90, 465, 500
Friedman, Rose, 500
full employment, 16
    benefits of, 546–52
    defined, 97
    potential GDP and, 93–98
Full Employment Act (1946), 546
full-employment deficit, 393
full-employment level of output, 98
functions:
    consumption, *see* consumption function
    housing demand, 328
    investment, *see* investment function
    money demand, *see* money demand func-
        tion
    pipeline, 330
    production, *see* production function
    social welfare, 544
futures markets, rational expectation and,
    376–77

G-7, 138, 561, 594–95
GATT (General Agreement on Trade and
    Tariffs), 110
GDP (gross domestic product), 31–49
    aggregate demand curve and, 250
    defined, 31
    disinflation and, 251–57
    disposable income and, 270–72
    exports and, 36–37, 353
    fiscal policy and, 435–37
    fluctuations in, *see* GDP fluctuation
    GNP and, 46–47
    government spending and, 166–68
    imports and, 36
    income and, 45–49, 50, 151, 158, 270–73
    inflation and, 220–24
    investment and, 166, 168, 309–10, 330–32
    LM curve and, 438
    in long run, 23, 129, 131
    monetary policy and, 191–92, 250–51,
        440–41
    national income vs., 46–47
    1991 breakdown of, 37–38
    nominal, *see* nominal GDP
    per capita, 38
    per worker, 43
    potential, *see* potential GDP
    price disturbances and, 241, 242
    production and, 151
    as productivity measure, 43
    quarterly data on, 42
    real, *see* real GDP
    savings and investment in, 50–55
    shares of, 130–31
    spending and, 32–43, 151

GDP (gross domestic product) (*continued*)
   spending balance and, 154–71
   targeting level of, 432, 434–35
   training and, 551
   unemployment and, 550–52
   value added and, 44–45
GDP fluctuation, 6–9, 509
   consumption and income fluctuation and,
      268–73
   investment fluctuations and, 309–10
GDP gap, 77, 252–57
GDP implicit price deflator, 69
General Agreement on Trade and Tariffs
      (GATT), 110
General Motors, 153–54
*General Theory of Employment, Interest and
      Money, The* (Keynes), 24, 422
Germany, 577, 597
   budget deficit in, 595
   European Monetary System and, 596
   inflation-output loops in, 528, 559–60
   IS-LM and, 195
   real GDP in, 42–43
GNP (gross national product), 46–47
Goldfield, Stephen, 428n, 430n
gold standard, 581–82
   departure from, 582
goods:
   durable, *see* durable goods
   final, 38
   intermediate, 38, 44
   investment, 177
   nondurable, 33, 269, 276
Governing the $5 Trillion Economy (Stein),
      130
government bonds, 50, 54–55, 414, 580
government budget:
   federal, 384–86
   state and local, 386–87
government budget identity, 55
government debt:
   deficit and, 395–97
   economic significance of, 398–401
government outlays, defined, 36, 384
government purchases, 36, 124–25, 126, 128,
      387–88
government saving, 51
government spending:
   accumulation of debt and, 397
   budget process reform and, 246–47
   and changes in income, 166
   deficit and, 229–30
   economic fluctuations and, 387–88
   GDP and, 166–68
   interest rate and, 192–94
   IS curve and, 401
   in 1991, 38
   price adjustment and, 361

   printing press in, 420
   reaction function and, 384
   and shifts in IS curve, 183, 185
   taxes and, 390–92
government transfers, 388–89
   taxes and, 385, 392
   unemployment and, 389
gradual price adjustment, 21
Gramm-Rudman-Hollings bill, 383
Gray, Jo Anna, 501n
Great Depression, 8, 22, 25, 582
Greece, 411
Greenspan, Alan, 199, 419
gross domestic product, *see* GDP
gross national product (GNP), 46–47
gross saving, 53
growth, 3–30, 88–93, 98–112
   balanced, *see* balanced growth
   endogenous theory of, 24, 110–11
   fluctuations and, 3–4
   long-run economic, 4–5, 13–19, 104,
      110–11
   negative, 3
   of potential GDP, 18–19, 22
   stimulation of, 105–12
growth formula, derivation of, 104–5
growth path:
   balanced, 99–103
   stability proof of, 101–2
   technological change and, 103
   transition period and, 102–3
   see also equilibrium
growth rate policy rules, activist vs. constant,
      541
growth rates:
   fixed, 243
   policy rules on, 541
   transition period and, 102–3
Gulf Oil, 38

Hall, Robert E., 115n, 291n, 293n, 297n,
      323n, 457n, 475n, 564n
Hamada, Koichi, 595n
Hansen, Lars Peter, 291n, 377n
Harberger, Arnold, 243
Haverylyshyn, Oleh, 598
Hayashi, Fumio, 288, 295n
Hayek, Friedrich, 598
Heller, Walter, 238
help-wanted advertising, index of, 76
Heston, Robert, 24
Hicks, J. R., 181
high-powered money, 416
Hirsch, Albert A., 332n
Hodrick, Robert, 377n
Hong Kong, 599
hours worked per week, 71–72
housing, 328–30

accelerator principle for, 328
demand function for, 328
desired stock of, 328–29
monetary policy and investment in,
   329–30
Hubbard, Glenn, 24
Humphrey-Hawkins Act (1978), 546

IBM PC MacroSolve program, 605–10
equipment required for, 606
installing of, 606–7
menus and options for, 608–10
starting of, 607–8
identity, 32
IMF (International Monetary Fund), 138
imperfect information model, Lucas supply
   curve in, 462–65
import, marginal propensity to, 169
imports, 36–37
defined, 36
demand for, 575
GDP and, 36
see also foreign trade
incentives, tax, 324–27
income, 31, 45–49, 50
anticipated vs. unanticipated changes in,
   285–86
consumption and temporary changes in,
   292–93
consumption as function of, 155–58
disposable, *see* disposable income
fluctuations in, 270–73
GDP and, 45–49, 50, 151, 158, 270–73
government spending and changes in, 166
interest rate and, 192
IS-LM approach to computation of,
   190–91
national, 46–47
net exports and, 352–55
output and, 31–65
permanent vs. transitory, 278
personal, 47
real interest rate and, 296–98
temporary vs. permanent changes in,
   282–85
value added and, 45
wage, *see* wages
income effect, 96, 297, 453
income identity, 124, 154, 158, 159
defined, 124
IS curve and, 182
net exports in, 138, 168
income tax, 20, 293–94
income tax brackets, 548
inconvertible currency, 578
indexing of contracts, 487, 489, 492–93,
   509–10, 566

indexing of tax system, 548
indexing to inflation, 487, 489
improvements in, 566
in price-adjustment model, 509–10
in union contracts, 487, 489, 492–93,
   509–10
indifference curves, 305–7
defined, 305
inflation, 4–5, 588–93
in Argentina vs. U.S., 592
contracts indexed to, 487, 489, 492–93,
   509–10, 566
countercyclical stabilization policy and, 239
current vs. lagged rates of, 509–10
defined, 137
employment and, 66–86
expected, *see* expected inflation
fluctuations and, 10–11
gains and losses due to, 548–50
GDP and, 220–24
indexing to, *see* indexing to inflation
measuring of, 67–70
monetary policy and, 543
nonadapting economic institutions and,
   549
output and, 217–19
pensions and, 549
policy frontier between unemployment
   and, 552–69
potential GDP and, 220–24
PPI as warning indicator of, 69
in price adjustment, 215–19
price disturbances and, 515, 596
public view of, 548–50
rate of, defined, 67
real GDP and, 10–11, 67
recession and, 10–11, 249–50, 253, 256–57
tax distortions and, 548, 549
wage setting and, 487
world, with floating exchange rates,
   592–93
zero, 547
see also disinflation; expectations-
   augmented Phillips curve
inflation differentials, exchange rate appreciation and, 592–93
inflation loss, defined, 547
inflation-output loops, 525–29, 559–60
information problems, 452, 462–65
inheritance, for next generation, 282
initial claims for unemployment benefits, 73
instruments and targets, 543–45
intercept, defined, 161
interest-rate differential, 379–82
interest-rate parity, 374-77
covered, 376
defined, 375
testing of, 376–77

interest rates, 4–5, 11–13
  bonds and, 427
  consumption and, 125–26, 127, 296–98
  deficits and, 394–95
  demand and, 17
  exchange rate and, 355–57, 374–76
  expansionary fiscal policy and, 575
  Fed and, 24
  government spending and, 192–94
  income and, 192
  investment and, 125–26, 127, 176–80
  investment demand and, 195
  IS-LM approach and, 165–68, 191
  money demand and, 132–34, 185–86,
    195
  money demand function and, 134n, 195
  money market and, 132–34
  money supply and, 12, 135, 192
  net exports and, 125–26, 127, 180, 195
  nominal, 179, 296
  as price indicator, 562
  as procyclical, 12
  real, see real interest rate
  short-term vs. long-term, 179
  targeting of, 432, 434, 439
interest-rate sensitivity, 125–26, 127, 296–98
intermediate goods, 38, 44
intermediate products, defined, 44
intermediate targets, 543
intermediation role of banks, 414
international financial and monetary system,
    576–79, 584–87
  Bretton Woods, see Bretton Woods System
  capital controls and, 581
  current system in, 584–87
  EMS in, 578
  exchange-rate policy of, 581
  free-market principles in, 578
  history of, 581–87
  inflation differentials and parity adjust-
    ments in, 592–93
  joining of, 578–79
  movement of capital controlled in, 578
international macro policy coordination,
    594–96
International Monetary Fund (IMF), 138
International Trade Commission (ITC), 364,
    365
intertemporal budget constraint, 279–81,
    286, 397
inventory investment, 34–35, 309–10,
    330–33
  buffer stock and, 331
  defined, 33
  GDP and, 330–32
  pipeline function of, 330
  square-root rule and, 425–26
inventory theory, 424–26

investment:
  accelerator and, 300, 303, 320
  business vs. residential, 309
  crowding out and, see crowding out
  defined, 33
  depreciation and, 321
  factors in volume of, 309–10, 311–12
  financial variables and, 177
  fixed, 33–34, 309–11, 312, 326
  flow of, 312
  fluctuations in, 166
  GDP and, 166, 168, 309–10, 330–32
  in housing, 328–30
  interest rate and, 125–26, 127, 176–80
  interest-rate sensitivity of, 125–26, 127
  inventory, see inventory investment
  lag in, 322
  macro, 35
  net, 34, 91
  nonresidential, see nonresidential fixed in-
    vestment
  output and, 320–21
  portfolio, 35
  as primary force in economy, 308
  real interest rate and, 333
  residential, see residential fixed investment
  saving and, 50–55
  taxes and, 323–27
  wage rate and, 321
investment demand, 308–44
  defined, 310
  interest rates and, 195
  Tobin's q in, 343–44
investment demand function, 177–79
  defined, 319
investment function, 178–80, 319–23
  defined, 320
  IS curve and, 182, 333–34
investment goods, 177
investment spending:
  fluctuations in, 309–11
  interest rate and, 125–26, 127
  see also inventory investment; nonresiden-
    tial fixed investment; residential fixed
    investment
investment supply, defined, 310
investment tax credits, 20, 324–27
  for research and development, 106, 108
Iran, 558
Iraq, 558
IS curves, 181–85, 361
  algebraic derivation of, 188–89, 358–59
  automatic stabilizers and, 401
  consumption and, 298–99
  exchange rate and, 368
  government and, 401
  graphical derivation of, 184
  investment function and, 182, 333–34

open-economy, 358–61
  shifts in, 183, 185
  slope of, 182–83, 196–97, 299, 401
  tariffs and, 365
  tax cuts and, 299–300
  unavoidable shocks to, 437–39
IS-LM approach, 181–200, 220, 222
  Fed in, 181, 194
  fiscal policy and, 192–94, 195–96, 198
  framework of, 191
  interest rates and, 165–68, 191
  monetary policy and, 191–92, 195–97, 359
  open-economy macro model in, *see* open-economy macroeconomics
  tariffs and, 365
  in U.S., Japan, and Germany, 194–95
Is the Business Cycle Obsolete? (Bronfenbrenner), 23
ITC (International Trade Commission), 364, 365
Ito, Takatoshi, 377

Japan, 345, 346, 360–61, 362–63
  exchange rate in, 58–59, 585–86
  IS-LM and, 194–95
  output fluctuations in, 526
  real GDP in, 42–43
  saving rate in, 288, 361
  SII and, 138
  synchronized wage decisions in, 494
  trade surplus of, 138
Johnson administration, 293
Jorgenson, Dale, 312, 317, 323n

Katz, Lawrence F., 490n
Kennedy, John F., 108, 238, 391
Keynes, John Maynard, 19, 22, 24, 87, 155, 166, 230, 308, 422, 424, 426–27, 484, 582
Keynesian consumption function, 273–77, 289, 291
Keynesian cross diagram, 158–59
Keynesian school, 22, 25
  new vs. traditional, 22
Klamer, Arjo, 25
Knetter, Michael, 363n
Krugman, Paul, 363n
Kurihara, K. K., 278n
Kuznets, Simon, 32
Kydland, Finn, 23, 113, 246, 248n, 454n, 540

labor, 88–91
  contracts for, 476, 484, 487
  defined, 88
  demand for, 94, 114, 456–58
  elasticity of, 477–79
  income effect in, 96, 453
  increasing supply of, 109

marginal product of, 93, 94, 456–58, 492
  natural rate of unemployment and, 89–93
  real interest rate and, 297–98, 458–62
  shifts in demand for, 114
  shifts in supply of, 452–56
  substitution effect in, 95, 453
  supply of, *see* labor supply
  supply schedule for, 452–56
  see also employment; unemployment; unions; wages
labor demand functions, 94–95
labor force, defined, 72
labor force participation rate, 73, 89
labor markets, 145–46
  equilibrium and, 97, 144–46
  expansions in, 76
  flexible-price theories of fluctuation and, 451–72
  sticky-wage, 484–86, 542
  streamlining of, 565–66
labor productivity, 79–81
labor supply, 95–97, 452–56
  and alternative activities in recessions, 454–55
  elasticity of, 477–79
  flat, 454, 456, 474
  increasing of, 109
  long-run vs. short-run, 452–54, 456
  marginal cost and, 480
  real business cycle model and, 458–59
  real interest rate and, 297–98, 458–62
  tax cuts and, 109, 111
labor supply curves, 109, 477–78
lags:
  investment, 322
  in monetary policy effect, 440–41
Lazear, Edward P., 475n
leakage, defined, 358
lean production, 92
lending, defined, 50
life-cycle theory of consumption, 278
Lilien, David M., 90n
line, spending, 158–59
liquid, defined, 422
liquid assets, 236, 422
liquidity-constrained consumers, 295
liquidity preference, defined, 422
LM curve, 181, 185–91
  algebraic derivation of, 188–90
  exchange rate and, 368
  Fed policy rule and, 432–35, 439
  fiscal expansion and, 437
  GDP and, 438
  graphical derivation of, 187
  money supply and, 185
  price level and, 185, 187
  shifts in, 186–87
  slope of, 185–86, 197

LM curve (*continued*)
    tariffs and, 365
    unavoidable shocks to, 437–39
loans, 414
    compensating balances for, 428
longitudinal surveys, 291
long run:
    economic growth in, 4–5, 13–19, 104,
        110–11
    GDP in, 23, 129, 131
    labor supply in, 452–54, 456
long-run assumption, importance of, 129,
    131
long-run growth model, 14–19, 87–120
    classical dichotomy and, 139–40
    complete model vs., 88
    convergence hypothesis of, 104
    defined, 87
    derivation of formula for, 119
    and determinants of economic growth,
        88–93
    effects of monetary and fiscal policies on,
        121–43
    endogenous growth theory vs., 110–11
    expenditure and, 18
    output shifting and, 18
long-run marginal propensity to consume
    (MPC), 275–76, 287
    defined, 275–76
    durables and, 276–77
    nondurables and, 276
    services and, 276
Lovell, Michael, 332*n*
Lucas, Robert, 22, 24, 25, 110, 238, 243,
    457*n*, 460, 462–65, 466, 482, 502*n*,
    512*n*, 539
Lucas supply curve, 462–65
    price-adjustment curve vs., 467
    Lyons, Richard, 458*n*

M_1, 412
    targeting level of, 432, 433-34, 438
M_2, 412, 419, 562
M_3, 412
McCallum, B. T., 470
Machine That Changed the World, The, 92
Macintosh MacroSolve program, 610–15
    from diskettes, 610–11
    equipment for, 610
    installing of, 615
    menus and options for, 611–13
    transporting data and graphs from, 613–15
McKinnon, Ronald I., 595*n*
macroeconomic model, *see* complete model
macroeconomic policy, 229–64, 535–615
    activist, 237, 541
    capital controls in, 581
    changing policy frontier in, 564–69

consumption function error and, 275
cooperative policy choice in, 594–96
countercyclical stabilization policy in,
    237–39
demand for currency and checking de-
    posits in, 421–32
design and maintenance of, 537–74
disinflation and, *see* disinflation
disturbances in, *see* disturbances
exchange rates and, 588–93
experiments in, 290, 293–94
floating exchange rate in, 588–89, 592–93
general principles in analysis of, 537–43
inflation and, 552–56, 588–93
instruments of, 538–39
international coordination of, 594–96
monetary union in, 596–600
noncooperative policy choice in, 594
output and unemployment loss in, 550–52
as policy rule, *see* Fed policy rule; policy
    rule
real GDP and, 122–24
social welfare function in, 544
targeting in, 250–51, 432, 439, 543–45,
    564
uncertainty and timing in, 545
unemployment and, 550–56
world economy and, 575–603
see also specific policies
macroeconomics:
    classical, 21–22
    currents of thought in, 21–25
    defined, 4–6
    introduction to, 3–30
    microeconomics vs., 4
    monetarist vs. Keynesian schools of
        thought in, 22
    new classical school of, 22, 26
    open-economy, *see* open-economy macro-
        economics
    recent advances in, 21–24
    study of economics and, 25
    supply side of, *see* output; potential GDP
macro investment, 35
MacroSolve, 605–15
    introduction to, 605–6
    see also IBM PC MacroSolve program;
        Macintosh MacroSolve program
Mankiw, N. Gregory, 22, 484*n*
marginal benefit:
    of capital, 314
    defined, 313
    rental price of capital and, 316–17, 321
    marginal cost, 313–14
    defined, 313
    price and, 477–80
marginal opportunity costs, 423
marginal product, diminishing, 314

marginal product of labor, 93, 456–58, 492
   wages and, 94
marginal propensity to consume (MPC), 156,
      157
   in consumption function, 272–73, 275–77
   decreased taxes and, 283–85
   in long run, 275–76, 287
   in short run, 276–77, 287
   temporary vs. permanent changes in in-
      come and, 282–85
marginal propensity to import, 169
marginal rate of substitution, 305
marginal social costs of unemployment, 551,
      552
marginal tax rate, 111
market conditions, price adjustment and, 214
market failures, recessions as, 243
markup ratio, 479
Matsushita, 364
maximum profit, point of, 94
means of payment, 410, 412
Medoff, James L., 487*n*
menu costs, 484
merchandise account, 56
merchandise deficit, 56
Michigan, University of, 291, 293
microeconomic demand curves, for rented
      capital, 314
microeconomics, 4
   aggregate demand founded in, 265–447
   first principle of, 267
   macroeconomics vs., 4
Mishkin, Frederic, 293*n*
misperceptions model, 462–67
Mitchell, Daniel J. B., 487*n*
models:
   complete, *see* complete model
   defined, 14
   with flexible prices, *see* flexible-price
      model
   long-run growth, *see* long-run growth
      model
   price-adjustment, *see* price-adjustment
      model
   rational expectation, *see* rational expecta-
      tions model
   real business cycle, *see* real business cycle
      model
   short-run, *see* short-run model
   staggered wage setting, 487, 494–97,
      511–12
   with sticky prices, *see* sticky-price model
Modigliani, Franco, 22, 25, 278, 287, 289, 290
Mohammed Reza Shah Pahlavi, 558
monetarists, 22
   on stabilization policy, 238–40
monetary base:
   borrowed reserves and, 418

defined, 414–15
   Fed control of, 413–21
   Fed policy rule for, *see* Fed policy rule
   foreign reserves and, 580
   targeting of, 432, 439
monetary base multiplier, 416
monetary expansion, 440–41
   fiscal expansion vs., 257
monetary policy:
   aggregate demand curve and, 201–3, 248,
      250–51
   central question of, 432
   contractionary, 257, 596
   defined, 122
   disinflation and, 250–57, 498–502
   expansionary, *see* expansionary monetary
      policy
   expected inflation and, 513
   Fed control of, 199, 250, 252
   fiscal policy coordination with, 359
   fiscal policy vs., 257–58, 419–21
   fixed exchange rate and, 590–91
   GDP and, 191–92, 250–51, 440–41
   housing investment and, 329–30
   inflation and, 543
   IS-LM approach and, 191–92, 195–97, 359
   lags in effect of, 440–41
   long-run growth and, 121–43
   rational expectations and, 199, 498–501
   sterilization in, 580–81
   strong, 196
   targeting in, 250–51, 432–35, 439, 543, 564
   trade-offs in, 544–45
   weak, 196
   see also Federal Reserve System; Fed pol-
      icy rule; policy rule
monetary policy ineffectiveness theorem,
      465
monetary system, 409–47
   defined, 409
   elements of, 410–12
   establishment of, 598
   international, *see* international financial
      and monetary system
   means of payment in, 410, 412
   unit of account in, 410, 412
monetary union, 596–600
monetization of deficit, 395
money:
   defined, 132–33, 411
   demand functions for, 428–32
   high-powered, 416
   M_1, *see* M_1
   neutrality of, 136
   nominal, 186
   opportunity costs of holding funds as,
      422–23, 428
   real, 12, 186

money (*continued*)
  as store of wealth, 426–27, 598
  as unit of value, 598
  see also capital
money demand, 421–32
  aggregate demand curve and, 236–37
  currency and checking deposits in, 421–32
  disturbances to, 231, 236, 237
  interest rates and, 132–34, 185–86, 195
  inventory theory of, 424–26
  precautionary motive in, 422, 426
  speculative motive in, 422, 426
  transaction motive in, 422, 424, 428
money demand function, 134
  interest rate for, 134n, 195
money market:
  equilibrium in, 135–37
  price level in, 132–37
money multiplier, 433
money supply, 134–35
  accommodative policy and rule and, 241, 248
  adjustment of, price disturbances and, 240–41, 242
  algebraic derivation of response to, 224
  for central banks, 580
  defined, 12
  as endogenous variable, 243
  exchange rate and, 595
  as exogenous variable, 242–43
  Fed control of, 413–21; *see also* Fed policy rule
  fixed growth rate rule for, 242
  interest rate and, 12, 135, 192
  LM curve and, 185
  nonaccommodative policies and, 241
  recession and, 12–13
  and shifts in LM curve, 186
money supply (M_1) target policy, 432, 433–34, 438
MPC, *see* marginal propensity to consume
Multifiber Agreement, 365
multiplier, 163–68
  decline of, 170
  leakage and, 358
  monetary base, 416
  money, 433
  open economy, 170–71
Muth, John, 538

NAFTA (North American Free Trade Area), 110
national debt, 398–401
national income, 46–47
  GDP vs., 46–47
national income and product accounts (NIPA), 32, 46, 47, 49, 54, 344

national saving, 53
natural rate of employment, 75–77, 89–93, 508
  defined, 77
natural rate property of price-adjustment model, 216, 508
negative assets, 280
negative growth, 3
Nelson, Richard, 344n
neoclassical growth model, *see* long-run growth model
net base, defined, 419
net export function, 169, 171, 353–55
net exports, 36–37, 38, 168–71
  determinants of, 352–55
  as endogenous variable, 355
  exchange rate and, 352–53, 354
  income and, 352–55
  in income identity, 138, 168
  interest rate and, 125–26, 127, 180, 195
  interest-rate sensitivity of, 125–26, 127
  trade deficit and, 138
  see also foreign trade
net foreign investment of U.S., 52
net investment:
  capital stock and, 91
  defined, 34
neutrality of money, 136
new classical school, 22, 26
New Keynesian Economics (Mankiw and Romer), 22–23
new Keynesian school, 22–23
Newsweek, 238n
New York Times, 199
NIPA (national income and product accounts), 32, 46, 47, 49, 54, 344
Nixon administration, 567, 584
nominal GDP, 39, 558–59, 560–61
  forecasts of, 563
  government debt and, 395–97
  as price indicator, 563
  targeting of, 560–61, 563–64
nominal interest rate, 179, 296
nominal money, defined, 186
nominal wage:
  price rigidity and, 482–86
  sticky, 484–86
nonaccommodative policies, 241
nonborrowed reserves, defined, 419
noncooperative policy choice, 594
nondurable goods, 33, 269
  long-run MPC and, 276
  short-run MPC and, 276
nonresidential fixed investment, 33, 309–11, 312
  residential investment vs., 308
nonunion sector, 489–93
normative perspective on policy,

defined, 384
North American Free Trade Area (NAFTA), 110

OECD (Organization for Economic Cooperation and Development), 138
Office of Management and Budget, U.S., 398
oil prices, 568–69
   disturbances to, 233–34, 524–25, 566
Okun, Arthur, 77, 243, 499–500
Okun's law, 77, 78, 212–13, 254, 509, 555, 562
OPEC (Organization of Petroleum Exporting Countries), 568
open-economy IS curve, 358–61
   algebraic derivation of, 358–59
open-economy macroeconomics, 168
   fixed exchange rate in, 590–91
   floating exchange rate in, 588–89, 592–93
   IS curve in, 361
   macro policy in, 588–93
   net exports and, 168–71
   spending balance in, 171
open-economy multiplier, 170–71
open-market operations, 414–17
   by Fed, 415, 432
open-market purchases, 508
opportunity costs:
   of holding funds as money, 422–23, 428
   marginal, 423
   "shoe-leather," 548, 549
Organization for Economic Cooperation and Development (OECD), 138
Organization of Petroleum Exporting Countries (OPEC), 568
Oudiz, Gilles, 595*n*
outlays, government, 36, 384–85
output, 31–65
   aggregate demands as determinant of, 148, 149, 210–12
   expected inflation and, 515–18
   fiscal policy and, 132
   fluctuations in, 526
   full-employment level of, 98
   income and, 31–65
   inflation and, 217–19
   investment and, 320–21
   potential, 16, 252
   price level and, 17
   in production function, 18
   real, 199–200, 252
   short-run fluctuations in, 212
   single-year inflation and, 514
   in sticky-price model, 209–12
output-inflation loops, 525–29, 559–60
output losses, cost of, 550–52

Pacific rim countries, 577–78, 586
panel data sets, 291

par value, 582, 583
passive policy rule, 541
Patinkin, D., 411*n*
pay-as-you-go rule, 247
payment, means of, 410, 412
peaks, 6
   prices and, 10
Pencavel, John, 96*n*
pensions, 549
permanent-income theory of consumption, 278
personal income:
   defined, 47
   disposable, *see* disposable income
personal income tax, 20, 293–94
Phelps, Edmund S., 22, 216–17, 238
Phillips, A. W., 215
Phillips curve, 215–16, 219, 507–9
   disinflation and, 249
   expectations-augmented, *see* expectations-augmented Phillips curve
   price adjustment and, 215–16
pipeline function, 330
Plosser, Charles, 112*n*
Policano, Andrew, 493*n*
policy experiments, 290, 293–94
policy frontier, 546
   changing of, 564–69
   controls and incentives in, 567–69
   between inflation and unemployment loss, 552–69
policy-makers, credibility of, 540
policy rule, 242–49
   activist, 237, 541
   aggregate demand curve and, 244–45, 250–51
   constant, 541
   defined, 243
   discretionary, 541
   and expectations of policy, 248
   of Fed, *see* Fed policy rule
   feedback and, 541
   fluctuations and, 439
   importance of, 248–49
   normative vs. positive perspectives on, 384
   passive, 541
   reaction function as, 384
   time inconsistency and, 246–47, 248
Poole, William, 438*n*
population, employment and, 73
portfolio investment, 35
positive perspective on policy, defined, 384
post-World War II period, high consumption levels in, 277, 289
potential GDP, 16–17
   defined, 16, 93, 98
   full employment and, 93–98

potential GDP, (*continued*)
  growth of, 18–19, 22
  inflation and, 220–24
  movement to, 224
  real GDP and, 76, 252
potential output, 16, 252
PPI (producer price index), 69, 70
precautionary motive, in money demand,
  422, 426
predatory pricing, 364
predetermined variables:
  endogenous vs., 181
  price level as, 181, 214
Prescott, Edward, 23, 113, 246, 248*n*, 454*n*,
  540
price:
  fixing of, 567
  marginal cost and, 477–80
  peaks and, 10
  troughs and, 10
  see also flexible–price model; sticky-price
    model
price adjustment, 23
  aggregate demand and, 219–24, 518–25
  aggregate demand curve and, 219
  aggregate demand disturbances and,
    232–35
  and changes in demand, 152–53
  complete model and, 214–23
  defined, 23
  equilibrium adjustment process and,
    214–19
  exchange rate and, 359, 361
  foreign trade and, 359, 361
  government spending and, 361
  gradual, 21
  inflation and, 215–19
  market conditions and, 214
  Phillips curve and, 215–16
price-adjustment curve, Lucas supply curve
  vs., 467
price-adjustment model, 219, 507–34, 553
  booms in, 522–24
  changes in coefficients of, 509–11
  indexing to inflation in, 509–10
  length and severity of business cycles in,
    510–11
  oil price shocks in, 524–25
  wage-price process in, 507–9
  wage-price spiral in, 510
price disturbances, 230–49
  adjustment of money supply in response
    to, 240–41, 242
  aggregate demand curve and, 240–41
  economic forecasting and, 235–36
  GDP and, 241, 242
  government creation of, 566–67
  inflation and, 515, 596

  optimal policy for, 556–64
  in petroleum-related industries, 232–34
  recession and, 232–33
  responding to, 240–41, 556–64
  unemployment and, 596
  from wage increases, 234
price fixing, 565
price indexes, 67–69, 70
price indicator:
  commodities as, 562
  exchange rates as, 562
  interest rates as, 562
  nominal GDP as, 563
price level:
  aggregate demand and, 200, 201–2
  and demand for money, 432
  disturbances to, 233–35
  exchange rate and, 362–63
  level of output and, 17
  LM curve and, 185, 187
  in money market, 132–37
  natural rate property of, 508
  as predetermined variable, 181, 214
  shifts in, 234
  unresponsiveness of, 152–53
price level indicators, 561–63, 599
price rigidities, 473–506, 541
  nominal wage and, 482–86
  real wage and, 474–82
  trade-off between unemployment and,
    546–52
  wage stickiness and, 482–86
  see also wage rigidities
price shocks, *see* price disturbances
price stability, 247*n*
price stickiness, *see* sticky-price model
printing press, in raising revenues, 420
private saving, 51
procyclical interest rates, 12
producer price index (PPI), 69, 70
production, 5–6, 31
  employment and, 9
  GDP and, 151
  lean, 92
  shifts in, 18
  technology and, 91–92, 106
  wage bargaining and, 491
production function:
  defined, 92
  output in, 18
  real business cycle model and, 112
productivity, 79–81
  defined, 79
  employment and, 79–81
  GDP as measure of, 43
  improvement of, 106–7
  labor, 79–81
  marginal, of labor, *see* marginal product

of labor
total factor, 79, 92
wages as components of, 78
products, contracts for, 476, 477
profits, maximization of, 94
protectionism:
dumping and, 364
free trade vs., 363–66
macroeconomic effects of, 365–66
stabilization policy and, 568–69
purchasing power parity:
defined, 351
exchange rate and, 351–52, 377–79

R&D (research and development), 106–7,
108
random walks, 292–93
rate of time preference, 297
rational expectations, 23–24, 26
in forward-looking theory of consumption,
290–91
futures markets and, 376–77
interest and exchange rates and, 374–76
monetary policy and, 199, 498–501
see also consumer behavior
rational expectations model, 26
reaction function, defined, 384
Reagan, Ronald, 255–57, 391
Reagan administration, 325
contractionary policies of, 595
real business cycle model, 112–16, 458–59
critique of, 114–16
fluctuations in, 112–16
and shifts in production function, 112
theory of, 116
real business cycle school, 23, 112–16
real disposable income, consumption and,
272–73
real exchange rate, defined, 350
real GDP, 6–14, 31, 39, 229
aggregate demand curve and, 212–13,
232–33
employment and, 9–10
Fed and, 252
in Germany, 42–43
inflation and, 10–11, 67
international comparisons of, 42–43
in Japan, 42–43
macroeconomic policy and, 122–24
1981–83, 40–41
1990–92, 40–41
percentage deviations of, 6–8
potential GDP and, 76, 252
quarterly data on, 42
recessions and, 39–42
and shifts in aggregate demand curve,
232–33
stability of, 247

target level of, 250–51
unemployment and, 77, 550–52
real interest rate, 12, 179
consumption and, 296–98
defined, 296
investment and, 333
labor and, 297–98, 458–62
rate of time preference and, 297
saving and, 296–98
work and, 297–98
real money, defined, 12, 186
real output, monetary and fiscal policies and,
199–200, 252
real wage, 77–79
in booms vs. recessions, 474, 481
employment and, 477–82
price rigidity and, 474–82
profit maximization and, 94
real wage rigidity, 474–75
recessions, 5, 6, 293, 474, 481
aggregate demand disturbances and,
232–33
automatic stabilizers and deficit in, 393
consumption in, 274, 287
currency holdings in, 429
defined, 6
demand-deficient, 520–21
disinflation and, 498
employment and, 9, 70–71, 113
inflation and, 10–11, 249–50, 253, 256–57
labor supply in, 454–55
as market failures, 243
money supply and, 12–13
price disturbances and, 232–33
real GDP and, 39–42
residential investment in, 309
and shifts in demand, 17
taxes in, 390–92
unemployment and, 70–71, 73–75
recovery, 520–22
price adjustment and aggregate demand
in, 520–24
from stagflation, 522
relative price setting, exchange rate and,
350–52
see also price adjustment
rental price:
residential investment and, 328–30
taxes and, 325
rented capital:
capital budgeting and, 317–18, 341–43
demand curve for, 314
determining price of, 312, 316–17
marginal benefit vs. price of, 316–17,
321
Tax Reform Act and, 324, 325
Tobin's q and, 343–44
required reserves, defined, 417

research and development (R&D),
    106–7, 108
Research and Experimentation Tax Credit,
    106–7
reserve inflow, 582
reserve outflow, 582
reserve ratio, 415–16
reserves:
    on balance sheet, 414
    borrowed, 418–19
    excess, 417
    in Fed, 417
    as monetary unit, 599
    nonborrowed, 419
    required, 417
residential fixed investment, 33, 309–11, 327,
    328–30
    nonresidential fixed investment vs., 308
    in recession, 309
    rental price and, 328–30
rest of world saving, 51–55
    defined, 51
rest of world (ROW) sector, 55–59, 350–51
retained earnings, defined, 48
retirement, 549
    consumption and, 282
Ricardian equivalence, 400
Rogerson, Richard, 454n, 455
Romer, David, 22–23
Romer, Paul 24, 110
Rothschild, Michael, 321n

Sachs, Jeffrey, 511, 595n
salary administrators, 489–90
Samuelson, Paul, 522n
Sargent, Thomas, 22, 256, 457n, 460, 465,
    466, 502
saving:
    balanced growth and, 98–103
    changes in assets and, 54–55
    consumption vs., real interest rate and,
        296–98
    defined, 50
    GDP and, 50–55
    government, 51
    gross, 53
    investment and, 50–55
    Japanese, 288, 361
    national, 53
    private, 51
    by rest of world sector, 51–55
saving rate, defined, 100
saving supply, defined, 310
scarcity, 544
schedules, defined, 161
services, 33
    consumption expenditures and, 270

long-run MPC and, 276
    short-run MPC and, 276
services trade account, 57
Shleifer, Andrei, 282n
shocks, see aggregate demand disturbances;
        disturbances
"shoe leather costs," 548, 549
short run, labor supply in, 452–54, 456
short-run marginal propensity to consume
        (MPC), 276–77, 287
    defined, 276
    durables and, 276–77
    nondurables and, 276
    services and, 276
short-run model:
    aggregate demand in, 147–54
    and economy out of equilibrium, 146–49
    fluctuations in, 144–75
    and labor market out of equilibrium, 146
    spending balance in, see spending balance
shunto, 494
SII (Structural Impediments Initiative), 138
Silk, Leonard, 199–200
Sims, Christopher, 539
Singleton, Kenneth, 291n
slope:
    of aggregate demand curve, 200
    defined, 161
    of 45-degree line, 159
    of IS curve, 182–83, 196–97, 299, 401
    of LM curve, 185–86, 197
Smith, Adam, 267
Smithsonian Institution, 584
SNA (system of national accounts), 46
social insurance, contributions for, 48
social security, COLA and, 68–69
social security tax, 47–48
social welfare function, 544
Solow, Robert M., 22, 24, 99–103, 110–11,
    511
Solow growth model, 103, 110, 111
South Africa, Republic of, 576
speculative motive, in money demand, 422,
    426
spending, 31
    GDP and, 32–43, 151
spending balance, 149–71
    aggregate demand and, 149–54
    algebraic solution of, 160, 162
    GDP and, 154–71
    graphical analysis of, 158–59
    maintenance of, 162–63
    net exports and, 168–71
    in open economy, 171
spending line, 158–59
squared error, 546
stabilization policy, 236–40
    countercyclical, 237–39, 392

disagreements on, 237–40
exchange rate and, 366–68
in international macro policy coordination, 594
protectionism and, 568–69
underlying objective of, 237
stabilizers, automatic, *see* automatic stabilizers
stagflation, 589
defined, 522
staggered wage setting, 487, 490–97
algebraic model of, 494–97
expected inflation and, 511–12
standard monetary policy, 584
statistical discrepancy, defined, 45
steel industry, 481
Stein, Herbert, 130–31
sterilized intervention, 580–81, 584
sticky-price model, 26, 209–28, 483
flexible-price model vs., 16
output in, 209–12
unemployment in, 212–14
sticky-wage labor markets, 484–86, 542
stochastic equilibrium, 541
stock market, random walks of, 292–93
structural deficits, cyclical deficits vs., 393–94
Structural Impediments Initiative (SII), 138
substitution:
consumption, 297
marginal rate of, 305
substitution effect, 95, 453
Summers, Lawrence H., 89n, 115n 282n, 327n
Summers, Robert, 24
supply:
investment, 310
of labor, *see* labor supply
saving, 310
tax cuts and, 109
supply curves:
labor, 109, 477–78
Lucas, 462–65, 467
Supreme Court, U.S., 364
surplus:
balance of payments, 582
trade, 37, 168
surveys, wage, 490, 493
system of national accounts (SNA), 46

targeting, 250–51, 432–35, 439, 564
instruments and, 543–45
tariffs, 363–66
IS curve and, 365
LM curve and, 365
tax brackets, 548
tax credits, investment, 20, 324–27
for research and development, 106, 108

tax cuts, 283–85, 391
IS curve and, 299–300
labor supply and, 109, 111
permanent vs. temporary, 299
of Reagan administration, 325
tax deductions, 548
taxed-based incomes policy, 568
taxes:
anticipated changes in, 325, 327
capital gains, 326–27
discretionary changes in, 390–91
distortions in, 548, 549
economic activity and, 390–92
government spending and, 390–92
government transfers and, 385, 392
income, 20, 293–94
investment and, 323–27
marginal rate of, 111
permanent changes in, 324–25
in recession, 390–92
rental price and, 325
social security, 47–48
unemployment and, 390, 391
value-added, 566–67
tax incentives, 324–27
tax law, discretionary vs. automatic changes in, 390–91
Tax Reform Act (1986), 111, 274, 324, 325
tax system:
flat, 111
indexing of, 548
modifications to, 548, 549
Taylor, John B., 327n, 489n, 499n, 512n, 538n, 556n, 564n, 595n
T-bills (U.S. Treasury bills), 582
technological change, growth path and, 103
technological growth, improvement of, 106–7
technology:
defined, 88
production and, 91–92, 106
terms of trade, 346
Thatcher, Margaret, 560
Thatcher government, 588
Thurow, Lester, 486, 489
time inconsistency, 246–47, 248
time preference, rate of, 297
Tinbergen, Jan, 544
Tobin, James, 22, 25, 238, 243, 344n, 422, 424n, 427, 564n
Tobin's q, 343–44
total factor productivity, 79, 92
trade:
barriers to, 363–66
foreign, *see* foreign trade
policy for, 568–69
quotas in, 568
terms of, 346

trade balance, 37
trade deficit, 5, 6, 345
    budget deficit and, 126, 129, 138, 360–61
    defined, 37, 168
    foreign saving and, 54
    net exports and, 138
trade-offs, 544–45
trade surplus, defined, 37, 168
trade-weighted exchange rate, 58, 349, 351
training, GDP and, 551
transaction motive, in money demand, 422,
        424, 428
transfers:
    government, *see* government transfers
    unilateral, 57
transition period, growth rate and, 102–3
Treasury Bills (T-bills), U.S., 582
Treasury Department, U.S., 414, 585
troughs, 6
    prices and, 10

UAW (United Automobile Workers), 218
UF (*Unidad de Fomento*), 483, 597
UMW (United Mine Workers), 487, 498
underground economy, 429
unemployment, 546–52
    disinflation and, 254, 257
    equilibrium and, 89, 90, 97
    frictional, 76–77, 89, 97
    government purchases and, 388
    government transfers and, 389
    marginal social costs of, 551, 552
    measuring of, 70, 72–77
    natural rate of, 75–77, 89–93, 508
    policy frontier between inflation and,
        552–69
    price disturbances and, 596
    price rigidity and, 546–52
    real GDP and, 77, 550–52
    recessions and, 70–71, 73–75
    in sticky-price model, 212–14
    taxes and, 390, 391
    wage bargaining and, 492
    wages and, 508–9
    see also employment; full employment
unemployment benefits, initial claims for, 73
unemployment compensation, reformation
        of, 565–66
unemployment loss, 550–52
    defined, 547
unemployment rate:
    defined, 10, 72
    natural, 75–77, 89–93, 508
Unidad de Fomento (UF), 483, 597
unilateral transfers, 57
union contracts, 486–89
    COLA and, 68–69
    complexity of, 490–93

    contingency clauses in, 490–93
    indexing to inflation in, 487, 489, 492–93,
        509–10
unions:
    in collective bargaining, 68–69, 486–89,
        491
    wage and price inflation forecasts by, 542
    wage setting and, 218–19, 486–89
United Automobile Workers (UAW), 218
United Kingdom:
    inflation-output loops in, 528–29, 559–60
    in 1989, 588–89
    value-added tax in, 566
United Mine Workers (UMW), 487, 498
unit of account, 410, 412
unused capacity, 456–57
unused shifts, 457
Uruguay Round, 110, 111
Uzawa, Hirofumi, 110

value, money as unit of, 598
value added:
    defined, 44
    GDP and, 44–45
value-added tax, 566–67
variables, 4–5
    endogenous, *see* endogenous variables
    exogenous, *see* exogenous variables
    financial, 176–208
    predetermined, *see* predetermined vari-
        ables
vault cash, 414n
Vietnam War, 293, 567
Volcker, Paul, 255, 256

wage administrators, 489–90
wage behavior, backward-looking, 488–89
    expected inflation and, 511–12
wage determination, 486–97
    contingencies in, 490–93
    expected inflation and, 218–19, 489,
        511–13, 542
    in nonunion sector, 489–93
    staggered, *see* staggered wage setting
    synchronization in, 493–94
    in union sector, 218–19, 486–89
wage-price spiral, defined, 510
wage rigidities, 473–506, 541
    nominal price and, 482–86
    policy implications of, 498–502
    temporary, 494
    trade-off between inflation and unemploy-
        ment and, 552–56
    wage determination and, *see* wage deter-
        mination
    see also price rigidities
wages, 77–79
    adjustment costs of, 491

bargaining and, 486–89, 491, 492
determination of, *see* wage determination
fixing of, 565
indexing of, *see* indexing to inflation
investment and, 321
marginal product of labor and, 94
measuring of, 70–71
nominal, 482–86
price disturbance from increases in, 234
productivity and, 78
real, *see* real wage
"under-the-table," 429
unemployment and, 508–9
see also labor
wage surveys, 490, 493
Wallace, Neil, 457*n*, 465, 466
Wall Street Journal, 229, 466, 502
Washington Post, 199
wealth, money as store of, 426–27, 598
Whitaker, J. K., 470

Williamson, John, 598
work, *see* employment; labor supply
world economy, 575–603
floating rates policies in, 584–87, 588–89
see also Bretton Woods System; international financial and monetary system;
policy frontier
World War II:
government deficit in, 395–97
prisoner-of-war camps in, 411
Wright, Randall, 454*n*
write-offs for fixed investments, 326

Yellen, Janet, 490*n*
yen, Japanese, 586, 596

Zenith Radio, 364
zero-deficit case, 399
zero inflation, 547